FORD | ESCORT/LYNX
1981-90 REPAIR MANUAL

CHILTON'S

President Dean F. Morgantini, S.A.E.
Vice President–Finance Barry L. Beck
Vice President–Sales Glenn D. Potere

Executive Editor Kevin M. G. Maher, A.S.E.
Production Manager Ben Greisler, S.A.E.
Production Assistant Melinda Possinger

Project Managers George B. Heinrich III, A.S.E., S.A.E., Will Kessler, A.S.E., S.A.E., James R. Marotta, A.S.E., S.T.S., Richard Schwartz, A.S.E., Todd W. Stidham, A.S.E.

Schematics Editor Christopher G. Ritchie

Editor Thomas A. Mellon, A.S.E., S.A.E.

CHILTON™ Automotive Books

PUBLISHED BY W. G. NICHOLS, INC.

Manufactured in
© 1998 W. G. N
1020 Andrew Dr
West Chester, PA
ISBN 0-8019-9093-9
Library of Congress Catalog Card No. 98-71365
1234567890 7654321098

Contents

629.287
C43FEM(2)

Contents

DRIVE TRAIN   **7**

SUSPENSION AND STEERING   **8**

BRAKES   **9**

BODY AND TRIM   **10**

GLOSSARY

MASTER INDEX

See last page for information on additional titles

SAFETY NOTICE

Proper service and repair procedures are vital to the safe, reliable operation of all motor vehicles, as well as the personal safety of those performing repairs. This manual outlines procedures for servicing and repairing vehicles using safe, effective methods. The procedures contain many NOTES, CAUTIONS and WARNINGS which should be followed, along with standard procedures to eliminate the possibility of personal injury or improper service which could damage the vehicle or compromise its safety.

It is important to note that repair procedures and techniques, tools and parts for servicing motor vehicles, as well as the skill and experience of the individual performing the work vary widely. It is not possible to anticipate all of the conceivable ways or conditions under which vehicles may be serviced, or to provide cautions as to all possible hazards that may result. Standard and accepted safety precautions and equipment should be used when handling toxic or flammable fluids, and safety goggles or other protection should be used during cutting, grinding, chiseling, prying, or any other process that can cause material removal or projectiles.

Some procedures require the use of tools specially designed for a specific purpose. Before substituting another tool or procedure, you must be completely satisfied that neither your personal safety, nor the performance of the vehicle will be endangered.

Although information in this manual is based on industry sources and is complete as possible at the time of publication, the possibility exists that some car manufacturers made later changes which could not be included here. While striving for total accuracy, NP/Chilton cannot assume responsibility for any errors, changes or omissions that may occur in the compilation of this data.

PART NUMBERS

Part numbers listed in this reference are not recommendations by Chilton for any product brand name. They are references that can be used with interchange manuals and aftermarket supplier catalogs to locate each brand supplier's discrete part number.

SPECIAL TOOLS

Special tools are recommended by the vehicle manufacturer to perform their specific job. Use has been kept to a minimum, but where absolutely necessary, they are referred to in the text by the part number of the tool manufacturer. These tools can be purchased, under the appropriate part number, from your local dealer or regional distributor, or an equivalent tool can be purchased locally from a tool supplier or parts outlet. Before substituting any tool for the one recommended, read the SAFETY NOTICE at the top of this page.

ACKNOWLEDGMENTS

NP/Chilton expresses appreciation to Ford Motor Company for their generous assistance.

A special thanks to the fine companies who supported the production of this book. Hand tools, supplied by Craftsman, were used during all phases of vehicle teardown and photography. Many of the fine specialty tools used in procedures were provided courtesy of Lisle Corporation. Lincoln Automotive Products has provided their industrial shop equipment including jacks, engine stands and shop presses. A Rotary lift, the largest automobile lift manufacturer in the world offering the biggest variety of surface and inground lifts available, was also used. Fel-Pro Incorporated supplied gasket sets for engine reassembly.

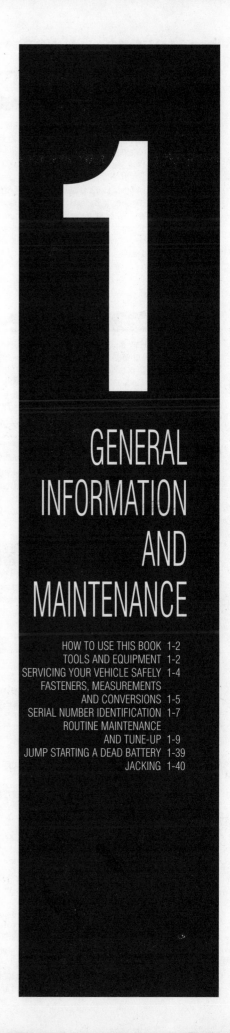

1

GENERAL INFORMATION AND MAINTENANCE

HOW TO USE THIS BOOK

Chilton's Total Car Care manual for the 1981–90 Ford Escort and Mercury Lynx is intended to help you learn more about the inner workings of your vehicle while saving you money on its upkeep and operation.

The beginning of the book will likely be referred to the most, since that is where you will find information for maintenance and tune-up. The other sections deal with the more complex systems of your vehicle. Systems (from engine through brakes) are covered to the extent that the average do-it-yourselfer can attempt. This book will not explain such things as rebuilding a differential because the expertise required and the special tools necessary make this uneconomical. It will, however, give you detailed instructions to help you change your own brake pads and shoes, replace spark plugs, and perform many more jobs that can save you money and help avoid expensive problems.

A secondary purpose of this book is a reference for owners who want to understand their vehicle and/or their mechanics better.

Where to Begin

Before removing any bolts, read through the entire procedure. This will give you the overall view of what tools and supplies will be required. So read ahead and plan ahead. Each operation should be approached logically and all procedures thoroughly understood before attempting any work.

If repair of a component is not considered practical, we tell you how to remove the part and then how to install the new or rebuilt replacement. In this way, you at least save labor costs.

Avoiding Trouble

Many procedures in this book require you to "label and disconnect . . ." a group of lines, hoses or wires. Don't be think you can remember where everything goes—you won't. If you hook up vacuum or fuel lines incorrectly, the vehicle may run poorly, if at all. If you hook up electrical wiring incorrectly, you may instantly learn a very expensive lesson.

You don't need to know the proper name for each hose or line. A piece of masking tape on the hose and a piece on its fitting will allow you to assign your own label. As long as you remember your own code, the lines can be reconnected by matching your tags. Remember that tape will dissolve in gasoline or solvents; if a part is to be washed or cleaned, use another method of identification. A permanent felt-tipped marker or a metal scribe can be very handy for marking metal parts. Remove any tape or paper labels after assembly.

Maintenance or Repair?

Maintenance includes routine inspections, adjustments, and replacement of parts which show signs of normal wear. Maintenance compensates for wear or deterioration. Repair implies that something has broken or is not working. A need for a repair is often caused by lack of maintenance. for example: draining and refilling automatic transmission fluid is maintenance recommended at specific intervals. Failure to do this can shorten the life of the transmission/transaxle, requiring very expensive repairs. While no maintenance program can prevent items from eventually breaking or wearing out, a general rule is true: MAINTENANCE IS CHEAPER THAN REPAIR.

Two basic mechanic's rules should be mentioned here. First, whenever the left side of the vehicle or engine is referred to, it means the driver's side. Conversely, the right side of the vehicle means the passenger's side. Second, screws and bolts are removed by turning counterclockwise, and tightened by turning clockwise unless specifically noted.

Safety is always the most important rule. Constantly be aware of the dangers involved in working on an automobile and take the proper precautions. Please refer to the information in this section regarding SERVICING YOUR VEHICLE SAFELY and the SAFETY NOTICE on the acknowledgment page.

Avoiding the Most Common Mistakes

Pay attention to the instructions provided. There are 3 common mistakes in mechanical work:

1. Incorrect order of assembly, disassembly or adjustment. When taking something apart or putting it together, performing steps in the wrong order usually just costs you extra time; however, it CAN break something. Read the entire procedure before beginning. Perform everything in the order in which the instructions say you should, even if you can't see a reason for it. When you're taking apart something that is very intricate, you might want to draw a picture of how it looks when assembled in order to make sure you get everything back in its proper position. When making adjustments, perform them in the proper order. One adjustment possibly will affect another.

2. Overtorquing (or undertorquing). While it is more common for overtorquing to cause damage, undertorquing may allow a fastener to vibrate loose causing serious damage. Especially when dealing with aluminum parts, pay attention to torque specifications and utilize a torque wrench in assembly. If a torque figure is not available, remember that if you are using the right tool to perform the job, you will probably not have to strain yourself to get a fastener tight enough. The pitch of most threads is so slight that the tension you put on the wrench will be multiplied many times in actual force on what you are tightening.

There are many commercial products available for ensuring that fasteners won't come loose, even if they are not torqued just right (a very common brand is Loctite®). If you're worried about getting something together tight enough to hold, but loose enough to avoid mechanical damage during assembly, one of these products might offer substantial insurance. Before choosing a threadlocking compound, read the label on the package and make sure the product is compatible with the materials, fluids, etc. involved.

3. Crossthreading. This occurs when a part such as a bolt is screwed into a nut or casting at the wrong angle and forced. Crossthreading is more likely to occur if access is difficult. It helps to clean and lubricate fasteners, then to start threading the bolt, spark plug, etc. with your fingers. If you encounter resistance, unscrew the part and start over again at a different angle until it can be inserted and turned several times without much effort. Keep in mind that many parts have tapered threads, so that gentle turning will automatically bring the part you're threading to the proper angle. Don't put a wrench on the part until it's been tightened a couple of turns by hand. If you suddenly encounter resistance, and the part has not seated fully, don't force it. Pull it back out to make sure it's clean and threading properly.

Be sure to take your time and be patient, and always plan ahead. Allow yourself ample time to perform repairs and maintenance.

TOOLS AND EQUIPMENT

♦ See Figures 1 thru 15

Without the proper tools and equipment it is impossible to properly service your vehicle. It would be virtually impossible to catalog every tool that you would need to perform all of the operations in this book. It would be unwise for the amateur to rush out and buy an expensive set of tools on the theory that he/she may need one or more of them at some time.

The best approach is to proceed slowly, gathering a good quality set of those tools that are used most frequently. Don't be misled by the low cost of bargain tools. It is far better to spend a little more for better quality. Forged wrenches, 6 or 12-point sockets and fine tooth ratchets are by far preferable to their less expensive counterparts. As any good mechanic can tell you, there are few worse experiences than trying to work on a vehicle with bad tools. Your monetary savings will be far outweighed by frustration and mangled knuckles.

Begin accumulating those tools that are used most frequently: those associated with routine maintenance and tune-up. In addition to the normal assortment of screwdrivers and pliers, you should have the following tools:

• Wrenches/sockets and combination open end/box end wrenches in sizes ⅛–¾ in. and/or 3mm-19mm ¹³⁄₁₆ in. or ⅝ in. spark plug socket (depending on plug type).

➥If possible, buy various length socket drive extensions. Universaljoint and wobble extensions can be extremely useful, but be careful when using them, as they can change the amount of torque applied to the socket.

• Jackstands for support.
• Oil filter wrench.

- Spout or funnel for pouring fluids.
- Grease gun for chassis lubrication (unless your vehicle is not equipped with any grease fittings)
- Hydrometer for checking the battery (unless equipped with a sealed, maintenance-free battery).
- A container for draining oil and other fluids.
- Rags for wiping up the inevitable mess.

In addition to the above items there are several others that are not absolutely necessary, but handy to have around. These include an equivalent oil absorbent gravel, like cat litter, and the usual supply of lubricants, antifreeze and fluids. This is a basic list for routine maintenance, but only your personal needs and desire can accurately determine your list of tools.

After performing a few projects on the vehicle, you'll be amazed at the other tools and non-tools on your workbench. Some useful household items are: a large turkey baster or siphon, empty coffee cans and ice trays (to store parts), a ball of twine, electrical tape for wiring, small rolls of colored tape for tagging lines or hoses, markers and pens, a note pad, golf tees (for plugging vacuum lines), metal coat hangers or a roll of mechanic's wire (to hold things out of the way), dental pick or similar long, pointed probe, a strong magnet, and a small mirror (to see into recesses and under manifolds).

A more advanced set of tools, suitable for tune-up work, can be drawn up easily. While the tools are slightly more sophisticated, they need not be outrageously expensive. There are several inexpensive tach/dwell meters on the market that are every bit as good for the average mechanic as a professional model. Just be sure that it goes to a least 1200–1500 rpm on the tach scale and that it works on 4, 6 and 8–cylinder engines. The key to these purchases is to make them with an eye towards adaptability and wide range. A basic list of tune-up tools could include:

- Tach/dwell meter.
- Spark plug wrench and gapping tool.
- Feeler gauges for valve adjustment.
- Timing light.

The choice of a timing light should be made carefully. A light which works on the DC current supplied by the vehicle's battery is the best choice; it should

Fig. 1 All but the most basic procedures will require an assortment of ratchets and sockets

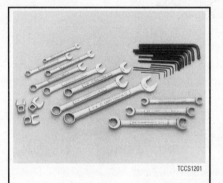

Fig. 2 In addition to ratchets, a good set of wrenches and hex keys will be necessary

Fig. 3 A hydraulic floor jack and a set of jackstands are essential for lifting and supporting the vehicle

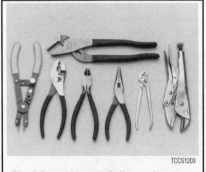

Fig. 4 An assortment of pliers, grippers and cutters will be handy for old rusted parts and stripped bolt heads

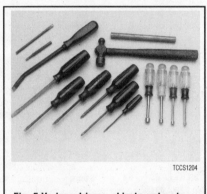

Fig. 5 Various drivers, chisels and prybars are great tools to have in your toolbox

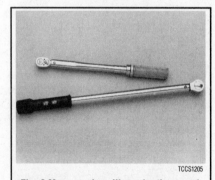

Fig. 6 Many repairs will require the use of a torque wrench to assure the components are properly fastened

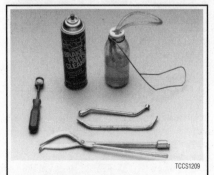

Fig. 7 Although not always necessary, using specialized brake tools will save time

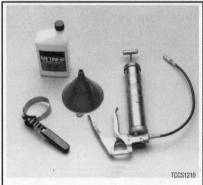

Fig. 8 A few inexpensive lubrication tools will make maintenance easier

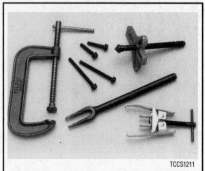

Fig. 9 Various pullers, clamps and separator tools are needed for many larger, more complicated repairs

Fig. 10 A variety of tools and gauges should be used for spark plug gapping and installation

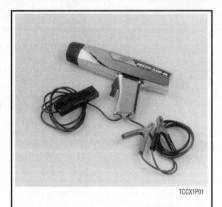

Fig. 11 Inductive type timing light

Fig. 12 A screw-in type compression gauge is recommended for compression testing

Fig. 13 A vacuum/pressure tester is necessary for many testing procedures

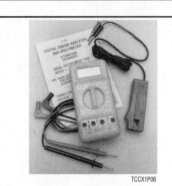

Fig. 14 Most modern automotive multimeters incorporate many helpful features

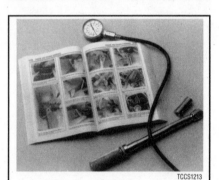

Fig. 15 Proper information is vital, so always have a Chilton Total Car Care manual handy

have a xenon tube for brightness. On any vehicle with an electronic ignition system, a timing light with an inductive pickup that clamps around the No. 1 spark plug cable is preferred.

In addition to these basic tools, there are several other tools and gauges you may find useful. These include:
- Compression gauge. The screw-in type is slower to use, but eliminates the possibility of a faulty reading due to escaping pressure.
- Manifold vacuum gauge.
- 12V test light.
- A combination volt/ohmmeter
- Induction Ammeter. This is used for determining whether or not there is current in a wire. These are handy for use if a wire is broken somewhere in a wiring harness.

As a final note, you will probably find a torque wrench necessary for all but the most basic work. The beam type models are perfectly adequate, although the newer click types (breakaway) are easier to use. The click type torque wrenches tend to be more expensive. Also keep in mind that all types of torque wrenches should be periodically checked and/or recalibrated. You will have to decide for yourself which better fits your pocketbook, and purpose.

Special Tools

Normally, the use of special factory tools is avoided for repair procedures, since these are not readily available for the do-it-yourself mechanic. When it is possible to perform the job with more commonly available tools, it will be pointed out, but occasionally, a special tool was designed to perform a specific function and should be used. Before substituting another tool, you should be convinced that neither your safety nor the performance of the vehicle will be compromised.

Special tools can usually be purchased from an automotive parts store or from your dealer. In some cases special tools may be available directly from the tool manufacturer.

SERVICING YOUR VEHICLE SAFELY

♦ See Figures 16, 17 and 18

It is virtually impossible to anticipate all of the hazards involved with automotive maintenance and service, but care and common sense will prevent most accidents.

The rules of safety for mechanics range from "don't smoke around gasoline," to "use the proper tool(s) for the job." The trick to avoiding injuries is to develop safe work habits and to take every possible precaution.

Do's

- Do keep a fire extinguisher and first aid kit handy.
- Do wear safety glasses or goggles when cutting, drilling, grinding or prying, even if you have 20–20 vision. If you wear glasses for the sake of vision, wear safety goggles over your regular glasses.

- Do shield your eyes whenever you work around the battery. Batteries contain sulfuric acid. In case of contact with, flush the area with water or a mixture of water and baking soda, then seek immediate medical attention.
- Do use safety stands (jackstands) for any undervehicle service. Jacks are for raising vehicles; jackstands are for making sure the vehicle stays raised until you want it to come down.
- Do use adequate ventilation when working with any chemicals or hazardous materials. Like carbon monoxide, the asbestos dust resulting from some brake lining wear can be hazardous in sufficient quantities.
- Do disconnect the negative battery cable when working on the electrical system. The secondary ignition system contains EXTREMELY HIGH VOLTAGE. In some cases it can even exceed 50,000 volts.
- Do follow manufacturer's directions whenever working with potentially hazardous materials. Most chemicals and fluids are poisonous.

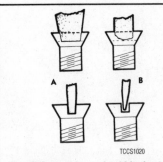

Fig. 16 Screwdrivers should be kept in good condition to prevent injury or damage which could result if the blade slips from the screw

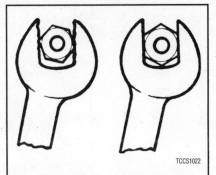

Fig. 17 Using the correct size wrench will help prevent the possibility of rounding off a nut

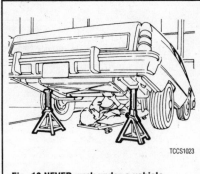

Fig. 18 NEVER work under a vehicle unless it is supported using safety stands (jackstands)

• Do properly maintain your tools. Loose hammerheads, mushroomed punches and chisels, frayed or poorly grounded electrical cords, excessively worn screwdrivers, spread wrenches (open end), cracked sockets, slipping ratchets, or faulty droplight sockets can cause accidents.

• Likewise, keep your tools clean; a greasy wrench can slip off a bolt head, ruining the bolt and often harming your knuckles in the process.

• Do use the proper size and type of tool for the job at hand. Do select a wrench or socket that fits the nut or bolt. The wrench or socket should sit straight, not cocked.

• Do, when possible, pull on a wrench handle rather than push on it, and adjust your stance to prevent a fall.

• Do be sure that adjustable wrenches are tightly closed on the nut or bolt and pulled so that the force is on the side of the fixed jaw.

• Do strike squarely with a hammer; avoid glancing blows.

• Do set the parking brake and block the drive wheels if the work requires a running engine.

Don'ts

• Don't run the engine in a garage or anywhere else without proper ventilation—EVER! Carbon monoxide is poisonous; it takes a long time to leave the human body and you can build up a deadly supply of it in your system by simply breathing in a little at a time. You may not realize you are slowly poisoning yourself. Always use power vents, windows, fans and/or open the garage door.

• Don't work around moving parts while wearing loose clothing. Short sleeves are much safer than long, loose sleeves. Hard-toed shoes with neoprene soles protect your toes and give a better grip on slippery surfaces. Watches and jewelry is not safe working around a vehicle. Long hair should be tied back under a hat or cap.

• Don't use pockets for toolboxes. A fall or bump can drive a screwdriver deep into your body. Even a rag hanging from your back pocket can wrap around a spinning shaft or fan.

• Don't smoke when working around gasoline, cleaning solvent or other flammable material.

• Don't smoke when working around the battery. When the battery is being charged, it gives off explosive hydrogen gas.

• Don't use gasoline to wash your hands; there are excellent soaps available. Gasoline contains dangerous additives which can enter the body through a cut or through your pores. Gasoline also removes all the natural oils from the skin so that bone dry hands will suck up oil and grease.

• Don't service the air conditioning system unless you are equipped with the necessary tools and training. When liquid or compressed gas refrigerant is released to atmospheric pressure it will absorb heat from whatever it contacts. This will chill or freeze anything it touches.

• Don't use screwdrivers for anything other than driving screws! A screwdriver used as an prying tool can snap when you least expect it, causing injuries. At the very least, you'll ruin a good screwdriver.

• Don't use an emergency jack (that little ratchet, scissors, or pantograph jack supplied with the vehicle) for anything other than changing a flat! These jacks are only intended for emergency use out on the road; they are NOT designed as a maintenance tool. If you are serious about maintaining your vehicle yourself, invest in a hydraulic floor jack of at least a 1½ ton capacity, and at least two sturdy jackstands.

FASTENERS, MEASUREMENTS AND CONVERSIONS

Bolts, Nuts and Other Threaded Retainers

▶ See Figures 19 and 20

Although there are a great variety of fasteners found in the modern car or truck, the most commonly used retainer is the threaded fastener (nuts, bolts, screws, studs, etc.). Most threaded retainers may be reused, provided that they are not damaged in use or during the repair. Some retainers (such as stretch bolts or torque prevailing nuts) are designed to deform when tightened or in use and should not be reinstalled.

Whenever possible, we will note any special retainers which should be replaced during a procedure. But you should always inspect the condition of a retainer when it is removed and replace any that show signs of damage. Check all threads for rust or corrosion which can increase the torque necessary to achieve the desired clamp load for which that fastener was originally selected. Additionally, be sure that the driver surface of the fastener has not been compromised by rounding or other damage. In some cases a driver surface may become only partially rounded, allowing the driver to catch in only one direction. In many of these occurrences, a fastener may be installed and tightened, but the driver would not be able to grip and loosen the fastener again.

If you must replace a fastener, whether due to design or damage, you must ALWAYS be sure to use the proper replacement. In all cases, a retainer of the

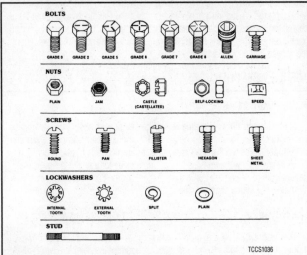

Fig. 19 There are many different types of threaded retainers found on vehicles

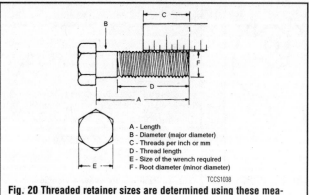

A - Length
B - Diameter (major diameter)
C - Threads per inch or mm
D - Thread length
E - Size of the wrench required
F - Root diameter (minor diameter)

TCCS1038

Fig. 20 Threaded retainer sizes are determined using these measurements

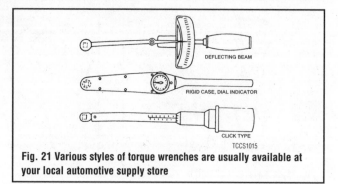

TCCS1015

Fig. 21 Various styles of torque wrenches are usually available at your local automotive supply store

same design, material and strength should be used. Markings on the heads of most bolts will help determine the proper strength of the fastener. The same material, thread and pitch must be selected to assure proper installation and safe operation of the vehicle afterwards.

Thread gauges are available to help measure a bolt or stud's thread. Most automotive and hardware stores keep gauges available to help you select the proper size. In a pinch, you can use another nut or bolt for a thread gauge. If the bolt you are replacing is not too badly damaged, you can select a match by finding another bolt which will thread in its place. If you find a nut which threads properly onto the damaged bolt, then use that nut to help select the replacement bolt.

※※ WARNING

Be aware that when you find a bolt with damaged threads, you may also find the nut or drilled hole it was threaded into has also been damaged. If this is the case, you may have to drill and tap the hole, replace the nut or otherwise repair the threads. NEVER try to force a replacement bolt to fit into the damaged threads.

Torque

Torque is defined as the measurement of resistance to turning or rotating. It tends to twist a body about an axis of rotation. A common example of this would be tightening a threaded retainer such as a nut, bolt or screw. Measuring torque is one of the most common ways to help assure that a threaded retainer has been properly fastened.

When tightening a threaded fastener, torque is applied in three distinct areas, the head, the bearing surface and the clamp load. About 50 percent of the measured torque is used in overcoming bearing friction. This is the friction between the bearing surface of the bolt head, screw head or nut face and the base material or washer (the surface on which the fastener is rotating). Approximately 40 percent of the applied torque is used in overcoming thread friction. This leaves only about 10 percent of the applied torque to develop a useful clamp load (the force which holds a joint together). This means that friction can account for as much as 90 percent of the applied torque on a fastener.

TORQUE WRENCHES

♦ See Figure 21

In most applications, a torque wrench can be used to assure proper installation of a fastener. Torque wrenches come in various designs and most automotive supply stores will carry a variety to suit your needs. A torque wrench should be used any time we supply a specific torque value for a fastener. Again, the general rule of "if you are using the right tool for the job, you should not have to strain to tighten a fastener" applies here.

Beam Type

The beam type torque wrench is one of the most popular types. It consists of a pointer attached to the head that runs the length of the flexible beam (shaft) to a scale located near the handle. As the wrench is pulled, the beam bends and the pointer indicates the torque using the scale.

Click (Breakaway) Type

Another popular design of torque wrench is the click type. To use the click type wrench you pre-adjust it to a torque setting. Once the torque is reached, the wrench has a reflex signaling feature that causes a momentary breakaway of the torque wrench body, sending an impulse to the operator's hand.

Pivot Head Type

♦ See Figure 22

Some torque wrenches (usually of the click type) may be equipped with a pivot head which can allow it to be used in areas of limited access. BUT, it must be used properly. To hold a pivot head wrench, grasp the handle lightly, and as you pull on the handle, it should be floated on the pivot point. If the handle comes in contact with the yoke extension during the process of pulling, there is a very good chance the torque readings will be inaccurate because this could alter the wrench loading point. The design of the handle is usually such as to make it inconvenient to deliberately misuse the wrench.

➡ It should be mentioned that the use of any U-joint, wobble or extension will have an effect on the torque readings, no matter what type of wrench you are using. For the most accurate readings, install the socket directly on the wrench driver. If necessary, straight extensions (which hold a socket directly under the wrench driver) will have the least effect on the torque reading. Avoid any extension that alters the length of the wrench from the handle to the head/driving point (such as a crow's foot). U-joint or wobble extensions can greatly affect the readings; avoid their use at all times.

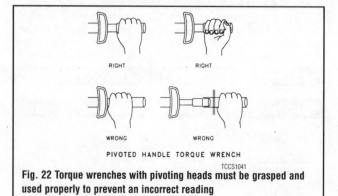

RIGHT   RIGHT

WRONG   WRONG

PIVOTED HANDLE TORQUE WRENCH

TCCS1041

Fig. 22 Torque wrenches with pivoting heads must be grasped and used properly to prevent an incorrect reading

Rigid Case (Direct Reading)

A rigid case or direct reading torque wrench is equipped with a dial indicator to show torque values. One advantage of these wrenches is that they can be held at any position on the wrench without affecting accuracy. These wrenches are often preferred because they tend to be compact, easy to read and have a great degree of accuracy.

TORQUE ANGLE METERS

Because the frictional characteristics of each fastener or threaded hole will vary, clamp loads which are based strictly on torque will vary as well. In most applications, this variance is not significant enough to cause worry. But, in certain applications, a manufacturer's engineers may determine that more precise clamp loads are necessary (such is the case with many aluminum cylinder heads). In these cases, a torque angle method of installation would be specified. When installing fasteners which are torque angle tightened, a predetermined seating torque and standard torque wrench are usually used first to remove any compliance from the joint. The fastener is then tightened the specified additional portion of a turn measured in degrees. A torque angle gauge (mechanical protractor) is used for these applications.

Standard and Metric Measurements

♦ See Figure 23

Throughout this manual, specifications are given to help you determine the condition of various components on your vehicle, or to assist you in their installation. Some of the most common measurements include length (in. or cm/mm), torque (ft. lbs., inch lbs. or Nm) and pressure (psi, in. Hg, kPa or mm Hg). In most cases, we strive to provide the proper measurement as determined by the manufacturer's engineers.

Though, in some cases, that value may not be conveniently measured with what is available in your toolbox. Luckily, many of the measuring devices which are available today will have two scales so the Standard or Metric measurements may easily be taken. If any of the various measuring tools which are available to you do not contain the same scale as listed in the specifications, use the accompanying conversion factors to determine the proper value.

The conversion factor chart is used by taking the given specification and multiplying it by the necessary conversion factor. For instance, looking at the first line, if you have a measurement in inches such as "free-play should be 2 in." but your ruler reads only in millimeters, multiply 2 in. by the conversion factor of 25.4 to get the metric equivalent of 50.8mm. Likewise, if the specification was given only in a Metric measurement, for example in Newton Meters (Nm), then look at the center column first. If the measurement is 100 Nm, multiply it by the conversion factor of 0.738 to get 73.8 ft. lbs.

CONVERSION FACTORS

LENGTH-DISTANCE

Inches (in.)	x 25.4	= Millimeters (mm)	x .0394	= Inches
Feet (ft.)	x .305	= Meters (m)	x 3.281	= Feet
Miles	x 1.609	= Kilometers (km)	x .0621	= Miles

VOLUME

Cubic Inches (in3)	x 16.387	= Cubic Centimeters	x .061	= in3
IMP Pints (IMP pt.)	x .568	= Liters (L)	x 1.76	= IMP pt.
IMP Quarts (IMP qt.)	x 1.137	= Liters (L)	x .88	= IMP qt.
IMP Gallons (IMP gal.)	x 4.546	= Liters (L)	x .22	= IMP gal.
IMP Quarts (IMP qt.)	x 1.201	= US Quarts (US qt.)	x .833	= IMP qt.
IMP Gallons (IMP gal.)	x 1.201	= US Gallons (US gal.)	x .833	= IMP gal.
Fl. Ounces	x 29.573	= Milliliters	x .034	= Ounces
US Pints (US pt.)	x .473	= Liters (L)	x 2.113	= Pints
US Quarts (US qt.)	x .946	= Liters (L)	x 1.057	= Quarts
US Gallons (US gal.)	x 3.785	= Liters (L)	x .264	= Gallons

MASS-WEIGHT

Ounces (oz.)	x 28.35	= Grams (g)	x .035	= Ounces
Pounds (lb.)	x .454	= Kilograms (kg)	x 2.205	= Pounds

PRESSURE

Pounds Per Sq. In. (psi)	x 6.895	= Kilopascals (kPa)	x .145	= psi
Inches of Mercury (Hg)	x .4912	= psi	x 2.036	= Hg
Inches of Mercury (Hg)	x 3.377	= Kilopascals (kPa)	x .2961	= Hg
Inches of Water (H_2O)	x .07355	= Inches of Mercury	x 13.783	= H_2O
Inches of Water (H_2O)	x .03613	= psi	x 27.684	= H_2O
Inches of Water (H_2O)	x .248	= Kilopascals (kPa)	x 4.026	= H_2O

TORQUE

Pounds-Force Inches (in-lb)	x .113	= Newton Meters (N·m)	x 8.85	= in-lb
Pounds-Force Feet (ft-lb)	x 1.356	= Newton Meters (N·m)	x .738	= ft-lb

VELOCITY

Miles Per Hour (MPH)	x 1.609	= Kilometers Per Hour (KPH)	x .621	= MPH

POWER

Horsepower (Hp)	x .745	= Kilowatts	x 1.34	= Horsepower

FUEL CONSUMPTION*

Miles Per Gallon IMP (MPG)	x .354	= Kilometers Per Liter (Km/L)	
Kilometers Per Liter (Km/L)	x 2.352	= IMP MPG	
Miles Per Gallon US (MPG)	x .425	= Kilometers Per Liter (Km/L)	
Kilometers Per Liter (Km/L)	x 2.352	= US MPG	

*It is common to covert from miles per gallon (mpg) to liters/100 kilometers (1/100 km), where mpg (IMP) x 1/100 km = 282 and mpg (US) x 1/100 km = 235.

TEMPERATURE

Degree Fahrenheit (°F)	= (°C x 1.8) + 32
Degree Celsius (°C)	= (°F – 32) x .56

TCCS1044

Fig. 23 Standard and metric conversion factors chart

SERIAL NUMBER IDENTIFICATION

Vehicle Identification Number

♦ See Figure 24

The Vehicle Identification Number (VIN) is located on the instrument panel, close to the windshield on the driver's side of the vehicle. It is visible from outside the vehicle.

The 17–character label contains the following information:
- Digits 1, 2 and 3: World manufacturer identifier
- Digit 4: Restraint system type
- Digit 5: Constant P
- Digits 6 and 7: Line, series and body type

86751305

Fig. 24 The VIN is visible through the driver's side of the windshield

VEHICLE IDENTIFICATION CHART

Engine Series (ID/VIN)	Engine Displacement Liters	Cubic Inches	No. of Cylinders	Fuel System	Eng. Mfg.	Code	Year
1	1.3	79	4	2-bbl	Ford	B	1981
2	1.6	98	4	2-bbl	Ford	C	1982
4	1.6 HO	98	4	2-bbl	Ford	D	1983
5	1.6 EFI	98	4	EFI	Ford	E	1984
8	1.6 EFI	98	4	EFI ①	Ford	F	1985
9	1.9	114	4	②	Ford	G	1986
J	1.9 HO	114	4	EFI	Ford	H	1987
						J	1988
						K	1989
						L	1990

HO—High Output
2-bbl—Two-barrel carburetor
CFI—Central Fuel Injection
EFI—Electronic Fuel Injection
① Turbocharged
② 1986-87 models: 2-bbl
1988-90 models: CFI

90931C01

- Digit 8: Engine type
- Digit 9: Check digit
- Digit 10: Vehicle model year
- Digit 11: Assembly plant
- Digits 12 through 17: Production sequence number

Vehicle Certification Label

▶ **See Figure 25**

A Vehicle Certification Label (VCL) is affixed on the left front door jamb. The VCL, which is used for warranty identification, contains the 17–digit Vehicle Identification Number (VIN) in addition to other data.

This label contains the following information:

- Manufacturer
- Type of restraint system
- Vehicle line
- Model series
- Body type
- Engine
- Model year
- Assembly plant
- Production sequence number
- Exterior color
- Interior trim type and color
- Radio type
- Transaxle ratio
- Transaxle type

Engine

The 8th character of the VIN designates the engine type installed in the vehicle. An engine identification label may also be attached to the engine timing cover.

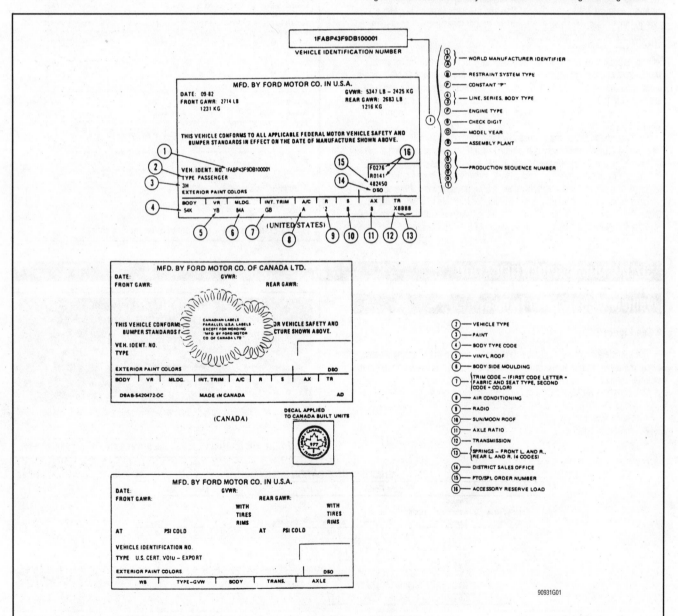

Fig. 25 Typical vehicle certification label used on 1981–89 models; 1990 models are similar

GENERAL ENGINE SPECIFICATIONS

Year	Model	Engine ID/VIN	Engine Displacement Liters (CI)	No. of Cyl.	Fuel System Type	Net Horsepower @ rpm	Net Torque @ rpm (ft. lbs.)	Com-pression Ratio	Oil Pressure (lbs. @ rpm)
1981	Escort/Lynx	1	1.3L (79)	4	2-bbl	58 @ 5700	63 @ 3600	8.0:1	35-45 psi @ 2000
		2	1.6L (98)	4	2-bbl	65 @ 5200	89 @ 3000	8.8:1	35-45 psi @ 2000
1982	Escort/Lynx	2	1.6L (98)	4	2-bbl	70 @ 4600	89 @ 3000	8.8:1	35-65 psi @ 2000
1983	Escort/Lynx	2	1.6L (98)	4	2-bbl	70 @ 4600	89 @ 3000	8.8:1	35-65 psi @ 2000
1984	Escort/Lynx	2	1.6 (98)	4	2-bbl	70 @ 4600	88 @ 2600	9.0:1	35-65 psi @ 2000
		4	1.6 HO (98)	4	2-bbl	80 @ 5400	88 @ 3000	9.0:1	35-65 psi @ 2000
		5	1.6 (98)	4	EFI	120 @ 5200	120 @ 3400	8.0:1	35-65 psi @ 2000
		8	1.6 (98)	4	EFI Turbo	84 @ 5200	90 @ 2800	9.0: 1	35-65 psi @ 2000
1985	Escort/Lynx	2	1.6 (98)	4	2-bbl	70 @ 4600	88 @ 2600	9.0:1	35-65 psi @ 2000
		4	1.6 HO (98)	4	2-bbl	80 @ 5400	88 @ 3000	9.0:1	35-65 psi @ 2000
		5	1.6 (98)	4	EFI	120 @ 5200	120 @ 3400	8.0:1	35-65 psi @ 2000
		8	1.6 (98)	4	EFI Turbo	84 @ 5200	90 @ 2800	9.0: 1	35-65 psi @ 2000
1986	Escort/Lynx	9	1.9 (114)	4	2-bbl	86 @ 4800	100 @ 3000	9.0:1	35-65 psi @ 2000
		J	1.9 HO (114)	4	EFI	108 @ 5200	114 @ 4000	9.0:1	35-65 psi @ 2000
1987	Escort/Lynx	9	1.9 (114)	4	2-bbl	86 @ 4800	100 @ 3000	9.0:1	35-65 psi @ 2000
		J	1.9 HO (114)	4	EFI	108 @ 5200	114 @ 4000	9.0:1	35-65 psi @ 2000
1988	Escort	9	1.9 (114)	4	CFI	90 @ 4600	106 @ 3400	9.0:1	35-65 psi @ 2000
		J	1.9 HO (114)	4	EFI	110 @ 5400	115 @ 4200	9.0:1	35-65 psi @ 2000
1989	Escort	9	1.9 (114)	4	CFI	90 @ 4600	106 @ 3400	9.0:1	35-65 psi @ 2000
		J	1.9 HO (114)	4	EFI	110 @ 5400	115 @ 4200	9.0:1	35-65 psi @ 2000
1990	Escort	9	1.9 (114)	4	CFI	90 @ 4600	106 @ 3400	9.0:1	35-65 psi @ 2000
		J	1.9 HO (114)	4	EFI	110 @ 5400	115 @ 4200	9.0:1	35-65 psi @ 2000

CI–Cubic Inches

HO–High Output

@–At

2-bbl–Two-barrel carburetor

CFI–Central Fuel Injection

EFI–Electronic Fuel Injection (also known as MFI or Multi-port Fuel Injection)

90931C02

Transaxle

♦ See Figure 26

The transaxle code is found on the Vehicle Certification Label (VCL), affixed to the left (driver's) side door lock post. The code is located in the lower right-hand corner of the VCL. This code designates the transaxle type installed in the vehicle. A transaxle identification tag may be affixed to the transaxle assembly.

Drive Axle

The drive axle code is found in the lower right-hand corner of the vehicle certification label. This code designate the transaxle ratio.

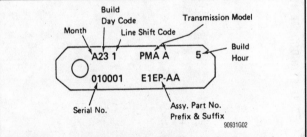

Fig. 26 Typical automatic transaxle identification tag that may be attached to the transaxle housing

ROUTINE MAINTENANCE AND TUNE-UP

Proper maintenance and tune-up is the key to long and trouble-free vehicle life, and the work can yield its own rewards. Studies have shown that a properly tuned and maintained vehicle can achieve better gas mileage than an out-of-tune vehicle. As a conscientious owner and driver, set aside a Saturday morning, say once a month, to check or replace items which could cause major problems later. Keep your own personal log to jot down which services you performed, how much the parts cost you, the date, and the exact odometer reading at the time. Keep all receipts for such items as engine oil and filters, so that they may be referred to in case of related problems or to determine operating expenses. As a do-it-yourselfer, these receipts are the only proof you have that the required maintenance was performed. In the event of a warranty problem, these receipts will be invaluable.

The literature provided with your vehicle when it was originally delivered includes the factory recommended maintenance schedule. If you no longer have this literature, replacement copies are usually available from the dealer. A maintenance schedule is provided later in this section, in case you do not have the factory literature.

Air Cleaner (Element)

The air cleaner element should be replaced every 30 months or 30,000 miles (48,300 km). More frequent changes are necessary if the car is operated in dusty conditions.

UNDERHOOD MAINTENANCE COMPONENT LOCATIONS

1. Fuel filter
2. Air filter element (under housing cover)
3. PCV valve
4. Engine oil filler cap
5. Coolant recovery tank
6. Serpentine belt
7. Radiator cap
8. Spark plug wire and plug
9. Brake master cylinder
10. Distributor assembly
11. Upper radiator hose
12. Battery
13. Engine oil dipstick
14. Automatic transaxle dipstick

REMOVAL & INSTALLATION

Carbureted Engines

▶ **See Figure 27**

➡ **The crankcase emission filter should be changed each time you replace the air cleaner element.**

1. Remove the wing nut and grommet that retains the air cleaner assembly to the carburetor.

➡ **To avoid dirt from falling into the carburetor, remove the air cleaner as an assembly from the engine compartment.**

2. Unfasten any engine-to-air cleaner support bracket bolts.
3. Unplug the air duct tubing, vacuum lines and heat tubes attached to the air cleaner.
4. Remove the air cleaner assembly from the vehicle.
5. Unfasten the spring clips that hold the top of the air cleaner to the body. Remove the cover.
6. Remove the air cleaner element.
7. Remove the crankcase filter.

To install:

8. Before installing the air cleaner or emission filters, clean the inside of the air cleaner housing by wiping it with a rag. Check the mounting gasket (gaskets, if the car is equipped with a spacer), and replace any gasket(s) that show wear.
9. Install a new emission filter and a new air cleaner element.
10. Install the housing cover and fasten the spring clips that hold the top of the air cleaner to the housing.
11. Install the air cleaner assembly onto the carburetor.
12. Install the grommet and wing nut that retains the air cleaner assembly to the carburetor.
13. If equipped, install any engine-to-air cleaner support bracket bolts.
14. Attach the air duct tubing, vacuum lines and heat tubes connected to the air cleaner.

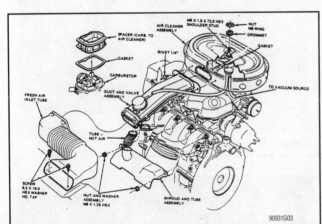

Fig. 27 Exploded view of the air cleaner and air intake system components—1.3L, 1.6L and 1.9L carbureted engines

Fuel Injected Engines

▶ **See Figures 28 thru 33**

1. Unclip the air intake tube and remove the tube from the air cleaner tray.
2. Unclip the air cleaner tray from the air cleaner assembly.
3. Pull the cleaner tray out to expose the air cleaner element.
4. Pull the air cleaner element from the tray.
5. Visually inspect the air cleaner tray and cover for signs of dust or leaking holes in the filter or past the seals.

To install:

6. Assemble the air cleaner element to the tray making sure the element is installed in its original position. Check to see that the seal is fully seated into the groove in the tray.
7. Clip the air intake tube to the air cleaner tray.

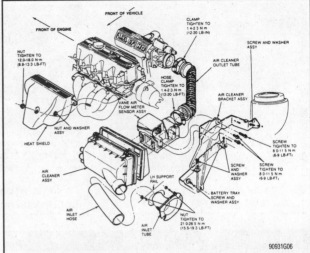

Fig. 28 Exploded view of the air cleaner and air intake system components—1.9L EFI engine; 1.6L EFI engine similar

Fig. 29 View of the engine bay and the air filter assembly—1.9L CFI engine

Fig. 30 Remove the wing nuts that retain the air cleaner cover

Fig. 31 Remove the cover to expose the air cleaner element inside

Fig. 32 Lift out the air cleaner element for inspection and replacement

Fig. 33 Here, the blow-by valve is also being removed for inspection while the air cleaner housing is open

Fuel Filter

REMOVAL & INSTALLATION

Carbureted Engines

▶ **See Figure 34**

1. Remove the air cleaner assembly.
2. Use a backup wrench on the fuel filter inlet hex nut (located in the carburetor inlet) to prevent the filter from turning. Loosen the fuel line nut with a flare wrench.
3. Remove the fuel line from the filter.
4. Unscrew the filter from the carburetor.

To install:

5. Apply a drop of Loctite® Hydraulic Sealant No. 069 or equivalent to the external threads of the fuel filter.
6. Hand-start the new filter into the carburetor, then use a wrench to tighten the fuel filter to 7–8 ft. lbs. (9–11 Nm).
7. Apply a drop of engine oil to the fuel supply tube nut and flare, and hand start the nut into the filter inlet approximately two threads.
8. Use a backup wrench on the fuel filter to prevent the filter from rotating while tightening. Tighten the nut to 15–18 ft. lbs. (20–24 Nm).
9. Start the engine and check for fuel leaks.
10. Install the air cleaner assembly.

Fig. 34 Location of the fuel filter—carbureted engines

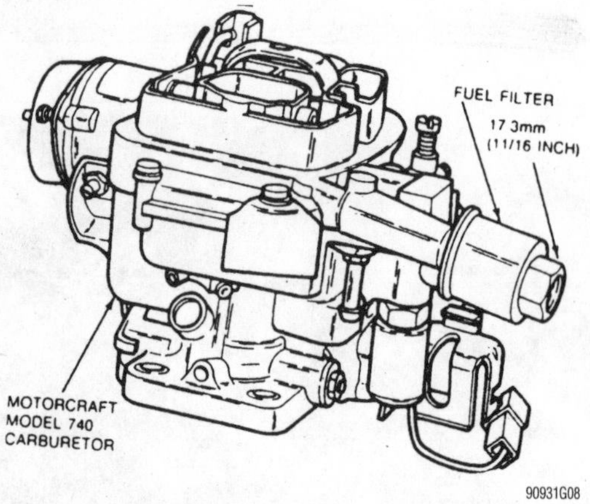

FUEL FILTER
17.3mm
(11/16 INCH)

MOTORCRAFT
MODEL 740
CARBURETOR

90931G08

Fuel Injected Engines

▶ **See Figures 35 and 36**

1. Disconnect the negative battery cable.
2. Properly relieve the fuel system pressure.
3. Remove the push connect fittings.

➡ **The flow arrow direction should be noted to ensure proper flow of fuel through the replacement filter.**

4. Remove the filter from the bracket by loosening the filter retaining clamp enough to allow the filter to pass through.

Fig. 35 Here, the hairpin-type clip is being removed from the push connector to access the fuel filter

Fig. 36 Note the direction of the flow arrow on the side of the filter, so you can install the filter right side up

To install:

5. Install the filter in the bracket, ensuring the proper direction of flow, as noted earlier. Tighten the clamp to 15–25 inch lbs. (1.7–2.8 Nm).

6. Install push-connect fittings at both ends of the filter.

7. Connect the negative battery cable.

8. Start the engine and inspect for leaks.

PCV Valve

REMOVAL & INSTALLATION

1. Pull the valve, with the hose still attached to the valve, from the rubber grommet in the rocker cover.

2. Use a pair of pliers to release the hose clamp, then remove the PCV valve from the hose.

3. Install the new valve into the hose, slide the clamp into position, and install the valve into the rubber grommet.

Evaporative Emission Canister

SERVICING

♦ See Figure 37

Since the canister is purged of fumes when the engine is operating, no real maintenance is required. However, the canister and hoses should be visually inspected for cracks, loose connections, etc. Replacement is simply a matter of disconnecting the hoses, loosening the mount and replacing the canister.

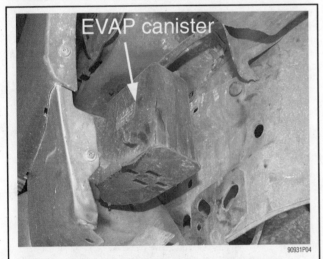

Fig. 37 The EVAP canister is located behind the left-hand inner fender—1988 1.9L engine shown

Battery

PRECAUTIONS

Always use caution when working on or near the battery. Never allow a tool to bridge the gap between the negative and positive battery terminals. Also, be careful not to allow a tool to provide a ground between the positive cable/terminal and any metal component on the vehicle. Either of these conditions will cause a short circuit, leading to sparks and possible personal injury.

Do not smoke, have an open flame or create sparks near a battery; the gases contained in the battery are very explosive and, if ignited, could cause severe injury or death.

All batteries, regardless of type, should be carefully secured by a battery hold-down device. If this is not done, the battery terminals or casing may crack from stress applied to the battery during vehicle operation. A battery which is not secured may allow acid to leak out, making it discharge faster; such leaking corrosive acid can also eat away at components under the hood.

Always visually inspect the battery case for cracks, leakage and corrosion. A white corrosive substance on the battery case or on nearby components would indicate a leaking or cracked battery. If the battery is cracked, it should be replaced immediately.

GENERAL MAINTENANCE

A battery that is not sealed must be checked periodically for electrolyte level. You cannot add water to a sealed maintenance-free battery (though not all maintenance-free batteries are sealed); however, a sealed battery must also be checked for proper electrolyte level, as indicated by the color of the built-in hydrometer "eye."

Always keep the battery cables and terminals free of corrosion. Check these components about once a year. Refer to the removal, installation and cleaning procedures outlined in this section.

Keep the top of the battery clean, as a film of dirt can help completely discharge a battery that is not used for long periods. A solution of baking soda and water may be used for cleaning, but be careful to flush this off with clear water. DO NOT let any of the solution into the filler holes. Baking soda neutralizes battery acid and will de-activate a battery cell.

Batteries in vehicles which are not operated on a regular basis can fall victim to parasitic loads (small current drains which are constantly drawing current from the battery). Normal parasitic loads may drain a battery on a vehicle that is in storage and not used for 6–8 weeks. Vehicles that have additional accessories such as a cellular phone, an alarm system or other devices that increase parasitic load may discharge a battery sooner. If the vehicle is to be stored for 6–8 weeks in a secure area and the alarm system, if present, is not necessary, the negative battery cable should be disconnected at the onset of storage to protect the battery charge.

Remember that constantly discharging and recharging will shorten battery life. Take care not to allow a battery to be needlessly discharged.

BATTERY FLUID

♦ See Figure 38

· Check the battery electrolyte level at least once a month, or more often in hot weather or during periods of extended vehicle operation. On non-sealed batteries, the level can be checked either through the case on translucent batteries or by removing the cell caps on opaque-cased types. The electrolyte level in each cell should be kept filled to the split ring inside each cell, or the line marked on the outside of the case.

If the level is low, add only distilled water through the opening until the level is correct. Each cell is separate from the others, so each must be checked and filled individually. Distilled water should be used, because the chemicals and minerals found in most drinking water are harmful to the battery and could significantly shorten its life.

If water is added in freezing weather, the vehicle should be driven several miles to allow the water to mix with the electrolyte. Otherwise, the battery could freeze.

Fig. 38 A typical location for the built-in hydrometer on maintenance-free batteries

Although some maintenance-free batteries have removable cell caps for access to the electrolyte, the electrolyte condition and level on all sealed maintenance-free batteries must be checked using the built-in 16 hydrometer "eye." The exact type of eye varies between battery manufacturers, but most apply a sticker to the battery itself explaining the possible readings. When in doubt, refer to the battery manufacturer's instructions to interpret battery condition using the built-in hydrometer.

→Although the readings from built-in hydrometers found in sealed batteries may vary, a green eye usually indicates a properly charged battery with sufficient fluid level. A dark eye is normally an indicator of a battery with sufficient fluid, but one which may be low in charge. And a light or yellow eye is usually an indication that electrolyte supply has dropped below the necessary level for battery (and hydrometer) operation. In this last case, sealed batteries with an insufficient electrolyte level must usually be discarded.

Checking the Specific Gravity

▶ **See Figures 39, 40 and 41**

A hydrometer is required to check the specific gravity on all batteries that are not maintenance-free. On batteries that are maintenance-free, the specific gravity is checked by observing the built-in hydrometer "eye" on the top of the battery case. Check with your battery's manufacturer for proper interpretation of its built-in hydrometer readings.

✳✳ CAUTION

Battery electrolyte contains sulfuric acid. If you should splash any on your skin or in your eyes, flush the affected area with plenty of clear water. If it lands in your eyes, get medical help immediately.

The fluid (sulfuric acid solution) contained in the battery cells will tell you many things about the condition of the battery. Because the cell plates must be kept submerged below the fluid level in order to operate, maintaining the fluid level is extremely important. And, because the specific gravity of the acid is an indication of electrical charge, testing the fluid can be an aid in determining if the battery must be replaced. A battery in a vehicle with a properly operating charging system should require little maintenance, but careful, periodic inspection should reveal problems before they leave you stranded.

As stated earlier, the specific gravity of a battery's electrolyte level can be used as an indication of battery charge. At least once a year, check the specific gravity of the battery. It should be between 1.20 and 1.26 on the gravity scale. Most auto supply stores carry a variety of inexpensive battery testing hydrometers. These can be used on any non-sealed battery to test the specific gravity in each cell.

The battery testing hydrometer has a squeeze bulb at one end and a nozzle at the other. Battery electrolyte is sucked into the hydrometer until the float is lifted from its seat. The specific gravity is then read by noting the position of the float. If gravity is low in one or more cells, the battery should be slowly charged and checked again to see if the gravity has come up. Generally, if after charging, the specific gravity between any two cells varies more than 50 points (0.50), the battery should be replaced, as it can no longer produce sufficient voltage to guarantee proper operation.

CABLES

▶ **See Figures 42, 43, 44 and 45**

Once a year (or as necessary), the battery terminals and the cable clamps should be cleaned. Loosen the clamps and remove the cables, negative cable first. On batteries with posts on top, the use of a puller specially made for this purpose is recommended. These are inexpensive and available in most auto parts stores. Side terminal battery cables are secured with a small bolt.

Clean the cable clamps and the battery terminal with a wire brush, until all corrosion, grease, etc., is removed and the metal is shiny. It is especially important to clean the inside of the clamp thoroughly (an old knife is useful here), since a small deposit of foreign material or oxidation there will prevent a sound electrical connection and inhibit either starting or charging. Special tools are available for cleaning these parts, one type for conventional top post batteries and another type for side terminal batteries. It is also a good idea to apply some dielectric grease to the terminal, as this will aid in the prevention of corrosion.

After the clamps and terminals are clean, reinstall the cables, negative cable last; DO NOT hammer the clamps onto battery posts. Tighten the clamps securely, but do not distort them. Give the clamps and terminals a thin external coating of grease after installation, to retard corrosion.

Check the cables at the same time that the terminals are cleaned. If the cable insulation is cracked or broken, or if the ends are frayed, the cable should be replaced with a new cable of the same length and gauge.

CHARGING

✳✳ CAUTION

The chemical reaction which takes place in all batteries generates explosive hydrogen gas. A spark can cause the battery to explode and splash acid. To avoid serious personal injury, be sure there is proper ventilation and take appropriate fire safety precautions when connecting, disconnecting, or charging a battery and when using jumper cables.

A battery should be charged at a slow rate to keep the plates inside from getting too hot. However, if some maintenance-free batteries are allowed to discharge until they are almost "dead," they may have to be charged at a high rate to bring them back to "life." Always follow the charger manufacturer's instructions on charging the battery.

REPLACEMENT

When it becomes necessary to replace the battery, select one with an amperage rating equal to or greater than the battery originally installed. Deterioration and just plain aging of the battery cables, starter motor, and associated wires makes the battery's job harder in successive years. The slow increase in electrical resistance over time makes it prudent to install a new battery with a greater capacity than the old.

TCCA1P07

Fig. 39 On non-maintenance-free batteries, the fluid level can be checked through the case on translucent models; the cell caps must be removed on other models

TCCA1P08

Fig. 40 If the fluid level is low, add only distilled water through the opening until the level is correct

TCCA1P09

Fig. 41 Check the specific gravity of the battery's electrolyte with a hydrometer

Fig. 42 The underside of this special battery tool has a wire brush to clean post terminals

Fig. 43 Place the tool over the battery posts and twist to clean until the metal is shiny

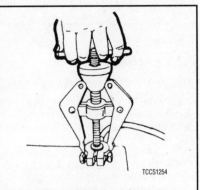

Fig. 44 A special tool is available to pull the clamp from the post

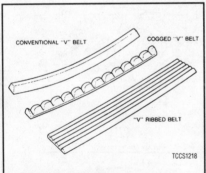

Fig. 45 The cable ends should be cleaned as well

Belts

INSPECTION

▶ See Figures 46, 47, 48, 49 and 50

Inspect the belts for signs of glazing or cracking. A glazed belt will be perfectly smooth from slippage, while a good belt will have a slight texture of fabric visible. Cracks will usually start at the inner edge of the belt and run outward. All worn or damaged drive belts should be replaced immediately. It is best to replace all drive belts at one time, as a preventive maintenance measure, during this service operation.

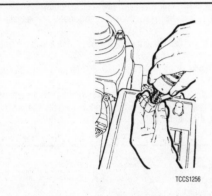

Fig. 46 There are typically 3 types of accessory drive belts found on vehicles today

Fig. 47 An example of a healthy drive belt

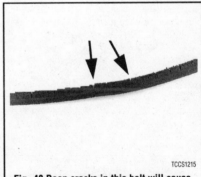

Fig. 48 Deep cracks in this belt will cause flex, building up heat that will eventually lead to belt failure

Fig. 49 The cover of this belt is worn, exposing the critical reinforcing cords to excessive wear

Fig. 50 Installing too wide a belt can result in serious belt wear and/or breakage

ADJUSTMENT

♦ **See Figure 51**

1981–86 Models

ALTERNATOR BELT WITH MODIFIED BRACKET

Some later models are equipped with a modified alternator bracket (high mount alternator). The bracket incorporates a slot that will accommodate a tapered prybar, such as a lug wrench, to give a place to apply leverage.

1. Loosen the accessory adjustment and pivot bolts.

Insert the tire lug wrench into the slot opening. Pry on the alternator until the correct belt tension is reached.

While maintaining belt tension, first tighten the ⅜ in. adjusting bolt to 24–30 ft. lbs. (32–40 Nm), then tighten the pivot bolt to 45–65 ft. lbs. (61–88 Nm).

1981–86 Models Except V-Ribbed Belts

1. Check the belt deflection using a belt tension gauge, if the deflection is not ⅛–¼ in. (3–6mm), the belt tension should be adjusted.
2. Loosen the accessory adjustment and pivot bolts.
3. Using the proper pry tool, pry against the necessary accessory in order to gain the proper belt tension.
4. Tighten the adjustment bolts. Release the pressure on the prybar. Tighten the pivot bolt.
5. Check the belt tension and reset it if not within specifications.

1987–90 1.9L Engines With V-Ribbed Belts

♦ **See Figure 52**

It is necessary to adjust the power steering belt prior to adjusting the air pump belt as follows:

1. From above the vehicle, loosen the pivot bolt and upper adjustment bolt.
2. From below the vehicle, loosen the lower adjustment bolt and apply pressure with a ½ in. drive ratchet. Tighten the lower bolts to 30–45 ft. lbs. (40–62 Nm).
3. From above the vehicle, tighten the pivot bolt to 30–45 ft. lbs. (40–62 Nm) and the upper adjustment bolts to 30–45 ft. lbs. (40–62 Nm).
4. To adjust the alternator belt on the 1987–88 models, loosen the pivot bolt and upper adjustment bolt.
5. Using the proper pry tool, pry against the necessary accessory in order to gain the proper belt tension.
6. Tighten the pivot bolt to 15–22 ft. lbs. (20–30 Nm) and the adjustment bolt to 24–34 ft. lbs. (33–46 Nm). Tighten the alternator through-bolts to 45–55 ft. lbs. (61–75 Nm).
7. On the 1989–90 models, adjust the alternator belt as follows:
    a. Install a ½ in. breaker bar or equivalent to the support bracket behind the alternator.
    b. Apply tension to the belt using the breaker bar. Using a suitable belt tension gauge set the proper belt tension.
    c. The tension should be 140–180 lbs. (623–801 N) for a new belt and 120–140 lbs. (534–623 Nm) for a used belt.

Secure the alternator pivot bolt, leaving it loose enough to allow the alternator to move. While maintaining the proper belt tension, tighten the alternator adjustment bolt to 30 ft. lbs. (40 Nm).

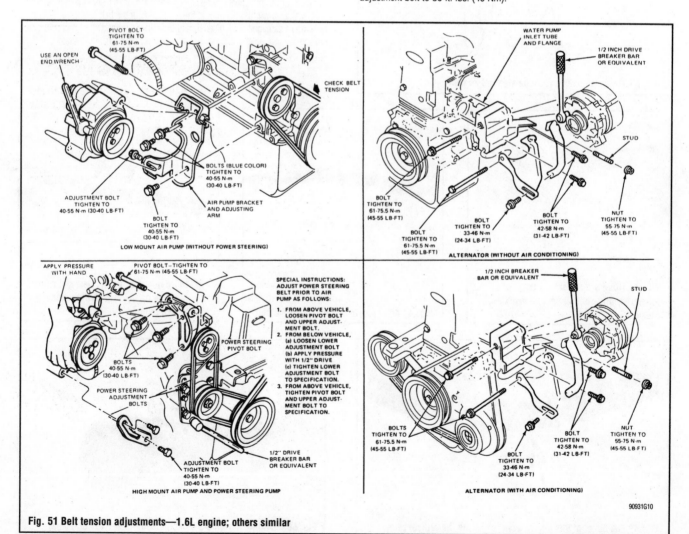

Fig. 51 Belt tension adjustments—1.6L engine; others similar

Fig. 52 Use a ½ in. ratchet to lever the alternator bracket in order to tension the belt

   d. Remove the belt tension gauge and breaker bar and idle the engine for 5 minutes.

   e. With the ignition switch in the **OFF** position, check the belt tension. If the tension is below 120 lbs., retension the belt with the tension gauge in place and tension being applied to the breaker bar so that the existing tension on the belt is not lost, then slowly loosen the alternator adjustment bolt to allow belt tension to increase to used belt specifications and tighten the adjustment bolt.

   f. Tighten the alternator pivot bolt to 50 ft. lbs. (68 Nm) and support bracket bolt to 35 ft. lbs. (47 Nm).

➡ The power steering pump belt on the 1989–90 models is adjusted in the same manner as the alternator belt.

REMOVAL & INSTALLATION

   1. Loosen the pivot bolt and/or the adjustment bolt on the accessories which need belts replaced.

   2. Move the driven unit (power steering pump, air pump, etc.) toward or away from the engine to loosen the belt. Remove the belt.

   To install:

   3. Install the new belt on the driven unit and either move the unit towards or away from the engine to put tension on the belt.

   4. Snug up the mounting and/or adjusting bolt to hold the driven unit, but do not completely tighten.

   5. Adjust the belt tension.

Timing Belts

SERVICING

   All engines covered in this manual utilizes a timing belt to drive the camshaft from the crankshaft's turning motion and to maintain proper valve timing. Some manufacturer's schedule periodic timing belt replacement to assure optimum engine performance, to make sure the motorist is never stranded should the belt break (as the engine will stop instantly) and for some (manufacturer's with interference motors) to prevent the possibility of severe internal engine damage should the belt break.

   Although the 1.3L and 1.9L engines are not listed as interference motors (they are not listed by the manufacturer as motors whose valves might contact the pistons if the camshaft was rotated separately from the crankshaft), the first 2 reasons for periodic replacement still apply. Ford does not publish a replacement interval for these motors, but most belt manufacturers recommend intervals anywhere from 45,000 miles (72,500 km) to 90,000 miles (145,000 km). You will have to decide for yourself if the peace of mind offered by a new belt is worth the cost on higher mileage engines.

   The 1.6L engine is listed as an interference motor. Ford recommends that the timing belt be replaced every 60,000 miles (96,000 km). It is far less expensive to replace the belt than to repair engine damage which can result from the belt breaking.

   Whether or not you decide to replace it, you would be wise to check it periodically to make sure it has not become damaged or worn. Generally speaking, a severely worn belt may cause engine performance to drop dramatically, but a damaged belt (which could give out suddenly) may not give as much warning. In general, any time the engine timing cover(s) is (are) removed you should inspect the belt for premature parting, severe cracks or missing teeth.

Hoses

INSPECTION

▶ **See Figures 53, 54, 55 and 56**

   Upper and lower radiator hoses along with the heater hoses should be checked for deterioration, leaks and loose hose clamps at least every 12,000 miles (19,000 km). It is also wise to check the hoses periodically in early spring and at the beginning of the fall or winter when you are performing other maintenance. A quick visual inspection could discover a weakened hose which might have left you stranded if it had remained unrepaired.

   Whenever you are checking the hoses, make sure the engine and cooling system are cold. Visually inspect for cracking, rotting or collapsed hoses, and replace as necessary. Run your hand along the length of the hose. If a weak or swollen spot is noted when squeezing the hose wall, the hose should be replaced.

REMOVAL & INSTALLATION

   1. Remove the radiator pressure cap.

✱✱ CAUTION

Never remove the pressure cap while the engine is running, or personal injury from scalding hot coolant or steam may result. If possible, wait until the engine has cooled to remove the pressure cap. If this is not possible, wrap a thick cloth around the pressure cap and turn it slowly to the stop. Step back while the pressure is released from the cooling system. When you are sure all the pressure has been released, use the cloth to turn and remove the cap.

   2. Position a clean container under the radiator and/or engine draincock or plug, then open the drain and allow the cooling system to drain to an appropriate level. For some upper hoses, only a little coolant must be drained. To remove hoses positioned lower on the engine, such as a lower radiator hose, the entire cooling system must be emptied.

Fig. 53 The cracks developing along this hose are a result of age-related hardening

Fig. 54 A hose clamp that is too tight can cause older hoses to separate and tear on either side of the clamp

TCCS1220

Fig. 55 A soft spongy hose (identifiable by the swollen section) will eventually burst and should be replaced

TCCS1221

Fig. 56 Hoses are likely to deteriorate from the inside if the cooling system is not periodically flushed

TCCS1222

✳✳ CAUTION

When draining coolant, keep in mind that cats and dogs are attracted by ethylene glycol antifreeze, and are quite likely to drink any that is left in an uncovered container or in puddles on the ground. This will prove fatal in sufficient quantity. Always drain coolant into a sealable container. Coolant may be reused unless it is contaminated or several years old.

3. Loosen the hose clamps at each end of the hose requiring replacement. Clamps are usually either of the spring tension type (which require pliers to squeeze the tabs and loosen) or of the screw tension type (which require screw or hex drivers to loosen). Pull the clamps back on the hose away from the connection.

4. Twist, pull and slide the hose off the fitting, taking care not to damage the neck of the component from which the hose is being removed.

➡ If the hose is stuck at the connection, do not try to insert a screwdriver or other sharp tool under the hose end in an effort to free it, as the connection and/or hose may become damaged. Heater connections especially may be easily damaged by such a procedure. If the hose is to be replaced, use a single-edged razor blade to make a slice along the portion of the hose which is stuck on the connection, perpendicular to the end of the hose. Do not cut deep so as to prevent damaging the connection. The hose can then be peeled from the connection and discarded.

5. Clean both hose mounting connections. Inspect the condition of the hose clamps and replace them, if necessary.

To install:

6. Dip the ends of the new hose into clean engine coolant to ease installation.

7. Slide the clamps over the replacement hose, then slide the hose ends over the connections into position.

8. Position and secure the clamps at least ¼ in. (6.35mm) from the ends of the hose. Make sure they are located beyond the raised bead of the connector.

9. Close the radiator or engine drains and properly refill the cooling system with the clean drained engine coolant or a suitable mixture of ethylene glycol coolant and water.

10. If available, install a pressure tester and check for leaks. If a pressure tester is not available, run the engine until normal operating temperature is reached (allowing the system to naturally pressurize), then check for leaks.

✳✳ CAUTION

If you are checking for leaks with the system at normal operating temperature, BE EXTREMELY CAREFUL not to touch any moving or hot engine parts. Once temperature has been reached, shut the engine OFF, and check for leaks around the hose fittings and connections which were removed earlier.

CV-Boots

INSPECTION

♦ See Figures 57 and 58

The CV (Constant Velocity) boots should be checked for damage each time the oil is changed and any other time the vehicle is raised for service. These boots keep water, grime, dirt and other damaging matter from entering the CV-joints. Any of these could cause early CV-joint failure which can be expensive to repair. Heavy grease thrown around the inside of the front wheel(s) and on the brake caliper/drum can be an indication of a torn boot. Thoroughly check the boots for missing clamps and tears. If the boot is damaged, it should be replaced immediately. Please refer to Section 7 for procedures.

Spark Plugs

♦ See Figure 59

A typical spark plug consists of a metal shell surrounding a ceramic insulator. A metal electrode extends downward through the center of the insulator and protrudes a small distance. Located at the end of the plug and attached to the side of the outer metal shell is the side electrode. The side electrode bends in at a 90° angle so that its tip is just past and parallel to the tip of the center electrode. The distance between these two electrodes (measured in thousandths of an inch or hundredths of a millimeter) is called the spark plug gap.

TCCS1011

Fig. 57 CV-boots must be inspected periodically for damage

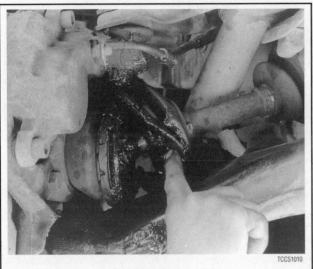

Fig. 58 A torn boot should be replaced immediately

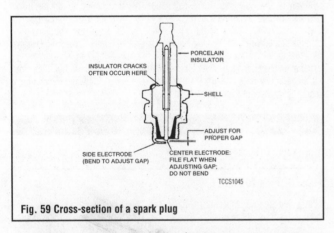

Fig. 59 Cross-section of a spark plug

The spark plug does not produce a spark, but instead provides a gap across which the current can arc. The coil produces anywhere from 20,000 to 50,000 volts (depending on the type and application) which travels through the wires to the spark plugs. The current passes along the center electrode and jumps the gap to the side electrode, and in doing so, ignites the air/fuel mixture in the combustion chamber.

SPARK PLUG HEAT RANGE

▶ **See Figure 60**

Spark plug heat range is the ability of the plug to dissipate heat. The longer the insulator (or the farther it extends into the engine), the hotter the plug will operate; the shorter the insulator (the closer the electrode is to the block's cooling passages) the cooler it will operate. A plug that absorbs little heat and remains too cool will quickly accumulate deposits of oil and carbon since it is not hot enough to burn them off. This leads to plug fouling and consequently to misfiring. A plug that absorbs too much heat will have no deposits but, due to the excessive heat, the electrodes will burn away quickly and might possibly lead to preignition or other ignition problems. Preignition takes place when plug tips get so hot that they glow sufficiently to ignite the air/fuel mixture before the actual spark occurs. This early ignition will usually cause a pinging during low speeds and heavy loads.

The general rule of thumb for choosing the correct heat range when picking a spark plug is: if most of your driving is long distance, high speed travel, use a colder plug; if most of your driving is stop and go, use a hotter plug. Original equipment plugs are generally a good compromise between the 2 styles and most people never have the need to change their plugs from the factory-recommended heat range.

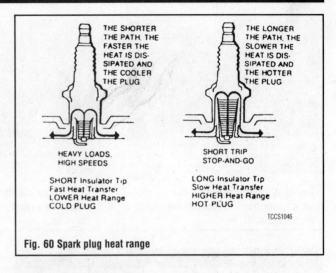

Fig. 60 Spark plug heat range

REMOVAL & INSTALLATION

▶ **See Figures 61, 62, 63 and 64**

A set of spark plugs usually requires replacement after about 20,000–30,000 miles (32,000–48,000 km), depending on your style of driving. In normal operation plug gap increases about 0.001 in. (0.025mm) for every 2500 miles (4000 km). As the gap increases, the plug's voltage requirement also increases. It requires a greater voltage to jump the wider gap and about two to three times as much voltage to fire the plug at high speeds than at idle. The improved air/fuel ratio control of modern fuel injection combined with the higher voltage output of modern ignition systems will often allow an engine to run significantly longer on a set of standard spark plugs, but keep in mind that efficiency will drop as the gap widens (along with fuel economy and power).

When you're removing spark plugs, work on one at a time. Don't start by removing the plug wires all at once, because, unless you number them, they may become mixed up. Take a minute before you begin and number the wires with tape.

1. Disconnect the negative battery cable, and if the vehicle has been run recently, allow the engine to thoroughly cool.

2. Carefully twist the spark plug wire boot to loosen it, then pull upward and remove the boot from the plug. Be sure to pull on the boot and not on the wire, otherwise the connector located inside the boot may become separated.

3. Using compressed air, blow any water or debris from the spark plug well to assure that no harmful contaminants are allowed to enter the combustion chamber when the spark plug is removed. If compressed air is not available, use a rag or a brush to clean the area.

➡**Remove the spark plugs when the engine is cold, if possible, to prevent damage to the threads. If removal of the plugs is difficult, apply a few drops of penetrating oil or silicone spray to the area around the base of the plug, and allow it a few minutes to work.**

4. Using a spark plug socket that is equipped with a rubber insert to properly hold the plug, turn the spark plug counterclockwise to loosen and remove the spark plug from the bore.

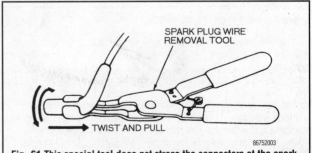

Fig. 61 This special tool does not stress the connectors at the spark plug boots, while making removal easier

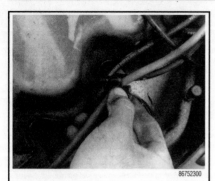

Fig. 62 Disconnect and reposition any plug wire separators that make it difficult to access the wire

Fig. 63 After cleaning around the spark plugs, use a spark plug socket to loosen the plugs

Fig. 64 Carefully remove the spark plug for inspection and replacement

✲✲ WARNING

Be sure not to use a flexible extension on the socket. Use of a flexible extension may allow a shear force to be applied to the plug. A shear force could break the plug off in the cylinder head, leading to costly and frustrating repairs.

To install:

5. Inspect the spark plug boot for tears or damage. If a damaged boot is found, the spark plug wire must be replaced.

6. Using a wire feeler gauge, check and adjust the spark plug gap. When using a gauge, the proper size should pass between the electrodes with a slight drag. The next larger size should not be able to pass while the next smaller size should pass freely.

7. Carefully thread the plug into the bore by hand. If resistance is felt before the plug is almost completely threaded, back the plug out and begin threading again. In small, hard to reach areas, an old spark plug wire and boot could be used as a threading tool. The boot will hold the plug while you twist the end of the wire and the wire is supple enough to twist before it would allow the plug to crossthread.

✲✲ WARNING

Do not use the spark plug socket to thread the plugs. Always carefully thread the plug by hand or using an old plug wire to prevent the possibility of crossthreading and damaging the cylinder head bore.

8. Carefully tighten the spark plug. If the plug you are installing is equipped with a crush washer, seat the plug, then tighten about ¼ turn to crush the washer. If you are installing a tapered seat plug, tighten the plug to specifications provided by the vehicle or plug manufacturer.

9. Apply a small amount of silicone dielectric compound to the end of the spark plug lead or inside the spark plug boot to prevent sticking, then install the boot to the spark plug and push until it clicks into place. The click may be felt or heard, then gently pull back on the boot to assure proper contact.

INSPECTION & GAPPING

▶ See Figures 65, 66, 67, 68 and 69

Check the plugs for deposits and wear. If they are not going to be replaced, clean the plugs thoroughly. Remember that any kind of deposit will decrease the efficiency of the plug. Plugs can be cleaned on a spark plug cleaning machine, which can sometimes be found in service stations, or you can do an acceptable job of cleaning with a stiff brush. If the plugs are cleaned, the electrodes must be filed flat. Use an ignition points file, not an emery board or the like, which will leave deposits. The electrodes must be filed perfectly flat with sharp edges; rounded edges reduce the spark plug voltage by as much as 50%.

Check spark plug gap before installation. The ground electrode (the L-shaped one connected to the body of the plug) must be parallel to the center electrode and the specified size wire gauge (please refer to the Tune-Up Specifications chart for details) must pass between the electrodes with a slight drag.

➡ **NEVER adjust the gap on a used platinum type spark plug.**

Always check the gap on new plugs as they are not always set correctly at the factory. Do not use a flat feeler gauge when measuring the gap on a used plug, because the reading may be inaccurate. A round-wire type gapping tool is the best way to check the gap. The correct gauge should pass through the electrode gap with a slight drag. If you're in doubt, try one size smaller and one larger. The smaller gauge should go through easily, while the larger one shouldn't go through at all. Wire gapping tools usually have a bending tool attached. Use that to adjust the side electrode until the proper distance is obtained. Absolutely never attempt to bend the center electrode. Also, be careful not to bend the side electrode too far or too often as it may weaken and break off within the engine, requiring removal of the cylinder head to retrieve it.

Spark Plug Wires

TESTING

▶ See Figures 70 and 71

At every tune-up/inspection, visually check the spark plug cables for burns cuts, or breaks in the insulation. Check the boots and the nipples on the distributor cap and/or coil. Replace any damaged wiring.

Every 50,000 miles (80,000 km) or 60 months, the resistance of the wires should be checked with an ohmmeter. Wires with excessive resistance will cause misfiring, and may make the engine difficult to start in damp weather.

To check resistance, an ohmmeter should be used on each wire to test resistance between the end connectors. Remove and install/replace the wires in order, one-by-one.

Resistance on these wires must not exceed 7,000 ohms per foot. To properly measure this, remove the wires from the plugs, coil, or the distributor cap. Do not pierce any ignition wire for any reason. Measure only from the two ends.

➡ **Whenever the high tension wires are removed from the plugs, coil, or distributor, silicone grease must be applied to the boot before reconnection. Coat the entire interior surface with Ford silicone grease D7AZ-19A331-A or its equivalent.**

REMOVAL & INSTALLATION

▶ See Figure 72

When you're removing spark plug wires, work on one at a time. Don't start by removing the plug wires all at once, because, unless you number them, they may become mixed up. Take a minute before you begin and number the wires with tape.

1. Disconnect the negative battery cable, and if the vehicle has been run recently, allow the engine to thoroughly cool.

2. Carefully twist the spark plug wire boot to loosen it, then pull upward and remove the boot from the plug. Be sure to pull on the boot and not on the wire, otherwise the connector located inside the boot may become separated.

3. Carefully twist the spark plug wire boot to loosen it, then pull upward and remove the boot from the distributor towers or coil tower. Be sure to pull on the

A normally worn spark plug should have light tan or gray deposits on the firing tip.

A carbon fouled plug, identified by soft, sooty, black deposits, may indicate an improperly tuned vehicle. Check the air cleaner, ignition components and engine control system.

This spark plug has been **left in the engine too long,** as evidenced by the extreme gap- Plugs with such an extreme gap can cause misfiring and stumbling accompanied by a noticeable lack of power.

An oil fouled spark plug indicates an engine with worn poston rings and/or bad valve seals allowing excessive oil to enter the chamber.

A physically damaged spark plug may be evidence of severe detonation in that cylinder. Watch that cylinder carefully between services, as a continued detonation will not only damage the plug, but could also damage the engine.

A bridged or almost bridged spark plug, identified by a build-up between the electrodes caused by excessive carbon or oil build-up on the plug.

TCCA1P40

Fig. 65 Inspect the spark plug to determine engine running conditions

TCCS1212
Fig. 66 A variety of tools and gauges are needed for spark plug service

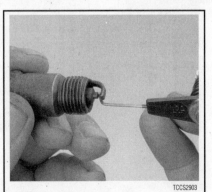
TCCS2903
Fig. 67 Checking the spark plug gap with a feeler gauge

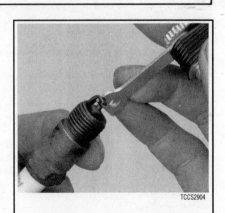
TCCS2904
Fig. 68 Adjusting the spark plug gap

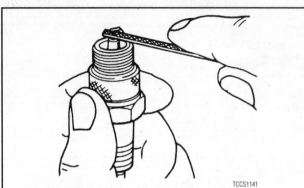

Fig. 69 If the standard plug is in good condition, the electrode may be filed flat—WARNING: do not file platinum plugs

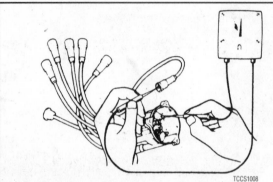

Fig. 70 Checking plug wire resistance through the distributor cap with an ohmmeter

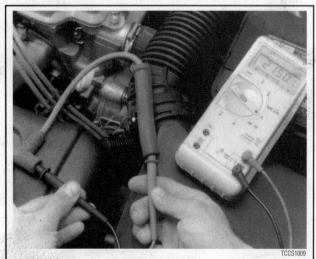

Fig. 71 Checking individual plug wire resistance with a digital ohmmeter

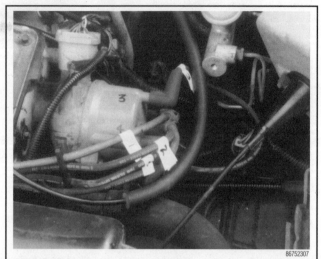

Fig. 72 Labeling the wires and the cap (if necessary) prevents confusion upon re-installation

Distributor Cap and Rotor

REMOVAL & INSTALLATION

1. Disconnect the negative battery cable.
2. Matchmark the spark plug wires to their respective towers on the distributor cap.
3. Disconnect the spark plug wires from the cap.
4. Loosen the distributor cap's hold-down screws.
5. Remove the distributor cap.
6. On models where the rotor is retained by screws, loosen the rotor retaining screws an remove the rotor.
7. On models were the rotor is not retained with screws, grasp the rotor and pull it from the shaft.

To install:

8. On models where the rotor is retained by screws, position the rotor with the square and round locator pins matched to the distributor weight plate. Tighten the screws until they are snug.
9. On models were the rotor is not retained with screws, align the rotor locating boss with the appropriate hole in the distributor, then press the rotor into position.
10. Position the cap on the distributor and fasten the hold-down screws.
11. Install the spark plug wires.
12. Start the vehicle and check for proper operation.

INSPECTION

1. Remove the distributor cap and rotor.
2. Wash the inside and outside of the cap, as well as the rotor, with soap and water, then dry them thoroughly with compressed air or a lint-free cloth.
3. Look closely at the distributor cap, inspecting it for signs of deterioration such as cracks, a broken carbon button or carbon tracks.
4. Inspect the terminals for dirt or corrosion.
5. Inspect the rotor for carbon build-up, cracks or damage to the blade or spring.
6. If damage is found, replace the distributor cap and/or rotor.

Ignition Timing

INSPECTION & ADJUSTMENT

The timing marks on the 1.3L, 1.6L and 1.9L engines consists of a notch on the crankshaft pulley and a graduated scale molded into the camshaft drive belt cover. The number of degrees before or after Top Dead Center (TDC) repre-

boot and not on the wire, otherwise the connector located inside the boot may become separated.

To install:

4. Apply a small amount of silicone dielectric compound to the end of the spark plug lead or inside the spark plug boot to prevent sticking, then install the boot to the spark plug and push until it clicks into place. The click may be felt or heard, then gently pull back on the boot to assure proper contact.
5. Push the boot onto the distributor tower or coil tower until it is firmly engaged.

sented by each mark can be interpreted according to the decal affixed to the top of the belt cover (emissions decal).

Carbureted Engines

▶ **See Figure 73**

1. Place the transaxle in the **P** or **N** position. Firmly apply the parking brake and block the wheels.
2. Turn **OFF** all accessories (A/C, heater, radio, etc.).
3. Once the timing marks are located, clean with a stiff brush or solvent, if necessary.
4. Remove the vacuum hoses from the distributor vacuum advance connection at the distributor and plug the hoses.
5. Connect a suitable inductive-type timing light to the No. 1 spark plug wire. Do not puncture an ignition wire with any type of probing device.
6. Connect a suitable tachometer to the engine.
7. If the vehicle is equipped with a barometric pressure switch, unplug it from the ignition module and place a jumper wire across the pins at the ignition module connector (yellow and black wires).
8. Start the engine and let it run until it reaches normal operating temperature.
9. Check the engine idle rpm if it is not within specifications, adjust as necessary. After the rpm has been adjusted or checked, aim the timing light at the timing marks. If they are not aligned, loosen the distributor clamp bolts slightly and rotate the distributor body until the marks are aligned under timing light illumination.
10. Tighten the distributor clamp bolts and recheck the ignition timing. Turn the engine **OFF**, remove all test equipment.
11. Unplug and reconnect the vacuum hoses.
12. Remove the jumper wire from the ignition module connector.
13. Attach the barometric pressure switch connector.

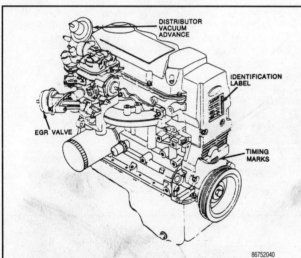

Fig. 73 Location of the ignition timing marks necessary to check and adjust timing—1.3L, 1.6L and 1.9L carbureted engines

Fuel Injected Engines

▶ **See Figure 74**

1. Place the transaxle in the **P** or **N** position. Firmly apply the parking brake and block the wheels.
2. Turn **OFF** all accessories (A/C, heater, etc.).
3. Locate the timing marks and if necessary, clean the marks with a stiff brush or solvent.
4. Connect a suitable inductive type timing light to the No. 1 spark plug wire. Do not puncture an ignition wire with any type of probing device.
5. Connect a suitable tachometer to the engine.
6. Unplug the single wire white connector near the distributor.
7. Start the engine and let it run until it reaches normal operating temperature.
8. Check the engine idle rpm if it is not within specifications, adjust as necessary. After the rpm has been adjusted or checked, aim the timing light at

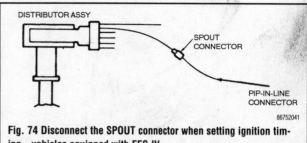

Fig. 74 Disconnect the SPOUT connector when setting ignition timing—vehicles equipped with EEC-IV

the timing marks. If they are not aligned, loosen the distributor clamp bolts slightly and rotate the distributor body until the marks are aligned under timing light illumination.

9. Tighten the distributor clamp bolts and recheck the ignition timing.
10. Attach the single wire white connector near the distributor and check the timing advance to verify the distributor is advancing beyond the initial setting.
11. Shut the engine **OFF**, remove all test equipment.

Valve Lash

ADJUSTMENT

The intake and exhaust valves are driven by the camshaft, working through hydraulic lash adjusters and stamped steel rocker arms. The lash adjusters eliminate the need for periodic valve lash adjustments.

Idle Speed and Mixture Adjustments

➡️Most carburetor adjustments are factory set, and are based on guidelines to reduce engine emissions and to improve performance. When performing any idle speed adjustments, a tachometer must be used. Follow the manufacturer's instructions for proper hook-up of the tachometer being used. Refer to the emissions decal for idle speed and specific instructions. If the decal instructions differ from the following procedures, use the decal procedures. They reflect planned production changes.

CURB IDLE

Carbureted Engines

740 CARBURETOR WITHOUT IDLE SPEED CONTROL

▶ **See Figures 75 and 76**

1. Place the transaxle in **P** or **N**. Set the parking brake and block the wheels.
2. Connect a tachometer to the engine.
3. Bring the engine to normal operating temperature.
4. Disconnect and plug the vacuum hose at the thermactor air control valve bypass sections.
5. Place the fast idle adjustment screw on the second highest step of the fast idle cam. Run the engine until the cooling fan comes on.
6. Slightly depress the throttle to allow the fast idle cam to rotate. On models with an automatic transaxle, place the transaxle in **D**, then check and adjust, if necessary, the curb idle speed to specification.

➡️**The engine cooling fan must be running when checking curb idle rpm. (Use of a jumper wire is necessary.)**

7. Place the transaxle in **P** or **N**. Increase the engine rpm momentarily. On models with an automatic transaxle, place the transaxle in **D** and recheck curb idle speed. Readjust if required.
8. If the vehicle is equipped with a dashpot, check/adjust the clearance to specification.
9. Remove the plug from the hose at the thermactor air control valve bypass sections and reconnect.
10. If the vehicle is equipped with an automatic transaxle and the required curb idle adjustment is more than 50 rpm, an automatic transaxle linkage adjustment may be necessary.

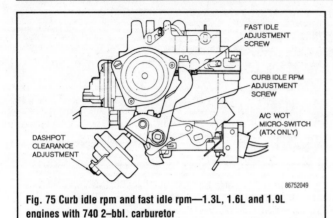

Fig. 75 Curb idle rpm and fast idle rpm—1.3L, 1.6L and 1.9L engines with 740 2-bbl. carburetor

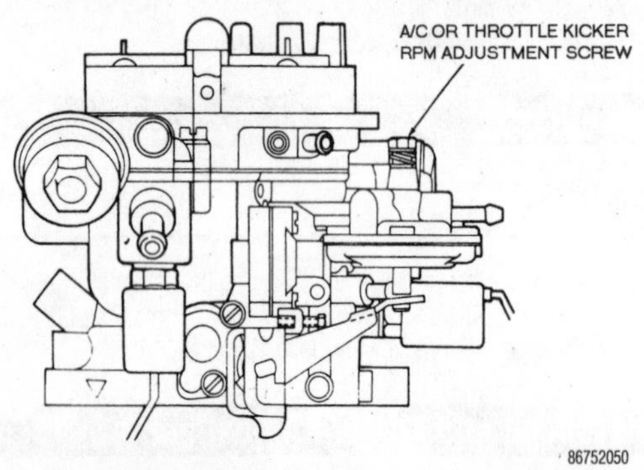

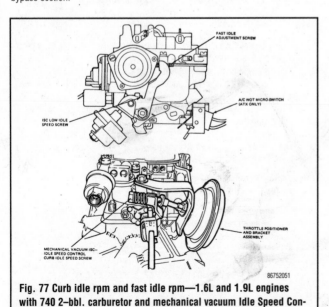

Fig. 76 A/C or throttle kicker rpm set—1.3L, 1.6L and 1.9L engines with 740 2-bbl. carburetor

740/5740 CARBURETOR WITH MECHANICAL VACUUM IDLE SPEED CONTROL (ISC)

▶ **See Figure 77**

1. Place the transaxle in **P** or **N**. Set the parking brake and block the wheels. Connect a tachometer to the engine.
2. Bring the engine to normal operating temperature.
3. Disconnect and plug the vacuum hose at the thermactor air control valve bypass section.

Fig. 77 Curb idle rpm and fast idle rpm—1.6L and 1.9L engines with 740 2-bbl. carburetor and mechanical vacuum Idle Speed Control (ISC)

4. Place the fast idle adjustment screw on the second highest step of the fast idle cam. Run the engine until the cooling fan comes on.
5. Slightly depress the throttle to allow the fast idle cam to rotate. Place the transaxle in **D** (fan on) and check curb idle rpm is within specification.

➡ **The engine cooling fan must be running when checking curb idle rpm.**

6. If adjustment is required:
   a. Place the transaxle in **P**. Deactivate the Idle Speed Control (ISC) by removing the vacuum hose at the ISC and plugging the hose.
   b. Turn the ISC adjusting screw until the ISC plunger is clear of the throttle lever.
   c. Place the transaxle in the **D** position; if rpm is not at the ISC retracted speed (fan on), adjust the rpm by turning the throttle stop adjusting screw.
   d. Place the transaxle in **P**. Remove the plug from the ISC vacuum line and reconnect the ISC.
   e. Place the transaxle in **D**. If rpm is not at the curb idle speed (fan on), adjust by turning the ISC adjustment screw.
7. Place the transaxle in **P** or **N**. Increase the engine rpm momentarily. Place the transaxle in the specified position and recheck the curb idle rpm. Readjust if necessary.
8. Remove the plug from the thermactor air control valve bypass section hose and reconnect.
9. If the vehicle is equipped with an automatic transaxle and the required curb idle adjustment is more than 50 rpm, an automatic transaxle linkage adjustment may be necessary.

740/5740 CARBURETOR WITH VACUUM OPERATED THROTTLE MODULATOR (VOTM)

▶ **See Figure 78**

1. Place the transaxle in **P** or **N**. Set the parking brake and block the wheels. Connect a tachometer to the engine.
2. Bring the engine to normal operating temperature.
3. To check or adjust Vacuum Operated Throttle Modulator (VOTM) rpm:
   a. Place the air conditioning heat selector in the Heat position, with the blower switch on High.
   b. Disconnect the vacuum hose from the VOTM and plug the hose, then install a slave vacuum hose from the intake manifold vacuum to the VOTM.
4. Disconnect and plug the vacuum hose at the thermactor air control valve bypass section.
5. Run the engine until the engine cooling fan comes on.
6. Place the transaxle in specified gear, and check/adjust VOTM rpm until it is within specification.

➡ **The engine cooling fan must be running when checking VOTM rpm. Adjust the rpm by turning the screw on the VOTM.**

7. Remove the slave vacuum hose.

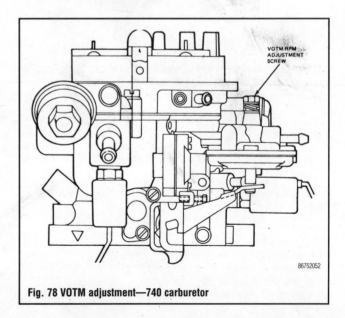

Fig. 78 VOTM adjustment—740 carburetor

8. Remove the plug from the VOTM vacuum hose and connect the hose to the VOTM.

9. Return the intake manifold vacuum supply source to its original location.

10. Remove the plug from the vacuum hose at the thermactor air control valve bypass section and reconnect the hose.

Fuel Injected Engines

1984–85 1.6L AND 1986 1.9L MODELS

➡Curb idle speed is controlled by the EEC-IV processor and the Idle Speed Control (ISC) device (part of the fuel charging assembly). The purpose of this procedure is to provide a means of verifying the initial engine rpm setting with the ISC disconnected. If engine idle rpm is not within specification after performing this procedure, it will be necessary to perform diagnostic procedures on the 1.6L or 1.9L MFI EEC-IV system.

1. Place the transaxle in **P** or **N**. Set the parking brake and block the wheels.
2. Connect a tachometer to the engine.
3. Bring the engine to the normal operating temperature and shut the engine **OFF**.
4. Unplug the vacuum connector at the EGR solenoids and plug both lines.
5. Unplug the Idle Speed Control (ISC) electrical connection.
6. The electric cooling fan must be on during the idle speed setting procedure.
7. Start the engine and operate it at 2000 rpm for 60 seconds.
8. Place transaxle in **P** (automatic) or **N** (manual). Check or adjust the initial engine rpm within 120 seconds by adjusting the throttle plate screw.
9. If idle adjustment is not completed within the 120 second time limit, turn the engine **OFF**, then restart it and repeat Steps 6 and 7.
10. If the vehicle is equipped with an automatic transaxle and the initial engine rpm adjustment increases or decreases by more than 50 rpm, an automatic transaxle linkage adjustment may be necessary.
11. Turn the engine **OFF**. Remove the plugs from the EGR vacuum lines at the EGR solenoid and connect the lines.
12. Attach the ISC electrical connection.

1987–90 MODELS WITH CENTRAL FUEL INJECTION (CFI)

▸ **See Figures 79 and 80**

➡The idle speed and idle mixture adjustments are controlled by on-board vehicle computerized engine controls. Also, in order to adjust the idle speed on this model, it is necessary to remove the Central Fuel Injection (CFI) assembly from the vehicle, in order to gain access to and remove the tamper resistant plug covering the throttle stop adjusting screw. This procedure should be performed by an authorized factory technician.

It is recommended that the Idle Speed Control (ISC) motor be checked to see if is functioning correctly, before performing the curb idle adjustment. This can be done as follows:

1. Start the engine and run it for at least 30 seconds, then turn the ignition switch to the **OFF** position. Visually inspect the ISC motor to see if it is retracting and repositioning.

➡**If, for any reason, the battery has been disconnected or the vehicle has been jump started, this procedure may need to be performed.**

2. Set the parking brake and block the wheels. Make all checks and/or adjustments at normal operating temperature with all accessories **OFF**. Only a suitable tachometer is needed for this procedure. Before any adjustments are made, check for vacuum leaks and repair as necessary.

3. Place the transaxle in **P** (automatic) or **N** (manual). Idle the engine for approximately 120 seconds, and check to see that the idle speed is within specifications. The engine speed should then increase by approximately 75 rpm, when the transaxle is put in **D** or **N**.

4. Lightly step on and off the accelerator pedal. The engine rpm should return to specification. If the rpm remains high, wait 120 seconds and repeat the sequence. Remember, it may take the computerized system 120 seconds to relearn the program.

➡**Curb and fast idle speeds are controlled by the on-board computer and the Idle Speed Control (ISC) device. If the control system is operating properly, these speeds are fixed and cannot be changed by traditional adjustment techniques.**

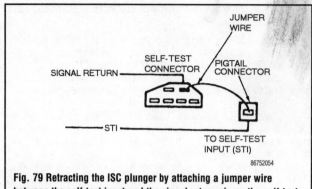

Fig. 79 Retracting the ISC plunger by attaching a jumper wire between the self-test input and the signal return pin on the self-test connector—1.9L CFI engine

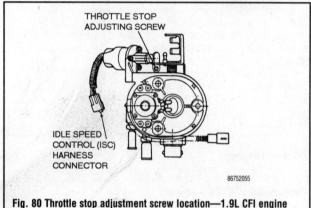

Fig. 80 Throttle stop adjustment screw location—1.9L CFI engine

Adjustments are sometimes required to establish the correct operating limit in which the ISC system can properly function. This adjustment, as outlined below, will normally have no direct effect on the actual idle speed, and generally will not be required unless the curb idle is higher than specified.

Misadjustment of the operating limit could restrict the operating range of the ISC system, so adjustment of this limit should never be made unless a specific causal factor exists. If the operating limit adjustment does not correct an out-of-specification curb idle speed, it will be necessary to take the vehicle to a factory authorized technician for further diagnostic evaluation. Perform the adjustment as follows:

5. With the engine **OFF**, remove the air cleaner assembly. Attach a jumper wire between the self-test input and the signal return pin on the self-test connector.

6. Turn the ignition to the **ON** position, but do not start the engine. The ISC plunger should retract within 10–15 seconds. If the plunger does not retract, there is a malfunction within the on-board diagnostic system, and the vehicle should be taken to a factory authorized technician for further diagnostic evaluation.

7. Unplug the ISC harness connector. Turn the ignition key **OFF** and remove the jumper wire.

8. Start the engine and check the idle rpm; if not within specification, perform the following procedure:

   a. With the engine **OFF**, remove the CFI assembly from the vehicle.
   b. Remove the tamper-resistant plug that covers the throttle stop adjusting screw.
   c. Remove the old throttle stop adjusting screw and install a new screw.
   d. Install the CFI assembly back on the intake manifold/engine.

9. Start the engine and let the idle stabilize. Adjust the throttle stop adjusting screw until the specified rpm is reached.

10. Turn the engine **OFF** and attach the ISC motor electrical connection. Make sure that the throttle plate is not binding in the bore or that the linkage is preventing the throttle plate from returning.

11. Install the air cleaner assembly.

12. Be sure to refer to the underhood emission/calibration sticker for the engine idle rpm specification. If the specifications on the sticker differ from the specifications in this manual, the specifications on the sticker should be followed.

1987–90 1.9L HIGH OUTPUT (HO) MODELS WITH ELECTRONIC FUEL INJECTION (EFI)

1. Apply the parking brake and block the wheels. Place the transaxle in **N** and start the engine. Allow the engine to run until it reaches normal operating temperature. Turn off all accessories and turn the engine **OFF**.

2. Unplug the Idle Speed Control (ISC) electrical connection.

3. Start the engine and run it at 2000 rpm for approximately one minute, then return it to idle.

4. Unplug the EGR vacuum connection at the EGR solenoid and plug both lines (if so equipped).

5. Unplug the idle speed control bypass air solenoid electrical connection (if so equipped).

6. With the transaxle in **D** (automatic) or **N** (manual), check to see that the idle speed is 900–1000 rpm. If the idle speed is not within specifications, go on to the next step.

7. Make sure that the cooling fan is **OFF**. Turn the throttle plate adjusting screw until the idle is within specifications. Adjustment must be made within 2 minutes after returning to idle.

8. If the idle speed adjustment was necessary, repeat Steps 2 through 6.

9. Once the idle has been set to specifications, turn the ignition **OFF**.

10. Attach the ISC electrical connection. Make sure that the throttle plate is not binding in the bore or that the linkage is preventing the throttle plate from returning.

11. To make sure that the proper adjustment was made, run the engine at 2000 rpm for approximately one minute and return it to idle. Be sure to refer to the underhood emission/calibration sticker for the engine idle speed specification.

FAST IDLE

Carbureted Engines

1. Place the transaxle in **P** or **N**. Set the parking brake and block the wheels. Connect a tachometer to the engine.

2. Bring the engine to normal operating temperature.

3. Disconnect the vacuum hose at the EGR and plug.

4. Place the fast idle adjustment screw on the second highest step of the fast idle cam. Run the engine until the cooling fan comes on.

5. Check, and if necessary, adjust fast idle rpm to specification. If adjustment is required, loosen the locknut, adjust and retighten.

➡**The engine cooling fan must be running when checking the fast idle rpm. (Use of a jumper wire is necessary).**

6. Remove the plug from the EGR hose and reconnect.

Fuel Injected Engines

➡**Curb and fast idle speeds are controlled by the on-board computer and the Idle Speed Control (ISC) device. If the control system is operating properly, these speeds are fixed and cannot be changed by traditional adjustment techniques.**

DASHPOT CLEARANCE

Carbureted Engines

If so equipped, the dashpot must be adjusted when the curb idle speed is adjusted.

1. With the engine **OFF**, push the dashpot plunger in as far as possible and check the clearance between the plunger and the throttle lever pad.

➡**Refer to the emissions decal for proper dashpot clearance. If not available, set the clearance to 0.118–0.158 in. (3–4mm).**

2. Adjust the dashpot clearance by loosening the mounting locknut and rotating the dashpot.

➡**If the locknut is very tight, remove the mounting bracket and hold it in a suitable device so that it will not bend, then loosen the locknut.**

TUNE-UP SPECIFICATIONS

Year	Engine ID/VIN	Engine Displacement Liters (CI)	Spark Plugs Gap (in.)	Ignition Timing (deg.) MT	AT	Fuel Pump (psi)	Idle Speed (rpm) MT	AT	Valve Clearance In.	Ex.
1981	1	1.3L (79)	0.044	10B	10B	4.5-6.5 ②	①	①	HYD	HYD
	2	1.6L (98)	0.044	10B	10B	4.5-6.5 ②	①	①	HYD	HYD
1982	2	1.6L (98)	0.044	10B	10B	4.5-6.5 ②	①	①	HYD	HYD
1983	2	1.6L (98)	0.044	10B	10B	4.5-6.5 ②	①	①	HYD	HYD
	4	1.6 HO (98)	0.044	10B	10B	4.5-6.5 ②	①	①	HYD	HYD
	5	1.6 (98)	0.044	10B	10B	30-45	①	①	HYD	HYD
1984	2	1.6 (98)	0.044	10B	10B	4.5-6.5 ②	①	①	HYD	HYD
	4	1.6 HO (98)	0.044	10B	10B	4.5-6.5 ②	①	①	HYD	HYD
	5	1.6 (98)	0.044	10B	10B	30-45	①	①	HYD	HYD
	8	1.6 Turbo (98)	0.044	10B	10B	30-45	①	①	HYD	HYD
1985	2	1.6 (98)	0.044	10B	10B	4.5-6.5 ②	①	①	HYD	HYD
	4	1.6 HO (98)	0.044	10B	10B	4.5-6.5 ②	①	①	HYD	HYD
	5	1.6 (98)	0.044	10B	10B	30-45	①	①	HYD	HYD
	8	1.6 Turbo (98)	0.044	10B	10B	30-45	①	①	HYD	HYD
1986	9	1.9 (114)	0.044	10B	10B	4.5-6.5 ②	①	①	HYD	HYD
	J	1.9 HO (114)	0.044	10B	10B	30-45	①	①	HYD	HYD
1987	9	1.9 (114)	0.044	10B	10B	4.5-6.5 ②	①	①	HYD	HYD
	J	1.9 HO (114)	0.044	10B	10B	30-45	①	①	HYD	HYD
1988	9	1.9 (114)	0.044	10B	10B	13-17	①	①	HYD	HYD
	J	1.9 HO (114)	0.044	10B	10B	30-45	①	①	HYD	HYD
1989	9	1.9 (114)	0.044	10B	10B	13-17	①	①	HYD	HYD
	J	1.9 HO (114)	0.044	10B	10B	30-45	①	①	HYD	HYD
1990	9	1.9 (114)	0.044	10B	10B	13-17	①	①	HYD	HYD
	J	1.9 HO (114)	0.044	10B	10B	30-45	①	①	HYD	HYD

HO–High Output

CI–Cubic Inches

HYD–Hydraulic

① Refer to the underhood sticker

② With fuel return line closed at filter

90931C03

3. Install the bracket and dashpot.

4. After gaining the required clearance, tighten the locknut and recheck adjustment.

THROTTLE KICKER

Carbureted Engines

1. Place the transaxle in **P** or **N**.

2. Bring engine to normal operating temperature.

3. Identify the vacuum source which goes to the air bypass section of the air supply control valve. If the vacuum hose is attached to the carburetor, disconnect and plug the hose at the air supply control valve. Attach the slave vacuum hose between the intake manifold and the air bypass connection on the air supply control valve.

4. To check or adjust the air conditioning or throttle kicker rpm:

   a. If the vehicle is equipped with air conditioning, place the selector to maximum cooling, with the blower switch on HIGH, and unplug the air conditioning compressor clutch wire.

   b. If the vehicle is equipped with the kicker and has no air conditioning, disconnect and plug the vacuum hose from the kicker. Attach the slave vacuum hose from the intake manifold vacuum to the kicker.

5. Run the engine until the engine cooling fan comes **ON**.

6. On models equipped with an automatic transaxle, place the transaxle in **D** and check/adjust the air conditioning or throttle kicker rpm until it is within specification.

➡**The engine cooling fan must be running when checking the air conditioning or throttle kicker rpm. Adjust the rpm by turning the screw on the kicker.**

7. If a slave vacuum hose was installed to check/adjust the kicker rpm, remove the slave vacuum hose.

8. Remove the plug from the kicker vacuum hose and reconnect the hose to the kicker.

9. Remove the slave vacuum hose. Return the intake manifold supply source to its original condition.

10. Remove the plug from the carburetor vacuum hose and reconnect the hose to the air bypass valve.

Air Conditioning System

SYSTEM SERVICE & REPAIR

➡**It is recommended that the A/C system be serviced by an EPA Section 609 certified automotive technician utilizing a refrigerant recovery/recycling machine.**

The do-it-yourselfer should not service his/her own vehicle's A/C system for many reasons, including legal concerns, personal injury, environmental damage and cost. The following are some of the reasons why you may decide not to service your own vehicle's A/C system.

According to the U.S. Clean Air Act, it is a federal crime to service or repair (involving the refrigerant) a Motor Vehicle Air Conditioning (MVAC) system for money without being EPA certified. It is also illegal to vent R-12 and R-134a refrigerants into the atmosphere. Selling or distributing A/C system refrigerant (in a container which contains less than 20 pounds of refrigerant) to any person who is not EPA 609 certified is also not allowed by law.

State and/or local laws may be more strict than the federal regulations, so be sure to check with your state and/or local authorities for further information. For further federal information on the legality of servicing your A/C system, call the EPA Stratospheric Ozone Hotline.

➡**Federal law dictates that a fine of up to $25,000 may be levied on people convicted of venting refrigerant into the atmosphere. Additionally, the EPA may pay up to $10,000 for information or services leading to a criminal conviction of the violation of these laws.**

When servicing an A/C system you run the risk of handling or coming in contact with refrigerant, which may result in skin or eye irritation or frostbite. Although low in toxicity (due to chemical stability), inhalation of concentrated refrigerant fumes is dangerous and can result in death; cases of fatal cardiac

arrhythmia have been reported in people accidentally subjected to high levels of refrigerant. Some early symptoms include loss of concentration and drowsiness.

➡**Generally, the limit for exposure is lower for R-134a than it is for R-12. Exceptional care must be practiced when handling R-134a.**

Also, refrigerants can decompose at high temperatures (near gas heaters or open flame), which may result in hydrofluoric acid, hydrochloric acid and phosgene (a fatal nerve gas).

R-12 refrigerant can damage the environment because it is a Chlorofluorocarbon (CFC), which has been proven to add to ozone layer depletion, leading to increasing levels of UV radiation. UV radiation has been linked with an increase in skin cancer, suppression of the human immune system, an increase in cataracts, damage to crops, damage to aquatic organisms, an increase in ground-level ozone, and increased global warming.

R-134a refrigerant is a greenhouse gas which, if allowed to vent into the atmosphere, will contribute to global warming (the Greenhouse Effect).

It is usually more economically feasible to have a certified MVAC automotive technician perform A/C system service on your vehicle. Some possible reasons for this are as follows:

• While it is illegal to service an A/C system without the proper equipment, the home mechanic would have to purchase an expensive refrigerant recovery/recycling machine to service his/her own vehicle.

• Since only a certified person may purchase refrigerant-according to the Clean Air Act, there are specific restrictions on selling or distributing A/C system refrigerant-it is legally impossible (unless certified) for the home mechanic to service his/her own vehicle. Procuring refrigerant in an illegal fashion exposes one to the risk of paying a $25,000 fine to the EPA.

R-12 Refrigerant Conversion

If your vehicle still uses R-12 refrigerant, one way to save A/C system costs down the road is to investigate the possibility of having your system converted to R-134a. The older R-12 systems can be easily converted to R-134a refrigerant by a certified automotive technician by installing a few new components and changing the system oil.

The cost of R-12 is steadily rising and will continue to increase, because it is no longer imported or manufactured in the United States. Therefore, it is often possible to have an R-12 system converted to R-134a and recharged for less than it would cost to just charge the system with R-12.

If you are interested in having your system converted, contact local automotive service stations for more details and information.

PREVENTIVE MAINTENANCE

▶ **See Figures 81 and 82**

Although the A/C system should not be serviced by the do-it-yourselfer, preventive maintenance can be practiced and A/C system inspections can be performed to help maintain the efficiency of the vehicle's A/C system. For preventive maintenance, perform the following:

• The easiest and most important preventive maintenance for your A/C system is to be sure that it is used on a regular basis. Running the system for five minutes each month (no matter what the season) will help ensure that the seals and all internal components remain lubricated.

➡**Some newer vehicles automatically operate the A/C system compressor whenever the windshield defroster is activated. When running, the compressor lubricates the A/C system components; therefore, the A/C system would not need to be operated each month.**

• In order to prevent heater core freeze-up during A/C operation, it is necessary to maintain proper antifreeze protection. Use a hand-held coolant tester (hydrometer) to periodically check the condition of the antifreeze in your engine's cooling system.

➡**Antifreeze should not be used longer than the manufacturer specifies.**

• For efficient operation of an air conditioned vehicle's cooling system, the radiator cap should have a holding pressure which meets manufacturer's specifications. A cap which fails to hold these pressures should be replaced.

• Any obstruction of or damage to the condenser configuration will restrict air flow which is essential to its efficient operation. It is, therefore, a good rule to keep this unit clean and in proper physical shape.

Fig. 81 A coolant tester can be used to determine the freezing and boiling levels of the coolant in your vehicle

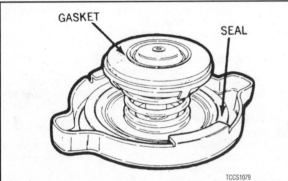

Fig. 82 To ensure efficient cooling system operation, inspect the radiator cap gasket and seal

➡Bug screens which are mounted in front of the condenser (unless they are original equipment) are regarded as obstructions.

• The condensation drain tube expels any water which accumulates on the bottom of the evaporator housing into the engine compartment. If this tube is obstructed, the air conditioning performance can be restricted and condensation buildup can spill over onto the vehicle's floor.

SYSTEM INSPECTION

♦ See Figure 83

Although the A/C system should not be serviced by the do-it-yourselfer, preventive maintenance can be practiced and A/C system inspections can be performed to help maintain the efficiency of the vehicle's A/C system. For A/C system inspection, perform the following:

The easiest and often most important check for the air conditioning system consists of a visual inspection of the system components. Visually inspect the air conditioning system for refrigerant leaks, damaged compressor clutch, abnormal compressor drive belt tension and/or condition, plugged evaporator drain tube, blocked condenser fins, disconnected or broken wires, blown fuses, corroded connections and poor insulation.

A refrigerant leak will usually appear as an oily residue at the leakage point in the system. The oily residue soon picks up dust or dirt particles from the surrounding air and appears greasy. Through time, this will build up and appear to be a heavy dirt impregnated grease.

For a thorough visual and operational inspection, check the following:
• Check the surface of the radiator and condenser for dirt, leaves or other material which might block air flow.
• Check for kinks in hoses and lines. Check the system for leaks.

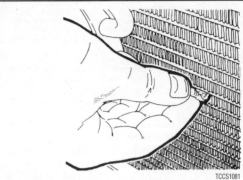

Fig. 83 Periodically remove any debris from the condenser and radiator fins

• Make sure the drive belt is properly tensioned. When the air conditioning is operating, make sure the drive belt is free of noise or slippage.
• Make sure the blower motor operates at all appropriate positions, then check for distribution of the air from all outlets with the blower on **HIGH** or **MAX**.

➡Keep in mind that under conditions of high humidity, air discharged from the A/C vents may not feel as cold as expected, even if the system is working properly. This is because vaporized moisture in humid air retains heat more effectively than dry air, thereby making humid air more difficult to cool.

• Make sure the air passage selection lever is operating correctly. Start the engine and warm it to normal operating temperature, then make sure the temperature selection lever is operating correctly.

Windshield Wipers

ELEMENT (REFILL) CARE & REPLACEMENT

♦ See Figures 84, 85 and 86

For maximum effectiveness and longest element life, the windshield and wiper blades should be kept clean. Dirt, tree sap, road tar and so on will cause streaking, smearing and blade deterioration if left on the glass. It is advisable to wash the windshield carefully with a commercial glass cleaner at least once a month. Wipe off the rubber blades with the wet rag afterwards. Do not attempt to move wipers across the windshield by hand; damage to the motor and drive mechanism will result.

To inspect and/or replace the wiper blade elements, place the wiper switch in the **LOW** speed position and the ignition switch in the **ACC** position. When the wiper blades are approximately vertical on the windshield, turn the ignition switch to **OFF**.

Examine the wiper blade elements. If they are found to be cracked, broken or torn, they should be replaced immediately. Replacement intervals will vary with usage, although ozone deterioration usually limits element life to about one year. If the wiper pattern is smeared or streaked, or if the blade chatters across the glass, the elements should be replaced. It is easiest and most sensible to replace the elements in pairs.

If your vehicle is equipped with aftermarket blades, there are several different types of refills and your vehicle might have any kind. Aftermarket blades and arms rarely use the exact same type blade or refill as the original equipment.

Regardless of the type of refill used, be sure to follow the part manufacturer's instructions closely. Make sure that all of the frame jaws are engaged as the refill is pushed into place and locked. If the metal blade holder and frame are allowed to touch the glass during wiper operation, the glass will be scratched.

Tires and Wheels

Common sense and good driving habits will afford maximum tire life. Make sure that you don't overload the vehicle or run with incorrect pressure in the tires. Either of these will increase tread wear. Fast starts, sudden stops and sharp cornering are hard on tires and will shorten their useful life span.

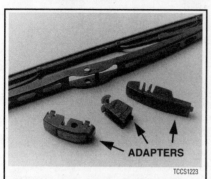

Fig. 84 Most aftermarket blades are available with multiple adapters to fit different vehicles

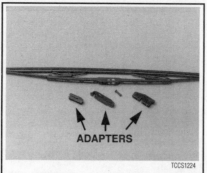

Fig. 85 Choose a blade which will fit your vehicle, and that will be readily available next time you need blades

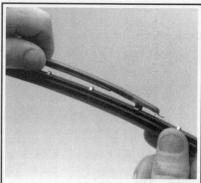

Fig. 86 When installed, be certain the blade is fully inserted into the backing

➡️**For optimum tire life, keep the tires properly inflated, rotate them often and have the wheel alignment checked periodically.**

Inspect your tires frequently. Be especially careful to watch for bubbles in the tread or sidewall, deep cuts or underinflation. Replace any tires with bubbles in the sidewall. If cuts are so deep that they penetrate to the cords, discard the tire. Any cut in the sidewall of a radial tire renders it unsafe. Also look for uneven tread wear patterns that may indicate the front end is out of alignment or that the tires are out of balance.

TIRE ROTATION

▶ **See Figure 87**

Tires must be rotated periodically to equalize wear patterns that vary with a tire's position on the vehicle. Tires will also wear in an uneven way as the front steering/suspension system wears to the point where the alignment should be reset.

Rotating the tires will ensure maximum life for the tires as a set, so you will not have to discard a tire early due to wear on only part of the tread. Regular rotation is required to equalize wear.

When rotating "unidirectional tires," make sure that they always roll in the same direction. This means that a tire used on the left side of the vehicle must not be switched to the right side and vice-versa. Such tires should only be rotated front-to-rear or rear-to-front, while always remaining on the same side of the vehicle. These tires are marked on the sidewall as to the direction of rotation; observe the marks when reinstalling the tire(s).

Some styled or "mag" wheels may have different offsets front to rear. In these cases, the rear wheels must not be used up front and vice-versa. Furthermore, if these wheels are equipped with unidirectional tires, they cannot be rotated unless the tire is remounted for the proper direction of rotation.

➡️**The compact or space-saver spare is strictly for emergency use. It must never be included in the tire rotation or placed on the vehicle for everyday use.**

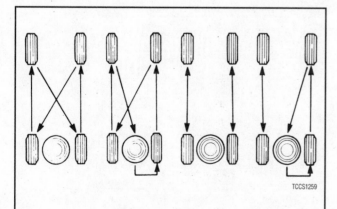

Fig. 87 Common tire rotation patterns for 4 and 5–wheel rotations

TIRE DESIGN

▶ **See Figure 88**

For maximum satisfaction, tires should be used in sets of four. Mixing of different brands or types (radial, bias-belted, fiberglass belted) should be avoided. In most cases, the vehicle manufacturer has designated a type of tire on which the vehicle will perform best. Your first choice when replacing tires should be to use the same type of tire that the manufacturer recommends.

When radial tires are used, tire sizes and wheel diameters should be selected to maintain ground clearance and tire load capacity equivalent to the original specified tire. Radial tires should always be used in sets of four.

❊❊ CAUTION

Radial tires should never be used on only the front axle.

When selecting tires, pay attention to the original size as marked on the tire. Most tires are described using an industry size code sometimes referred to as P-Metric. This allows the exact identification of the tire specifications, regardless of the manufacturer. If selecting a different tire size or brand, remember to check the installed tire for any sign of interference with the body or suspension while the vehicle is stopping, turning sharply or heavily loaded.

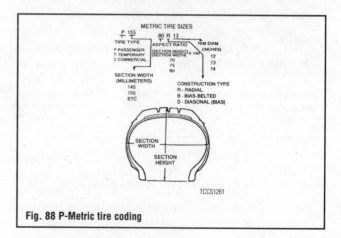

Fig. 88 P-Metric tire coding

Snow Tires

Good radial tires can produce a big advantage in slippery weather, but in snow, a street radial tire does not have sufficient tread to provide traction and control. The small grooves of a street tire quickly pack with snow and the tire behaves like a billiard ball on a marble floor. The more open, chunky tread of a snow tire will self-clean as the tire turns, providing much better grip on snowy surfaces.

To satisfy municipalities requiring snow tires during weather emergencies, most snow tires carry either an M + S designation after the tire size stamped on the sidewall, or the designation "all-season." In general, no change in tire size is necessary when buying snow tires.

Most manufacturers strongly recommend the use of 4 snow tires on their vehicles for reasons of stability. If snow tires are fitted only to the drive wheels, the opposite end of the vehicle may become very unstable when braking or turning on slippery surfaces. This instability can lead to unpleasant endings if the driver can't counteract the slide in time.

Note that snow tires, whether 2 or 4, will affect vehicle handling in all non-snow situations. The stiffer, heavier snow tires will noticeably change the turning and braking characteristics of the vehicle. Once the snow tires are installed, you must re-learn the behavior of the vehicle and drive accordingly.

➠**Consider buying extra wheels on which to mount the snow tires. Once done, the "snow wheels" can be installed and removed as needed. This eliminates the potential damage to tires or wheels from seasonal removal and installation. Even if your vehicle has styled wheels, see if inexpensive steel wheels are available. Although the look of the vehicle will change, the expensive wheels will be protected from salt, curb hits and pothole damage.**

TIRE STORAGE

If they are mounted on wheels, store the tires at proper inflation pressure. All tires should be kept in a cool, dry place. If they are stored in the garage or basement, do not let them stand on a concrete floor; set them on strips of wood, a mat or a large stack of newspaper. Keeping them away from direct moisture is of paramount importance. Tires should not be stored upright, but in a flat position.

INFLATION & INSPECTION

◆ **See Figures 89 thru 94**

The importance of proper tire inflation cannot be overemphasized. A tire employs air as part of its structure. It is designed around the supporting strength of the air at a specified pressure. For this reason, improper inflation drastically reduces the tire's ability to perform as intended. A tire will lose some air in day-to-day use; having to add a few pounds of air periodically is not necessarily a sign of a leaking tire.

Two items should be a permanent fixture in every glove compartment: an accurate tire pressure gauge and a tread depth gauge. Check the tire pressure (including the spare) regularly with a pocket type gauge. Too often, the gauge on the end of the air hose at your corner garage is not accurate because it suffers too much abuse. Always check tire pressure when the tires are cold, as pressure increases with temperature. If you must move the vehicle to check the tire inflation, do not drive more than a mile before checking. A cold tire is generally one that has not been driven for more than three hours.

A plate or sticker is normally provided somewhere in the vehicle (door post, hood, tailgate or trunk lid) which shows the proper pressure for the tires. Never counteract excessive pressure build-up by bleeding off air pressure (letting some air out). This will cause the tire to run hotter and wear quicker.

❋❋ CAUTION

Never exceed the maximum tire pressure embossed on the tire! This is the pressure to be used when the tire is at maximum loading, but it is rarely the correct pressure for everyday driving. Consult the owner's manual or the tire pressure sticker for the correct tire pressure.

Once you've maintained the correct tire pressures for several weeks, you'll be familiar with the vehicle's braking and handling personality. Slight adjustments in tire pressures can fine-tune these characteristics, but never change the cold pressure specification by more than 2 psi. A slightly softer tire pressure will give a softer ride but also yield lower fuel mileage. A slightly harder tire will give crisper dry road handling but can cause skidding on wet surfaces. Unless you're fully attuned to the vehicle, stick to the recommended inflation pressures.

TCCS1095

Fig. 89 Tires with deep cuts, or cuts which bulge, should be replaced immediately

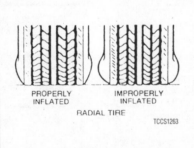

PROPERLY INFLATED   IMPROPERLY INFLATED

RADIAL TIRE

TCCS1263

Fig. 90 Radial tires have a characteristic sidewall bulge; don't try to measure pressure by looking at the tire. Use a quality air pressure gauge

TCCS1265

Fig. 91 Tread wear indicators will appear when the tire is worn

CONDITION	RAPID WEAR AT SHOULDERS	RAPID WEAR AT CENTER	CRACKED TREADS	WEAR ON ONE SIDE	FEATHERED EDGE	BALD SPOTS	SCALLOPED WEAR
EFFECT							
CAUSE	UNDER-INFLATION OR LACK OF ROTATION	OVER-INFLATION OR LACK OF ROTATION	UNDER-INFLATION OR EXCESSIVE SPEED*	EXCESSIVE CAMBER	INCORRECT TOE	UNBALANCED WHEEL OR TIRE DEFECT *	LACK OF ROTATION OF TIRES OR WORN OR OUT-OF-ALIGNMENT SUSPENSION.
CORRECTION	ADJUST PRESSURE TO SPECIFICATIONS WHEN TIRES ARE COOL ROTATE TIRES			ADJUST CAMBER TO SPECIFICATIONS	ADJUST TOE-IN TO SPECIFICATIONS	DYNAMIC OR STATIC BALANCE WHEELS	ROTATE TIRES AND INSPECT SUSPENSION

*HAVE TIRE INSPECTED FOR FURTHER USE.

TCCS1267

Fig. 92 Common tire wear patterns and causes

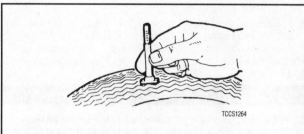

Fig. 93 Accurate tread depth indicators are inexpensive and handy

Fig. 94 A penny works well for a quick check of tread depth

All automotive tires have built-in tread wear indicator bars that show up as ½ in. (13mm) wide smooth bands across the tire when ¹⁄₁₆ in. (1.5mm) of tread remains. The appearance of tread wear indicators means that the tires should be replaced. In fact, many states have laws prohibiting the use of tires with less than this amount of tread.

You can check your own tread depth with an inexpensive gauge or by using a Lincoln head penny. Slip the Lincoln penny (with Lincoln's head upside-down) into several tread grooves. If you can see the top of Lincoln's head in 2 adjacent grooves, the tire has less than ¹⁄₁₆ in. (1.5mm) tread left and should be replaced. You can measure snow tires in the same manner by using the "tails" side of the Lincoln penny. If you can see the top of the Lincoln memorial, it's time to replace the snow tire(s).

Fluid Disposal

Used fluids such as engine oil, transmission fluid, antifreeze and brake fluid are hazardous wastes and must be disposed of properly. Before draining any fluids, consult with your local authorities; in many areas, waste oil, antifreeze, etc. is being accepted as a part of recycling programs. A number of service stations and auto parts stores are also accepting waste fluids for recycling.

Be sure of the recycling center's policies before draining any fluids, as many will not accept different fluids that have been mixed together.

Fuel and Engine Oil Recommendations

FUEL

Your vehicle is designed to operate using regular unleaded fuel with an 87 octane. Ford advises that using gasoline with an octane rating lower than 87 can cause persistent and heavy knocking, and may cause internal engine damage.

If your vehicle is having problems with rough idle or hesitation when the engine is cold, it may be caused by low volatility fuel. If this occurs, try a different grade or brand of fuel.

OIL

▶ **See Figure 95**

Gasoline engines are required to use engine oil meeting API classification SG, such as SG/CC or SG/CD, or the latest superseding version. Viscosity grade 10W-30 or 10W-40 is recommended for use in pre-1984 models; 5W-30 or 10W-30 is recommended for use in 1984 and later models. See the viscosity-to-temperature relationship chart in this section.

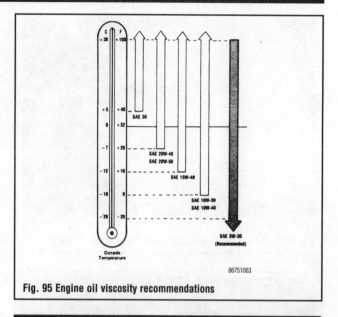

Fig. 95 Engine oil viscosity recommendations

Engine

OIL LEVEL CHECK

▶ **See Figures 96, 97 and 98**

✳✳ CAUTION

The EPA warns that prolonged contact with used engine oil may cause a number of skin disorders, including cancer! You should make every effort to minimize your exposure to used engine oil. Protective gloves should be worn when changing the oil. Wash your hands and any other exposed skin areas as soon as possible after exposure to used engine oil. Soap and water, or waterless hand cleaner should be used.

✳✳ WARNING

Operating the engine without the proper amount and type of engine oil will result in severe engine damage.

Check the engine oil level every time you fill the gas tank. To obtain a true reading, the car should be on level ground when checking the oil.

1. Turn the car off and wait several minutes. This will allow the oil to return to the oil pan, thereby permitting an accurate reading.

Fig. 96 Check the oil level on the dipstick at every gasoline stop

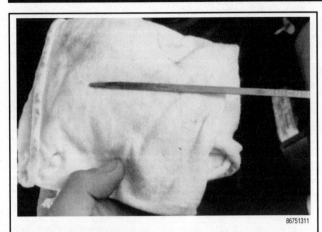

Fig. 97 Hold the dipstick horizontal while reading the oil level

Fig. 98 If the level is low, pour oil through the filler cap on the rocker arm cover

2. Locate the engine oil dipstick and withdraw it from the tube.

3. Wipe the dipstick with a clean rag and reinsert it in the dipstick tube.

4. Remove the dipstick again, hold it horizontally and observe the level of the oil.

5. The oil level should be at the **FULL** mark on the dipstick.

6. If the level is at or near the **LOW** mark, replace the dipstick and add fresh oil to bring the level up to the **FULL** mark. Do not overfill.

7. Recheck the oil level and close the hood.

OIL & FILTER CHANGE

▶ See Figures 99, 100, 101 and 102

➡The engine oil and oil filter should be changed at the recommended intervals on the Maintenance Intervals chart. Although some manufacturers have at times recommended changing the filter only at every other oil change, we recommend that you always change the filter with the oil. The benefit of fresh oil is quickly lost if the old filter is clogged and unable to do its job. Also, leaving the old filter in place leaves a significant amount of dirty oil in the system.

The oil should be changed more frequently if the vehicle is being operated in a very dusty area. Before draining the oil, make sure that the engine is at operating temperature. Hot oil will hold more impurities in suspension and will flow better, allowing the removal of more oil and dirt.

➡It is usually a good idea to place your ignition key in the box or bag with the bottles of fresh engine oil. In this way, it will be VERY HARD to forget to refill the engine crankcase before you go to start the engine.

1. Raise and support the vehicle safely on jackstands.

2. Before you crawl under the car, take a look at where you will be working and gather all the necessary tools such as: a few wrenches or a ratchet and strip of sockets, a drain pan and clean rags. If the oil filter is more accessible from underneath the vehicle, you will also want to grab a bottle of oil, the new filter and a filter wrench at this time.

✳✳ CAUTION

The EPA warns that prolonged contact with used engine oil may cause a number of skin disorders, including cancer! You should make every effort to minimize your exposure to used engine oil. Protective gloves should be worn when changing the oil. Wash your hands and any other exposed skin areas as soon as possible after exposure to used engine oil. Soap and water, or waterless hand cleaner, should be used.

✳✳ WARNING

Operating the engine without the proper amount and type of engine oil will result in severe engine damage.

3. Position the drain pan beneath the oil pan drain plug. Keep in mind that the fast flowing oil, which will spill out as you pull the plug from the pan, will flow with enough force that it could miss the pan. Position the drain pan accordingly and be ready to move the pan more directly beneath the plug as the oil flow lessens to a trickle.

4. Loosen the drain plug with a wrench (or socket and driver), then carefully unscrew the plug with your fingers. Use a rag to shield your fingers from the heat. Push in on the plug as you unscrew it so you can feel when all of the screw threads are out of the hole (and so you will keep the oil from seeping past the threads until you are ready to remove the plug). You can then remove the plug quickly to avoid having hot oil run down your arm. This will also help assure that have the plug in your hand, not in the bottom of a pan of hot oil.

✳✳ CAUTION

Be careful of the oil; when at operating temperature, it is hot enough to cause a severe burn.

5. Allow the oil to drain until nothing but a few drops come out of the drain hole. Check the drain plug to make sure the threads and sealing surface are not damaged. Clean the plug and install a new seal if it is missing or damaged.

6. Carefully thread the plug into position and tighten it with a torque wrench to 15–25 ft. lbs. (20–34 Nm). If a torque wrench is not available, snug the drain plug and give a slight additional turn. You don't want the plug to fall out (as you would quickly become stranded), but the pan threads are EASILY stripped from overtightening (and this can be time consuming and/or costly to fix).

7. Position the drain pan beneath the filter. To remove the filter, you may need an oil filter wrench, since the filter may have been fitted too tightly and/or the heat from the engine may have made it even tighter. A filter wrench can be obtained at any auto parts store and is well worth the investment. Loosen the filter with the filter wrench. With a rag wrapped around the filter, unscrew the filter from the boss on the engine. Be careful of hot oil that will run down the side of the filter. Make sure that your drain pan is under the filter before you start to remove it from the engine; should some of the hot oil happen to get on you, there will be a place to dump the filter in a hurry, and the filter will usually spill a good bit of dirty oil as it is removed.

8. Wipe the base of the mounting boss with a clean, dry cloth. When you install the new filter, smear a small amount of fresh oil on the gasket with your finger, just enough to coat the entire contact surface. When you tighten the filter, rotate it about a half-turn after it contacts the mounting boss (or follow any instructions which are provided on the filter or parts box).

✳✳ WARNING

Never operate the engine without engine oil, otherwise SEVERE engine damage will be the result.

9. Remove the jackstands and carefully lower the vehicle, then IMMEDIATELY refill the engine crankcase with the proper amount of oil. DO NOT WAIT TO DO THIS, because if you forget and someone tries to start the car, severe engine damage will occur.

Fig. 99 With the vehicle level, drain the oil completely from the pan

Fig. 100 Remove the filter and let the oil drain from this location as well

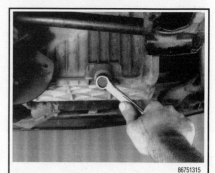

Fig. 101 Tighten the drain plug bolt, but to not overtorque—be especially careful with aluminum oil pans

Fig. 102 Before installing a new oil filter, lightly coat the rubber gasket with clean engine oil

10. Refill the engine crankcase slowly, checking the level often. You may notice that it usually takes less than the amount of oil listed in the Capacities Chart to refill the crankcase. But, that is only until the engine is run and the oil filter is filled with oil. To make sure the proper level is obtained, run the engine to normal operating temperature. While the engine is warming, look under the vehicle for any oil leakage; if any leakage is found, shut the engine **OFF** immediately, then fix the leak.

11. Shut the engine **OFF**, allow the oil to drain back into the oil pan, and recheck the level. Top off the oil at this time to the FULL mark.

➡If the vehicle is not resting on level ground, the oil level reading on the dipstick may be slightly off. Be sure to check the level only when the car is sitting level.

12. Drain your used oil into a suitable container for recycling and clean up your tools, as you will be needing them again in a few thousand more miles (kilometers).

Manual Transaxle

FLUID RECOMMENDATIONS

• 1981–82 models with a manual transaxle: Type F Automatic Transmission Fluid (ATF)
• 1983–88 models with a manual transaxle: Type F Automatic Transmission Fluid (ATF) or Motorcraft Dexron® II Automatic Transmission Fluid (ATF)
• 1989–90 models with a manual transaxle: Type F Automatic Transmission Fluid (ATF) or MERCON® Automatic Transmission Fluid (ATF)

FLUID LEVEL CHECK

Each time the engine oil is changed, the fluid level of the transaxle should be checked.

1. Raise the vehicle and evenly support it by placing jackstands on the front and back, or on a lift, if available.

2. Remove the transaxle filler plug, located on the upper front (driver's side) of the transaxle with a ⁷⁄₁₆ in. wrench or a ⅜ inch. extension and ratchet.

➡The filler plug has a hex-head or it has a flat surface with a cut-in ⅜ in. square box. Do not mistake any other bolts for the filler. Damage to the transaxle could occur if the wrong plug is removed.

3. The oil level should be even with the edge of the filler hole or within ¼ in. (6mm) of the hole. If the oil level is not as specified, add the recommended lubricant until the proper level is reached.

➡A rubber bulb syringe, such as a turkey baster, will be helpful in adding the recommended lubricant.

4. After the transaxle is filled to the correct fluid level, install the filler plug and tighten the plug to 9–15 ft. lbs. (12–20 Nm).

DRAIN & REFILL

Changing the fluid in a manual transaxle is not necessary under normal operating conditions. However, the fluid levels should be checked at normal intervals. The only two ways to drain the oil from the transaxle is by removing it and then turning the transaxle on its side to drain or by using a suction tool. When refilling the transaxle, the lubricant level should be even with the edge of the filler hole or within ¼ inch. (6mm) of the hole.

Automatic Transaxle

FLUID RECOMMENDATIONS

• 1981–85 models with an automatic transaxle: Dexron_ II Automatic Transmission Fluid (ATF)
• 1985 ½–87 models with an automatic transaxle: Type H Automatic Transmission Fluid (ATF)
• 1988–90 models with an automatic transaxle: MERCON_ Automatic Transmission Fluid (ATF)

FLUID LEVEL CHECK

▶ **See Figures 103, 104, 105 and 106**

A dipstick is provided in the engine compartment to check the level of the automatic transaxle.

It is very important to maintain the proper fluid level in an automatic transaxle. If the level is either too high or too low, poor shifting operation and internal damage are likely to occur. For this reason, a regular check of the fluid level is essential.

It is best to check fluid at normal operating temperature.

1. Drive the vehicle for 15–20 minutes or idle it at a fast idle speed (about 1200 rpm), allowing the transaxle to reach operating temperature. When the fluid is warm allow the engine to idle normally.

2. Park the car on a level surface, apply the parking brake and leave the engine idling. Make sure the parking brake is FIRMLY ENGAGED.

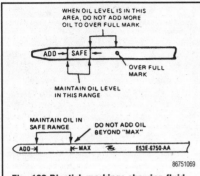

Fig. 103 Dipstick markings showing fluid expansion from "room" to normal operating temperature

Fig. 104 Check the automatic transmission fluid level when the engine is running and warmed up

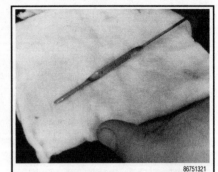

Fig. 105 Wipe the dipstick, re-insert it and read the fluid level against the dipstick markings

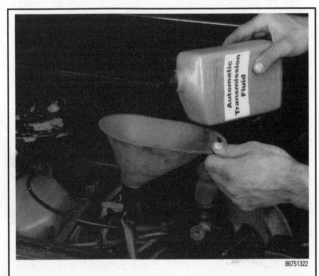

Fig. 106 Add ATF using a long funnel to reach the dipstick tube/filler

3. Depress the brake pedal and shift the transaxle engaging each gear, then place the selector in **P** (PARK) position.

4. Keep the engine running and open the hood. Locate the transaxle dipstick. Wipe away any dirt in the area of the dipstick to prevent it from falling into the filler tube. Withdraw the dipstick, wipe it with a clean, lint-free rag and reinsert it until it fully seats.

5. Withdraw the dipstick and hold it horizontally while noting the fluid level. It should be between the **L** and the **F** marks when the temperature of the fluid is 149–170F (65–77C).

6. If the level is below the lower mark, use a funnel and add fluid in small quantities through the dipstick filler neck. Keep the engine running while adding fluid and check the level after each small amount. DO NOT overfill, as this could lead to foaming and transaxle damage or seal leaks.

➡Since the transaxle fluid is added through the dipstick tube, if you check the fluid too soon after adding fluid, an incorrect reading may occur. After adding fluid, wait a few minutes to allow it to fully drain into the transaxle.

PAN & FILTER SERVICE

▶ **See Figures 107 and 108**

➡Although not a required service, transaxle fluid changing can help assure a trouble-free transaxle. Likewise, changing the transaxle filter at this time is also added insurance.

1. Raise the car and support it securely on jackstands.
2. Place a large drain pan under the transaxle.
3. Loosen all the pan bolts except the bolts on the four corners.

4. Loosen the front two bolts about three turns and the rear two bolts about six turns.

✳✳ CAUTION

DO NOT force the pan while breaking the gasket seal. DO NOT allow the pan flange to become bent or otherwise damaged.

5. Use a prytool to gently separate the pan from the transaxle.
6. As the fluid drains from the pan, keep loosening the bolts in the same two-to-one ratio allowing all the fluid to completely drain.
7. When fluid has drained, remove the pan bolts and the pan, doing your best to drain the rest of the fluid into the drain pan.
8. Loosen the transaxle fluid filter mounting bolts.
9. Remove the filter by pulling it down and off of the valve body. Make sure any gaskets or seals are removed with the old filter.

To install:

10. Install the new oil filter screen, making sure all gaskets or seals are in place, then tighten the retaining bolts to 7–9 ft lbs. (9–12 Nm).
11. Place a new gasket on the fluid pan, then install the pan to the transaxle. Tighten the attaching bolts to 15–19 ft lbs. (20–26 Nm).
12. Remove the jackstands and lower the vehicle.
13. Add the proper type and quantity of fluid through the dipstick tube.
14. The level should always just be below the **F** mark.
15. Start the engine and move the gear selector through all gears in the shift pattern. Allow the engine to reach normal operating temperature.
16. Check the transaxle fluid level. Add fluid, as necessary, to obtain the correct level.

Fig. 107 Remove the bolts supporting the transaxle fluid pan (which in this case is damaged and leaking)

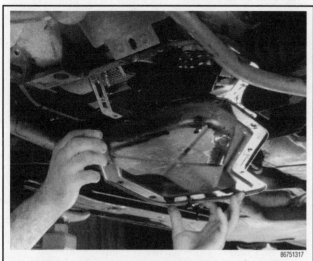

Fig. 108 Carefully lower the pan to drain the fluid into a suitable container

Cooling System

FLUID RECOMMENDATIONS

The recommended coolant for all vehicles covered by this manual is a 50/50 mixture of ethylene glycol and water for year-round use. Choose an aluminum compatible, good quality antifreeze with water pump lubricants, rust inhibitors and other corrosion inhibitors, along with acid neutralizers.

INSPECTION

▶ See Figures 109 and 110

Any time you have the hood open, glance at the coolant recovery tank to make sure it is properly filled. Top off the cooling system using the recovery tank and its markings as a guideline. If you top off the system, make a note of it to check again soon. A coolant level that consistently drops is usually a sign of a small, hard to detect leak, although in the worst case it could be a sign of an internal engine leak (blown head gasket/cracked block? . . . check the engine oil for coolant contamination). In most cases, you will be able to trace the leak to a loose fitting or damaged hose (and you might solve a problem before it leaves you stranded). Evaporating ethylene glycol antifreeze will leave small, white (salt-like) deposits, which can be helpful in tracing a leak.

At least annually or every 15,000 miles (25,000 km), all hoses, fittings and cooling system connections should be inspected for damage, wear or leaks. Hose clamps should be checked for tightness, and soft or cracked hoses should be replaced. Damp spots, or accumulations of rust or dye near hoses or fittings indicate possible leakage. These must be corrected before filling the system with fresh coolant. The pressure cap should be examined for signs of deterioration and aging. The water pump drive belt(s) should be inspected and adjusted to the proper tension. Refer to the information on drive belts found earlier in this section. Finally, if everything looks good, obtain an antifreeze/coolant testing hydrometer in order to check the freeze and boil-over protection capabilities of the coolant currently in your engine. Old or improperly mixed coolant should be replaced.

❋❋ CAUTION

Never open, service or drain the radiator or cooling system when hot; serious burns can occur from the steam and hot coolant. Also, when draining engine coolant, keep in mind that cats and dogs are attracted to ethylene glycol antifreeze and could drink any that is left in an uncovered container or in puddles on the ground. This will prove fatal in sufficient quantities. Always drain coolant into a sealable container. Coolant 8be reused unless it is contaminated or is several years old.

At least once every 3 years or 36,000 miles (48,000 km), the engine cooling system should be inspected, flushed and refilled with fresh coolant. If the

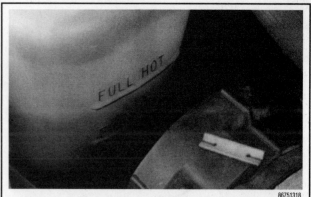

Fig. 109 Check the coolant overflow tank by reading the appropriate markings on the bottle

Fig. 110 Check the fluid level in the radiator by removing the cap once the engine is cold

coolant is left in the system too long, it loses its ability to prevent rust and corrosion. If the coolant has too much water, it won't protect against freezing.

If you experience problems with your cooling system, such as overheating or boiling over, check for a simple cause before expecting the complicated. Make sure the system can fully pressurize (are all the connections tight/is the radiator cap on properly, is the cap seal intact?). Ideally, a pressure tester should be connected to the radiator opening and the system should be pressurized and inspected for leaks. If no obvious problems are found, use a hydrometer antifreeze/coolant tester (available at most automotive supply stores) to check the condition and concentration of the antifreeze in your cooling system. Excessively old coolant or the wrong proportions of water and coolant will adversely affect the coolant's boiling and freezing points.

Check the Radiator Cap

▶ See Figure 111

While you are checking the coolant level, check the radiator cap for a worn or cracked gasket. If the cap doesn't seal properly, fluid will be lost and the engine will overheat. Worn caps should be replaced with new ones.

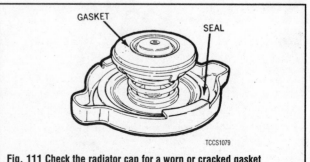

Fig. 111 Check the radiator cap for a worn or cracked gasket

Clean Radiator of Debris

▶ See Figure 112

Periodically, clean any debris-leaves, paper, insects, etc.-from the radiator fins. Pick the large pieces off by hand. The smaller pieces can be washed away with water pressure from a hose.

Carefully straighten any bent radiator fins with a pair of needle-nosed pliers. Be careful; the fins are very soft. Don't wiggle the fins back and forth too much. Straighten them once and try not to move them again.

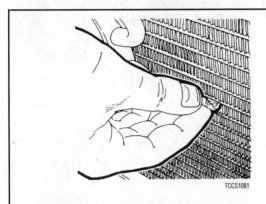

TCCS1081

Fig. 112 Periodically remove all debris from the radiator fins

DRAIN & REFILL

▶ See Figures 113, 114, 115 and 116

Connect an 18 in. (457mm) long, ⅜ in. (9.5mm) inside diameter hose to the nipple on the drain valve located on the bottom of the radiator.

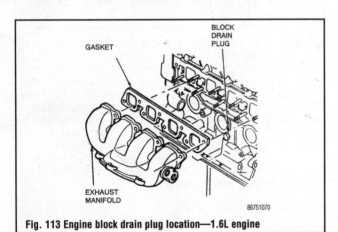

86751070

Fig. 113 Engine block drain plug location—1.6L engine

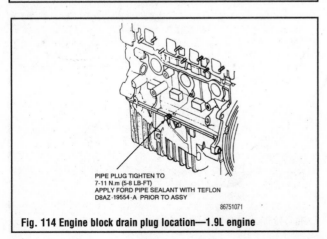

PIPE PLUG TIGHTEN TO
7-11 N.m (5-8 LB-FT)
APPLY FORD PIPE SEALANT WITH TEFLON
D8AZ-19554-A PRIOR TO ASSY

86751071

Fig. 114 Engine block drain plug location—1.9L engine

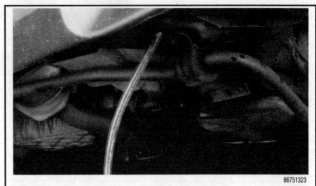

86751323

Fig. 115 Drain the coolant from the radiator using a ⅜ in. (9.5mm) inside diameter hose

1. With the engine cool, set the heater control to the maximum heat position.
2. Place a suitable drain pan under the drain valve.
3. Remove the radiator cap and open the drain valve.
4. When all of the coolant is drained, remove the ⅜ in. (9.5mm) hose and close the drain valve.
5. On some 1.9L engines some coolant may remain in the engine block. To drain this coolant, place a suitable drain pan under the drain valve, remove the Allen® head pipe plug using a ³⁄₁₆ in. Allen® wrench and allow the coolant to completely drain.
6. Before installing drain valves be sure to coat the threads of the pipe plug with a suitable thread sealer or Teflon® tape. Install the plug and tighten it to 5–8 ft. lbs. (7–11 Nm).

➡ If there is any evidence of rust or scaling in the cooling system, the system should be flushed thoroughly before refilling.

7. With the engine in the **OFF** position, add 50 percent of system's capacity of specified coolant to the radiator. Then add water until the radiator is full.

➡ Be sure to wait several minutes as the coolant level in the radiator drops, continue to slowly add coolant until the radiator remains full (approximately 10–15 minutes are required to fill the system).

8. Reinstall the radiator cap to the pressure relief position by installing the cap to the fully installed position and then backing off to the first stop.
9. Start and idle the engine until the upper radiator hose is warm.
10. Immediately shut **OFF** the engine. Cautiously remove radiator cap and add water until the radiator is full. Reinstall radiator cap securely.
11. Add coolant to the ADD mark on the reservoir, then fill to the **FULL HOT** mark with water.
12. Check system for leaks and return the heater temperature control to normal position.

86751324

Fig. 116 Refill the radiator using a funnel to direct the flow of the coolant and prevent spills

FLUSHING & CLEANING THE SYSTEM

✳✳ CAUTION

Never open, service or drain the radiator or cooling system when hot; serious burns can occur from the steam and hot coolant. Also, when draining engine coolant, keep in mind that cats and dogs are attracted to ethylene glycol antifreeze and could drink any that is left in an uncovered container or in puddles on the ground. This will prove fatal in sufficient quantities. Always drain coolant into a sealable container. Coolant should be reused unless it is contaminated or is several years old.

1. Drain the cooling system.
2. Add water until the radiator is full.
3. Reinstall the radiator cap to the pressure relief position by installing the cap to the fully installed position and then backing off to the first stop.
4. Start and idle the engine until the upper radiator hose is warm.
5. Immediately shut off the engine. Cautiously drain the water by opening the draincock.
6. Repeat Steps 2–5 as many times as necessary until nearly clear water comes out of the radiator. Allow remaining water to drain and then close the petcock.
7. Disconnect the overflow hose from the radiator filler neck nipple.
8. Remove the coolant recovery reservoir from the fender apron and empty the fluid. Flush the reservoir with clean water, drain and install the reservoir and overflow hose and clamp to the radiator filler neck.
9. Refill the coolant system as outlined in this section.
10. If the radiator has been removed, it is possible to back-flush the system as follows:
    a. Back-flush the radiator, ensuring the radiator cap is in position. Turn the radiator upside down. Position a high pressure water hose in the bottom hose location and backflush. The radiator internal pressure must not exceed 20 psi (138 kPa).
    b. Remove the thermostat housing and thermostat.
11. Positioning a high pressure hose into the engine through the thermostat location and back-flush the engine.

➡ **If the radiator is showing signs of rust and wear, it may be a good idea while the radiator is out of the vehicle, to thoroughly clean and get the cooling fins free from debris. Then using a suitable high temperature rustproof engine paint, paint the exterior of the radiator assembly.**

Brake Master Cylinder

The brake master cylinder reservoir is located under the hood, attached to the firewall on the driver's side of the engine compartment.

FLUID RECOMMENDATIONS

✳✳ WARNING

BRAKE FLUID EATS PAINT. Take great care not to splash or spill brake fluid on painted surfaces. Should you spill a small amount on the car's finish, don't panic, just flush the area with plenty of water.

When adding fluid to the system, ONLY use fresh DOT 3 brake fluid from a sealed container. DOT 3 brake fluid will absorb moisture when it is exposed to the atmosphere, which will lower its boiling point. A container that has been opened once, closed and placed on a shelf will allow enough moisture to enter over time to contaminate the fluid within. If your brake fluid is contaminated with water, you could boil the brake fluid under hard braking conditions and lose all or some braking ability. Don't take the risk, buy fresh brake fluid whenever you must add to the system.

LEVEL CHECK

◆ See Figures 117 and 118

1. Before removing the master cylinder reservoir cap, make sure the vehicle is positioned on a level surface.

2. Wipe clean the cover and the area around the master cylinder, before opening it up. When satisfied nothing will contaminate the fluid, then open the master cylinder to inspect the fluid.
3. On early model vehicles without translucent (see through) reservoirs, open the master cylinder cover by prying the retaining clip off to the side and remove the master cylinder cover.
4. If the level of the brake fluid is within ¼ in. (6mm) of the top, the fluid level is OK. If the level is less than half the volume of the reservoir, check the brake system for leaks. Leaks in the brake system most commonly occur at the wheel cylinders or at the front calipers. Leaks at brake lines or the master cylinder can also be cause brake fluid loss.

➡ **There is a rubber diaphragm at the top of the master cylinder cap. As the fluid level lowers due to normal brake shoe wear or leakage, the diaphragm takes up the space. This is to prevent the loss of brake fluid from the vented cap and to help stop contamination by dirt.**

5. After filling the master cylinder to the proper level with brake fluid (Type DOT 3), but before replacing the cap, fold the rubber diaphragm up into the cap, then replace the cap on the reservoir and snap the retaining clip back in place.
6. On later model vehicles with the translucent master cylinder reservoir, check the brake fluid by visually inspecting the fluid level against the level markings on its side.
7. The fluid level should be between the MIN and the MAX level marks embossed on the side of the reservoir. If the level is low, remove the reservoir cap and fill to the MAX level with DOT 3 brake fluid.
8. When the fluid is at the correct level, replace the reservoir cap.

Fig. 117 View the brake fluid level through the translucent reservoir, on cars so equipped

Fig. 118 Wipe away any dirt, then unscrew the reservoir cap and add fresh brake fluid

➡The fluid level will decrease with accumulated mileage. This is a normal condition associated with the wear of the disc brake linings. If the fluid is excessively low, have the brake system checked.

❋❋ CAUTION

To avoid the possibility of brake failure that could result in property damage or personal injury, do not allow the master cylinder to run dry. Never reuse brake fluid that has been drained from the hydraulic system or fluid that has been allowed to stand in an open container for an extended period of time.

Power Steering Pump

FLUID RECOMMENDATION

Use only power steering fluid that meets Ford Specifications such as Motorcraft Type **F** Automatic Transmission and Power Steering Fluid.

FLUID LEVEL CHECK

◆ **See Figures 119, 120 and 121**

1. Run the engine until it reaches normal operating temperature.
2. While the engine is idling, turn the steering wheel all the way to the right and then to the left, and repeat several times.
3. Turn the engine **OFF**.
4. Open the hood and remove the power steering pump dipstick.
5. Wipe the dipstick clean and reinstall into the pump reservoir.
6. Withdraw the dipstick and note the fluid level shown. The level must show between the COLD FULL mark and the HOT FULL mark.
7. Add fluid if necessary, but do not overfill. Remove any excess fluid with a suction bulb or suction gun.

Steering Gear

The steering gear is factory-filled with steering gear grease. Changing of this lubricant should not be performed and the housing should not be drained; periodic lubrication is not required for the steering gear.

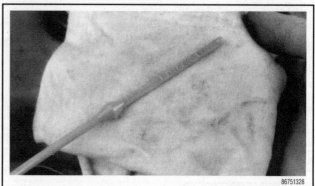

Fig. 119 Clean the power steering dipstick, then reinsert and withdraw to check the fluid level

Fig. 120 Add power steering fluid through the dipstick tube using a long funnel

Item	Part Name	Ford Part No.	Ford Specification
*Hinges, Hinge Checks and Pivots	Polyethylene Grease	D7AZ-19584-A	ESB-M1C106-B
Hood Latch and Auxilliary Catch	Polyethylene Grease	D7AZ-19584-A	ESB-M1C106-B
Lock Cylinders	Lock Lubricant	D8AZ-19587-A	ESB-M2C20-A
Steering Gear Housing (Manual)	Steering Gear Grease	D8AZ-19578-A	ESA-M1C175-A
Steering Gear (Power)	Grease	C3AZ-19578-A	ESW-M1C87-A
Steering-Power (Pump Reservoir)	Motorcraft Auto. Trans. Fluid — Type F	XT-1-QF	ESW-M2C33-F
Speedometer Cable	Speedometer Cable Lube	D2AZ-19581-A	ESF-M1C160-A
Engine Coolant	Cooling System Fluid	E2FZ-19549-A	ESE-M97B44-A
Front Wheel Bearings and Hubs Front Wheel Bearing Seals Rear Wheel Bearings	Long Life Lubricant	C1AZ-19590-B	ESA-M1C75-B
Brake Master Cylinder	H.D. Brake Fluid	C6AZ-19542-A	ESA-M6C25-A
Brake Master Cylinder Push Rod and Bushing	Motorcraft SAE 10W-30 Engine Oil	XO-10W30-QP	ESE-M2C153-B
Drum Brake Shoe Ledges	Disc Brake Caliper Slide Grease	D7AZ-19590-A	ESA-M1C172-A
Parking Brake Cable	Polyethylene Grease	D0AZ-19584-A	ESB-M1C93-B
Brake Pedal Pivot Bushing	Motorcraft SAE 10W-30 Engine Oil	XO-10W30-QP	ESE-M2C153-B
Tire Mounting Bead (of Tire)	Tire Mounting Lube	D9AZ-19583-A	ESA-M1B6-A
Clutch Pedal Pivot Bushing	Motorcraft SAE 10W-30 Engine Oil	XO-10W30-QP	ESE-M2C153-B
Clutch Pedal Quadrant and Pawl Pivot Holes			
Clutch Cable Connection Transmission End			
Clutch Release Lever — At Fingers (Both Sides and Fulcrum)	Long Life Lubricant	C1AZ-19590-B	ESA-M1C75-B
Clutch Release Bearing Retainer			

*For door hinges, use Disc Brake Caliper slide grease D7AZ-19590-A.
DEXRON* is a registered trademark of General Motors Corporation.

Fig. 121 Chassis and body lubricant specifications

Chassis Lubrication

Chassis lubrication should be performed at least once a year, depending on the conditions under which the vehicle is operated.

The primary components that need lubrication are:
- Rear wheel bearings: Premium long-life grease
- Parking brake linkage: Multi-purpose grease
- Clutch linkage: Premium long-life grease

Body Lubrication

Whenever you take care of chassis greasing it is also advised that you walk around the vehicle and give attention to a number of other surfaces which require a variety of lubrication/protection.

Lubricate the door and tailgate hinges, door locks, door latches, and the hood latch when they become noisy or difficult to operate. A high quality multi-purpose grease should be used as a lubricant.

HOOD/DOOR LATCH & HINGES

Wipe clean any exposed surfaces of the door latches and hinges and hood latch, liftgate hinges and latches. Then, treat the surfaces using a multi-purpose grease spray that meets Ford's D7AZ-19584–A specification.

LOCK CYLINDERS

These should be treated with Ford penetrating lubricant, part no. E8AZ-19A501–B or equivalent. Consult your local parts supplier for equivalent lubricants.

DOOR WEATHERSTRIPPING

Spray or wipe the door weatherstripping using a silicone lubricant to help preserve the rubber.

Wheel Bearings

REPACKING

Front

The front wheel bearings are sealed units and are not serviceable. If the bearings are damaged, they must be replaced.

Rear

▶ **See Figure 122**

Use a long-life lubricant that meets Ford specification ESA-M1C75–B or equivalent to pack the rear wheel bearings.

1. Remove the wheel bearings. Refer to Section 8 of this manual for the procedure.
2. Wash all the old grease or axle lubricant out of the wheel hub, using a suitable solvent.
3. Wash the bearing cups and rollers and inspect them for pitting, galling, and uneven wear patterns. Inspect the roller for end wear.
4. Pack each bearing cone and roller with a bearing packer.
5. If a bearing packer is not available, pack the inner and outer bearing cone with a quality wheel bearing grease by hand, working the grease through the cage behind the roller.
6. Install and adjust the wheel bearing as outlined in Section 8 of this manual.

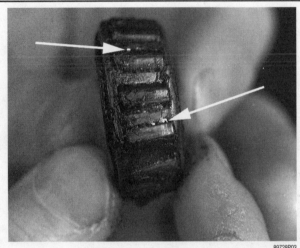

Fig. 122 Inspect the wheel bearing assembly for signs of damage, as indicated by the arrows

JUMP STARTING A DEAD BATTERY

▶ **See Figure 123**

Whenever a vehicle is jump started, precautions must be followed in order to prevent the possibility of personal injury. Remember that batteries contain a small amount of explosive hydrogen gas which is a by-product of battery charging. Sparks should always be avoided when working around batteries, especially when attaching jumper cables. To minimize the possibility of accidental sparks, follow the procedure carefully.

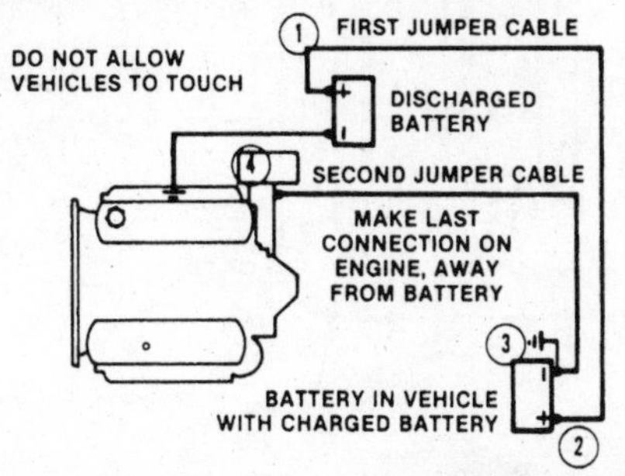

❋❋ CAUTION

NEVER hook the batteries up in a series circuit or the entire electrical system will go up in smoke, including the starter!

Jump Starting Precautions

- Be sure that both batteries are of the same voltage. Vehicles covered by this manual and most vehicles on the road today utilize a 12 volt charging system.
- Be sure that both batteries are of the same polarity (have the same terminal, in most cases NEGATIVE grounded).
- Be sure that the vehicles are not touching or a short could occur.
- On serviceable batteries, be sure the vent cap holes are not obstructed.
- Do not smoke or allow sparks anywhere near the batteries.
- In cold weather, make sure the battery electrolyte is not frozen. This can occur more readily in a battery that has been in a state of discharge.
- Do not allow electrolyte to contact your skin or clothing.

MAKE CONNECTIONS IN NUMERICAL ORDER

FIRST JUMPER CABLE

DO NOT ALLOW VEHICLES TO TOUCH

DISCHARGED BATTERY

SECOND JUMPER CABLE

MAKE LAST CONNECTION ON ENGINE, AWAY FROM BATTERY

BATTERY IN VEHICLE WITH CHARGED BATTERY

TCCS1080

Fig. 123 Connect the jumper cables to the batteries and engine in the order shown

Jump Starting Procedure

1. Make sure that the voltages of the 2 batteries are the same. Most batteries and charging systems are of the 12 volt variety.

2. Pull the jumping vehicle (with the good battery) into a position so the jumper cables can reach the dead battery and that vehicle's engine. Make sure that the vehicles do NOT touch.

3. Place the transaxles of both vehicles in **Neutral** (MT) or **P** (AT), as applicable, then firmly set their parking brakes.

➡**If necessary for safety reasons, the hazard lights on both vehicles may be operated throughout the entire procedure without significantly increasing the difficulty of jumping the dead battery.**

4. Turn all lights and accessories OFF on both vehicles. Make sure the ignition switches on both vehicles are turned to the **OFF** position.

5. Cover the battery cell caps with a rag, but do not cover the terminals.

6. Make sure the terminals on both batteries are clean and free of corrosion or proper electrical connection will be impeded. If necessary, clean the battery terminals before proceeding.

7. Identify the positive and negative terminals on both batteries.

8. Connect the first jumper cable to the positive terminal of the dead battery, then connect the other end of that cable to the positive terminal of the booster (good) battery.

9. Connect one end of the other jumper cable to the negative terminal on the booster battery and the final cable clamp to an engine bolt head, alternator bracket or other solid, metallic point on the engine with the dead battery. Try to pick a ground on the engine that is positioned away from the battery in order to minimize the possibility of the 2 clamps touching should one loosen during the procedure. DO NOT connect this clamp to the negative (f) terminal of the bad battery.

Be very careful to keep the jumper cables away from moving parts (cooling fan, belts, etc.) on both engines.

10. Check to make sure that the cables are routed away from any moving parts, then start the donor vehicle's engine. Run the engine at moderate speed for several minutes to allow the dead battery a chance to receive some initial charge.

11. With the donor vehicle's engine still running slightly above idle, try to start the vehicle with the dead battery. Crank the engine for no more than 10 seconds at a time and let the starter cool for at least 20 seconds between tries. If the vehicle does not start in 3 tries, it is likely that something else is also wrong or that the battery needs additional time to charge.

12. Once the vehicle is started, allow it to run at idle for a few seconds to make sure that it is operating properly.

13. Turn ON the headlights, heater blower and, if equipped, the rear defroster of both vehicles in order to reduce the severity of voltage spikes and subsequent risk of damage to the vehicles' electrical systems when the cables are disconnected. This step is especially important to any vehicle equipped with computer control modules.

14. Carefully disconnect the cables in the reverse order of connection. Start with the negative cable that is attached to the engine ground, then the negative cable on the donor battery. Disconnect the positive cable from the donor battery and finally, disconnect the positive cable from the formerly dead battery. Be careful when disconnecting the cables from the positive terminals not to allow the alligator clips to touch any metal on either vehicle or a short and sparks will occur.

JACKING

◆ **See Figures 124, 125, 126, 127 and 128**

Your vehicle was supplied with a jack for emergency road repairs. This jack is fine for changing a flat tire or other short term procedures not requiring you to go beneath the vehicle. If it is used in an emergency situation, carefully follow the instructions provided either with the jack or in your owner's manual. Do not attempt to use the jack on any portions of the vehicle other than specified by the vehicle manufacturer. Always block the diagonally opposite wheel when using a jack.

A more convenient way of jacking is the use of a garage or floor jack. You may use the floor jack to raise the car in the positions indicated in the accompanying illustration and photographs.

Never place the jack under the radiator, engine or transaxle components. Severe and expensive damage will result when the jack is raised. Additionally, never jack under the floorpan or bodywork; the metal will deform.

Whenever you plan to work under the vehicle, you must support it on jackstands or ramps. Never use cinder blocks or stacks of wood to support the vehicle, even if you're only going to be under it for a few minutes. Never crawl under the vehicle when it is supported only by the tire-changing jack or other floor jack.

➡**Always position a block of wood or small rubber pad on top of the jack or jackstand to protect the lifting point's finish when lifting or supporting the vehicle.**

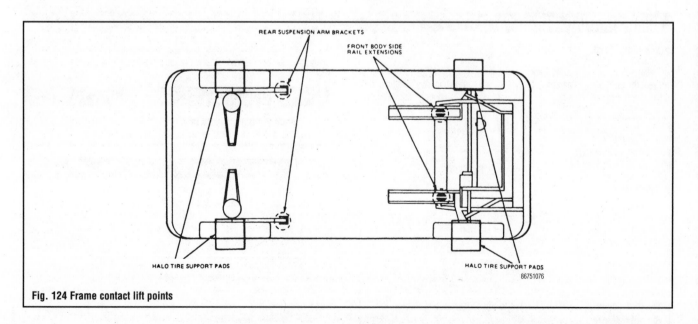

Fig. 124 Frame contact lift points

86751330

Fig. 125 Front rocker flange jacking point

86751331

Fig. 126 Front body rail jacking point

86751332

Fig. 127 A jackstand is necessary for any service in which the car must be raised

86751333

Fig. 128 Rear rocker flange jacking point

Small hydraulic, screw, or scissors jacks are satisfactory for raising the vehicle. Drive-on trestles or ramps are also a handy and safe way to both raise and support the vehicle. Be careful though, some ramps may be too steep to drive your vehicle onto without scraping the front bottom panels. Never support the vehicle on any suspension member (unless specifically instructed to do so by a repair manual) or by an underbody panel.

Jacking Precautions

The following safety points cannot be overemphasized:
- Always block the opposite wheel or wheels to keep the vehicle from rolling off the jack.
- When raising the front of the vehicle, firmly apply the parking brake.
- When the drive wheels are to remain on the ground, leave the vehicle in gear to help prevent it from rolling.
- Always use jackstands to support the vehicle when you are working underneath. Place the stands beneath the vehicle's jacking brackets. Before climbing underneath, rock the vehicle a bit to make sure it is firmly supported.

Normal Maintenance Schedule

SERVICE INTERVAL Perform at the months or distances shown, whichever comes first.	Miles x 1000	3	6	9	12	15	18	21	24	27	30	33	36	39	42	45	48	51	54	57	60
	Kilometers x 1000	4.8	9.6	14.4	19.2	24	28.8	33.6	38.4	43.2	48	52.8	57.6	62.4	67.2	72	76.8	81.6	86.4	91.2	96
EMISSION CONTROL SERVICE																					
Change Engine Oil and Oil Filter (every 3 months) or		X	X	X	X	X	X	X	X	X	X	X	X	X	X	X	X	X	X	X	X
Spark Plugs: Replace											X										
Inspect Accessory Drive Belt(s)											X										X
Replace Air Cleaner Filter ①											X①										X①
Replace Crankcase Emission Filter ①											X①										X①
Replace Engine Coolant (every 36 months) or											X										X
Check Engine Coolant Protection, Hoses and Clamps		ANNUALLY																			
GENERAL MAINTENANCE																					
Inspect Exhaust Heat Shields											X										X
Change Automatic Transaxle Fluid ②											X										X
Inspect Disc Brake Pads and Rotors (Front) ③											X										X
Inspect Brake Linings and Drums (Rear) ③											X										X
Inspect and Repack Rear Wheel Bearings											X										X

① If operating in severe dust, more frequent intervals may be required — consult your dealer.

② Change automatic transaxle fluid if your driving habits frequently include one or more of the following conditions:
- Operation during HOT WEATHER (above 32°C (90°F).
- Towing a trailer or using a car top carrier.
- Police, taxi or door-to-door delivery service.

③ If your driving includes continuous stop and go driving or driving in mountainous areas, more frequent intervals may be required.

90931C05

Severe Maintenance Schedule

SERVICE INTERVALS Perform at the months or distances shown, whichever comes first.	Miles x 1000	7.5	15	22.5	30	37.5	45	52.5	60
	Kilometers x 1000	12	24	36	48	60	72	84	96
EMISSIONS CONTROL SERVICE									
Change Engine Oil and Oil Filter (Every 6 Months) or 7500 miles whichever occurs first		X	X	X	X	X	X	X	X
Replace Spark Plugs					X				X
Change Crankcase Emission Filter ①					X①				X①
Inspect Accessory Drive Belt(s)					X				X
Replace Air Cleaner Filter ①					X①				X①
Change Engine Coolant Every 36 Months or					X				X
Check Engine Coolant Protection, Hoses and Clamps					ANNUALLY				
GENERAL MAINTENANCE									
Check Exhaust Heat Shields					X				X
Inspect Disc Brake Pads and Rotors (Front) ②					X②				X②
Inspect Brake Linings and Drums (Rear) ②					X②				X②
Inspect and Replace Rear Wheel Bearings					X				X

① If operating in severe dust, more frequent intervals may be required. Consult your dealer.
② If your driving includes continuous stop-and-go driving or driving in mountainous areas, more frequent intervals may be required.

90931C06

CAPACITIES

Year	Model	Engine ID/VIN	Engine Displacement Liters (CI)	Engine Oil with Filter (qts.)	Transaxle (pts.)			Fuel Tank (gal.)	Cooling System (qts.)
					4-Spd	5-Spd	Auto.		
1981	Escort/Lynx	1	1.3 (79)	4.0	5.0	–	①	②	7.4
		2	1.6 (98)	4.0	5.0	–	①	②	8.0
1982	Escort/Lynx	2	1.6 (98)	4.0	5.0	–	①	②	8.0
1983	Escort/Lynx	2	1.6 (98)	4.0	5.0	6.1	①	③	6.3
1984	Escort/Lynx	2	1.6 (98)	4.0	5.0	6.1	①	③	④
		4	1.6 HO (98)	4.0	5.0	6.1	①	③	④
		5	1.6 (98)	4.0	5.0	6.1	①	③	④
		8	1.6 Turbo (98)	4.0	5.0	6.1	①	③	④
1985	Escort/Lynx	2	1.6 (98)	4.0	5.0	6.1	①	③	④
		4	1.6 HO (98)	4.0	5.0	6.1	①	③	④
		5	1.6 (98)	4.0	5.0	6.1	①	③	④
		8	1.6 Turbo (98)	4.0	5.0	6.1	①	③	④
1986	Escort/Lynx	9	1.9 (114)	4.0	4.0	6.1	①	③	⑤
		J	1.9 HO (114)	4.0	6.1	6.1	①	③	⑤
1987	Escort/Lynx	9	1.9 (114)	4.0	6.1	6.1	①	③	⑤
		J	1.9 HO (114)	4.0	6.1	6.1	①	③	⑤
1988	Escort	9	1.9 (114)	4.0	6.1	6.1	①	③	⑤
		J	1.9 HO (114)	4.0	6.1	6.1	①	③	⑤
1989	Escort	9	1.9 (114)	4.0	6.1	6.1	①	③	⑤
		J	1.9 HO (114)	4.0	6.1	6.1	①	③	⑤
1990	Escort	9	1.9 (114)	4.0	6.1	6.1	①	③	⑤
		J	1.9 HO (114)	4.0	6.1	6.1	①	③	⑤

These capacities are approximate. It is advisable to check the level as you fill the component.

CI—Cubic Inches

① Total dry capacity—converter, cooler and sump drained.
    1981-82 models: 19.6 pints
    1983-90 models: 16.6 pints

② 10 gal. with auto transaxle
    9 gal. with manual transaxle
    11.3 gal. Extended range

③ 10 gal. FE models
    13 gal. Standard models, EXP/LN7

④ Manual transaxle without A/C: 6.5 qts.
    Automatic transaxle without A/C: 7.0 qts.
    Manual transaxle with A/C: 6.3 qts.
    Automatic transaxle with A/C: 7.1 qts

⑤ Automatic and manual transaxle without A/C: 7.3 qts.
    Manual transaxle with A/C: 6.8 qts.
    Automatic transaxle with A/C: 7.3 qts

90931C07

ENGLISH TO METRIC CONVERSION: MASS (WEIGHT)

Current mass measurement is expressed in pounds and ounces (lbs. & ozs.). The metric unit of mass (or weight) is the kilogram (kg). Even although this table does not show conversion of masses (weights) larger than 15 lbs, it is easy to calculate larger units by following the data immediately below.

To convert ounces (oz.) to grams (g): multiply th number of ozs. by 28
To convert grams (g) to ounces (oz.): multiply the number of grams by .035

To convert pounds (lbs.) to kilograms (kg): multiply the number of lbs. by .45
To convert kilograms (kg) to pounds (lbs.): multiply the number of kilograms by 2.2

lbs	kg	lbs	kg	oz	kg	oz	kg
0.1	0.04	0.9	0.41	0.1	0.003	0.9	0.024
0.2	0.09	1	0.4	0.2	0.005	1	0.03
0.3	0.14	2	0.9	0.3	0.008	2	0.06
0.4	0.18	3	1.4	0.4	0.011	3	0.08
0.5	0.23	4	1.8	0.5	0.014	4	0.11
0.6	0.27	5	2.3	0.6	0.017	5	0.14
0.7	0.32	10	4.5	0.7	0.020	10	0.28
0.8	0.36	15	6.8	0.8	0.023	15	0.42

ENGLISH TO METRIC CONVERSION: TEMPERATURE

To convert Fahrenheit (°F) to Celsius (°C): take number of °F and subtract 32; multiply result by 5; divide result by 9

To convert Celsius (°C) to Fahrenheit (°F): take number of °C and multiply by 9; divide result by 5; add 32 to total

Fahrenheit (F)	Celsius (C)			Fahrenheit (F)	Celsius (C)			Fahrenheit (F)	Celsius (C)		
°F	°C	°C	°F	°F	°C	°C	°F	°F	°C	°C	°F
−40	−40	−38	−36.4	80	26.7	18	64.4	215	101.7	80	176
−35	−37.2	−36	−32.8	85	29.4	20	68	220	104.4	85	185
−30	−34.4	−34	−29.2	90	32.2	22	71.6	225	107.2	90	194
−25	−31.7	−32	−25.6	95	35.0	24	75.2	230	110.0	95	202
−20	−28.9	−30	−22	100	37.8	26	78.8	235	112.8	100	212
−15	−26.1	−28	−18.4	105	40.6	28	82.4	240	115.6	105	221
−10	−23.3	−26	−14.8	110	43.3	30	86	245	118.3	110	230
−5	−20.6	−24	−11.2	115	46.1	32	89.6	250	121.1	115	239
0	−17.8	−22	−7.6	120	48.9	34	93.2	255	123.9	120	248
1	−17.2	−20	−4	125	51.7	36	96.8	260	126.6	125	257
2	−16.7	−18	−0.4	130	54.4	38	100.4	265	129.4	130	266
3	−16.1	−16	3.2	135	57.2	40	104	270	132.2	135	275
4	−15.6	−14	6.8	140	60.0	42	107.6	275	135.0	140	284
5	−15.0	−12	10.4	145	62.8	44	112.2	280	137.8	145	293
10	−12.2	−10	14	150	65.6	46	114.8	285	140.6	150	302
15	−9.4	−8	17.6	155	68.3	48	118.4	290	143.3	155	311
20	−6.7	−6	21.2	160	71.1	50	122	295	146.1	160	320
25	−3.9	−4	24.8	165	73.9	52	125.6	300	148.9	165	329
30	−1.1	−2	28.4	170	76.7	54	129.2	305	151.7	170	338
35	1.7	0	32	175	79.4	56	132.8	310	154.4	175	347
40	4.4	2	35.6	180	82.2	58	136.4	315	157.2	180	356
45	7.2	4	39.2	185	85.0	60	140	320	160.0	185	365
50	10.0	6	42.8	190	87.8	62	143.6	325	162.8	190	374
55	12.8	8	46.4	195	90.6	64	147.2	330	165.6	195	383
60	15.6	10	50	200	93.3	66	150.8	335	168.3	200	392
65	18.3	12	53.6	205	96.1	68	154.4	340	171.1	205	401
70	21.1	14	57.2	210	98.9	70	158	345	173.9	210	410
75	23.9	16	60.8	212	100.0	75	167	350	176.7	215	414

ENGLISH TO METRIC CONVERSION: LENGTH

To convert inches (ins.) to millimeters (mm): multiply number of inches by 25.4

To convert millimeters (mm) to inches (ins.): multiply number of millimeters by .04

Inches	Decimals	Milli-meters	inches	mm	Inches	Decimals	Milli-meters	inches	mm
	1/64 0.051625	0.3969	0.0001	0.00254		33/64 0.515625	13.0969	0.6	15.24
1/32	0.03125	0.7937	0.0002	0.00508	17/32	0.53125	13.4937	0.7	17.78
	3/64 0.046875	1.1906	0.0003	0.00762		35/64 0.546875	13.8906	0.8	20.32
1/16	0.0625	1.5875	0.0004	0.01016	9/16	0.5625	14.2875	0.9	22.86
	5/64 0.078125	1.9844	0.0005	0.01270		37/64 0.578125	14.6844	1	25.4
3/32	0.09375	2.3812	0.0006	0.01524	19/32	0.59375	15.0812	2	50.8
	7/64 0.109375	2.7781	0.0007	0.01778		39/64 0.609375	15.4781	3	76.2
1/8	0.125	3.1750	0.0008	0.02032	5/8	0.625	15.8750	4	101.6
	9/64 0.140625	3.5719	0.0009	0.02286		41/64 0.640625	16.2719	5	127.0
5/32	0.15625	3.9687	0.001	0.0254	21/32	0.65625	16.6687	6	152.4
	11/64 0.171875	4.3656	0.002	0.0508		43/64 0.671875	17.0656	7	177.8
3/16	0.1875	4.7625	0.003	0.0762	11/16	0.6875	17.4625	8	203.2
	13/64 0.203125	5.1594	0.004	0.1016		45/64 0.703125	17.8594	9	228.6
7/32	0.21875	5.5562	0.005	0.1270	23/32	0.71875	18.2562	10	254.0
	15/64 0.234375	5.9531	0.006	0.1524		47/64 0.734375	18.6531	11	279.4
1/4	0.25	6.3500	0.007	0.1778	3/4	0.75	19.0500	12	304.8
	17/64 0.265625	6.7469	0.008	0.2032		49/64 0.765625	19.4469	13	330.2
9/32	0.28125	7.1437	0.009	0.2286	25/32	0.78125	19.8437	14	355.6
	19/64 0.296875	7.5406	0.01	0.254		51/64 0.796875	20.2406	15	381.0
5/16	0.3125	7.9375	0.02	0.508	13/16	0.8125	20.6375	16	406.4
	21/64 0.328125	8.3344	0.03	0.762		53/64 0.828125	21.0344	17	431.8
11/32	0.34375	8.7312	0.04	1.016	27/32	0.84375	21.4312	18	457.2
	23/64 0.359375	9.1281	0.05	1.270		55/64 0.859375	21.8281	19	482.6
3/8	0.375	9.5250	0.06	1.524	7/8	0.875	22.2250	20	508.0
	25/64 0.390625	9.9219	0.07	1.778		57/64 0.890625	22.6219	21	533.4
13/32	0.40625	10.3187	0.08	2.032	29/32	0.90625	23.0187	22	558.8
	27/64 0.421875	10.7156	0.09	2.286		59/64 0.921875	23.4156	23	584.2
7/16	0.4375	11.1125	0.1	2.54	15/16	0.9375	23.8125	24	609.6
	29/64 0.453125	11.5094	0.2	5.08		61/64 0.953125	24.2094	25	635.0
15/32	0.46875	11.9062	0.3	7.62	31/32	0.96875	24.6062	26	660.4
	31/64 0.484375	12.3031	0.4	10.16		63/64 0.984375	25.0031	27	690.6
1/2	0.5	12.7000	0.5	12.70					

ENGLISH TO METRIC CONVERSION: TORQUE

To convert foot-pounds (ft. lbs.) to Newton-meters: multiply the number of ft. lbs. by 1.3

To convert inch-pounds (in. lbs.) to Newton-meters: multiply the number of in. lbs. by .11

in lbs	N-m	in lbs	N-m	in lbs	N-m	in lbs	N-m	in lbs	N-m
0.1	0.01	1	0.11	10	1.13	19	2.15	28	3.16
0.2	0.02	2	0.23	11	1.24	20	2.26	29	3.28
0.3	0.03	3	0.34	12	1.36	21	2.37	30	3.39
0.4	0.04	4	0.45	13	1.47	22	2.49	31	3.50
0.5	0.06	5	0.56	14	1.58	23	2.60	32	3.62
0.6	0.07	6	0.68	15	1.70	24	2.71	33	3.73
0.7	0.08	7	0.78	16	1.81	25	2.82	34	3.84
0.8	0.09	8	0.90	17	1.92	26	2.94	35	3.95
0.9	0.10	9	1.02	18	2.03	27	3.05	36	4.0

TCCS1C02

ENGLISH TO METRIC CONVERSION: TORQUE

Torque is now expressed as either foot-pounds (ft./lbs.) or inch-pounds (in./lbs.). The metric measurement unit for torque is the Newton-meter (Nm). This unit—the Nm—will be used for all SI metric torque references, both the present ft./lbs. and in./lbs.

ft lbs	N-m	ft lbs	N-m	ft lbs	N-m	ft lbs	N-m
0.1	0.1	33	44.7	74	100.3	115	155.9
0.2	0.3	34	46.1	75	101.7	116	157.3
0.3	0.4	35	47.4	76	103.0	117	158.6
0.4	0.5	36	48.8	77	104.4	118	160.0
0.5	0.7	37	50.7	78	105.8	119	161.3
0.6	0.8	38	51.5	79	107.1	120	162.7
0.7	1.0	39	52.9	80	108.5	121	164.0
0.8	1.1	40	54.2	81	109.8	122	165.4
0.9	1.2	41	55.6	82	111.2	123	166.8
1	1.3	42	56.9	83	112.5	124	168.1
2	2.7	43	58.3	84	113.9	125	169.5
3	4.1	44	59.7	85	115.2	126	170.8
4	5.4	45	61.0	86	116.6	127	172.2
5	6.8	46	62.4	87	118.0	128	173.5
6	8.1	47	63.7	88	119.3	129	174.9
7	9.5	48	65.1	89	120.7	130	176.2
8	10.8	49	66.4	90	122.0	131	177.6
9	12.2	50	67.8	91	123.4	132	179.0
10	13.6	51	69.2	92	124.7	133	180.3
11	14.9	52	70.5	93	126.1	134	181.7
12	16.3	53	71.9	94	127.4	135	183.0
13	17.6	54	73.2	95	128.8	136	184.4
14	18.9	55	74.6	96	130.2	137	185.7
15	20.3	56	75.9	97	131.5	138	187.1
16	21.7	57	77.3	98	132.9	139	188.5
17	23.0	58	78.6	99	134.2	140	189.8
18	24.4	59	80.0	100	135.6	141	191.2
19	25.8	60	81.4	101	136.9	142	192.5
20	27.1	61	82.7	102	138.3	143	193.9
21	28.5	62	84.1	103	139.6	144	195.2
22	29.8	63	85.4	104	141.0	145	196.6
23	31.2	64	86.8	105	142.4	146	198.0
24	32.5	65	88.1	106	143.7	147	199.3
25	33.9	66	89.5	107	145.1	148	200.7
26	35.2	67	90.8	108	146.4	149	202.0
27	36.6	68	92.2	109	147.8	150	203.4
28	38.0	69	93.6	110	149.1	151	204.7
29	39.3	70	94.9	111	150.5	152	206.1
30	40.7	71	96.3	112	151.8	153	207.4
31	42.0	72	97.6	113	153.2	154	208.8
32	43.4	73	99.0	114	154.6	155	210.2

TCCS1C03

ENGLISH TO METRIC CONVERSION: FORCE

Force is presently measured in pounds (lbs.). This type of measurement is used to measure spring pressure, specifically how many pounds it takes to compress a spring. Our present force unit (the pound) will be replaced in SI metric measurements by the Newton (N). This term will eventually see use in specifications for electric motor brush spring pressures, valve spring pressures, etc.

To convert pounds (lbs.) to Newton (N): multiply the number of lbs. by 4.45

lbs	N	lbs	N	lbs	N	oz	N
0.01	0.04	21	93.4	59	262.4	1	0.3
0.02	0.09	22	97.9	60	266.9	2	0.6
0.03	0.13	23	102.3	61	271.3	3	0.8
0.04	0.18	24	106.8	62	275.8	4	1.1
0.05	0.22	25	111.2	63	280.2	5	1.4
0.06	0.27	26	115.6	64	284.6	6	1.7
0.07	0.31	27	120.1	65	289.1	7	2.0
0.08	0.36	28	124.6	66	293.6	8	2.2
0.09	0.40	29	129.0	67	298.0	9	2.5
0.1	0.4	30	133.4	68	302.5	10	2.8
0.2	0.9	31	137.9	69	306.9	11	3.1
0.3	1.3	32	142.3	70	311.4	12	3.3
0.4	1.8	33	146.8	71	315.8	13	3.6
0.5	2.2	34	151.2	72	320.3	14	3.9
0.6	2.7	35	155.7	73	324.7	15	4.2
0.7	3.1	36	160.1	74	329.2	16	4.4
0.8	3.6	37	164.6	75	333.6	17	4.7
0.9	4.0	38	169.0	76	338.1	18	5.0
1	4.4	39	173.5	77	342.5	19	5.3
2	8.9	40	177.9	78	347.0	20	5.6
3	13.4	41	182.4	79	351.4	21	5.8
4	17.8	42	186.8	80	355.9	22	6.1
5	22.2	43	191.3	81	360.3	23	6.4
6	26.7	44	195.7	82	364.8	24	6.7
7	31.1	45	200.2	83	369.2	25	7.0
8	35.6	46	204.6	84	373.6	26	7.2
9	40.0	47	209.1	85	378.1	27	7.5
10	44.5	48	213.5	86	382.6	28	7.8
11	48.9	49	218.0	87	387.0	29	8.1
12	53.4	50	224.4	88	391.4	30	8.3
13	57.8	51	226.9	89	395.9	31	8.6
14	62.3	52	231.3	90	400.3	32	8.9
15	66.7	53	235.8	91	404.8	33	9.2
16	71.2	54	240.2	92	409.2	34	9.4
17	75.6	55	244.6	93	413.7	35	9.7
18	80.1	56	249.1	94	418.1	36	10.0
19	84.5	57	253.6	95	422.6	37	10.3
20	89.0	58	258.0	96	427.0	38	10.6

TCCS1C04

2

ENGINE
ELECTRICAL

ELECTRONIC IGNITION

All vehicles covered by this manual are equipped with some type of electronic ignition system. Such ignition systems eliminate the deterioration of spark quality associated with older breaker point type ignition systems, as the breaker points wore. Electronic ignition also extends maintenance intervals, while providing a more intense and reliable spark at every firing impulse, in order to ignite the leaner gas mixtures necessary to control emissions.

The breaker points, point actuating cam and condenser have been eliminated in the solid state distributor. They are replaced by an ignition module and magnetic pulse-signal generator (pick-up).

Your vehicle is likely equipped with one of the following ignition systems, depending on the year and engine combination:
- 1981–82 1.3L and 1.6L engines: Dura Spark II Ignition System
- 1982–87 1.6L carbureted and 1.9L carbureted engines: Thick Film Ignition I (TFI-I) System
- 1984–90 1.6L EFI and 1.9L CFI/EFI engines: Thick Film Ignition IV (TFI-IV) System

Refer to the appropriate portion of this section for your particular electronic ignition system.

DURA SPARK II IGNITION SYSTEM

General Information

▶ See Figure 1

The Dura Spark II ignition system features a tang-driven distributor assembly with a top weight centrifugal advance mechanism, a concentric vacuum advance mechanism, and a concentric coil stator assembly.

The Dura Spark II ignition system is a solid state ignition system. The system uses 14mm spark plugs, which have a screw-on gasket. The spark plug boots includes a seal for the spark plug cavity to keep it clean and dry. The Dura Spark II ignition systems consist of the typical electronic primary and conventional secondary circuits, designed to carry higher voltages. The primary and secondary circuits consists of the following components:

Primary Circuit
- Battery
- Ignition switch
- Ballast resistor (start bypass wire)
- Ignition coil primary winding
- Ignition module
- Distributor stator assembly

Secondary Circuit
- Battery
- Ignition switch
- Ignition coil secondary winding
- Distributor rotor
- Distributor cap
- High voltage wires (spark plug and coil wires)
- Spark plugs

The basic operation of the distributor is the same as a solid state distributor. With the ignition switch in the **RUN** position, the primary circuit current is directed from the battery, through the ignition switch, the ballast resistor, the ignition coil primary, the ignition module and back to the battery through the ignition system ground in the distributor. When the engine is being cranked, the rotating armature induces a signal in the stator assembly. This current flow causes a magnetic field to be built up in the ignition coil. When the poles on the armature and the stator assembly align, the ignition module turns the primary current flow off, collapsing the magnetic field in the ignition coil. The collapsing field induces a high voltage in the ignition coil secondary windings. The ignition coil wire then conducts the high voltage to the distributor where the cap and rotor distributes it to the appropriate spark plug.

Diagnosis and Testing

Before performing any component testing, check for and, if necessary, repair the following:
- Damaged, corroded, contaminated, carbon tracked or worn distributor cap and rotor
- Damaged, fouled, improperly seated or gapped spark plug(s)
- Damaged or improperly engaged electrical connections, spark plug wires, etc.
- Discharged battery
- Blown fuses

SECONDARY SPARK TEST

▶ See Figure 2

The best way to perform this procedure is to use a spark tester (available at most automotive parts stores). Two types of spark testers are commonly available. The neon bulb type is connected to the spark plug wire and flashes with each ignition pulse. The air gap type must be adjusted to the individual spark plug gap specified for the engine. This type of tester allows the user to not only detect the presence of spark, but also the intensity (orange/yellow is weak, blue is strong).

1. Disconnect a spark plug wire at the spark plug end.
2. Connect the plug wire to the spark tester and ground the tester to an appropriate location on the engine.
3. Crank the engine and check for spark at the tester.
4. If a spark did occur, inspect the distributor cap, adapter, rotor for cracks,

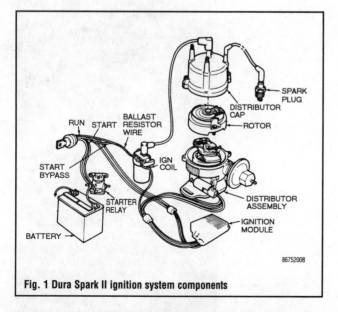

Fig. 1 Dura Spark II ignition system components

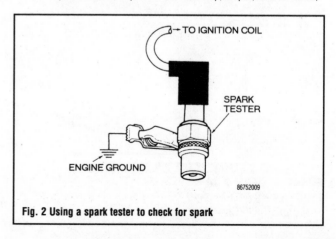

Fig. 2 Using a spark tester to check for spark

carbon tracking, or lack of silicone compound. Also, check that the roll pin is securing the armature to the sleeve in the distributor.

5. If spark does not exist at the spark plug wire, remove the distributor cap and ensure that the rotor is turning when the engine is cranked.

6. If no spark occurs, check the following:

a. Using an ohmmeter, measure the resistance of the ignition coil secondary wire (high voltage wire). The reading should not exceed 5,000 ohms per foot.

b. Inspect the ignition coil for damage or carbon tracking.

c. Also, check that the distributor shaft is rotating while the engine is being cranked.

7. If no spark occurs, go to the module voltage test in this section.

MODULE VOLTAGE

♦ See Figure 3

1. Turn the ignition switch **OFF**.
2. Measure the battery voltage.

➡**Do not allow the straight pin to contact electrical ground, while performing this test.**

3. Carefully insert a small straight pin in the **RED** module wire.
4. Attach the negative lead of a voltmeter to the distributor base.
5. Attach the positive lead of the voltmeter the straight pin and measure the voltage, with the ignition switch in **RUN** position.
6. Turn the ignition switch **OFF** and remove the straight pin.
7. If the results are within 90% of battery voltage, go to the ballast resistor test in this section.
8. If the results are not within 90% of battery voltage, inspect the wiring harness between the module and ignition switch. Also, check for a faulty ignition switch.

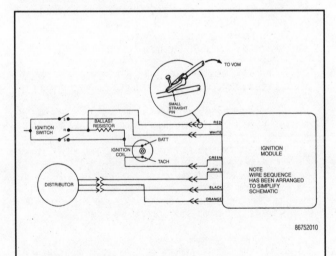

Fig. 3 Use a straight pin and a digital volt ohmmeter to check module voltage—1981–82 Dura Spark II system

BALLAST RESISTOR

♦ See Figure 4

1. Unplug and inspect the ignition module 2–wire connector (RED and WHITE).
2. Unplug and inspect the ignition coil connector.
3. Using an ohmmeter, measure the ballast resistor resistance between the battery terminal of the ignition coil connector and the wiring harness connector mating with the **RED** module wire. The results should be between 0.6–1.6 ohms.
4. If the result is less than 0.6 ohms, or greater than 1.6 ohms, replace the ballast resistor.
5. If the result is okay, the problem is either intermittent or not in the ignition system.

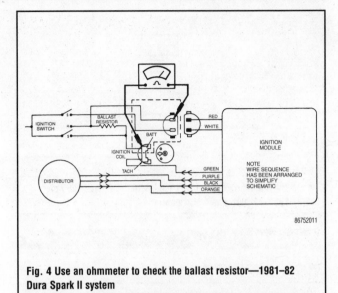

Fig. 4 Use an ohmmeter to check the ballast resistor—1981–82 Dura Spark II system

Ignition Coil

TESTING

♦ See Figures 5 and 6

1. Verify that the ignition switch is in the **OFF** position.
2. Remove the primary connector, clean and inspect the connector for dirt or corrosion.
3. Using an ohmmeter, measure the secondary resistance between the **BATT** terminal to the **HIGH VOLTAGE** terminal of the coil.
4. The resistance should be 7,700–9, 600 ohms.
5. Measure the primary resistance from the **BATT** terminal to the **TACH** terminal of the coil. The resistance should be 1–2 ohms.
6. Replace the coil, if either readings are not within specifications.

REMOVAL & INSTALLATION

1. Disconnect the negative battery cable.
2. Unplug the spark plug wire from the coil.
3. Unpug the coil electrical connector(s).
4. Unfasten the coil bracket retainer(s).
5. Remove the ignition coil.
6. Installation is the reverse of removal.

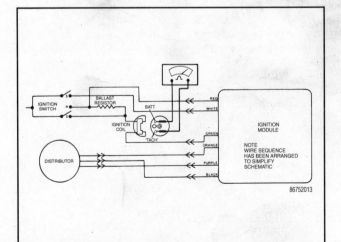

Fig. 5 Use an ohmmeter to check the ignition coil primary circuit—1981–82 Dura Spark II system

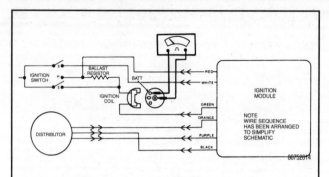

Fig. 6 Use an ohmmeter to check the ignition coil secondary circuit—1981–82 Dura Spark II system

Ignition Module

REMOVAL & INSTALLATION

1. Disconnect the negative battery cable.
2. Unplug all ignition module electrical connections.
3. Unfasten the module retainers and remove the module.
4. Installation is the reverse of removal.

Distributor

REMOVAL & INSTALLATION

♦ **See Figure 7**

1. Disconnect the negative battery cable.
2. Remove the distributor cap and position the cap and wires out of the way.
3. If the distributor unit is not being replaced, matchmark the distributor base to the engine block and also mark the direction the rotor is pointing on the distributor housing.

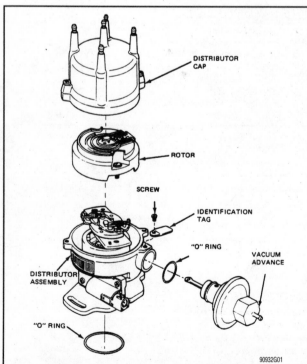

Fig. 7 Exploded view of Dura Spark II system distributor assembly components—1.3L and 1.6L engines

4. Remove the rotor.
5. Disconnect and plug the vacuum hose at the vacuum diaphragm.
6. Disconnect the wiring harness to the distributor.

➡**Some engines are equipped with a security type distributor hold-down bolt. Use tool T82L12270A or equivalent to remove the distributor.**

7. Unfasten the two distributor hold-down bolts and remove the distributor from the engine.

To install:

Engine Not Disturbed

1. Check that the base O-ring and the drive coupling spring is in place.
2. Position the distributor in the engine. Make certain the offset tang of the drive coupling is in the groove on the end of the camshaft.
3. Loosely install the distributor hold-down bolts.
4. Install the distributor rotor.
5. Attach the distributor wiring harness.
6. Install the cap.
7. Reconnect the negative battery cable, start the engine and check the ignition timing.
8. Once the ignition timing is correct, tighten the distributor hold-down to 4–5 ft. lbs. (5–7 Nm).
9. Recheck the ignition timing and readjust as necessary.
10. Install the vacuum hose.

Engine Disturbed

1. Position the distributor in the engine. Make certain the offset tang of the drive coupling is in the groove on the end of the camshaft.
2. Make sure that the engine is still with the No. 1 piston up on TDC of its compression stroke.
3. If the engine was disturbed while the distributor was removed, it will be necessary to remove the No. 1 spark plug and rotate the engine clockwise until the No. 1 piston is on the compression stroke as follows:
    a. Remove the No. 1 spark plug.
    b. Place a socket and breaker bar on the crankshaft pulley bolt.
    c. Place your thumb over the No. 1 spark plug hole.
    d. Rotate the engine clockwise using the breaker bar and socket attached to the crankshaft pulley bolt until you feel air pressure pushing on your thumb.
    e. When you feel the pressure on your thumb, stop turning the crankshaft and check that the timing marks are aligned. If the timing marks are not aligned, turn the crankshaft slowly until the marks align.
    f. If you go past the alignment marks, repeat the procedure.
    g. Remove the breaker bar and socket.
4. If installing the old distributor:
    a. Install the distributor and align the marks made before removal and ensure the rotor points toward the mark on the distributor housing made previously. Make certain the rotor is pointing to the No. 1 mark on the distributor base.
5. If installing a new distributor:
    a. Install the rotor and cap (with wires still attached) on the distributor, follow the No. 1 spark plug wire from the plug to the cap, this will be the No.1 tower on the cap. Mark the location of the tower on the distributor housing, then remove the cap.
    b. Install the distributor and make sure the rotor aligns with the No.1 tower mark made on the distributor.
6. When all the marks are aligned, loosely install the distributor hold-down bolts.
7. Install the distributor rotor.
8. Attach the distributor wiring harness.
9. Install the cap.
10. Reconnect the negative battery cable, start the engine and check the ignition timing.
11. Once the ignition timing is correct, tighten the distributor hold-down to 4–5 ft. lbs. (5–7 Nm).
12. Recheck the ignition timing and readjust as necessary.
13. Install the vacuum hose.

THICK FILM IGNITION (TFI) SYSTEMS

General Information

▶ **See Figures 8, 9, 10 and 11**

The Thick Film Integrated (TFI) ignition system was incorporated on 1.6L engines, in late 1982. In 1983, two versions of the Thick Film Ignition system were used. The original version from 1982, also known as TFI-I, was carried over for carbureted 1.6L and 1.9L engines; another version, known as TFI-IV, was used on all engines equipped with Electronic Fuel Injection (EFI) or Central Fuel Injection (CFI). Engines equipped with TFI-IV use redesigned spark plugs which have an extended reach 14mm tapered seat, a multi-point rotor and a universal distributor, which eliminates the conventional centrifugal and vacuum advance mechanisms, used on the earlier Dura Spark II Ignition System.

The distributor used on carbureted 1.6L and 1.9L engines is a carry-over design with a top weight centrifugal advance mechanism and concentric coil stator assembly. The distributor used on 1.6L EFI engines is a universal distributor design which has a tang-driven die cast base. This distributor incorporates an integrally mounted TFI-IV module, a vane switch stator assembly which replaces the current coil stator. The distributor also contains a provision for fix octane adjustment. The overall design of this distributor eliminates the conventional centrifugal and vacuum advance mechanisms.

The basic operation of the distributor (with concentric coil stator assembly) is the same as the Dura Spark II ignition system. The rotating armature induces

a signal in the stator assembly, causing the ignition module to turn the ignition coil current **ON** and **OFF**.

During model years 1986–90, operation of the universal distributor assembly used on 1.9L CFI/EFI engines is accomplished through a Hall effect vane switch assembly, which causes the ignition coil to be switched **OFF** and **ON** by the Electronic Engine Control-IV (EEC-IV) computer and TFI-IV module. The vane switch is an encapsulated package consisting of a Hall sensor on one side and a permanent magnet on the other side. The distributor contains a provision to change the basic distributor calibration with the use of a replaceable octane rod, from the standard of 0⁻ to either 3⁻ or 6⁻ retard rods. No other calibration changes are possible. The TFI-IV system featured a ``push start'' mode which allows manual transaxle vehicles to be push started. Automatic transaxle vehicles cannot be push started.

A rotary armature, made of ferrous metal, is used to trigger the Hall effect switch. When the window of the armature is between the magnet and the Hall effect device, a magnetic flux field is completed from the magnet through the Hall effect device, and back to the magnet. As the vane passes through the opening, the flux lines are shunted through the vane and back to the magnet. A voltage is produced while the vane passes through the opening. When the vane clears the opening, the window causes the signal to go to 0 volts. The signal is then used by the EEC-IV system for crankshaft position sensing and the computation of the desired spark advance based on the engine demand and calibration. The voltage distribution is accomplished through a conventional rotor, cap and ignition wires.

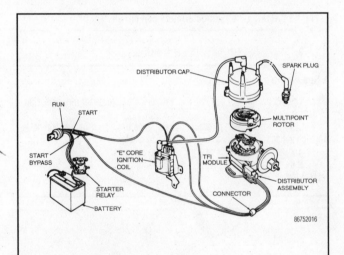

Fig. 8 Thick Film Integrated Ignition System (TFI-I)—1982–85 1.6L carbureted and 1986–87 1.9L carbureted engines

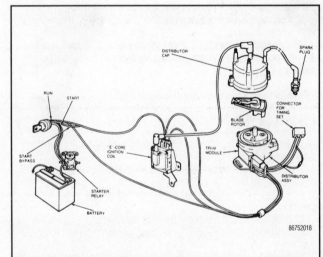

Fig. 10 Thick Film Integrated Ignition System (TFI-IV)—1.9L CFI/EFI engines

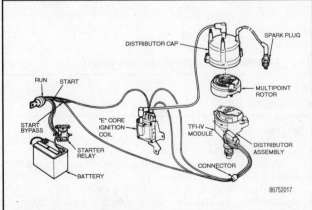

Fig. 9 Thick Film Integrated (TFI-IV) Ignition System—1984–85 1.6L EFI engine

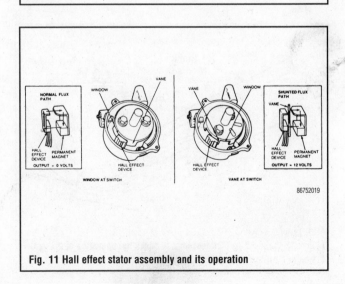

Fig. 11 Hall effect stator assembly and its operation

Diagnosis and Testing-TFI-I System

Before performing any component testing, check for and, if necessary, repair the following:
- Damaged, corroded, contaminated, carbon tracked or worn distributor cap and rotor
- Damaged, fouled, improperly seated or gapped spark plug(s)
- Damaged or improperly engaged electrical connections, spark plug wires, etc.
- Discharged battery
- Blown fuses

SECONDARY SPARK TEST

The best way to perform this procedure is to use a spark tester (available at most automotive parts stores). Two types of spark testers are commonly available. The neon bulb type is connected to the spark plug wire and flashes with each ignition pulse. The air gap type must be adjusted to the individual spark plug gap specified for the engine. This type of tester allows the user to not only detect the presence of spark, but also the intensity (orange/yellow is weak, blue is strong).

1. Disconnect a spark plug wire at the spark plug end.
2. Connect the plug wire to the spark tester and ground the tester to an appropriate location on the engine.
3. Crank the engine and check for spark at the tester.
4. If spark exists at the tester, the ignition system is functioning properly.
5. If spark does not exist at the spark plug wire, remove the distributor cap and ensure that the rotor is turning when the engine is cranked.
6. If the rotor is turning, perform the spark test again using the ignition coil wire.
7. If spark does not exist at the ignition coil wire, test the ignition coil, and other distributor related components or wiring. Repair or replace components as necessary.

IGNITION COIL PRIMARY CIRCUIT SWITCHING

♦ **See Figure 12**

1. Unplug the wiring harness from the ignition coil. Check the harness for dirt, corrosion or damage.
2. Carefully insert a small straight pin into the wire that runs from the coil negative terminal to the TFI-I module about one inch (25mm) from the module.
3. Attach a 12 volt DC test light between the test pin and a good engine ground.
4. If the light flashes proceed to the next test.
5. If the test lamp lights but does not flash, proceed to the wiring harness test.
6. If there is no light or a very dim light, proceed to the primary coil continuity test.
7. Remove the pin and seal the wire with a silicone sealer.

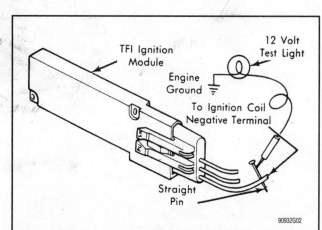

Fig. 12 Use a 12 volt DC test light to check the operation of the ignition coil primary circuit switching

IGNITION COIL PRIMARY RESISTANCE

♦ **See Figure 13**

1. Turn the ignition switch to the **OFF** position.
2. Unplug the ignition coil connector. Check the harness for dirt, corrosion or damage.
3. Using an ohmmeter, measure the resistance from the positive to negative terminals of the coil.
4. The resistance should be 0.3–1.0 ohms.
5. If the resistance is less than 0.3 ohms or greater than 1.0 ohms, replace the coil.

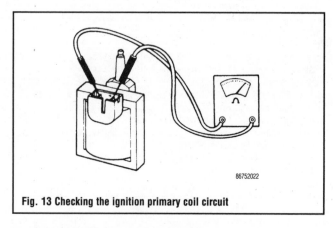

Fig. 13 Checking the ignition primary coil circuit

IGNITION COIL SECONDARY RESISTANCE

♦ **See Figure 14**

1. Unplug the ignition coil connector. Check the harness for dirt, corrosion or damage.
2. Using an ohmmeter, measure the resistance from the negative terminal to the high voltage terminal of the ignition coil connector.
3. The resistance should be 6,500–11,500 ohms.
4. If the resistance is less than 6,500 ohms or greater than 11,500 ohms, replace the coil.

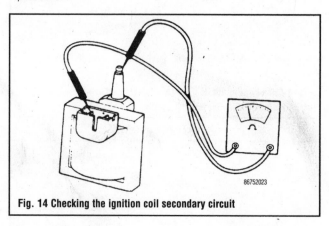

Fig. 14 Checking the ignition coil secondary circuit

WIRING HARNESS

♦ **See Figure 15**

1. Measure and note the battery voltage.
2. Unplug the wiring harness connector from the TFI-I module. Check the harness for dirt, corrosion or damage.
3. Disconnect the wire from the **S** terminal of the starter relay.
4. Attach the negative lead of a voltmeter to the base of the distributor.
5. Insert a small straight pin into the No. 1 terminal of the wiring harness and turn the ignition switch to the **RUN** position.

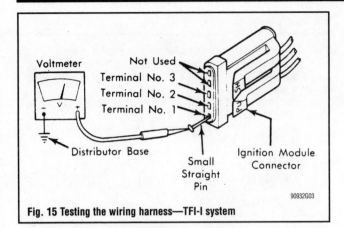

Fig. 15 Testing the wiring harness—TFI-I system

6. Attach the positive lead to the straight pin and note the voltage reading which should be at least 90% of the battery voltage.

7. Move the straight pin to the No. 2 terminal of the wiring harness and with the ignition switch in the **RUN** position, measure the voltage. The voltage should be at least 90% of the battery voltage.

8. Move the straight pin to the No. 3 terminal of the wiring harness and turn the ignition switch to the **START** position, measure the voltage. The voltage should be at least 90% of the battery voltage.

9. If any of the voltage readings are less than 90% of the battery voltage, inspect the wiring, connectors and/or the ignition switch for problems.

10. Turn the ignition switch to the **OFF** position. Remove the straight pin and attach the module electrical connector.

11. Attach the wire to the **S** terminal of the starter relay

STATOR ASSEMBLY AND MODULE

▶ **See Figure 16**

1. Remove the distributor assembly from the engine.
2. Remove the TFI-I module from the distributor.
3. Check the distributor terminals, ground screw and the stator wires for damage.
4. Using an ohmmeter, measure the resistance of the stator as shown in the accompanying illustration.
5. The resistance reading should be between 650–1,300 ohms.
6. If the reading is within specifications, replace the TFI-I module.
7. If the resistance is less than 650 ohms or more than 1,300 ohms, the TFI-I module is good, but the stator assembly must be replaced.
8. Install the TFI-I module and the distributor assembly.

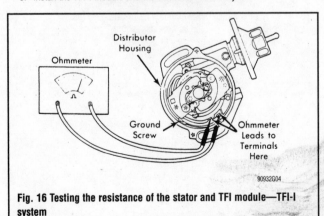

Fig. 16 Testing the resistance of the stator and TFI module—TFI-I system

PRIMARY CIRCUIT CONTINUITY

1. Seperate the wiring harness connector from the ignition module.
2. Attach the negative lead of a voltmeter to the base of the distributor and the positive lead to the battery positive terminal. Measure and note the battery voltage reading.

3. Insert a straight pin into connector terminal No. 1, attach the positive lead of the voltmeter to the straight pin and the negative lead to the distributor base.

4. Turn the ignition key to the **RUN** position and measure the voltage. The voltage reading should be at least 90% of the battery voltage.

5. If the voltage reading is less than 90% battery voltage, perform the ignition coil primary voltage test in this section.

6. Turn the ignition switch **OFF** and remove the straight pin.

IGNITION COIL PRIMARY VOLTAGE

1. Attach the negative lead of a voltmeter to the base of the distributor and the positive lead to the battery positive terminal. Measure and note the battery voltage reading.

2. Turn the ignition key to the **RUN** position and attach the positive lead of the voltmeter to the negative ignition coil terminal and the negative lead to the distributor base. Note the voltage reading and turn the ignition **OFF**.

3. If the voltage reading is less than 90% battery voltage, inspect the wiring between the ignition module and the negative coil terminal.

IGNITION COIL SUPPLY VOLTAGE

1. Attach the negative lead of a voltmeter to the base of the distributor.

2. Turn the ignition key to the **ON** position and attach the positive lead of the voltmeter to the positive ignition coil terminal and the negative lead to the distributor base. Note the voltage reading and turn the ignition **OFF**.

3. If the voltage reading is at least 90% of the battery voltage and the engine will not run, check the ignition coil connector and terminals for damage, corrosion and dirt. If the terminals and connector are in good condition, replace the ignition switch.

Diagnosis and Testing-TFI-IV System

Before performing any component testing, check for and, if necessary, repair the following:
• Damaged, corroded, contaminated, carbon tracked or worn distributor cap and rotor
• Damaged, fouled, improperly seated or gapped spark plug(s)
• Damaged or improperly engaged electrical connections, spark plug wires, etc.
• Discharged battery
• Blown fuses

SECONDARY SPARK TEST

The best way to perform this procedure is to use a spark tester (available at most automotive parts stores). Two types of spark testers are commonly available. The neon bulb type is connected to the spark plug wire and flashes with each ignition pulse. The air gap type must be adjusted to the individual spark plug gap specified for the engine. This type of tester allows the user to not only detect the presence of spark, but also the intensity (orange/yellow is weak, blue is strong).

1. Disconnect a spark plug wire at the spark plug end.
2. Connect the plug wire to the spark tester and ground the tester to an appropriate location on the engine.
3. Crank the engine and check for spark at the tester.
4. If spark exists at the tester, the ignition system is functioning properly.
5. If spark does not exist at the spark plug wire, remove the distributor cap and ensure that the rotor is turning when the engine is cranked.
6. If the rotor is turning, perform the spark test again using the ignition coil wire.
7. If spark does not exist at the ignition coil wire, test the ignition coil, and other distributor related components or wiring. Repair or replace components as necessary.

IGNITION COIL PRIMARY CIRCUIT SWITCHING

1. Unplug the wiring harness from the ignition coil. Check the harness for dirt, corrosion or damage.
2. Attach a 12 volt DC test light between the coil **TACH** terminal and a good engine ground.

3. Crank the engine and observe the lamp.

4. If the lamp flashes or lights without flashing, go to the ignition coil primary resistance test in this section.

5. If there is no light or a very dim light, perform the primary circuit continuity test in this section.

IGNITION COIL PRIMARY RESISTANCE

♦ **See Figure 13**

1. Turn the ignition switch to the **OFF** position.
2. Unplug the ignition coil connector. Check the harness for dirt, corrosion or damage.
3. Using an ohmmeter, measure the resistance from the positive to negative terminals of the coil.
4. The resistance should be 0.3–1.0 ohms.
5. If the resistance is less than 0.3 ohms or greater than 1.0 ohms, replace the coil.

IGNITION COIL SECONDARY RESISTANCE

♦ **See Figure 14**

1. Unplug the ignition coil connector. Check the harness for dirt, corrosion or damage.
2. Using an ohmmeter, measure the resistance from the negative terminal to the high voltage terminal of the ignition coil connector.
3. The resistance should be 6,500–11,500 ohms.
4. If the resistance is less than 6,500 ohms or greater than 11,500 ohms, replace the coil.

WIRING HARNESS

♦ **See Figure 17**

1. Disconnect the wiring harness from the ignition module.
2. Disconnect the wire at the **S** terminal of the starter relay.
3. Measure the battery voltage.
4. Carefully insert a small straight pins in the appropriate terminal.

➡**Do not allow the straight pins to contact an electrical ground, while performing this test.**

5. Measure the voltage at the following points:
   a. Terminal No. 2 with the ignition switch in the **RUN** position.
   b. Terminal No. 3 with the ignition switch in the **RUN** position.
   c. Terminal No. 4 with the ignition switch in the **START** position.
6. Turn the ignition switch **OFF** and remove the straight pin.
7. Reconnect the **S** terminal wire at the starter relay.
8. If the results are not within 90% of battery voltage, inspect the wiring harness and connectors in the faulty circuit. Also, check for a faulty ignition switch.

PRIMARY CIRCUIT CONTINUITY

1. Seperate the wiring harness connector from the ignition module.
2. Attach the negative lead of a voltmeter to the base of the distributor and the positive lead to the battery positive terminal. Measure and note the battery voltage reading.
3. Insert a straight pin into connector terminal No. 2, attach the positive lead of the voltmeter to the straight pin and the negative lead to the distributor base.
4. Turn the ignition key to the **RUN** position and measure the voltage. The voltage reading should be at least 90% of the battery voltage.
5. If the voltage reading is less than 90% battery voltage, perform the ignition coil primary voltage test in this section.
6. Turn the ignition switch **OFF** and remove the straight pin.

IGNITION COIL PRIMARY VOLTAGE

1. Attach the negative lead of a voltmeter to the base of the distributor and the positive lead to the battery positive terminal. Measure and note the battery voltage reading.
2. Turn the ignition key to the **RUN** position and attach the positive lead of the voltmeter to the negative ignition coil terminal. Note the voltage reading and turn the ignition **OFF**.
3. If the voltage reading is less than 90% battery voltage, inspect the wiring between the ignition module and the negative coil terminal.

IGNITION COIL SUPPLY VOLTAGE

1. Attach the negative lead of a voltmeter to the base of the distributor.
2. Turn the ignition key to the **RUN** position and attach the positive lead of the voltmeter to the positive ignition coil terminal. Note the voltage reading and turn the ignition **OFF**.
3. If the voltage reading is at least 90% of the battery voltage and the engine will not run, check the ignition coil connector and terminals for damage, corrosion and dirt. If the terminals and connector are in good condition, replace the ignition switch.

STATOR

♦ **See Figure 18**

1. Remove the distributor from the engine. Remove the TFI-IV module from the distributor.
2. Using an ohmmeter, measure the resistance between the TFI-I module terminals, as follows:
   a. GND ƒ PIP In: should be greater than 500 ohms.
   b. PIP PWR ƒ PIP In: should be less than 2 kilohms.
   c. PIP PWR ƒ TFI-IV PWR: should be less than 200 ohms.
   d. GND ƒ IGN GND: should be less than 2 ohms.
   e. PIP In ƒ PIP: should be less than 200 ohms.
3. If the readings are within the specified value, replace the stator.
4. If the readings are not as specified, replace the TFI module.

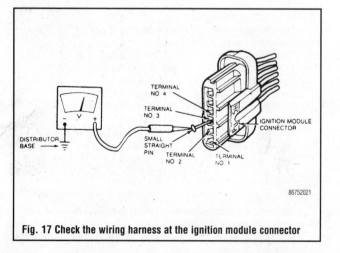

Fig. 17 Check the wiring harness at the ignition module connector

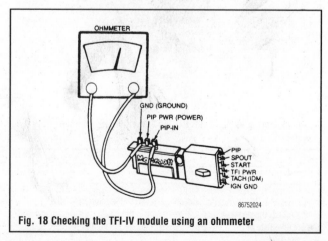

Fig. 18 Checking the TFI-IV module using an ohmmeter

Ignition Module

REMOVAL & INSTALLATION

1. Disconnect the negative battery cable.
2. Remove the distributor from the engine.
3. Place the distributor assembly on a workbench.
4. Remove the two TFI ignition module retaining screws.
5. Pull the right side of the module down the distributor mounting flange and then back up to disengage the module terminals from the connector in the distributor base. The module may then be pulled toward the flange and away from the distributor.

➡**Do not attempt to lift the module from the mounting surface, except as explained in Step 3, as the pins will break at the distributor module connector.**

To install:

6. Coat the baseplate of the TFI ignition module uniformly with a $FR1/32 in. (0.8mm) of silicone dielectric compound WA-10 or equivalent.
7. Position the module on the distributor base mounting flange. Carefully position the module toward the distributor bowl and engage the three connector pins securely.
8. Install the retaining screws. Tighten to 15–35 inch lbs. (1.7–4.0 Nm), starting with the upper right screw.
9. Install the distributor into the engine. Install the cap and wires.
10. Reconnect the negative battery cable.
11. Recheck the initial timing. Adjust the timing, if necessary.

Distributor

REMOVAL & INSTALLATION

▸ **See Figures 19, 20, 21 and 22**

1. Disconnect the negative battery cable.
2. Remove the distributor cap and position the cap and wires out of the way. You may opt to mark the wires or the cap so as to avoid confusion when replacing the wires on the cap.
3. Disconnect and plug the vacuum hose at the vacuum diaphragm (carbureted engines only).
4. Disconnect the wiring harness to the distributor.

➡**Some engines are equipped with a security-type distributor hold-down bolt. Use tool T82L-12270—A or equivalent to remove the distributor.**

5. Matchmark the distributor base to the rocker arm cover to allow more accurate timing upon reinstallation.
6. Unfasten the two distributor hold-down bolts and remove the distributor from the engine.

To install:

Engine Not Disturbed

1. Check that the base O-ring and the drive coupling spring is in place.
2. Position the distributor in the engine. Make certain the offset tang of the drive coupling is in the groove on the end of the camshaft.
3. Loosely install the distributor hold-down bolts.
4. Install the distributor rotor.
5. Attach the distributor wiring harness.
6. Install the cap.
7. Reconnect the negative battery cable, start the engine and check the ignition timing.
8. Once the ignition timing is correct, tighten the distributor hold-down to 4–5 ft. lbs. (5–7 Nm).
9. Recheck the ignition timing and readjust as necessary.
10. Install the vacuum hose (carbureted only).

Engine Disturbed

1. Position the distributor in the engine. Make certain the offset tang of the drive coupling is in the groove on the end of the camshaft.
2. Make sure that the engine is still with the No. 1 piston up on TDC of its compression stroke.
3. If the engine was disturbed while the distributor was removed, it will be necessary to remove the No. 1 spark plug and rotate the engine clockwise until the No. 1 piston is on the compression stroke as follows:
   a. Remove the No. 1 spark plug.
   b. Place a socket and breaker bar on the crankshaft pulley bolt.
   c. Place your thumb over the No. 1 spark plug hole.
   d. Rotate the engine clockwise using the breaker bar and socket attached to the crankshaft pulley bolt until you feel air pressure pushing on your thumb.
   e. When you feel the pressure on your thumb, stop turning the crankshaft and check that the timing marks are aligned. If the timing marks are not aligned, turn the crankshaft slowly until the marks align.
   f. If you go past the alignment marks, repeat the procedure.
   g. Remove the breaker bar and socket.
4. If installing the old distributor:
   a. Install the distributor and align the marks made before removal and ensure the rotor points toward the mark on the distributor housing made previously. Make certain the rotor is pointing to the No. 1 mark on the distributor base.
5. If installing a new distributor:
   a. Install the rotor and cap (with wires still attached) on the distributor, follow the No. 1 spark plug wire from the plug to the cap, this will be the No.1 tower on the cap. Mark the location of the tower on the distributor housing, then remove the cap.
   b. Install the distributor and make sure the rotor aligns with the No.1 tower mark made on the distributor.
6. When all the marks are aligned, loosely install the distributor hold-down bolts.

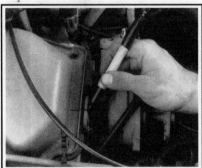

Fig. 19 Matchmark the distributor to the rocker cover, in order to assure installation in the original position

Fig. 20 After detaching the wiring, remove the hold-down bolts using a ratchet and socket

Fig. 21 Remove the distributor assembly (with the rotor still attached) for inspection

Fig. 22 Inspect the O-ring and replace if dry, cracked or compressed

7. Install the distributor rotor.
8. Attach the distributor wiring harness.
9. Install the cap.
10. Reconnect the negative battery cable, start the engine and check the ignition timing.
11. Once the ignition timing is correct, tighten the distributor hold-down to 48–60 inch lbs. (5–7 Nm).
12. Recheck the ignition timing and readjust as necessary.
13. Install the vacuum hose (carbureted engines only).

FIRING ORDERS

▶ **See Figures 23 and 24**

➡ **To avoid confusion, remove and tag the spark plug wires one at a time, for replacement.**

If a distributor is not keyed for installation with only one orientation, it could have been removed previously and rewired. The resultant wiring would hold the correct firing order, but could change the relative placement of the plug towers in relation to the engine. For this reason, it is imperative that you label all wires before disconnecting any of them. Also, before removal, compare the current wiring with the accompanying illustrations. If the current wiring does not match, make notes in your book to reflect how your engine is wired.

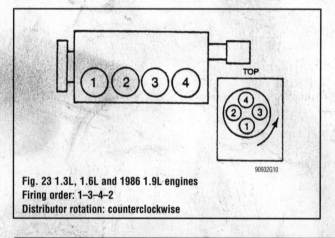

Fig. 23 1.3L, 1.6L and 1986 1.9L engines
Firing order: 1–3–4–2
Distributor rotation: counterclockwise

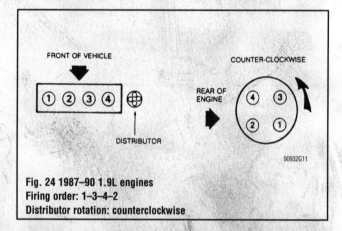

Fig. 24 1987–90 1.9L engines
Firing order: 1–3–4–2
Distributor rotation: counterclockwise

CHARGING SYSTEM

Alternator Precautions

To prevent damage to the alternator and voltage regulator, the following precautionary measures must be taken when working with the electrical system:
- NEVER ground or short out the alternator or regulator terminals.
- NEVER operate the alternator with any of its or the battery's lead wires disconnected.
- NEVER use a fast battery charger to jump start a dead battery.
- NEVER attempt to polarize an alternator.
- NEVER subject the alternator to excessive heat or dampness (for instance, steam cleaning the engine).
- NEVER use arc welding equipment on the car with the alternator connected.
- ALWAYS observe proper polarity of the battery connections; be especially careful when jump starting the car.
- ALWAYS remove the battery or at least disconnect the ground cable while charging.
- ALWAYS disconnect the battery ground cable while repairing or replacing an electrical components.

Alternator

TESTING

Rectifier and Stator Grounded Tests

▶ **See Figures 25 and 26**

1. Check the drive belt tension and ensure that it is properly adjusted.
2. Check the battery terminals and make sure they are clean and tight.
3. Check all the charging system wires for insulation damage, corrosion at the connections and make sure they are properly engaged.
4. Start the engine and check that the battery voltage is approximately 14.1–14.7 volts.
5. If the battery voltage is not within specification, remove the alternator from the vehicle.

➡**These tests cannot be performed using a Digital Volt Ohmmeter (DVOM).**

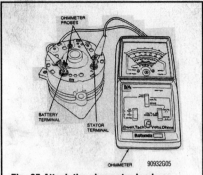

Fig. 25 Attach the ohmmeter leads as illustrated to check the rectifier and stator—rear terminal alternator

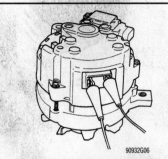

Fig. 26 Attach the ohmmeter leads as illustrated to check the rectifier and stator—alternator with integral regulator and external fan

Fig. 27 Attach the ohmmeter leads as illustrated to test for an open field or short circuit—rear terminal alternator

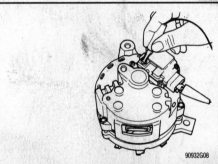

Fig. 28 Attach the ohmmeter leads as illustrated to test for an field open or short circuit—alternator with integral regulator and external fan

6. Using an analog ohmmeter, contact the **B+** terminal with one lead and the **STA** terminal with the other lead.

7. Reverse the leads and repeat the test.

8. There should be no needle movement in one direction, which indicates that the rectifier diodes are being checked in the reverse current direction and are not being shorted. A low reading of about 6.5 ohms with the leads reversed indicates that the rectifier positive diodes are being checked in the forward current direction. If there is a reading in both directions, this indicates a bad positive diode or a shorted radio suppression capacitor.

9. Attach one lead to the **STA** terminal and the other lead to the alternator rear housing.

10. Reverse the leads and repeat the test.

11. A reading in both directions indicates a either a grounded stator wiring, damaged negative diode, grounded stator lead wire or a shorted radio suppression capacitor.

12. If there is no needle movement with the leads in one direction and no needle movement or high resistance (significantly more than 6.5 ohms) in the opposite direction. The rectifier is damaged and the alternator must be replaced.

Field Open or Short Circuit Test

♦ See Figures 27 and 28

1. Place your ohmmeter on the multiply by 1 setting.

2. On models with a rear terminal alternator, attach one lead from the meter to the **FIELD** terminal and the other lead to the **GROUND>** terminal.

3. On models with an integral regulator and external fan, attach one lead from the meter to the **F** screw head and the other lead to the **A** blade terminal.

4. Spin the alternator pulley and note the reading, the reading should fluctuate between 2.2–100 ohms.

5. Reverse the leads, spin the pulley and note the reading. The reading should be 2.2–9 ohms

6. If there is no reading in one direction and a reading of 9 ohms in the other direction, replace the alternator.

7. If you have a reading of less than 2.2 ohms in either direction replace the alternator.

8. Attach one lead to the **F** terminal or screw and the other lead to the alternator rear housing.

9. Reverse the leads and repeat the test.

10. The reading in one direction should be infinite and approximately 9 ohms in the other. If the readings are not within specification, replace the alternator.

REMOVAL & INSTALLATION

♦ See Figures 29, 30, 31, 32 and 33

1. Disconnect the negative battery cable.

2. If equipped with a pulley cover shield, remove the shield at this time.

3. Loosen the alternator pivot bolt. Remove the adjustment arm to alternator bolt. Pivot the alternator to gain slack in the drive belt and remove the belt.

4. Disconnect and label (for correct installation) the alternator wiring.

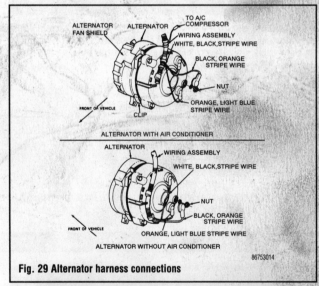

Fig. 29 Alternator harness connections

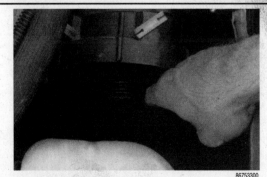

Fig. 30 Remove and set aside the alternator belt

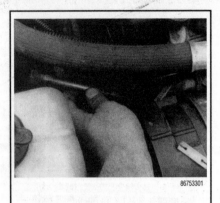

Fig. 31 Remove the alternator pivot bolt

Fig. 32 Tag and disconnect the wiring harness connector

Fig. 33 Remove the alternator when it is completely detached

➡**Some models use a push-on wiring connector on the field and stator connections. Pull or push straight when removing or installing, or damage to the connectors may occur.**

   5. Remove the pivot bolt and the alternator.

To install:

   6. Position the alternator assembly onto the vehicle. Install the alternator pivot and adjuster arm bolts, but do not tighten them at this time.

   7. Install the alternator drive belt and adjust the drive belt tension.

   8. Once the proper belt tension is reached, tighten the adjuster bolt to 24–40 ft. lbs. (33–54 Nm) and the pivot bolt to 40–50 ft. lbs. (54–67 Nm).

   9. Reconnect the alternator wiring.

   10. Install the pulley shield, if equipped.

   11. Connect the negative battery cable.

Regulator

➡**Two different types of regulators were used; which one depends on the model, engine, alternator output and type of dash mounted charging indicator (light or ammeter). The regulators are 100 percent solid state, and are calibrated and preset by the manufacturer. No readjustment is required or possible on these regulators.**

SERVICE

Whenever system components are being replaced, the following precautions should be followed so that the charging system will work properly and the components will not be damaged.

• Always use the proper alternator.

• The electronic regulators are color coded for identification. Never install a different coded regulator for the one being replaced. If the regulator removed is not the color mentioned, identify the output of the alternator and method of charging indication, then consult the parts department of a Ford/Mercury dealer, or an automotive parts store to obtain the correct regulator. A black coded regulator is used in systems which use a signal lamp for charging indication. Gray coded regulators are used with an ammeter gauge.

• Models using a charging lamp indicator are equipped with a 500 ohms resistor on the back of the instrument panel.

REMOVAL & INSTALLATION

Except External Fan Type

   1. Disconnect the negative battery cable.

   2. Unplug the wiring harness from the regulator.

   3. Remove the regulator mounting screws and remove the regulator assembly.

To install:

   4. Place the regulator into position and install the retaining screws.

   5. Reconnect the wiring harness.

   6. Reconnect the negative battery cable.

External Fan Type

   1. Disconnect the negative battery cable.

   2. Disconnect the wiring harness from the alternator/regulator assembly.

   3. Remove the four screws (T20 Torx® head type) attaching the regulator to the alternator rear housing.

   4. Remove the regulator, with brush holder attached, from the alternator.

To install:

   5. Fit the regulator assembly to the alternator rear housing and install the retaining (T20 Torx® head type) screws.

   6. Reconnect the alternator wiring harness.

   7. Reconnect the negative battery cable.

STARTING SYSTEM

Starter

TESTING

Starter Cranks Slowly

   1. Place the transaxle in **N** (MT) or **P** (AT).

   2. If equipped, unplug the vacuum line from the thermactor bypass valve.

   3. Clean and tighten the battery terminals and posts.

   4. Check the battery voltage, making sure that it is fully charged.

   5. Clean and tighten the connections at the starter relay and the battery ground on the engine. Eyelet terminals should be tight and not easily rotated. Also check the wires for a short to ground.

   6. If after completing the above steps the starter still cranks slowly, replace the starter motor.

Relay Operates (Clicks), But Starter Does Not Crank

   1. Clean and tighten the electrical connections at the starter and relay.

   2. Make sure the wire strands are secure in the eyelets.

   3. If after completing the above steps the starter still does not operate, replace the starter motor.

Relay Chatters or Does Not Click, and Starter Does Not Crank

   1. Clean and tighten the battery terminals and posts.

   2. Check the battery voltage, making sure that it is fully charged.

   3. Remove the push on connector from the relay (red wire with a blue stripe).

   4. Make sure the connection is clean and tight, also check that the relay bracket is grounded.

   5. If the connection is good check the operation of the relay using a jumper as follows:

a. Place the transaxle in Neutral (MT) or Park (AT).

b. Remove the push on connector from the relay.

c. Connect the jumper wire from the terminal on the starter relay to the main terminal (battery side or battery positive post).

d. If this does not correct the problem, replace the relay.

e. If this corrects the problem, check the ignition switch, neutral start switch and the starting circuit wiring for damage, dirty or loose connections.

Starter Spins (Humming Noise), But Does Not Crank Engine

1. Remove the starter and check the armature shaft for corrosion.

2. If corrosion is present, clean or replace the armature and install the starter.

3. If no corrosion is found, replace the armature or starter.

Starter Cranking Circuit Test

▶ **See Figure 34**

1. Attach the connections to the components as shown in the accompanying illustration.

2. Unplug the ignition coil electrical connector to prevent the vehicle from starting.

3. Attach a remote starter from the battery terminal of the starter relay to the **S** terminal of the starter relay.

4. Use a voltmeter set at the 0–2 volt range. The maximum allowable voltage drop is as follows:

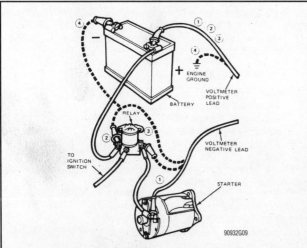

Fig. 34 Attach the voltmeter leads to components in the order shown to test the starter cranking circuit

a. 0.5 volt with the voltmeter negative lead attached to the starter terminal and the positive lead attached to the battery positive terminal (connection 1).

b. 0.1 volt with the voltmeter negative lead attached to the starter relay (battery side) and the positive lead attached to the positive terminal of the battery (connection 2).

c. 0.3 volt with the voltmeter negative lead attached to the starter relay (starter side) and the positive lead attached to the positive terminal of the battery (connection 3).

d. 0.3 volt with the voltmeter negative lead attached to the negative battery terminal and the positive lead attached to the engine ground (connection 4).

REMOVAL & INSTALLATION

▶ **See Figures 35, 36 and 37**

1. Disconnect the negative battery cable.

2. Raise and safely support the vehicle.

3. Disconnect the wiring harness from the starter motor.

4. On models that are equipped with a manual transaxle, remove the three nuts that attach the roll restrictor brace to the starter mounting studs at the transaxle. Remove the brace. On models that are equipped with an automatic transaxle, remove the nose bracket mounted on the starter studs.

5. Unfasten the two bolts attaching the rear starter support bracket, remove the retaining nut from the rear of the starter motor and remove the support bracket.

6. On models equipped with a manual transaxle, remove the three starter mounting studs and the starter motor.

7. On models equipped with an automatic transaxle, remove the two starter mounting studs and the starter motor.

To install:

8. Position the starter to the transaxle housing. Install the attaching studs or bolts. Tighten the studs or bolts to 30–40 ft. lbs. (41–54 Nm).

9. On vehicles equipped with a roll restrictor brace, install the brace on the starter mounting studs at the transaxle housing.

10. Position the starter rear support bracket to the starter. Install the two attaching bolts.

11. Connect the starter cable to the starter terminal.

12. Lower the vehicle and connect the negative battery cable.

RELAY REPLACEMENT

1. Disconnect the negative battery cable.

2. Remove the nuts securing the battery-to-relay lead and relay-to-starter lead.

3. Unfasten the relay mounting bolts and remove the relay.

4. Install the new relay, bolt it in place and re-connect the leads.

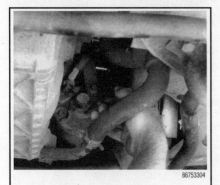

Fig. 35 Remove the two bolts attaching the rear starter bracket

Fig. 36 Disconnect the wiring harness from the terminal on the starter motor

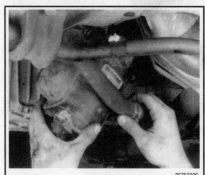

Fig. 37 Once disconnected, remove the starter

SENDING UNITS

➡**This section describes the operating principles of sending units, warning lights and gauges. Sensors which provide information to the Electronic Control Module (ECM) are covered in Section 4 of this manual.**

Instrument panels contain a number of indicating devices (gauges and warning lights). These devices are composed of two separate components. One is the sending unit, mounted on the engine or other remote part of the vehicle, and the other is the actual gauge or light in the instrument panel.

Several types of sending units exist; however, most can be characterized as being either a pressure type or a resistance type. Pressure type sending units convert liquid pressure into an electrical signal which is sent to the gauge. Resistance type sending units are most often used to measure temperature and use variable resistance to control the current flow back o the indicating device. Both types of sending units are connected in series by a wire to the battery (through the ignition switch). When the ignition is turned **ON**, current flows from the battery through the indicating device and on to the sending unit.

Coolant Temperature Sender

TESTING

Gauge Type

1. Make sure the engine-to-ground body strap is clean and tight.
2. Start the engine and let it idle until it reaches normal operating temperature and check the cooling system operation. If the cooling system is not functioning properly, repair the problem before continuing with the test.
3. Check the gauge operation, if the gauge is functioning the sender is working properly.
4. If the gauge is not operating, turn the engine **OFF**.
5. Locate the sender and unplug the lead wire from the sender.
6. Ground the sender lead wire. The gauge should go to the full hot position.
7. If the gauge does not go to the full hot position it may be faulty.
8. If the gauge goes to the full hot position, replace the sender.

Lamp Type

♦ **See Figure 38**

1. Turn the ignition switch **ON**. The temperature lamp should illuminate.
2. If the lamp does not illuminate, replace the bulb and check the lamp wiring.
3. Start the engine and let it idle until it reaches normal operating temperature and check the cooling system operation. If the cooling system is not functioning properly, repair the problem before continuing with the test.
4. Once the engine is started, the lamp should go off.
5. If the lamp remains on and the coolant temperature is less than 121˜C (249˜F), unplug the light lead from the sender.
6. If the light goes out, replace the sender.
7. If the light stays on, repair the ground circuit from the sender to the bulb.
8. In some cases the engine lamp is controlled by the temperature and oil pressure sending units. If the light stays illuminated while the engine is running, check the lamp wiring circuit, then test the sending units and their wiring as outlined, to see if the light will operate properly.

REMOVAL & INSTALLATION

✳✳ CAUTION

Never open, service or drain the radiator or cooling system when hot; serious burns can occur from the steam and hot coolant. Also, when draining engine coolant, keep in mind that cats and dogs are attracted to ethylene glycol antifreeze and could drink any that is left in an uncovered container or in puddles on the ground. This will prove fatal in sufficient quantities. Always drain coolant into a sealable container. Coolant should be reused unless it is contaminated or is several years old.

1. Locate the coolant temperature sending unit on the engine.
2. Disconnect the sending unit electrical harness.

3. If necessary, drain the engine coolant below the level of the switch.
4. If it is not necessary to drain the coolant, remove the radiator cap to relieve system pressure.
5. Unfasten and remove the sending unit from the engine.
To install:
6. Coat the new sending unit with Teflon® tape or an equivalent water resistant, electrically conductive sealer.
7. Install and tighten the sending unit.
8. Attach the sending unit's electrical connector.
9. If drained, fill the engine with coolant.
10. If removed, install the radiator cap.
11. Start the engine, allow it to reach operating temperature and check for leaks.
12. Check for proper sending unit operation.

Oil Pressure Sender

The oil pressure sensor is threaded into an oil passage on the engine block.

TESTING

♦ **See Figure 39**

1. Turn the ignition switch to the **ON** position but do not start the engine. The warning lamp should come on.
2. If the lamp does not illuminate, remove the wire from the sender and ground the wire.
3. If the lamp now operates, the sender should be replaced or it is not properly sealed to the engine.
4. If the lamp does not illuminate with the wire grounded, replace the bulb and repeat the test.

REMOVAL & INSTALLATION

1. Raise the car and support it with safety stands.
2. Locate the oil pressure sending unit on the engine.
3. Unplug the sending unit electrical connection.
4. Unfasten and remove the sending unit from the engine.
To install:
5. Coat the new sending unit with Teflon® tape or an equivalent water resistant, electrically conductive sealer.
6. Install the sending unit and tighten to 8–18 ft. lbs. (10–24 Nm).
7. Attach the sending unit's electrical connector.
8. Remove the safety stands and lower the car.
9. Start the engine, allow it to reach operating temperature and check for leaks.
10. Check for proper sending unit operation.

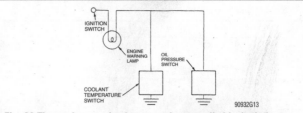

Fig. 38 The engine warning lamp may be controlled by both the temperature and oil pressure sending units

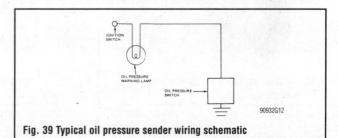

Fig. 39 Typical oil pressure sender wiring schematic

3

ENGINE AND ENGINE OVERHAUL

ENGINE MECHANICAL

1.3L and 1.6L ENGINE MECHANICAL SPECIFICATIONS

Description	English Specifications	Metric Specifications
General Information		
Engine type	Single Overhead Camshaft	
Displacement		
1.3L engine	79 cu. in.	1.3L (1300cc)
1.6L engine	98 cu. in.	1.6L (1606cc)
Number of cylinders	4	
Bore and stroke		
1.3L engine	3.15 x 2.4 in.	80 x 64.5mm
1.6L engine	3.15 x 3.13 in.	80 x 79.5mm
Firing order	1-3-4-2	
Oil pressure (hot @ 2000 rpm)		
1981 models	40 psi	275 kPa
1982-85 models	30-50 psi	206-344 kPa
Cylinder Head and Valve Train ① ②		
Combustion chamber volume	53.01-56.21cc	
Valve guide bore diameter		
Intake	0.531-0.532 in.	13.481-13.519mm
Exhaust	0.531-0.532 in.	13.481-13.519mm
Valve guide I.D.		
Intake	0.3174-0.3187 in.	8.063-8.094mm
Exhaust	0.3174-0.3187 in.	8.063-8.094mm
Valve seat		
Intake width	0.069-0.091 in.	1.75-2.32mm
Exhaust width	0.069-0.091 in.	1.75-2.32mm
Angle	45°	
Run-out (TIR)	0.03 in. (Max.)	0.076mm (Max.)
Bore diameter (insert counterbore diameter)		
Intake	1.723 in. (Min.)	43.763mm (Min.)
	1.724 in. (Max.)	43.788mm (Max.)
Exhaust		
1981 models	1.428 in. (Min.)	38.265mm (Min.)
	1.453 in. (Max.)	38.288mm (Max.)
1982-85 models	1.506 in. (Min.)	38.263mm (Min.)
	1.507 in. (Max.)	38.288mm (Max.)
Valve stem-to-guide clearance		
Intake	0.0008-0.0027 in.	0.020-0.069mm
Exhaust	0.0015-0.0032 in.	0.046-0.095mm
Valve head diameter		
1981 models		
Intake	1.654 in.	42.0mm
Exhaust	1.457 in.	37.0mm
1982-85 models		
Intake	1.66-1.65 in.	42.1-41.9mm
Exhaust	1.50-1.42 in.	37.1-36.9mm
Valve face run-out limit		
Intake	0.002 in.	0.05mm
Exhaust	0.002 in.	0.05mm
Valve face angle		
1981 models	91°	
1982-85 models	45.6°	

90933C01

1.3L and 1.6L ENGINE MECHANICAL SPECIFICATIONS

Description	English Specifications	Metric Specifications
Cylinder Head and Valve Train (cont.) ① ②		
Valve stem diameter		
Standard		
1981 models		
Intake	0.316 in.	8.034mm
Exhaust	0.315 in.	8.008mm
Oversize		
Intake	0.331 in.	8.414mm
Exhaust	0.330 in.	8.388mm
Oversize		
Intake	0.348 in.	8.834mm
Exhaust	0.348 in.	8.828mm
1982–85 models		
Intake	0.3167–0.3159 in.	8.043–8.025mm
Exhaust	0.3156–0.3149 in.	8.017–7.996mm
Oversize		
Intake	0.3316–0.3309 in.	8.423–8.405mm
Exhaust	0.3306–0.3298 in.	8.397–8.378mm
Oversize		
Intake	0.3481–0.3474 in.	8.843–8.825mm
Exhaust	0.3479–0.347 in.	8.777–8.759mm
Valve springs		
1981 models		
Compression pressure @ specified length		
Loaded	180 lbs. @ 1.09 in.	81.6kg @ 27.71mm
Unloaded	75 lbs. @ 1.461 in.	34kg @ 37.71mm
Free length (approximate)	1.724 in.	43.79mm
Assembled height	1.504–1.417 in.	38.19–35.99mm
Service limit	10% pressure loss @ specified height	
Out of square limit	0.060 in.	1.53mm
Base engine		
Compression pressure @ specified length		
Loaded	200 lbs. @ 1.09 in.	892.7 N @ 27.71mm
Unloaded	95 lbs. @ 1.461 in.	422 N @ 37.1mm
Free length (approximate)	1.86 in.	47.2mm
EFI engine		
Compression pressure @ specified length		
Loaded	200 lbs. @ 1.09 in.	892.7 N @ 27.71mm
Unloaded	95 lbs. @ 1.461 in.	422 N @ 37.1mm
Free length (approximate)	1.86 in.	47.2mm
EFI–HO engine		
Compression pressure @ specified length		
Loaded	216 lbs. @ 1.016 in.	960 N @ 25.8mm
Unloaded	94 lbs. @ 1.461 in.	417 N @ 37.1mm
Free length (approximate)	1.90 in.	48.3mm
Assembled height	1.48–1.44 in.	37.5–36.9mm
Service limit	5% pressure loss @ specified height	
Out-of-square limit	0.060 in.	1.53mm

90933C02

1.3L and 1.6L ENGINE MECHANICAL SPECIFICATIONS

Description	English Specifications	Metric Specifications
Cylinder Head and Valve Train (cont.) ① ②		
Rocker arm ratio	1.65	
Valve tappet (hydraulic)		
Diameter (standard)		
1981 models	0.874 in.	22.206mm
1982-85 models	0.8745-0.8740 in.	22.212-22.200mm
Clearance-to-bore	0.0009-0.0026 in.	0.023-0.065mm
Roundness	0.0005 in.	0.013mm
Run-out	0.1	
Finish	8 micro in.	0.2 micro mm
Service limit	0.005 in.	0.127mm
Collapsed tappet gap	0.059-0.194 in.	1.50-4.93mm
Distributor shaft bearing bore diameter	1.852-1.854 in.	47.05-47.10mm
Tappet bore diameter	0.8754-0.8766 in.	22.235-22.265mm
Camshaft bore inside diameter		
1981 models		
No. 1	1.803-1.763 in.	45.808-44.783mm
No. 2	1.774-1.773 in.	45.058-45.033mm
No. 3	1.784-1.783 in.	45.308-45.283mm
No. 4	1.794-1.793 in.	45.558-45.553mm
No. 5	1.803-1.802 in.	45.808-45.783mm
1982-85 models		
No. 1	1.7636-1.7646 in.	44.796-44.821mm
No. 2	1.7735-1.7745 in.	45.046-45.071mm
No. 3	1.7833-1.7843 in.	45.298-45.321mm
No. 4	1.7931-1.7941 in.	45.546-45.571mm
No. 5	1.8030-1.8040 in.	45.796-45.821mm
Camshaft bore inside diameter–Oversize (not applicable to HO, EFI or Turbo)		
No. 1	1.7796-1.7786 in.	45.201-45.176mm
No. 2	1.7894-1.7884 in.	45.451-45.426mm
No. 3	1.7993-1.7983 in.	45.701-45.676mm
No. 4	1.8091-1.8081 in.	45.951-45.926mm
No. 5	1.8189-1.8179 in.	46.201-46.176mm
Camshaft		
Base engine		
Lobe lift		
Intake	0.229 in.	5.805mm
Exhaust	0.229 in.	5.805mm
Allowable lobe lift loss	0.005 in.	0.127mm
Theoretical valve maximum lift		
Intake	0.377 in.	9.58mm
Exhaust	0.377 in.	9.58mm
HO and EFI engine		
Lobe lift		
Intake	0.240 in.	6.094mm
Exhaust	0.240 in.	6.094mm
Theoretical valve maximum lift		
Intake	0.036 in.	10.06mm
Exhaust	0.036 in.	10.06mm

1.3L and 1.6L ENGINE MECHANICAL SPECIFICATIONS

Description	English Specifications	Metric Specifications
Camshaft (cont.)		
End-play	0.006-0.0018 in.	0.152-0.046mm
Service limit	0.0078 in.	0.20mm
Journal-to-bearing clearance	0.0008-0.0028 in.	0.0205-0.0705mm
Journal diameter		
Standard		
No. 1	1.7623-1.7613 in.	44.7625-44.7375mm
No. 2	1.7721-1.7712 in.	45.0125-44.9875mm
No. 3	1.7820-1.7810 in.	45.2624-45.2375mm
No. 4	1.7918-1.7979 in.	45.5125-45.4875mm
No. 5	1.8017-1.7979 in.	45.765-45.7375mm
Oversize (not applicable to HO)		
No. 1	1.7730-1.7763 in.	45.1425-45.1175mm
No. 2	1.7871-1.7861 in.	45.3925-45.3675mm
No. 3	1.7969-1.7960 in.	45.6425-45.6175mm
No. 4	1.8091-1.8081 in.	45.8925-45.8675mm
No. 5	1.8166-1.8156 in.	46.1425-46.1175mm
Run-out limit (run-out of center bearing, relative to bearings 1 and 5)	0.005 in.	0.127mm
Out-of-round limit	0.0003 in.	0.008mm
Camshaft Drive		
Assembled gear face run-out		
Crankshaft	0.026 in.	0.65mm
Camshaft	0.011 in.	0.275mm
Cylinder Block		
Head gasket surface flatness	0.003 in.	0.076mm
Cylinder bore		
Diameter	3.15 in.	80mm
Out-of-round limit		
1981 models	0.001 in.	0.025mm
1982-85 models	0.0015 in.	0.04mm
Out-of-round service limit	0.005 in.	0.127mm
Taper limit (positive)	0.001 in.	0.025mm
Main bearing bore diameter		
@ + or - 30° PF bearing cap P/L	2.4521-2.4533 in.	62.2835-62.3145mm
Other than above	2.4525 in. (+ or - 0.00025 in.)	62.2935mm (+ or - 0.0065 mm)
Crankshaft and Flywheel		
Main bearing journal diameter	2.2834-2.2826 in.	58.0-57.98mm
Out-of-round limit	0.0005 in.	0.013mm
Taper limit (per 1 inch: 25.4mm)	0.008 in./1 in.	0.008mm/25.4mm
Journal run-out limit (run-out of bearings 2, 3 and 4, relative to bearings 1 and 5)	0.005 in.	0.13mm
Surface finish	12 micro in.	0.3 micro mm
Thrust bearing journal		
Length	1.135-1.136 in.	28.825-28.854mm
Connecting rod journal		
Diameter	1.886-1.885 in.	47.91-47.89mm
Out-of-round limit	0.0005 in.	0.013mm
Taper limit (per 1 inch or 25.4mm)	0.0003 in.	0.008mm
Surface limit	12 micro in.	0.3 micro mm

90933C04

1.3L and 1.6L ENGINE MECHANICAL SPECIFICATIONS

Description	English Specifications	Metric Specifications
Crankshaft and Flywheel (cont.)		
Main bearing thrust face		
Surface finish		
Front	25 micro in.	0.6 micro mm
Rear	35 micro in.	0.9 micro mm
Front run-out limit	0.001 in.	0.025mm
Flywheel clutch face		
Run-out limit (TIR)	0.007 in.	0.180mm
Flywheel ring gear lateral run-out (TIR)		
Manual transaxle	0.025 in.	0.64mm
Automatic transaxle	0.05 in.	1.5mm
Crankshaft end-play	0.004-0.008 in.	0.100-0.200mm
Connecting rod bearings		
Clearance-to-crankshaft		
Desired		
1981 models	0.0002-0.0003 in.	0.006-0.0064mm
1982-85 models	0.0008-0.0015 in.	0.020-0.038mm
Allowable		
1981 models	0.0002-0.0025 in.	0.006-0.0064mm
1982-85 models	0.0008-0.0026 in.	0.020-0.066mm
Bearing wall thickness (standard)		
1981 models	0.0581-0.0586 in.	1.476-1.488mm
1982-85 models	0.00016-0.0028 in.	0.004-0.072mm
Main bearings		
Clearance of crankshaft		
Desired	0.0008-0.0015 in.	0.020-0.028mm
Allowable	0.0008-0.0026 in.	0.020-0.016mm
Bearing wall thickness	0.0837-0.084 in.	2.128-2.138mm
Connecting Rod, Piston and Rings		
Connecting rod		
Piston pin bore diameter	0.8106-0.8114 in.	20.589-20.609mm
Crankshaft bearing bore diameter	2.0035-2.0043 in.	50.89-50.91mm
Out-of-round limit—piston pin bore		
1981 models	0.0003 in.	0.008mm
1982-85 models	0.0004 in.	0.010mm
Taper limit—piston pin bore		
1981 models	0.00015 in./1 in.	0.0038mm/25.4mm
1982-85 models	0.0004 in.	0.010mm
Length (center-to-center)		
1.3L	4.285-4.288 in.	108.845-108.915mm
1.6L	5.193-5.196 in.	131.905-131.975mm
Out-of-round limit—bearing bore	0.0004 in.	0.010mm
Alignment bore-to-bore (max. differential)		
Twist	0.002 in.	0.05mm
1981 models	0.003 in./1 in.	0.076/25.4mm
1982-85 models	0.002 in.	0.05mm
Bend		
1981 models	0.0015 in./1 in.	0.038/25.4mm
1982-85 models	0.0015 in.	0.038mm

90933C05

1.3L and 1.6L ENGINE MECHANICAL SPECIFICATIONS

Description	English Specifications	Metric Specifications
Connecting Rod, Piston and Rings (cont.)		
Side clearance (assembled-to-crankshaft)		
Standard	0.004-0.011 in.	0.092-0.268mm
Service limit	0.014 in.	0.356mm
Piston Diameter		
1981 models		
Coded red	3.1466-3.1461 in.	79.925-79.910mm
Coded blue	3.1478-3.1472 in.	79.955-79.940mm
0.004 in. (0.1mm) oversize	3.1506-3.15 in.	80.025-80.010mm
1982-85 models		
Coded red	3.1463-3.157 in.	79.915-79.900mm
Coded blue	3.1474-3.1468 in.	79.945-79.930mm
0.004 in. (0.1mm) oversize	3.1502-3.1496 in.	80.015-80.000mm
Piston-to-bore clearance		
1981 models	0.0008-0.0016 in.	0.020-0.040mm
1982-85 models	0.0018-0.0026 in.	0.045-0.065mm
Piston bore diameter		
1981 models	0.8122-0.8127 in.	20.630-20.642mm
1982-85 models	0.8123-0.8128 in.	20.632-20.644mm
Ring groove width		
Compression (top)	0.0653-0.0645 in.	1.660-1.640mm
Compression (bottom)	0.0812-0.0802 in.	2.062-2.038mm
Oil	0.1587-0.1578 in.	4.032-4.008mm
Piston pin		
Length	2.606-2.638 in.	66.2-67.0mm
Diameter		
Standard	0.8119-0.8124 in.	20.622-20.634mm
Pin-to-piston clearance		
1981 models	0.0003-0.0005 in.	0.007-0.013mm
1982-85 models	0.0002-0.0004 in.	0.005-0.011mm
Pin-to-rod clearance	Press fit-8 kilonewtons	
Piston rings		
Ring width		
1981 models		
Compression (top)	0.0634-0.0621 in.	1.61-1.578mm
Compression (bottom)	0.0786-0.078 in.	1.998-1.982mm
Oil ring	Side seal (snug fit)	
Service limit (side clearance)	0.006 in.	0.15mm
1982-85 models		
Compression (top)	0.0626-0.0621 in.	1.59-1.578mm
Compression (bottom)	0.0574-0.0586 in.	1.998-1.982mm
Oil ring	Side seal (snug fit)	
Service limit (side clearance)	0.006 in. (Max.)	0.15mm (Max.)
Ring gap		
Compression (top)	0.012-0.020 in.	0.30-0.50mm
Compression (bottom)	0.012-0.020 in.	0.30-0.50mm
Oil ring (steel ring)	0.016-0.055 in.	0.04-1.4mm

90933C06

1.3L and 1.6L ENGINE MECHANICAL SPECIFICATIONS

Description	English Specifications	Metric Specifications
Connecting Rod, Piston and Rings (cont.)		
Side clearance		
1981 models		
1st ring	0.002-0.0032 in.	0.05-0.82mm
2nd ring	0.0016-0.0032 in.	0.04-0.08mm
1982-85 models		
1st ring	0.001-0.003 in.	0.030-0.082mm
2nd ring	0.002-0.003 in.	0.049-0.084mm
Lubrication System		
Oil pump		
Relief valve spring tension		
1981 models	42.6-47.1 @ 0.921 in.	42.6-47.1 @ 23.4mm
1982-85 models	5.3-4.7 lbs. @ 1.65 in.	23.6-20.9 N @ 42.5mm
Relief valve-to-bore clearance	0.0007-0.0031 in.	0.02-0.08mm
Rotor clearance		
Outer gear-to-housing clearance	0.0029-0.0063 in.	0.0074-0.161mm
Inner and outer gear-to-cover clearance (end-play)	0.0005-0.0035 in.	0.013-0.089mm
Inner-to-outer gear tip clearance	0.002-0.007 in.	0.05-0.18mm
Fuel Pump		
Static pressure	5-6.5 psi	34-49 kPa
Minimum volume flow (curb idle with return line plugged)	1 pint	4.732 liters
Eccentric total lift	0.189-0.209 in.	4.8-5.3mm

① Some engines may have O/S tappets (All eight). The cylinder head assemblies will be identified by metal stamping .254 OT on the machined pad

below the rocker arm rail and above the No. 1 exhaust port.

② Some engines may have O/S tappets 1 and/or O/S camshaft. The cylinder head assemblies will be identified by a metal stamping on the cover rail tug

on the No. 4 exhaust port .38 O/C. The camshaft will also be stamped .38 O/S on the distributor drive end

TIR: Total Indicated Run-out

Max: Maximum

Min: Minimum

@: At

90933C07

1.9L ENGINE MECHANICAL SPECIFICATIONS

Description	English Specifications	Metric Specifications
General Information		
Engine type	Single Overhead Camshaft	
Displacement	114 cu. in.	1.9L (1901cc)
Number of cylinders	4	
Bore and stroke	3.23 x 3.46 in.	82 x 88mm
Firing order	1-3-4-2	
Oil pressure (hot @ 2000 rpm)	35-65 psi	240-450 kPa
Cylinder Head and Valve Train ① ②		
Combustion chamber volume	44.4-47.6cc	
1985-87 models		
1988-90 models		
EFI-HO engines	39.1-40.7cc	
EFI engines	53.4-56.6cc	
Valve guide bore diameter		
Intake	0.531-0.5324 in.	13.481-13.519mm
Exhaust	0.531-0.5324 in.	13.481-13.519mm
Valve guide I.D.		
Intake	0.3174-0.3187 in.	8.063-8.094mm
Exhaust	0.3174-0.3187 in.	8.063-8.094mm
Valve seat		
Intake width	0.069-0.091 in.	1.75-2.32mm
Exhaust width	0.069-0.091 in.	1.75-2.32mm
Angle	45°	
Run-out (TIR)	0.03 in. (Max.)	0.076mm (Max.)
Bore diameter (insert counterbore diameter)	1.573 in. (Max.)	39.965mm (Max.)
1985-87 models		
Intake	1.723 in. (Min.)	43.763mm (Min.)
	1.724 in. (Max.)	43.788mm (Max.)
Exhaust	1.506 in. (Min.)	38.263mm (Min.)
	1.507 in. (Max.)	38.288mm (Max.)
1988-90 models		
EFI-HO engines		
Intake	1.723 in. (Min.)	43.763mm (Min.)
	1.724 in. (Max.)	43.788mm (Max.)
Exhaust	1.506 in. (Min.)	38.263mm (Min.)
	1.507 in. (Max.)	38.288mm (Max.)
EFI engines		
Intake	1.572 in. (Min.)	39.940mm (Min.)
	1.573 in. (Max.)	39.965mm (Max.)
Exhaust	1.375 in. (Min.)	34.940mm (Min.)
	1.573 in. (Max.)	39.965mm (Max.)
Valve stem-to-guide clearance		
Intake	0.0008-0.0027 in.	0.020-0.069mm
Exhaust	0.0018-0.0037 in.	0.046-0.095mm
Valve head diameter		
Intake	1.66-1.65 in.	42.1-41.9mm
Exhaust	1.50-1.42 in.	37.1-36.9mm
Valve face run-out limit		
Intake	0.002 in.	0.05mm
Exhaust	0.002 in.	0.05mm
Valve face angle	45.6°	

90933C08

1.9L ENGINE MECHANICAL SPECIFICATIONS

Description	English Specifications	Metric Specifications
Cylinder Head and Valve Train (cont.) ① ②		
Valve stem diameter		
Standard		
Intake	0.3167-0.3159 in.	8.043-8.025mm
Exhaust	0.3156-0.3149 in.	8.017-7.996mm
Oversize		
Intake	0.3316-0.3309 in.	8.423-8.405mm
Exhaust	0.3306-0.3298 in.	8.397-8.378mm
Oversize		
Intake	0.3481-0.3474 in.	8.843-8.825mm
Exhaust	0.3479-0.347 in.	8.777-8.759mm
Valve springs		
Base Engine		
Compression pressure @ specified length		
Loaded	200 lbs. @ 1.09 in.	892.7 N @ 27.71mm
Unloaded	95 lbs. @ 1.461 in.	422 N @ 37.1mm
Free length (approximate)	1.86 in.	47.2mm
EFI engine		
Compression pressure @ specified length		
Loaded	200 lbs. @ 1.09 in.	892.7 N @ 27.71mm
Unloaded	95 lbs. @ 1.461 in.	422 N @ 37.1mm
Free length (approximate)	1.86 in.	47.2mm
EFI–HO engine		
Compression pressure @ specified length		
Loaded	216 lbs. @ 1.016 in.	960 N @ 25.8mm
Unloaded	94 lbs. @ 1.461 in.	417 N @ 37.1mm
Free length (approximate)	1.90 in.	48.3mm
Assembled height	1.48-1.44 in.	37.5-36.9mm
Service limit	5% pressure loss @ specified height	
Out of square limit	0.060 in.	1.53mm
Rocker arm ratio		
Base	1.65	
EFI engine	1.65-1.68	
EFI–HO engine	1.68	
Valve tappet (hydraulic)		
Diameter (standard)	0.8745-0.8740 in.	22.212-22.200mm
Clearance to bore	0.0009-0.0026 in.	0.023-0.065mm
Roundness	0.0005 in.	0.013mm
Run-out	0.1	
Finish	8 micro in.	0.2 micro mm
Service limit	0.005 in.	0.127mm
Collapsed tappet gap		
Base	0.059-0.194 in.	1.50-4.93mm
EFI	0.04-1.3 in.	1.2-3.5mm
EFI–HO	0.5-1.4 in.	1.5-3.8mm
Tappet bore diameter	0.8754-0.8766 in.	22.235-22.265mm
Camshaft bore inside diameter		
Nos. 1, 2, 3, 4 and 5	1.8030-1.8040 in.	45.796-45.821mm
Camshaft bore inside diameter (Oversize)		
No. 1	1.7796-1.7786 in.	45.201-45.176mm
No. 2	1.7894-1.7884 in.	45.451-45.426mm
No. 3	1.7993-1.7983 in.	45.701-45.676mm
No. 4	1.8091-1.8081 in.	45.951-45.926mm
No. 5	1.8189-1.8179 in.	46.201-46.176mm

90933C09

1.9L ENGINE MECHANICAL SPECIFICATIONS

Description	English Specifications	Metric Specifications
Camshaft		
Base/EFI engine		
Lobe lift		
Intake	0.240 in.	6.096mm
Exhaust	0.240 in.	6.096mm
Allowable lobe face lift	0.005 in.	0.127mm
Theoretical valve maximum lift		
Intake	0.468 in.	10.06mm
Exhaust	0.468 in.	10.06mm
EFI-HO engine		
Lobe lift		
Intake	0.240 in.	6.731mm
Exhaust	0.240 in.	6.731mm
Theoretical valve maximum lift		
Intake	0.396 in.	11.31mm
Exhaust	0.396 in.	11.31mm
All engines		
End-play	0.006-0.0018 in.	0.152-0.046mm
Service limit	0.0078 in.	0.20mm
Journal-to-bearing clearance	0.0013-0.0033 in.	0.0335-0.0835mm
Journal diameter (standard)	1.8017-1.8007 in.	45.7625-45.7375mm
Oversize (not applicable to EFI)	1.8166-1.8156 in.	46.1425-46.1175mm
Run-out limit (run-out of center bearing relative to bearing Nos. 1 and 5)	0.005 in.	0.127mm
Out-of-round limit	0.003 in.	0.08mm
Camshaft drive		
Assembled gear face run-out		
Crankshaft	0.026 in.	0.65mm
Camshaft	0.011 in.	0.275mm
Cylinder Block		
Head gasket surface flatness	0.003 in.	0.076mm
Roughness height cutoff	0.31 in.	0.8mm
Cylinder bore		
Diameter		
1985-87 models	3.23 in.	83mm
1988-90 models	3.15 in.	80mm
Out-of-round limit	0.001 in.	0.025mm
Out-of-round service limit	0.005 in.	0.127mm
Taper limit (positive)	0.001 in.	0.025mm
Main bearing bore diameter		
@ + or - 30° PF bearing cap P/L	2.4521-2.4533 in.	62.2835-62.3145mm
Other than above	2.45225-2.45275 in.	62.287-62.30mm
Crankshaft and Flywheel		
Main bearing journal diameter	2.2835-2.2827 in.	58.0-57.98mm
Out-of-round limit	0.00032 in.	0.008mm
Taper limit (per 1 inch: 25.4mm)	0.0003 in.	0.008mm
Journal run-out limit (run-out of bearings 2, 3 and 4, relative to bearings 1 and 5)	0.002 in.	0.05mm
Surface finish	12 micro in.	0.3 micro mm
Thrust bearing journal		
Length	1.135-1.136 in.	28.825-28.854mm
Connecting rod journal		
Diameter		
1985-87 models	1.8862-1.8854 in.	47.91-47.98mm
1988-90 models	1.7287-1.7279 in.	43.91-43.89mm

1.9L ENGINE MECHANICAL SPECIFICATIONS

Description	English Specifications	Metric Specifications
Crankshaft and Flywheel (cont.)		
Out-of-round limit	0.00032 in.	0.008mm
Taper limit (per 1 inch: 25.4mm)	0.0003 in.	0.008mm
Surface limit	12 micro in.	0.3 micro mm
Main bearing thrust face		
Surface finish	25 micro in.	0.6 micro mm
Rear	35 micro in.	0.9 micro mm
Front run-out limit	0.001 in.	0.025mm
Flywheel clutch face		
Run-out limit (TIR)	0.007 in.	0.180mm
Flywheel ring gear lateral run-out (TIR)		
Manual transaxle	0.025 in.	0.64mm
Automatic transaxle	0.06 in.	1.5mm
Crankshaft end-play	0.004-0.008 in.	0.100-0.200mm
Connecting rod bearings		
Clearance-to-crankshaft		
Desired	0.0008-0.0015 in.	0.020-0.038mm
Allowable	0.0008-0.0026 in.	0.020-0.066mm
Bearing wall thickness (standard)	0.0581-0.0586 in.	1.476-1.488mm
Clearance of crankshaft		
Without the cylinder head		
Desired	0.0018-0.0026 in.	0.0457-0.0660mm
Allowable	0.0018-0.0034 in.	0.0461-0.0859mm
With the cylinder head		
Desired	0.0011-0.0019 in.	0.0279-0.0483mm
Allowable	0.0011-0.0027 in.	0.0276-0.0674mm
Bearing wall thickness	0.0838-0.0833 in.	2.129-2.117mm
Connecting Rod, Piston and Rings		
Connecting rod		
Piston pin bore diameter	0.8106-0.8114 in.	20.589-20.609mm
Crankshaft bearing bore diameter		
1985-87 models	2.0035-2.0043 in.	50.89-50.91mm
1988-90 models	1.8460-1.8468 in.	46.89-46.91mm
Out-of-round limit—piston pin bore	0.0003 in.	0.008mm
Taper limit piston pin bore	0.00015 in./1 in.	0.0038mm/25.4mm
Length (center-to-center)	5.193-5.196 in.	131.905-131.975mm
Out-of-round limit—bearing bore	0.0004 in.	0.010mm
Alignment bore-to-bore (max. differential)		
Twist	0.002 in.	0.05mm
Bend	0.0015 in.	0.038mm
Side clearance (assembled to crankshaft)		
Standard	0.004-0.011 in.	0.092-0.268mm
Service limit	0.014 in.	0.356mm
Piston Diameter		
Coded red	3.224-3.225 in.	81.90-81.92mm
Coded blue	3.225-3.226 in.	81.92-81.94mm
0.004 in. (0.1mm) oversize	3.226-3.227 in.	81.94-81.96mm
Piston-to-bore clearance	0.0016-0.0024 in.	0.040-0.060mm
Piston bore diameter	0.8123-0.8128 in.	20.632-20.644mm
Ring groove width		
Compression (Top)	0.0602-0.061 in.	1.53-1.55mm
Compression (Bottom)	0.0602-0.061 in.	1.53-1.55mm
Oil	0.1587-0.1578 in.	4.032-4.008mm

1.9L ENGINE MECHANICAL SPECIFICATIONS

Description	English Specifications	Metric Specifications
Connecting Rod, Piston and Rings (cont.)		
Piston pin		
Length	2.606-2.638 in.	66.2-67.0mm
Diameter		
Standard	0.8119-0.8124 in.	20.622-20.634mm
Pin-to-piston clearance	0.0003-0.0005 in.	0.007-0.013mm
Pin-to-rod clearance	Press fit-8 kilonewtons	
Piston rings		
Ring width		
Compression (top)	0.0578-0.0582 in.	1.47-1.49mm
Compression (bottom)	0.0574-0.0586 in.	1.46-1.49mm
Oil ring	Side seal (snug fit)	
Service limit (side clearance)	0.006 in. (max.)	0.15mm (max.)
Ring gap		
Compression (top)	0.010-0.020 in.	0.25-0.50mm
Compression (bottom)	0.010-0.020 in.	0.25-0.50mm
Oil ring (steel ring)	0.016-0.055 in.	0.04-1.4mm
Side clearance		
1st ring	0.0015-0.0032 in.	0.04-0.08mm
2nd ring	0.0015-0.0035 in.	0.04-0.09mm
Lubrication System		
Oil pump		
Relief valve spring tension	10.3-9.3 lbs. @ 1.11 in.	45.8-41.4 N @ 28.1mm
Relief valve-to-bore clearance	0.0008-0.0031 in.	0.02-0.08mm
Rotor clearance		
Outer gear-to-housing clearance	0.0029-0.0063 in.	0.0074-0.161mm
Inner and outer gear-to-cover clearance (end-play)	0.0005-0.0035 in.	0.013-0.089mm
Inner-to-outer gear tip clearance	0.002-0.007 in.	0.05-0.18mm

① Some engines may have O/S tappets (All eight). The cylinder head assemblies will be Identified by metal stamping 0.254 OT on the machined pad

below the rocker arm rail and above the No. 1 exhaust port.

② Some engines may have O/S tappaets 1 and/or O/S camshaft. The cylinder head assemblies will be identified by a metal stamping on the cover rail tug

on the No. 4 exhaust port 0.38 O/C. The camshaft will also be stamped 0.38 O/S on the distributor drive end

TIR: Total Indicated Run-out

Max: Maximum

Min: Minimum

@: At

90933C12

Engine

REMOVAL & INSTALLATION

In the process of removing the engine, you will come across a number of steps which call for the removal of a separate component or system, such as "disconnect the exhaust system" or "remove the radiator." In most instances, a detailed removal procedure can be found elsewhere in this manual.

It is virtually impossible to list each individual wire and hose which must be disconnected, simply because so many different model and engine combinations have been manufactured. Careful observation and common sense are the best possible approaches to any repair procedure.

Removal and installation of the engine can be made easier if you follow these basic points:

- If you have to drain any of the fluids, use a suitable container.
- Always tag any wires or hoses and, if possible, the components they came from before disconnecting them.
- Because there are so many bolts and fasteners involved, store and label the retainers from components separately in muffin pans, jars or coffee cans. This will prevent confusion during installation.
- After unbolting the transmission or transaxle, always make sure it is properly supported.
- If it is necessary to disconnect the air conditioning system, have this service performed by a qualified technician using a recovery/recycling station. If the system does not have to be disconnected, unbolt the compressor and set it aside.
- When unbolting the engine mounts, always make sure the engine is properly supported. When removing the engine, make sure that any lifting devices are properly attached to the engine. It is recommended that if your engine is supplied with lifting hooks, your lifting apparatus be attached to them.
- Lift the engine from its compartment slowly, checking that no hoses, wires or other components are still connected.
- After the engine is clear of the compartment, place it on an engine stand or workbench.
- After the engine has been removed, you can perform a partial or full teardown of the engine using the procedures outlined in this manual.

➡When removing some 1.3L and 1.6L engines, the engine and transaxle will be removed as an assembly.

1. Disconnect the negative battery cable.
2. Mark the position of the hinges on the hood underside and remove the hood.
3. Remove the air cleaner assembly. Remove the air feed duct and the heat tube. Remove the air duct to the alternator.
4. If equipped with air conditioning, remove compressor with the lines still connected and position it out of the way.

✳✳ CAUTION

Never open, service or drain the radiator or cooling system when hot; serious burns can occur from the steam and hot coolant. Also, when draining engine coolant, keep in mind that cats and dogs are attracted to ethylene glycol antifreeze and could drink any that is left in an uncovered container or in puddles on the ground. This will prove fatal in sufficient quantities. Always drain coolant into a sealable container. Coolant should be reused unless it is contaminated or is several years old.

5. Drain the cooling system.
6. Remove the drive belts from the alternator and if equipped, the thermactor pump.
7. If equipped, disconnect the thermactor air supply hose.
8. Disconnect the wiring harness at the alternator.
9. Remove alternator and if equipped, the thermactor.
10. Disconnect and remove the upper and lower radiator hoses.
11. If equipped with an automatic transaxle, disconnect and plug the fluid cooler lines at the radiator.
12. Disconnect the heater hoses from the engine.
13. Unplug the electric cooling fan wiring harness.
14. Remove the fan and radiator shroud as an assembly.

15. Remove the radiator.
16. Label and disconnect all electrical connections, vacuum lines, linkages and hoses that would interfere with engine removal.
17. If equipped with fuel injection, relieve the fuel system pressure.
18. Disconnect the fuel supply and return fuel lines to the fuel pump. Plug the lines.
19. Raise and safely support the car on jackstands.
20. Disconnect the battery cable from the starter motor.
21. Remove the starter motor.
22. Disconnect the exhaust system from the exhaust manifold.

✳✳ CAUTION

The EPA warns that prolonged contact with used engine oil may cause a number of skin disorders, including cancer! You should make every effort to minimize your exposure to used engine oil. Protective gloves should be worn when changing the oil. Wash your hands and any other exposed skin areas as soon as possible after exposure to used engine oil. Soap and water, or waterless hand cleaner should be used.

23. Drain the engine oil.
24. Remove the brace in front of the bell housing (flywheel or converter) inspection cover.
25. Remove the inspection cover.
26. Remove the crankshaft pulley.
27. If equipped with a manual transaxle, remove the timing belt cover lower attaching bolts.
28. If equipped with an automatic transaxle, and if you are removing the engine but not the transaxle, remove the torque converter-to-flywheel mounting nuts.
29. Remove the lower engine to transaxle attaching bolts.
30. Remove the engine mount retainers.
31. Lower the car from the jackstands.
32. Attach an engine lifting sling to the engine. Connect a chain hoist to the lifting sling and remove all slack.
33. Remove the through-bolt from the right front engine mount and remove the insulator.
34. If the car is equipped with a manual transaxle, remove the timing belt cover upper mounting bolts and remove the cover.
35. Remove the right front insulator attaching bracket from the engine.
36. If you are removing the engine, but not the transaxle:
    a. Position a floor jack under the transaxle. Raise the jack just enough to take the weight of the transaxle.
    b. Remove the upper bolts connecting the engine and transaxle. Unfasten any oil pan-to-transaxle bolts.
    c. Slowly raise the engine and separate it from the transaxle.
    d. If the engine will not move, check that all mounts and brackets that would interfere with engine removal are disconnected, also check for any wires or hoses that are still connected, then continue to remove the engine.
    e. Make sure the torque converter stays on the transaxle.
    f. Remove the engine from the car. On models equipped with a manual transaxle, the engine must be separated from the input shaft of the transaxle before raising.
37. If removing the engine and transaxle as an assembly:
    a. Remove the halfshafts.
    b. Disconnect all linkages, wires, lines and hoses from the transaxle.
    c. Remove the engine and transaxle from the vehicle.

To install:
38. If only the engine was removed:
    a. Slowly lower the engine and connect it to the transaxle.
    b. Install the upper bolts connecting the engine and transaxle.
    c. Lower the jack under the transaxle.
39. If the engine and transaxle were removed as an assembly:
    a. Install the engine and transaxle assembly in the vehicle.
    b. Connect all linkages, wires, lines and hoses to the transaxle.
    c. Install the halfshafts.
40. Install the right front insulator attaching bracket to the engine.
41. If the car is equipped with a manual transaxle, install the timing belt cover upper mounting bolts and install the cover.
42. Remove the engine sling from the engine. Install the through-bolt to the right front engine mount and install the insulator.

43. Raise the car and support it safely on jackstands.

44. Install the bolt and nut attaching the right front mount insulator to the engine bracket.

45. Install the bypass hose to the intake manifold and tighten the clamps.

46. If the engine and transaxle were removed as an assembly:

   a. Install the lower engine-to-transaxle attaching bolts.

   b. If equipped with an automatic transaxle, install the torque converter to the flywheel.

47. Install the crankshaft pulley.

48. If equipped with a manual transaxle, install the timing belt cover lower attaching bolts.

49. Install the brace in front of the bell housing (flywheel or converter) inspection cover. Install the inspection cover.

50. Reconnect the exhaust system to the exhaust manifold. Refill the engine oil.

51. Reconnect the battery cable to the starter motor. Install the brace or bracket to the back of the starter and install the starter.

52. Lower the car from the jackstands. Install the clamp to the heater supply and return tubes.

53. If equipped with fuel injection, install the supply and return fuel lines.

54. Install the radiator.

55. Attach all vacuum lines, hoses, electrical connections and linkages that were removed to facilitate engine removal.

56. Install the fan and radiator shroud as an assembly.

57. If equipped with an automatic transaxle, reconnect the fluid cooler lines at the radiator.

58. Refill the cooling system.

59. Install alternator and thermactor.

60. Install the drive belts.

61. Reconnect the negative battery cable.

62. If equipped with air conditioning, install the compressor.

63. Install the air cleaner assembly.

64. Install the air feed duct and the heat tube.

65. Install the air duct to the alternator.

66. Install the hood.

Rocker Arm (Valve) Cover

REMOVAL & INSTALLATION

♦ **See Figures 1 and 2**

1. Disconnect the negative battery cable.
2. Place fender covers on the aprons.
3. Remove the air cleaner.
4. Tag and disconnect all vacuum hoses from the rocker arm cover.
5. Remove the rocker arm cover retaining screws and washers.

Fig. 1 Remove the rocker arm cover bolts with an appropriate ratchet and socket . . .

86753308

Fig. 2 . . . then lift off the rocker arm cover

6. Loosen the PCV oil separator and allow the hoses to clear the rocker cover.

7. Remove the rocker arm cover and gasket.

8. Clean the head and rocker arm cover mating surfaces.

To install:

9. Install the guide pins into the cylinder head and position the gasket and rocker arm cover over the guide pins.

10. Start two retaining screw and washer assemblies into the cylinder head and remove the guide pins.

11. Install all retaining screw and washer assemblies and tighten the retainers as follows:

   a. On 1981–88 models, tighten all retainers to 72–96 inch lbs. (8–11 Nm).

   b. On 1989–90 models, tighten the bolts to 84–120 inch lbs. (9–13 Nm) and all studs to 72–96 inch lbs. (8–11 Nm).

12. Connect all vacuum hoses and install the air cleaner assembly.

13. Connect the negative battery cable, start the engine and check for leaks.

Rocker Arms

REMOVAL & INSTALLATION

1.3L and 1.6L Engines

♦ **See Figure 3**

1. Disconnect the negative battery cable. 4
2. Place fender covers on the aprons.
3. Remove the rocker arm cover.

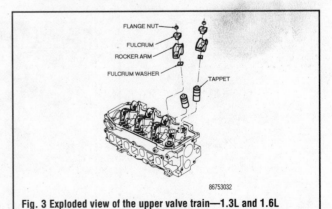

86753032

Fig. 3 Exploded view of the upper valve train—1.3L and 1.6L engines

4. Mark the location of the rocker arms so that they can be installed in their original positions.

5. Remove the rocker arm nuts.

6. Remove the rocker arms, fulcrums and if equipped the fulcrum washer.

To install:

7. Coat the valve tips and the rocker arm contact areas with Lubriplate® or the equivalent.

8. Install the fulcrum washers.

9. Rotate the camshaft as necessary to position the camshaft sprocket keyway at the 12 o'clock position.

➡ **The tappets are numbered one through 8 with the No. 1 tappet at the front of the head.**

10. Install the rocker arms and fulcrums at tappet positions 3–6–7–8.

11. Install the attaching nuts and tighten them to 15–19 ft. lbs. (21–25 Nm).

12. Rotate the camshaft to position the camshaft sprocket keyway at the 6 o'clock position.

13. Install the rocker arms and fulcrums at tappet positions 1–2–4–5.

14. Make sure each fulcrum is properly seated in the rocker arm pedestal slot before tightening the attaching nut.

15. Install the attaching nuts and tighten them to 15–19 ft. lbs. (21–25 Nm).

16. Install the valve the cover.

17. Connect the negative battery cable.

1.9L Engines

▶ **See Figures 4, 5 and 6**

1. Disconnect the negative battery cable.

2. Place fender covers on the aprons.

3. Remove the rocker arm cover.

4. Mark the location of the rocker arms so that they can be installed in their original positions.

5. Remove the rocker arm bolts.

6. Remove the rocker arms, fulcrums and tappet guide retainers.

To install:

7. Rotate the camshaft as necessary to position the camshaft sprocket keyway at the 12 o'clock position.

8. Install the tappet guide retainers into the rocker arm fulcrum slots, in both the intake and exhaust sides. Align the notch with the exhaust valve tappet.

9. Install four rocker arms in tappet positions 3, 6, 7 and 8.

10. Lubricate the rocker arm surface that contacts the fulcrum with heavy engine oil.

11. Install the four fulcrums making sure they are fully seated in the slots of the cylinder head.

12. Install the bolts and tighten them to 17–22 ft. lbs. (23–30 Nm).

13. Rotate the camshaft to position the camshaft sprocket keyway at the 6 o'clock position.

14. Install the rocker arms and fulcrums at tappet positions 1, 2, 4 and 5.

15. Lubricate the rocker arm surface that contacts the fulcrum with heavy engine oil.

16. Install the four fulcrums making sure they are fully seated in the slots of the cylinder head.

17. Install the bolts and tighten them to 17–22 ft. lbs. (23–30 Nm).

18. Install the valve the cover.

19. Connect the negative battery cable.

Thermostat

REMOVAL & INSTALLATION

▶ **See Figures 7, 8, 9, 10 and 11**

✳✳ CAUTION

Never open, service or drain the radiator or cooling system when hot; serious burns can occur from the steam and hot coolant. Also, when draining engine coolant, keep in mind that cats and dogs are attracted to ethylene glycol antifreeze and could drink any that is left in an uncovered container or in puddles on the ground. This will prove fatal in sufficient quantities. Always drain coolant into a sealable container. Coolant should be reused unless it is contaminated or is several years old.

1. Disconnect the negative battery cable.

2. Place fender covers on the aprons.

3. Drain the cooling system to a level below the thermostat.

4. Loosen the top radiator hose clamp at the radiator.

5. Remove the thermostat housing mounting bolts and lift up the housing.

6. Remove the thermostat by turning counterclockwise.

7. Clean the thermostat housing and engine gasket mounting surfaces.

To install:

8. Install a new mounting gasket, and fully insert the thermostat to compress the mounting gasket. Turn the thermostat clockwise to secure it in the housing.

9. Position the housing onto the engine. Install the mounting bolts and tighten to 72–96 inch lbs. 7–11 Nm) on 1981–87 models. On 1988–90 models, tighten the mounting bolts to 10–16 ft. lbs. (13–19 Nm).

10. Refill the cooling system.

11. Connect the negative battery cable, start the engine and check for leaks.

Intake Manifold

REMOVAL & INSTALLATION

✳✳ CAUTION

Never open, service or drain the radiator or cooling system when hot; serious burns can occur from the steam and hot coolant. Also, when draining engine coolant, keep in mind that cats and dogs are attracted to ethylene glycol antifreeze and could drink any that is left in an uncovered container or in puddles on the ground. This will prove fatal in sufficient quantities. Always drain coolant into a sealable container. Coolant should be reused unless it is contaminated or is several years old.

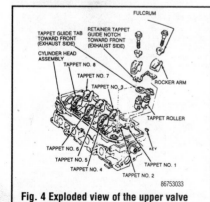

Fig. 4 Exploded view of the upper valve train—1.9L engines

Fig. 5 A single bolt holds the rocker arm to its mounting

Fig. 6 When installing the rocker arms, use a torque wrench and tighten to the proper specification

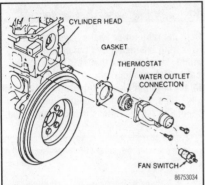

Fig. 7 Exploded view of the thermostat mounting—1.9L engines; others similar

Fig. 8 For thermostat removal, unplug the wiring from the thermal switch in the housing . . .

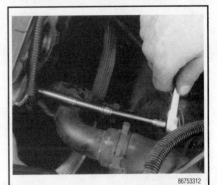

Fig. 9 . . . then unfasten the water outlet retaining bolts and remove the outlet

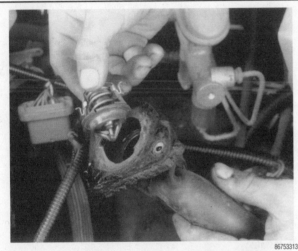

Fig. 10 Once the outlet is off, rotate the thermostat counterclockwise to remove it

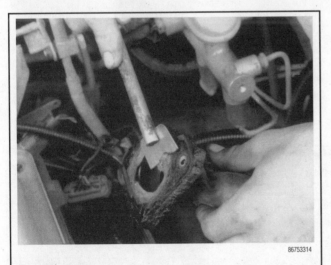

Fig. 11 To install, first remove all the old gasket with a scraper, but be sure not to gouge the mating surface

Carbureted Engines

▶ See Figure 12

1. Disconnect the negative battery terminal.
2. Remove the air cleaner housing.

3. Partially drain the cooling system and disconnect the heater hose from under the intake manifold.
4. Disconnect and label all vacuum and electrical connections that would interfere with the manifold removal.
5. Disconnect the EGR supply tube.
6. Raise the vehicle and support it using safely stands.
7. Using tool T-81P-8564-A or equivalent, tag and disconnect the Ported Vacuum Switch (PVS) hose connectors.
8. Remove the three bottom intake manifold nuts.
9. Lower the vehicle.
10. Disconnect the fuel line at the filter and the fuel line at the carburetor.
11. Disconnect the accelerator cable and if equipped the speed control cable.
12. If equipped with automatic transaxle disconnect the throttle valve linkage at the carburetor and remove the cable bracket attaching bolts.
13. If equipped with power steering, remove the thermactor pump drive belt, the pump, the mounting bracket, and the bypass hose.
14. Remove the fuel pump.
15. Remove the remaining intake manifold bolts.
16. Remove the intake manifold, and gasket.

➡Do not lay the intake manifold flat as the gasket surfaces may become damaged.

To install:
17. Clean the intake manifold-to-cylinder head mating surfaces.
18. Install the intake manifold, and gasket.
19. Install and tighten the intake manifold nuts to 12–15 ft. lbs. (16–20 Nm). Use wrench T-81P-9425-A or equivalent to tighten nut No. 1 to specification.

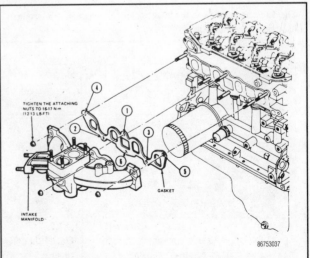

Fig. 12 Exploded view of the intake manifold mounting—carbureted engines

20. Install the fuel pump.
21. Install the thermactor pump drive belt, the pump, the mounting bracket, and the by-pass hose, as required.
22. If equipped with automatic transaxle reconnect the throttle valve linkage at the carburetor and install the cable bracket attaching bolts.
23. Disconnect the accelerator cable and if equipped the speed control cable.
24. Connect the fuel line at the filter and the fuel line at the carburetor.
25. Raise the vehicle and support it with safely stands.
26. Using tool T-81P-8564-A or equivalent, connect the PVS hose connectors.
27. Reconnect the heater hose to under the intake manifold.
28. Lower the vehicle.
29. Reconnect the EGR vacuum tube.
30. Attach all vacuum and electrical connections.
31. Refill the cooling system.
32. Install the air cleaner housing.
33. Reconnect the negative battery terminal.

Fuel Injected Engines

EXCEPT 1988–90 1.9L HO ENGINES

♦ See Figures 13 thru 18

➡Although the throttle body is missing in some of the photos, it need not be removed to perform this procedure.

1. Raise and secure the hood in the open position.
2. Install protective fender covers.
3. Properly relieve the fuel system pressure.
4. Disconnect the negative battery cable.

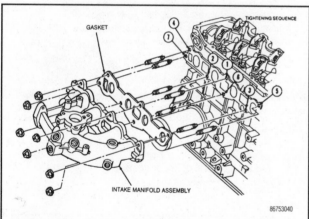

Fig. 13 Exploded view of the intake manifold mounting and torque sequence—1.9L CFI engine

Never open, service or drain the radiator or cooling system when hot; serious burns can occur from the steam and hot coolant. Also, when draining engine coolant, keep in mind that cats and dogs are attracted to ethylene glycol antifreeze and could drink any that is left in an uncovered container or in puddles on the ground. This will prove fatal in sufficient quantities. Always drain coolant into a sealable container. Coolant should be reused unless it is contaminated or is several years old.

5. Partially drain the cooling system and disconnect the heater hose at the fitting located on the side of the intake manifold.

➡If equipped with an automatic transaxle, removing the ATF dipstick and its housing may provide a little extra room to work.

6. Remove the air cleaner assembly.
7. Identify, tag and disconnect the vacuum hoses.
8. Identify, tag and unplug the wiring connectors at the following points:
   a. Coolant temperature sensor
   b. Air charge temperature sensor
9. Remove the Exhaust Gas Recirculation (EGR) supply tube.
10. Raise and safely support the vehicle.
11. Using tool T-81P-8564-A or equivalent, remove the Ported Vacuum Switch (PVS) hose connectors. Label the connectors and set aside.
12. Remove the bottom four intake manifold retaining nuts (locations 2, 3, 6 and 7).
13. Lower the vehicle.
14. Disconnect the fuel lines at the throttle body.
15. Disconnect the accelerator and, if equipped, the speed control cable.
16. Disconnect the throttle valve linkage at the throttle body and remove the cable bracket attaching bolts on vehicles equipped with an automatic transaxle.
17. Remove the remaining three intake manifold attaching nuts, intake manifold and gasket.

➡Do not lay the intake manifold flat, as the gasket surfaces may be damaged.

To install:
18. Make sure the mating surfaces on the intake manifold and the cylinder head are clean and free of gasket material.
19. Install a new intake manifold gasket.
20. Position the intake manifold on the engine and install the attaching nuts. Tighten the nuts to 12–15 ft. lbs. (16–20 Nm), in the following sequence:
   a. No. 1, then No. 6.
   b. Nos. 2 and 3 together
   c. Nos. 4, 5 and 7 together
21. Connect the throttle valve linkage and install the cable bracket attaching bolts, if removed, on vehicles with an automatic transaxle.
22. Connect the accelerator cable and, if equipped, the speed control cable.
23. Connect fuel lines at the fuel charging assembly.
24. Raise and safely support the vehicle with jackstands.

Fig. 14 Remove the cable bracket attaching bolts on vehicles equipped with an automatic transaxle

Fig. 15 On automatic transaxle vehicles, removing the ATF dipstick housing may provide extra clearance

Fig. 16 Disconnect the heater hose at the fitting on the side of the intake manifold

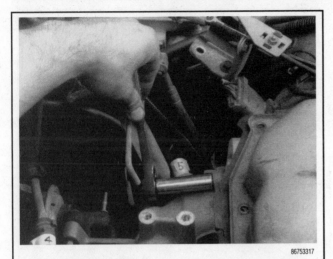

Fig. 17 With everything disconnected, remove the intake manifold mounting nuts . . .

Fig. 18 . . . then carefully pull the manifold and gasket from the cylinder head

25. Connect the heater hose to the fitting located on side of the intake manifold.
26. Lower the vehicle.
27. Connect the EGR supply tube.
28. Attach the wiring connectors at the following points:
    a. Coolant the temperature sensor
    b. Air charge temperature sensor
29. Connect all vacuum hoses.
30. Install the air cleaner assembly.
31. Fill the cooling system to specified level.
32. Connect the negative battery cable.
33. Start the engine and check for fuel and coolant leaks. Bring the engine to normal operating temperature and check again for coolant leaks.

1988–90 1.9L HO ENGINES—UPPER INTAKE MANIFOLD ASSEMBLY

1. Disconnect the negative battery cable.
2. Disconnect the engine air cleaner outlet tube from the air intake throttle body.
3. Unplug the Throttle Position (TP) sensor electrical connection.
4. Tag and disconnect the vacuum lines from the upper intake manifold and the throttle body assembly.
5. Disconnect the EGR tube at the manifold connection by supporting the connector while loosening the compression nut.
6. Unplug the air bypass valve connector.

7. Remove the manifold upper support bracket top bolt.
8. Unfasten the five upper manifold retaining bolts.
9. Remove the upper manifold assembly.
10. Remove and discard the gasket from the manifold.

➡If scraping is necessary, be careful not to damage the gasket surfaces of the upper or lower manifolds, or allow material to fall into the manifold.

11. Clean and inspect the mounting faces of the manifold assembly. Both surfaces must be clean, dry and flat.
To install:
12. Install a new gasket on the lower manifold and mount the upper manifold into position.
13. Install and tighten the upper manifold bolts to 15–22 ft. lbs. (20–30 Nm).
14. Install the manifold upper support bracket top bolt. Tighten the bolt to 15–22 ft. lbs. (20–30 Nm).
15. Install the EGR tube with an oil-coated compression nut and tighten to 30–40 ft. lbs. (40–55 Nm).
16. Attach the electrical connections and vacuum lines.
17. Install the air supply tube. Tighten the clamps to 12–20 inch lbs. (1.4–2.3 Nm).
18. Connect the negative battery cable.

1988–90 1.9L HO ENGINES—LOWER INTAKE MANIFOLD ASSEMBLY

♦ See Figure 19

1. Disconnect the negative battery cable.
2. Properly relieve the fuel system pressure.
3. Disconnect the engine air cleaner outlet tube from the air intake throttle body.
4. Tag and unplug the Throttle Position (TP) sensor electrical connection.
5. Disconnect and remove the accelerator and speed control cables, if equipped, from the accelerator mounting bracket and throttle lever.
6. Unfasten the top manifold vacuum fitting connections by disconnecting the rear vacuum line to the dash panel vacuum tree and the vacuum line at the intake manifold tee.
7. Disconnect the PCV system by disconnecting the hoses from the PCV valve at the intake manifold connection.
8. Disconnect the EGR vacuum line at the EGR valve. Disconnect the EGR tube from the upper intake manifold by supporting the connector while loosening the compression nut.
9. Disconnect the upper support manifold bracket by removing the top bolt only. Leave the bottom bolts attached.
10. If necessary, remove the upper intake manifold.
11. Disconnect the electrical connectors at the main engine harness, near the No. 1 runner, and at the ECT sensor located in the heater supply tube.
12. Remove the fuel supply and return lines.
13. Remove the six manifold mounting nuts.
14. Disconnect the lower support manifold bracket by removing the top bolt only. Leave the bottom bolts attached.

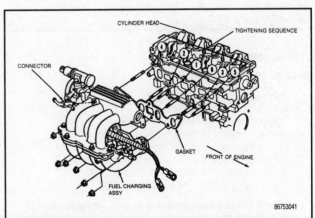

Fig. 19 Exploded view of the intake manifold and torque sequence—1988–90 1.9L HO EFI engine

15. Remove the manifold with the wiring harness and gasket.

16. If necessary, at this time remove subassemblies from the intake manifold such as the throttle body, fuel rail, fuel injectors, etc.

17. Clean and inspect the mounting faces of the manifold assembly and cylinder head. Both surfaces must be clean, dry and flat.

To install:

18. Clean the manifold stud threads with a wire brush. If excessively corroded, replace them with new studs. Coat the threads with a suitable anti-seize compound, or clean oil.

19. Install a new gasket.

20. Install the manifold assembly to the cylinder head and secure with the top middle nut. Tighten the nut finger-tight only at this time.

21. Install the fuel return line to the fitting in the fuel supply manifold. Install the two manifold mounting nuts, finger-tight.

22. Install the remaining three manifold mounting nuts. Tighten all six nuts to 12–15 ft. lbs. (16–20 Nm) in the proper sequence.

23. If removed, install the upper intake manifold.

24. Connect the upper and lower manifold support brackets and tighten the bolts to 15–22 ft. lbs. (20–30 Nm).

25. Install the EGR tube with oil-coated compression nut tightened to 30–40 ft. lbs. (40–55 Nm).

26. Attach the vacuum line to the throttle body port and connect the large PCV vacuum line to the upper manifold fitting.

27. Attach the rear manifold vacuum connections at the dash panel vacuum tree and connect the vacuum line(s) to the upper manifold.

28. Connect the accelerator and, if equipped, speed control cables.

29. Install the air supply tube. Tighten the clamps to 12–20 inch lbs. (1.4–2.3 Nm).

30. Connect the wiring harness at the coolant temperature sensor in the heater supply tube and the main engine harness, near the No. 1 runner.

31. Connect the fuel supply and return lines.

32. Reconnect the spring-lock coupling retaining clips on the fuel inlet and return fittings.

33. Fill the cooling system.

34. Connect the negative battery cable.

35. Start the engine and bring to normal operating temperature. Check for leaks. Stop the engine and check the coolant level.

Exhaust Manifold

REMOVAL & INSTALLATION

❊❊ CAUTION

Never open, service or drain the radiator or cooling system when hot; serious burns can occur from the steam and hot coolant. Also, when draining engine coolant, keep in mind that cats and dogs are attracted to ethylene glycol antifreeze and could drink any that is left in an uncovered container or in puddles on the ground. This will prove fatal in sufficient quantities. Always drain coolant into a sealable container. Coolant should be reused unless it is contaminated or is several years old.

Non-Turbocharged Engines

▶ **See Figures 20 thru 28**

1. Disconnect the negative battery cable.
2. Remove the air cleaner assembly.
3. Disconnect the electric fan wire.
4. Remove the radiator shroud bolts and radiator shroud.
5. Remove the air conditioning hose bracket.
6. Remove the oxygen sensor from the exhaust manifold.
7. Remove the exhaust manifold heat shield.
8. Disconnect the EGR tube at the exhaust manifold.

➡**The exhaust manifold retainers tend to become heavily corroded. If so, spray them with some penetrating lubricant and allow it to dissolve the rust.**

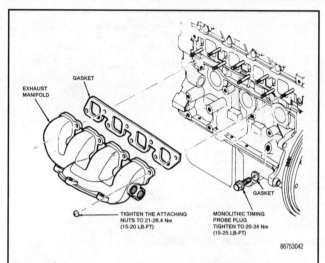

Fig. 20 Exploded view of the intake manifold mounting and torque sequence

Fig. 21 Either remove the header pipe at the exhaust manifold . . .

Fig. 22 . . . or remove the ground strap and detach the header at the catalytic converter

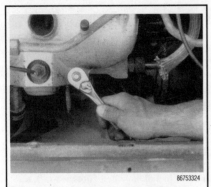

Fig. 23 Remove the A/C hose bracket to make room for heat shield removal

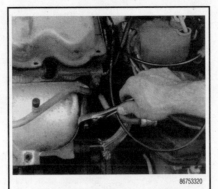

Fig. 24 Unbolt the exhaust manifold heat shield using the correct (metric) socket

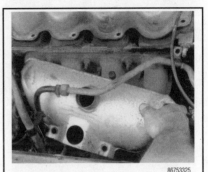

Fig. 25 After the oxygen sensor has been removed, the unbolted heat shield is clear for removal

Fig. 26 Disconnect the EGR tube at the exhaust manifold

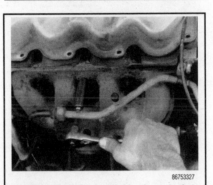

Fig. 27 Unbolt the manifold using a socket and extension—take care with heavily corroded fasteners

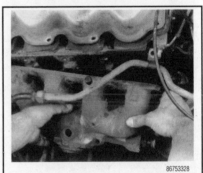

Fig. 28 Carefully remove the exhaust manifold and, if attached, header pipe assembly

9. Remove the exhaust manifold retaining nuts.
10. Raise and safely support the vehicle.
11. Remove the anti-roll brace.
12. Disconnect the water tube brackets.
13. Disconnect the exhaust pipe at the catalytic converter.

➡️**The exhaust pipe may also be unbolted from the manifold instead of the catalytic converter.**

14. Remove the exhaust manifold and gasket. Discard the gasket and replace with a new one.

To install:

15. Clean the exhaust manifold gasket contact areas.
16. Position the gasket and exhaust manifold.
17. Install the exhaust pipe to the catalyst.
18. Install the anti-roll brace. Install the water tube brackets.
19. Lower the vehicle.
20. Install the exhaust manifold retaining nuts. Tighten to 15–20 ft. lbs. (21–26 Nm).
21. Install the exhaust manifold heat shield.
22. Install the oxygen sensor in exhaust manifold. Tighten to 30–40 ft. lbs. (40–50 Nm).
23. Connect the EGR tube.
24. Install the air conditioning hose brackets.
25. Position the shroud and fan assembly on radiator and install bolts.
26. Connect the electric fan wire.
27. Connect the battery cable.
28. Install the air cleaner assembly.

1.6L Turbocharged Engine

♦ **See Figure 29**

1. Disconnect the negative battery cable.
2. Remove the cooling fan finger shield from the radiator support.
3. Loosen the compressor outlet hose clamp at the throttle housing.

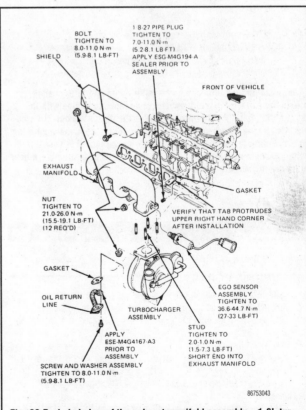

Fig. 29 Exploded view of the exhaust manifold assembly—1.6L turbocharged engines

4. Remove the hose from the turbocharger compressor outlet and rotate the hose up out of the way.

5. Disconnect the compressor inlet hose from the turbocharger.

6. Remove the alternator bracket along with the alternator.

7. Unplug the oxygen sensor electrical connector.

8. Raise and safely support the vehicle with jackstands.

9. Disconnect the oil supply line at the coolant outlet and at the turbocharger.

10. Disconnect the oil return line from the bottom of the turbocharger center housing and the cylinder block.

11. Lower the vehicle. Remove the exhaust pipe-to-turbocharger attaching nuts and move the exhaust pipe away from the studs.

12. Remove the bolt attaching the exhaust shield to the water outlet connector.

13. Remove the nuts attaching the exhaust manifold to the cylinder head. Slide the exhaust manifold and turbocharger away from the cylinder head enough to remove the exhaust shield.

14. Remove the turbocharger and exhaust manifolds as an assembly.

15. If the exhaust manifold is being replaced, remove the exhaust oxygen sensor.

To install:

16. Ensure the mating surfaces on the exhaust manifold and the cylinder head are clean and free of gasket material. The exhaust manifold gasket has a top and a bottom to it, be sure to install it correctly.

17. Position the exhaust manifold and turbocharger assembly onto the cylinder head studs. The exhaust manifold studs for the turbocharged engine are different than the studs for a non-turbocharger engine.

18. Raise and safely support the vehicle.

19. Reconnect the oil supply line at the coolant outlet and at the turbocharger.

20. Reconnect the oil return line to the bottom of the turbocharger center housing and the cylinder block.

21. Install the exhaust manifold nuts and tighten them to 16–19 ft. lbs. (21–26 Nm).

22. Lower the vehicle. Install the bolt attaching the exhaust shield to the water outlet connector.

23. Install the exhaust pipe-to-turbocharger attaching nuts. Tighten the nuts to 6–8 ft. lbs. (8–12 Nm).

24. Attach the oxygen sensor electrical connector.

25. Install the alternator bracket along with the alternator.

26. Connect the compressor inlet hose from the turbocharger.

27. Install the hose to the turbocharger compressor outlet.

28. Tighten the compressor outlet hose clamp at the throttle housing.

➡️After installing the turbocharger, or after an oil and filter change, disconnect the coil wire to the distributor and crank the engine with the starter motor until the oil pressure light on the dash goes out. Oil pressure must be up before starting the engine. Also always make sure that you use Turbo-approved motor oil when changing the oil in your turbocharged vehicle. Failure to use such an oil can cause premature bearing failure in your turbocharger assembly.

29. Install the cooling fan finger shield to the radiator support. Reconnect the negative battery cable.

Turbocharger

REMOVAL & INSTALLATION

1. Remove the turbocharger and exhaust manifold as an assembly.

2. Unfasten the four turbocharger retaining bolts and remove the turbocharger assembly. If the exhaust manifold is being replaced, remove the oxygen sensor.

To install:

3. Install the four turbocharger retaining bolts and tighten them to 16–19 ft. lbs. (21–26 Nm). Ensure the mating surfaces on the exhaust manifold and the cylinder head are clean and free of gasket material. The exhaust manifold gasket has a top and a bottom to it, be sure to install it correctly.

4. Install the exhaust manifold and turbocharger assembly onto the cylinder head studs.

Radiator

REMOVAL & INSTALLATION

▶ See Figures 30 thru 40

❊❊ CAUTION

Never open, service or drain the radiator or cooling system when hot; serious burns can occur from the steam and hot coolant. Also, when draining engine coolant, keep in mind that cats and dogs are attracted to ethylene glycol antifreeze and could drink any that is left in an uncovered container or in puddles on the ground. This will prove fatal in sufficient quantities. Always drain coolant into a sealable container. Coolant should be reused unless it is contaminated or is several years old.

1. Disconnect the negative battery cable.

2. Place fender covers on the aprons.

3. Drain the cooling system.

4. If equipped, remove the air intake tube(s) from the radiator.

5. Remove the upper hose from the radiator.

6. Remove the two fasteners retaining the upper end of the fan shroud to the radiator and sight shield.

7. If applicable, disconnect the electric cooling fan motor wires and air conditioning discharge line (if A/C equipped) from the shroud and remove the fan shroud from the vehicle.

8. Loosen the hose clamp and disconnect the radiator lower hose from the radiator.

9. Disconnect the overflow hose from the radiator filler neck.

10. If equipped with an automatic transaxle, disconnect the oil cooler hoses at the transaxle using a line disconnect tool, part No. T82-9500-AH, or equivalent. Cap the oil tubes and plug the oil cooler hoses.

11. Remove the two nuts retaining the top of the radiator to the radiator support. If the stud loosens, make sure it is tightened before the radiator is installed. Tilt the top of the radiator rearward to allow clearance with the upper mounting stud and lift the radiator from the vehicle. Make sure the mounts do not stick to the radiator lower mounting brackets.

To install:

12. Make sure the lower radiator mounts are installed over the bolts on the radiator support.

13. Position the radiator to the support making sure the lower brackets are positioned properly on the lower mounts.

14. Position the top of the radiator to the mounting studs on the radiator support and install two retaining nuts. Tighten to 5–7 ft. lbs. (7–9 Nm).

15. Connect the radiator lower hose to the engine water pump inlet tube. Install the hose clamp between the alignment marks on the hose.

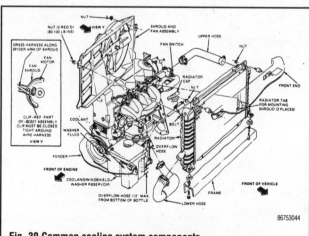

Fig. 30 Common cooling system components

Fig. 31 Remove the clamp and then the upper hose from the radiator

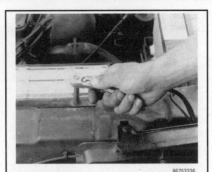

Fig. 32 Remove the cover from the radiator support to provide access to the cooling system components

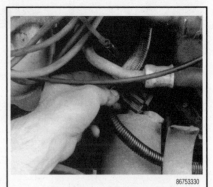

Fig. 33 Unplug the cooling fan wire connector

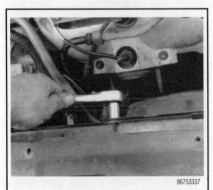

Fig. 34 Unbolt the radiator shroud from the radiator

Fig. 35 Once free, remove the radiator shroud and cooling fan as an assembly, then position aside

Fig. 36 Disconnect the overflow hose from the radiator filler neck

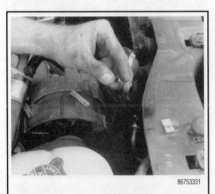

Fig. 37 If equipped with air conditioning, unscrew the coupling to the oil cooler line

Fig. 38 When disconnected, pull the oil cooler line away from the radiator

Fig. 39 Remove the two nuts retaining the top of the radiator to the radiator support

Fig. 40 When completely free, carefully angle the radiator out from its mounting position

16. Check to make sure the lower radiator hose is properly positioned on the outlet tank and install the hose clamp.

17. Connect the oil cooler hoses to the automatic transaxle oil cooler lines, if equipped. Use an appropriate oil resistant sealer.

18. Position the fan shroud to the radiator lower mounting bosses. Install the two nuts and bolts that retain the upper end of the fan shroud to the radiator. Tighten the nuts to 35–41 inch lbs. (4–5 Nm). Do not overtighten.

19. Connect the electric cooling fan motor wires to the wire harness.

20. Connect the upper hose to the radiator inlet tank fitting and install the constant tension hose clamp.

21. Connect the overflow hose to the nipple just below the radiator filler neck.

22. Install the air intake tube or sight shield.

23. Connect the negative battery cable.

24. Refill the cooling system. Start the engine and allow to come to normal operating temperature. Check for leaks. Confirm the operation of the electric cooling fan.

Electric Cooling Fan

REMOVAL & INSTALLATION

1. Disconnect the negative battery cable.
2. Place fender covers on the aprons.
3. Unplug the wiring connector from the fan motor. Disconnect the wire loom from the clip on the shroud by pushing down on the lock fingers and pulling the connector from the motor end.
4. Unfasten the fan motor and shroud assembly retainers and remove the fan and shroud from the vehicle.
5. Unfasten the retaining clip from the motor shaft and remove the fan.

➡**A metal burr may be present on the motor shaft after the retaining clip has been removed. If necessary, remove the burr to facilitate fan removal.**

6. Unbolt and withdraw the fan motor from the shroud.
   To install:
7. Install the fan motor in position in the fan shroud. Install the retaining nuts and washers or screws and tighten to 44–66 inch lbs. (5–8 Nm).
8. Position the fan assembly on the motor shaft and install the retaining clip.
9. Position the fan, motor and shroud as an assembly in the vehicle. Install the retaining nuts or screws and tighten nuts to 35–41 inch lbs. (4–5 Nm) and screws to 23–33 inch lbs. (3–4 Nm).
10. Install the fan motor wire loom in the clip provided on the fan shroud. Attach the wiring connector to the fan motor. Be sure the lock fingers on the connector snap firmly into place.
11. Reconnect the battery cable.
12. Check the fan for proper operation.

TESTING

1. Check the fuse or circuit breaker for power to the cooling fan motor.
2. Remove the connector(s) at the cooling fan motor(s). Connect a jumper wire and apply battery voltage to the positive terminal of the cooling fan motor.
3. Using an ohmmeter, check for continuity in the cooling fan motor.

➡**Remove the cooling fan connector at the fan motor before performing continuity checks. Check continuity of the motor windings only. The cooling fan control circuit is connected electrically to the ECM through the cooling fan relay center. Ohmmeter battery voltage must not be applied to the ECM.**

4. Ensure proper continuity of the cooling fan motor ground circuit at the chassis ground connector.

Water Pump

REMOVAL & INSTALLATION

▶ See Figures 41 thru 47

※※ CAUTION

Never open, service or drain the radiator or cooling system when hot; serious burns can occur from the steam and hot coolant. Also, when draining engine coolant, keep in mind that cats and dogs are attracted to ethylene glycol antifreeze and could drink any that is left in an uncovered container or in puddles on the ground. This will prove fatal in sufficient quantities. Always drain coolant into a sealable container. Coolant should be reused unless it is contaminated or is several years old.

1. Disconnect the negative battery cable.
2. Place fender covers on the aprons.
3. Drain the cooling system.
4. Remove the accessory drive belts.
5. Remove the timing belt cover.

Fig. 41 If equipped, remove the cover from the water pump

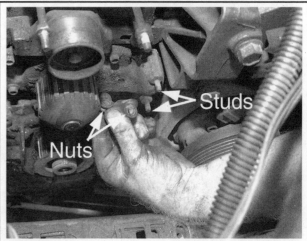

Fig. 42 Unfasten and remove the water pump inlet tube nuts from the studs

Fig. 43 Location of the water pump mounting bolts—1.9L engine

Fig. 44 After unfastening its retaining bolts, remove the water pump from the engine compartment

Fig. 45 If you are reusing the old water pump, remove the gasket . . .

Fig. 46 . . . and carefully clean both of the water pump mating surfaces with a gasket scraper

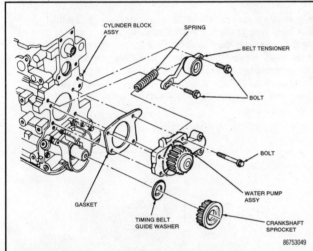

Fig. 47 Exploded view of the water pump assembly and related components—1.9L engine

➡For further information on timing belt cover and belt removal/installation, refer to the procedures later in this section.

6. Use a wrench on the crankshaft pulley to rotate the engine until No. 1 piston is at TDC of the compression stroke.

➡Turn the engine only in the direction of normal rotation. Backward rotation will cause the timing belt to slip or lose teeth.

7. Loosen the belt tensioner attaching bolts, then secure the tensioner away from the belt.

8. Pull the timing belt from the camshaft sprocket, tensioner, and water pump sprocket. Do not remove it from, or allow it to change its position on, the crankshaft sprocket.

✲✲ WARNING

Do not rotate the engine with the timing belt removed or serious engine damage could occur. The 1.3L and 1.6L engines are of the "interference type," meaning it is possible for the valves to contact the pistons if their reciprocation is not carefully timed and controlled. An engine allowed to spin freely without the timing belt could bend valves and scuff pistons almost instantly.

9. Remove the camshaft sprocket.
10. Remove the rear timing cover stud. If equipped, remove the cover from the water pump.
11. Remove the heater return tube hose connection at the water pump inlet tube.
12. Remove the water pump inlet tube fasteners, along with the inlet tube and gasket.

13. Unfasten the water pump-to-cylinder block bolts, then remove the water pump and its gasket.

To install:

14. Make sure the mating surfaces on the pump and the block are clean.
15. Using a new gasket and sealer, install the water pump. Tighten the bolts to 30–40 ft. lbs. (40–55 Nm) on 1981–87 models, or to 15–22 ft. lbs. (20–30 Nm) on 1988–90 models. Make sure the pump impeller is able to turn freely.
16. Install the water pump inlet tube and the inlet tube gasket and fasteners.
17. Install the rear timing cover stud and, if applicable, the water pump cover.
18. Fasten the heater return tube hose connection at the water pump inlet tube.
19. Properly position and install the camshaft sprocket.

✲✲ WARNING

The camshaft and crankshaft must not be turned until the timing sprockets and belt are installed. If the camshaft or crankshaft rotate before the timing belt is in place, severe piston and valve damage could occur.

20. With the camshaft sprocket, timing belt tensioner, and water pump sprocket properly aligned, install and route the timing belt.
21. Tighten the belt tensioner attaching bolts, and then release the tensioner against the belt.
22. Install the timing belt cover.
23. Install the accessory drive belts.
24. Refill the cooling system and reconnect the negative battery cable.

Cylinder Head

REMOVAL & INSTALLATION

◆ See Figures 48 thru 55

✲✲ WARNING

To reduce the possibility of cylinder head warpage and/or distortion, do not remove the cylinder head while the engine is warm. Always, allow the engine to cool entirely before disassembly.

1. Disconnect the negative battery cable.
2. Drain the cooling system.
3. Disconnect the heater hose under the intake manifold
4. Disconnect the upper radiator hose at the cylinder head.
5. Disconnect the wiring from the cooling fan switch.
6. Remove the air cleaner assembly
7. Remove the PCV hose.
8. Tag and disconnect all vacuum hoses that would interfere with cylinder head removal.
9. Remove the rocker arm cover and all accessory drive belts.
10. Remove the crankshaft pulley and the timing belt cover.

11. Set the No.1 cylinder to the Top Dead Center (TDC) compression stroke.

12. Remove the distributor cap and spark plug wires as an assembly.

13. Loosen both belt tensioner attaching bolts using special Ford tool T81P-6254-A or the equivalent. Secure the belt tensioner as far left as possible. Remove the timing belt and discard.

➡️ Once the tension on the timing belt has been released, the belt cannot be used again.

14. For 1.6L engines: disconnect the tube at the EGR valve, then remove the PVS hose connectors using tool T81P-8564-A or equivalent. Label the connectors and set them aside.

15. Disconnect the choke wire, the fuel supply and return lines, the accelerator cable and speed control cable (if equipped).

16. If equipped with power steering, remove the thermactor pump drive belt, the pump and its bracket.

17. Disconnect the altitude compensator, if equipped, from the dash panel and place on the heater/air conditioner air intake.

✳✳ WARNING

Exercise care not to damage the compensator.

18. Remove the alternator and its bracket.

19. If equipped with a turbocharger, disconnect the following components:
   a. Turbocharger inlet hose.
   b. Turbocharger oil supply tube at the turbocharger coolant outlet and at the engine block. Remove the oil supply line from the vehicle.

20. Raise the vehicle and disconnect the exhaust pipe from the manifold or if equipped, the turbocharger.

21. If equipped with a turbocharger, disconnect the oil drain at the turbocharger.

22. Lower the vehicle and remove the cylinder head bolts and washers. Discard the bolts, they cannot be used again.

23. Remove the cylinder head with the manifolds and if equipped, turbocharger still attached.

24. Remove and discard the head gasket.

✳✳ CAUTION

Do not place the cylinder head with its combustion chambers down, or damage to the spark plugs or gasket surfaces may result.

To install:

✳✳ WARNING

Before installing the cylinder head on a turbocharged engine, check the piston squish height.

25. Clean all gasket material from the mating surfaces of the block and cylinder head, then rotate the crankshaft so that the No.1 piston is 90 Before Top Dead Center (BTDC). In this position, the crankshaft pulley keyway will be at 9 o'clock.

26. Turn the camshaft so its keyway is at 6 o'clock. When installing the timing belt, turn the crankshaft keyway back to 12 o'clock but do not turn the camshaft from its 6 o'clock position. The crankshaft is turned 90° BTDC to prevent the valves from hitting the pistons when the cylinder head is installed.

➡️ To ensure proper squish height upon reassembly, no cylinder block deck machining or use of a replacement crankshaft, piston or connecting rod that causes the squish height to be over or under specification, is permitted. If only the head gasket is replaced, the squish height should be within specification. If parts other than the head gasket are replaced, check the squish height. If the squish height is out of specification, replace the parts again and recheck the squish height.

27. Position the cylinder head gasket on the block and install the cylinder head using new bolts and washers. Apply a coating of light oil to the head bolts,

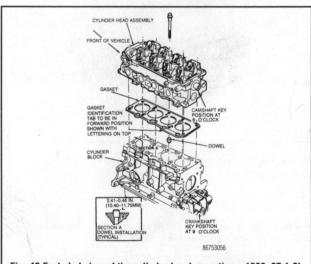

Fig. 49 Exploded view of the cylinder head mounting—1986–87 1.9L engines

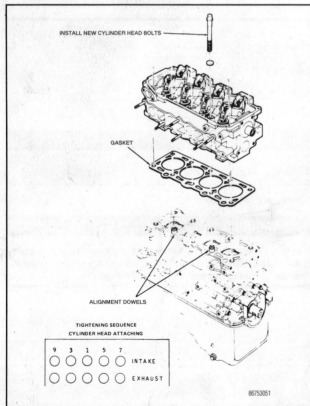

Fig. 48 Exploded view of the cylinder head mounting and tightening sequence—1.3L and 1.6L engines

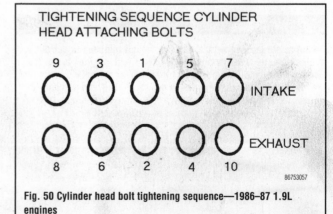

Fig. 50 Cylinder head bolt tightening sequence—1986–87 1.9L engines

Fig. 51 Remove the cylinder head bolts and washers—1988 1.9L engine shown

Fig. 52 As you untighten them, pull out the long cylinder head bolts and discard them

Fig. 53 Remove the cylinder head and attached manifolds

Fig. 54 Use a scraper to remove old gasket material before installing the cylinder head and new gasket

Fig. 55 A torque wrench is essential to properly tighten the cylinder head bolts

then tighten the bolts to 44 ft. lbs. (60 Nm) in the sequence shown. Back the bolts off two turns and retighten to 44 ft. lbs. (60 Nm). After tightening, turn the bolts an additional 90° in the same sequence. Complete the bolt tightening by turning an additional 90° in the same sequence. Always use new head bolts when reinstalling the cylinder head.

☼☼ WARNING

The camshaft and crankshaft must not be turned until the timing sprockets and belt are installed. If the camshaft or crankshaft rotate before the timing belt is in place, severe piston and valve damage could occur.

28. Raise the vehicle and safely support it on jackstands.
29. Connect the exhaust system at the exhaust pipe.
30. If equipped with a turbocharger, connect the oil drain at the turbocharger.
31. Lower the vehicle.
32. Install the thermactor pump mounting bracket, pump and drive belt (if removed). Apply Loctite® or equivalent to the attaching bolts.
33. If equipped with a turbocharger, disconnect the following components:
    a. Turbocharger oil supply tube at the turbocharger coolant outlet and at the engine block.
    b. Turbocharger inlet hose.
34. Install the alternator bracket, the alternator and connect the wiring harness and alternator air intake tube.
35. Connect the altitude compensator (if equipped).
36. Connect the accelerator cable and, if equipped, the speed control cable.
37. Connect the fuel supply and return lines at the metal connector, located on the right side of the engine.

38. Connect the choke cap.
39. Connect the EGR tube to the EGR valve.
40. Install the timing belt and timing belt cover.
41. Install the crankshaft pulley.
42. Replace the distributor cap and spark plug wires.
43. Install the rocker arm cover.
44. Attach all vacuum hoses that were removed. Plug in the wiring terminal to the cooling fan switch.
45. Connect the upper radiator hose at the cylinder head.
46. Connect the heater hose to the fitting located below the intake manifold.
47. Fill the cooling system with an approved coolant.
48. Connect the negative ground cable.
49. Start the engine and check for vacuum, coolant and oil leaks. After the engine has reached operating temperature, carefully check the coolant level and add coolant, if necessary.
50. Adjust the ignition timing and connect the distributor line.
51. Install the PCV hose and the air cleaner assembly.
52. Remove the protective aprons. Close the hood.

PISTON SQUISH HEIGHT

1.9L Engines

▶ See Figures 56, 57 and 58

Before final installation of the cylinder head to the engine, piston "squish height" must be checked. Squish height is the clearance of the piston dome to the cylinder head dome at piston TDC. No rework of the head gasket surfaces (slabbing) or use of replacement parts (crankshaft, piston and connecting rod) that causes the assembled squish height to be over or under the tolerance specification is permitted.

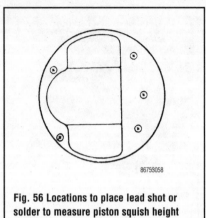

Fig. 56 Locations to place lead shot or solder to measure piston squish height

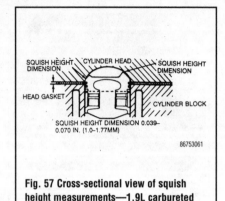

Fig. 57 Cross-sectional view of squish height measurements—1.9L carbureted and EFI (HO) engines

Fig. 58 Cross-sectional view of squish height measurements—1.9L CFI engines

➡If no parts other than the head gasket are replaced, the piston squish height should be within specification. If parts other than the head gasket are replaced, check the squish height. If out of specification, replace the parts again and recheck the squish height.

1. Clean all gasket material from the mating surfaces on the cylinder head and engine block.
2. Place a small amount of soft lead solder or lead shot of an appropriate thickness on the piston spherical areas.
3. Rotate the crankshaft to lower the piston in the bore and install the head gasket and cylinder head.

➡A compressed (used) head gasket is preferred for checking squish height.

4. Install used head bolts and tighten the head bolts to 30–44 ft. lbs. (40–60 Nm) following proper sequence.
5. Rotate the crankshaft to move the piston through its TDC position.
6. Remove the cylinder head and measure the thickness of the compressed solder to determine squish height at TDC. For all 1.9L carbureted and EFI (HO) engines, the compressed lead piece should be 0.039–0.070 in. (1.0–1.77mm). For 1.9L CFI engines, the compressed lead piece should be 0.046–0.060 in. (1.156–1.527mm).

Oil Pan

REMOVAL & INSTALLATION

☀☀ CAUTION

The EPA warns that prolonged contact with used engine oil may cause a number of skin disorders, including cancer! You should make every effort to minimize your exposure to used engine oil. Protective gloves should be worn when changing the oil. Wash your hands and any other exposed skin areas as soon as possible after exposure to used engine oil. Soap and water, or waterless hand cleaner should be used.

1.3L and 1.6L Engines

▶ See Figure 59

1. Disconnect the negative cable at the battery.
2. Raise the vehicle and support it with safety stands.
3. Remove the drain plug and drain the engine oil into a suitable container.

➡It may be necessary to disconnect coolant lines to allow clearance for the oil pan.

4. Disconnect the starter cable at its terminal on the starter.
5. Remove the knee-brace located at the front of the starter.
6. Remove the starter attaching bolts and starter.
7. Remove the knee-braces at the transaxle.

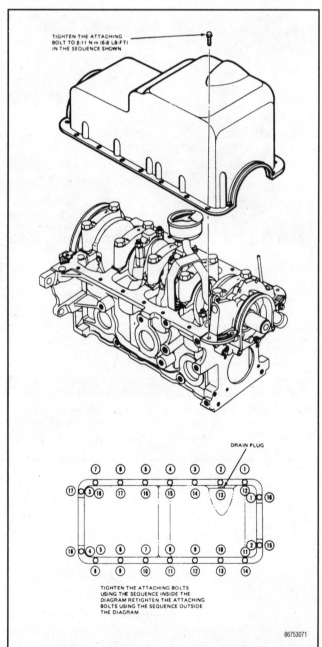

Fig. 59 Exploded, inverted view of the oil pan mounting and bolt tightening/retightening sequence—1.3L and 1.6L engines

8. On turbocharged engines only, remove the EGR tubes from the exhaust inlet pipe.

9. Disconnect the exhaust inlet pipe at the manifold and catalytic converter. On turbocharged engines, remove the exhaust inlet pipe support bracket. Remove the pipe.

10. Remove the oil pan retaining bolts and oil pan.

11. Remove the oil pan front and rear seals.

12. Remove the oil pan gasket(s) and discard.

To install:

13. Clean the oil pan gasket surface and the mating surface on the cylinder block. Wipe the oil pan rail with a solvent-soaked, lint-free cloth to remove all traces of oil.

14. Remove to clean the oil pump pick up tube and screen assembly. Install tube and screen assembly using a new gasket.

15. Apply a bead of suitable silicone rubber sealer at the corner of the oil pan front and rear seals and at the seating point of the oil pump to the block retainer joint.

16. Install the pan front oil seal by pressing it firmly into the oil pump slot cut into the bottom of the oil pump.

17. Install the pan rear oil seal by pressing it into the slot cut into the rear retainer assembly.

18. Apply a bead of suitable silicone rubber sealer evenly to the pan flange and the pan side of the gaskets and allow the sealer to dry past the "wet" stage. Do not allow the sealer to dry for more than 10 minutes before installing the pan.

19. Install the oil pan gasket on the pan.

20. Install the oil pan on the engine block.

21. Install the oil pan attaching bolts. Tighten the oil pan to 6–8 ft. lbs. (8–11 Nm) in the sequence illustrated.

22. Install the transaxle inspection plate and the rear section of the knee brace on the transaxle and tighten the attaching bolts.

23. Install the starter, knee brace at the starter and connect the starter cable.

24. Install the exhaust inlet pipe at the manifold or if equipped, the turbocharger. On turbocharged engines install the exhaust inlet pipe support bracket.

25. On turbocharged engines only, install the EGR tubes from the exhaust inlet pipe.

26. On turbocharged engines only, connect the EGR tubes to the exhaust inlet pipe.

27. Lower the vehicle and fill the crankcase.

28. Connect negative battery cable.

29. Start the engine and check for oil leaks.

1.9L Engines

♦ **See Figures 60 thru 68**

1. Disconnect the negative cable at the battery.

2. Raise the vehicle and support it with safely stands.

3. Remove the drain plug and drain the engine oil into a suitable container.

4. If necessary, disconnect the coolant line to make way for lowering the oil pan.

5. Disconnect the starter cable at its terminal on the starter.

6. Remove the starter brace from the front of the starter.

7. Remove the starter attaching bolts and starter.

8. Remove the two oil pan-to-transaxle bolts.

9. Disconnect the exhaust pipe from the manifold and converter.

10. Remove the oil pan retaining bolts and oil pan.

11. Remove the oil pan gasket and discard.

To install:

12. Clean the oil pan gasket surface and the mating surface on the cylinder block. Wipe the oil pan rail with a solvent-soaked, lint-free cloth to remove all traces of oil.

13. Remove to clean the oil pump pick up tube and screen assembly. Install tube and screen assembly using a new gasket.

14. Apply a bead of suitable silicone rubber sealer at the corner of the oil pan front and rear seals and at the seating point of the oil pump to the block retainer joint.

15. Install the oil pan gasket in the pan ensuring the press fit tabs are fully engaged in the gasket channel.

16. Install the oil pan attaching bolts. Tighten the bolts lightly until the two oil pan-to-transaxle bolts can be installed.

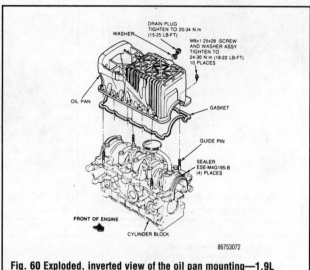

Fig. 60 Exploded, inverted view of the oil pan mounting—1.9L engines

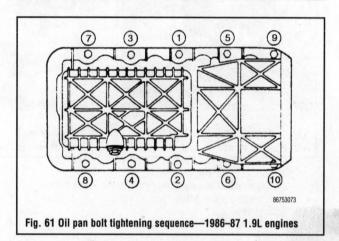

Fig. 61 Oil pan bolt tightening sequence—1986–87 1.9L engines

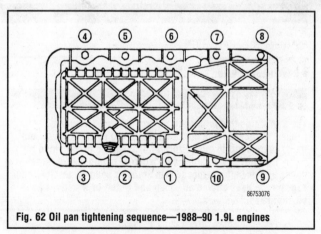

Fig. 62 Oil pan tightening sequence—1988–90 1.9L engines

➡If the oil pan is installed on the engine outside of the vehicle, a transaxle case or equivalent, the fixture must be bolted to the block to line-up the oil pan flush with the rear face of the block.

17. Tighten the two pan-to-transaxle bolts to 30–40 ft. lbs. (40–54 Nm), then back off the bolts one half turn.

18. Tighten the oil pan flange-to-cylinder block bolts to 15–22 ft. lbs. (20–30 Nm) in the proper sequence.

19. Install the transaxle inspection plate.

20. Install the starter, the brace at the front of the starter and connect the starter cable.

Fig. 63 If necessary, disconnect the coolant line to provide sufficient clearance

Fig. 64 Unbolt the oil-pan-to-transaxle fasteners

Fig. 65 Disconnect the exhaust pipe at the manifold and the rear flange (shown)

Fig. 66 Remove the exhaust pipe to provide room for oil pan removal

Fig. 67 Unbolt the oil pan after all obstructions have been removed

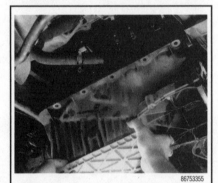

Fig. 68 Lower the oil pan carefully from the engine

21. Install the exhaust inlet pipe. Lower the vehicle and fill the crankcase.
22. If removed, connect the coolant line.
23. Connect negative battery cable.
24. Start the engine and check for oil leaks.

Oil Pump

REMOVAL & INSTALLATION

♦ See Figures 69 and 70

✳✳ CAUTION

The EPA warns that prolonged contact with used engine oil may cause a number of skin disorders, including cancer! You should make every effort to minimize your exposure to used engine oil. Protective gloves should be worn when changing the oil. Wash your hands and any other exposed skin areas as soon as possible after exposure to used engine oil. Soap and water, or waterless hand cleaner should be used.

1. Disconnect the negative cable at the battery.
2. Drain the engine oil.
3. Remove the oil pan retaining bolts.
4. Remove the oil pan, seals and gaskets.
5. Remove the oil pump attaching bolts, oil pump and gasket.
6. Remove the oil pump seal.
7. Make sure the mating surfaces on the cylinder block and the oil pump are clean and free of gasket material.
8. Remove the oil pick-up tube and screen assembly from the pump for cleaning.

   To install:
9. Lubricate the outside diameter of the oil pump seal with engine oil.

10. Install the oil pump seal using seal installer T81P-6700-A or equivalent.
11. Install the pick-up tube and screen assembly on the oil pump. Tighten attaching bolts to 6–9 ft. lbs. (8–12 Nm).
12. Lubricate the oil pump seal lip with light engine oil.
13. Position the oil pump gasket over the locating dowels. Install attaching bolts and tighten to 5–7 ft. lbs. (7–9 Nm).
14. Install the oil pan.
15. Fill the crankcase with the recommended motor oil.
16. Connect the negative battery cable.
17. Start the engine and check for oil leaks.

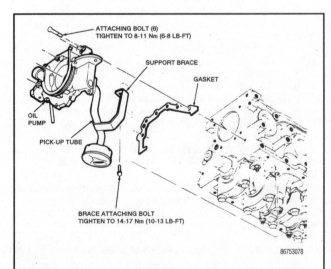

Fig. 69 Exploded view of the oil pump mounting—1.3L and 1.6L engines

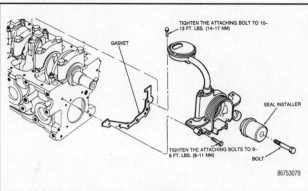

Fig. 70 Exploded, inverted view of the oil pump mounting—1.9L engines

Crankshaft Damper

REMOVAL & INSTALLATION

Except 1988–90 1.9L Engines

1. Disconnect the negative battery cable.
2. Remove the drive belt(s) from the crankshaft pulley.
3. Using a suitable crankshaft holding device such as tool T81P-6312-A or equivalent, hold the crankshaft pulley and loosen the pulley retaining bolt.
4. Remove the drive plate and the pulley.

To install:

5. Install the pulley and drive plate.
6. Hold the pulley in place using the holding device and tighten the pulley bolt to 74–90 ft. lbs. (100–122 Nm).
7. Install the drive belt(s).
8. Connect the negative battery cable.

1988–90 1.9L Engines

▶ See Figures 71, 72, 73 and 74

1. Disconnect the negative battery cable.
2. Remove the accessory drive belts.
3. Connect an engine support tool, such as part No. D79P-6000-B, or equivalent to the engine. A hydraulic jack with a block of wood can also be used to support and/or lower and raise the engine as needed.
4. With the engine supported, remove the right-hand side engine mount bolt.

Fig. 71 Use a hydraulic jack with a block of wood to support and/or lower and raise the engine as needed

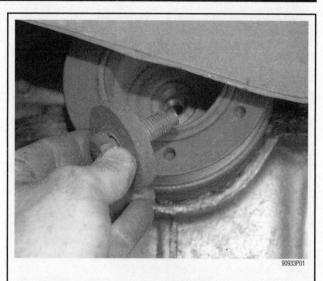

Fig. 72 Unfasten and remove the crankshaft damper retaining bolt

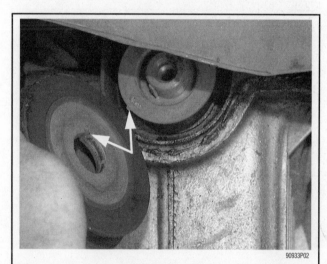

Fig. 73 Remove the crankshaft damper. Note the keyway (arrows) which must be aligned for proper installation

Fig. 74 The crankshaft pulley may have the word FRONT stamped into it. Make sure this faces outward when installing the damper

5. Lower the right side of the engine until the crankshaft damper bolt is past the frame rail and unfasten the bolt.

6. Raise the engine and remove the crankshaft damper (pulley).

To install:

7. Position the crankshaft damper (pulley) on the crankshaft.

8. Lower the engine, making sure that the damper clears the frame rail and install the damper bolt. Tighten the bolt to 81–96 ft. lbs. (110–130 Nm).

9. Install the right-hand side engine mount bolt.

10. Install the accessory drive belt(s).

11. Connect the negative battery cable.

Timing Belt Cover

REMOVAL & INSTALLATION

♦ **See Figures 71, 75, 76 and 77**

1. Disconnect the negative battery cable.

2. Place a block wood on a hydraulic jack, position the jack under the engine and raise the jack until it supports the weight of the engine.

3. Unfasten the upper left-hand engine mount retainers and remove the mount.

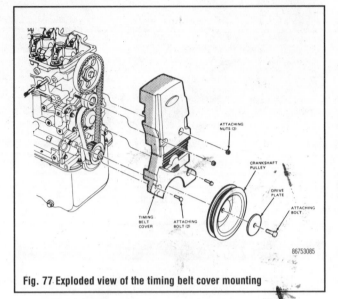

Fig. 77 Exploded view of the timing belt cover mounting

4. Remove the accessory drive belt(s).

5. Remove the crankshaft pulley.

6. Remove the timing belt cover attaching bolts.

7. Remove the timing belt cover.

To install:

8. Place the timing belt cover into position and install the attaching bolts.

9. Install the crankshaft pulley.

10. Install the left-hand engine mount and its retainers.

11. Install the accessory drive belt(s).

12. Connect the negative battery cable.

Timing Belt and Sprockets

REMOVAL & INSTALLATION

♦ **See Figures 78 thru 85**

1. Disconnect the negative battery cable.

2. Remove the timing belt cover.

➡ **Align the timing mark on the camshaft sprocket with the timing mark on the cylinder head.**

Fig. 75 With the engine supported, remove the upper left-hand engine mount

Fig. 76 Unfasten the timing belt cover retainers and remove the cover

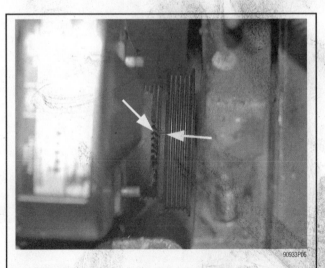

Fig. 78 Confirm that the timing mark on the crankshaft pulley aligns with the TDC mark on the front cover (arrows)

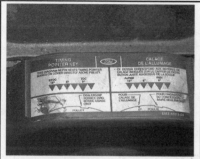

Fig. 79 A sticker on the timing cover identifies the timing marks and also shows the 0 degree mark on the crankshaft pulley

Fig. 80 Loosen the timing belt tensioner bolts (arrows), pry the tensioner to one side and retighten one of the bolts to hold the tensioner aside

Fig. 81 Slide the timing belt off the sprockets and remove it from the engine compartment

Fig. 82 Remove the camshaft sprocket attaching bolt, washer and sprocket

3. Temporarily install the timing belt cover and confirm that the timing mark on the crankshaft pulley aligns with the TDC mark on the cover.

4. Again remove the timing belt cover.

5. Loosen both timing belt tensioner attaching bolts using a torque wrench adapter (T81P-6254-A or equivalent).

6. Pry the belt tensioner away from the belt as far as possible and tighten one of the tensioner attaching bolts.

7. Remove the crankshaft pulley.

8. Remove the timing belt.

➡ With the timing belt removed and pistons at TDC, do not rotate the engine.

9. Remove the camshaft sprocket attaching bolt, washer, camshaft sprocket and sprocket key.

10. Remove the crankshaft sprocket.

To install:

11. Install the camshaft sprocket, key and attaching bolt and washer. Tighten to 37–46 ft. lbs. (50–62 Nm) on 1981–88 models or 71–84 ft. lbs. (95–115 Nm) on 1989–90 vehicles.

12. Install the crankshaft sprocket.

13. Install the timing belt over the sprockets in the counterclockwise direction, starting at the crankshaft. Keep the belt span from the crankshaft to the camshaft tight while the belt is installed over the remaining sprockets.

14. Loosen the belt tensioner attaching bolts and allow the tensioner to snap against the belt.

15. Tighten one of the tensioner attaching bolts.

16. Install the crankshaft pulley and pulley attaching bolt.

17. To seat the belt on the sprocket teeth, complete the following:

a. Connect the negative battery terminal.

b. Crank the engine several revolutions.

c. Disconnect the negative battery terminal.

d. Turn the crankshaft, as necessary, to align the timing pointer on the camshaft sprocket with the timing mark on the cylinder head.

➡ Do not turn the engine counterclockwise to align the timing marks.

e. Position the timing belt cover on the engine and check to see that the timing mark on the crankshaft aligns with the TDC pointer on the cover. If the timing marks do not align, remove the belt, align the timing marks and return to Step 9.

18. Loosen the belt tensioner attaching bolt that was tightened in Step 11.

19. On 1988 vehicles, proceed as follows:

a. Hold the crankshaft stationary and position a suitable torque wrench onto the camshaft sprocket bolt.

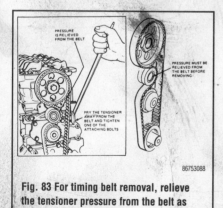

Fig. 83 For timing belt removal, relieve the tensioner pressure from the belt as shown

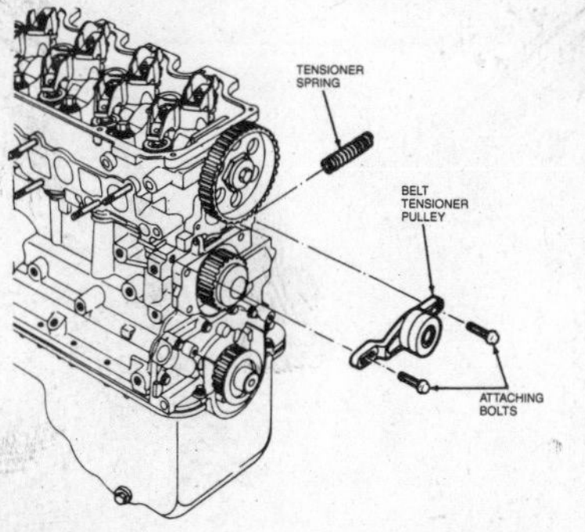

Fig. 84 Exploded view of the timing belt tensioner mounting position

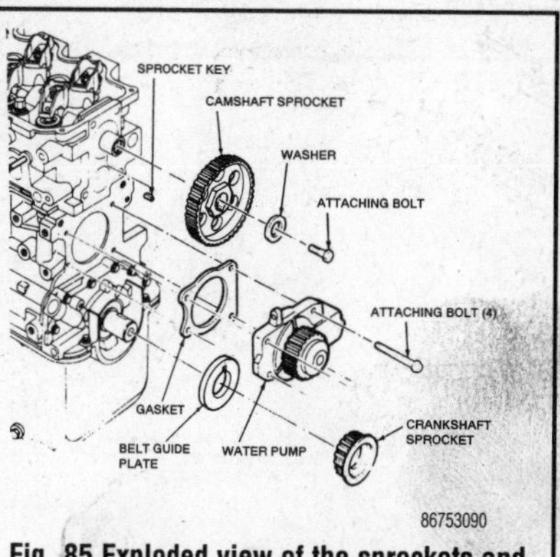

Fig. 85 Exploded view of the sprockets and other timing belt-related components

b. Turn the camshaft sprocket counterclockwise. Tighten the belt tensioner attaching bolt until the torque wrench reads: 27–32 ft. lbs. (36–43 Nm). For a used belt (in service for 30 days or more), tighten to 10 ft. lbs. (13 Nm).

20. On 1989–90 vehicles, the tensioner spring will apply the proper load on the belt. Tighten the belt tensioner bolt.

➡ **The engine must be at room temperature. Do not set belt tension on a hot engine.**

21. Install the timing belt cover.
22. Install the accessory drive belts.
23. Connect the negative battery cable.

Front Oil Seal

REMOVAL & INSTALLATION

1. Disconnect the negative battery cable.
2. Remove the accessory drive belts.
3. Remove the timing belt cover.
4. Remove the timing belt.

➡ **With the timing belt removed and pistons at TDC, do not rotate the engine. If the camshaft must be rotated, align the crankshaft pulley to 90 BTDC.**

5. Remove the crankshaft damper.
6. Remove the crankshaft sprocket.
7. Remove the crankshaft front seal.

To install:

8. Coat the new seal with clean engine oil.
9. Install the crankshaft front seal using a suitable seal installer tool.
10. Install the crankshaft sprocket and the crankshaft damper.
11. Install the timing belt and the timing belt cover.
12. Install the accessory drive belts, then adjust the tension of the drive belts.
13. Connect the negative battery cable.

Camshaft

REMOVAL & INSTALLATION

1.3L and 1.6L Engines

▸ **See Figures 86, 87 and 88**

1. Disconnect the negative battery cable.
2. Remove the air cleaner assembly and the PCV hose.
3. Remove the accessory drive belts.
4. Remove the crankshaft pulley.
5. Remove the timing belt cover.
6. Remove the valve cover.
7. Remove the distributor.

8. Remove the rocker arms.
9. Remove the hydraulic valve lash adjusters. Keep the parts in order, as they must be returned to their original positions.
10. Remove and discard the timing belt.
11. Remove the camshaft sprocket and key.
12. Remove the camshaft thrust plate.
13. Remove the fuel pump.
14. Remove the ignition coil and coil bracket.
15. Remove the camshaft through the back of the head towards the transaxle.
16. Inspect the camshaft seal for wear or damage.

To install:

17. Clean all the bearing surfaces thoroughly.
18. Before installing the camshaft, coat the bearing journals, cam lobe surfaces, the seal and thrust plate groove with engine oil.
19. Install the camshaft through the rear of the cylinder head. Rotate the camshaft during installation.
20. Install the camshaft thrust plate and tighten the two attaching bolts to 7–11 ft. lbs. (10–15 Nm).
21. Install the camshaft sprocket and key.
22. Install a new timing belt.
23. Install the timing belt cover.
24. Install the fuel pump.
25. Install the hydraulic valve lash adjusters in their original positions.
26. Install the rocker arm assembly.
27. Install the distributor assembly, then the rocker arm cover.
28. Install the PCV hose and air cleaner assembly.
29. Connect the negative battery cable.
30. Start the engine and check the ignition timing.

1.9L Engine

1. Disconnect the negative battery cable.
2. Remove the air cleaner or air intake duct.
3. Remove the accessory drive belts and the crankshaft pulley.
4. Remove the timing belt cover and the rocker arm cover.
5. Set the engine No. 1 cylinder at TDC prior to removing the timing belt.

➡ **Make sure the crankshaft is positioned at TDC. Do not turn the crankshaft until the timing belt is installed.**

6. Remove the rocker arms and lifters.
7. Remove the distributor assembly.
8. Remove the timing belt.
9. Remove the camshaft sprocket and key.
10. Remove the camshaft thrust plate.
11. Remove the ignition coil and coil bracket.
12. Remove the camshaft through the back of the head toward the transaxle.
13. Remove and discard the camshaft seal.

To install:

14. Thoroughly coat the camshaft bearing journals, cam lobe surfaces and thrust plate groove with a suitable lubricant.

➡ **Before installing the camshaft, apply a thin film of lubricant to the lip of the camshaft seal.**

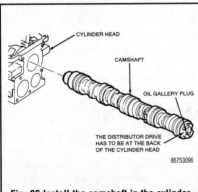

Fig. 86 Install the camshaft in the cylinder head as shown

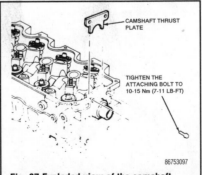

Fig. 87 Exploded view of the camshaft thrust plate mounting—1.3L and 1.6L engines

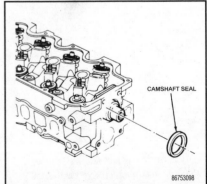

Fig. 88 The camshaft seal mounts in the end of the cylinder head as shown

15. Install a new camshaft seal.

16. Install the camshaft through the rear of the cylinder head. Rotate the camshaft during installation.

17. Install the camshaft thrust plate. Tighten the attaching bolts to 7–11 ft. lbs. (10–15 Nm).

18. Align and install the camshaft sprocket over the camshaft key. Install the attaching washer and bolt.

19. Install the ignition coil and coil bracket.

20. Install the timing belt.

21. Install the timing belt cover.

22. Install the distributor assembly.

23. Install a new rocker arm cover gasket, if required.

➡**Make sure the surfaces on the cylinder head and rocker arm cover are clean and free of sealant material.**

24. Install the valve cover.

25. Install the air intake duct or the air cleaner assembly.

26. Connect the negative battery cable.

INSPECTION

▶ **See Figures 89, 90 and 91**

Degrease the camshaft using safe solvent, clean all oil grooves. Visually inspect the cam lobes and bearing journals for excessive wear. If a lobe is questionable, check all lobes and journals with a micrometer.

Measure the lobes from nose to base and again at 90. The lift is determined by subtracting the second measurement from the first. If all exhaust lobes and all intake lobes are not identical, the camshaft must be reground or replaced. Measure the bearing journals and compare to the specifications. If a journal is worn there is a good chance that the cam bearings are worn too, requiring replacement.

If the lobes and journals appear intact, place the front and rear cam journals in V-blocks and rest a dial indicator on the center journal. Rotate the camshaft

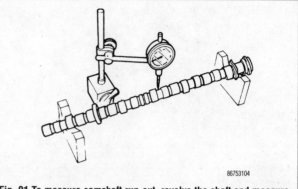

Fig. 91 To measure camshaft run-out, revolve the shaft and measure with a dial indicator

to check for straightness; if deviation exceeds 0.001 in. (0.025mm), replace the camshaft.

Valve Lifters

REMOVAL & INSTALLATION

▶ **See Figures 92 and 93**

1. Disconnect the negative battery cable.

2. Remove the air cleaner assembly.

3. Remove rocker arm cover and gasket.

➡**Mark the location of the valve lifters, so that they can be returned to their original bores.**

4. Remove the rocker arms, lifter guides, lifter retainers and lifters.

To install:

➡**Always return the lifters to their original bores unless they are being replaced.**

5. Lubricate each lifter bore with heavy duty, clean engine oil.

6. If equipped with flat bottom lifters, install with the oil hole in the plunger upward. If equipped with roller lifters, install with the plunger upward and position the guide flats of lifters to be parallel with the centerline of the camshaft. The color orientation dots on the lifters should be opposite the oil feed holes in the cylinder head.

7. For roller lifters only, install the lifter guide plates over the tappet guide flats with the notch toward the exhaust side. For flat lifters, no guide plate is required.

8. Lubricate the lifter plunger cap and valve tip with engine oil.

9. Install the lifter guide plate retainers into rocker arm fulcrum slots, in both the intake and exhaust side. Align the notch to be with the exhaust valve lifter.

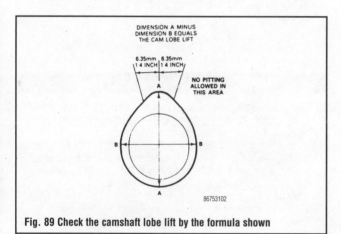

Fig. 89 Check the camshaft lobe lift by the formula shown

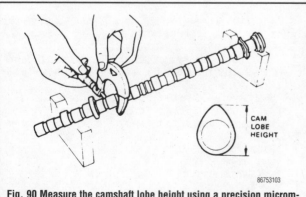

Fig. 90 Measure the camshaft lobe height using a precision micrometer

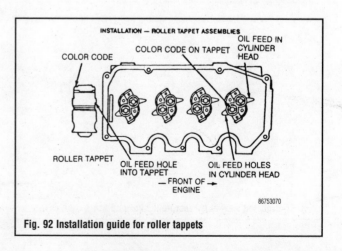

Fig. 92 Installation guide for roller tappets

Fig. 93 Once the way is clear, pull the lifter from its bore—ALWAYS return lifters to their original bores

10. Install four rocker arms in lifter position Nos. 3, 6, 7 and 8.

11. Lubricate the rocker arm surface that will contact the fulcrum surface with engine oil.

12. Install four fulcrums. The fulcrums must be fully seated in the slots of cylinder head.

13. Install the rocker arm retainers. Tighten to 15–19 ft. lbs. (21–25 Nm) on 1.3L and 1.6L engines. On 1.9L engines, tighten the retainers to 17–22 ft. lbs. (23–30 Nm).

14. Rotate the engine until the camshaft sprocket keyway is in the 6 o'clock position.

15. Repeat Steps 9–12 in lifter position Nos. 1, 2, 4 and 5.

16. Install the rocker arm cover and gasket. Install the air cleaner assembly.

17. Connect the negative battery cable.

INSPECTION

Inspect the lifter assembly and discard the entire lifter if any part shows pitting, scoring, galling, excessive wear or evidence of non-rotation.

Rear Main Seal

REMOVAL & INSTALLATION

♦ **See Figures 94, 95 and 96**

1. Disconnect the negative battery cable.
2. Remove the transaxle assembly.

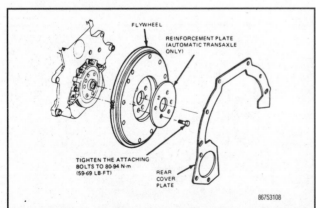

Fig. 94 Exploded view of the rear main seal's adjacent components

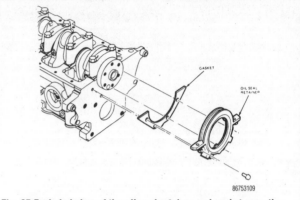

Fig. 95 Exploded view of the oil seal retainer and gasket mounting

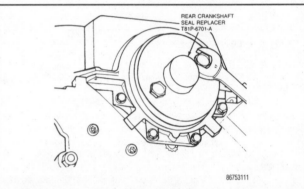

Fig. 96 Use a rear crankshaft seal replacer to correctly press the seal into place—1.3L and 1.6L engines

3. Remove the rear cover plate.

4. Install a suitable flywheel holding tool and unfasten the flywheel retaining bolts. Remove the flywheel.

❊❊ WARNING

Be careful not to damage the seal surface. Gouging it could make an oil-tight seal impossible and could necessitate replacement of the crankshaft.

5. With a sharp awl, punch a hole into the seal's metal surface between the lip and the block. Screw in the threaded end of the slide hammer removal tool, part No. T77L-9533-B or equivalent, and remove the seal.

To install:

6. Inspect the crankshaft seal area for any damage which may cause the seal to leak. If there is damage evident, you will have to service or replace the crankshaft as necessary.

7. Clean the seal mounting surfaces. Coat the crankshaft seal area and seal lip with engine oil.

8. On 1.3L and 1.6L engines, use seal installer T81P-6703-A or equivalent to install a new rear seal.

9. On 1.9L engines, install the seal as follows:

a. Place crankshaft rear seal pilot T88P-6703-B2, or equivalent, into rear crankshaft seal replacer T88P-6701-B1, or equivalent, and lubricate the pilot replacer with clean engine oil.

b. Slide the rear oil seal over the pilot and onto the replacer tool.

c. Remove the rear seal pilot from the seal replacer.

d. Place the rear oil seal and replacer tool over the crankshaft and install the seal.

e. Remove the seal installer tool.

10. Install the flywheel.

11. Install the cover plate.

12. Install the transaxle.

13. Connect the negative battery cable. Start the engine and check for oil leaks.

Flywheel/Flexplate

REMOVAL & INSTALLATION

▶ See Figure 97

1. Disconnect the negative battery cable.
2. Remove the transaxle assembly.
3. Remove the clutch assembly, if equipped.
4. Remove the rear cover plate, if so equipped.
5. Install a suitable holding tool and remove the flywheel (manual transaxle) or flexplate (automatic transaxle) retaining bolts. Remove the flywheel/flexplate.

To install:

6. Inspect the flywheel (manual transaxle) or flexplate (automatic transaxle) for cracks, heat checks or other damage that would make it unfit for further service. Replace with a new one, if required.
7. Install the flywheel (manual transaxle) or flexplate (automatic transaxle). Use a suitable holding tool, tighten the retaining bolts to 54–6 ft. lbs. (73–87 Nm) using the correct tightening sequence.
8. Install the rear cover plate, if so equipped.

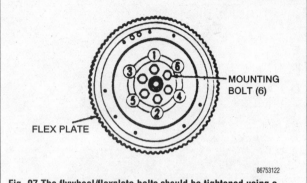

Fig. 97 The flywheel/flexplate bolts should be tightened using a crisscross sequence

9. Install the clutch assembly, if equipped.
10. Install the transaxle assembly.
11. Reconnect the negative battery cable. Start the engine and check for proper starter gear meshing.

EXHAUST SYSTEM

Inspection

▶ See Figures 98 thru 104

➡Safety glasses should be worn at all times when working on or near the exhaust system. Older exhaust systems will almost always be covered with loose rust particles which will shower you when disturbed. These particles are more than a nuisance and could injure your eye.

✷✷ CAUTION

DO NOT perform exhaust repairs or inspection with the engine or exhaust hot. Allow the system to cool completely before attempting any work. Exhaust systems are noted for sharp edges, flaking metal and rusted bolts. Gloves and eye protection are required. A healthy supply of penetrating oil and rags is highly recommended.

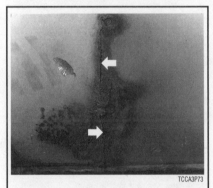

Fig. 98 Cracks in the muffler are a guaranteed leak

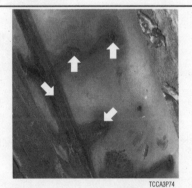

Fig. 99 Check the muffler for rotted spot welds and seams

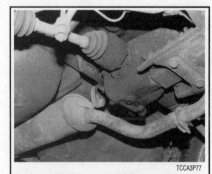

Fig. 100 Make sure the exhaust components are not contacting the body or suspension

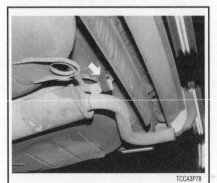

Fig. 101 Check for overstretched or torn exhaust hangers

Fig. 102 Example of a badly deteriorated exhaust pipe

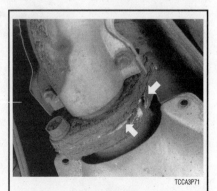

Fig. 103 Inspect flanges for gaskets that have deteriorated and need replacement

Fig. 104 Some systems, like this one, use large O-rings ("donuts") in between the flanges

Your vehicle must be raised and supported safely to inspect the exhaust system properly. By placing 4 safety stands under the vehicle for support should provide enough room for you to slide under the vehicle and inspect the system completely. Start the inspection at the exhaust manifold or turbocharger pipe where the header pipe is attached and work your way to the back of the vehicle. On dual exhaust systems, remember to inspect both sides of the vehicle. Check the complete exhaust system for open seams, holes loose connections, or other deterioration which could permit exhaust fumes to seep into the passenger compartment. Inspect all mounting brackets and hangers for deterioration, some models may have rubber O-rings that can be overstretched and non-supportive. These components will need to be replaced if found. It has always been a practice to use a pointed tool to poke up into the exhaust system where the deterioration spots are to see whether or not they crumble. Some models may have heat shield covering certain parts of the exhaust system , it will be necessary to remove these shields to have the exhaust visible for inspection also.

REPLACEMENT

▶ See Figure 105

There are basically two types of exhaust systems. One is the flange type where the component ends are attached with bolts and a gasket in-between. The

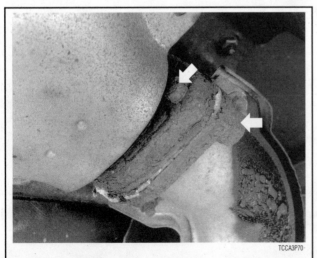

Fig. 105 Nuts and bolts will be extremely difficult to remove when deteriorated with rust

other exhaust system is the slip joint type. These components slip into one another using clamps to retain them together.

✳✳ CAUTION

Allow the exhaust system to cool sufficiently before spraying a solvent exhaust fasteners. Some solvents are highly flammable and could ignite when sprayed on hot exhaust components.

Before removing any component of the exhaust system, ALWAYS squirt a liquid rust dissolving agent onto the fasteners for ease of removal. A lot of knuckle skin will be saved by following this rule. It may even be wise to spray the fasteners and allow them to sit overnight.

Flange Type

▶ See Figure 106

✳✳ CAUTION

Do NOT perform exhaust repairs or inspection with the engine or exhaust hot. Allow the system to cool completely before attempting any work. Exhaust systems are noted for sharp edges, flaking metal and rusted bolts. Gloves and eye protection are required. A healthy supply of penetrating oil and rags is highly recommended. Never spray liquid rust dissolving agent onto a hot exhaust component.

Fig. 106 Example of a flange type exhaust system joint

Before removing any component on a flange type system, ALWAYS squirt a liquid rust dissolving agent onto the fasteners for ease of removal. Start by unbolting the exhaust piece at both ends (if required). When unbolting the headpipe from the manifold, make sure that the bolts are free before trying to remove them. if you snap a stud in the exhaust manifold, the stud will have to be removed with a bolt extractor, which often means removal of the manifold itself. Next, disconnect the component from the mounting; slight twisting and turning may be required to remove the component completely from the vehicle. You may need to tap on the component with a rubber mallet to loosen the component. If all else fails, use a hacksaw to separate the parts. An oxy-acetylene cutting torch may be faster but the sparks are DANGEROUS near the fuel tank, and at the very least, accidents could happen, resulting in damage to the under-car parts, not to mention yourself.

Slip Joint Type

▶ See Figure 107

Before removing any component on the slip joint type exhaust system, ALWAYS squirt a liquid rust dissolving agent onto the fasteners for ease of

Fig. 107 Example of a common slip joint type system

removal. Start by unbolting the exhaust piece at both ends (if required). When unbolting the headpipe from the manifold, make sure that the bolts are free before trying to remove them. if you snap a stud in the exhaust manifold, the stud will have to be removed with a bolt extractor, which often means removal of the manifold itself. Next, remove the mounting U-bolts from around the exhaust pipe you are extracting from the vehicle. Don't be surprised if the U-bolts break while removing the nuts. Loosen the exhaust pipe from any mounting brackets retaining it to the floor pan and separate the components.

ENGINE RECONDITIONING

Determining Engine Condition

Anything that generates heat and/or friction will eventually burn or wear out (for example, a light bulb generates heat, therefore its life span is limited). With this in mind, a running engine generates tremendous amounts of both; friction is encountered by the moving and rotating parts inside the engine and heat is created by friction and combustion of the fuel. However, the engine has systems designed to help reduce the effects of heat and friction and provide added longevity. The oiling system reduces the amount of friction encountered by the moving parts inside the engine, while the cooling system reduces heat created by friction and combustion. If either system is not maintained, a break-down will be inevitable. Therefore, you can see how regular maintenance can affect the service life of your vehicle. If you do not drain, flush and refill your cooling system at the proper intervals, deposits will begin to accumulate in the radiator, thereby reducing the amount of heat it can extract from the coolant. The same applies to your oil and filter; if it is not changed often enough it becomes laden with contaminates and is unable to properly lubricate the engine. This increases friction and wear.

There are a number of methods for evaluating the condition of your engine. A compression test can reveal the condition of your pistons, piston rings, cylinder bores, head gasket(s), valves and valve seats. An oil pressure test can warn you of possible engine bearing, or oil pump failures. Excessive oil consumption, evidence of oil in the engine air intake area and/or bluish smoke from the tail pipe may indicate worn piston rings, worn valve guides and/or valve seals. As a general rule, an engine that uses no more than one quart of oil every 1000 miles is in good condition. Engines that use one quart of oil or more in less than 1000 miles should first be checked for oil leaks. If any oil leaks are present, have them fixed before determining how much oil is consumed by the engine, especially if blue smoke is not visible at the tail pipe.

COMPRESSION TEST

▶ See Figure 108

A noticeable lack of engine power, excessive oil consumption and/or poor fuel mileage measured over an extended period are all indicators of internal engine wear. Worn piston rings, scored or worn cylinder bores, blown head gaskets, sticking or burnt valves, and worn valve seats are all possible culprits. A check of each cylinder's compression will help locate the problem.

➡A screw-in type compression gauge is more accurate than the type you simply hold against the spark plug hole. Although it takes slightly longer to use, it's worth the effort to obtain a more accurate reading.

1. Make sure that the proper amount and viscosity of engine oil is in the crankcase, then ensure the battery is fully charged.

2. Warm-up the engine to normal operating temperature, then shut the engine **OFF**.

3. Disable the ignition system.

4. Label and disconnect all of the spark plug wires from the plugs.

5. Thoroughly clean the cylinder head area around the spark plug ports, then remove the spark plugs.

6. Set the throttle plate to the fully open (wide-open throttle) position. You can block the accelerator linkage open for this, or you can have an assistant fully depress the accelerator pedal.

7. Install a screw-in type compression gauge into the No. 1 spark plug hole until the fitting is snug.

✳✳ WARNING

Be careful not to crossthread the spark plug hole.

8. According to the tool manufacturer's instructions, connect a remote starting switch to the starting circuit.

9. With the ignition switch in the **OFF** position, use the remote starting switch to crank the engine through at least five compression strokes (approximately 5 seconds of cranking) and record the highest reading on the gauge.

Fig. 108 A screw-in type compression gauge is more accurate and easier to use without an assistant

10. Repeat the test on each cylinder, cranking the engine approximately the same number of compression strokes and/or time as the first.

11. Compare the highest readings from each cylinder to that of the others. The indicated compression pressures are considered within specifications if the lowest reading cylinder is within 75 percent of the pressure recorded for the highest reading cylinder. For example, if your highest reading cylinder pressure was 150 psi (1034 kPa), then 75 percent of that would be 113 psi (779 kPa). So the lowest reading cylinder should be no less than 113 psi (779 kPa).

12. If a cylinder exhibits an unusually low compression reading, pour a tablespoon of clean engine oil into the cylinder through the spark plug hole and repeat the compression test. If the compression rises after adding oil, it means that the cylinder's piston rings and/or cylinder bore are damaged or worn. If the pressure remains low, the valves may not be seating properly (a valve job is needed), or the head gasket may be blown near that cylinder. If compression in any two adjacent cylinders is low, and if the addition of oil doesn't help raise compression, there is leakage past the head gasket. Oil and coolant in the combustion chamber, combined with blue or constant white smoke from the tail pipe, are symptoms of this problem. However, don't be alarmed by the normal white smoke emitted from the tail pipe during engine warm-up or from cold weather driving. There may be evidence of water droplets on the engine dipstick and/or oil droplets in the cooling system if a head gasket is blown.

OIL PRESSURE TEST

Check for proper oil pressure at the sending unit passage with an externally mounted mechanical oil pressure gauge (as opposed to relying on a factory installed dash-mounted gauge). A tachometer may also be needed, as some specifications may require running the engine at a specific rpm.

1. With the engine cold, locate and remove the oil pressure sending unit.

2. Following the manufacturer's instructions, connect a mechanical oil pressure gauge and, if necessary, a tachometer to the engine.

3. Start the engine and allow it to idle.

4. Check the oil pressure reading when cold and record the number. You may need to run the engine at a specified rpm, so check the specifications chart located earlier in this section.

5. Run the engine until normal operating temperature is reached (upper radiator hose will feel warm).

6. Check the oil pressure reading again with the engine hot and record the number. Turn the engine **OFF**.

7. Compare your hot oil pressure reading to that given in the chart. If the reading is low, check the cold pressure reading against the chart. If the cold pressure is well above the specification, and the hot reading was lower than the specification, you may have the wrong viscosity oil in the engine. Change the oil, making sure to use the proper grade and quantity, then repeat the test.

Low oil pressure readings could be attributed to internal component wear, pump related problems, a low oil level, or oil viscosity that is too low. High oil pressure readings could be caused by an overfilled crankcase, too high of an oil viscosity or a faulty pressure relief valve.

Buy or Rebuild?

Now that you have determined that your engine is worn out, you must make some decisions. The question of whether or not an engine is worth rebuilding is largely a subjective matter and one of personal worth. Is the engine a popular one, or is it an obsolete model? Are parts available? Will it get acceptable gas mileage once it is rebuilt? Is the car it's being put into worth keeping? Would it be less expensive to buy a new engine, have your engine rebuilt by a pro, rebuild it yourself or buy a used engine from a salvage yard? Or would it be simpler and less expensive to buy another car? If you have considered all these matters and more, and have still decided to rebuild the engine, then it is time to decide how you will rebuild it.

➡ **The editors at Chilton feel that most engine machining should be performed by a professional machine shop. Don't think of it as wasting money, rather, as an assurance that the job has been done right the first time. There are many expensive and specialized tools required to perform such tasks as boring and honing an engine block or having a valve job done on a cylinder head. Even inspecting the parts requires expensive micrometers and gauges to properly measure wear and clearances. Also, a machine shop can deliver to you clean, and ready to assemble parts, saving you time and aggravation. Your maximum savings will come from performing the removal, disassembly, assembly and instal-**lation of the engine and purchasing or renting only the tools required to perform the above tasks. Depending on the particular circumstances, you may save 40 to 60 percent of the cost doing these yourself.

A complete rebuild or overhaul of an engine involves replacing all of the moving parts (pistons, rods, crankshaft, camshaft, etc.) with new ones and machining the non-moving wearing surfaces of the block and heads. Unfortunately, this may not be cost effective. For instance, your crankshaft may have been damaged or worn, but it can be machined undersize for a minimal fee.

So, as you can see, you can replace everything inside the engine, but, it is wiser to replace only those parts which are really needed, and, if possible, repair the more expensive ones. Later in this section, we will break the engine down into its two main components: the cylinder head and the engine block. We will discuss each component, and the recommended parts to replace during a rebuild on each.

Engine Overhaul Tips

Most engine overhaul procedures are fairly standard. In addition to specific parts replacement procedures and specifications for your individual engine, this section is also a guide to acceptable rebuilding procedures. Examples of standard rebuilding practice are given and should be used along with specific details concerning your particular engine.

Competent and accurate machine shop services will ensure maximum performance, reliability and engine life. In most instances it is more profitable for the do-it-yourself mechanic to remove, clean and inspect the component, buy the necessary parts and deliver these to a shop for actual machine work.

Much of the assembly work (crankshaft, bearings, piston rods, and other components) is well within the scope of the do-it-yourself mechanic's tools and abilities. You will have to decide for yourself the depth of involvement you desire in an engine repair or rebuild.

TOOLS

The tools required for an engine overhaul or parts replacement will depend on the depth of your involvement. With a few exceptions, they will be the tools found in a mechanic's tool kit (see in-depth work will require some or all of the following:

- A dial indicator (reading in thousandths) mounted on a universal base
- Micrometers and telescope gauges
- Jaw and screw-type pullers
- Scraper
- Valve spring compressor
- Ring groove cleaner
- Piston ring expander and compressor
- Ridge reamer
- Cylinder hone or glaze breaker
- Plastigage®
- Engine stand

The use of most of these tools is illustrated in this section. Many can be rented for a one-time use from a local parts jobber or tool supply house specializing in automotive work.

Occasionally, the use of special tools is called for. See the information on Special Tools and the Safety Notice in the front of this book before substituting another tool.

OVERHAUL TIPS

Aluminum has become extremely popular for use in engines, due to its low weight. Observe the following precautions when handling aluminum parts:

- Never hot tank aluminum parts (the caustic hot tank solution will eat the aluminum.
- Remove all aluminum parts (identification tag, etc.) from engine parts prior to the tanking.
- Always coat threads lightly with engine oil or anti-seize compounds before installation, to prevent seizure.
- Never overtighten bolts or spark plugs, especially in aluminum threads.

When assembling the engine, any parts that will be exposed to frictional contact must be prelubed to provide lubrication at initial start-up. Any product specifically formulated for this purpose can be used, but engine oil is not recommended as a prelube in most cases.

When semi-permanent (locked, but removable) installation of bolts or nuts is desired, threads should be cleaned and coated with Loctite® or another similar, commercial non-hardening sealant.

CLEANING

◆ **See Figures 109, 110, 111 and 112**

Before the engine and its components are inspected, they must be thoroughly cleaned. You will need to remove any engine varnish, oil sludge and/or carbon deposits from all of the components to insure an accurate inspection. A crack in the engine block or cylinder head can easily become overlooked if hidden by a layer of sludge or carbon.

Most of the cleaning process can be carried out with common hand tools and readily available solvents or solutions. Carbon deposits can be chipped away using a hammer and a hard wooden chisel. Old gasket material and varnish or sludge can usually be removed using a scraper and/or cleaning solvent. Extremely stubborn deposits may require the use of a power drill with a wire brush. If using a wire brush, use extreme care around any critical machined surfaces (such as the gasket surfaces, bearing saddles, cylinder bores, etc.). USE OF A WIRE BRUSH IS NOT RECOMMENDED ON ANY ALUMINUM COMPONENTS. Always follow any safety recommendations given by the manufacturer of the tool and/or solvent. You should always wear eye protection during any cleaning process involving scraping, chipping or spraying of solvents.

An alternative to the mess and hassle of cleaning the parts yourself is to drop them off at a local garage or machine shop. They will, more than likely, have the necessary equipment to properly clean all of the parts for a nominal fee.

✳✳ CAUTION

Always wear eye protection during any cleaning process involving scraping, chipping or spraying of solvents.

Remove any oil galley plugs, freeze plugs and/or pressed-in bearings and carefully wash and degrease all of the engine components including the fasteners and bolts. Small parts such as the valves, springs, etc., should be placed in a metal basket and allowed to soak. Use pipe cleaner type brushes, and clean all passageways in the components. Use a ring expander and remove the rings from the pistons. Clean the piston ring grooves with a special tool or a piece of broken ring. Scrape the carbon off of the top of the piston. You should never use a wire brush on the pistons. After preparing all of the piston assemblies in this manner, wash and degrease them again.

✳✳ WARNING

Use extreme care when cleaning around the cylinder head valve seats. A mistake or slip may cost you a new seat.

When cleaning the cylinder head, remove carbon from the combustion chamber with the valves installed. This will avoid damaging the valve seats.

Fig. 110 Use a ring expander tool to remove the piston rings

Fig. 111 Clean the piston ring grooves using a ring groove cleaner tool, or . . .

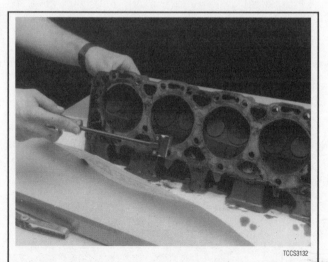

Fig. 109 Use a gasket scraper to remove the old gasket material from the mating surfaces

Fig. 112 . . . use a piece of an old ring to clean the grooves. Be careful, the ring can be quite sharp

REPAIRING DAMAGED THREADS

▶ **See Figures 113, 114, 115, 116 and 117**

Several methods of repairing damaged threads are available. Heli-Coil® (shown here), Keenserts® and Microdot® are among the most widely used. All involve basically the same principle—drilling out stripped threads, tapping the hole and installing a prewound insert—making welding, plugging and oversize fasteners unnecessary.

Two types of thread repair inserts are usually supplied: a standard type for most inch coarse, inch fine, metric course and metric fine thread sizes and a spark lug type to fit most spark plug port sizes. Consult the individual tool manufacturer's catalog to determine exact applications. Typical thread repair kits will contain a selection of prewound threaded inserts, a tap (corresponding to the outside diameter threads of the insert) and an installation tool. Spark plug inserts usually differ because they require a tap equipped with pilot threads and

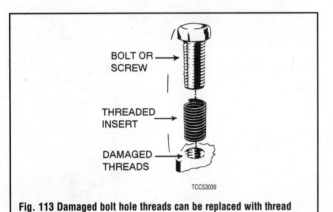

Fig. 113 Damaged bolt hole threads can be replaced with thread repair inserts

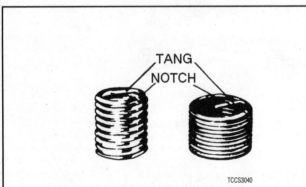

Fig. 114 Standard thread repair insert (left), and spark plug thread insert

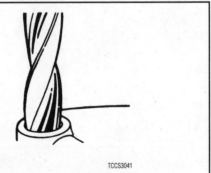

Fig. 115 Drill out the damaged threads with the specified size bit. Be sure to drill completely through the hole or to the bottom of a blind hole

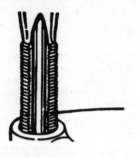

Fig. 116 Using the kit, tap the hole in order to receive the thread insert. Keep the tap well oiled and back it out frequently to avoid clogging the threads

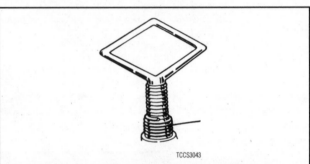

Fig. 117 Screw the insert onto the installer tool until the tang engages the slot. Thread the insert into the hole until it is ¼–½ turn below the top surface, then remove the tool and break off the tang using a punch

a combined reamer/tap section. Most manufacturers also supply blister-packed thread repair inserts separately in addition to a master kit containing a variety of taps and inserts plus installation tools.

Before attempting to repair a threaded hole, remove any snapped, broken or damaged bolts or studs. Penetrating oil can be used to free frozen threads. The offending item can usually be removed with locking pliers or using a screw/stud extractor. After the hole is clear, the thread can be repaired, as shown in the series of accompanying illustrations and in the kit manufacturer's instructions.

Engine Preparation

To properly rebuild an engine, you must first remove it from the vehicle, then disassemble and diagnose it. Ideally you should place your engine on an engine stand. This affords you the best access to the engine components. Follow the manufacturer's directions for using the stand with your particular engine. Remove the flywheel or flexplate before installing the engine to the stand.

Now that you have the engine on a stand, and assuming that you have drained the oil and coolant from the engine, it's time to strip it of all but the necessary components. Before you start disassembling the engine, you may want to take a moment to draw some pictures, or fabricate some labels or containers to mark the locations of various components and the bolts and/or studs which fasten them. Modern day engines use a lot of little brackets and clips which hold wiring harnesses and such, and these holders are often mounted on studs and/or bolts that can be easily mixed up. The manufacturer spent a lot of time and money designing your vehicle, and they wouldn't have wasted any of it by haphazardly placing brackets, clips or fasteners on the vehicle. If it's present when you disassemble it, put it back when you assemble, you will regret not remembering that little bracket which holds a wire harness out of the path of a rotating part.

You should begin by unbolting any accessories still attached to the engine, such as the water pump, power steering pump, alternator, etc. Then, unfasten any manifolds (intake or exhaust) which were not removed during the engine removal procedure. Finally, remove any covers remaining on the engine such as the rocker arm, front or timing cover and oil pan. Some front covers may require the vibration damper and/or crank pulley to be removed beforehand. The idea is to reduce the engine to the bare necessities (cylinder head(s), valve train, engine block, crankshaft, pistons and connecting rods), plus any other `in block' components such as oil pumps, balance shafts and auxiliary shafts.

Finally, remove the cylinder head(s) from the engine block and carefully place on a bench. Disassembly instructions for each component follow later in this section.

Cylinder Head

There are two basic types of cylinder heads used on today's automobiles: the Overhead Valve (OHV) and the Overhead Camshaft (OHC). The latter can also be broken down into two subgroups: the Single Overhead Camshaft (SOHC) and the Dual Overhead Camshaft (DOHC). Generally, if there is only a single camshaft on a head, it is just referred to as an OHC head. Also, an engine with an OHV cylinder head is also known as a pushrod engine.

Most cylinder heads these days are made of an aluminum alloy due to its light weight, durability and heat transfer qualities. However, cast iron was the material of choice in the past, and is still used on many vehicles today. Whether made from aluminum or iron, all cylinder heads have valves and seats. Some use two valves per cylinder, while the more hi-tech engines will utilize a multi-valve configuration using 3, 4 and even 5 valves per cylinder. When the valve contacts the seat, it does so on precision machined surfaces, which seals the combustion chamber. All cylinder heads have a valve guide for each valve. The guide centers the valve to the seat and allows it to move up and down within it. The clearance between the valve and guide can be critical. Too much clearance and the engine may consume oil, lose vacuum and/or damage the seat. Too little, and the valve can stick in the guide causing the engine to run poorly if at all, and possibly causing severe damage. The last component all cylinder heads have are valve springs. The spring holds the valve against its seat. It also returns the valve to this position when the valve has been opened by the valve train or camshaft. The spring is fastened to the valve by a retainer and valve locks (sometimes called keepers). Aluminum heads will also have a valve spring shim to keep the spring from wearing away the aluminum.

An ideal method of rebuilding the cylinder head would involve replacing all of the valves, guides, seats, springs, etc. with new ones. However, depending on how the engine was maintained, often this is not necessary. A major cause of valve, guide and seat wear is an improperly tuned engine. An engine that is running too rich, will often wash the lubricating oil out of the guide with gasoline, causing it to wear rapidly. Conversely, an engine which is running too lean will place higher combustion temperatures on the valves and seats allowing them to wear or even burn. Springs fall victim to the driving habits of the individual. A driver who often runs the engine rpm to the redline will wear out or break the springs faster then one that stays well below it. Unfortunately, mileage takes it toll on all of the parts. Generally, the valves, guides, springs and seats in a cylinder head can be machined and re-used, saving you money. However, if a valve is burnt, it may be wise to replace all of the valves, since they were all operating in the same environment. The same goes for any other component on the cylinder head. Think of it as an insurance policy against future problems related to that component.

Unfortunately, the only way to find out which components need replacing, is to disassemble and carefully check each piece. After the cylinder head(s) are disassembled, thoroughly clean all of the components.

DISASSEMBLY

OHC Heads

▶ See Figures 118 and 119

Whether it is a single or dual overhead camshaft cylinder head, the disassembly procedure is relatively unchanged. One aspect to pay attention to is careful labeling of the parts on the dual camshaft cylinder head. There will be an intake camshaft and followers as well as an exhaust camshaft and followers and they must be labeled as such. In some cases, the components are identical and could easily be installed incorrectly. DO NOT MIX THEM UP! Determining which is which is very simple; the intake camshaft and components are on the same side of the head as was the intake manifold. Conversely, the exhaust camshaft and components are on the same side of the head as was the exhaust manifold.

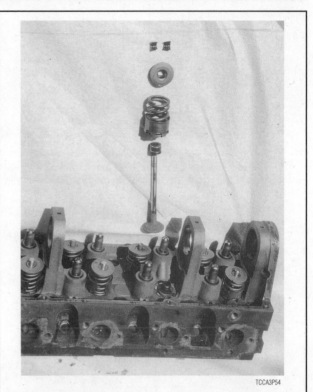

TCCA3P54

Fig. 118 Exploded view of a valve, seal, spring, retainer and locks from an OHC cylinder head

TCCA3P62

Fig. 119 Example of a multi-valve cylinder head. Note how it has 2 intake and 2 exhaust valve ports

CUP TYPE CAMSHAFT FOLLOWERS

▶ **See Figures 120, 121 and 122**

Most cylinder heads with cup type camshaft followers will have the valve spring, retainer and locks recessed within the follower's bore. You will need a C-clamp style valve spring compressor tool, an OHC spring removal tool (or equivalent) and a small magnet to disassemble the head.

1. If not already removed, remove the camshaft(s) and/or followers. Mark their positions for assembly.
2. Position the cylinder head to allow use of a C-clamp style valve spring compressor tool.

➡**It is preferred to position the cylinder head gasket surface facing you with the valve springs facing the opposite direction and the head laying horizontal.**

3. With the OHC spring removal adapter tool positioned inside of the follower bore, compress the valve spring using the C-clamp style valve spring compressor.
4. Remove the valve locks. A small magnetic tool or screwdriver will aid in removal.
5. Release the compressor tool and remove the spring assembly.
6. Withdraw the valve from the cylinder head.
7. If equipped, remove the valve seal.

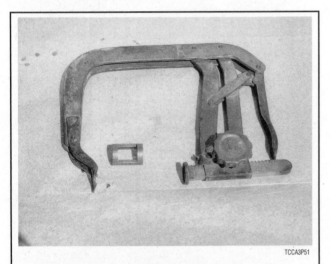

Fig. 120 C-clamp type spring compressor and an OHC spring removal tool (center) for cup type followers

TCCA3P51

Fig. 121 Most cup type follower cylinder heads retain the camshaft using bolt-on bearing caps

TCCA3P63

TCCA3P65

Fig. 122 Position the OHC spring tool in the follower bore, then compress the spring with a C-clamp type tool

➡**Special valve seal removal tools are available. Regular or needlenose type pliers, if used with care, will work just as well. If using ordinary pliers, be sure not to damage the follower bore. The follower and its bore are machined to close tolerances and any damage to the bore will effect this relationship.**

8. If equipped, remove the valve spring shim. A small magnetic tool or screwdriver will aid in removal.
9. Repeat Steps 3 through 8 until all of the valves have been removed.

ROCKER ARM TYPE CAMSHAFT FOLLOWERS

▶ **See Figures 123 thru 131**

Most cylinder heads with rocker arm-type camshaft followers are easily disassembled using a standard valve spring compressor. However, certain models may not have enough open space around the spring for the standard tool and may require you to use a C-clamp style compressor tool instead.

1. If not already removed, remove the rocker arms and/or shafts and the camshaft. If applicable, also remove the hydraulic lash adjusters. Mark their positions for assembly.
2. Position the cylinder head to allow access to the valve spring.
3. Use a valve spring compressor tool to relieve the spring tension from the retainer.

➡**Due to engine varnish, the retainer may stick to the valve locks. A gentle tap with a hammer may help to break it loose.**

4. Remove the valve locks from the valve tip and/or retainer. A small magnet may help in removing the small locks.

Fig. 123 Example of the shaft mounted rocker arms on some OHC heads

Fig. 124 Another example of the rocker arm type OHC head. This model uses a follower under the camshaft

Fig. 125 Before the camshaft can be removed, all of the followers must first be removed . . .

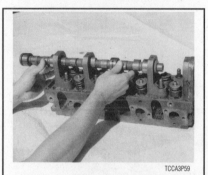

Fig. 126 . . . then the camshaft can be removed by sliding it out (shown), or unbolting a bearing cap (not shown)

Fig. 127 Compress the valve spring . . .

Fig. 128 . . . then remove the valve locks from the valve stem and spring retainer

Fig. 129 Remove the valve spring and retainer from the cylinder head

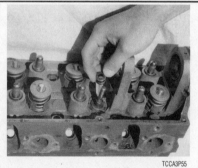

Fig. 130 Remove the valve seal from the guide. Some gentle prying or pliers may help to remove stubborn ones

Fig. 131 All aluminum and some cast iron heads will have these valve spring shims. Remove all of them as well

5. Lift the valve spring, tool and all, off of the valve stem.

6. If equipped, remove the valve seal. If the seal is difficult to remove with the valve in place, try removing the valve first, then the seal. Follow the steps below for valve removal.

7. Position the head to allow access for withdrawing the valve.

➡Cylinder heads that have seen a lot of miles and/or abuse may have mushroomed the valve lock grove and/or tip, causing difficulty in removal of the valve. If this has happened, use a metal file to carefully remove the high spots around the lock grooves and/or tip. Only file it enough to allow removal.

8. Remove the valve from the cylinder head.

9. If equipped, remove the valve spring shim. A small magnetic tool or screwdriver will aid in removal.

10. Repeat Steps 3 though 9 until all of the valves have been removed.

INSPECTION

Now that all of the cylinder head components are clean, it's time to inspect them for wear and/or damage. To accurately inspect them, you will need some specialized tools:

- A 0–1 in. micrometer for the valves
- A dial indicator or inside diameter gauge for the valve guides
- A spring pressure test gauge

If you do not have access to the proper tools, you may want to bring the components to a shop that does.

Valves

▶ See Figures 132 and 133

The first thing to inspect are the valve heads. Look closely at the head, margin and face for any cracks, excessive wear or burning. The margin is the best place to look for burning. It should have a squared edge with an even width all around the diameter. When a valve burns, the margin will look melted and the edges rounded. Also inspect the valve head for any signs of tulipping. This will show as a lifting of the edges or dishing in the center of the head and will usually not occur to all of the valves. All of the heads should look the same, any that seem dished more than others are probably bad. Next, inspect the valve lock grooves and valve tips. Check for any burrs around the lock grooves, especially if you had to file them to remove the valve. Valve tips should appear flat, although slight rounding with high mileage engines is normal. Slightly worn valve tips will need to be machined flat. Last, measure the valve stem diameter with the micrometer. Measure the area that rides within the guide, especially towards the tip where most of the wear occurs. Take several measurements along its length and compare them to each other. Wear should be even along the length with little to no taper. If no minimum diameter is given in the specifications, then the stem should not read more than 0.001 in. (0.025mm) below the specification. Any valves that fail these inspections should be replaced.

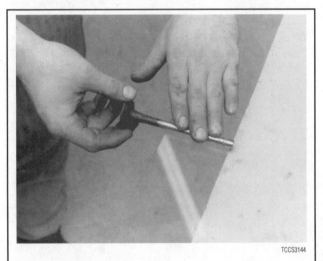

TCCS3144

Fig. 132 Valve stems may be rolled on a flat surface to check for bends

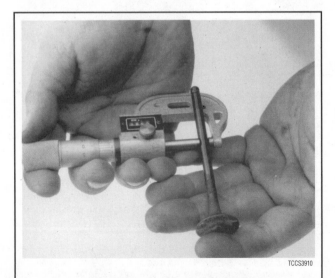

TCCS3910

Fig. 133 Use a micrometer to check the valve stem diameter

Springs, Retainers and Valve Locks

▶ See Figures 134 and 135

The first thing to check is the most obvious, broken springs. Next check the free length and squareness of each spring. If applicable, insure to distinguish between intake and exhaust springs. Use a ruler and/or carpenters square to measure the length. A carpenters square should be used to check the springs for squareness. If a spring pressure test gauge is available, check each springs rating and compare to the specifications chart. Check the readings against the specifications given. Any springs that fail these inspections should be replaced.

The spring retainers rarely need replacing, however they should still be checked as a precaution. Inspect the spring mating surface and the valve lock retention area for any signs of excessive wear. Also check for any signs of cracking. Replace any retainers that are questionable.

Valve locks should be inspected for excessive wear on the outside contact area as well as on the inner notched surface. Any locks which appear worn or broken and its respective valve should be replaced.

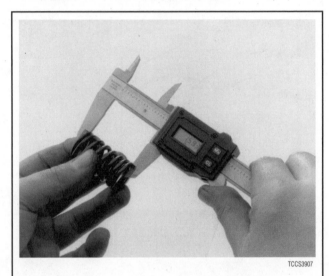

TCCS3907

Fig. 134 Use a caliper to check the valve spring free-length

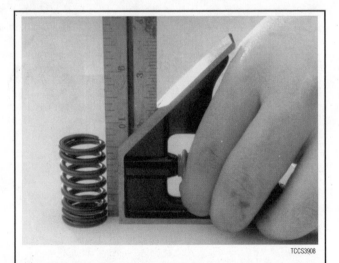

TCCS3908

Fig. 135 Check the valve spring for squareness on a flat surface; a carpenter's square can be used

Cylinder Head

There are several things to check on the cylinder head: valve guides, seats, cylinder head surface flatness, cracks and physical damage.

VALVE GUIDES

▶ See Figure 136

Now that you know the valves are good, you can use them to check the guides, although a new valve, if available, is preferred. Before you measure anything, look at the guides carefully and inspect them for any cracks, chips or breakage. Also if the guide is a removable style (as in most aluminum heads), check them for any looseness or evidence of movement. All of the guides should appear to be at the same height from the spring seat. If any seem lower (or higher) from another, the guide has moved. Mount a dial indicator onto the spring side of the cylinder head. Lightly oil the valve stem and insert it into the cylinder head. Position the dial indicator against the valve stem near the tip and zero the gauge. Grasp the valve stem and wiggle towards and away from the dial indicator and observe the readings. Mount the dial indicator 90 degrees from the initial point and zero the gauge and again take a reading. Compare the two readings for an out-of-round condition. Check the readings against the specifications given. An Inside Diameter (I.D.) gauge designed for valve guides will give you an accurate valve guide bore measurement. If the I.D. gauge is used, compare the readings with the specifications given. Any guides that fail these inspections should be replaced or machined.

Fig. 136 A dial gauge may be used to check valve stem-to-guide clearance; read the gauge while moving the valve stem

VALVE SEATS

A visual inspection of the valve seats should show a slightly worn and pitted surface where the valve face contacts the seat. Inspect the seat carefully for severe pitting or cracks. Also, a seat that is badly worn will be recessed into the cylinder head. A severely worn or recessed seat may need to be replaced. All cracked seats must be replaced. A seat concentricity gauge, if available, should be used to check the seat run-out. If run-out exceeds specifications the seat must be machined (if no specification is given use 0.002 in. or 0.051mm).

CYLINDER HEAD SURFACE FLATNESS

▶ See Figures 137 and 138

After you have cleaned the gasket surface of the cylinder head of any old gasket material, check the head for flatness.

Place a straightedge across the gasket surface. Using feeler gauges, determine the clearance at the center of the straightedge and across the cylinder head at several points. Check along the centerline and diagonally on the head surface. If the warpage exceeds 0.003 in. (0.076mm) within a 6.0 in. (15.2cm) span, or 0.006 in. (0.152mm) over the total length of the head, the cylinder head must be resurfaced. After resurfacing the heads of a V-type engine, the intake manifold flange surface should be checked, and if necessary, milled proportionally to allow for the change in its mounting position.

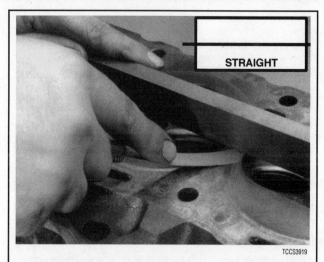

Fig. 137 Check the head for flatness across the center of the head surface using a straightedge and feeler gauge

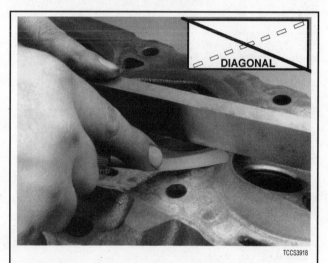

Fig. 138 Checks should also be made along both diagonals of the head surface

CRACKS AND PHYSICAL DAMAGE

Generally, cracks are limited to the combustion chamber, however, it is not uncommon for the head to crack in a spark plug hole, port, outside of the head or in the valve spring/rocker arm area. The first area to inspect is always the hottest: the exhaust seat/port area.

A visual inspection should be performed, but just because you don't see a crack does not mean it is not there. Some more reliable methods for inspecting for cracks include Magnaflux®, a magnetic process or Zyglo®, a dye penetrant. Magnaflux® is used only on ferrous metal (cast iron) heads. Zyglo® uses a spray on fluorescent mixture along with a black light to reveal the cracks. It is strongly recommended to have your cylinder head checked professionally for cracks, especially if the engine was known to have overheated and/or leaked or consumed coolant. Contact a local shop for availability and pricing of these services.

Physical damage is usually very evident. For example, a broken mounting ear from dropping the head or a bent or broken stud and/or bolt. All of these defects should be fixed or, if unrepairable, the head should be replaced.

Camshaft and Followers

Inspect the camshaft(s) and followers as described earlier in this section.

REFINISHING & REPAIRING

Many of the procedures given for refinishing and repairing the cylinder head components must be performed by a machine shop. Certain steps, if the inspected part is not worn, can be performed yourself inexpensively. However, you spent a lot of time and effort so far, why risk trying to save a couple bucks if you might have to do it all over again?

Valves

Any valves that were not replaced should be refaced and the tips ground flat. Unless you have access to a valve grinding machine, this should be done by a machine shop. If the valves are in extremely good condition, as well as the valve seats and guides, they may be lapped in without performing machine work.

It is a recommended practice to lap the valves even after machine work has been performed and/or new valves have been purchased. This insures a positive seal between the valve and seat.

LAPPING THE VALVES

➡**Before lapping the valves to the seats, read the rest of the cylinder head section to insure that any related parts are in acceptable enough condition to continue.**

➡**Before any valve seat machining and/or lapping can be performed, the guides must be within factory recommended specifications.**

1. Invert the cylinder head.
2. Lightly lubricate the valve stems and insert them into the cylinder head in their numbered order.
3. Raise the valve from the seat and apply a small amount of fine lapping compound to the seat.
4. Moisten the suction head of a hand-lapping tool and attach it to the head of the valve.
5. Rotate the tool between the palms of both hands, changing the position of the valve on the valve seat and lifting the tool often to prevent grooving.
6. Lap the valve until a smooth, polished circle is evident on the valve and seat.
7. Remove the tool and the valve. Wipe away all traces of the grinding compound and store the valve to maintain its lapped location.

❊❊ WARNING

Do not get the valves out of order after they have been lapped. They must be put back with the same valve seat with which they were lapped.

Springs, Retainers and Valve Locks

There is no repair or refinishing possible with the springs, retainers and valve locks. If they are found to be worn or defective, they must be replaced with new (or known good) parts.

Cylinder Head

Most refinishing procedures dealing with the cylinder head must be performed by a machine shop. Read the sections below and review your inspection data to determine whether or not machining is necessary.

VALVE GUIDE

➡**If any machining or replacements are made to the valve guides, the seats must be machined.**

Unless the valve guides need machining or replacing, the only service to perform is to thoroughly clean them of any dirt or oil residue.

There are only two types of valve guides used on automobile engines: the replaceable-type (all aluminum heads) and the cast-in integral-type (most cast iron heads). There are four recommended methods for repairing worn guides.

- Knurling
- Inserts
- Reaming oversize
- Replacing

Knurling is a process in which metal is displaced and raised, thereby reducing clearance, giving a true center, and providing oil control. It is the least expensive way of repairing the valve guides. However, it is not necessarily the best, and in some cases, a knurled valve guide will not stand up for more than a short time. It requires a special knurlizer and precision reaming tools to obtain proper clearances. It would not be cost effective to purchase these tools, unless you plan on rebuilding several of the same cylinder head.

Installing a guide insert involves machining the guide to accept a bronze insert. One style is the coil-type which is installed into a threaded guide. Another is the thin-walled insert where the guide is reamed oversize to accept a split-sleeve insert. After the insert is installed, a special tool is then run through the guide to expand the insert, locking it to the guide. The insert is then reamed to the standard size for proper valve clearance.

Reaming for oversize valves restores normal clearances and provides a true valve seat. Most cast-in type guides can be reamed to accept an valve with an oversize stem. The cost factor for this can become quite high as you will need to purchase the reamer and new, oversize stem valves for all guides which were reamed. Oversizes are generally 0.003 to 0.030 in. (0.076 to 0.762mm), with 0.015 in. (0.381mm) being the most common.

To replace cast-in type valve guides, they must be drilled out, then reamed to accept replacement guides. This must be done on a fixture which will allow centering and leveling off of the original valve seat or guide, otherwise a serious guide-to-seat misalignment may occur making it impossible to properly machine the seat.

Replaceable-type guides are pressed into the cylinder head. A hammer and a stepped drift or punch may be used to install and remove the guides. Before removing the guides, measure the protrusion on the spring side of the head and record it for installation. Use the stepped drift to hammer out the old guide from the combustion chamber side of the head. When installing, determine whether or not the guide also seals a water jacket in the head, and if it does, use the recommended sealing agent. If there is no water jacket, grease the valve guide and its bore. Use the stepped drift, and hammer the new guide into the cylinder head from the spring side of the cylinder head. A stack of washers the same thickness as the measured protrusion may help the installation process.

VALVE SEATS

➡**Before any valve seat machining can be performed, the guides must be within factory recommended specifications.**

➡**If any machining or replacements were made to the valve guides, the seats must be machined.**

If the seats are in good condition, the valves can be lapped to the seats, and the cylinder head assembled. See the valves section for instructions on lapping.

If the valve seats are worn, cracked or damaged, they must be serviced by a machine shop. The valve seat must be perfectly centered to the valve guide, which requires very accurate machining.

CYLINDER HEAD SURFACE

If the cylinder head is warped, it must be machined flat. If the warpage is extremely severe, the head may need to be replaced. In some instances, it may be possible to straighten a warped head enough to allow machining. In either case, contact a professional machine shop for service.

➡**Any OHC cylinder head that shows excessive warpage should have the camshaft bearing journals align bored after the cylinder head has been resurfaced.**

❊❊ WARNING

Failure to align bore the camshaft bearing journals could result in severe engine damage including but not limited to: valve and piston damage, connecting rod damage, camshaft and/or crankshaft breakage.

CRACKS AND PHYSICAL DAMAGE

Certain cracks can be repaired in both cast iron and aluminum heads. For cast iron, a tapered threaded insert is installed along the length of the crack. Aluminum can also use the tapered inserts, however welding is the preferred method. Some physical damage can be repaired through brazing or welding. Contact a machine shop to get expert advice for your particular dilemma.

ASSEMBLY

The first step for any assembly job is to have a clean area in which to work. Next, thoroughly clean all of the parts and components that are to be assembled. Finally, place all of the components onto a suitable work space and, if necessary, arrange the parts to their respective positions.

OHC Engines

▶ See Figure 139

CUP TYPE CAMSHAFT FOLLOWERS

To install the springs, retainers and valve locks on heads which have these components recessed into the camshaft follower's bore, you will need a small screwdriver-type tool, some clean white grease and a lot of patience. You will also need the C-clamp style spring compressor and the OHC tool used to disassemble the head.

1. Lightly lubricate the valve stems and insert all of the valves into the cylinder head. If possible, maintain their original locations.
2. If equipped, install any valve spring shims which were removed.
3. If equipped, install the new valve seals, keeping the following in mind:
• If the valve seal presses over the guide, lightly lubricate the outer guide surfaces.
• If the seal is an O-ring type, it is installed just after compressing the spring but before the valve locks.
4. Place the valve spring and retainer over the stem.
5. Position the spring compressor and the OHC tool, then compress the spring.
6. Using a small screwdriver as a spatula, fill the valve stem side of the lock with white grease. Use the excess grease on the screwdriver to fasten the lock to the driver.
7. Carefully install the valve lock, which is stuck to the end of the screwdriver, to the valve stem then press on it with the screwdriver until the grease squeezes out. The valve lock should now be stuck to the stem.
8. Repeat Steps 6 and 7 for the remaining valve lock. 51
9. Relieve the spring pressure slowly and insure that neither valve lock becomes dislodged by the retainer.
10. Remove the spring compressor tool.
11. Repeat Steps 2 through 10 until all of the springs have been installed.
12. Install the followers, camshaft(s) and any other components that were removed for disassembly.

TCCA3P64

Fig. 139 Once assembled, check the valve clearance and correct as needed

ROCKER ARM TYPE CAMSHAFT FOLLOWERS

1. Lightly lubricate the valve stems and insert all of the valves into the cylinder head. If possible, maintain their original locations.
2. If equipped, install any valve spring shims which were removed.

3. If equipped, install the new valve seals, keeping the following in mind:
• If the valve seal presses over the guide, lightly lubricate the outer guide surfaces.
• If the seal is an O-ring type, it is installed just after compressing the spring but before the valve locks.
4. Place the valve spring and retainer over the stem.
5. Position the spring compressor tool and compress the spring.
6. Assemble the valve locks to the stem.
7. Relieve the spring pressure slowly and insure that neither valve lock becomes dislodged by the retainer.
8. Remove the spring compressor tool.
9. Repeat Steps 2 through 8 until all of the springs have been installed.
10. Install the camshaft(s), rockers, shafts and any other components that were removed for disassembly.

Engine Block

GENERAL INFORMATION

A thorough overhaul or rebuild of an engine block would include replacing the pistons, rings, bearings, timing belt/chain assembly and oil pump. For OHV engines also include a new camshaft and lifters. The block would then have the cylinders bored and honed oversize (or if using removable cylinder sleeves, new sleeves installed) and the crankshaft would be cut undersize to provide new wearing surfaces and perfect clearances. However, your particular engine may not have everything worn out. What if only the piston rings have worn out and the clearances on everything else are still within factory specifications? Well, you could just replace the rings and put it back together, but this would be a very rare example. Chances are, if one component in your engine is worn, other components are sure to follow, and soon. At the very least, you should always replace the rings, bearings and oil pump. This is what is commonly called a "freshen up".

Cylinder Ridge Removal

Because the top piston ring does not travel to the very top of the cylinder, a ridge is built up between the end of the travel and the top of the cylinder bore.

Pushing the piston and connecting rod assembly past the ridge can be difficult, and damage to the piston ring lands could occur. If the ridge is not removed before installing a new piston or not removed at all, piston ring breakage and piston damage may occur.

➡**It is always recommended that you remove any cylinder ridges before removing the piston and connecting rod assemblies. If you know that new pistons are going to be installed and the engine block will be bored oversize, you may be able to forego this step. However, some ridges may actually prevent the assemblies from being removed, necessitating its removal.**

There are several different types of ridge reamers on the market, none of which are inexpensive. Unless a great deal of engine rebuilding is anticipated, borrow or rent a reamer.

1. Turn the crankshaft until the piston is at the bottom of its travel.
2. Cover the head of the piston with a rag.
3. Follow the tool manufacturers instructions and cut away the ridge, exercising extreme care to avoid cutting too deeply. 52
4. Remove the ridge reamer, the rag and as many of the cuttings as possible. Continue until all of the cylinder ridges have been removed.

DISASSEMBLY

▶ See Figures 140 and 141

The engine disassembly instructions following assume that you have the engine mounted on an engine stand. If not, it is easiest to disassemble the engine on a bench or the floor with it resting on the bell housing or transmission/transaxle mounting surface. You must be able to access the connecting rod fasteners and turn the crankshaft during disassembly. Also, all engine covers (timing, front, side, oil pan, whatever) should have already been removed. Engines which are seized or locked up may not be able to be completely disassembled, and a core (salvage yard) engine should be purchased.

OHC Engines

If not done during the cylinder head removal, remove the timing chain/belt and/or gear/sprocket assembly. Remove the oil pick-up and pump assembly and, if necessary, the pump drive. If equipped, remove any balance or auxiliary shafts. If necessary, remove the cylinder ridge from the top of the bore. See the cylinder ridge removal procedure earlier in this section.

All Engines

Rotate the engine over so that the crankshaft is exposed. Use a number punch or scribe and mark each connecting rod with its respective cylinder number. The cylinder closest to the front of the engine is always number 1. However, depending on the engine placement, the front of the engine could either be the flywheel or damper/pulley end. Generally the front of the engine faces the front of the vehicle. Use a number punch or scribe and also mark the main bearing caps from front to rear with the front most cap being number 1 (if there are five caps, mark them 1 through 5, front to rear).

✳✳ WARNING

Take special care when pushing the connecting rod up from the crankshaft because the sharp threads of the rod bolts/studs will score the crankshaft journal. Insure that special plastic caps are installed over them, or cut two pieces of rubber hose to do the same.

Again, rotate the engine, this time to position the number one cylinder bore (head surface) up. Turn the crankshaft until the number one piston is at the bottom of its travel, this should allow the maximum access to its connecting rod. Remove the number one connecting rods fasteners and cap and place two lengths of rubber hose over the rod bolts/studs to protect the crankshaft from damage. Using a sturdy wooden dowel and a hammer, push the connecting rod up about 1 in. (25mm) from the crankshaft and remove the upper bearing insert. Continue pushing or tapping the connecting rod up until the piston rings are out of the cylinder bore. Remove the piston and rod by hand, put the upper half of the bearing insert back into the rod, install the cap with its bearing insert installed, and hand-tighten the cap fasteners. If the parts are kept in order in this manner, they will not get lost and you will be able to tell which bearings came form what cylinder if any problems are discovered and diagnosis is necessary. Remove all the other piston assemblies in the same manner. On V-style engines, remove all of the pistons from one bank, then reposition the engine with the other cylinder bank head surface up, and remove that banks piston assemblies.

The only remaining component in the engine block should now be the crankshaft. Loosen the main bearing caps evenly until the fasteners can be turned by hand, then remove them and the caps. Remove the crankshaft from the engine block. Thoroughly clean all of the components.

Fig. 140 Place rubber hose over the connecting rod studs to protect the crankshaft and cylinder bores from damage

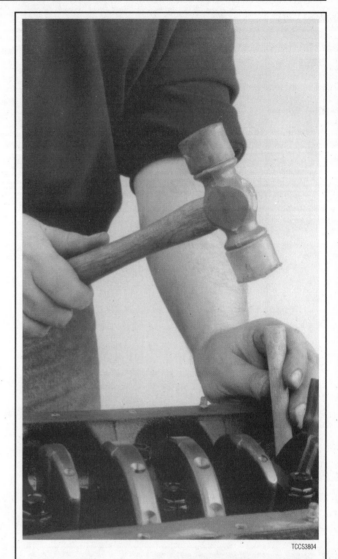

Fig. 141 Carefully tap the piston out of the bore using a wooden dowel

INSPECTION

Now that the engine block and all of its components are clean, it's time to inspect them for wear and/or damage. To accurately inspect them, you will need some specialized tools:

• Two or three separate micrometers to measure the pistons and crankshaft journals
• A dial indicator
• Telescoping gauges for the cylinder bores
• A rod alignment fixture to check for bent connecting rods

If you do not have access to the proper tools, you may want to bring the components to a shop that does.

Generally, you shouldn't expect cracks in the engine block or its components unless it was known to leak, consume or mix engine fluids, it was severely overheated, or there was evidence of bad bearings and/or crankshaft damage. A visual inspection should be performed on all of the components, but just because you don't see a crack does not mean it is not there. Some more reliable methods for inspecting for cracks include Magnaflux®, a magnetic process or Zyglo®, a dye penetrant. Magnaflux® is used only on ferrous metal (cast iron). Zyglo® uses a spray on fluorescent mixture along with a black light to reveal the cracks. It is strongly recommended to have your engine block checked professionally for cracks, especially if the engine was known to have overheated and/or leaked or consumed coolant. Contact a local shop for availability and pricing of these services.

Engine Block

ENGINE BLOCK BEARING ALIGNMENT

Remove the main bearing caps and, if still installed, the main bearing inserts. Inspect all of the main bearing saddles and caps for damage, burrs or high spots. If damage is found, and it is caused from a spun main bearing, the block will need to be align-bored or, if severe enough, replacement. Any burrs or high spots should be carefully removed with a metal file.

Place a straightedge on the bearing saddles, in the engine block, along the centerline of the crankshaft. If any clearance exists between the straightedge and the saddles, the block must be align-bored.

Align-boring consists of machining the main bearing saddles and caps by means of a flycutter that runs through the bearing saddles.

DECK FLATNESS

The top of the engine block where the cylinder head mounts is called the deck. Insure that the deck surface is clean of dirt, carbon deposits and old gasket material. Place a straightedge across the surface of the deck along its centerline and, using feeler gauges, check the clearance along several points. Repeat the checking procedure with the straightedge placed along both diagonals of the deck surface. If the reading exceeds 0.003 in. (0.076mm) within a 6.0 in. (15.2cm) span, or 0.006 in. (0.152mm) over the total length of the deck, it must be machined.

CYLINDER BORES

▶ See Figure 142

The cylinder bores house the pistons and are slightly larger than the pistons themselves. A common piston-to-bore clearance is 0.0015–0.0025 in. (0.0381mm–0.0635mm). Inspect and measure the cylinder bores. The bore should be checked for out-of-roundness, taper and size. The results of this inspection will determine whether the cylinder can be used in its existing size and condition, or a rebore to the next oversize is required (or in the case of removable sleeves, have replacements installed).

The amount of cylinder wall wear is always greater at the top of the cylinder than at the bottom. This wear is known as taper. Any cylinder that has a taper of 0.0012 in. (0.305mm) or more, must be rebored. Measurements are taken at a number of positions in each cylinder: at the top, middle and bottom and at two points at each position; that is, at a point 90 degrees from the crankshaft centerline, as well as a point parallel to the crankshaft centerline. The measurements are made with either a special dial indicator or a telescopic gauge and micrometer. If the necessary precision tools to check the bore are not available, take the block to a machine shop and have them mike it. Also if you don't have the tools to check the cylinder bores, chances are you will not have the necessary devices to check the pistons, connecting rods and crankshaft. Take these components with you and save yourself an extra trip.

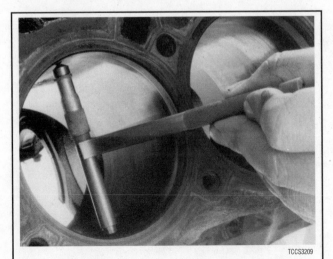

TCCS3209

Fig. 142 Use a telescoping gauge to measure the cylinder bore diameter—take several readings within the same bore

For our procedures, we will use a telescopic gauge and a micrometer. You will need one of each, with a measuring range which covers your cylinder bore size.

1. Position the telescopic gauge in the cylinder bore, loosen the gauges lock and allow it to expand.

➡**Your first two readings will be at the top of the cylinder bore, then proceed to the middle and finally the bottom, making a total of six measurements.**

2. Hold the gauge square in the bore, 90 degrees from the crankshaft centerline, and gently tighten the lock. Tilt the gauge back to remove it from the bore.
3. Measure the gauge with the micrometer and record the reading.
4. Again, hold the gauge square in the bore, this time parallel to the crankshaft centerline, and gently tighten the lock. Again, you will tilt the gauge back to remove it from the bore.
5. Measure the gauge with the micrometer and record this reading. The difference between these two readings is the out-of-round measurement of the cylinder.
6. Repeat steps 1 through 5, each time going to the next lower position, until you reach the bottom of the cylinder. Then go to the next cylinder, and continue until all of the cylinders have been measured.

The difference between these measurements will tell you all about the wear in your cylinders. The measurements which were taken 90 degrees from the crankshaft centerline will always reflect the most wear. That is because at this position is where the engine power presses the piston against the cylinder bore the hardest. This is known as thrust wear. Take your top, 90 degree measurement and compare it to your bottom, 90 degree measurement. The difference between them is the taper. When you measure your pistons, you will compare these readings to your piston sizes and determine piston-to-wall clearance.

Crankshaft

Inspect the crankshaft for visible signs of wear or damage. All of the journals should be perfectly round and smooth. Slight scores are normal for a used crankshaft, but you should hardly feel them with your fingernail. When measuring the crankshaft with a micrometer, you will take readings at the front and rear of each journal, then turn the micrometer 90 degrees and take two more readings, front and rear. The difference between the front-to-rear readings is the journal taper and the first-to-90 degree reading is the out-of-round measurement. Generally, there should be no taper or out-of-roundness found, however, up to 0.0005 in. (0.0127mm) for either can be overlooked. Also, the readings should fall within the factory specifications for journal diameters.

If the crankshaft journals fall within specifications, it is recommended that it be polished before being returned to service. Polishing the crankshaft insures that any minor burrs or high spots are smoothed, thereby reducing the chance of scoring the new bearings.

Pistons and Connecting Rods

PISTONS

▶ See Figure 143

The piston should be visually inspected for any signs of cracking or burning (caused by hot spots or detonation), and scuffing or excessive wear on the skirts. The wristpin attaches the piston to the connecting rod. The piston should move freely on the wrist pin, both sliding and pivoting. Grasp the connecting rod securely, or mount it in a vise, and try to rock the piston back and forth along the centerline of the wristpin. There should not be any excessive play evident between the piston and the pin. If there are C-clips retaining the pin in the piston then you have wrist pin bushings in the rods. There should not be any excessive play between the wrist pin and the rod bushing. Normal clearance for the wrist pin is approx. 0.001–0.002 in. (0.025mm–0.051mm).

Use a micrometer and measure the diameter of the piston, perpendicular to the wrist pin, on the skirt. Compare the reading to its original cylinder measurement obtained earlier. The difference between the two readings is the piston-to-wall clearance. If the clearance is within specifications, the piston may be used as is. If the piston is out of specification, but the bore is not, you will need a new piston. If both are out of specification, you will need the cylinder rebored and oversize pistons installed. Generally if two or more pistons/bores are out of

Fig. 143 Measure the piston's outer diameter, perpendicular to the wrist pin, with a micrometer

specification, it is best to rebore the entire block and purchase a complete set of oversize pistons.

CONNECTING RODS

You should have the connecting rod checked for straightness at a machine shop. If the connecting rod is bent, it will unevenly wear the bearing and piston, as well as place greater stress on these components. Any bent or twisted connecting rods must be replaced. If the rods are straight and the wrist pin clearance is within specifications, then only the bearing end of the rod need be checked. Place the connecting rod into a vice, with the bearing inserts in place, install the cap to the rod and torque the fasteners to specifications. Use a telescoping gauge and carefully measure the inside diameter of the bearings. Compare this reading to the rods original crankshaft journal diameter measurement. The difference is the oil clearance. If the oil clearance is not within specifications, install new bearings in the rod and take another measurement. If the clearance is still out of specifications, and the crankshaft is not, the rod will need to be reconditioned by a machine shop.

➡You can also use Plastigage® to check the bearing clearances. The assembling section has complete instructions on its use.

Camshaft

Inspect the camshaft and lifters/followers as described earlier in this section.

Bearings

All of the engine bearings should be visually inspected for wear and/or damage. The bearing should look evenly worn all around with no deep scores or pits. If the bearing is severely worn, scored, pitted or heat blued, then the bearing, and the components that use it, should be brought to a machine shop for inspection. Full-circle bearings (used on most camshafts, auxiliary shafts, balance shafts, etc.) require specialized tools for removal and installation, and should be brought to a machine shop for service.

Oil Pump

➡The oil pump is responsible for providing constant lubrication to the whole engine and so it is recommended that a new oil pump be installed when rebuilding the engine.

Completely disassemble the oil pump and thoroughly clean all of the components. Inspect the oil pump gears and housing for wear and/or damage. Insure that the pressure relief valve operates properly and there is no binding or sticking due to varnish or debris. If all of the parts are in proper working condition, lubricate the gears and relief valve, and assemble the pump.

REFINISHING

▶ **See Figure 144**

Almost all engine block refinishing must be performed by a machine shop. If the cylinders are not to be rebored, then the cylinder glaze can be removed with a ball hone. When removing cylinder glaze with a ball hone, use a light or penetrating type oil to lubricate the hone. Do not allow the hone to run dry as this may cause excessive scoring of the cylinder bores and wear on the hone. If new pistons are required, they will need to be installed to the connecting rods. This should be performed by a machine shop as the pistons must be installed in the correct relationship to the rod or engine damage can occur.

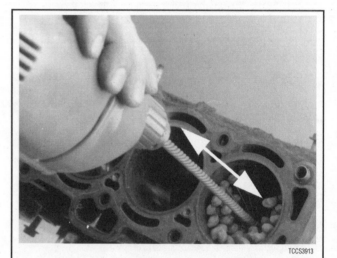

Fig. 144 Use a ball type cylinder hone to remove any glaze and provide a new surface for seating the piston rings

Pistons and Connecting Rods

▶ **See Figure 145**

Only pistons with the wrist pin retained by C-clips are serviceable by the home-mechanic. Press fit pistons require special presses and/or heaters to remove/install the connecting rod and should only be performed by a machine shop.

All pistons will have a mark indicating the direction to the front of the engine and the must be installed into the engine in that manner. Usually it is a notch or

Fig. 145 Most pistons are marked to indicate positioning in the engine (usually a mark means the side facing the front)

arrow on the top of the piston, or it may be the letter F cast or stamped into the piston.

C-CLIP TYPE PISTONS

1. Note the location of the forward mark on the piston and mark the connecting rod in relation.
2. Remove the C-clips from the piston and withdraw the wrist pin.

➡**Varnish build-up or C-clip groove burrs may increase the difficulty of removing the wrist pin. If necessary, use a punch or drift to carefully tap the wrist pin out.**

3. Insure that the wrist pin bushing in the connecting rod is usable, and lubricate it with assembly lube.
4. Remove the wrist pin from the new piston and lubricate the pin bores on the piston.
5. Align the forward marks on the piston and the connecting rod and install the wrist pin.
6. The new C-clips will have a flat and a rounded side to them. Install both C-clips with the flat side facing out.
7. Repeat all of the steps for each piston being replaced.

ASSEMBLY

Before you begin assembling the engine, first give yourself a clean, dirt free work area. Next, clean every engine component again. The key to a good assembly is cleanliness.

Mount the engine block into the engine stand and wash it one last time using water and detergent (dishwashing detergent works well). While washing it, scrub the cylinder bores with a soft bristle brush and thoroughly clean all of the oil passages. Completely dry the engine and spray the entire assembly down with an anti-rust solution such as WD-40® or similar product. Take a clean lint-free rag and wipe up any excess anti-rust solution from the bores, bearing saddles, etc. Repeat the final cleaning process on the crankshaft. Replace any freeze or oil galley plugs which were removed during disassembly.

Crankshaft

▶ **See Figures 146, 147, 148 and 149**

1. Remove the main bearing inserts from the block and bearing caps.
2. If the crankshaft main bearing journals have been refinished to a definite undersize, install the correct undersize bearing. Be sure that the bearing inserts and bearing bores are clean. Foreign material under inserts will distort bearing and cause failure.
3. Place the upper main bearing inserts in bores with tang in slot.

➡**The oil holes in the bearing inserts must be aligned with the oil holes in the cylinder block.**

4. Install the lower main bearing inserts in bearing caps.
5. Clean the mating surfaces of block and rear main bearing cap.
6. Carefully lower the crankshaft into place. Be careful not to damage bearing surfaces.
7. Check the clearance of each main bearing by using the following procedure:

    a. Place a piece of Plastigage® or its equivalent, on bearing surface across full width of bearing cap and about ¼ in. off center.

    b. Install cap and tighten bolts to specifications. Do not turn crankshaft while Plastigage® is in place.

    c. Remove the cap. Using the supplied Plastigage® scale, check the width of Plastigage® at its widest point to get maximum clearance. The difference between readings is the taper of the journal.

    d. If clearance exceeds specified limits, try a 0.001 in. or 0.002 in. undersize bearing in combination with the standard bearing. Bearing clearance must be within specified limits. If standard and 0.002 in. undersize bearing does not bring clearance within desired limits, refinish crankshaft journal, then install undersize bearings.

8. Install the rear main seal.
9. After the bearings have been fitted, apply a light coat of engine oil to the journals and bearings. Install the rear main bearing cap. Install all bearing caps except the thrust bearing cap. Be sure that main bearing caps are installed in original locations. Tighten the bearing cap bolts to specifications.

10. Install the thrust bearing cap with bolts finger-tight.
11. Pry the crankshaft forward against the thrust surface of upper half of bearing.
12. Hold the crankshaft forward and pry the thrust bearing cap to the rear. This aligns the thrust surfaces of both halves of the bearing.
13. Retain the forward pressure on the crankshaft. Tighten the cap bolts to specifications.
14. Measure the crankshaft end-play as follows:

    a. Mount a dial gauge to the engine block and position the tip of the gauge to read from the crankshaft end.

    b. Carefully pry the crankshaft toward the rear of the engine and hold it there while you zero the gauge.

    c. Carefully pry the crankshaft toward the front of the engine and read the gauge.

    d. Confirm that the reading is within specifications. If not, install a new thrust bearing and repeat the procedure. If the reading is still out of specifications with a new bearing, have a machine shop inspect the thrust surfaces of the crankshaft, and if possible, repair it.

15. Rotate the crankshaft so as to position the first rod journal to the bottom of its stroke.

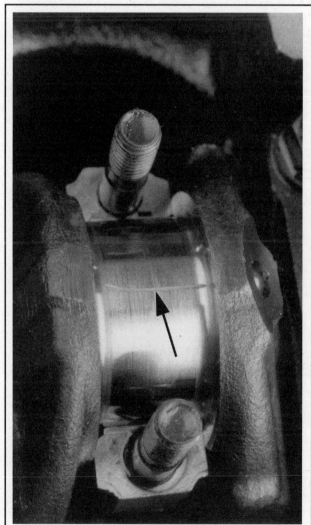

TCCS3243

Fig. 146 Apply a strip of gauging material to the bearing journal, then install and torque the cap

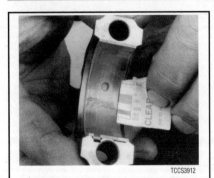

Fig. 147 After the cap is removed again, use the scale supplied with the gauging material to check the clearance

Fig. 148 A dial gauge may be used to check crankshaft end-play

Fig. 149 Carefully pry the crankshaft back and forth while reading the dial gauge for end-play

Pistons and Connecting Rods

▶ See Figures 150, 151, 152 and 153

1. Before installing the piston/connecting rod assembly, oil the pistons, piston rings and the cylinder walls with light engine oil. Install connecting rod bolt protectors or rubber hose onto the connecting rod bolts/studs. Also perform the following:

a. Select the proper ring set for the size cylinder bore.

b. Position the ring in the bore in which it is going to be used.

c. Push the ring down into the bore area where normal ring wear is not encountered.

Fig. 150 Checking the piston ring-to-ring groove side clearance using the ring and a feeler gauge

d. Use the head of the piston to position the ring in the bore so that the ring is square with the cylinder wall. Use caution to avoid damage to the ring or cylinder bore.

e. Measure the gap between the ends of the ring with a feeler gauge. Ring gap in a worn cylinder is normally greater than specification. If the ring gap is greater than the specified limits, try an oversize ring set.

f. Check the ring side clearance of the compression rings with a feeler gauge inserted between the ring and its lower land according to specification. The gauge should slide freely around the entire ring circumference without binding. Any wear that occurs will form a step at the inner portion of the lower land. If the lower lands have high steps, the piston should be replaced.

2. Unless new pistons are installed, be sure to install the pistons in the cylinders from which they were removed. The numbers on the connecting rod and bearing cap must be on the same side when installed in the cylinder bore. If a connecting rod is ever transposed from one engine or cylinder to another, new bearings should be fitted and the connecting rod should be numbered to correspond with the new cylinder number. The notch on the piston head goes toward the front of the engine.

3. Install all of the rod bearing inserts into the rods and caps.

4. Install the rings to the pistons. Install the oil control ring first, then the second compression ring and finally the top compression ring. Use a piston ring expander tool to aid in installation and to help reduce the chance of breakage.

5. Make sure the ring gaps are properly spaced around the circumference of the piston. Fit a piston ring compressor around the piston and slide the piston and connecting rod assembly down into the cylinder bore, pushing it in with the wooden hammer handle. Push the piston down until it is only slightly below the top of the cylinder bore. Guide the connecting rod onto the crankshaft bearing journal carefully, to avoid damaging the crankshaft.

6. Check the bearing clearance of all the rod bearings, fitting them to the crankshaft bearing journals. Follow the procedure in the crankshaft installation above.

7. After the bearings have been fitted, apply a light coating of assembly oil to the journals and bearings.

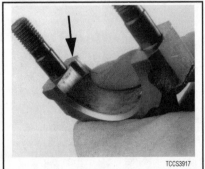

Fig. 151 The notch on the side of the bearing cap matches the tang on the bearing insert

Fig. 152 Most rings are marked to show which side of the ring should face up when installed to the piston

Fig. 153 Install the piston and rod assembly into the block using a ring compressor and the handle of a hammer

8. Turn the crankshaft until the appropriate bearing journal is at the bottom of its stroke, then push the piston assembly all the way down until the connecting rod bearing seats on the crankshaft journal. Be careful not to allow the bearing cap screws to strike the crankshaft bearing journals and damage them.

9. After the piston and connecting rod assemblies have been installed, check the connecting rod side clearance on each crankshaft journal.

10. Prime and install the oil pump and the oil pump intake tube.

OHC Engines

CYLINDER HEAD(S)

1. Install the cylinder head(s) using new gaskets.
2. Install the timing sprockets/gears and the belt/chain assemblies.

Engine Covers and Components

Install the timing cover(s) and oil pan. Refer to your notes and drawings made prior to disassembly and install all of the components that were removed. Install the engine into the vehicle.

Engine Start-up and Break-in

STARTING THE ENGINE

Now that the engine is installed and every wire and hose is properly connected, go back and double check that all coolant and vacuum hoses are connected. Check that you oil drain plug is installed and properly tightened. If not already done, install a new oil filter onto the engine. Fill the crankcase with the proper amount and grade of engine oil. Fill the cooling system with a 50/50 mixture of coolant/water.

1. Connect the vehicle battery.
2. Start the engine. Keep your eye on your oil pressure indicator; if it does not indicate oil pressure within 10 seconds of starting, turn the vehicle off.

❈❈ WARNING

Damage to the engine can result if it is allowed to run with no oil pressure. Check the engine oil level to make sure that it is full. Check for any leaks and if found, repair the leaks before continuing. If there is still no indication of oil pressure, you may need to prime the system.

3. Confirm that there are no fluid leaks (oil or other).
4. Allow the engine to reach normal operating temperature (the upper radiator hose will be hot to the touch).
5. If necessary, set the ignition timing.
6. Install any remaining components such as the air cleaner (if removed for ignition timing) or body panels which were removed.

BREAKING IT IN

Make the first miles on the new engine, easy ones. Vary the speed but do not accelerate hard. Most importantly, do not lug the engine, and avoid sustained high speeds until at least 100 miles. Check the engine oil and coolant levels frequently. Expect the engine to use a little oil until the rings seat. Change the oil and filter at 500 miles, 1500 miles, then every 3000 miles past that.

KEEP IT MAINTAINED

Now that you have just gone through all of that hard work, keep yourself from doing it all over again by thoroughly maintaining it. Not that you may not have maintained it before, heck you could have had one to two hundred thousand miles on it before doing this. However, you may have bought the vehicle used, and the previous owner did not keep up on maintenance. Which is why you just went through all of that hard work. See?

TORQUE SPECIFICATIONS

Components	Ft. Lbs.	Nm
Valve/Rocker Arm Cover		
1981-88 models		
Cover retainers	72-96 inch lbs.	8-11
1989-90 models		
Bolts	7-10	9-13
Studs	72-96 inch lbs.	8-11
Rocker Arms		
1.3L and 1.6L engines		
Nuts	15-19	21-25
1.9L engines		
Bolts	17-22	23-30
Thermostat		
1981-87 models		
Mounting bolts	72-96 inch lbs.	7-11
1988-90 models		
Mounting bolts	10-16	13-19
Intake Manifold		
Non-MFI/CFI engines		
Intake manifold nuts	12-15	16-20
CFI and MFI engines		
Except 1988-90 MFI/HO engines		
Intake manifold nuts	12-15	16-20
1988-90 1.9L MFI/HO engines		
Upper Intake manifold assembly		
Upper manifold bolts	15-22	20-30
Manifold upper support bracket top bolt	15-22	20-30
EGR tube compression nut	30-40	40-55
Air supply tube clamps	12-20 inch lbs.	1.4-2.3
Lower intake manifold assembly		
Manifold mounting nuts	12-15	16-20
Upper and lower manifold support bracket bolts	15-22	20-30
EGR tube compression nut	30-40	40-55
Air supply tube clamps	12-20 inch lbs.	1.4-2.3
Exhaust Manifold		
1.6L turbocharged engine		
Exhaust manifold nuts	16-19	21-26
Exhaust pipe-to-turbocharger attaching nuts	72-96 inch lbs.	8-12
1.3L, 1.6L (except turbo) and 1.9L engines		
Exhaust manifold retaining nuts	15-20	21-26
Oxygen sensor	30-40	40-50
Turbocharger		
Turbocharger bolts	16-19	21-26
Radiator		
Radiator mounting nuts	60-84 inch lbs.	7-9
Electric Cooling Fan		
Fan motor-to-fan shroud nuts	44-66 inch lbs.	5-8
Fan assembly		
Nuts	35-41 inch lbs.	4-5
Screws	23-33 inch lbs.	3-4
Water Pump		
Water pump bolts		
1981-87 models	30-40	40-50
1988-90 models	15-22	20-30

90933C16

TORQUE SPECIFICATIONS

Components	Ft. Lbs.	Nm
Cylinder Head		
Cylinder head bolts	①	①
Oil Pan		
1.3L and 1.6L engines		
Oil pan bolts	72-96 ②	8-11 ②
1.9L engines		
Oil pan-to-transaxle bolts	30-40 ③	40-54 ③
Oil pan flange-to-cylinder block bolts	15-22	20-30
Oil Pump		
Pick-up tube and screen assembly bolts	72-108 inch lbs.	8-12
Oil pump bolts	60-84 inch lbs.	7-10
Crankshaft Damper		
1.3L, 1.6L and 1985-87 1.9L engines		
Pulley bolt	74-90	100-122
1988-89 1.9L engines		
Damper bolt	81-96	110-130
Timing Belt and Sprockets		
Camshaft sprocket bolt		
1981-88 models	37-46	50-62
1989-90 models	71-84	95-115
Belt tensioner attaching bolt		
1988 models		
New belt	27-32	36-43
Used belt	10	13
Camshaft		
Camshaft thrust plate bolts	84-132 inch lbs.	10-15
Connecting Rods		
Rod cap-to-rod retainers	19-25	26-34
Flywheel/Flexplate		
Flywheel/Flexplate bolts	54-64	73-87

① Step 1: Tighten bolts to 44 ft. lbs. (60 Nm) in the correct sequence

  Step 2: Back the bolts off two turns in the correct sequence

  Step 3: Retighten bolts to 44 ft. lbs. (60 Nm) in the correct sequence

  Step 3: Turn the bolts an additional 90° in the correct sequence

  Step 4: Turn the bolts additional 90° in the correct sequence

② Tighten in the correct sequence

③ After the bolt has been tightened, back it off 1/2 a turn

90933C17

USING A VACUUM GAUGE

White needle = steady needle   *Dark needle = drifting needle*

The vacuum gauge is one of the most useful and easy-to-use diagnostic tools. It is inexpensive, easy to hook up, and provides valuable information about the condition of your engine.

Indication: Normal engine in good condition

Gauge reading: Steady, from 17-22 in./Hg.

Indication: Sticking valve or ignition miss

Gauge reading: Needle fluctuates from 15-20 in./Hg. at idle

Indication: Late ignition or valve timing, low compression, stuck throttle valve, leaking carburetor or manifold gasket.

Gauge reading: Low (15-20 in./Hg.) but steady

Indication: Improper carburetor adjustment, or minor intake leak at carburetor or manifold

NOTE: Bad fuel injector O-rings may also cause this reading.

Gauge reading: Drifting needle

Indication: Weak valve springs, worn valve stem guides, or leaky cylinder head gasket (vibrating excessively at all speeds).

NOTE: A plugged catalytic converter may also cause this reading.

Gauge reading: Needle fluctuates as engine speed increases

Indication: Burnt valve or improper valve clearance. The needle will drop when the defective valve operates.

Gauge reading: Steady needle, but drops regularly

Indication: Choked muffler or obstruction in system. Speed up the engine. Choked muffler will exhibit a slow drop of vacuum to zero.

Gauge reading: Gradual drop in reading at idle

Indication: Worn valve guides

Gauge reading: Needle vibrates excessively at idle, but steadies as engine speed increases

TCCS3C01

Troubleshooting Engine Mechanical Problems

Problem	Cause	Solution
External oil leaks	• Cylinder head cover RTV sealant broken or improperly seated	• Replace sealant; inspect cylinder head cover sealant flange and cylinder head sealant surface for distortion and cracks
	• Oil filler cap leaking or missing	• Replace cap
	• Oil filter gasket broken or improperly seated	• Replace oil filter
	• Oil pan side gasket broken, improperly seated or opening in RTV sealant	• Replace gasket or repair opening in sealant; inspect oil pan gasket flange for distortion
	• Oil pan front oil seal broken or improperly seated	• Replace seal; inspect timing case cover and oil pan seal flange for distortion
	• Oil pan rear oil seal broken or improperly seated	• Replace seal; inspect oil pan rear oil seal flange; inspect rear main bearing cap for cracks, plugged oil return channels, or distortion in seal groove
	• Timing case cover oil seal broken or improperly seated	• Replace seal
	• Excess oil pressure because of restricted PCV valve	• Replace PCV valve
	• Oil pan drain plug loose or has stripped threads	• Repair as necessary and tighten
	• Rear oil gallery plug loose	• Use appropriate sealant on gallery plug and tighten
	• Rear camshaft plug loose or improperly seated	• Seat camshaft plug or replace and seal, as necessary
Excessive oil consumption	• Oil level too high	• Drain oil to specified level
	• Oil with wrong viscosity being used	• Replace with specified oil
	• PCV valve stuck closed	• Replace PCV valve
	• Valve stem oil deflectors (or seals) are damaged, missing, or incorrect type	• Replace valve stem oil deflectors
	• Valve stems or valve guides worn	• Measure stem-to-guide clearance and repair as necessary
	• Poorly fitted or missing valve cover baffles	• Replace valve cover
	• Piston rings broken or missing	• Replace broken or missing rings
	• Scuffed piston	• Replace piston
	• Incorrect piston ring gap	• Measure ring gap, repair as necessary
	• Piston rings sticking or excessively loose in grooves	• Measure ring side clearance, repair as necessary
	• Compression rings installed upside down	• Repair as necessary
	• Cylinder walls worn, scored, or glazed	• Repair as necessary

TCCS3C02

Troubleshooting Engine Mechanical Problems

Problem	Cause	Solution
Excessive oil consumption (cont.)	• Piston ring gaps not properly staggered • Excessive main or connecting rod bearing clearance	• Repair as necessary • Measure bearing clearance, repair as necessary
No oil pressure	• Low oil level • Oil pressure gauge, warning lamp or sending unit inaccurate • Oil pump malfunction • Oil pressure relief valve sticking • Oil passages on pressure side of pump obstructed • Oil pickup screen or tube obstructed • Loose oil inlet tube	• Add oil to correct level • Replace oil pressure gauge or warning lamp • Replace oil pump • Remove and inspect oil pressure relief valve assembly • Inspect oil passages for obstruction • Inspect oil pickup for obstruction • Tighten or seal inlet tube
Low oil pressure	• Low oil level • Inaccurate gauge, warning lamp or sending unit • Oil excessively thin because of dilution, poor quality, or improper grade • Excessive oil temperature • Oil pressure relief spring weak or sticking • Oil inlet tube and screen assembly has restriction or air leak • Excessive oil pump clearance • Excessive main, rod, or camshaft bearing clearance	• Add oil to correct level • Replace oil pressure gauge or warning lamp • Drain and refill crankcase with recommended oil • Correct cause of overheating engine • Remove and inspect oil pressure relief valve assembly • Remove and inspect oil inlet tube and screen assembly. (Fill inlet tube with lacquer thinner to locate leaks.) • Measure clearances • Measure bearing clearances, repair as necessary
High oil pressure	• Improper oil viscosity • Oil pressure gauge or sending unit inaccurate • Oil pressure relief valve sticking closed	• Drain and refill crankcase with correct viscosity oil • Replace oil pressure gauge • Remove and inspect oil pressure relief valve assembly
Main bearing noise	• Insufficient oil supply • Main bearing clearance excessive • Bearing insert missing • Crankshaft end-play excessive • Improperly tightened main bearing cap bolts • Loose flywheel or drive plate • Loose or damaged vibration damper	• Inspect for low oil level and low oil pressure • Measure main bearing clearance, repair as necessary • Replace missing insert • Measure end-play, repair as necessary • Tighten bolts with specified torque • Tighten flywheel or drive plate attaching bolts • Repair as necessary

TCCS3C03

Troubleshooting Engine Mechanical Problems

Problem	Cause	Solution
Connecting rod bearing noise	· Insufficient oil supply · Carbon build-up on piston · Bearing clearance excessive or bearing missing · Crankshaft connecting rod journal out-of-round · Misaligned connecting rod or cap · Connecting rod bolts tightened improperly	· Inspect for low oil level and low oil pressure · Remove carbon from piston crown · Measure clearance, repair as necessary · Measure journal dimensions, repair or replace as necessary · Repair as necessary · Tighten bolts with specified torque
Piston noise	· Piston-to-cylinder wall clearance excessive (scuffed piston) · Cylinder walls excessively tapered or out-of-round · Piston ring broken · Loose or seized piston pin · Connecting rods misaligned · Piston ring side clearance excessively loose or tight · Carbon build-up on piston is excessive	· Measure clearance and examine piston · Measure cylinder wall dimensions, rebore cylinder · Replace all rings on piston · Measure piston-to-pin clearance, repair as necessary · Measure rod alignment, straighten or replace · Measure ring side clearance, repair as necessary · Remove carbon from piston
Valve actuating component noise	· Insufficient oil supply · Rocker arms or pivots worn · Foreign objects or chips in hydraulic tappets · Excessive tappet leak-down · Tappet face worn · Broken or cocked valve springs · Stem-to-guide clearance excessive · Valve bent · Loose rocker arms · Valve seat runout excessive · Missing valve lock · Excessive engine oil	· Check for: (a) Low oil level (b) Low oil pressure (c) Wrong hydraulic tappets (d) Restricted oil gallery (e) Excessive tappet to bore clearance · Replace worn rocker arms or pivots · Clean tappets · Replace valve tappet · Replace tappet; inspect corresponding cam lobe for wear · Properly seat cocked springs; replace broken springs · Measure stem-to-guide clearance, repair as required · Replace valve · Check and repair as necessary · Regrind valve seat/valves · Install valve lock · Correct oil level

TCCS3C04

Troubleshooting Engine Performance

Problem	Cause	Solution
Hard starting (engine cranks normally)	• Faulty engine control system component	• Repair or replace as necessary
	• Faulty fuel pump	• Replace fuel pump
	• Faulty fuel system component	• Repair or replace as necessary
	• Faulty ignition coil	• Test and replace as necessary
	• Improper spark plug gap	• Adjust gap
	• Incorrect ignition timing	• Adjust timing
	• Incorrect valve timing	• Check valve timing; repair as necessary
Rough idle or stalling	• Incorrect curb or fast idle speed	• Adjust curb or fast idle speed (If possible)
	• Incorrect ignition timing	• Adjust timing to specification
	• Improper feedback system operation	• Refer to Chapter 4
	• Faulty EGR valve operation	• Test EGR system and replace as necessary
	• Faulty PCV valve air flow	• Test PCV valve and replace as necessary
	• Faulty TAC vacuum motor or valve	• Repair as necessary
	• Air leak into manifold vacuum	• Inspect manifold vacuum connections and repair as necessary
	• Faulty distributor rotor or cap	• Replace rotor or cap (Distributor systems only)
	• Improperly seated valves	• Test cylinder compression, repair as necessary
	• Incorrect ignition wiring	• Inspect wiring and correct as necessary
	• Faulty ignition coil	• Test coil and replace as necessary
	• Restricted air vent or idle passages	• Clean passages
	• Restricted air cleaner	• Clean or replace air cleaner filter element
Faulty low-speed operation	• Restricted idle air vents and passages	• Clean air vents and passages
	• Restricted air cleaner	• Clean or replace air cleaner filter element
	• Faulty spark plugs	• Clean or replace spark plugs
	• Dirty, corroded, or loose ignition secondary circuit wire connections	• Clean or tighten secondary circuit wire connections
	• Improper feedback system operation	• Refer to Chapter 4
	• Faulty ignition coil high voltage wire	• Replace ignition coil high voltage wire (Distributor systems only)
	• Faulty distributor cap	• Replace cap (Distributor systems only)
Faulty acceleration	• Incorrect ignition timing	• Adjust timing
	• Faulty fuel system component	• Repair or replace as necessary
	• Faulty spark plug(s)	• Clean or replace spark plug(s)
	• Improperly seated valves	• Test cylinder compression, repair as necessary
	• Faulty ignition coil	• Test coil and replace as necessary

Troubleshooting Engine Performance

Problem	Cause	Solution
Faulty acceleration (cont.)	• Improper feedback system operation	• Refer to Chapter 4
Faulty high speed operation	• Incorrect ignition timing • Faulty advance mechanism	• Adjust timing (if possible) • Check advance mechanism and repair as necessary (Distributor systems only)
	• Low fuel pump volume • Wrong spark plug air gap or wrong plug	• Replace fuel pump • Adjust air gap or install correct plug
	• Partially restricted exhaust manifold, exhaust pipe, catalytic converter, muffler, or tailpipe	• Eliminate restriction
	• Restricted vacuum passages • Restricted air cleaner	• Clean passages • Cleaner or replace filter element as necessary
	• Faulty distributor rotor or cap	• Replace rotor or cap (Distributor systems only)
	• Faulty ignition coil • Improperly seated valve(s)	• Test coil and replace as necessary • Test cylinder compression, repair as necessary
	• Faulty valve spring(s)	• Inspect and test valve spring tension, replace as necessary
	• Incorrect valve timing	• Check valve timing and repair as necessary
	• Intake manifold restricted	• Remove restriction or replace manifold
	• Worn distributor shaft	• Replace shaft (Distributor systems only)
	• Improper feedback system operation	• Refer to Chapter 4
Misfire at all speeds	• Faulty spark plug(s) • Faulty spark plug wire(s) • Faulty distributor cap or rotor	• Clean or relace spark plug(s) • Replace as necessary • Replace cap or rotor (Distributor systems only)
	• Faulty ignition coil • Primary ignition circuit shorted or open intermittently • Improperly seated valve(s)	• Test coil and replace as necessary • Troubleshoot primary circuit and repair as necessary • Test cylinder compression, repair as necessary
	• Faulty hydraulic tappet(s) • Improper feedback system operation • Faulty valve spring(s)	• Clean or replace tappet(s) • Refer to Chapter 4 • Inspect and test valve spring tension, repair as necessary
	• Worn camshaft lobes • Air leak into manifold	• Replace camshaft • Check manifold vacuum and repair as necessary
	• Fuel pump volume or pressure low • Blown cylinder head gasket • Intake or exhaust manifold passage(s) restricted	• Replace fuel pump • Replace gasket • Pass chain through passage(s) and repair as necessary
Power not up to normal	• Incorrect ignition timing • Faulty distributor rotor	• Adjust timing • Replace rotor (Distributor systems only)

TCCS3C06

Troubleshooting Engine Performance

Problem	Cause	Solution
Power not up to normal (cont.)	• Incorrect spark plug gap	• Adjust gap
	• Faulty fuel pump	• Replace fuel pump
	• Faulty fuel pump	• Replace fuel pump
	• Incorrect valve timing	• Check valve timing and repair as necessary
	• Faulty ignition coil	• Test coil and replace as necessary
	• Faulty ignition wires	• Test wires and replace as necessary
	• Improperly seated valves	• Test cylinder compression and repair as necessary
	• Blown cylinder head gasket	• Replace gasket
	• Leaking piston rings	• Test compression and repair as necessary
	• Improper feedback system operation	• Refer to Chapter 4
Intake backfire	• Improper ignition timing	• Adjust timing
	• Defective EGR component	• Repair as necessary
	• Defective TAC vacuum motor or valve	• Repair as necessary
Exhaust backfire	• Air leak into manifold vacuum	• Check manifold vacuum and repair as necessary
	• Faulty air injection diverter valve	• Test diverter valve and replace as necessary
	• Exhaust leak	• Locate and eliminate leak
Ping or spark knock	• Incorrect ignition timing	• Adjust timing
	• Distributor advance malfunction	• Inspect advance mechanism and repair as necessary (Distributor systems only)
	• Excessive combustion chamber deposits	• Remove with combustion chamber cleaner
	• Air leak into manifold vacuum	• Check manifold vacuum and repair as necessary
	• Excessively high compression	• Test compression and repair as necessary
	• Fuel octane rating excessively low	• Try alternate fuel source
	• Sharp edges in combustion chamber	• Grind smooth
	• EGR valve not functioning properly	• Test EGR system and replace as necessary
Surging (at cruising to top speeds)	• Low fuel pump pressure or volume	• Replace fuel pump
	• Improper PCV valve air flow	• Test PCV valve and replace as necessary
	• Air leak into manifold vacuum	• Check manifold vacuum and repair as necessary
	• Incorrect spark advance	• Test and replace as necessary
	• Restricted fuel filter	• Replace fuel filter
	• Restricted air cleaner	• Clean or replace air cleaner filter element
	• EGR valve not functioning properly	• Test EGR system and replace as necessary
	• Improper feedback system operation	• Refer to Chapter 4

TCCS3C07

4

DRIVEABILITY AND EMISSION CONTROLS

EMISSION CONTROLS

Crankcase Ventilation System

OPERATION

▶ **See Figures 1, 2 and 3**

The Positive Crankcase Ventilation (PCV) system cycles crankcase gases back through the engine, where they are burned.

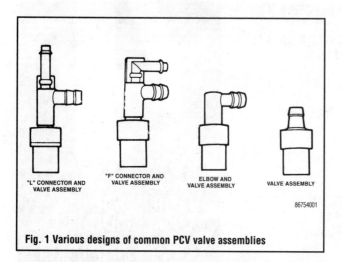

"L" CONNECTOR AND VALVE ASSEMBLY | "F" CONNECTOR AND VALVE ASSEMBLY | ELBOW AND VALVE ASSEMBLY | VALVE ASSEMBLY

86754001

Fig. 1 Various designs of common PCV valve assemblies

The vent system for the 1.6L and 1.9L engines does not depend on a flow of scavenging air, as do most other engines. On the 1.3L and 1.6L engine, the vent system evacuates the crankcase vapors drawn into the intake manifold in metered amounts according to the manifold depression and the fixed orifice as they become available. If availability is low, air may be drawn in along with the vapors. If the availability is high, some vapors will be delivered to the intake manifold and any amount over that will go into the air cleaner. The fixed orifice is the critical point of this system. On 1.9L engines, the vent system evacuates the crankcase vapors drawn into the intake manifold in metered amounts through a dual orifice valve assembly.

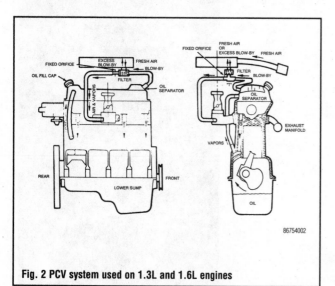

86754002

Fig. 2 PCV system used on 1.3L and 1.6L engines

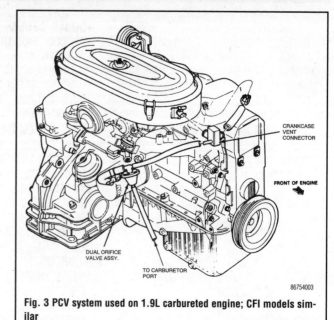

CRANKCASE VENT CONNECTOR

FRONT OF ENGINE

DUAL ORIFICE VALVE ASSY.

TO CARBURETOR PORT

86754003

Fig. 3 PCV system used on 1.9L carbureted engine; CFI models similar

TESTING

1.3L and 1.6L Engines

1. Start the engine and allow it to idle.
2. Locate the PCV hose leading from the air cleaner to the intake manifold. Pinch it closed with a pair of pliers.
3. If the idle speed decreases, the system is functioning properly.

1.9L Engines

1. Remove the vacuum control hose at the dual orifice valve assembly. This leads to the carburetor/throttle body.
2. Apply manifold vacuum to the port.
3. If no significant change in engine rpm is noticed, replace the dual orifice valve assembly.
4. If there is a significant change in engine rpm, the system is functioning properly.

REMOVAL & INSTALLATION

To remove the PCV valve, simply pull it out of the valve cover and/or hose. On models not equipped with these valves, remove the PCV hoses by pulling and twisting them from their ports. Always check the hoses for clogging, breaks and deterioration.

Evaporative Emission Controls (EVAP)

OPERATION

Fuel Tank Venting

Trapped fuel vapors inside the fuel tank are vented through an orifice to the vapor valve assembly on top of the tank. These vapors leave the valve assembly through a single vapor line and continue to the canister, for storage, until they are purged to the engine for burning.

Carburetor Venting

The vapors from the fuel bowl are vented to the carbon canister when the engine is stopped. When the engine is started and a specified engine temperature is reached, the vapors will be drawn into the engine for burning. These vapors are controlled by the canister purge solenoid, the canister purge valve, the carburetor fuel bowl solenoid vent valve and the carburetor fuel bowl thermal vent valve (if used).

Canister Purging

♦ See Figure 4

Purging the carbon canister removes the fuel vapor stored in the carbon. With a computer controlled EVAP system, the flow of vapors from the canister to the engine is controlled by a purge solenoid (CANP). Others use a vacuum controlled purge valve. Purging occurs when the engine is at operating temperature and off idle.

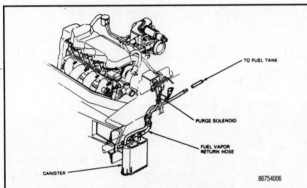

Fig. 4 Canister purging system—1.9L EFI engine shown; others similar

Heater/Spacer Assembly

This component is a heater that warms the air/fuel mixture below the carburetor for better fuel evaporation when the engine is cold. The fuel evaporation heater consists of a spacer, upper and lower gaskets and a 12 volt grid-type heater attached to the bottom side of the primary bore of the spacer. The offset design of the heater mounting bracket positions the heater in the intake manifold inlet opening.

Fuel Evaporative Heater Switch

The evaporative heater switch is mounted at the rear of the engine, on the bottom of the intake manifold. It controls the relay and the heater element in the early fuel evaporative emission system, based on engine temperature. The normally closed switch will activate the relay and the heater at low engine temperature and will open at the specified calibration of the temperature switch. This will open the control relay, which in turn will shut off the early fuel evaporation heater after the engine has warmed up.

Fuel/Vacuum Separator

The fuel/vacuum separator is used in carbureted systems in order to prevent fuel travel to a vacuum operated device. This component requires positive orientation to insure that any fuel collected will drain back to the carburetor. If the separator becomes clogged or cracked, it must be replaced.

TESTING

Thermostatic Bowl Vent Valve

♦ See Figure 5

1. Check the vacuum vent valve, at engine temperatures of 120°F (49C) or more. Air should flow between the carburetor port and canister port when no vacuum is applied to the vacuum signal nipple.

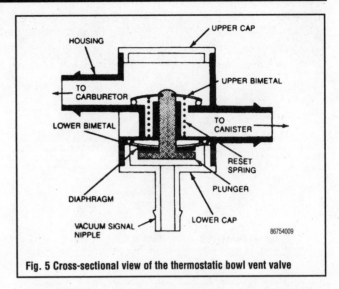

Fig. 5 Cross-sectional view of the thermostatic bowl vent valve

2. It should not allow the flow of air with a vacuum applied at the vacuum signal nipple.
3. At a temperature of 90°F (32C) or less, the valve should have an air flow or be very restrictive to air flow.

Vacuum Bowl Vent Valve

♦ See Figure 6

The vacuum bowl vent valve should have an air flow between the carburetor port and the canister port when no vacuum is applied to the vacuum signal nipple, and should not have an air flow with vacuum applied at the vacuum signal nipple.

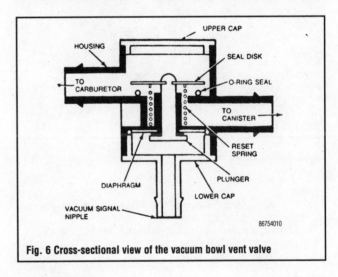

Fig. 6 Cross-sectional view of the vacuum bowl vent valve

Purge Control Valve

♦ See Figure 7

1. Apply vacuum to port A (only), there should be no air flow. If air flow occurs, replace the valve.
2. Apply vacuum to port B (only), there should no air flow. The valve should be closed. If air flow occurs, replace the valve.
3. Apply and maintain 16 in. Hg (110 kPa) of vacuum to port A, and apply vacuum to port B. Air should pass.

Fuel Bowl Vent Solenoid Valve

♦ See Figure 8

Apply 9–14 volts DC to the fuel bowl vent solenoid valve. The valve should close, not allowing air to pass. If the valve does not close or leaks when voltage and 1 in. Hg (68 kPa) of vacuum is applied to the carburetor port, replace the valve.

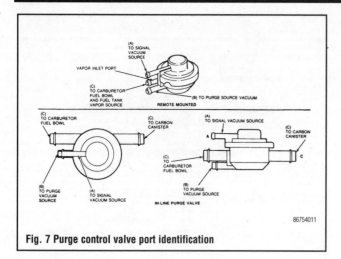

Fig. 7 Purge control valve port identification

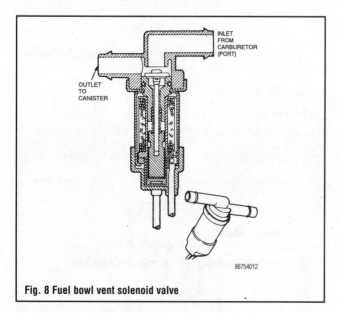

Fig. 8 Fuel bowl vent solenoid valve

Heater/Spacer Assembly

1. When the engine coolant temperature is below 128°F (53°C), the switch should be closed.
2. When the heater relay is energized, the relay contacts close allowing current to flow through the relay and to the heater.
3. The heater operates for approximately the first three minutes of cold engine operation which aids in a leaner choke calibration for improved emissions without cold drive-away problems.
4. At ambient temperatures of less than 40°F (4°C), the leaner choke calibrations reduce loading and spark plug fouling.
5. The heater grid is functioning if radiant heat can be detected when the heater grid is energized.

➡️Do not probe the heater grid while the grid is in the heat mode, as it is possible to cause a direct short in the circuit. The heater is designed to operate at a constant temperature of approximately 320–383°F (160–195°C), and could result in burns if touched.

REMOVAL & INSTALLATION

Removal and installation of the evaporative emission control system components consists of locating the component, labeling and disconnecting hoses,

loosening retaining screws and removing the part which is to be replaced from its mounting point.

➡️When replacing any EVAP system hose, always use hoses that are fuel-resistant or marked EVAP. Use of hoses which are not fuel-resistant will lead to premature hose failure.

Exhaust Gas Recirculation System

OPERATION

The Exhaust Gas Recirculation (EGR) system is designed to reintroduce small amounts of exhaust gas into the combustion cycle, thus reducing the generation of Nitrous Oxides (NOx). The amount of exhaust gas reintroduced and the timing of the cycle varies by calibration and is controlled by various factors such as engine speed, altitude, engine vacuum, exhaust system backpressure, coolant temperature and throttle angle.

➡️A malfunctioning EGR valve can cause one or more of the following:

- Detonation
- Rough idle or stalling on deceleration
- Hesitation or surge
- Abnormally low power at wide-open throttle

Basic Poppet or Tapered Stem Design

▶ See Figure 9

The basic EGR valve has two passages in the base connecting the exhaust system to the intake manifold. These passages are blocked by a valve that is opened by vacuum and closed by spring pressure. Both the poppet or the tapered stem design function in the same manner.

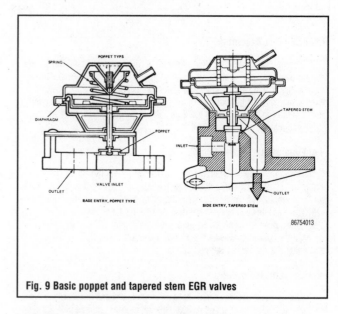

Fig. 9 Basic poppet and tapered stem EGR valves

Integral Backpressure Transducer EGR Valve

▶ See Figure 10

This poppet-type or tapered (pintle) valve cannot be opened by vacuum until the bleed hole is closed by exhaust backpressure. Once the valve opens, it seeks a level dependent upon exhaust backpressure flowing through the orifice and in so doing, oscillates at that level. The higher the signal vacuum and exhaust backpressure, the more the valve opens.

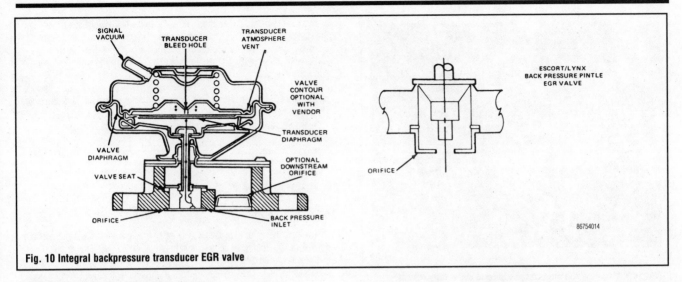

Fig. 10 Integral backpressure transducer EGR valve

Backpressure Variable Transducer EGR Valve

▶ See Figure 11

This system consists of three components: a vacuum regulator, an EGR valve and a flow control orifice. The regulator modulates the vacuum signal to the EGR valve using two backpressure inputs. One input is standard vehicle backpressure and the other is backpressure downstream of the flow control orifice. The control chamber pick-up is in the EGR tube and the flow control orifice is integral with the upstream EGR tube connector.

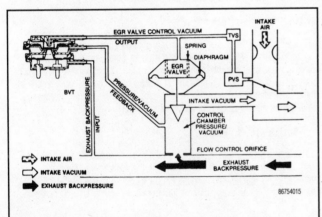

Fig. 11 Exhaust gas flow in the backpressure variable transducer EGR system

TESTING

Exhaust Gas Recirculation (EGR) Valve

▶ See Figure 12

1. Start the car and let the engine reach normal operating temperature.
2. Turn the engine **OFF** and connect a vacuum tester (pump) to the EGR valve vacuum source port.
3. Turn the engine **ON** and idle the engine.
4. Slowly apply 5–10 in. Hg (16–33 kPa) of vacuum; if the engine idles roughly or stalls, the EGR valve is functioning properly.
5. If the engine does not idle roughly, replace the EGR valve.

REMOVAL & INSTALLATION

▶ See Figures 13 and 14

1. Unplug the vacuum hose from the EGR valve.

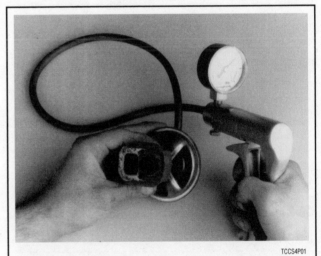

Fig. 12 Some EGR valves may be tested using a vacuum pump by watching for diaphragm movement

Fig. 13 Unbolt the EGR valve from its base, then remove the valve and old gasket

Fig. 14 If installing the old valve, be sure to clean the gunk and build-up from all the passages

2. If applicable, unplug the electrical connector and remove the Exhaust Valve Position (EVP) sensor. It may be secured by small screws.

3. If equipped, unfasten the nut that attaches the EGR tube to the valve, then separate the tube from the valve.

4. Unfasten the nuts/bolts securing the EGR valve and remove the valve. Discard the gasket.

To install:

5. Clean the EGR valve gasket mating surfaces.

6. Install a new gasket and the EGR valve.

7. Install and tighten the EGR valve nuts/bolts to 18 ft. lbs. (25 Nm).

8. If equipped, attach the EGR tube to the valve and tighten the valve-to-tube nut.

9. If equipped, install the EVP sensor and attach its electrical connection.

Air Injection Systems

OPERATION

▶ **See Figures 15 and 16**

The thermactor (air injection) exhaust emission control system reduces the hydrocarbon and carbon monoxide content of the exhaust gases. This is accomplished by continuing the combustion of unburned gases after they leave the combustion chamber, by injecting fresh air into the hot exhaust stream leaving the exhaust ports or into the catalyst. At this point, the fresh air mixes with hot exhaust gases. This promotes further oxidation of both the hydrocarbons and carbon monoxide, reducing their concentration and converting some of them into harmless carbon dioxide and water.

During some modes of operation (highway cruise/wide open throttle), the thermactor air is dumped to atmosphere to prevent overheating in the exhaust system.

The following components are typical of an air injection system:

- Air supply pump and centrifugal filter or remote filter
- Air bypass valve
- Check valves
- Air manifold
- Air hoses
- Air control valve

Air Bypass Valves

There are two types of air bypass valves: normally closed valves and normally opened valves. Both types are available in remote (inline) versions or pump mounted (installed directly on the air pump) versions. Normally closed valves supply air to the exhaust system during medium and high vacuum signals during normal engine operating modes and short idles with some accelerations. With low or no vacuum applied, the pumped air is dumped through the silencer ports of the valve. Normally open air bypass valves are available with or without vacuum vents. Normally open valves using a vacuum vent provide a timed air dump during decelerations and also dump when a vacuum pressure difference is maintained between the signal port and the vent port. The signal port must have 3 in. Hg (10 kPa) or more vacuum than the vent port to hold the dump. This mode is required in order to protect the catalyst from overheating. Normally open air bypass valves without a vacuum vent provide a timed dump of air for 1.0 or 2.8 seconds when a sudden high vacuum of about 20 in. Hg (67.5 kPa) is applied to the signal port. This prevents backfire during deceleration.

Air Check Valve/Pulse Air Valve

The air check valve is a one-way valve that allows the thermactor air to pass into the exhaust system while preventing exhaust gases from passing in the opposite direction. The pulse air valve replaces the air pump in some thermactor systems. It draws air into the exhaust system on vacuum exhaust pulses and blocks the backflow of high pressure exhaust pulses. The fresh air completes the oxidation of exhaust gas components.

Anti-Backfire (Gulp) Valve

The anti-backfire (gulp) valve is located downstream from the air bypass valve. Its function is to divert a portion of the thermactor air to the intake manifold when it is triggered by intake manifold vacuum signals on deceleration. This helps prevent an overly rich mixture from entering the catalytic converter.

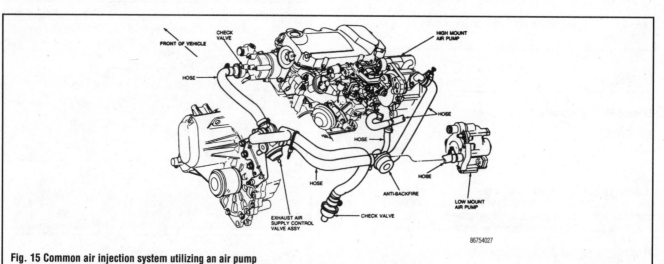

Fig. 15 Common air injection system utilizing an air pump

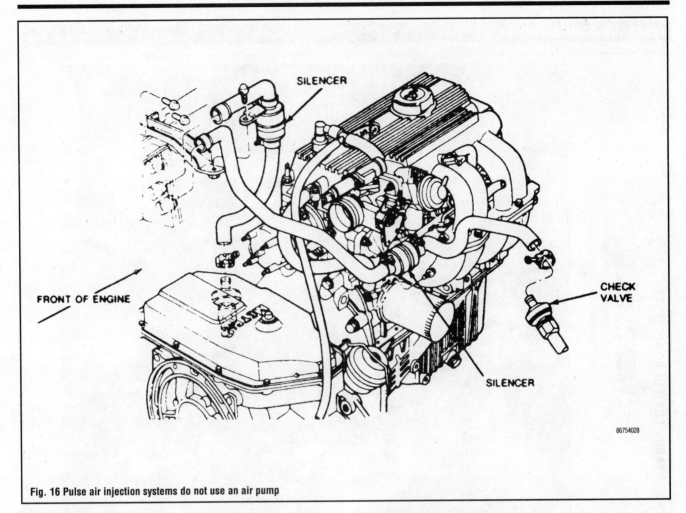

Fig. 16 Pulse air injection systems do not use an air pump

Air Supply Pump

➤This pump is only utilized by air injection systems, not pulse air systems.

The air supply is a belt driven, positive engagement vane-type pump, that supplies air for the thermactor system. The pump is available in two sizes: 11 cubic inch (180cc) and 19 cubic inch (311cc), depending on the particular vehicle application. The 11 cubic inch pump receives air through a remote filter that is attached to the air inlet nipple or through an impeller-type centrifugal air filter fan. The 19 cubic inch pump uses an impeller-type centrifugal air filter fan which separates dirt, dust and other contaminants from the intake air, using centrifugal force. The air supply pump does not have a built in pressure relief valve, but the system does use a bypass valve.

TESTING

Anti-Backfire (Gulp) Valve

1. Disconnect the air supply hose from the air pump side of the anti-backfire valve.
2. Look inside the valve through the disconnect port and observe the valve pintle.
3. Accelerate the engine to about 3000 rpm. Release the throttle, the pintle should open and then close. 7
4. If it does not perform as indicated, replace the defective valve.

Air Supply Pump

1. Check the belt tension. If not within specification, adjust it properly.
2. Disconnect the air supply hose from the bypass control valve.
3. If the air flow is felt at the pump outlet and flow increases, as the engine speed increases, the pump is functioning properly.
4. If the pump does not perform properly, replace as required.

Check Valves

1. Disconnect the air supply at the pump side of the valve.
2. Blow through the check valve, toward the manifold, then attempt to suck back through the valve. Air should pass in the direction of the exhaust manifold only. Replace the valve if air flows both ways.

REMOVAL & INSTALLATION

Air Supply Pump

1. Loosen the pivot mounting and adjustment bolt. Relax the drive belt tension and remove the belt. Disconnect the air hoses.
2. Remove the adjuster and pivot nuts and bolts. Remove the air pump.
3. Installation is in the reverse order of removal. Adjust the belt to its proper tension (refer to Section 1 under Belts.

ELECTRONIC ENGINE CONTROLS

TYPICAL EMISSION AND ELECTRONIC ENGINE CONTROL COMPONENTS

1. Data Link Connector (DLC)
2. Manifold Absolute Pressure (MAP) sensor
3. Idle Speed Control (ISC) motor assembly (under air cleaner housing)
4. Engine Coolant Temperature (ECT) sensor
5. Air Charge Temperature (ACT) sensor
6. Heated Oxygen (HO2S) sensor
7. Throttle Position (TP) sensor (under air cleaner housing)
8. Exhaust Gas Recirculation (EGR) valve

General Information

➡When the term Powertrain Control Module (PCM) is used in this manual, it refers to the engine control computer, regardless of whether it is a Microprocessor Control Unit (MCU) or Electronic Engine Control-Four (EEC-IV) module.

There are two types of engine control systems used on the Escort/Lynx vehicles. The two systems are the Microprocessor Control Unit (MCU) System and the Electronic Engine Control-Four (EEC-IV) system.

The Microprocessor Control Unit (MCU) System was used on 1981–83 models. The MCU system uses a large six-sided connector, identical to the one used with EEC-IV systems. The MCU system does NOT use the small, single-wire connector, found on the EEC-IV system.

The MCU system has limited ability to diagnose a malfunction within itself. Through the use of trouble codes, the system will indicate where to test. When an analog voltmeter or special tester is connected to the diagnostic link connector and the system is triggered, the self-test simulates a variety of engine operating conditions and evaluates all the responses received from the various MCU components, so any abnormal operating conditions can be detected.

Ford's fourth generation engine control system is centered around a microprocessor called the Electronic Engine Control-Four (EEC-IV) system. The EEC-IV module receives and sends electronic signals relaying pertinent engine management information (data) to and from a number of sensors and other electronic components. The EEC-IV module contains a specific calibration for maintaining optimum emissions, fuel economy and driveability. By comparing the input signals to its own calibrated program, the module generates output signals to the various relays, solenoids and actuators.

The EEC-IV module is usual located under the instrument panel left of the steering column, and communicates service information to the outside world by way of service codes. The service codes are two or three-digit numbers representing the result of the self-test.

The service codes are transmitted through the Self-Test Output (STO) terminal, found in the self-test connector.

The module stores the self-test program in its permanent memory. When activated, it checks the system by testing its memory and processing capability.

The self-test also verifies if the various sensors and actuators are connected and operating properly. The self-test is divided into three specialized tests:

- Key On, Engine Off (KOEO) is a static check of the processor inputs and outputs with the power **ON**, but the engine **OFF**.
- Engine Running self-test is a dynamic check with the engine in operation and the vehicle at rest.
- Continuous self-test is a check of the sensor inputs for opens and shorts while the vehicle is in operation.

The KOEO and Engine Running tests are functional tests which only detect faults present at the time of the self-test. Continuous testing is an ongoing test that stores fault information for retrieval at a later time, during the self-test.

Powertrain Control Module

REMOVAL & INSTALLATION

➡When the term Powertrain Control Module (PCM) is used in this manual, it refers to the engine control computer, regardless of whether it is a Microprocessor Control Unit (MCU) or Electronic Engine Control-Four (EEC-IV) module.

Microprocessor Control Unit (MCU)

The Microprocessor Control Unit (MCU) assembly is located in the engine compartment or under the instrument panel, to the left of the steering column.
1. Disconnect the negative battery cable.
2. Tag and disengage all electrical connections from the MCU assembly.
3. Unfasten the retainers and remove the MCU from the vehicle.
4. Installation is the reverse of removal.

Electronic Engine Control-Four (EEC-IV) Module

The EEC-IV module is usually located in the passenger compartment, under the front section of the center console.

1. Disconnect the negative battery cable.
2. Remove the center console to access the module.
3. Unplug the module's electrical connections.
4. Unfasten the retainers and remove the module from the vehicle.
5. Installation is the reverse of removal.

Oxygen Sensor

OPERATION

An Oxygen Sensor (O2S) is used on some of the vehicles covered in this manual. The sensor is mounted in the exhaust manifold. The sensor protrudes into the exhaust stream and monitors the oxygen content of the exhaust gases. The difference between the oxygen content of the exhaust gases and that of the outside air generates a voltage signal to the PCM. The PCM monitors this voltage and, depending upon the value of the signal received, issues a command to adjust for a rich or a lean condition.

TESTING

1. Perform a visual inspection on the sensor as follows:
   a. Remove the sensor from the exhaust.
   b. If the sensor tip has a black/sooty deposit, this may indicate a rich fuel mixture.
   c. If the sensor tip has a white gritty deposit, this may indicate an internal anti-freeze leak.
   d. If the sensor tip has a brown deposit, this could indicate oil consumption.

➡All these contaminants can destroy the sensor; if the problem is not repaired, the new sensor will also be damaged.

2. Reinstall the sensor and disengage its electrical connection.
3. Connect jumper wires from the sensor connector to the wiring harness. This permits the engine to operate normally while you check the engine.

✳✳ WARNING

Never disengage any sensor while the ignition is ON.

4. Start the engine and allow it to reach normal operating temperature. This will take around ten minutes.
5. Engage the positive lead of a high impedance Digital Volt Ohmmeter (DVOM) to the sensor signal wire and the negative lead to a good known engine ground, such as the negative battery terminal.

➡For specific information on the wire terminals refer to the accompanying illustrations.

6. The voltage reading should fluctuate as the sensor detects varying levels of oxygen in the exhaust stream.
7. If the sensor voltage does not fluctuate, the sensor may be defective or the fuel mixture could be extremely out of range.
8. If the sensor reads above 550 millivolts constantly, the fuel mixture may be too lean or you could have an exhaust leak near the sensor.
9. Under normal conditions, the sensor should fluctuate high and low. Prior to condemning the sensor, try forcing the system to have a rich fuel mixture by restricting the air intake or lean by removing a vacuum line. If this causes the sensor to respond, look for problems in other areas of the system.

REMOVAL & INSTALLATION

1. Disconnect the negative battery cable.
2. Unplug the oxygen sensor electrical connection.
3. Remove the exhaust manifold heat shield.
4. Raise the front of the car and support it with safety stands.
5. Using the appropriate size wrench, remove the oxygen sensor.
To install:
6. Install the new sensor and tighten it to 22–36 ft. lbs. (29–49 Nm).
7. Lower the car and install the heat shield.
8. Attach the oxygen sensor electrical connection.
9. Connect the negative battery cable.

Heated Oxygen Sensor

OPERATION

The Heated Oxygen Sensor (HO2S) monitors the oxygen content in the three-way catalytic converter and then transmits this information to the Powertrain Control Module (PCM). The PCM then adjusts the air/fuel ratio to provide a rich (more fuel) or lean (less fuel) condition.

TESTING

▶ **See Figures 17 and 18**

1. Perform a visual inspection on the sensor as follows:
   a. Remove the sensor from the exhaust.
   b. If the sensor tip has a black/sooty deposit, this may indicate a rich fuel mixture.

Fig. 17 Inspect the oxygen sensor tip for abnormal deposits

TCCA4P01

Fig. 18 Testing the resistance of the HO2S heater element using a DVOM

90934P07

   c. If the sensor tip has a white gritty deposit, this may indicate an internal anti-freeze leak.
   d. If the sensor tip has a brown deposit, this could indicate oil consumption.

➡**All these contaminants can destroy the sensor; if the problem is not repaired, the new sensor will also be damaged.**

2. Reinstall the sensor.
3. Disconnect the Heated Oxygen Sensor (HO2S). Measure the resistance between PWR and GND (heater) terminals of the sensor.
4. With the engine hot-to-warm, the resistance should be 5.0–30.0 ohms.
5. At room temperature, the resistance should be 2.0–5.0 ohms. If the readings are within specification, the sensor's heater element is okay.
6. With the O2S connected and engine running, measure voltage with a DVOM by backprobing the **SIG RTN** wire of the oxygen sensor connector. The voltage readings at idle should stay below 1.0 volts. When the speed is increased or decreased the voltage should fluctuate between 0–1.0 volts, if so the sensor is okay.

REMOVAL & INSTALLATION

1. Open and support the hood with the prop rod.
2. Disconnect the negative battery cable.
3. If equipped, remove the exhaust manifold heat shield.
4. Unplug the Heated Oxygen Sensor (HO2S) electrical connection.
5. Using the appropriate size wrench or socket, remove the oxygen sensor.
To install:
6. Install and tighten the new sensor.
7. If removed, install the heat shield.
8. Attach the oxygen sensor electrical connection.
9. Connect the negative battery cable.

Knock Sensor

OPERATION

Located in the engine block, the Knock Sensor (KS) retards ignition timing during a spark knock condition to allow the PCM to maintain maximum timing advance under most conditions.

TESTING

1. Connect a timing light to the vehicle and start the engine.
2. Check that the timing is correct before testing knock sensor operation.
3. If timing is correct, tap on the front of the engine block with a metal object while observing the timing to see 11 if the timing retards.
4. If the timing does not retard, the knock sensor may be defective.

REMOVAL & INSTALLATION

1. Disconnect the negative battery cable.
2. Disengage the wiring harness connector from the knock sensor.
3. Remove the knock sensor from the engine block.
To install:
4. Apply a water base caulk to the knock sensor threads and install the sensor in the engine block.

❊❊ WARNING

Do not use silicone tape to coat the knock sensor threads, as this will insulate the sensor from the engine block.

5. Engage the wiring harness connector.
6. Connect the negative battery cable.

Idle Tracking Switch

TESTING

MCU Systems

▶ See Figure 19

1. Check that the idle tracking switch contacts are open when the switch is actuated (closed throttle) and that the contacts are closed when the switch is not actuated (part throttle).

2. If the switch contacts are open when the switch is actuated (closed throttle), the switch is functioning properly.

3. If the contacts are closed when the switch is not actuated (part throttle), proceed as follows:

   a. Turn the ignition key **OFF**.

   b. Disconnect the module from the harness.

   c. Use a Digital Volt Ohmmeter (DVOM) to measure the resistance between circuits 189 and 687 (refer to the accompanying illustration). The resistance should be between 280–380 ohms.

4. If the resistance is not in range, replace the resistor and the switch.

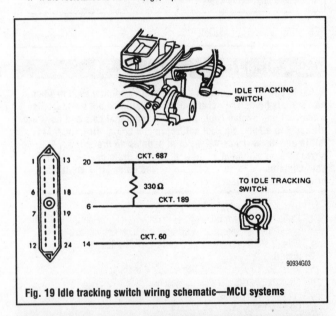

Fig. 19 Idle tracking switch wiring schematic—MCU systems

Idle Speed Control/Idle Tracking Switch

TESTING

EEC-IV Systems

▶ See Figures 20 and 21

1. Turn the ignition key **OFF** and wait about ten seconds before starting the testing procedure.

2. Unplug the harness connector from the ISC motor.

3. Connect a jumper wire from the ISC motor positive terminal to the battery positive terminal and attach a jumper wire from the ISC motor negative terminal to the negative battery terminal for about four seconds. Measure the distance the motor shaft protrudes when it reaches the end of its travel.

4. Connect a jumper wire from the ISC motor positive terminal to the battery positive negative and attach a jumper wire from the ISC motor negative terminal to the battery positive terminal for about four seconds. Measure the distance the motor shaft protrudes when it reaches the end of its travel.

5. The motor shaft should have extended to greater than 2 inches (50.8mm) and retracted to less than 1 ¾ inches (44.45mm) from the mounting bracket.

Fig. 20 Use a Vernier caliper or comparable tool to measure the ISC motor shaft when retracted. The reading should be approximately 1.75 inches (44.45mm) . . .

Fig. 21 . . . then use the caliper to measure the ISC motor shaft when fully extended. The reading should be approximately 2.0 inches (50.8mm)

6. If the motor does shaft does not meet the specification or is completely inoperative, replace the motor.

Air Charge Temperature Sensor

OPERATION

The Air Charge Temperature (ACT) sensor measures the intake air temperature or manifold air temperature. As the air temperature becomes colder, the sensor signals the air temperature change to the Powertrain Control Module (PCM). The PCM then increases fuel injector pulse width, increases cold-enrichment fuel flow, and can also advance the ignition timing, as necessary.

TESTING

▶ See Figures 22 and 23

1. Unplug the sensor electrical connection.

2. Using a Digital Volt Ohmmeter (DVOM) set on the resistance scale, measure across the sensor terminals.

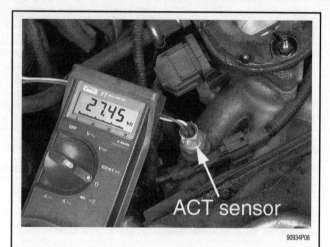

Fig. 22 Measure the resistance across the ACT sensor terminals and compare your readings to the temperature versus resistance values in the accompanying chart

Fig. 24 Measure the resistance across the ECT sensor terminals and compare your readings to the temperature versus resistance values in the accompanying chart

Temperature		Engine Coolant/Air Charge Temperature Sensor Values	
°F	°C	Voltage—(volts)	Resistance—(K ohms)
248	120	.27	1.18
230	110	.35	1.55
212	100	.46	2.07
194	90	.60	2.80
176	80	.78	3.84
158	70	1.02	5.37
140	60	1.33	7.70
122	50	1.70	10.97
104	40	2.13	16.15
86	30	2.60	24.27
68	20	3.07	37.30
50	10	3.51	58.75

90934G04

Fig. 23 Temperature versus resistance chart—ECM systems

3. If the readings are not within the temperature versus resistance specifications shown in the accompanying chart, replace the sensor.

Engine Coolant Temperature Sensor

OPERATION

The Engine Coolant Temperature (ECT) sensor is a thermistor (changes resistance or voltage as temperature changes). The sensor detects the temperature of engine coolant and provides a corresponding signal to the PCM.

TESTING

▶ See Figures 23 and 24

1. Disengage the temperature sensor electrical connection.
2. Connect jumper wires from the sensor connector to the wiring harness. This permits the engine to operate normally while you check the sensor.
3. Connect a Digital Volt Ohmmeter (DVOM) between the sensor terminals.
4. Measure the voltage or resistance with the engine off and cool and with the engine running and warmed up. Compare the temperature versus voltage or resistance values obtained with the chart.
5. Replace the sensor if the readings are incorrect.

REMOVAL & INSTALLATION

✻✻ CAUTION

Never open, service or drain the radiator or cooling system when hot; serious burns can occur from the steam and hot coolant. Also, when draining engine coolant, keep in mind that cats and dogs are attracted to ethylene glycol antifreeze and could drink any that is left in an uncovered container or in puddles on the ground. This will prove fatal in sufficient quantities. Always drain coolant into a sealable container. Coolant should be reused unless it is contaminated or is several years old.

1. Disconnect the negative battery cable.
2. Partially drain the cooling system until the level is below the ECT sensor.
3. Locate the ECT sensor and unplug its electrical connection.
4. Using a suitable size wrench, remove the ECT sensor.
To install:
5. Install the new sensor and tighten until it is snug.
6. Attach the sensor electrical connection.
7. Fill the cooling system.
8. Connect the negative battery cable.
9. Start the vehicle, check for coolant leaks around the sensor and repair as necessary.

Barometric/Manifold Absolute Pressure Sensors

OPERATION

The Barometric (BARO) sensor signals the PCM of changes in atmospheric pressure and density to regulate calculated air flow into the engine. The Manifold Absolute Pressure (MAP) sensor monitors and signals the PCM of changes in intake manifold pressure which result from engine load, speed and atmospheric pressure changes.

TESTING

▶ See Figures 25 and 26

1. Connect jumper wires from the sensor connector to the wiring harness. This permits the engine to operate normally while you check the sensor.

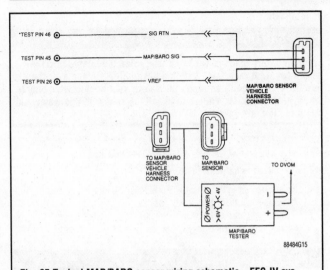

Fig. 25 Typical MAP/BARO sensor wiring schematic—EEC-IV systems

2. Connect a Digital Volt Ohmmeter (DVOM) between the VREF and SIG RTN terminals of the MAP sensor harness connector. The voltage should be between 4–6 volts.

3. If the voltage is not within specification, check the VREF wiring and circuit.

4. Probe the SIG RTN and MAP/SIG RTN terminals with the DVOM.

5. Unplug the sensor vacuum hose and attach a vacuum testing pump to the sensor.

6. With the ignition **ON** and engine **OFF**, apply varying amounts of vacuum to the sensor and use the DVOM to measure voltage across terminals.

7. If the DVOM voltage reading varies with the varying vacuum, the sensor is functioning properly.

Approximate Altitude (Ft.)	Voltage Output (±.04 Volts)
0	1.59
1000	1.56
2000	1.53
3000	1.50
4000	1.47
5000	1.44
6000	1.41
7000	1.39

90934G05

Fig. 26 Measure across the MAP/BARO sensor terminals with a DVOM, and compare the voltage readings with the specifications for your altitude

REMOVAL & INSTALLATION

1. Disconnect the negative battery cable.

2. Disengage the electrical connector and the vacuum line from the sensor.

3. Unfasten the sensor mounting bolts and remove the sensor.

To install:

4. Install the sensor with the mounting bolts and tighten.

5. Attach the electrical wiring lead to the sensor.

6. Attach the vacuum line to the sensor.

7. Connect the negative battery cable.

Throttle Position Sensor

OPERATION

The Throttle Position (TP) sensor detects the throttle plate opening angle and supplies the PCM with an input signal indicating throttle position.

The TP sensor is a rotary potentiometer which consists of either a rigid or flexible thick film resistive substrate and a moving wiper that is mounted on a rotor.

TESTING

▶ **See Figures 27, 28, 29 and 30**

1. Connect jumper wires from the sensor connector to the wiring harness. This permits the engine to operate normally while you check the sensor.

2. Turn the ignition key **OFF** and wait for about ten seconds before conducting the test.

3. Using the jumper wires, probe the VREF and SIG RTN terminals at the TP sensor connector, with a Digital Volt Ohmmeter (DVOM).

4. The voltage should be between 4–6 volts.

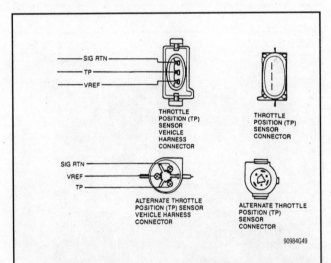

Fig. 27 Typical TP sensor wiring schematic. Also shown is an alternate TP sensor schematic used on some engines

Fig. 28 Probe the VREF and SIG RTN terminals at the TP sensor connector; the reading should be 4–6 volts

Fig. 29 Connect a DVOM to the TP sensor connector and note the voltage reading when the throttle plate is fully closed. . .

Fig. 30 . . . and when the throttle plate is fully open. The voltage should rise evenly and should not jump erratically

5. If the voltage is not within specification, check the VREF wiring and circuit.

6. Probe the SIG RTN and TP terminals with the DVOM.

7. Have an assistant turn the ignition key **ON** and depress the accelerator pedal in small smooth increments from the fully closed to the wide open position.

8. Observe the voltmeter at each of these positions and note the voltage displayed.

9. The voltage at the closed position should be approximately 0 volts. As the throttle is moved slowly through its travel, the voltage should rise evenly until you reach the fully open position, where the voltage should be approximately 5 volts.

10. If the voltage does not meet specifications, or jumps around erratically when moving the throttle through its travel, the sensor may be defective and should be replaced.

REMOVAL & INSTALLATION

1. Disconnect the negative battery cable.
2. Remove the air cleaner-to-intake manifold tube.
3. Unplug the TP sensor electrical connection.
4. Unfasten the sensor retaining screws and remove the sensor.

To install:

✖✖✖ CAUTION

Slide the rotary tangs of the TP sensor, rotated 90 degrees clockwise away from their final installed position, into place over the throttle shaft blade, then rotate the sensor counterclockwise only to the installed position. Failure to install the sensor in this way could result in high idle speeds.

5. Place the sensor on the throttle body. Make sure the tangs on the sensor are properly aligned and the wires are pointing down.

➡**The TP sensor is not adjustable.**

6. Install and tighten the sensor retainers to 25–30 inch lbs. (2.8–3.4 Nm).
7. Attach the TP sensor electrical connection.
8. Install the air cleaner-to-intake manifold tube.
9. Connect the negative battery cable.

Vane Air Flow Meter

OPERATION

The Vane Air Flow (VAF) meter measures the air flowing into the engine (1.6L EFI engines only). The meter contains a movable vane which is connected to a potentiometer. As air flows through the meter, the movable vane and potentiometer change position and provide an input to the PCM. The PCM can then translate the vane position into the volume of air flowing into the engine.

TESTING

▶ **See Figure 31**

1. Make sure the ignition key is **OFF**.
2. Connect jumper wires from the sensor connector to the wiring harness. This permits the engine to operate normally while you check the sensor.
3. Connect a Digital Volt Ohmmeter (DVOM) set to read voltage, between sensor terminals VAF and SIG RTN.
4. Turn the key **ON** and access the VAF meter measuring vane.
5. With the vane fully closed, the voltage reading should be 4.5–5 volts.
6. Slowly move the vane to the fully open position. As the vane moves through its travel the voltage should drop slowly and smoothly. When the vane reaches the end of its travel the voltage reading should be 0.5–1.5 volts.
7. If the voltage readings are not within specifications, replace the VAF meter.

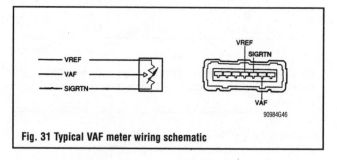

Fig. 31 Typical VAF meter wiring schematic

REMOVAL & INSTALLATION

➡**Only 1.6L EFI engines are equipped with a Vane Air Flow (VAF) meter.**

1. Disconnect the negative battery cable.
2. Unfasten the hose clamp from the VAF meter outlet hose, then detach the outlet hose from the meter and position it out of the way.
3. Remove the air intake hose from the air cleaner.
4. Unfasten the two spring clamps and position the air cleaner cover and the filter element aside.
5. Unfasten the four screw and washer assemblies from the flange of the

air cleaner tray where it is attached to the VAF meter assembly. Pull the air cleaner tray away from the VAF. If the tray-to-VAF meter gasket is deteriorated, replace the gasket.

6. Unplug the VAF meter electrical connection.

➡The VAF meter-to-mounting bracket screws are different sizes. Make a note of the locations of the screws; doing so will aid during installation.

7. Hold the VAF meter with one hand, and unfasten the three screws and washers which attach the meter to the bracket, then remove the meter assembly.

To install:

8. Clean the mounting surfaces of the air cleaner outlet flange and the VAF meter housing.

9. Place the retaining screws in the holes in the air cleaner outlet flange and, if necessary install a new gasket over the screws.

10. Attach the air cleaner to the VAF meter using the screws. Tighten the screws to 33–49 inch lbs.(4–5 Nm). Make sure the gasket is seated and aligned properly.

11. Attach the VAF meter to its mounting bracket using the screws, then tighten the screws to 6–9 ft. lbs. (8–12 Nm).

12. Attach the VAF meter outlet tube to the VAF meter assembly and tighten the hose clamp.

13. Install the air cleaner element and cover.

14. Attach the air intake duct to the air cleaner.

TROUBLE CODES—MICROPROCESSOR CONTROL UNIT (MCU) SYSTEMS

General Information

Diagnosis of a driveability problem requires attention to detail and following the diagnostic procedures in the correct order. Resist the temptation to begin extensive testing before completing the preliminary diagnostic steps. The preliminary or visual inspection must be completed in detail before diagnosis begins. In many cases, this will shorten diagnostic time and often cure the problem without electronic testing.

VISUAL INSPECTION

This is possibly the most critical step of diagnosis. A detailed examination of all connectors, wiring and vacuum hoses can often lead to a repair without further diagnosis. Performance of this step relies on the skill of the technician performing it; a careful inspector will check the undersides of hoses as well as the integrity of hard-to-reach hoses blocked by the air cleaner or other components. Wiring should be checked carefully for any sign of strain, burning, crimping or terminal pull-out from a connector.

Checking connectors at components or in harnesses is required; usually, pushing them together will reveal a loose fit. Pay particular attention to ground circuits, making sure they are not loose or corroded. Remember to inspect connectors and hose fittings at components not mounted on the engine, such as the evaporative canister or relays mounted on the fender aprons. Any component or wiring in the vicinity of a fluid leak or spillage should be given extra attention during inspection. Additionally, inspect maintenance items such as belt condition and tension, battery charge and condition and the radiator cap carefully. Any of these very simple items may affect the system enough to set a fault.

PREPARATION FOR READING CODES

1. Turn **OFF** all electrical equipment and accessories in the vehicle.
2. Follow all safety precautions during testing.
3. Make sure all the fluids are at the proper level.
4. Perform a visual inspection of the system.
5. Start the engine and let it idle, until the engine reaches normal operating temperature. This is when the upper radiator hose is hot and engine rpm has dropped to its normal warm idle speed.
6. Turn ignition switch **OFF**.

✳ CAUTION

Always operate the vehicle in well ventilated area. Exhaust gases are very poisonous.

7. On engines with canister control valves, remove the hose that goes to the carbon canister (this simulates a clean carbon canister). Do NOT plug this hose for the remainder of the test procedure. Make certain the throttle linkage is off of the high choke cam setting.

MCU SYSTEM TROUBLE CODES

The code definitions listed are general for Ford vehicles using the Microprocessor Control Unit (MCU) engine control system. A diagnostic code does not neccesarily mean that the component is defective. For example, Code 44 is an oxygen sensor code (rich oxygen sensor signal). This code may set if a carburetor is flooding or has a very restricted air cleaner. Replacing the oxygen sensor would not fix the problem. This list is for reference purposes and does not necessarily mean that a component is defective.

➡When the term Powertrain Control Module (PCM) is used in this manual, it refers to the engine control computer, regardless of whether it is a Microprocessor Control Unit (MCU) or Electronic Engine Control-Four (EEC-IV) module.

- Code 11: System Pass-(except high altitude) or Altitude (ALT) circuit is open (high altitude)
- Code 12: RPM out of specification (throttle kicker system)
- Code 25: Knock Sensor (KS) signal is not detected during Key On Engine Running (KOER) self-test
- Code 33: Key On Engine Running (KOER) self-test not initiated
- Code 41: Oxygen sensor voltage signal always lean (low value) does not switch
- Code 42: Oxygen sensor voltage signal always rich (high value) does not switch
- Code 44: Oxygen sensor signal indicates rich excessive fuel, restricted air intake or inoperative thermactor system
- Code 45: Thermactor air flow is always upstream (going into exhaust manifold)
- Code 46: Thermactor air system is unable to bypass air (vent to atmosphere)
- Code 51: Low or mid temperature vacuum switch circuit is open when engine is hot
- Code 52: Idle Tracking Switch (ITS) voltage does not change from closed to open throttle (closed throttle checked during KOEO condition)
- Code 53: Wide Open Throttle (WOT) vacuum switch circuit is always open
- Code 54: Mid-temperature switch circuit is always open
- Code 55: Road load vacuum switch circuit is always open
- Code 56: Closed throttle vacuum switch circuit is always open
- Code 61: Hi/Low vacuum switch circuit is always closed
- Code 62: Idle Tracking Switch (ITS) circuit is closed at idle or idle/decel vacuum switch circuit is always closed
- Code 63: Wide Open Throttle (WOT) vacuum switch circuit is always closed
- Code 65: System pass (high altitude vehicles) or Altitude (ALT) circuit is open (except high altitude vehicles)
- Code 66: Closed Throttle Vacuum (CTV) switch circuit is always closed

Reading Codes

USING AN ANALOG VOLTMETER

Key ON Engine OFF Test

▶ **See Figure 32**

1. With the ignition switch in the **OFF** position, connect a jumper wire between circuits 60 and 201 on the self-test connector.
2. Connect the analog voltmeter from the battery positive post to the self-test output connector.

3. Self the voltmeter scale to 0–15 volt range.

4. Turn the ignition switch **ON**, but do NOT start the engine. One quick initialization pulse may occur. The output codes will follow in about 5 seconds.

5. Count the voltmeter sweeps, to determine which codes are being transmitted.

6. The MCU system uses 2-digit codes with the pause between each digit being about 2 seconds long. The pause between the two different codes is about 4 seconds long. The code group is sent twice. This allow you to check the accuracy of the codes as you record them.

7. Once this test has been performed and all fault codes recorded, you can refer to the "Code Descriptions" in this manual for the meaning of the fault code(s).

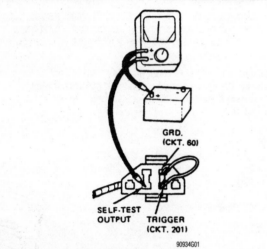

Fig. 32 Connect a jumper wire between circuits 60 and 201 on the self-test connector—MCU system

Key ON Engine Running (KOER) Test

▶ **See Figure 33**

1. Turn **OFF** all electrical equipment and accessories in the vehicle.
2. Follow all safety precautions during testing.
3. Make sure all fluids are at the proper levels.
4. Perform a "Visual Inspection" as detailed earlier in this manual.
5. The following steps involve servicing the engine with the engine running. Observe all safety precautions and perform the steps as follows:
   • Apply the parking brake.
   • Put the shift lever in **P** (automatic transaxle) or **N** (manual transaxle).
   • Block the drive wheels.
   • Always operate the vehicle in a well ventilated area. Exhaust gases are very poisonous.
   • Stay clear of hot and moving engine parts.

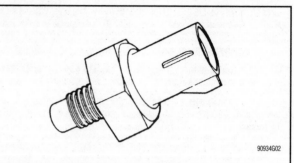

Fig. 33 If your vehicle is equipped with a knock sensor (shown), you must simulate a spark knock for the self-test—MCU systems

6. The engine should be at normal operating temperature for this test. If not, start the engine and let it idle, until the engine reaches normal operating temperature. This is when the upper radiator hose is Hot and engine RPM has dropped to its normal warm idle speed and repeat Key ON Engine OFF test again.

7. If engine is warm, after the codes have been retrieved, Start the engine.

❋❋ CAUTION

Always operate vehicle in well ventilated area. Exhaust gases are very poisonous.

8. Extract the fault codes as follows:
   a. Start the engine and raise idle to 3000 rpm within 20 seconds of starting vehicle.
   b. Hold the idle at 3000 rpm until codes are sent.
   c. When codes are sent release throttle and let engine return to idle speed.

9. If your vehicle is equipped with a knock sensor perform the following test, if not skip to Step 10. Simulate a spark knock by placing a ⅜ inch socket extension (or similar tool) on the manifold near the base of knock sensor. Tap on the end of extension lightly with a 2–6oz. hammer for approximately 15 seconds. Do NOT hit on the knock sensor itself. Count the voltmeter's needle sweeps to determine which codes are being sent.

10. The first series of sweeps should be the engine ID code; ignore any sweeps that last any longer than 1 second. The engine ID code will be ½ the number of cylinders. Specifically, confirmation of a 4-cylinder engine would appear as 2 needle sweeps.

11. If no sweeps occur, repeat KOER test procedures, starting with Step 1. If the meter still does not sweep, you have a problem which must be repaired before proceeding.

12. Count the sweeps on the meter to find out which codes are being sent. All codes are 2 digits long and will appear the same way as in KOEO Self-Test. Ignore any sweeps lasting more than 1 second. Write codes down on a piece of paper; codes will be sent twice so you can check your list for accuracy. Write codes down in the order they appear. Turn the ignition switch **OFF** when codes are finished and remove the jumper wire.

TROUBLE CODES—EEC-IV SYSTEMS

General Information

➡**When the term Powertrain Control Module (PCM) is used in this manual, it refers to the engine control computer, regardless of whether it is a Microprocessor Control Unit (MCU) or Electronic Engine Control-Four (EEC-IV) module.**

One part of the EEC-IV module is devoted to monitoring both input and output functions within the system. This ability forms the core of the self-diagnostic system. If a problem is detected within a circuit, the controller will recognize the fault, assign it an identification code, and store the code in a memory section. Depending on the year and model, the fault code(s) may be represented by two or three-digit numbers. The stored code(s) may be retrieved during diagnosis.

While the EEC-IV system is capable of recognizing many internal faults, certain faults will not be recognized. Because the computer system sees only electrical signals, it cannot sense or react to mechanical or vacuum faults affecting engine operation. Some of these faults may affect another component which will set a code. For example, the PCM monitors the output signal to the fuel injectors, but cannot detect a partially clogged injector. As long as the output driver responds correctly, the computer will read the system as functioning correctly. However, the improper flow of fuel may result in a lean mixture. This would, in turn, be detected by the oxygen sensor and noticed as a constantly lean signal by the PCM. Once the signal falls outside the pre-programmed limits, the engine control assembly would notice the fault and set an identification code.

The PCM contains back-up programs which allow the engine to operate if a sensor signal is lost. If a sensor input is seen to be out of range—either high or low—the Failure Mode Effects Management (FMEM) program is used. The processor substitutes a fixed value for the missing sensor signal. The engine will continue to operate, although performance and driveability may be noticeably reduced. This function of the controller is sometimes referred to as the limp-in or fail-safe mode. If the missing sensor signal is restored, the FMEM system immediately returns the system to normal operation. The dashboard warning lamp will be lit when FMEM is in effect.

If the fault is too extreme for the FMEM circuit to handle, the system enters what is known as Hardware Limited Operation Strategy (HLOS). In this mode, the processor has ceased all computation and control; the entire system is run on fixed values. The vehicle may be operated but performance and driveability will be greatly reduced. The fixed or default settings provide minimal calibration, allowing the vehicle to be carefully driven in for service. The dashboard warning lamp will be lit when HLOS is engaged. Codes cannot be read while the system is operating in this mode.

Code Reading Tools

HAND-HELD SCAN TOOLS

▶ **See Figure 34**

Although stored codes may be read through the flashing of the CHECK ENGINE or SERVICE ENGINE SOON lamp, the use of hand-held scan tools such as Ford's Self-Test Automatic Readout (STAR) tester or the second generation SUPER STAR II tester or their equivalent is highly recommended. There are many manufacturers of these tools; the purchaser must be certain that the tool is proper for the intended use.

The scan tool allows any stored faults to be read from the engine controller memory. Use of the scan tool provides additional data during troubleshooting, but does not eliminate the use of the charts. The scan tool makes collecting information easier, but the data must be correctly interpreted by an operator familiar with the system.

TCCS4P11

Fig. 34 Inexpensive scan tools, such as this Auto Xray®, are available to interface with your Ford vehicle

ELECTRICAL TOOLS

The most commonly required electrical diagnostic tool is the Digital Multimeter, allowing voltage, ohmmage (resistance) and amperage to be read by one instrument. Many of the diagnostic charts require the use of a volt or ohmmeter during diagnosis. The multimeter must be a high impedance unit, with 10 megohms of impedance in the voltmeter. This type of meter will not place an additional load on the circuit it is testing; this is extremely important in low voltage circuits.

The multimeter must be of high quality in all respects. It should be handled carefully and protected from impact or damage. Replace the batteries frequently in the unit.

Additionally, an analog (needle type) voltmeter may be used to read stored fault codes if the STAR tester is not available. The codes are transmitted as visible needle sweeps on the face of the instrument.

Almost all diagnostic procedures will require the use of a Breakout Box, a device which connects into the EEC-IV harness and provides testing ports for the 60 wires in the harness. Direct testing of the harness connectors at the terminals or by backprobing is not recommended; damage to the wiring and terminals is almost certain to occur.

Other necessary tools include a quality tachometer with inductive (clip-on) pickup, a fuel pressure gauge with system adapters and a vacuum gauge with an auxiliary source of vacuum.

Reading Codes

Diagnosis of a driveability problem requires attention to detail and following the diagnostic procedures in the correct order. Resist the temptation to begin extensive testing before completing the preliminary diagnostic steps. The preliminary or visual inspection must be completed in detail before diagnosis begins. In many cases this will shorten diagnostic time and often cure the problem without electronic testing.

VISUAL INSPECTION

This is possibly the most critical step of diagnosis. A detailed examination of all connectors, wiring and vacuum hoses can often lead to a repair without further diagnosis. Performance of this step relies on the skill of the technician performing it; a careful inspector will check the undersides of hoses as well as the integrity of hard-to-reach hoses blocked by the air cleaner or other components. Wiring should be checked carefully for any sign of strain, burning, crimping or terminal pull-out from a connector.

Checking connectors at components or in harnesses is required; usually, pushing them together will reveal a loose fit. Pay particular attention to ground circuits, making sure they are not loose or corroded. Remember to inspect connectors and hose fittings at components not mounted on the engine, such as the evaporative canister or relays mounted on the fender aprons. Any component or wiring in the vicinity of a fluid leak or spillage should be given extra attention during inspection.

Additionally, inspect maintenance items such as belt condition and tension, battery charge and condition and the radiator cap carefully. Any of these very simple items may affect the system enough to set a fault.

ELECTRONIC TESTING

If a code was set before a problem self-corrected (such as a momentarily loose connector), the code will be erased if the problem does not reoccur within 80 warm-up cycles. Codes will be output and displayed as numbers on the hand-held scan tool, such as 23. If the codes are being read on an analog voltmeter, the needle sweeps indicate the code digits. code 23 will appear as two needle pulses (sweeps) then, after a 1.6 second pause, the needle will pulse (sweep) three times.

USING AN ANALOG VOLTMETER

▶ **See Figures 35 and 36**

In the absence of a scan tool, an analog voltmeter may be used to retrieve stored fault codes. Set the meter range to read 0–15 volts DC. Connect the + lead of the meter to the battery positive terminal and connect the - lead of the meter to the self-test output pin of the diagnostic connector.

Follow the directions given previously for performing the KOEO and KOER tests. To activate the tests, use a jumper wire to connect the signal return pin on the diagnostic connector to the self-test input connector. The self-test input line is the separate wire and connector with or near the diagnostic connector.

The codes will be transmitted as groups of needle sweeps. This method may be used to read either 2 or 3-digit codes. The Continuous Memory codes are separated from the KOEO codes by 6 seconds, a single sweep and another 6 second delay.

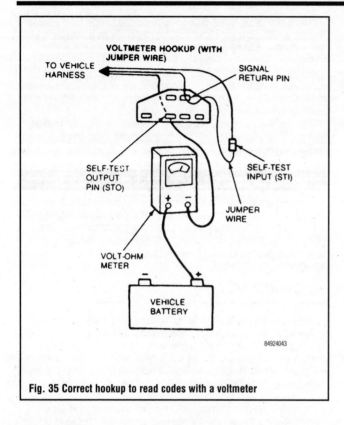

Fig. 35 Correct hookup to read codes with a voltmeter

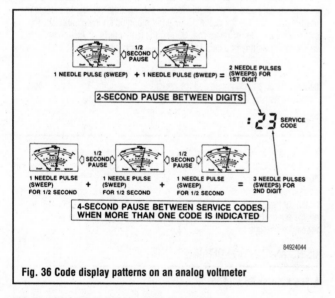

Fig. 36 Code display patterns on an analog voltmeter

MALFUNCTION INDICATOR LAMP (MIL) METHOD

▶ **See Figures 37 and 38**

The Malfunction Indicator Lamp (MIL) on the dashboard may also be used to retrieve the stored codes. This method displays only the stored codes and does

not allow any system investigation. It should only be used in field conditions where a quick check of stored codes is needed.

Follow the directions given previously for performing the scan tool procedure. To activate the tests, use a jumper wire to connect the signal return pin on the diagnostic connector to the Self-Test Input (STI) connector. The self-test input line is the separate wire and connector with or near the diagnostic connector.

Codes are transmitted by place value with a pause between the digits; for example, code 32 would be sent as 3 flashes, a pause and 2 flashes. A slightly longer pause divides codes from each other. Be ready to count and record codes; the only way to repeat a code is to recycle the system. This method may be used to read either 2 or 3-digit codes. The Continuous Memory codes are separated from the other codes by 6 seconds, a single flash and another 6-second delay.

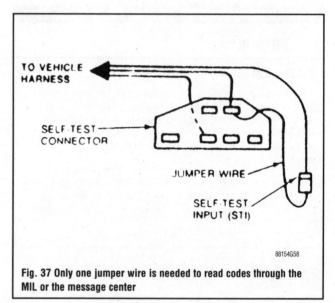

Fig. 37 Only one jumper wire is needed to read codes through the MIL or the message center

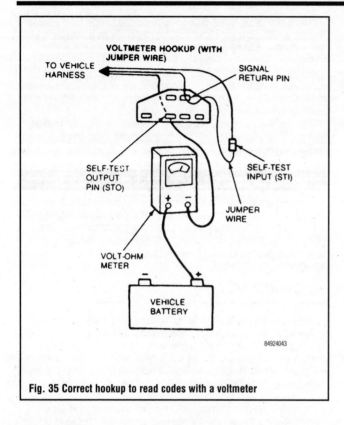

Fig. 38 Code display pattern using the dashboard warning lamp

EEC-IV SYSTEM TROUBLE CODES

Year—1983
Model—Escort/Lynx, EXP/LN7
Engine—1.6L EFI (98 cid)
Engine Code—5

ECA SERVICE CODES

Code		Explanation
11	O/R/C	System pass
12	R	Idle Speed Control (ISC)—failed at elevated rpm
13	R	Idle Speed Control (ISC)—failed at idle rpm
21		Engine coolant
23		Throttle Position (TP) sensor
24		Vane Air Temperature (VAT) sensor
26		Vane Air Flow (VAF) meter
41		Fuel always lean
42		Fuel always rich
56	O/C	Vane Air Flow (VAF) sensor
61	O/C	Engine Coolant Temperature (ECT) sensor
63	O/C	Throttle Position (TP) sensor
64	O/C	Vane Air Temperature (VAT) sensor
66	O/C	Vane Air Flow (VAF) sensor
73	R	Throttle Position (TP) sensor
76	R	Vane Air Flow (VAF) sensor
77	R	Dynamic response test

Year—1984
Model—Escort, Lynx and EXP
Engine—1.6L EFI
Engine Code—5

ECA SERVICE CODES

Code		Explanation
11	O/R/C	System pass
12	R	Idle speed control, bypass air
13	R	Idle speed control, bypass air
14	C	Erratic ignition
15	O	Replace processor, repeat quick test
18	C	Ignition Diagnostic Monitor (IDM)
21	O/R/C	Engine Coolant Temperature (ECT) sensor
22	O/R/C	Barometric Pressure (BP) sensor
23	O/R	Throttle Position (TP) sensor
24	O/R	Vane Air Temperature (VAT) sensor
25	R	Knock sensor
26	O/R	Vane Air Flow (VAF) sensor
34	R	EGR on/off control
41	R/C	Fuel control, EFI
42	R/C	Fuel control, EFI
51	O/C	Engine Coolant Temperature (ECT) sensor
53	O/C	Throttle Position (TP) sensor
54	O/C	Vane Air Temperature (VAT) sensor

Year—1984
Model—Escort, Lynx and EXP
Engine—1.6L EFI TC
Engine Code—8

ECA SERVICE CODES

Code		Explanation
11	O/R/C	System pass
12	R	Idle speed control, bypass air
13	R	Idle speed control, bypass air
14	C	Erratic ignition
15	O	Replace processor, repeat quick test
18	C	Ignition Diagnostic Monitor (IDM)
21	O/R/C	Engine Coolant Temperature (ECT) sensor
22	O/R/C	Barometric Pressure (BP) sensor
23	O/R	Throttle Position (TP) sensor
24	O/R	Vane Air Temperature (VAT) sensor
25	R	Knock sensor
26	O/R	Vane Air Flow (VAF) sensor
34	R	EGR on/off control
41	R/C	Fuel control, EFI
42	R/C	Fuel control, EFI
51	O/C	Engine Coolant Temperature (ECT) sensor
53	O/C	Throttle Position (TP) sensor
54	O/C	Vane Air Temperature (VAT) sensor
56	O/C	Vane Air Flow (VAF) sensor
61	O/C	Engine Coolant Temperature (ECT) sensor
63	O/C	Throttle Position (TP) sensor
64	O/C	Vane Air Temperature (VAT) sensor
66	O/C	Vane Air Flow (VAF) sensor
73	R	Throttle Position (TP) sensor
76	R	Vane Air Flow (VAF) sensor
77	R	Dynamic response test

Year—1985
Model—Escort, Lynx and EXP
Engine—1.6L EFI
Engine Code—5

ECA SERVICE CODES

Code		Explanation
11	O/R/C	System pass
12	R	Idle speed control, bypass air
13	R	Idle speed control, bypass air
14	C	Erratic ignition
18	C	Ignition Diagnostic Monitor (IDM)
21	O/R/C	Engine Coolant Temperature (ECT) sensor
22	O/R/C	Manifold Absolute Pressure/Barometric Pressure (MAP/BP)
23	O/R	Throttle Position Sensor (TPS)
24	O/R	Air Charge Temperature (ACT) sensor, VAT in meter
25	R	Knock sensor
26	O/R	Vane Air Flow (VAF) sensor
34	R	EGR on-off check
41	R/C	Fuel control, EFI
42	R/C	Fuel control, EFI
51	O/C	Engine Coolant Temperature (ECT) sensor
53	O/C	Throttle Position Sensor (TPS)
54	O/C	Air Charge Temperature (ACT) sensor, VAT in meter
56	O/C	Vane Air Flow (VAF) sensor
61	O/C	Engine Coolant Temperature (ECT) sensor
63	O/C	Throttle Position Sensor (TPS)
64	O/C	Air Charge Temperature (ACT) sensor, VAT in meter
66	O/C	Vane Air Flow (VAF) sensor
67	O	A/C and/or neutral drive switch
73	R	Throttle Position Sensor (TPS)
76	R	Vane Air Flow (VAF) sensor
77	R	Dynamic response test

86754214

Year—1985
Model—Escort, Lynx and EXP
Engine—1.6L EFI TC
Engine Code—8

ECA SERVICE CODES

Code		Explanation
11	O/R/C	System pass
12	R	Idle speed control, bypass air
13	R	Idle speed control, bypass air
14	C	Erratic ignition
18	C	Ignition Diagnostic Monitor (IDM)
21	O/R/C	Engine Coolant Temperature (ECT) sensor
22	O/R/C	Manifold Absolute Pressure/Barometric Pressure (MAP/BP)
23	O/R	Throttle Position Sensor (TPS)
24	O/R	Air Charge Temperature (ACT) sensor, VAT in meter
25	R	Knock sensor
26	O/R	Vane Air Flow (VAF) sensor
34	R	EGR on-off check
41	R/C	Fuel control, EFI
42	R/C	Fuel control, EFI
51	O/C	Engine Coolant Temperature (ECT) sensor
53	O/C	Throttle Position Sensor (TPS)
54	O/C	Air Charge Temperature (ACT) sensor, VAT in meter
56	O/C	Vane Air Flow (VAF) sensor
61	O/C	Engine Coolant Temperature (ECT) sensor
63	O/C	Throttle Position Sensor (TPS)
64	O/C	Air Charge Temperature (ACT) sensor, VAT in meter
66	O/C	Vane Air Flow (VAF) sensor
67	O	A/C and/or neutral drive switch
73	R	Throttle Position Sensor (TPS)
76	R	Vane Air Flow (VAF) sensor
77	R	Dynamic response test

86754215

Year–1986
Model–Escort and Lynx
Engine–1.9L EFI
Engine Code–9

ECA SERVICE CODES

Code		Explanation
11	O/R/C	System pass
12	R	Cannot control rpm during high rpm check
13	R	Cannot control rpm during low rpm check
14	C	PIP circuit failure
15	O	ECA read only memory (ROM) test failed
17	R	Rpm below self-test limit, set too low
18	C	Loss of tach input to ECU
21	O/R/C	ECT out of range
22	O/R/C	Barometric Pressure (BP) sensor out of test range
23	O/R	TP sensor out of self-test range
24	O/R	VAT sensor input out of test range
26	O/R	VAF sensor input out of self-test range
34	R	Insufficient EGR flow
41	R	Fuel system at adaptive limits, no HEGO switch system shows lean
41	C	Lack of EGO/HEGO switching detected system indicates lean
42	R	Lack of EGO/HEGO switches, indicates rich
42	C	No EGO/HEGO switches, indicates rich
51	O/C	ECT sensor indicated test maximum or open circuit
53	O/C	TP sensor circuit above maximum voltage
54	O/C	VAT sensor input exceeds test maximum
56	O/C	VAF circuit above maximum voltage
61	O/C	ECT sensor input below test minimum
63	O/C	TP sensor circuit below minimum voltage
64	O/C	VAT sensor input below test minimum
66	O/C	VAF below test minimum
67	O	Neutral switch open or A/C input high
73	R	Insufficient TP change, dynamic response test
76	R	Insufficient VAF output change, dynamic response test
77	R	Operator error, WOT not sensed during test

86754216

Year–1987
Model–Escort/Lynx
Body VIN–1 and 2
Engine–1.9L   Cylinder–4
Fuel System–Multi-Point Injection (EFI)
Engine VIN–J

ECA SERVICE CODES

Code		Explanation
11	O/R/C	System pass
12	R	Rpm unable to reach upper test limit
13	R	Rpm unable to reach lower test limit
14	C	PIP circuit failure
15	O/C	Power interrupted to keep alive memory
16	R	Rpm unable to reach lower test limit
17	C	Curb idle–Idle Speed Control (Bypass air)
18	C	Loss of ignition signal to ECU–ignition grounded, spout, PIP, IDM
21	O/R	ECT sensor input out of test range
22	O/R/C	MAP sensor out of test range
23	O/R	TP sensor out of test range
26	O/R	VAF sensor out of self-test range
28	O/R	VAT sensor out of self-test range
41	R	Fuel Control–always lean
41	C	HEGO shows fuel system lean
42	R	HEGO shows system rich
42	C	HEGO shows fuel system lean
43	C	HEGO shows fuel system lean
47	R	Airflow at base idle
48	R	Airflow high at base idle
51	O/C	ECT sensor input exceeds test maximum
53	O/C	TP sensor input exceeds test maximum
56	O/C	VAF sensor input exceeds test maximum
58	O/C	VAT sensor input exceeds test maximum
61	O/C	ECT test sensor input below test minimum
63	O/C	TP sensor below test minimum
66	O/C	VAF sensor input below test minimum
67	O/C	Neutral drive switch open. A/C input high
68	O/C	VAT sensor input below test minimum
71	C	Re-initialization check–check EEC IV wiring position to secondary wiring
72	C	Power interrupt detected
73	R	Insufficient TP output change during test
76	R	Insufficient VAF output change during test
77	R	Wide open throttle not sensed during test
No Code		Unable to run self-test or output codes
Code not listed		Does not apply to vehicle being tested

O–Key On, Engine Off   C–Continuous Memory
R–Engine running   1 Refer to system diagnostics

86754217

Year–1987
Model–Escort/Lynx
Body VIN–1 and 2
Engine–1.9L CFI   Cylinder–4
Fuel System–Central Fuel Injection (CFI)
Engine VIN–9

ECA SERVICE CODES

Code		Explanation
11	O/R/C	System pass
12	R	Rpm unable to reach upper test limit
13	R	Rpm unable to reach lower test limit
14	C	PIP circuit failure
15	O/C	Power interrupted to keep alive memory
16	R	Rpm unable to reach lower test limit
18	C	Loss of ignition signal to ECU—ignition grounded, spout, PIP, IDM
21	O/R	ECT sensor input out of test range
22	O/R/C	MAP sensor out of test range
23	O/R	TP sensor out of test range
24	O/R	ACT sensor out of self-test range
31	O/R/C	PFE sensor out of self-test range
32	R/C	PFE sensor sense a lack of pressure in exhaust system
33	R/C	PFE valve not opening
34	O	PFE sensor out of range
34	R/C	Defective PFE sensor
35	O/R/C	PFE circuit above maximum voltage
38	C	Idle track switch circuit open
41	R	EGO/HEGO circuit shows system lean
41	C	No EGO/HEGO switching detected, system lean
42	R	EGO/HEGO shows system rich
51	O/C	ECT sensor input exceeds test maximum
53	O/C	TP sensor input exceeds test maximum
54	O/C	ACT sensor input exceeds test maximum
55	R	Key power input to processor is open
58	R	Idle tracking switch circuit closed
58	O	Idle tracking switch circuit open
61	O/C	ECT test sensor input below test minimum
63	O/C	TP sensor below test minimum
64	O/C	ACT sensor input below test minimum
67	O/R	Neutral drive switch open. A/C input high
68	R	Idle tracking switch circuit open
66	O	Idle tracking switch closed
71	C	Idle tracking switch closed on pre-position
73	O	Insufficient TP change
84	O/R	EGR VAC regulator circuit failure
85	O/R	Canister purge circuit failure

ECA SERVICE CODES

Code		Explanation
87	O/R/C	Fuel pump primary circuit failure
93	O	TP sensor input low at max DC motor extension
98	R	Hard fault is present
99	R	EEC system has not learned to control idle
No Code		Unable to run self-test or output codes [1]
Code not listed		Does not apply to vehicle being tested [1]

O–Key On, Engine Off
R–Engine running
C–Continuous Memory
1 Refer to system diagnostics

Year–1988
Model–Escort
Body VIN–1 and 2
Engine–1.9L   Cylinder–4
Fuel System–Multi-Point Injection (EFI)
Engine VIN–J

ECA SERVICE CODES

Code		Explanation
11	O/R/C	System pass
12	R	Rpm unable to reach upper test limit
13	R	Rpm unable to reach lower test limit
14	C	PIP circuit failure
15	O	ROM test failure
15	C	Power interrupted to keep alive memory
16	R	Rpm above self test limit, set too high (ISC off)
17	R	Rpm below self-test limit, set too low (ISC off)
18	C	Loss of tach input to ECU, spout grounded
18	R	Spout circuit open
19	R	Erratic rpm during test or rpm too low (ISC off)
21	O/R	ECT sensor input out of test range
22	O/R/C	MAP sensor input out of test range
23	O/R	TP sensor input out of test range
26	O/R	VAF sensor input out of self-test range
28	O/R	VAT sensor input out of self-test range
41	O/R	EGO/HEGO circuit shows system lean
41	C	No EGO/HEGO switching detected, system lean
42	R	EGO/HEGO shows system rich
42	C	No EGO/HEGO switching detected, system rich
43	C	EGO/HEGO lean at wide open throttle
47	R	Airflow at base idle

86754219

86754218

ECA SERVICE CODES

Code		Explanation
48	R	Airflow high at base idle
51	O/C	ECT sensor input exceeds test maximum
53	O/C	TP sensor input exceeds test maximum
56	O/C	VAF sensor input exceeds test maximum
58	O/C	VAT sensor input exceeds test maximum
61	O/C	ECT test sensor input below test minimum
63	O/C	TP sensor below test minimum
65	C	Failed to enter self-test mode
66	O/C	VAF sensor input below test minimum
67	O	Neutral drive switch open. A/C input high
67	O/C	Clutch switch circuit failure
68	O/C	VAT sensor input below test minimum
72	C	Power interrupt detected
73	R	Insufficient TP output change during test
76	R	Insufficient VAF output change during test
77	R	Wide open throttle not sensed during test
85	C	Adaptive lean limit reached
86	C	Adaptive rich limit reached
95	O/C	Fuel pump secondary circuit failure
96	O/C	Fuel pump secondary circuit failure
No Code		Unable to run self-test or output codes ¹
Code not listed		Does not apply to vehicle being tested ¹

O – Key On, Engine Off
R – Engine running
C – Continuous Memory
1 Refer to system diagnostics

Year – 1988
Model – Escort
Body VIN – 1 and 2   Cylinder – 4
Engine – 1.9L
Fuel System – Central Fuel Injection (CFI)
Engine VIN – 9

ECA SERVICE CODES

Code		Explanation
11	O/R/C	System pass
12	R	Rpm unable to reach upper test limit
13	R	Rpm unable to reach lower test limit
13	O	DC motor did not follow dashpot
14	C	PIP circuit failure
15	O	ROM test failure
15	C	Power interrupted to keep alive memory

ECA SERVICE CODES

Code		Explanation
17	R	Rpm below self-test limit, set too low
18	C	Loss of tach input to ECU, spout grounded
18	R	Spout circuit open
19	R	Erratic rpm during test or rpm too low
21	O/R	ECT sensor input out of test range
22	O/R/C	MAP sensor input out of test range
23	O/R/C	TP sensor input out of test range
24	O/R	ACT sensor input out of test range
31	O/R/C	EVP circuit below minimum voltage
32	R/C	EGR valve not seated
33	R/C	EGR valve not opening
34	O	Defective PFE sensor
34	R/C	Excess exhaust back pressure
35	O/R/C	PFE circuit above maximum voltage
38	C	Idle track switch circuit open
41	R	EGO/HEGO circuit shows system lean
41	C	No EGO/HEGO switching detected, system lean
42	R	EGO/HEGO shows system rich
51	O/C	ECT sensor input exceeds test maximum
53	O/C	TP sensor input exceeds test maximum
54	O/C	ACT sensor input exceeds test maximum
55	R	Key power input to processor is open
58	R	Idle tracking switch circuit closed
58	O	Idle tracking switch circuit open
61	O/C	ECT test sensor input below test minimum
63	O/C	TP sensor below test minimum
64	O/C	ACT sensor input below test minimum
67	O/R	Neutral drive switch open. A/C input high
68	R	Idle tracking switch circuit open
68	O	Idle tracking switch closed
71	C	Idle tracking switch closed on pre-position
73	O	Insufficient TP change
84	O/R	EGR VAC regulator circuit failure
85	O/R	Canister purge circuit failure
87	O/R/C	Fuel pump primary circuit failure
93	O	TP sensor input low at max DC motor extension
95	O/C	Fuel pump secondary circuit failure
96	O/C	Fuel pump secondary circuit failure
98	R	Hard fault is present
99	R	EEC system has not learned to control idle ¹
No Code		Unable to run self-test or output codes ¹
Code not listed		Does not apply to vehicle being tested ¹

O – Key On, Engine Off
R – Engine running
C – Continuous Memory
1 Refer to system diagnostics

Year—1989
Model—Escort
Body VIN—1 and 2
Engine—1.9L HO Cylinder—4
Fuel System—Multi-Point Injection (EFI)
Engine VIN—J

ECA SERVICE CODES

Code		Explanation
11	O/R/C	System pass
12	R	Rpm unable to reach upper test limit
13	R	Rpm unable to reach lower test limit
14	C	PIP circuit failure
15	O	ROM test failure
15	C	Power interrupted to keep alive memory
16	R	Rpm above self test limit, set too high (ISC off)
17	R	Rpm below self-test limit, set too low (ISC off)
18	C	Loss of tach input to ECU, spout grounded
19	R	Spout circuit open
21	R	Erratic rpm during test or rpm too low (ISC off)
21	O/R	ECT sensor input out of test range
22	O/R/C	MAP sensor input out of test range
23	O/R	TP sensor input out of test range
26	O/R	VAF sensor input out of self-test range
28	O/R	VAT sensor input out of self-test range
41	R	EGO/HEGO circuit shows system lean
41	C	No EGO/HEGO switching detected, system lean
42	R	EGO/HEGO shows system rich
42	C	No EGO/HEGO switching detected, system rich
43	C	EGO/HEGO lean at wide open throttle
47	R	Airflow at base idle
48	R	Airflow high at base idle
51	O/C	ECT sensor input exceeds test maximum
53	O/C	TP sensor input exceeds test maximum
56	O/C	VAF sensor input exceeds test maximum
58	O/C	VAT sensor input exceeds test maximum
61	O/C	ECT test sensor input below test minimum
63	O/C	TP sensor below test minimum
65	C	Failed to enter self-test mode
66	O/C	VAF sensor input below test minimum
67	O	Neutral drive switch open. A/C input high
67	C	Clutch switch circuit failure
68	O/C	VAT sensor input below test minimum
71	C	Software re-initialization detected
72	C	Power interrupt detected
73	R	Insufficient TP output change during test

Year—1989
Model—Escort
Body VIN—1 and 2
Engine—1.9L Cylinder—4
Fuel System—Central Fuel Injection (CFI)
Engine VIN—9

ECA SERVICE CODES

Code		Explanation
11	O/R/C	System pass
12	R	Rpm unable to reach upper test limit
13	R	Rpm unable to reach lower test limit
13	O	DC motor did not follow dashpot
14	C	PIP circuit failure
15	O	ROM test failure
15	C	Power interrupted to keep alive memory
17	R	Rpm below self-test limit, set too low
18	C	Loss of tach input to ECU, spout grounded
18	R	Spout circuit open
19	R	Erratic rpm during test or rpm too low
21	O/R	ECT sensor input out of test range
22	O/R/C	MAP sensor input out of test range
23	O/R/C	TP sensor input out of test range
24	O/R	ACT sensor input out of test range
31	O/R/C	EVP circuit below minimum voltage
32	R/C	EGR valve not seated
33	R/C	EGR valve not opening
34	O	Defective PFE sensor
34	R/C	Excess exhaust back pressure
35	O/R/C	PFE circuit above maximum voltage
76	R	Insufficient VAF output change during test
77	R	Wide open throttle not sensed during test
85	C	Adaptive lean limit reached
86	C	Adaptive rich limit reached
95	O/C	Fuel pump secondary circuit failure
96	O/C	Fuel pump secondary circuit failure [1]
No Code		Unable to run self-test or output codes [1]
Code not listed		Does not apply to vehicle being tested [1]

O—Key On, Engine Off
R—Engine running
C—Continuous Memory
1 Refer to system diagnostics

Year—1990
Model—Escort
Body VIN—1 and 2
Engine—1.9L Cylinder—4
Fuel System—Central Fuel Injection (CFI)
Engine VIN—9

ECA SERVICE CODES

Code		Explanation
11	O/R/C	System pass
12	R	Cannot control rpm during self-test high rpm check
13	R	Cannot control rpm during self-test low rpm check
13	O	DC motor movement not detected
13	C	DC motor did not follow dashpot
14	C	PIP circuit failure
15	O	ECA ROM test failure
15	C	ECA KAM test failure
16	R	Idle rpm high with ISC off
17	R	Idle rpm low with ISC off
18	R	SPOUT circuit open
18	C	IDM circuit failure/SPOUT circuit grounded
19	R	Rpm for EGR test not achieved
21	O/R	ECT sensor input out of test range
22	O/R/C	MAP sensor input out of test range
23	O/R/C	TP sensor input out of test range
24	O/R	ACT sensor input out of test range
31	R/C	PFE circuit is below minimum voltage
32	R/C	EPT circuit voltage low (PFE)
33	R/C	EGR valve opening (PFE) not detected
34	O	Defective PFE sensor
34	R/C	EPT sensor voltage high (PFE)
35	O/R/C	PFE circuit above maximum voltage
38	C	Idle track switch circuit open
41	R	HEGO circuit shows system lean
41	C	No HEGO switching detected, system lean
42	R	HEGO shows system rich
51	O/C	ECT sensor circuit open
53	O/C	TP sensor input exceeds test maximum
54	O/C	ACT sensor circuit open
55	R	Keypower circuit open
58	R	Idle tracking switch circuit closed
58	O	Idle tracking switch circuit open
61	O/C	ECT test sensor input below test minimum
63	O/C	TP sensor below. test minimum
64	O/C	ACT sensor input below test minimum
67	O/R	Neutral drive switch open. A/C input high

86754225

ECA SERVICE CODES

Code		Explanation
38	C	Idle track switch circuit open
41	R	EGO/HEGO circuit shows system lean
41	C	No EGO/HEGO switching detected, system lean
42	R	EGO/HEGO shows system rich
51	O/C	ECT sensor input exceeds test maximum
53	O/C	TP sensor input exceeds test maximum
54	O/C	ACT sensor input exceeds test maximum
55	R	Key power input to processor is open
58	R	Idle tracking switch circuit closed
58	O	Idle tracking switch circuit open
61	O/C	ECT test sensor input below test minimum
63	O/C	TP sensor below test minimum
64	O/C	ACT sensor input below test minimum
67	O/R	Neutral drive switch open. A/C input high
68	R	Idle tracking switch circuit open
68	O	Idle tracking switch closed
71	C	Idle tracking switch closed on pre-position
73	O	Insufficient TP change
84	O/R	EGR VAC regulator circuit failure
85	O/R	Canister purge circuit failure
87	O/R/C	Fuel pump primary circuit failure
93	O	TP sensor input low at max DC motor extension
95	O/C	Fuel pump secondary circuit failure
96	O/C	Fuel pump secondary circuit failure
98	R	Hard fault is present
99	R	EEC system has not learned to control idle
No Code		Unable to run self-test or output codes [1]
Code not listed		Does not apply to vehicle being tested [1]

O—Key On, Engine Off
R—Engine running
C—Continuous Memory
1 Refer to system diagnostics

86754224

ECA SERVICE CODES

Code		Explanation
31	O/R/C	PFE circuit is below minimum voltage
32	R/C	PFE circuit voltage low
33	R/C	EGR valve opening not detected
34	O	PFE sensor voltage out of range
34	R/C	EPT sensor voltage high (PFE)
35	O/R/C	PFE circuit above maximum voltage
41	R	HEGO circuit shows system lean
41	C	No HEGO switching detected, system lean
42	R	HEGO shows system rich
45	C	Coil 1 primary circuit failure
46	C	Coil 2 primary circuit failure
51	O/C	ECT sensor circuit open
53	O/C	TP sensor input exceeds test maximum
54	O/C	ACT sensor circuit open
56	O/R/C	MAF circuit above maximum voltage
61	O/C	ECT indicates circuit grounded
63	O/C	TP sensor below test minimum
64	O/C	ACT indicates circuit grounded
66	R/C	MAF circuit below minimum voltage
67	O/R	Neutral drive switch open
67	C	Clutch switch circuit failure
72	R	Insufficient MAF change during dynamic response test
73	O	Insufficient TP change
74	R	Brake ON/OFF circuit failure/not actuated during self-test
77	R	Brief WOT not sensed during self-test/operator error
79	O	A/C ON/defrost on during self-test
83	O	High speed electro drive fan circuit failure
84	O/R	EGR VAC regulator circuit failure
87	O/C	Fuel pump primary circuit failure
88	O	Electro drive fan circuit failure
95	O/C	Fuel pump secondary circuit failure
96	O/C	Fuel pump secondary circuit failure
98	R	Hard fault is present—FMEM mode
No Code		unable to run self-test or output codes[1]
Code not listed		does not apply to vehicle being tested[1]

O—Key On, Engine Off
R—Engine running
C—Continuous Memory

ECA SERVICE CODES

Code		Explanation
68	R	Idle tracking switch circuit open
68	O	Idle tracking switch closed
71	C	Idle tracking switch closed on pre-position
73	O	Insufficient TP change
84	O	EGR VAC regulator circuit failure
85	O/R	Canister purge circuit failure
87	O/R/C	Fuel pump primary circuit failure
93	O	TP sensor input low at max DC motor extension
95	O/C	Fuel pump circuit open—ECA to motor ground
96	O/C	Fuel pump circuit open—battery to ECA
98	R	Hard fault is present
99	R	EEC system has not learned to control idle
No Code		unable to run self-test or output codes[1]
Code not listed		does not apply to vehicle being tested[1]

O—Key On, Engine Off
R—Engine running
C—Continuous Memory

Year—1990
Model—Escort
Body VIN—4
Engine—1.9L MA Cylinder—4
Fuel System—Sequential Electronic Fuel (SEFI)
Engine VIN—9

ECA SERVICE CODES

Code		Explanation
11	O/R/C	System pass
12	R	Cannot control rpm during self-test high rpm check
13	R	Cannot control rpm during self-test low rpm check
14	C	PIP circuit failure
15	O	ECA ROM test failure
15	C	ECA KAM test failure
18	R	SAW circuit failure
18	C	IDM circuit failure/SPOUT circuit grounded
19	O	Failure in ECA internal voltage
19	C	CID circuit failure
21	O/R	ECT sensor input out of test range
23	O/R	TP sensor input out of test range
24	O/R	ACT sensor input out of test range
26	O/R	MAF sensor out of self-test range
29	C	Insufficient input from VSS

TEST MODES

Key On Engine Off (KOEO) Test

▶ See Figures 39, 40 and 41

1. Connect the scan tool to the self-test connectors. Make certain the test button is unlatched or up.
2. Start the engine and run it until normal operating temperature is reached.
3. Turn the engine **OFF** for 10 seconds.
4. Activate the test button on the STAR tester.
5. Turn the ignition switch **ON**, but do not start the engine.
6. The KOEO codes will be transmitted. Six to nine seconds after the last KOEO code, a single separator pulse will be transmitted. Six to nine seconds after this pulse, the codes from the Continuous Memory will be transmitted.
7. Record all service codes displayed. Do not depress the throttle during the test.

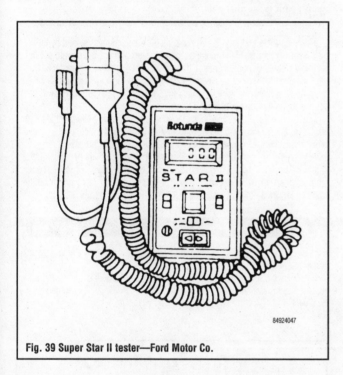

Fig. 39 Super Star II tester—Ford Motor Co.

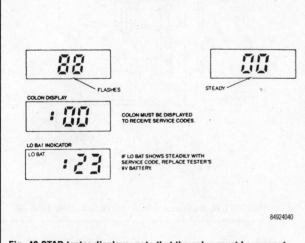

Fig. 40 STAR tester displays; note that the colon must be present before codes can be received

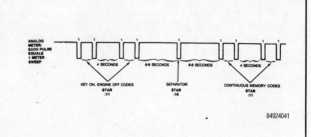

Fig. 41 Code transmission during KOEO test. Note that the continuous memory codes are transmitted after a pause and a separator pulse

Key On Engine Running (KOER) Test

▶ See Figures 39, 40 and 42

1. Make certain the self-test button is released or de-activated on the STAR tester.
2. Start the engine and run it at 2000 rpm for two minutes. This action warms up the oxygen sensor.
3. Turn the ignition switch **OFF** for 10 seconds.
4. Activate or latch the self-test button on the scan tool.
5. Start the engine. The engine identification code will be transmitted. This is a single digit number representing ½ the number of cylinders in a gasoline engine. On the STAR tester, this number may appear with a zero, such as 20 = 2. The code is used to confirm that the correct processor is installed and that the self-test has begun.
6. If the vehicle is equipped with a Brake On/Off (BOO) switch, the brake

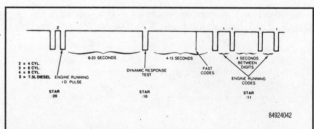

Fig. 42 Code transmission during KOER testing begins with the engine identification pulse and may include a dynamic response prompt

pedal must be depressed and released after the ID code is transmitted.
7. If the vehicle is equipped with a Power Steering Pressure Switch (PSPS), the steering wheel must be turned at least ½ turn and released within 2 seconds after the engine ID code is transmitted.
8. Certain Ford vehicles will display a Dynamic Response code 6–20 seconds after the engine ID code. This will appear as one pulse on a meter or as a 10 on the STAR tester. When this code appears, briefly take the engine to wide open throttle. This allows the system to test the throttle position, MAF and MAP sensors.
9. All relevant codes will be displayed and should be recorded. Remember that the codes refer only to faults present during this test cycle. Codes stored in Continuous Memory are not displayed in this test mode.
10. Do not depress the throttle during testing unless a dynamic response code is displayed.

Other Test Modes

CONTINUOUS MONITOR OR WIGGLE TEST

Once entered, this mode allows the operator to attempt to recreate intermittent faults by wiggling or tapping components, wiring or connectors. The test may be performed during either KOEO or KOER procedures. The test requires the use of either an analog voltmeter or a hand-held scan tool.

To enter the continuous monitor mode during KOEO testing, turn the ignition switch **ON**. Activate the test, wait 10 seconds, then deactivate and reactivate the test; the system will enter the continuous monitor mode. Tap, move or wiggle the harness, component or connector suspected of causing the problem; if a fault is detected, the code will store in the memory. When the fault occurs, the dash warning lamp will illuminate, the STAR tester will light a red indicator (and possibly beep) and the analog meter needle will sweep once.

To enter this mode in the KOER test:

1. Start the engine and run it at 2000 rpm for two minutes. This action warms up the oxygen sensor. 25

2. Turn the ignition switch **OFF** for 10 seconds.

3. Start the engine.

4. Activate the test, wait 10 seconds, then deactivate and reactivate the test; the system will enter the continuous monitor mode.

5. Tap, move or wiggle the harness, component or connector suspected of causing the problem; if a fault is detected, the code will store in the memory.

6. When the fault occurs, the dash warning lamp will illuminate, the STAR tester will light a red indicator (and possibly beep) and the analog meter needle will sweep once.

OUTPUT STATE CHECK

This testing mode allows the operator to energize and de-energize most of the outputs controlled by the EEC-IV system. Many of the outputs may be checked at the component by listening for a click or feeling the item move or engage by a hand placed on the case. To enter this check:

1. Enter the KOEO test mode.

2. When all codes have been transmitted, depress the accelerator all the way to the floor and release it.

3. The output actuators are now all ON. Depressing the throttle pedal to the floor again switches the all the actuator outputs OFF.

4. This test may be performed as often as necessary, switching between ON and OFF by depressing the throttle.

5. Exit the test by turning the ignition switch **OFF**, disconnecting the jumper at the diagnostic connector or releasing the test button on the scan tool.

Clearing Codes

CONTINUOUS MEMORY CODES

These codes are retained in memory for 40 warm-up cycles. To clear the codes for purposes of testing or confirming repair, perform the code reading procedure. When the fault codes begin to be displayed, de-activate the test either by disconnecting the jumper wire (if using a meter, MIL or message center) or by releasing the test button on the hand scanner. Stopping the test during code transmission will erase the Continuous Memory. Do not disconnect the negative battery cable to clear these codes; the Keep Alive memory will be cleared and a new code, 19, will be stored for loss of PCM power.

KEEP ALIVE MEMORY

The Keep Alive Memory (KAM) contains the adaptive factors used by the processor to compensate for component tolerances and wear. It should not be routinely cleared during diagnosis. If an emissions related part is replaced during repair, the KAM must be cleared. Failure to clear the KAM may cause severe driveability problems since the correction factor for the old component will be applied to the new component.

To clear the Keep Alive Memory, disconnect the negative battery cable for at least 5 minutes. After the memory is cleared and the battery reconnected, the vehicle must be driven at least 10 miles (16 km) so that the processor may relearn the needed correction factors. The distance to be driven depends on the engine and vehicle, but all drives should include steady-throttle cruise on open roads. Certain driveability problems may be noted during the drive because the adaptive factors are not yet functioning.

VACUUM DIAGRAMS

Following is a listing of vacuum diagrams for most of the engine and emissions package combinations covered by this manual. Because vacuum circuits will vary based on various engine and vehicle options, always refer first to the vehicle emission control information label, if present. Should the label be missing, or should the vehicle be equipped with a different engine from the car's

original equipment, refer to the diagrams below for the same or similar configuration.

If you wish to obtain a replacement emissions label, most manufacturers make the labels available for purchase. The labels can usually be ordered from a local dealer.

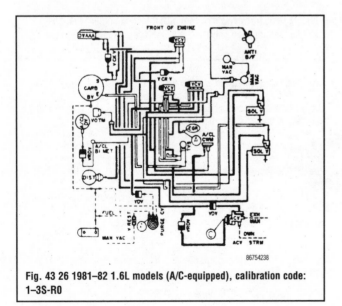

Fig. 43 26 1981–82 1.6L models (A/C-equipped), calibration code: 1–3S-R0

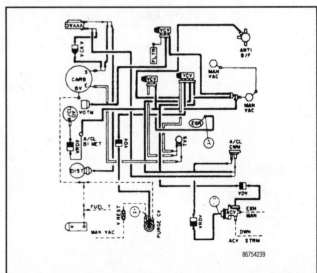

Fig. 44 1981–82 1.6L models (non-A/C), calibration code: 1–3S-R0

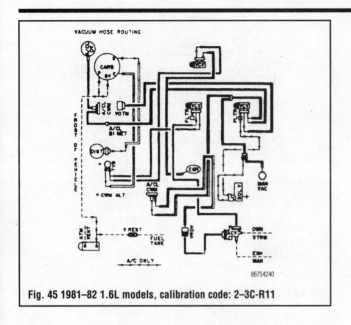

Fig. 45 1981–82 1.6L models, calibration code: 2–3C-R11

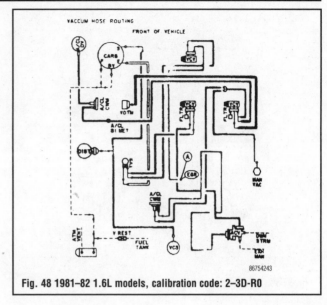

Fig. 48 1981–82 1.6L models, calibration code: 2–3D-R0

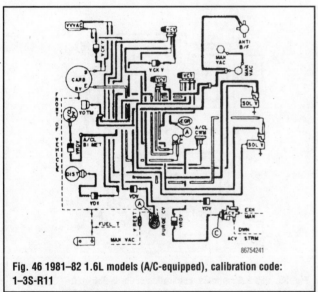

Fig. 46 1981–82 1.6L models (A/C-equipped), calibration code: 1–3S-R11

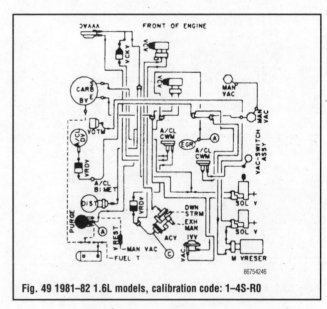

Fig. 49 1981–82 1.6L models, calibration code: 1–4S-R0

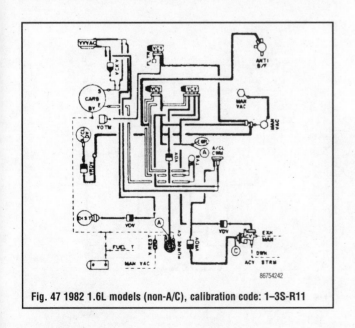

Fig. 47 1982 1.6L models (non-A/C), calibration code: 1–3S-R11

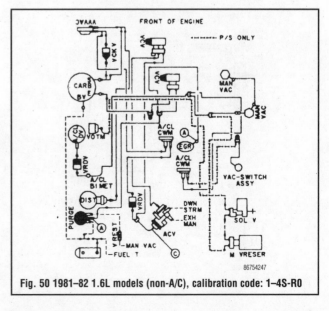

Fig. 50 1981–82 1.6L models (non-A/C), calibration code: 1–4S-R0

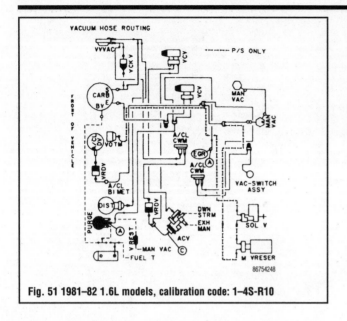

Fig. 51 1981–82 1.6L models, calibration code: 1–4S-R10

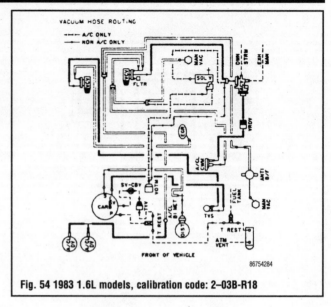

Fig. 54 1983 1.6L models, calibration code: 2–03B-R18

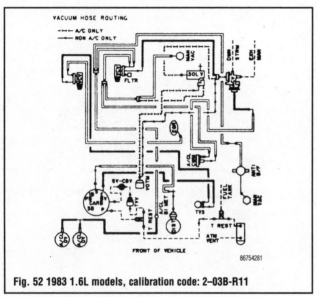

Fig. 52 1983 1.6L models, calibration code: 2–03B-R11

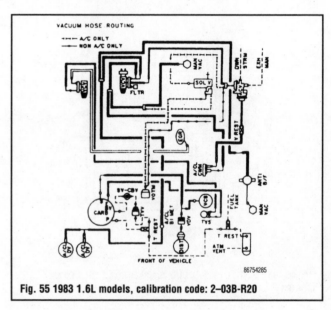

Fig. 55 1983 1.6L models, calibration code: 2–03B-R20

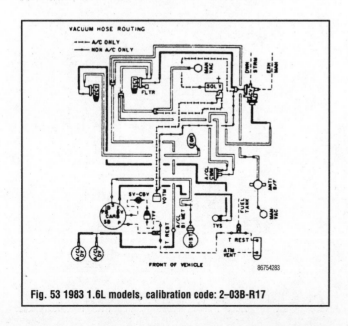

Fig. 53 1983 1.6L models, calibration code: 2–03B-R17

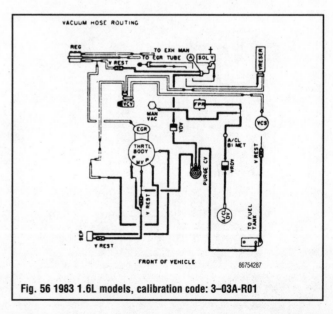

Fig. 56 1983 1.6L models, calibration code: 3–03A-R01

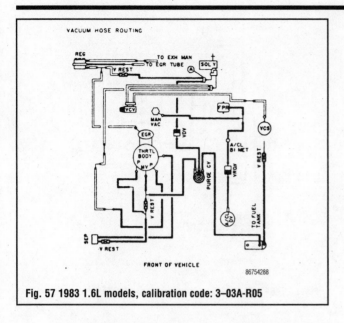

Fig. 57 1983 1.6L models, calibration code: 3–03A-R05

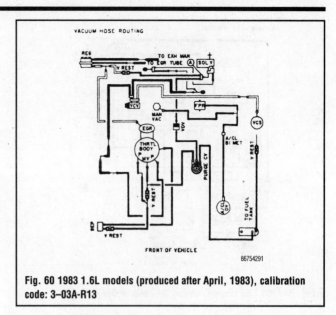

Fig. 60 1983 1.6L models (produced after April, 1983), calibration code: 3–03A-R13

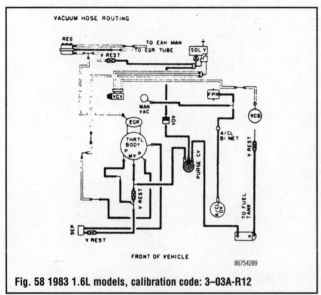

Fig. 58 1983 1.6L models, calibration code: 3–03A-R12

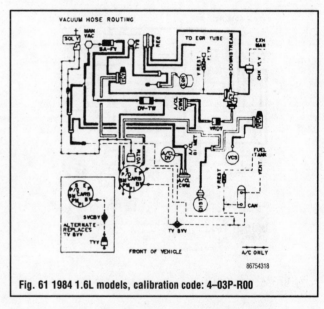

Fig. 61 1984 1.6L models, calibration code: 4–03P-R00

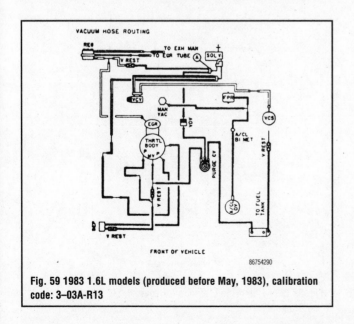

Fig. 59 1983 1.6L models (produced before May, 1983), calibration code: 3–03A-R13

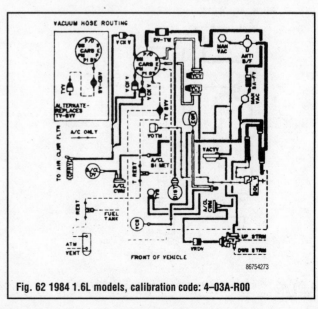

Fig. 62 1984 1.6L models, calibration code: 4–03A-R00

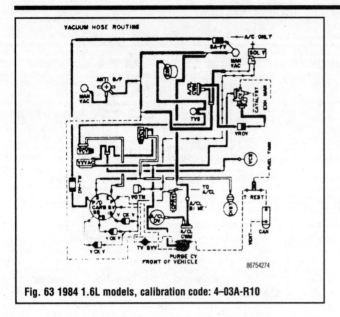

Fig. 63 1984 1.6L models, calibration code: 4–03A-R10

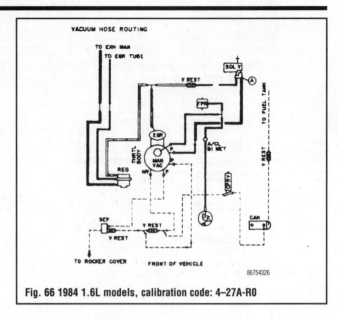

Fig. 66 1984 1.6L models, calibration code: 4–27A-R0

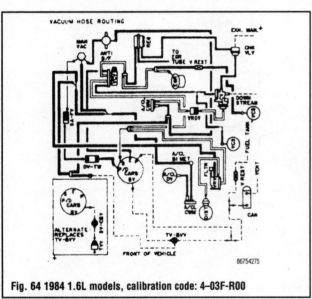

Fig. 64 1984 1.6L models, calibration code: 4–03F-R00

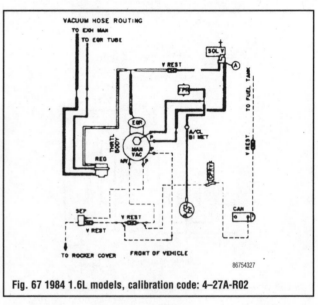

Fig. 67 1984 1.6L models, calibration code: 4–27A-R02

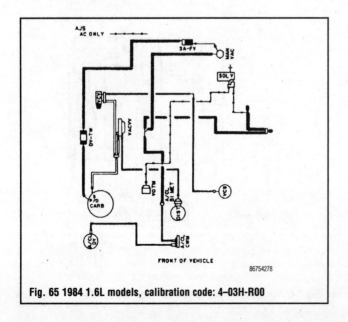

Fig. 65 1984 1.6L models, calibration code: 4–03H-R00

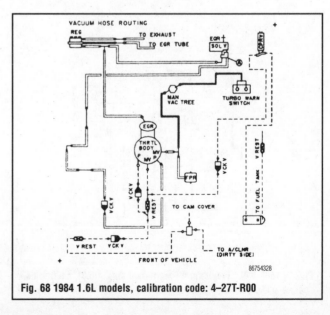

Fig. 68 1984 1.6L models, calibration code: 4–27T-R00

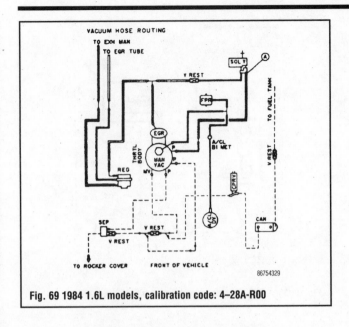

Fig. 69 1984 1.6L models, calibration code: 4–28A-R00

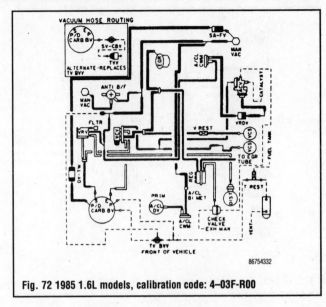

Fig. 72 1985 1.6L models, calibration code: 4–03F-R00

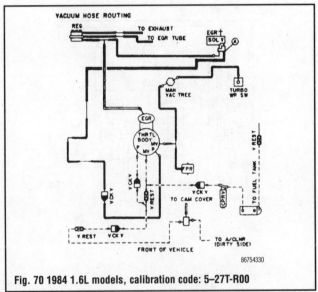

Fig. 70 1984 1.6L models, calibration code: 5–27T-R00

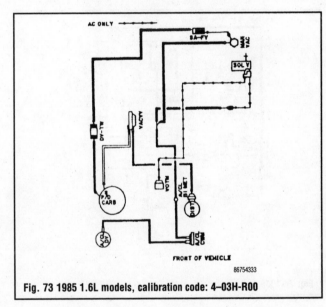

Fig. 73 1985 1.6L models, calibration code: 4–03H-R00

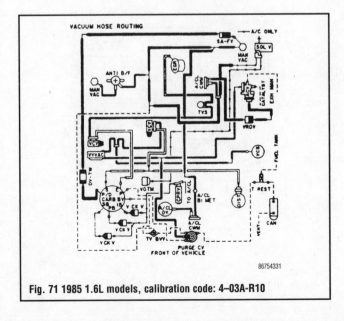

Fig. 71 1985 1.6L models, calibration code: 4–03A-R10

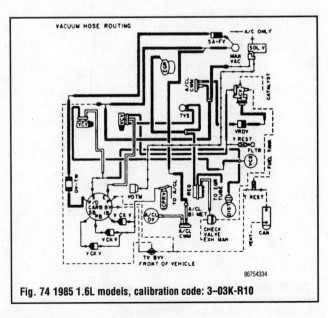

Fig. 74 1985 1.6L models, calibration code: 3–03K-R10

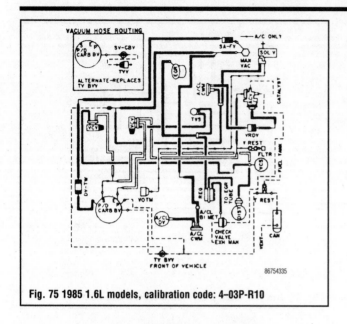

Fig. 75 1985 1.6L models, calibration code: 4–03P-R10

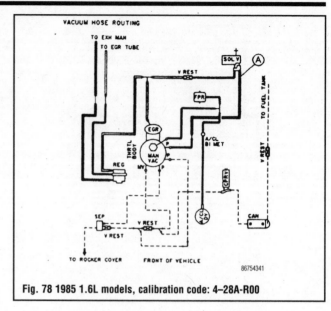

Fig. 78 1985 1.6L models, calibration code: 4–28A-R00

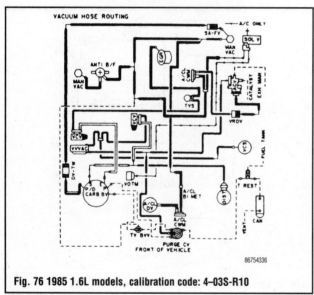

Fig. 76 1985 1.6L models, calibration code: 4–03S-R10

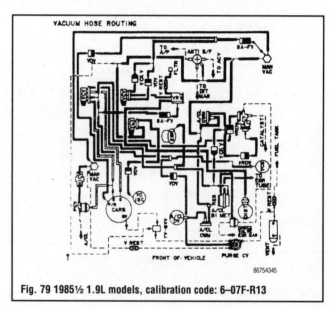

Fig. 79 1985½ 1.9L models, calibration code: 6–07F-R13

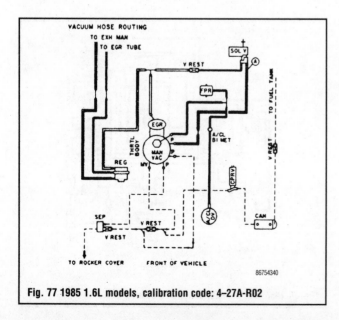

Fig. 77 1985 1.6L models, calibration code: 4–27A-R02

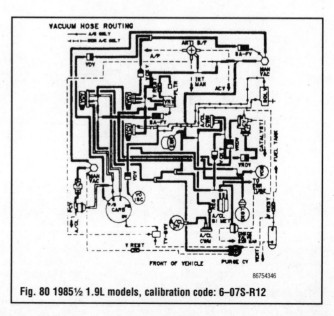

Fig. 80 1985½ 1.9L models, calibration code: 6–07S-R12

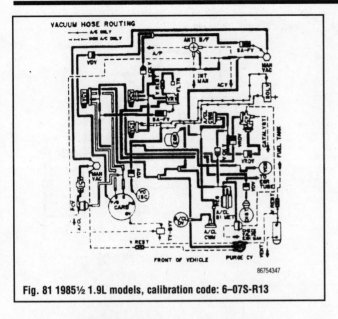

Fig. 81 1985½ 1.9L models, calibration code: 6–07S-R13

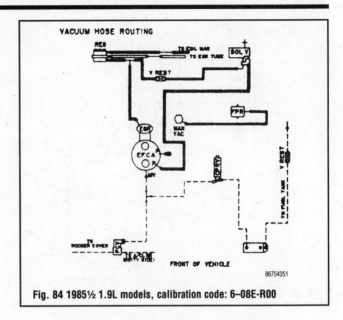

Fig. 84 1985½ 1.9L models, calibration code: 6–08E-R00

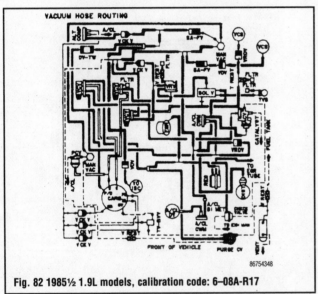

Fig. 82 1985½ 1.9L models, calibration code: 6–08A-R17

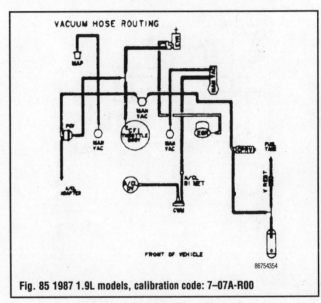

Fig. 85 1987 1.9L models, calibration code: 7–07A-R00

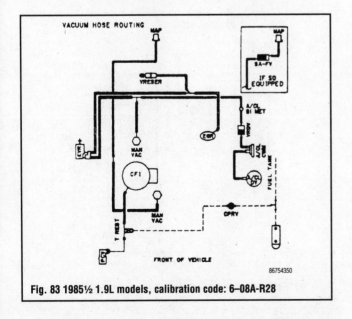

Fig. 83 1985½ 1.9L models, calibration code: 6–08A-R28

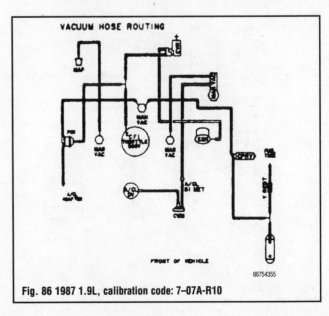

Fig. 86 1987 1.9L, calibration code: 7–07A-R10

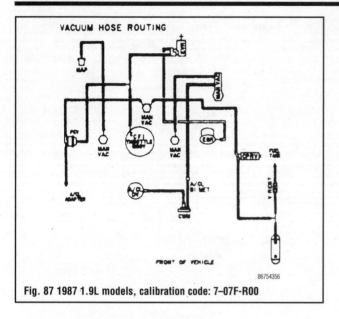

Fig. 87 1987 1.9L models, calibration code: 7–07F-R00

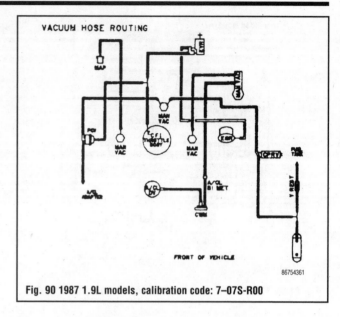

Fig. 90 1987 1.9L models, calibration code: 7–07S-R00

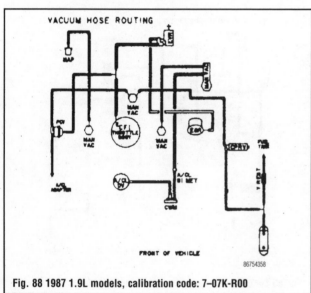

Fig. 88 1987 1.9L models, calibration code: 7–07K-R00

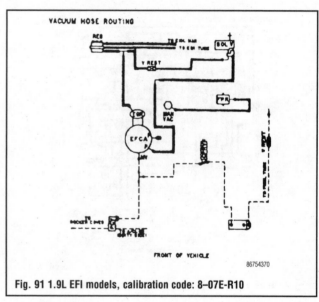

Fig. 91 1.9L EFI models, calibration code: 8–07E-R10

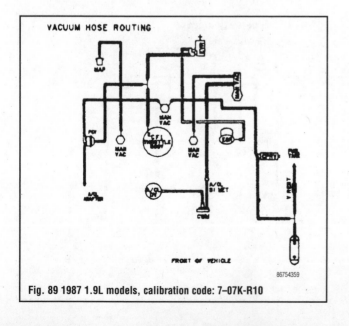

Fig. 89 1987 1.9L models, calibration code: 7–07K-R10

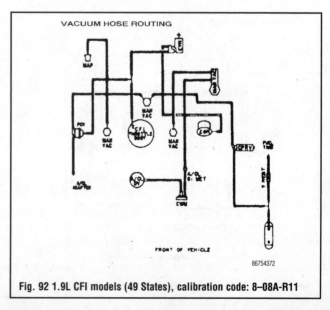

Fig. 92 1.9L CFI models (49 States), calibration code: 8–08A-R11

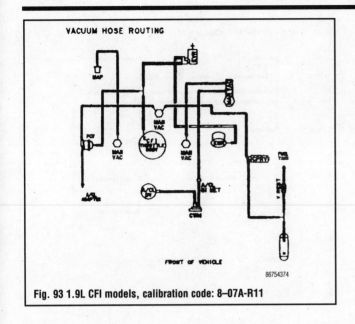

Fig. 93 1.9L CFI models, calibration code: 8-07A-R11

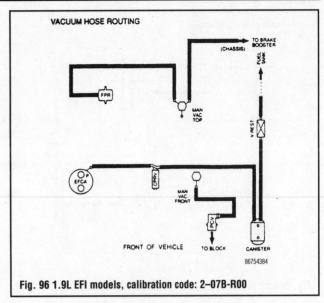

Fig. 96 1.9L EFI models, calibration code: 2-07B-R00

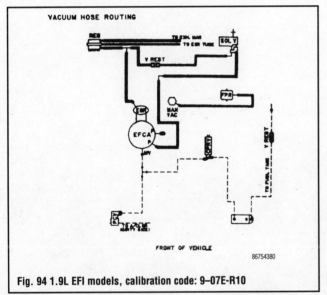

Fig. 94 1.9L EFI models, calibration code: 9-07E-R10

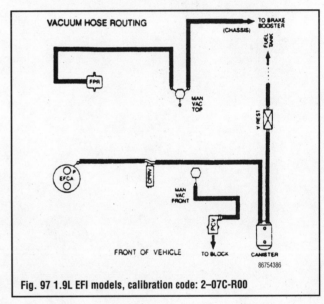

Fig. 97 1.9L EFI models, calibration code: 2-07C-R00

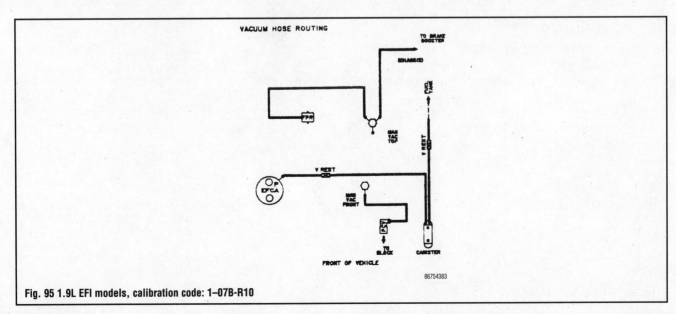

Fig. 95 1.9L EFI models, calibration code: 1-07B-R10

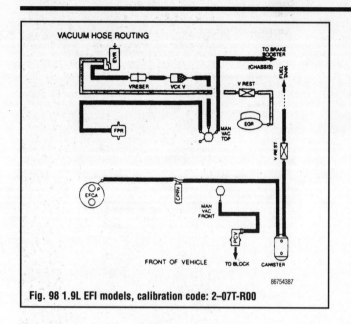

Fig. 98 1.9L EFI models, calibration code: 2–07T-R00

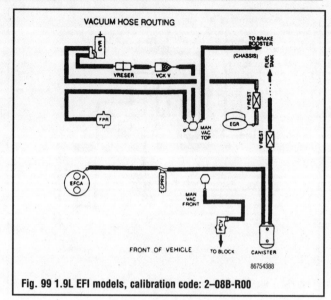

Fig. 99 1.9L EFI models, calibration code: 2–08B-R00

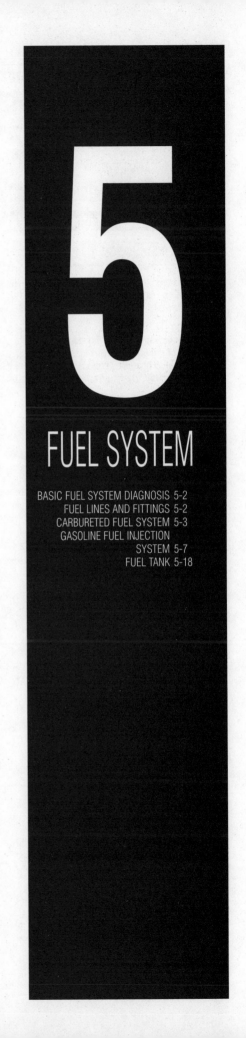

5

FUEL SYSTEM

BASIC FUEL SYSTEM DIAGNOSIS

When there is a problem starting or driving a vehicle, two of the most important checks involve the ignition and the fuel systems. The questions most mechanics attempt to answer first, "is there spark?" and "is there fuel?" will often lead to solving most basic problems. For ignition system diagnosis and testing, please refer to the information on engine electrical components and ignition systems found earlier in this manual. If the ignition system checks out (there is spark), then you must determine if the fuel system is operating properly (is there fuel?).

FUEL LINES AND FITTINGS

Quick-Connect Line Fittings

REMOVAL & INSTALLATION

The fuel system, depending on model year of the vehicle, may be equipped with push type connectors or spring lock couplings. When removing the fuel lines on these vehicles, it will be necessary to use Fuel Line Coupling Disconnect Tool D87L-9280-A or -B, or equivalent.

➡**Quick-Connect (push) type fittings must be disconnected using proper procedures or the fitting may be damaged. Two types of retainers are used on the push connect fittings. Line sizes of ⅜ in. and 5⁄16 in. use a hairpin clip retainer. ¼ in. line connectors use a Duck bill clip retainer.**

Push Connect (Steel) Fittings

▸ See Figures 1, 2, 3 and 4

1. Relieve the fuel system pressure.
2. Open the safety clip and fit tool T90T-9550-B (5⁄16 in.) or T90T-9550-C (⅜ in.) to the coupling so that the tool enters the female fitting.
3. Push the tool into the female fitting so that it releases the retaining fingers from the male tube end.
4. Pull the fittings apart and remove the tool.
5. Inspect the lines and fittings for damage.

To install:
6. Push the two ends of the fittings together until an audible click is heard.

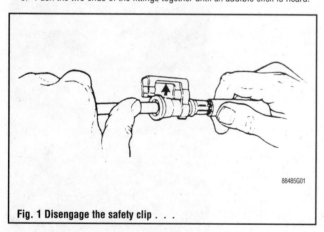

Fig. 1 Disengage the safety clip . . .

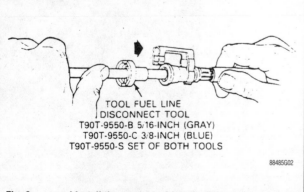

TOOL FUEL LINE
DISCONNECT TOOL
T90T-9550-B 5/16-INCH (GRAY)
T90T-9550-C 3/8-INCH (BLUE)
T90T-9550-S SET OF BOTH TOOLS

Fig. 2 . . . and install the correct tool into the fitting

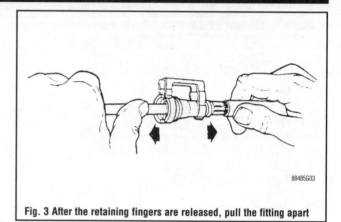

Fig. 3 After the retaining fingers are released, pull the fitting apart

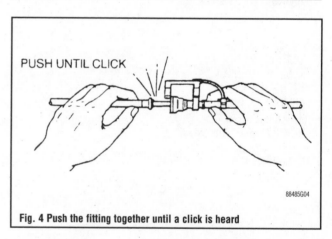

PUSH UNTIL CLICK

Fig. 4 Push the fitting together until a click is heard

7. Pull on the fitting to make sure that it is properly connected.
8. Lock the assembly with a safety clip, start the van and check for leaks

Spring Lock Couplings

▸ See Figure 5

If the fuel system is equipped with spring lock couplings, remove the retaining clip from the spring lock coupling by hand only. Do not use any sharp tool or screwdriver as it may damage the spring lock coupling.
1. Relieve the fuel system pressure.
2. Twist the fitting to free it from any adhesion at the O-ring seals.

➡**Inspect the condition of the O-ring seals and replace them with the correct parts if necessary.**

3. Fit Spring Lock Coupling Tool T81P-9623-G1 or G2 or their equivalent to the coupling.
4. Close the tool and push it into the open side of the cage to expand garter spring and release the female fitting.
5. After the garter spring is expanded, pull the fittings apart.
6. Remove the tool from the disconnected coupling.

To install:
7. Lubricate the O-rings with refrigerant oil and insert the white indicator ring into the cage of the male fitting.
8. Push the fitting together with a slight twisting motion until the white indicator ring pops free.

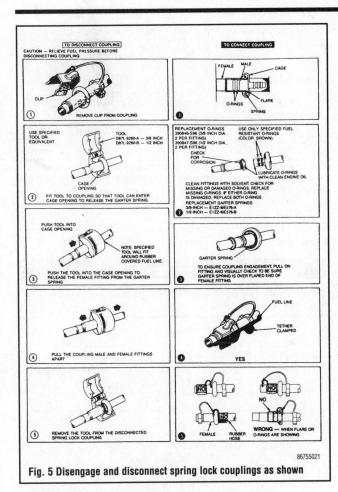

Fig. 5 Disengage and disconnect spring lock couplings as shown

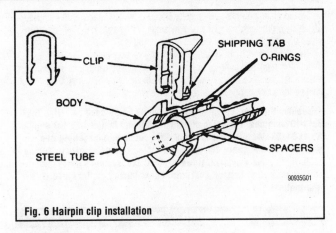

Fig. 6 Hairpin clip installation

Hairpin Clip

▶ See Figure 6

1. Clean all dirt and/or grease from the fittings. Spread the two clip legs about an $FR1/8in. each to disengage from the fitting and pull the clip outward from the fitting. Use finger pressure only, do not use any tools.

✳✳ CAUTION

Never smoke when working around gasoline! Avoid all sources of sparks or ignition. Gasoline vapors are EXTREMELY volatile!

2. Grasp the fittings and hose assembly and pull away from the steel line. Twist the fitting and hose assembly slightly while pulling, if necessary, when a sticking condition exists.
3. Inspect the hairpin clip for damage, replace the clip if necessary. Reinstall the clip in position on the fitting.
4. Inspect the fitting and inside of the connector to ensure freedom of dirt or obstruction. Install fitting into the connector and push together. A click will be heard when the hairpin snaps into proper connection. Pull on the line to insure full engagement.

Duck Bill Clip

▶ See Figure 7

1. A special tool is available for Ford for removing the retaining clip (Ford Tool No. T82L-957-AH). If the tool is not available, see Step 2. Align the slot on the push connector disconnect tool with either tab on the retaining clip. Pull the line from the connector.

✳✳ CAUTION

Never smoke when working around gasoline! Avoid all sources of sparks or ignition. Gasoline vapors are EXTREMELY volatile!

2. If the special clip tool is not available, use a pair of narrow 6 in. (152mm) locking pliers with a jaw width of 0.2 in. (5mm) or less. Align the jaws of the pliers with the openings of the fitting case and compress the part of the retaining clip that engages the case. Compressing the retaining clip will release the fitting which may be pulled from the connector. Both sides of the clip must be compressed at the same time to disengage.
3. Inspect the retaining clip, fitting end and connector. Replace the clip if any damage is apparent.
4. Push the line into the steel connector until a click is heard, indicating the clip is in place. Pull on the line to check engagement.

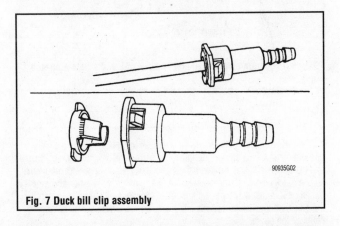

Fig. 7 Duck bill clip assembly

CARBURETED FUEL SYSTEM

Carbureted vehicles which employ the Motorcraft model 740 and 5740 carburetors utilize five basic metering systems to control engine operating conditions. These five basic metering systems are as follows:

- Choke system
- Idle system
- Main metering system
- Acceleration system
- Power enrichment system

The choke system is used for cold starting. It incorporates a bimetal spring and an electric heater for faster cold weather starts and improved driveability during warm-up.

The idle system is a separate and adjustable system for the correct air/fuel mixture at both idle and low speed operation.

The main metering system provides the necessary air/fuel mixture for normal driving speeds. A main metering system is provided for both primary and secondary stages of operation.

The accelerating system is operated from the primary stage throttle linkage. The system provides fuel to the primary stage during acceleration. Fuel is provided by a diaphragm pump located on the carburetor.

The power enrichment system consists of a vacuum operated power valve and airflow regulated pullover system for the secondary carburetor barrel. The system is used in conjunction with the main metering system to provide acceptable performance during mid and heavy acceleration.

➡**Besides the more common gasoline fueled 1.6L base and High Output (HO) engines, Ford also offered a methanol fueled 1.6L HO engine for 1984–85. With the exception of different carburetor jetting and alcohol-resistant seals, the methanol fueled vehicles utilize a comparable fuel delivery system. However, their fuel system service specifications may vary. Consult your local Ford/Mercury dealer for further information.**

Mechanical Fuel Pump

♦ **See Figure 8**

The fuel pump is bolted to the left rear side of the cylinder head. It is mechanically operated by an eccentric lobe on the camshaft. A pushrod between the eccentric lobe and the rocker arm drives the pump.

The pump cannot be disassembled for any type of service. If testing indicates it is not within performance specifications, the pump assembly must be replaced.

➡**The fuel pump has a rollover check valve in accordance with Federal Motor Vehicle Safety Standards (FMVSS). In the event of an accident in which the car rolls upside down, the valve is intended to prevent unwanted fuel spillage. When replacement of the fuel pump is necessary, the new pump must meet the same FMVSS requirement.**

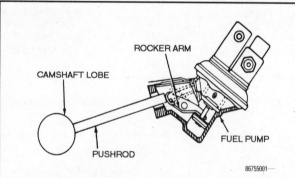

Fig. 8 A common mechanical fuel pump—1.6L and 1.9L carbureted engines

TESTING

The fuel pump can fail in two ways: it can fail to provide a sufficient volume of gasoline under the proper pressure to the carburetor, or it can develop an internal or external leak. An external leak will be evident; not so with an internal leak. A quick check for an internal leak is to remove the oil dipstick and examine the oil on it. A fuel pump with an internal leak will leak fuel into the oil pan. If the oil on the dipstick is very thin and smells of gas, a defective fuel pump could be the cause.

➡**If the engine is excessively hot, allow it to cool for approximately 20–30 minutes.**

Capacity (Volume) Test

1. Remove the carburetor air cleaner.
2. Wrap a shop rag around the fuel line and slowly disconnect the fuel line. Use an $FR11/16 in. backup wrench on the hex of the filter to prevent damage.
3. Connect a suitable rubber hose and clamp it to the fuel line.
4. Place a non-breakable 1 pint (473ml) minimum container at the end of the rubber hose.
5. Crank the engine 10 revolutions. If little or no fuel flows from the hose

during the 10th revolution, the fuel pump is inoperative. Replace the fuel pump.
6. If the fuel flow is adequate, proceed to the following pressure test.

Pressure Test

1. Connect a suitable pressure gauge, 0–15 psi (0–103 kPa), to the fuel filter end of the fuel line. No tee is required.
2. Start the engine and read the pressure after 10 seconds. The pressure should read 4.5–6.5 psi (31–45 kPa) with the fuel return line closed at the fuel filter.
3. Replace the fuel pump if the pressure is above or below specification.
4. Disconnect the fuel pump and connect fuel line to fuel filter. Use a backup wrench on the filter and tighten the fuel line to 15–18 ft. lbs. (20–24 Nm).

REMOVAL & INSTALLATION

♦ **See Figure 9**

✻ CAUTION

When working near the fuel system, do not smoke or have an open flame of any type nearby.

1. Disconnect the negative battery cable.
2. Loosen the threaded fuel line connection(s) a small amount. Do not remove lines at this time.
3. Loosen the mounting bolts approximately two turns. Apply force manually to loosen the fuel pump if gasket is stuck.
4. Rotate the engine until the fuel pump camshaft lobe is near its low position. The tension on the fuel pump will be greatly reduced at the low camshaft position.
5. Disconnect the fuel pump inlet and outlet lines.
6. Unfasten the fuel pump attaching bolts and remove the pump and gasket. Discard the old gasket and replace with a new one.
7. Measure the fuel pump pushrod length. It should be at least 2.36 in. (60mm) in length. Replace if it is out of specification.

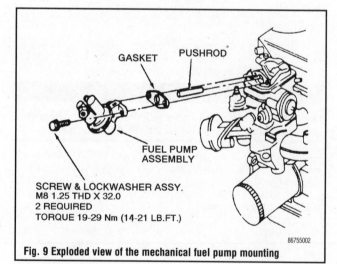

Fig. 9 Exploded view of the mechanical fuel pump mounting

To install:

8. Remove all fuel pump gasket material from the engine and the fuel pump if installing the original pump.
9. Install the attaching bolts into the fuel pump and install a new gasket.
10. Position the fuel pump on the mounting pad. Tighten the attaching bolts alternately and evenly and tighten to 11–19 ft. lbs. (15–25 Nm).
11. Install fuel lines to fuel pump. Start the threaded fitting by hand to avoid cross-threading. Tighten the outlet nut to 15–18 ft. lbs. (20–24 Nm).
12. Start the engine and inspect for fuel leaks.
13. Stop the engine and check all fuel pump fuel line connections for fuel leaks by running a finger under the connections. Check for oil leaks at the fuel pump mounting gasket.

Carburetor

ADJUSTMENTS

Motorcraft Models 740 and 5740

◆ **See Figures 10, 11 and 12**

Most carburetor adjustments are factory-set to reduce engine emissions and improve performance.

FAST IDLE

1. Place the transaxle in **P** or **N**.
2. Bring the engine to normal operating temperature.
3. Disconnect and plug the vacuum hose at the EGR and purge valves.
4. Identify the vacuum source to the air bypass section of the air supply control valve. If a vacuum hose is connected to the carburetor, disengage the hose and plug the hose at the air supply control valve.
5. Place the fast idle adjustment on the second step of the fast idle cam.
6. Run the engine until the cooling fan comes on.
7. While the cooling fan is on, check the fast idle rpm.
8. If adjustment is necessary, loosen the locknut and adjust to the specification on the under-hood decal.
9. Remove all plugs and reconnect the hoses to their original position.

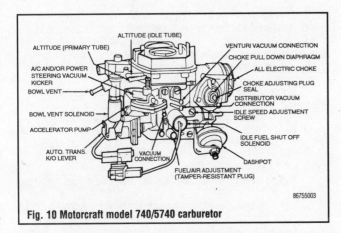

Fig. 10 Motorcraft model 740/5740 carburetor

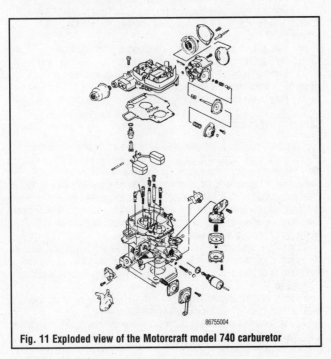

Fig. 11 Exploded view of the Motorcraft model 740 carburetor

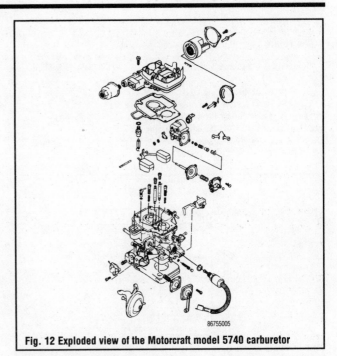

Fig. 12 Exploded view of the Motorcraft model 5740 carburetor

FAST IDLE CAM

1. Set the fast idle screw on the kickdown step of the cam against the shoulder of the top step.
2. Manually close the primary choke plate, and measure the distance between the downstream side of the choke plate and the air horn wall.
3. Adjust the right fork of the choke bimetal shaft, which engages the fast idle cam, by bending the fork up and down to obtain the required clearance.

DASHPOT

1. Set the throttle to the curb idle position.
2. Fully depress the dashpot stem.
3. Measure the distance between the stem and the throttle lever.
4. Adjust by loosening the locknut and turning the dashpot.

FLOAT LEVEL

◆ **See Figure 13**

1. Unfasten the screws which fasten the air horn to the main body of the carburetor.
2. Remove the air horn from the carburetor.
3. Hold the air horn upside down, at about a 45° angle with the air horn gasket in position.
4. Use the gauge supplied with the rebuilding kit to measure the clearance between the float toe and air horn casting.
5. Adjust, if necessary, by removing the float and bending the adjusting tang. Use care when handling the float.

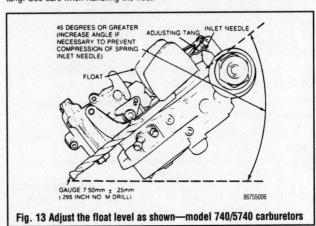

Fig. 13 Adjust the float level as shown—model 740/5740 carburetors

FLOAT DROP

▶ **See Figure 14**

1. Unfasten the screws which fasten the air horn to the main body of the carburetor.
2. Remove the air horn from the carburetor.
3. Hold the air horn in its normal installed position.
4. Measure the clearance from the gasket to the bottom of the float. This distance should be 1.38–2.00 in. (35–51mm).
5. Adjust, if necessary, by removing the float and bending the float drop adjusting tab.

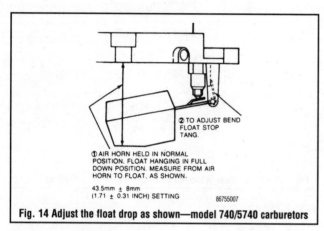

② TO ADJUST BEND FLOAT STOP TANG.

① AIR HORN HELD IN NORMAL POSITION. FLOAT HANGING IN FULL DOWN POSITION. MEASURE FROM AIR HORN TO FLOAT, AS SHOWN.

43.5mm ± 8mm
(1.71 ± 0.31 INCH) SETTING

86755007

Fig. 14 Adjust the float drop as shown—model 740/5740 carburetors

REMOVAL & INSTALLATION

> ✲✲ **CAUTION**
>
> **When working near the fuel system, do not smoke or have any open flame of any type nearby.**

Motorcraft Models 740 and 5740

1. Disconnect the negative battery cable.
2. Remove the air cleaner assembly.
3. Disconnect the throttle cable and speed control cable, if equipped.
4. Tag, then disconnect the bowl vent tube, altitude compensator tubes (idle, primary and secondary, if so equipped), air conditioning and/or power steering vacuum kicker (if so equipped).
5. Tag, then disconnect the EGR vacuum tube, venturi vacuum tube, distributor vacuum tube, Idle Speed Control (ISC) vacuum tube (if so equipped), choke pulldown motor vacuum tube, and fuel inlet line at filter.
6. Unplug the idle solenoid wire and choke cap terminal connectors.
7. Remove the automatic transaxle Throttle Valve (TV) linkage, if so equipped.
8. Remove the four carburetor flange mounting nuts, using Tool T74P-95–10-A or equivalent. Remove the Wide Open Throttle (WOT) A/C cut-out switch, if so equipped.
9. Remove the carburetor assembly from the manifold.

To install:

10. Clean all gasket surfaces. Replace any gasket(s) as necessary.
11. Position the carburetor on the spacer and install the WOT A/C cut-out switch and attaching nuts, if so equipped.

➡ **To prevent leakage, distortion or damage to the carburetor body flange, alternately tighten each nut to specifications.**

12. Install the automatic transaxle throttle valve (TV) linkage, if so equipped. Perform the TV adjustment.
13. Attach the choke cap and the idle solenoid terminal connectors.
14. Connect the fuel inlet line at the filter.
15. Reconnect: EGR vacuum tube, venturi vacuum tube, distributor vacuum tube, ISC vacuum tube (if so equipped), choke pulldown motor vacuum tube, and fuel inlet line at filter.

16. Reconnect: bowl vent tube, altitude compensator tubes (idle, primary and secondary if so equipped), air conditioning and/or power steering vacuum kicker (if so equipped).
17. Reconnect the throttle cable and speed control cable.
18. Connect the negative battery cable.
19. Start the engine and check for leaks. If any leaks are detected, shut off the engine immediately and correct the problem.
20. Install the air cleaner assembly.
21. Check and/or adjust the curb idle and fast idle speed as necessary.

OVERHAUL

Overhaul the carburetor in a clean, dust free area. Carefully disassembly the carburetor, referring often to the exploded views. Keep all similar and look-alike parts segregated during disassembly and cleaning to avoid accidental interchange during assembly. Make a note of all jet sizes.

➡ **To avoid damage to the carburetor or throttle plates, install carburetor legs on the base before disassembling or use an EGR spacer as a holding fixture. If legs are not available, install four bolts approximately 2¼ inch (57mm) long to the correct diameter, and eight nuts on the carburetor base.**

Disassembly

1. Remove the fuel filter.
2. Remove the six air horn screws and washers.
3. Carefully remove the air horn and invert it.
4. Remove the float hinge pin, float and needle, needle seat and gasket.
5. Remove the choke cap and housing shield. Unfasten the choke housing retaining screws and remove the housing, disengaging the primary choke link.
6. Remove the choke pulldown cover retaining screws and remove the cover and spring.
7. Remove the choke housing shaft nut and lockwasher. Pull the lever assembly outward. Carefully slide the diaphragm assembly out.
8. Remove the idle speed control assembly, if equipped.
9. Remove the accelerator pump retaining screws, pump cover, diaphragm and return spring. Remove the pump nozzle with a pair of needle nose pliers.
10. Using Tool T81P-9510-A or equivalent, remove the idle fuel shut-off solenoid and gasket.
11. Remove the power valve retaining screws, power valve cover, spring and diaphragm.
12. Remove the dashpot assembly, vacuum throttle kicker and/or Idle Speed Control (ISC), if equipped.
13. Remove the idle jet retainer clips and float bowl gasket.
14. Drill and remove the idle mixture plugs. Count and note the number of turns required to lightly seat the idle mixture screws. Remove the mixture screws and O-ring.
15. Note and remove the primary and secondary discharge nozzles.
16. Note and remove the primary and secondary idle jet holders and jets.
17. Remove the high speed air bleeds, main well tubes and main jets. This assembly is press fitted, but can usually be removed by hand.
18. Refer to the following cleaning and inspection procedure.

Cleaning and Inspection

When the carburetor is disassembled, wash all parts (except diaphragms, electric choke units. pump plunger, and any other plastic, leather, fiber, or rubber parts) in clean carburetor solvent. Do not leave parts in the solvent any longer than is necessary to sufficiently loosen the deposits. Excessive cleaning may remove the special finish from the float bowl and choke valve bodies, leaving these parts unfit for service. Rinse all parts in clean solvent and blow them dry with compressed air or allow them to air dry. Wipe clean all cork, plastic, leather, and fiber parts with a clean, lint free cloth.

Blow out all passages and jets with compressed air and be sure that there are no restrictions or blockages. Never use wire or similar tools to clean jets, fuel passages, or air bleeds. Clean all jets and valves separately to avoid accidental interchange.

Carefully examine all parts for wear or damage. If wear or damage is found, replace the defective parts. Especially inspect the following:

1. Check the float needle and seat for wear. If wear is found, replace the complete assembly.

2. Inspect the float hinge pin for wear and the float(s) for dents or distortion. Replace the float if fuel has leaked into it.

3. Check the throttle and choke shaft bores for wear or an out-of-round condition. Damage or wear to the throttle arm, shaft, shaft bore will often require replacement of the throttle body. These parts require a close 8 tolerance; wear may allow air leakage, which could affect starting and idling.

➡**Throttle shafts and bushings are usually not included in overhaul kits. They can be purchased separately.**

4. Inspect the idle mixture adjusting needles for burrs or grooves. Any such condition requires replacement of the needle, since you will not be able to obtain a satisfactory idle.

5. Test the accelerator pump check valves. They should pass air in one direction but not the other. Test for proper seating by blowing and sucking on the valve. Replace the valve if necessary. If the valve is satisfactory, wash the valve again to remove breath moisture.

6. Check the bowl cover for warped surfaces with a straightedge.

7. Closely inspect the valves and seats for wear and damage, replacing as necessary.

After cleaning and checking all components, re-assemble the carburetor, using new parts. When re-assembling, make sure that all screw and jets are tight in their seats, but do not overtighten, as the tips will be distorted. Tighten all screws gradually, in rotation. Do not tighten needle valves into their seat; uneven jetting will result. Always use new gaskets. Be sure to adjust the float level when re-assembling.

Assembly

1. Install the high speed air bleeds, main well tubes and main jets.
2. Install the primary and secondary idle jet holders and jets.

3. Install the primary and secondary discharge nozzles.

4. Lubricate and install the mixture screws and O-ring. Lightly seat the idle mixture screws, then back them out the number of turns recorded during disassembly.

5. Install the idle jet retainer clips and float bowl gasket.

6. Install the dashpot assembly, vacuum throttle kicker and/or ISC, if equipped.

7. Install the power valve spring, diaphragm, cover and retaining screws.

8. Install the idle fuel shut-off solenoid and gasket.

9. Install the accelerator pump diaphragm, return spring, cover and retaining screws.

10. Install the idle speed control assembly, if equipped.

11. Install the choke assembly. Pay attention to the following:
   a. Use caution not to roll or damage the Teflon® bushing.
   b. Both shaft arms must be to the left of the fast idle cam molded plastic steps.
   c. The cam spring tab must be located to the left of the fast idle cam lever.
   d. Check for freedom of movement of the choke mechanism.

12. Install a new air horn gasket.

13. Install the needle seat and gasket.

14. Install the inlet needle float and float hinge pin. Perform the float level and float drop adjustments.

15. Install the air horn assembly to the main body.

16. Install a new fuel filter.

17. Install the carburetor and perform the adjustments described earlier in this section.

18. After all adjustments are completed, install the idle mixture concealment plugs.

GASOLINE FUEL INJECTION SYSTEM

General Information

There are two types of fuel injection systems used on the Ford Escort and Mercury Lynx:
- Central Fuel Injection (CFI)
- Multi-port Fuel Injection (MFI)

CENTRAL FUEL INJECTION (CFI) SYSTEM

◆ **See Figures 15 and 16**

The Central Fuel Injection (CFI) system, used on 1987–90 1.9L CFI fuel injected engines, is classified as a single-point, pulse time, modulated injection

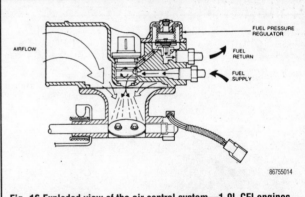

Fig. 16 Exploded view of the air control system—1.9L CFI engines

system. Fuel is metered into the intake air stream according to engine demand by a single solenoid injection valve, mounted in a throttle body on the intake manifold.

The fuel charging assembly is comprised of five individual components which perform the air/fuel metering function to the engine. The throttle body assembly mounts to the conventional carburetor pad of the intake manifold and provides for packaging of:
- Air control is through a single butterfly vane mounted to the throttle body.
- Fuel injector nozzles an electro-mechanical device which meters and atomizes the fuel delivered to the engine.
- Fuel pressure regulator maintains the fuel supply pressure upon engine and fuel pump shut down.
- Fuel pressure diagnostic valve
- Cold engine speed control.
- Throttle position sensor used by the computer Electronic Engine Control (EEC) module to determine the operating modes (closed throttle, part throttle and wide open throttle).

The system is supplied with fuel, by an in-tank mounted low pressure electric fuel pump. After being filtered, the fuel is sent to the fuel charging assembly

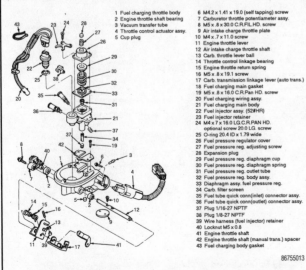

1 Fuel charging throttle body
2 Engine throttle shaft bearing
3 Vacuum transfer tube
4 Throttle control actuator assy.
5 Cup plug
6 M4.2 x 1.41 x 19.0 (self tapping) screw
7 Carburetor throttle potentiameter assy.
8 M5 x .8 x 30.0 C.R.FIL.HD. screw
9 Air intake charge throttle plate
10 M4 x .7 x 11.0 screw
11 Engine throttle lever
12 Air intake charge throttle shaft
13 Carb. throttle lever ball
14 Throttle control linkage bearing
15 Engine throttle return spring
16 M5 x .8 x 19.1 screw
17 Carb. transmission linkage lever (auto trans.)
18 Fuel charging main gasket
19 M5 x .8 x 16.0 C.R.Pan HD. screw
20 Fuel charging wiring assy.
21 Fuel charging main body
22 Fuel injector assy. (52#HR)
23 Fuel injector retainer
24 M4 x 7 x 16.0 LG.C.R.PAN HD. optional screw 20.0 LG. screw
25 O-ring 20.4 ID x 1.79 wide
26 Fuel pressure regulator cover
27 Fuel pressure reg. adjusting screw
28 Expansion plug
29 Fuel pressure reg. diaphragm cup
30 Fuel pressure reg. diaphragm spring
31 Fuel pressure reg. outlet tube
32 Fuel pressure reg. body assy.
33 Diaphragm assy. fuel pressure reg.
34 Carb. filter screen
35 Fuel tube quick conn(inlet) connector assy.
36 Fuel tube quick conn(outlet) connector assy.
37 Plug 1/16-27 NPTF
38 Plug 1/8-27 NPTF
39 Wire harness (fuel injector) retainer
40 Locknut M5 x 0.8
41 Engine throttle shaft
42 Engine throttle shaft (manual trans.) spacer
43 Fuel charging body gasket

86755013

Fig. 15 Exploded view of the fuel injection system—1.9L CFI engines

injector fuel cavity and then to the regulator where the fuel delivery pressure is maintained at a nominal value of 14.5 psi (100 kPa). Excess fuel is returned to the fuel tank by a steel fuel return line.

The electrical system also incorporates an inertia switch. In the event of a collision, the electrical contacts in the inertia switch will open and the fuel pump will automatically shut OFF (even if the engine continues to operate).

✻✻ CAUTION

If the inertia switch is tripped, never reset the switch without first inspecting the fuel system for leaks.

MULTI-PORT FUEL INJECTION (MFI)

➡Ford Motor Co. also refers to this system as Electronic Fuel Injection (EFI).

The Multi-port Fuel Injection (MFI) system is classified as a multi-point, pulse time, mass airflow fuel injection system. Fuel is metered into the intake air stream in accordance with engine demand through four injectors mounted on a tuned intake manifold.

The MFI system can be sub-divided into four distinct categories:

- Fuel Delivery
- Air Induction
- Sensors
- Electronic Control Unit

1.6L MFI Engine

➧ See Figure 17

The Multi-port Fuel Injection (MFI) system, used on the 1.6L MFI engine, utilizes a fuel tank with a different design than those on CFI vehicles, along with a fuel sender mounted pick-up tube, and an externally mounted high pressure electrical fuel pump. The fuel sender and pick-up tube rest in an internal pump cavity inside the fuel tank, allowing satisfactory pump operation during extreme vehicle maneuvers.

The electrical system has a fuel pump control relay controlled by the Electronic Engine Control (EEC) module. This provides power to the fuel pump under various operating conditions. The system pressure is controlled by a pressure regulator on the engine.

The electrical system also incorporates an inertia switch. In the event of a collision, the electrical contacts in the inertia switch will open and the fuel pump will automatically shut off (even if the engine continues to operate).

✻✻ CAUTION

If the inertia switch is tripped, never reset the switch without first inspecting the fuel system for leaks.

1986–90 1.9L MFI Engine

➧ See Figure 18

The Multi-port Fuel Injection (MFI) system, used on 1986–90 1.9L MFI engines, supplies the engine with its air/fuel mixture by metering fuel into the intake air stream according to engine demand, through four injectors mounted on a tuned intake manifold.

An on-board Electronic Engine Control (EEC) computer accepts electronic input signals from various engine sensors to compute the required fuel flow rate necessary to maintain a predetermined air/fuel ratio throughout all engine operating ranges.

The fuel charging manifold assembly incorporates four electrically actuated fuel injectors directly above each of the engine's intake ports. Each injector, when energized, sprays a metered quantity of fuel into the intake air stream.

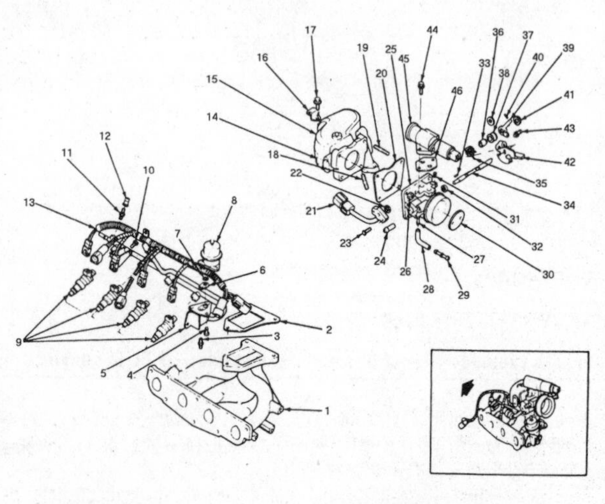

1 Intake lower manifold
2 Intake manifold upper gasket
3 1/4 flareless x 1/8 external pipe connector
4 M5 x .8 x 10 socket head screw
5 Fuel injection fuel supply manifold assembly
6 Fuel pressure regulator gasket
7 5/16 x .070 "O"ring seal
8 Fuel pressure regulator assembly
9 Fuel injector assembly
10 M8 x 1.25 x 20 HEX flange head bolt
11 Fuel pressure relief valve assembly
12 Fuel pressure relief cap
13 Fuel charging wiring harness
14 Carburetor identification decal
15 Intake upper manifold
16 Wiring harness retainer
17 M8 x 1.25 x 30 HEX flange head bolt
18 M6 x 1.0 x 1.0 x 40 stud
19 M8 x 1.25 x 1.25 x 47.5 stud
20 Air intake charge to intake manifold gasket
21 Throttle position potentiometer
22 Carburetor throttle shaft bushing
23 Screw and washer assembly M4 x 22
24 Emission inlet tube
25 Air intake charge throttle body
26 M8 x 1.25 nut
27 Tube
28 Vacuum hose
29 Connector
30 Air intake charge throttle plate
31 M4 x .7 x 8 screw
32 Throttle control shaft seal
33 Spring coiled 1/16 x .42 pin
34 Shaft
35 Throttle return spring
36 Accelerator pump over travel spring bushing
37 Throttle control linkage bearing
38 Throttle control torsion spring (MTX only) spacer
39 Carburetor transmission linkage lever
40 M5 x .8 x 16.25 slot head screw
41 Carburetor throttle shaft spacer
42 Carburetor throttle lever
43 Carburetor throttle lever ball
44 M6 x 1.0 x 20 HEX flange head bolt
45 Throttle air bypass valve assembly
46 Air bypass valve gasket

86755010

Fig. 17 Exploded view of the fuel injection system—1.6L MFI engines

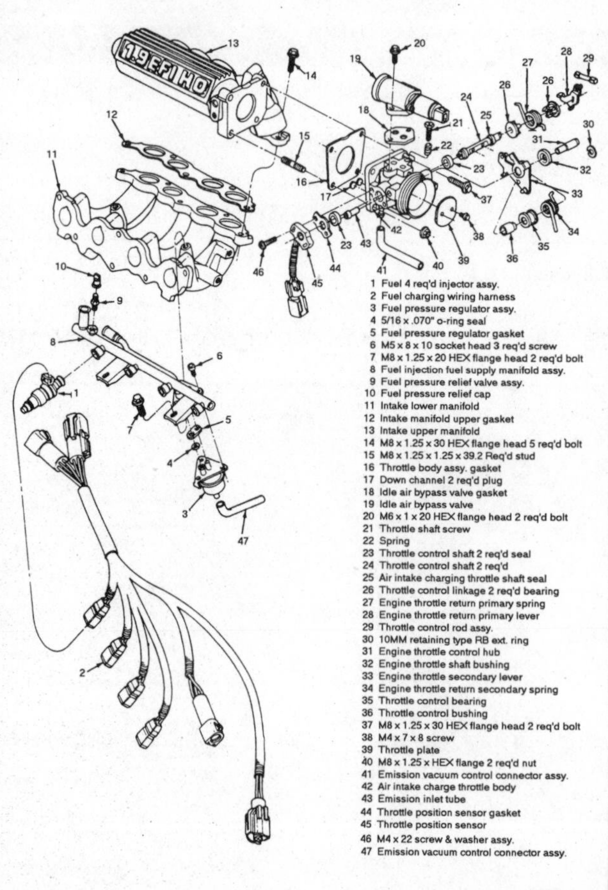

1 Fuel 4 req'd injector assy.
2 Fuel charging wiring harness
3 Fuel pressure regulator assy.
4 5/16 x .070" o-ring seal
5 Fuel pressure regulator gasket
6 M5 x 8 x 10 socket head 3 req'd screw
7 M8 x 1.25 x 20 HEX flange head 2 req'd bolt
8 Fuel injection fuel supply manifold assy.
9 Fuel pressure relief valve assy.
10 Fuel pressure relief cap
11 Intake lower manifold
12 Intake manifold upper gasket
13 Intake upper manifold
14 M8 x 1.25 x 30 HEX flange head 5 req'd bolt
15 M8 x 1.25 x 1.25 x 39.2 Req'd stud
16 Throttle body assy. gasket
17 Down channel 2 req'd plug
18 Idle air bypass valve gasket
19 Idle air bypass valve
20 M6 x 1 x 20 HEX flange head 2 req'd bolt
21 Throttle shaft screw
22 Spring
23 Throttle control shaft 2 req'd seal
24 Throttle control shaft 2 req'd
25 Air intake charging throttle shaft seal
26 Throttle control linkage 2 req'd bearing
27 Engine throttle return primary spring
28 Engine throttle return primary lever
29 Throttle control rod assy.
30 10MM retaining type RB ext. ring
31 Engine throttle control hub
32 Engine throttle shaft bushing
33 Engine throttle secondary lever
34 Engine throttle return secondary spring
35 Throttle control bearing
36 Throttle control bushing
37 M8 x 1.25 x 30 HEX flange head 2 req'd bolt
38 M4 x 7 x 8 screw
39 Throttle plate
40 M8 x 1.25 x HEX flange 2 req'd nut
41 Emission vacuum control connector assy.
42 Air intake charge throttle body
43 Emission inlet tube
44 Throttle position sensor gasket
45 Throttle position sensor
46 M4 x 22 screw & washer assy.
47 Emission vacuum control connector assy.

86755012

Fig. 18 Exploded view of the fuel injection system—1986–90 1.9L MFI engines

The system pressure is controlled by a pressure regulator connected in series with the fuel injectors. It is positioned downstream from the injectors. Excess fuel (not used by the engine) passes through the regulator and returns to the fuel tank through a fuel return line.

The fuel pump, used on 1986–90 1.9L MFI engine, is located at the rear of the vehicle in front of the fuel tank.

Service Precautions

Safety is the most important factor when performing not only fuel system maintenance but any type of maintenance. Failure to conduct maintenance and repairs in a safe manner may result in serious personal injury or death. Maintenance and testing of the vehicle's fuel system components can be accomplished safely and effectively by adhering to the following rules and guidelines.

• To avoid the possibility of fire and personal injury, always disconnect the negative battery cable unless the repair or test procedure requires that battery voltage be applied.

• Always relieve the fuel system pressure prior to disconnecting any fitting, fuel line connection or fuel system component (fuel injector, fuel rail, pressure regulator, etc.). Exercise extreme caution whenever relieving fuel system pressure to avoid exposing skin, face and eyes to fuel spray. Be advised that fuel under pressure may penetrate the skin or any part of the body that it contacts.

• Always place a shop towel or cloth around the fitting or connection prior to loosening to absorb any excess fuel due to spillage. Ensure that all fuel spillage (should it occur) is quickly removed from engine surfaces. Ensure that all fuel soaked cloths or towels are deposited into a suitable waste container.

• Always keep a dry chemical (Class B) fire extinguisher near the work area.

• Do not allow fuel spray or fuel vapors to come into contact with a spark or open flame.

• Always use a backup wrench when loosing and tightening fuel line connection fittings. This will prevent unnecessary stress and torsion to fuel line piping. Always follow the proper torque specifications.

• Always replace worn fuel fitting O-rings with new. Do not substitute fuel hose or equivalent, where fuel pipe is installed.

Relieving Fuel System Pressure

MFI AND CFI ENGINES

▶ See Figure 19

✳✳ WARNING

The fuel system will remain pressurized for long periods of time after the engine is shut off. This pressure must be relieved before servicing the fuel system. A fuel diagnostic valve is provided for this purpose.

1. Locate the fuel diagnostic valve (pressure relief valve) on the fuel rail assembly.
2. Remove the air cleaner assembly.

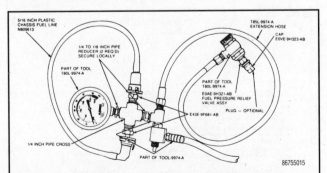

5/16 INCH PLASTIC
CHASSIS FUEL LINE
N809613

1/4 TO 1/8 INCH PIPE
REDUCER (2 REQ'D)
SECURE LOCALLY

PART OF TOOL
T80L-9974-A

PART OF TOOL
T80L-9974-A

1/4 INCH PIPE CROSS

PART OF TOOL-9974-A

T85L-9974-A
EXTENSION HOSE
CAP
E0VE-9H323-AB

E0AE-9H321-AB
FUEL PRESSURE RELIEF
VALVE ASSY

PLUG - OPTIONAL

E43E-9F681-AB

86755015

Fig. 19 A special tool, such as part no. T80L-9974-A, is recommended to properly relieve fuel system pressure

➡ **Always place a shop towel or cloth around the fitting or connection prior to loosening, in order to absorb any excess fuel due to spillage.**

3. Attach a pressure gauge tool (T80L-9974-A or equivalent) to the fuel diagnostic valve.
4. Operate the tool according to the manufacturer's instructions to relieve the fuel system pressure.

Alternate Method

1. Locate the inertia switch in the luggage compartment, then disconnect its electrical lead.
2. Crank the engine for a minimum of 15 seconds to reduce the pressure in the fuel system.

Electric Fuel Pump

The fuel pump used on 1.6L MFI engines is an externally mounted high pressure electrical fuel pump. The fuel tank has an internal pump cavity in which the fuel sender and pick-up tube rest.

The fuel pump used on 1986–90 vehicles equipped with 1.9L MFI engines is externally mounted; it is located at the rear of the vehicle in front of the fuel tank.

On 1987–90 vehicles equipped with the 1.9L CFI engine the fuel pump is located inside the fuel tank.

TESTING

1.6L MFI Engine

ELECTRICAL CIRCUIT

1. Ensure that the fuel tank contains a supply of fuel adequate for this procedure.
2. Make certain the ignition switch is **OFF**.
3. Check for signs of fuel leakage at all fittings and lines.
4. Disconnect the electrical connector just forward of the fuel pump inlet.
5. Attach a voltmeter to the wiring harness connector. Observe the voltmeter reading, when the ignition key is turned to the **ON** position. The voltage should rise to battery voltage and return to zero (0) volt after approximately one second.
6. If the voltage is not as specified, check the inertia switch for an open circuit. The switch may need to be reset.
7. Connector an ohmmeter to the pump wiring harness connector. If no continuity is present, check directly at the pump terminals.
8. If no continuity is present across the terminals, then replace the fuel pump.

PUMP OPERATION

1. Relieve the fuel system pressure.
2. Disconnect the fuel return line at the fuel rail. Try to avoid fuel spillage.
3. Connect a hose from the fuel return fitting to a calibrated container, at least 1 quart (0.95 L) minimum.
4. Attach the pressure gauge to the fuel diagnostic valve on the fuel rail.
5. Disconnect the electrical connector to the electric fuel pump, located just forward of the pump outlet.
6. Connect auxiliary wiring harness (jumpers) from a fully charged 12 volts battery to the electrical connector to the fuel pump. Energize the fuel pump for 10 seconds. Check the fuel pressure while energized.
7. If there is no pressure, check for proper polarity made at the wiring harness. Also, check the connections to the fuel pump. Correct, if necessary.

   a. The gauge should indicate a reading between 35–45 psi (241–310 kPa).

   b. Check that the fuel flow is a minimum of 7.5 ounces (221 ml.) in 10 seconds and fuel pressure remains at a minimum of 30 psi (207 kPa) immediately after shutdown.

   c. If these conditions are met, the pump is operating properly.

   d. If pressure is met, but fuel flow quantity is not within specification, check for a blocked fuel filter or fuel line. If fuel flow is still not correct, replace the fuel pump.

   e. If both pressure and flow conditions are met, but pressure will not maintain after shutdown, check for a leaking regulator or injectors. If both check okay, replace the fuel pump.

1986–87 1.9L MFI Engine

ELECTRICAL CIRCUIT

♦ See Figure 20

1. Ensure that the fuel tank contains a supply of fuel adequate for this procedure.
2. Make certain the ignition switch is **OFF**.
3. Check for signs of fuel leakage at all fittings and lines.
4. Locate the inertia switch in the luggage compartment.
5. Disconnect the electrical connector from the inertia switch and connect an ohmmeter to one of the leads at the wiring harness. Check for continuity between either of the wires and ground.
6. If continuity is not present at either wire, the fuel tank must be removed from the vehicle and continuity must be checked between the wiring harness and the switch leads.
7. If the leads check okay, check for continuity across the pump terminals.
8. If no continuity is present across terminals, then replace the fuel pump and sender assembly.

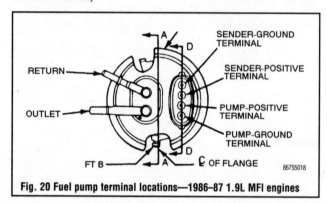

Fig. 20 Fuel pump terminal locations—1986–87 1.9L MFI engines

9. If continuity is present across the pump terminals, check the ground circuit or the connections to the pump form the body connector.
10. Reconnect the inertia switch. Attach a voltmeter to the wiring harness on the pump side of the switch. (This would be the side which did indicate continuity.)
11. Observe the voltmeter reading, when the ignition key is turn to the **ON** position. The voltmeter should read over 10 volts for one second and then return to zero (0).
12. If the voltage is not as specified, check the inertia switch for an open circuit. The switch may need to be reset. If okay, check the electrical circuit to find fault.

PUMP OPERATION

♦ See Figure 21

This test requires the use of a pressure gauge tool (T80L-9974-A or equivalent), which is attached to the diagnostic pressure tap fitting (fuel diagnostic valve). It also requires that the fuel system relay be modified, using one of the following relays: E3EB-9345-BA, CA, DA or E3TF-9345-AA.

1. Relieve the fuel system pressure.
2. Disconnect the fuel return line at the fuel rail. Try to avoid fuel spillage.
3. Connect a hose from the fuel return fitting to a calibrated container, at least 1 quart (0.95 L) minimum.
4. Attach the pressure gauge to the fuel diagnostic valve on the fuel rail.
5. Locate the fuel pump relay (left side of instrument panel, near the EEC-IV module) and remove it. The ground lead should be brought outside the vehicle and located nearby.
   a. Using the appropriate relay indicated above, modify the relay case by drilling a ⅛ in. (3mm) hole and cutting the skirt as indicated.
   b. Add 1618 gauge jumper wire between pins 2 and 4 (refer to the accompanying illustration).
   c. Add 8 ft. (2.4m) of flexible wire through the hole in the case to point B, as shown. Add a ground to the end of the added wire.

➡The leads should be soldered in place and as close to the base as possible, to permit insertion of the relay into socket with minimum interference.

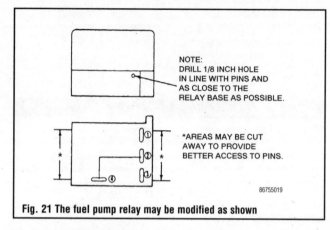

Fig. 21 The fuel pump relay may be modified as shown

6. Energize the fuel pump for 10 seconds by attaching a jumper to close the ground lead from the relay. Check the fuel pressure while energized. If there is no pressure, check that there is voltage pass the inertia switch. Correct, if necessary.
   a. The gauge should indicate a reading of 35–45 psi (241–310 kPa).
   b. Check that the fuel flow is a minimum of 7.5 ounces (221ml) in 10 seconds and fuel pressure remains at a minimum of 30 psi (207 kPa) immediately after shutdown.
   c. If these conditions are met, the pump is operating properly.
   d. If both pressure and flow conditions are met, but pressure will not maintain after shutdown, check for a leaking regulator or injectors. If both check okay, replace the fuel pump.
7. After testing, replace the modified fuel pump relay with the original relay.

1987–90 MFI and CFI Engines

♦ See Figures 22, 23, 24 and 25

Generally, any faults related to the electric fuel pump will result in a loss or reduction of fuel flow volume and/or pressure. The following diagnostic procedures will help determine if the electric fuel pump is functioning properly.

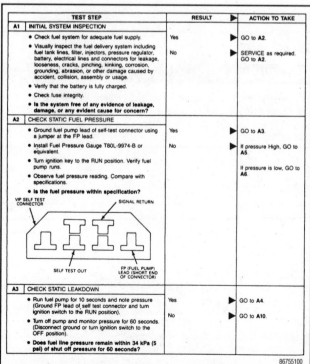

Fig. 22 Fuel pump diagnostic flow chart—1988–90 1.9L MFI and CFI engines

TEST STEP		RESULT	▶	ACTION TO TAKE
A4	CHECK VEHICLE UNDER LOAD CONDITIONS			
	• Remove and block vacuum line to pressure regulator.	Yes	▶	Fuel system is OK. DISCONNECT all test connections. RECONNECT vacuum line to regulator.
	• Run vehicle at idle and then increase engine speed to 2000 RPM or more in short bursts.			
	• Does fuel system pressure remain within chart limits? NOTE: Operating vehicle under load (road test) should give same results.	No	▶	GO to A12.
A5	CHECK FUEL PRESSURE			
	• Disconnect return line at fuel pressure regulator. Connect outlet of regulator to appropriate receptacle to catch return fuel.	Yes	▶	CHECK return fuel line for restrictions. SERVICE as required. REPEAT A2. GO to A3.
	• Turn on fuel pump (ground FP lead and turn ignition to the ON position) and monitor pressure.			
	• Is fuel pressure within chart limits?	No	▶	SERVICE or REPLACE fuel regulator as required. REPEAT A2. GO to A3.
A6	CHECK FUEL PUMP OPERATION			
	• Turn on fuel pump (ground FP lead and turn ignition to the RUN position).	Yes	▶	GO to A9.
	• Raise vehicle on hoist and use stethoscope to listen at fuel tank to monitor fuel pump noise, or listen at filler neck for fuel pump sound.	No	▶	GO to A7.
	• Is fuel pump running?			
A7	CHECK INERTIA SWITCH AND FUEL PUMP GROUND CONNECTOR			
	• Check if inertia switch is tripped.	Yes	▶	GO to A8.
	• Check fuel pump ground connection in vehicle.	No	▶	SERVICE switch or ground connection as required. REPEAT A2 and GO to A3.
	• Is inertia switch and ground connection OK?			

86755101

Fig. 23 Fuel pump diagnostic flow chart (continued)—1988–90 1.9L MFI and CFI engines

TEST STEP		RESULT	▶	ACTION TO TAKE
A8	CHECK VOLTAGE AT FUEL PUMP			
	• Check for continuity through fuel pump to ground by connecting meter to pump power wire lead as close to pump as possible.	Yes	▶	REPLACE fuel pump. REPEAT A2. If pressure OK GO to A3. If pressure not OK CHECK fuel pump connector for oversize connectors or other sources of open electrical circuit. SERVICE as required. REPEAT A3.
	• Check voltage as close to fuel pump as possible (turn on pump as outlined in A6).			
	• Is voltage within 0.5 Volts of battery voltage and is there continuity through pump?	No	▶	If voltage not present, CHECK fuel pump relay, EEC relay, and wiring for problem. If no ground, CHECK connection at fuel tank, etc. SERVICE as required. REPEAT A2 and A3.
A9	CHECK FUEL PRESSURE REGULATOR			
	• Replace fuel filter (if not replaced previously) and recheck pressure as in A2. If pressure not OK, continue. If pressure OK, go to A3.	Yes	▶	SERVICE or REPLACE regulator as required. REPEAT A2 and A3.
	• Open return line at pressure regulator. Attach return fitting from regulator to suitable container to catch gasoline.	No	▶	RECHECK systems for pressure restrictions. SERVICE as required. If no problem found, REPLACE fuel pump. GO to A2 and A3.
	• Turn on fuel pump as in A2.			
	• Is fuel being returned from regulator with low pressure in system?			
A10	CHECK FUEL PRESSURE FOR LEAKS			
	• Open return line at pressure regulator and attach suitable container to catch return fuel. Line should be clear to observe fuel flow.	Yes	▶	REPLACE regulator. REPEAT A2 and A3. If OK, GO to A4. If not OK, REPEAT A2 and follow procedure.
	• Run fuel pump as in A2.			
	• Turn off fuel pump by removing ground from self test connector or turning ignition to the OFF position.	No	▶	GO to A11.
	• Observe fuel return flow from regulator and system pressure when pump is off.			
	• Is there return flow when pump is turned off and system pressure is dropping?			

86755102

Fig. 24 Fuel pump diagnostic flow chart (continued)—1988–90 1.9L MFI and CFI engines

➥**Exercise care when disconnecting fuel lines or when installing gauges, to avoid fuel spillage.**

Unless otherwise stated, turn the fuel pump off at the conclusion of each step, by disconnecting the jumper or by turning the ignition switch **OFF**.

Normal fuel pressure specifications are as follows:
• 1987–90 1.9L CFI engines: 13–17 psi (90–117 kPa)
• 1988–90 1.9L MFI engines: 35–45 psi (241–310 kPa)

TEST STEP		RESULT	▶	ACTION TO TAKE
A11	CHECK FUEL PUMP CHECK VALVE			
	• Open pressure line from fuel pump and attach pressure gauge to line and block line to allow pressure build up.	Yes	▶	CHECK injectors for leakage or regulator for internal leakage. SERVICE as required. Fuel pump check valve is OK. GO to A4.
	• Operate pump momentarily as in A2 and bring pressure to about system pressure.			
	• Observe fuel pressure for one minute.			
	• Does pressure remain within 34 kPa (5 psi) of starting pressure over one minute period?	No	▶	CHECK lines and fittings from pump to rail for leakage, if none found REPLACE pump assembly. REPEAT A2. When OK go to A4.
A12	CHECK FUEL FILTER FOR RESTRICTIONS			
	• Replace fuel filter (if not previously replaced during this procedure) and repeat test A5.	Yes	▶	System is OK. DISCONNECT all test connections and RECONNECT all loosened or removed parts and lines.
	• Does system pressure remain within chart limits?	No	▶	CHECK pressure lines for kinks or restrictions. CHECK at fuel pump for low voltage. CHECK for wrong size injectors (too large). If no problem found, REPLACE pump and REPEAT A4. If problem found, SERVICE as required. REPEAT A4.

86755103

Fig. 25 Fuel pump diagnostic flow chart (continued)—1988–90 1.9L MFI and CFI engines

REMOVAL & INSTALLATION

1.6L and 1.9L MFI Engines

▶ **See Figure 26**

1. Properly relieve the fuel system pressure.
2. Raise the vehicle and support it with safety stands.
3. Unfasten bolt **A** (refer to the accompanying illustration) until the assembly can be removed from its mounting bracket.
4. Remove the parking brake cable from the clip on the pump.
5. Unplug the electrical connector and disengage the pump outlet fitting at point **C** (refer to the accompanying illustration).
6. Disconnect the pump outlet fitting at point **B** (refer to the accompanying illustration).

⚙ **CAUTION**

Drain the fuel tank or raise the end of the fuel line above the fuel level to avoid siphoning action.

7. Remove the fuel pump.

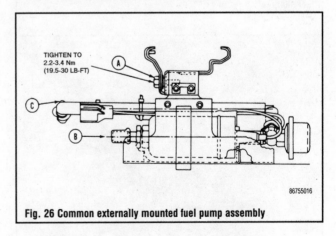

TIGHTEN TO 2.2–3.4 Nm (19.5–30 LB-FT)

86755016

Fig. 26 Common externally mounted fuel pump assembly

To install:
8. Attach the fuel pump to the fuel tank support bracket. Tighten the mounting bolt to 19.5–30 inch lbs. (2.2–3.4 Nm).
9. Attach the parking brake cable to its retaining clip on the pump.
10. Attach the fuel lines to the pump.
11. Lower the vehicle.

12. Attach a fuel pressure gauge to the fitting on the fuel rail.
13. Turn the ignition key **ON** and **OFF** in 2-second intervals until the fuel pressure reads at least 35 psi (241 kPa).
14. Check for leaks at the pump and the fuel lines.
15. Remove the gauge, start the engine and recheck for leaks.

1.9L CFI Engines

▶ See Figures 27, 28 and 29

1. Properly relieve the fuel system pressure.
2. Remove the fuel from the tank by using a pump or siphon.
3. Raise and safely support the rear of the vehicle using jackstands.
4. Remove the fuel tank.
5. Using an appropriate fuel tank sender wrench, unfasten the fuel pump locking ring.
6. Remove the fuel pump and bracket.
7. Remove the gasket seal and discard it.

To install:

8. Clean the pump mounting flange and seal ring groove.
9. Coat the new gasket seal with a long life lubricant.
10. Install the fuel pump assembly. Make sure the locating keys are in the keyways and that seal remains in position.
11. Install and fasten the pump locking ring.
12. Install the fuel tank in the vehicle.
13. Fill the fuel tank and check for leaks.
14. Start the vehicle and check for proper pump operation and leaks.

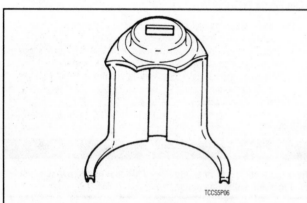

TCCS5P06

Fig. 27 A special tool is usually available to remove or install the fuel pump locking cam

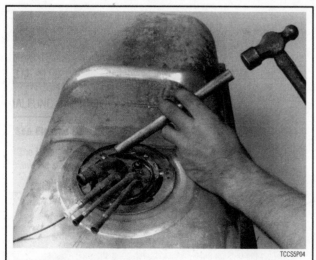

TCCS5P04

Fig. 28 A brass drift and a hammer can be used to loosen the fuel pump locking cam

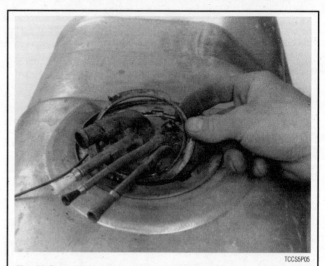

TCCS5P05

Fig. 29 Once the locking cam is released, it can be removed to free the fuel pump

Throttle Body

REMOVAL & INSTALLATION

1.6L and 1.9L MFI Engines

1. Properly relieve the fuel system pressure.
2. Disconnect the negative battery cable.
3. Disconnect the air cleaner outlet tube.
4. Unplug the electrical connections from the throttle body.
5. Unfasten the four throttle body mounting bolts.
6. Disconnect the vacuum hose from the throttle body.
7. Discoonect the throttle cable and if equipped, the speed control cable.
8. Remove the throttle bracket.
9. Carefully separate the throttle body from the upper intake manifold.
10. Remove the throttle body-to-intake manifold gasket and discard.

➡ **If scraping is necessary to remove any gasket residue, be careful not to damage the gasket mating surfaces.**

11. Clean the gasket mating surfaces.

To install:

12. Place the throttle body into position and install the mounting bolts. Tighten the bolts to 15–22 ft. lbs. (20–30 Nm).
13. Install the throttle bracket and tighten the retaining nuts to 12–15 ft. lbs. (1620 Nm).
14. Attach all electrical connections and the vacuum lines.
15. Attach the air cleaner outlet tube. Tighten the tube clamp to 12–20 inch lbs. (1.4–2.3 Nm).

1.9L CFI Engine

▶ See Figures 30 thru 37

1. Properly relieve the fuel system pressure.
2. Disconnect the negative battery cable.
3. Remove the air cleaner assembly
4. If equipped, remove the air tube clamp at the fuel charging assembly air inlet.
5. Disconnect the throttle cable, and also the transaxle Throttle Valve (TV) lever on automatic transaxle vehicles (if equipped).
6. Label, then unplug the electrical connector at the Idle Speed Control (ISC), Throttle Position (TP) sensor and fuel injector.
7. Disengage the fuel inlet and outlet connections, and PCV vacuum line at the fuel charging assembly.
8. Remove the three fuel charging assembly retaining fasteners and remove the fuel charging assembly.
9. Remove the mounting gasket from the intake manifold.

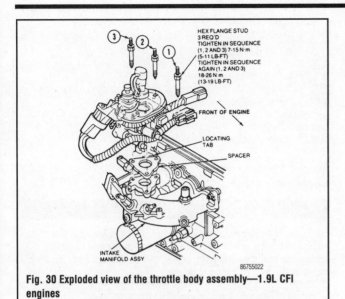

Fig. 30 Exploded view of the throttle body assembly—1.9L CFI engines

Fig. 33 Detach the fuel inlet hose from the throttle body

Fig. 31 Unplug all electrical connectors prior to throttle body removal

Fig. 34 Remove all retaining clips and disengage the throttle linkage

Fig. 32 Remove the fuel inlet coupling retainer to allow disconnection of the line

Fig. 35 Remove the three mounting bolts from the throttle body

Fig. 36 Remove the throttle body assembly and set it in a clean location

Fig. 37 Ensure that the mounting surface is clean prior to mounting the throttle body

To install:

10. Clean the mounting surface and position a new gasket on the intake manifold.

11. Position the fuel charging assembly on the intake manifold. Install the retaining nuts and tighten to specifications. Refer to the accompanying illustration.

12. Attach all electrical connectors, fuel and vacuum lines.

13. Connect the throttle cable, and TV cable, if equipped.

14. Start the engine and check for leaks. If any are detected, turn off the engine immediately and correct the leak(s).

15. Install the air cleaner assembly.

16. If equipped, attach the air tube clamp to the fuel charging assembly air inlet.

Fuel Injectors

REMOVAL & INSTALLATION

1.9L CFI Engines

1. Unplug the electrical connector from the injector.
2. Unfasten the injector retaining screw and remove the retainer.
3. Remove the injector and the lower O-ring. Discard the O-ring.

To install:

4. Lubricate a new O-ring with a small amount of clean engine oil.
5. Install the O-ring on the injector.
6. Lubricate the throttle body O-ring seat and the exterior of the injector O-ring ring with a small amount of clean engine oil.
7. Install the injector by centering and applying a steady downward pressure with a slight rotational force.
8. Install the injector retainer and screw(s). Tighten the screw(s) to 28–32 inch lbs. (3.2–3.6 Nm).
9. Attach the injector electrical connector.

1.6L and 1.9L MFI Engines

▶ See Figures 38 and 39

> **✳✳ CAUTION**
>
> **Fuel injection systems remain under pressure, even after the engine has been turned OFF. The fuel system pressure must be relieved before disconnecting any fuel lines. Failure to do so may result in fire and/or personal injury.**

1. Relieve the fuel system pressure.
2. Disconnect the negative battery cable.

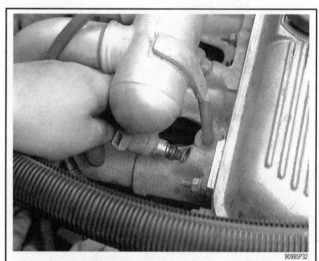

Fig. 38 Grasp the fuel injector's body and pull up while gently rocking the fuel injector from side-to-side

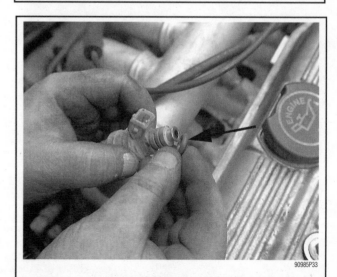

Fig. 39 Remove and discard the fuel injector O-rings

3. Disconnect fuel supply and return lines using the proper tool for spring lock coupling removal.

4. Unplug the fuel injector electrical connectors.

5. Remove the two fuel injection supply manifold (fuel rail) retaining bolts.

6. Carefully disengage the fuel injection supply manifold from the fuel injectors.

7. Disconnect the vacuum line from the fuel pressure regulator and set the fuel injection supply manifold aside.

8. Grasp the fuel injector's body and pull up while gently rocking the fuel injector from side to side.

9. Once removed, inspect the fuel injector end caps and washers for signs of deterioration. Replace as required.

10. Remove the O-rings and discard. If an O-ring or end cap is missing, look in the intake manifold for the missing part.

To install:

11. Install two new O-rings onto each injector and apply a small amount of clean engine oil to the O-rings.

12. Install the fuel injectors using a light twisting, pushing motion into the intake manifold.

13. Carefully position the fuel injection supply manifold on top of the fuel injectors. Push the fuel injection supply manifold down onto the injectors to fully seat the O-rings.

14. Install the two fuel injection supply manifold retaining bolts and tighten to 15–22 ft. lbs. (20–30 Nm).

15. Connect the fuel supply and return lines making sure the spring lock couplings are fully engaged and that the fuel tube clips are properly installed.

16. Connect the vacuum line to the fuel pressure regulator.

17. Attach the fuel injector electrical harness connectors.

18. Connect the negative battery cable and turn the ignition to the **ON** position to allow the fuel pump to pressurize the system.

19. Check for any fuel leaks. If any are found, immediately turn the ignition switch to the **OFF** position and disconnect the negative battery cable. Correct any leaks found.

20. Connect the fuel injector wiring harness.

21. Connect the negative battery cable.

22. Run the engine at idle for 2 minutes, then turn the engine **OFF** and check for fuel leaks and proper operation.

TESTING

CFI Engines

▶ **See Figure 40**

1. Remove the air cleaner assembly
2. Have an assistant crank the engine.
3. Observe the fuel injector and ensure that it is evenly spraying fuel.

4. If the injector spray is not even, or the injector is dripping or leaking, replace the injector.

5. If the injector is not spraying fuel, unplug the electrical connector from the injector.

6. Attach a noid light to the injector electrical harness and have an assistant crank the engine.

7. If the noid light operates, replace the injector.

8. If the noid light does not operate, check the injector wiring harness for damage and repair as necessary. If the noid light still does not operate, check the Throttle Position (TP) sensor and its circuit.

9. Measure the resistance of the injector by probing one terminal with the positive lead of an ohmmeter (or multimeter set to check resistance) and the other terminal with the meter's negative lead.

10. Resistance should be 12–16 ohms at 68°F (20°C).

11. If the resistance is not within specification, the fuel injector may be faulty.

12. If resistance is within specification, install a noid light and check for injector pulse from the PCM while cranking the engine.

13. If injector pulse is present check for proper fuel pressure.

MFI Engines

▶ **See Figures 41, 42 and 43**

1. Start the car and let the engine idle.
2. Connect a tachometer to the engine.
3. Disconnect each injector one at a time and note the rpm drop. All the readings should be similar.
4. If the rpm does not drop after unplugging an injector there could be a problem with that injector.
5. Connect and operate a fuel injection tester according to the manufacturers instructions.
6. Check that the leakage and flow is within specifications according to the tool manufacturer.
7. If the leakage and flow is not within specifications, replace the injector(s).

➡**Do not connect a test light to the injector harness as this may cause damage to the Powertrain Control Module (PCM).**

8. Disconnect the engine wiring harness from the injector.

➡**This may require removing the upper intake manifold or other engine components.**

9. Measure the resistance of the injector by probing one terminal with the positive lead of an ohmmeter (or multimeter set to check resistance) and the other terminal with the meter's negative lead.

10. Resistance should be between 12–16 ohms at 68°F (20°C).

11. If the resistance is not within specification, the fuel injector may be faulty.

Fig. 40 Measure the fuel injector's resistance by probing its two terminals with the leads of an ohmmeter

Fig. 41 Fuel injector testers can be purchased or sometimes rented

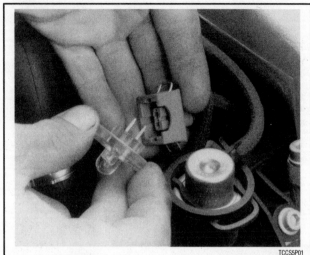

Fig. 42 A noid light can be attached to the fuel injector harness in order to test for injector pulse

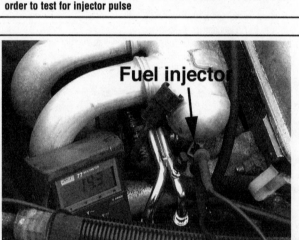

Fuel injector

Fig. 43 Measure fuel injector's resistance by probing one terminal with the positive lead of an ohmmeter and the other terminal with the negative lead

12. If resistance is within specification, install a noid light and check for injector pulse from the PCM while cranking the engine.

13. If injector pulse is present check for proper fuel pressure.

Fuel Charging Assembly (Fuel Rail)

REMOVAL & INSTALLATION

1.9L Engine

▶ See Figures 44 thru 51

☀ CAUTION

Fuel injection systems remain under pressure, even after the engine has been turned OFF. The fuel system pressure must be relieved before disconnecting any fuel lines. Failure to do so may result in fire and/or personal injury.

1. Disconnect the negative battery cable.
2. Relieve the fuel system pressure.
3. Disconnect fuel supply and return lines using the proper tool for spring lock coupling removal.

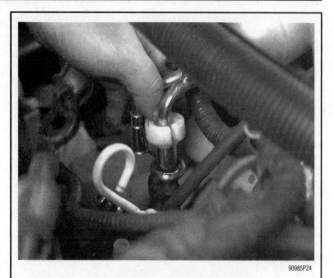

Fig. 44 Install the fuel line disconnect tool on the fuel line

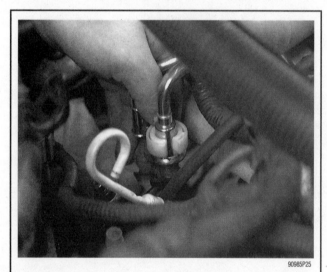

Fig. 45 Press the tool into the spring lock coupling . . .

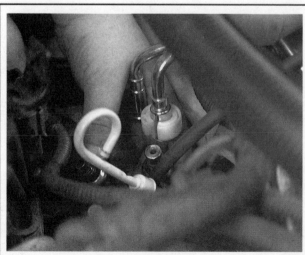

Fig. 46 . . . and separate the fuel line fitting from the hose

Fig. 47 Unplug the fuel injector electrical connectors

Fig. 48 Remove the two fuel injection supply manifold (fuel rail) retaining bolts

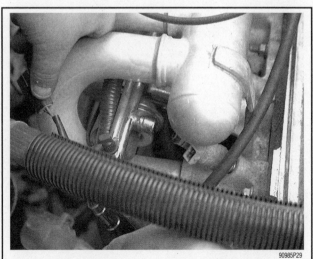

Fig. 49 Carefully disengage the fuel injection supply manifold from the fuel injectors

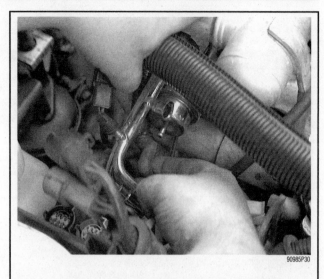

Fig. 50 Unplug the vacuum hose from the fuel pressure regulator

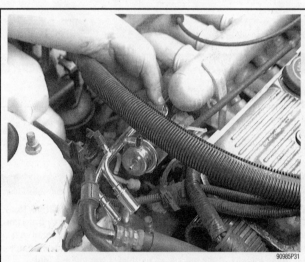

Fig. 51 Remove the fuel injection supply manifold (fuel rail) from the engine compartment

4. Unplug the fuel injector electrical connectors.
5. Remove the two fuel injection supply manifold (fuel rail) retaining bolts.
6. Carefully disengage the fuel injection supply manifold from the fuel injectors.
7. Disconnect the vacuum line from the fuel pressure regulator and set the fuel injection supply manifold aside.

To install:

8. Carefully position the fuel injection supply manifold on top of the fuel injectors. Push the fuel injection supply manifold down onto the injectors to fully seat the O-rings.
9. Install the two fuel injection supply manifold retaining bolts and tighten to 15–22 ft. lbs. (20–30 Nm).
10. Connect the fuel supply and return lines making sure the spring lock couplings are fully engaged and that the fuel tube clips are properly installed.
11. Connect the vacuum line to the fuel pressure regulator.
12. Attach the fuel injector electrical harness connectors.
13. Connect the negative battery cable and turn the ignition to the **ON** position to allow the fuel pump to pressurize the system.
14. Check for any fuel leaks. If any are found, immediately turn the ignition switch to the **OFF** position and disconnect the negative battery cable. Correct any leaks that are found.
15. Connect the fuel injector wiring harness.
16. Connect the negative battery cable.

17. Run the engine at idle for 2 minutes, then turn the engine **OFF** and check for fuel leaks and proper operation.

Fuel Pressure Regulator

REMOVAL & INSTALLATION

MFI Engines

1. Properly relieve the fuel system pressure.
2. Disconnect the negative battery cable.
3. Remove the Allen head retainers that attach the fuel pressure regulator to the fuel rail.
4. Remove the fuel pressure regulator, gasket and the O-ring. Discard the gasket and O-ring.
5. Clean any dirt and gasket residue from the fuel pressure regulator retaining screws.
To install:
6. Lubricate the new O-ring with a light engine oil.
7. Install a new gasket and O-ring on the fuel pressure regulator.
8. Place the fuel pressure regulator into position and install the retainers. Tighten the retainers to 27–40 inch lbs. (34 Nm).

9. Connect the negative battery cable.

CFI Engines

1. Properly relieve the fuel system pressure.
2. Disconnect the negative battery cable.
3. Unfasten the four pressure regulator retaining screws.

✳✳ CAUTION

The fuel pressure regulator cover is spring loaded. Apply a downward pressure when removing the cover to contain the assembly pieces.

4. Remove the cover assembly, cup, spring and diaphragm assembly.
5. Remove the pressure regulator valve seat.
To install:
6. Install the fuel pressure regulator valve seat.
7. Install the pressure regulator diaphragm assembly, spring, cup and cover.
8. Apply downward pressure to the pressure regulator cover and install the screws. Tighten the screws to 28–32 inch lbs. (3.2–3.6 Nm).

FUEL TANK

Tank Assembly

REMOVAL & INSTALLATION

This procedure will require a new flange gasket for installation. Be sure to have the necessary part(s) prior to starting this procedure. Also read the entire procedure prior to beginning to anticipate the need of any chemicals, tools or other items.

✳✳ CAUTION

Extreme caution should be taken when removing the fuel tank from the vehicle. Do not smoke and keep any open flame away from the work area. Ensure that all removal procedures are conducted in a well-ventilated area. Have a sufficient amount of absorbent material in the vicinity of the work area to quickly contain any fuel spillage. Never store waste fuel in an open container, as it presents a serious fire hazard.

1. Relieve the fuel system pressure, then disconnect the negative battery cable.

2. Remove the fuel from the fuel tank by pumping it out through the filler neck. Clean up any fuel spillage immediately.
3. Raise and safely support the rear of the vehicle, then remove the fuel filler tube (neck).
4. Support the fuel tank and remove the fuel tank straps, then lower the fuel tank enough to remove the fuel lines, electrical connectors and vent lines from the tank.
5. Remove the fuel tank from under the vehicle and place it on a suitable workbench.
To install:
6. Move the tank from the bench to the vehicle and support the tank, then properly attach the fuel lines, vent line and electrical connectors.
7. Install the tank in the vehicle and secure with its retaining straps.
8. Lower the vehicle and pour fresh fuel into the tank. Check for leaks and, if any are found, repair before proceeding.
9. Connect the negative battery cable.
10. Using a pressure gauge, check the fuel system pressure.
11. Remove the pressure gauge, then start the engine and recheck for fuel leaks. Correct any fuel leaks immediately.

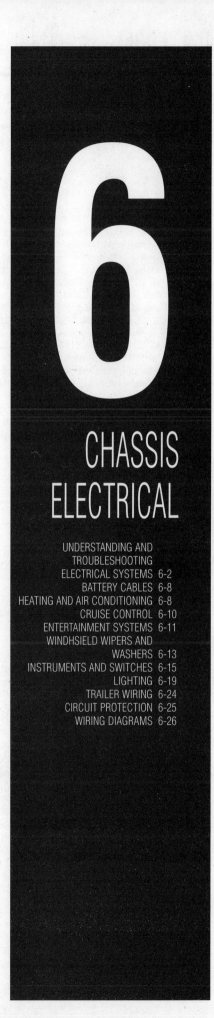

6

CHASSIS
ELECTRICAL

UNDERSTANDING AND TROUBLESHOOTING ELECTRICAL SYSTEMS

Basic Electrical Theory

♦ **See Figure 1**

For any 12 volt, negative ground, electrical system to operate, the electricity must travel in a complete circuit. This simply means that current (power) from the positive (+) terminal of the battery must eventually return to the negative (-) terminal of the battery. Along the way, this current will travel through wires, fuses, switches and components. If, for any reason, the flow of current through the circuit is interrupted, the component fed by that circuit will cease to function properly.

Perhaps the easiest way to visualize a circuit is to think of connecting a light bulb (with two wires attached to it) to the battery—one wire attached to the negative (-) terminal of the battery and the other wire to the positive (+) terminal. With the two wires touching the battery terminals, the circuit would be complete and the light bulb would illuminate. Electricity would follow a path from the battery to the bulb and back to the battery. It's easy to see that with longer wires on our light bulb, it could be mounted anywhere. Further, one wire could be fitted with a switch so that the light could be turned on and off.

The normal automotive circuit differs from this simple example in two ways. First, instead of having a return wire from the bulb to the battery, the current travels through the frame of the vehicle. Since the negative (-) battery cable is attached to the frame (made of electrically conductive metal), the frame of the vehicle can serve as a ground wire to complete the circuit. Secondly, most automotive circuits contain multiple components which receive power from a single circuit. This lessens the amount of wire needed to power components on the vehicle.

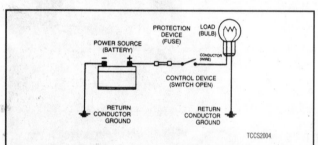

TCCS2004

Fig. 1 This example illustrates a simple circuit. When the switch is closed, power from the positive (+) battery terminal flows through the fuse and the switch, and then to the light bulb. The light illuminates and the circuit is completed through the ground wire back to the negative (-) battery terminal. In reality, the two ground points shown in the illustration are attached to the metal frame of the vehicle, which completes the circuit back to the battery

HOW DOES ELECTRICITY WORK: THE WATER ANALOGY

Electricity is the flow of electrons—the subatomic particles that constitute the outer shell of an atom. Electrons spin in an orbit around the center core of an atom. The center core is comprised of protons (positive charge) and neutrons (neutral charge). Electrons have a negative charge and balance out the positive charge of the protons. When an outside force causes the number of electrons to unbalance the charge of the protons, the electrons will split off the atom and look for another atom to balance out. If this imbalance is kept up, electrons will continue to move and an electrical flow will exist.

Many people have been taught electrical theory using an analogy with water. In a comparison with water flowing through a pipe, the electrons would be the water and the wire is the pipe.

The flow of electricity can be measured much like the flow of water through a pipe. The unit of measurement used is amperes, frequently abbreviated as amps (a). You can compare amperage to the volume of water flowing through a pipe. When connected to a circuit, an ammeter will measure the actual amount of current flowing through the circuit. When relatively few electrons flow through a circuit, the amperage is low. When many electrons flow, the amperage is high.

Water pressure is measured in units such as pounds per square inch (psi); The electrical pressure is measured in units called volts (v). When a voltmeter is connected to a circuit, it is measuring the electrical pressure.

The actual flow of electricity depends not only on voltage and amperage, but also on the resistance of the circuit. The higher the resistance, the higher the force necessary to push the current through the circuit. The standard unit for measuring resistance is an ohm Ω. Resistance in a circuit varies depending on the amount and type of components used in the circuit. The main factors which determine resistance are:

• Material—some materials have more resistance than others. Those with high resistance are said to be insulators. Rubber materials (or rubber-like plastics) are some of the most common insulators used in vehicles as they have a very high resistance to electricity. Very low resistance materials are said to be conductors. Copper wire is among the best conductors. Silver is actually a superior conductor to copper and is used in some relay contacts, but its high cost prohibits its use as common wiring. Most automotive wiring is made of copper.

• Size—the larger the wire size being used, the less resistance the wire will have. This is why components which use large amounts of electricity usually have large wires supplying current to them.

• Length—for a given thickness of wire, the longer the wire, the greater the resistance. The shorter the wire, the less the resistance. When determining the proper wire for a circuit, both size and length must be considered to design a circuit that can handle the current needs of the component.

• Temperature—with many materials, the higher the temperature, the greater the resistance (positive temperature coefficient). Some materials exhibit the opposite trait of lower resistance with higher temperatures (negative temperature coefficient). These principles are used in many of the sensors on the engine.

OHM'S LAW

There is a direct relationship between current, voltage and resistance. The relationship between current, voltage and resistance can be summed up by a statement known as Ohm's law.

Voltage (E) is equal to amperage (I) times resistance (R): $E = I \times R$
Other forms of the formula are $R = E/I$ and $I = E/R$

In each of these formulas, E is the voltage in volts, I is the current in amps and R is the resistance in ohms. The basic point to remember is that as the resistance of a circuit goes up, the amount of current that flows in the circuit will go down, if voltage remains the same.

The amount of work that the electricity can perform is expressed as power. The unit of power is the watt (w). The relationship between power, voltage and current is expressed as:

Power (w) is equal to amperage (I) times voltage (E): $W = I \times E$

This is only true for direct current (DC) circuits; The alternating current formula is a tad different, but since the electrical circuits in most vehicles are DC type, we need not get into AC circuit theory.

Electrical Components

POWER SOURCE

Power is supplied to the vehicle by two devices: The battery and the alternator. The battery supplies electrical power during starting or during periods when the current demand of the vehicle's electrical system exceeds the output capacity of the alternator. The alternator supplies electrical current when the engine is running. Just not does the alternator supply the current needs of the vehicle, but it recharges the battery.

The Battery

In most modern vehicles, the battery is a lead/acid electrochemical device consisting of six 2 volt subsections (cells) connected in series, so that the unit is capable of producing approximately 12 volts of electrical pressure. Each subsection consists of a series of positive and negative plates held a short distance apart in a solution of sulfuric acid and water.

The two types of plates are of dissimilar metals. This sets up a chemical reaction, and it is this reaction which produces current flow from the battery when its positive and negative terminals are connected to an electrical load . The power removed from the battery is replaced by the alternator, restoring the battery to its original chemical state.

The Alternator

On some vehicles there isn't an alternator, but a generator. The difference is that an alternator supplies alternating current which is then changed to direct current for use on the vehicle, while a generator produces direct current. Alternators tend to be more efficient and that is why they are used.

Alternators and generators are devices that consist of coils of wires wound together making big electromagnets. One group of coils spins within another set and the interaction of the magnetic fields causes a current to flow. This current is then drawn off the coils and fed into the vehicles electrical system.

GROUND

Two types of grounds are used in automotive electric circuits. Direct ground components are grounded to the frame through their mounting points. All other components use some sort of ground wire which is attached to the frame or chassis of the vehicle. The electrical current runs through the chassis of the vehicle and returns to the battery through the ground (-) cable; if you look, you'll see that the battery ground cable connects between the battery and the frame or chassis of the vehicle.

➡**It should be noted that a good percentage of electrical problems can be traced to bad grounds.**

PROTECTIVE DEVICES

◗ **See Figure 2**

It is possible for large surges of current to pass through the electrical system of your vehicle. If this surge of current were to reach the load in the circuit, the surge could burn it out or severely damage it. It can also overload the wiring, causing the harness to get hot and melt the insulation. To prevent this, fuses, circuit breakers and/or fusible links are connected into the supply wires of the electrical system. These items are nothing more than a built-in weak spot in the system. When an abnormal amount of current flows through the system, these protective devices work as follows to protect the circuit:

• Fuse—when an excessive electrical current passes through a fuse, the fuse "blows" (the conductor melts) and opens the circuit, preventing the passage of current.

• Circuit Breaker—a circuit breaker is basically a self-repairing fuse. It will open the circuit in the same fashion as a fuse, but when the surge subsides, the circuit breaker can be reset and does not need replacement.

• Fusible Link—a fusible link (fuse link or main link) is a short length of special, high temperature insulated wire that acts as a fuse. When an excessive electrical current passes through a fusible link, the thin gauge wire inside the link melts, creating an intentional open to protect the circuit. To repair the circuit, the link must be replaced. Some newer type fusible links are housed in plug-in modules, which are simply replaced like a fuse, while older type fusible links must be cut and spliced if they melt. Since this link is very early in the electrical path, it's the first place to look if nothing on the vehicle works, yet the battery seems to be charged and is properly connected.

> **❋❋ CAUTION**
>
> **Always replace fuses, circuit breakers and fusible links with identically rated components. Under no circumstances should a component of higher or lower amperage rating be substituted.**

SWITCHES & RELAYS

◗ **See Figures 3 and 4**

Switches are used in electrical circuits to control the passage of current. The most common use is to open and close circuits between the battery and the various electric devices in the system. Switches are rated according to the amount of amperage they can handle. If a sufficient amperage rated switch is not used in a circuit, the switch could overload and cause damage.

Some electrical components which require a large amount of current to operate use a special switch called a relay. Since these circuits carry a large amount of current, the thickness of the wire in the circuit is also greater. If this large wire

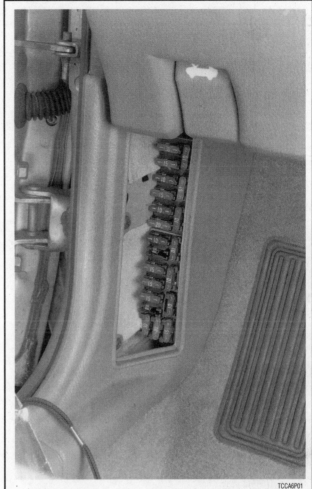

Fig. 2 Most vehicles use one or more fuse panels. This one is located on the driver's side kick panel

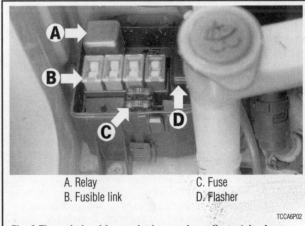

A. Relay   C. Fuse
B. Fusible link   D. Flasher

Fig. 3 The underhood fuse and relay panel usually contains fuses, relays, flashers and fusible links

were connected from the load to the control switch, the switch would have to carry the high amperage load and the fairing or dash would be twice as large to accommodate the increased size of the wiring harness. To prevent these problems, a relay is used.

Relays are composed of a coil and a set of contacts. When the coil has a cur-

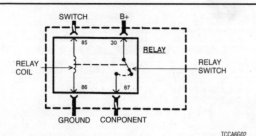

Fig. 4 Relays are composed of a coil and a switch. These two components are linked together so that when one operates, the other operates at the same time. The large wires in the circuit are connected from the battery to one side of the relay switch (B+) and from the opposite side of the relay switch to the load (component). Smaller wires are connected from the relay coil to the control switch for the circuit and from the opposite side of the relay coil to ground

rent passed though it, a magnetic field is formed and this field causes the contacts to move together, completing the circuit. Most relays are normally open, preventing current from passing through the circuit, but they can take any electrical form depending on the job they are intended to do. Relays can be considered "remote control switches." They allow a smaller current to operate devices that require higher amperages. When a small current operates the coil, a larger current is allowed to pass by the contacts. Some common circuits which may use relays are the horn, headlights, starter, electric fuel pump and other high draw circuits.

LOAD

Every electrical circuit must include a "load" (something to use the electricity coming from the source). Without this load, the battery would attempt to deliver its entire power supply from one pole to another. This is called a "short circuit." All this electricity would take a short cut to ground and cause a great amount of damage to other components in the circuit by developing a tremendous amount of heat. This condition could develop sufficient heat to melt the insulation on all the surrounding wires and reduce a multiple wire cable to a lump of plastic and copper.

WIRING & HARNESSES

The average vehicle contains meters and meters of wiring, with hundreds of individual connections. To protect the many wires from damage and to keep them from becoming a confusing tangle, they are organized into bundles, enclosed in plastic or taped together and called wiring harnesses. Different harnesses serve different parts of the vehicle. Individual wires are color coded to help trace them through a harness where sections are hidden from view.

Automotive wiring or circuit conductors can be either single strand wire, multi-strand wire or printed circuitry. Single strand wire has a solid metal core and is usually used inside such components as alternators, motors, relays and other devices. Multi-strand wire has a core made of many small strands of wire twisted together into a single conductor. Most of the wiring in an automotive electrical system is made up of multi-strand wire, either as a single conductor or grouped together in a harness. All wiring is color coded on the insulator, either as a solid color or as a colored wire with an identification stripe. A printed circuit is a thin film of copper or other conductor that is printed on an insulator backing. Occasionally, a printed circuit is sandwiched between two sheets of plastic for more protection and flexibility. A complete printed circuit, consisting of conductors, insulating material and connectors for lamps or other components is called a printed circuit board. Printed circuitry is used in place of individual wires or harnesses in places where space is limited, such as behind instrument panels.

Since automotive electrical systems are very sensitive to changes in resistance, the selection of properly sized wires is critical when systems are repaired. A loose or corroded connection or a replacement wire that is too small for the circuit will add extra resistance and an additional voltage drop to the circuit.

The wire gauge number is an expression of the cross-section area of the conductor. Vehicles from countries that use the metric system will typically describe the wire size as its cross-sectional area in square millimeters. In this method, the larger the wire, the greater the number. Another common system for expressing wire size is the American Wire Gauge (AWG) system. As gauge num-

ber increases, area decreases and the wire becomes smaller. An 18 gauge wire is smaller than a 4 gauge wire. A wire with a higher gauge number will carry less current than a wire with a lower gauge number. Gauge wire size refers to the size of the strands of the conductor, not the size of the complete wire with insulator. It is possible, therefore, to have two wires of the same gauge with different diameters because one may have thicker insulation than the other.

It is essential to understand how a circuit works before trying to figure out why it doesn't. An electrical schematic shows the electrical current paths when a circuit is operating properly. Schematics break the entire electrical system down into individual circuits. In a schematic, usually no attempt is made to represent wiring and components as they physically appear on the vehicle; switches and other components are shown as simply as possible. Face views of harness connectors show the cavity or terminal locations in all multi-pin connectors to help locate test points.

CONNECTORS

♦ See Figures 5 and 6

Three types of connectors are commonly used in automotive applications—weatherproof, molded and hard shell.

• Weatherproof—these connectors are most commonly used where the connector is exposed to the elements. Terminals are protected against moisture and dirt by sealing rings which provide a weathertight seal. All repairs require the use of a special terminal and the tool required to service it. Unlike standard

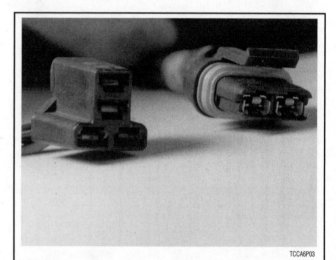

Fig. 5 Hard shell (left) and weatherproof (right) connectors have replaceable terminals

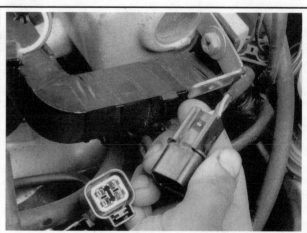

Fig. 6 Weatherproof connectors are most commonly used in the engine compartment or where the connector is exposed to the elements

blade type terminals, these weatherproof terminals cannot be straightened once they are bent. Make certain that the connectors are properly seated and all of the sealing rings are in place when connecting leads.

• Molded—these connectors require complete replacement of the connector if found to be defective. This means splicing a new connector assembly into the harness. All splices should be soldered to insure proper contact. Use care when probing the connections or replacing terminals in them, as it is possible to create a short circuit between opposite terminals. If this happens to the wrong terminal pair, it is possible to damage certain components. Always use jumper wires between connectors for circuit checking and NEVER probe through weatherproof seals.

• Hard Shell—unlike molded connectors, the terminal contacts in hard-shell connectors can be replaced. Replacement usually involves the use of a special terminal removal tool that depresses the locking tangs (barbs) on the connector terminal and allows the connector to be removed from the rear of the shell. The connector shell should be replaced if it shows any evidence of burning, melting, cracks, or breaks. Replace individual terminals that are burnt, corroded, distorted or loose.

Test Equipment

Pinpointing the exact cause of trouble in an electrical circuit is most times accomplished by the use of special test equipment. The following describes different types of commonly used test equipment and briefly explains how to use them in diagnosis. In addition to the information covered below, the tool manufacturer's instructions booklet (provided with the tester) should be read and clearly understood before attempting any test procedures.

JUMPER WIRES

✳✳ CAUTION

Never use jumper wires made from a thinner gauge wire than the circuit being tested. If the jumper wire is of too small a gauge, it may overheat and possibly melt. Never use jumpers to bypass high resistance loads in a circuit. Bypassing resistance's, in effect, creates a short circuit. This may, in turn, cause damage and fire. Jumper wires should only be used to bypass lengths of wire or to simulate switches.

Jumper wires are simple, yet extremely valuable, pieces of test equipment. They are basically test wires which are used to bypass sections of a circuit. Although jumper wires can be purchased, they are usually fabricated from lengths of standard automotive wire and whatever type of connector (alligator clip, spade connector or pin connector) that is required for the particular application being tested. In cramped, hard-to-reach areas, it is advisable to have insulated boots over the jumper wire terminals in order to prevent accidental grounding. It is also advisable to include a standard automotive fuse in any jumper wire. This is commonly referred to as a "fused jumper". By inserting an in-line fuse holder between a set of test leads, a fused jumper wire can be used for bypassing open circuits. Use a 5 amp fuse to provide protection against voltage spikes.

Jumper wires are used primarily to locate open electrical circuits, on either the ground (-) side of the circuit or on the power (+) side. If an electrical component fails to operate, connect the jumper wire between the component and a good ground. If the component operates only with the jumper installed, the ground circuit is open. If the ground circuit is good, but the component does not operate, the circuit between the power feed and component may be open. By moving the jumper wire successively back from the component toward the power source, you can isolate the area of the circuit where the open is located. When the component stops functioning, or the power is cut off, the open is in the segment of wire between the jumper and the point previously tested.

You can sometimes connect the jumper wire directly from the battery to the "hot" terminal of the component, but first make sure the component uses 12 volts in operation. Some electrical components, such as fuel injectors or sensors, are designed to operate on about 4 to 5 volts, and running 12 volts directly to these components will cause damage.

TEST LIGHTS

♦ **See Figure 7**

The test light is used to check circuits and components while electrical current is flowing through them. It is used for voltage and ground tests. To use a

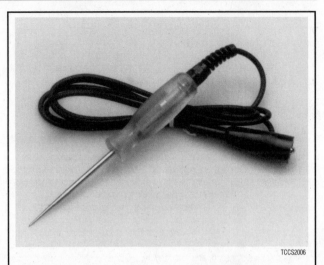

TCCS2006

Fig. 7 A 12 volt test light is used to detect the presence of voltage in a circuit

12 volt test light, connect the ground clip to a good ground and probe wherever necessary with the pick. The test light will illuminate when voltage is detected. This does not necessarily mean that 12 volts (or any particular amount of voltage) is present; it only means that some voltage is present. It is advisable before using the test light to touch its ground clip and probe across the battery posts or terminals to make sure the light is operating properly.

✳✳ WARNING

Do not use a test light to probe electronic ignition, spark plug or coil wires. Never use a pick-type test light to probe wiring on computer controlled systems unless specifically instructed to do so. Any wire insulation that is pierced by the test light probe should be taped and sealed with silicone after testing.

Like the jumper wire, the 12 volt test light is used to isolate opens in circuits. But, whereas the jumper wire is used to bypass the open to operate the load, the 12 volt test light is used to locate the presence of voltage in a circuit. If the test light illuminates, there is power up to that point in the circuit; if the test light does not illuminate, there is an open circuit (no power). Move the test light in successive steps back toward the power source until the light in the handle illuminates. The open is between the probe and a point which was previously probed.

The self-powered test light is similar in design to the 12 volt test light, but contains a 1.5 volt penlight battery in the handle. It is most often used in place of a multimeter to check for open or short circuits when power is isolated from the circuit (continuity test).

The battery in a self-powered test light does not provide much current. A weak battery may not provide enough power to illuminate the test light even when a complete circuit is made (especially if there is high resistance in the circuit). Always make sure that the test battery is strong. To check the battery, briefly touch the ground clip to the probe; if the light glows brightly, the battery is strong enough for testing.

➡**A self-powered test light should not be used on any computer controlled system or component. The small amount of electricity transmitted by the test light is enough to damage many electronic automotive components.**

MULTIMETERS

Multimeters are an extremely useful tool for troubleshooting electrical problems. They can be purchased in either analog or digital form and have a price range to suit any budget. A multimeter is a voltmeter, ammeter and ohmmeter (along with other features) combined into one instrument. It is often used when testing solid state circuits because of its high input impedance (usually 10 megaohms or more). A brief description of the multimeter main test functions follows:

• Voltmeter—the voltmeter is used to measure voltage at any point in a circuit, or to measure the voltage drop across any part of a circuit. Voltmeters usually have various scales and a selector switch to allow the reading of different voltage ranges. The voltmeter has a positive and a negative lead. To avoid damage to the meter, always connect the negative lead to the negative (-) side of the circuit (to ground or nearest the ground side of the circuit) and connect the positive lead to the positive (+) side of the circuit (to the power source or the nearest power source). Note that the negative voltmeter lead will always be black and that the positive voltmeter will always be some color other than black (usually red).

• Ohmmeter—the ohmmeter is designed to read resistance (measured in ohms) in a circuit or component. Most ohmmeters will have a selector switch which permits the measurement of different ranges of resistance (usually the selector switch allows the multiplication of the meter reading by 10, 100, 1,000 and 10,000). Some ohmmeters are "auto-ranging" which means the meter itself will determine which scale to use. Since the meters are powered by an internal battery, the ohmmeter can be used like a self-powered test light. When the ohmmeter is connected, current from the ohmmeter flows through the circuit or component being tested. Since the ohmmeter's internal resistance and voltage are known values, the amount of current flow through the meter depends on the resistance of the circuit or component being tested. The ohmmeter can also be used to perform a continuity test for suspected open circuits. In using the meter for making continuity checks, do not be concerned with the actual resistance readings. Zero resistance, or any ohm reading, indicates continuity in the circuit. Infinite resistance indicates an opening in the circuit. A high resistance reading where there should be none indicates a problem in the circuit. Checks for short circuits are made in the same manner as checks for open circuits, except that the circuit must be isolated from both power and normal ground. Infinite resistance indicates no continuity, while zero resistance indicates a dead short.

✳✳ WARNING

Never use an ohmmeter to check the resistance of a component or wire while there is voltage applied to the circuit.

• Ammeter—an ammeter measures the amount of current flowing through a circuit in units called amperes or amps. At normal operating voltage, most circuits have a characteristic amount of amperes, called "current draw" which can be measured using an ammeter. By referring to a specified current draw rating, then measuring the amperes and comparing the two values, one can determine what is happening within the circuit to aid in diagnosis. An open circuit, for example, will not allow any current to flow, so the ammeter reading will be zero. A damaged component or circuit will have an increased current draw, so the reading will be high. The ammeter is always connected in series with the circuit being tested. All of the current that normally flows through the circuit must also flow through the ammeter; if there is any other path for the current to follow, the ammeter reading will not be accurate. The ammeter itself has very little resistance to current flow and, therefore, will not affect the circuit, but it will measure current draw only when the circuit is closed and electricity is flowing. Excessive current draw can blow fuses and drain the battery, while a reduced current draw can cause motors to run slowly, lights to dim and other components to not operate properly.

Troubleshooting Electrical Systems

When diagnosing a specific problem, organized troubleshooting is a must. The complexity of a modern automotive vehicle demands that you approach any problem in a logical, organized manner. There are certain troubleshooting techniques, however, which are standard:

• Establish when the problem occurs. Does the problem appear only under certain conditions? Were there any noises, odors or other unusual symptoms? Isolate the problem area. To do this, make some simple tests and observations, then eliminate the systems that are working properly. Check for obvious problems, such as broken wires and loose or dirty connections. Always check the obvious before assuming something complicated is the cause.

• Test for problems systematically to determine the cause once the problem area is isolated. Are all the components functioning properly? Is there power going to electrical switches and motors. Performing careful, systematic checks will often turn up most causes on the first inspection, without wasting time checking components that have little or no relationship to the problem.

• Test all repairs after the work is done to make sure that the problem is fixed. Some causes can be traced to more than one component, so a careful verification of repair work is important in order to pick up additional malfunctions that may cause a problem to reappear or a different problem to arise. A blown fuse, for example, is a simple problem that may require more than another fuse to repair. If you don't look for a problem that caused a fuse to blow, a shorted wire (for example) may go undetected.

Experience has shown that most problems tend to be the result of a fairly simple and obvious cause, such as loose or corroded connectors, bad grounds or damaged wire insulation which causes a short. This makes careful visual inspection of components during testing essential to quick and accurate troubleshooting.

Testing

OPEN CIRCUITS

▶ **See Figure 8**

This test already assumes the existence of an open in the circuit and it is used to help locate the open portion.
1. Isolate the circuit from power and ground.
2. Connect the self-powered test light or ohmmeter ground clip to the ground side of the circuit and probe sections of the circuit sequentially.
3. If the light is out or there is infinite resistance, the open is between the probe and the circuit ground.
4. If the light is on or the meter shows continuity, the open is between the probe and the end of the circuit toward the power source.

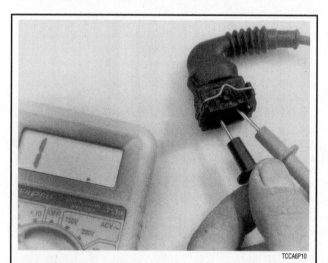

TCCA6P10

Fig. 8 The infinite reading on this multimeter (1 .) indicates that the circuit is open

SHORT CIRCUITS

➡**Never use a self-powered test light to perform checks for opens or shorts when power is applied to the circuit under test. The test light can be damaged by outside power.**

1. Isolate the circuit from power and ground.
2. Connect the self-powered test light or ohmmeter ground clip to a good ground and probe any easy-to-reach point in the circuit.
3. If the light comes on or there is continuity, there is a short somewhere in the circuit.
4. To isolate the short, probe a test point at either end of the isolated circuit (the light should be on or the meter should indicate continuity).
5. Leave the test light probe engaged and sequentially open connectors or switches, remove parts, etc. until the light goes out or continuity is broken.
6. When the light goes out, the short is between the last two circuit components which were opened.

VOLTAGE

This test determines voltage available from the battery and should be the first step in any electrical troubleshooting procedure after visual inspection. Many electrical problems, especially on computer controlled systems, can be caused by a low state of charge in the battery. Excessive corrosion at the battery cable terminals can cause poor contact that will prevent proper charging and full battery current flow.

1. Set the voltmeter selector switch to the 20V position.

2. Connect the multimeter negative lead to the battery's negative (-) post or terminal and the positive lead to the battery's positive (+) post or terminal.

3. Turn the ignition switch **ON** to provide a load.

4. A well charged battery should register over 12 volts. If the meter reads below 11.5 volts, the battery power may be insufficient to operate the electrical system properly.

VOLTAGE DROP

♦ **See Figure 9**

When current flows through a load, the voltage beyond the load drops. This voltage drop is due to the resistance created by the load and also by small resistance's created by corrosion at the connectors and damaged insulation on the wires. The maximum allowable voltage drop under load is critical, especially if there is more than one load in the circuit, since all voltage drops are cumulative.

1. Set the voltmeter selector switch to the 20 volt position.

2. Connect the multimeter negative lead to a good ground.

3. Operate the circuit and check the voltage prior to the first component (load).

4. There should be little or no voltage drop in the circuit prior to the first component. If a voltage drop exists, the wire or connectors in the circuit are suspect.

5. While operating the first component in the circuit, probe the ground side of the component with the positive meter lead and observe the voltage readings. A small voltage drop should be noticed. This voltage drop is caused by the resistance of the component.

6. Repeat the test for each component (load) down the circuit.

7. If a large voltage drop is noticed, the preceding component, wire or connector is suspect.

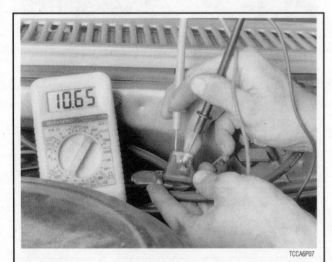

Fig. 9 This voltage drop test revealed high resistance (low voltage) in the circuit

RESISTANCE

♦ **See Figures 10 and 11**

✳✳ WARNING

Never use an ohmmeter with power applied to the circuit. The ohmmeter is designed to operate on its own power supply. The normal 12 volt electrical system voltage could damage the meter!

1. Isolate the circuit from the vehicle's power source.

2. Ensure that the ignition key is **OFF** when disconnecting any components or the battery.

3. Where necessary, also isolate at least one side of the circuit to be checked, in order to avoid reading parallel resistance's. Parallel circuit resistance's will always give a lower reading than the actual resistance of either of the branches.

Fig. 10 Checking the resistance of a coolant temperature sensor with an ohmmeter. Reading is 1.04 kilohms

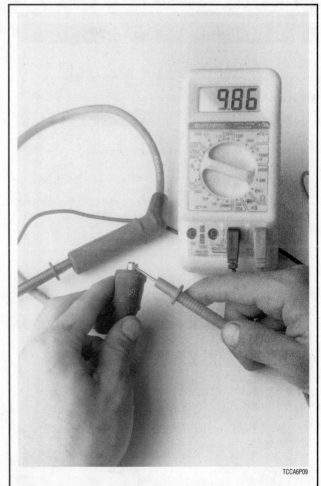

Fig. 11 Spark plug wires can be checked for excessive resistance using an ohmmeter

4. Connect the meter leads to both sides of the circuit (wire or component) and read the actual measured ohms on the meter scale. Make sure the selector switch is set to the proper ohm scale for the circuit being tested, to avoid misreading the ohmmeter test value.

Wire and Connector Repair

Almost anyone can replace damaged wires, as long as the proper tools and parts are available. Wire and terminals are available to fit almost any need. Even the specialized weatherproof, molded and hard shell connectors are now available from aftermarket suppliers.

Be sure the ends of all the wires are fitted with the proper terminal hardware and connectors. Wrapping a wire around a stud is never a permanent solution and will only cause trouble later. Replace wires one at a time to avoid confusion. Always route wires exactly the same as the factory.

➡ **If connector repair is necessary, only attempt it if you have the proper tools. Weatherproof and hard shell connectors require special tools to release the pins inside the connector. Attempting to repair these connectors with conventional hand tools will damage them.**

BATTERY CABLES

Disconnecting the Cables

When working on any electrical component on the vehicle, it is always a good idea to disconnect the negative (-) battery cable. This will prevent potential damage to many sensitive electrical components such as the Engine Control Module (ECM), radio, alternator, etc.

➡ **Any time you disengage the battery cables, it is recommended that you disconnect the negative (-) battery cable first. This will prevent your accidentally grounding the positive (+) terminal to the body of the vehicle when disconnecting it, thereby preventing damage to the above mentioned components.**

Before you disconnect the cable(s), first turn the ignition to the **OFF** position. This will prevent a draw on the battery which could cause arcing (electricity trying to ground itself to the body of a vehicle, just like a spark plug jumping the gap) and, of course, damaging some components such as the alternator diodes.

When the battery cable(s) are reconnected (negative cable last), be sure to check that your lights, windshield wipers and other electrically operated safety components are all working correctly. If your vehicle contains an Electronically Tuned Radio (ETR), don't forget to also reset your radio stations. Ditto for the clock.

HEATING AND AIR CONDITIONING

Blower Motor

REMOVAL & INSTALLATION

With Air Conditioning

◆ **See Figures 12, 13 and 14**

1. Disconnect the negative battery cable.
2. Remove the glove compartment door and glove compartment.
3. Disconnect the blower motor wires from the blower motor resistor.
4. Loosen the instrument panel at the lower right-hand side prior to removing the motor through the glove compartment opening.
5. Remove the blower motor and mounting plate from the evaporator case.
6. Rotate the motor until the mounting plate flat clears the edge of the glove compartment opening and remove the motor.
7. Remove the hub clamp spring from the blower wheel hub. Then remove the blower wheel from the motor shaft.
   To install:
8. If removed, assemble the blower wheel to the motor shaft and install the hub clamp.

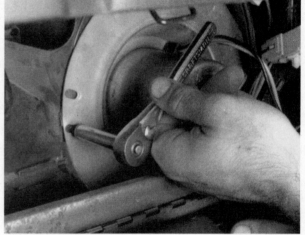

Fig. 13 Unbolt the mounting plate from the case

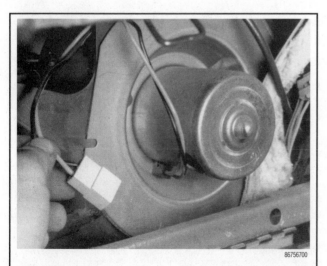

Fig. 12 Disconnect the blower motor wires from the blower motor resistor

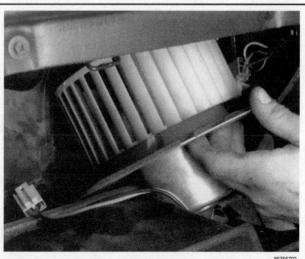

Fig. 14 The motor can now be removed from the case

9. Install the motor and blower wheel assembly.
10. Secure the instrument panel at the lower right-hand side.
11. Connect the blower motor wires at the blower motor resistor.
12. Install the glove compartment door and the glove compartment.
13. Connect the negative battery cable.
14. Check the system for proper operation.

Without Air Conditioning

1. Disconnect the negative battery cable.
2. Remove the air inlet duct assembly.
3. Remove the hub clamp spring from the blower wheel hub. Pull the blower wheel from the blower motor shaft.
4. Remove the blower motor flange attaching screws located inside the blower housing.
5. Pull the blower motor out from the blower housing (heater case) and disconnect the blower motor wires from the motor.

To install:
6. Connect the wires to the blower motor and position the motor in the blower housing.
7. Install the blower motor attaching screws.
8. Position the blower wheel on the motor shaft and install the hub clamp spring.
9. Install the air inlet duct assembly and the right ventilator assembly.
10. Connect negative battery cable.
11. Check the system for proper operation.

Heater Core

Vehicles may be equipped with either a brass or an aluminum heater core. It is important to positively identify the type of core being used because aluminum cores use different heater core-to-heater case seals than the copper/brass cores. Having the proper seal is necessary for proper sealing and heating system performance.

Identification can be made by looking at one of the core tubes after one of the hoses is disconnected. An aluminum core will have a silver colored tube. A brass core will have a brass colored tube.

If the vehicle is equipped with a copper/brass core, the old core seal may be used for the replacement core, providing that it is not damaged.

If the vehicle is equipped with an aluminum core, a new seal will be required for the replacement core.

REMOVAL & INSTALLATION

Without Air Conditioning

▶ See Figure 15

✳ CAUTION

Never open, service or drain the radiator or cooling system when hot; serious burns can occur from the steam and hot coolant. Also, when draining engine coolant, keep in mind that cats and dogs are attracted to ethylene glycol antifreeze and could drink any that is left in an uncovered container or in puddles on the ground. This will prove fatal in sufficient quantities. Always drain coolant into a sealable container. Coolant should be reused unless it is contaminated or is several years old.

1. Disconnect the negative battery cable.
2. Drain the coolant.
3. Disconnect the heater hoses from the core tubes at the firewall, inside the engine compartment. Plug the core tubes to prevent coolant spillage when the core is removed.
4. Open the glove compartment. Remove the glove compartment, the glove compartment liner and lower reinforcement
5. Move the temperature control lever to the warm position.
6. Remove the screws attaching the heater core cover and remove the cover.
7. Working under the hood, remove the two nuts attaching the heater assembly case to the dash panel.

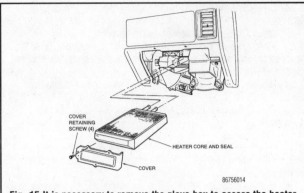

Fig. 15 It is necessary to remove the glove box to access the heater core

8. Push the heater core tubes towards the passenger compartment.
9. Pull the core through the glove compartment opening.

To install:
10. Install the core through the glove compartment opening.
11. Working under the hood, install the two nuts attaching the heater assembly case to the dash panel.
12. Install the heater core cover and tighten the screws securely.
13. Reconnect the heater hoses to the core tubes at the firewall, inside the engine compartment.
14. Refill the cooling system with coolant.
15. Reconnect the negative battery cable.
16. Start the engine and check for leaks.
17. Install the lower reinforcement, glove compartment door, and liner.

With Air Conditioning

▶ See Figure 16

✳ CAUTION

Never open, service or drain the radiator or cooling system when hot; serious burns can occur from the steam and hot coolant. Also, when draining engine coolant, keep in mind that cats and dogs are attracted to ethylene glycol antifreeze and could drink any that is left in an uncovered container or in puddles on the ground. This will prove fatal in sufficient quantities. Always drain coolant into a sealable container. Coolant should be reused unless it is contaminated or is several years old.

Fig. 16 Remove the heater core and cover from the plenum

1. Disconnect the negative battery cable and drain the cooling system.
2. Disconnect the heater hoses from the heater core.
3. Working inside the vehicle, remove the two screws and separate the floor duct from the plenum. On some later model vehicles, unfasten the instrument panel screw and evaporator screw.
4. Unfasten the four screws attaching the heater core cover to the plenum.
5. Remove the cover and the heater core.

To install:
6. Install the heater core and the cover.
7. Install the four screws attaching the heater core cover to the plenum. If equipped, tighten the instrument panel screw and evaporator screw.
8. Working inside the vehicle, Install the floor duct to the plenum with the two screws.
9. Reconnect the heater hoses to the heater core.
10. Reconnect the negative battery cable and refill the cooling system.

Air Conditioning Components

REMOVAL & INSTALLATION

Repair or service of air conditioning components is not covered by this manual, because of the risk of personal injury or death, and because of the legal ramifications of servicing these components without the proper EPA certification and experience. Cost, personal injury or death, environmental damage, and legal considerations (such as the fact that it is a federal crime to vent refrigerant into the atmosphere), dictate that the A/C components on your vehicle should be serviced only by a Motor Vehicle Air Conditioning (MVAC) trained, and EPA certified automotive technician.

➡**If your vehicle's A/C system uses R-12 refrigerant and is in need of recharging, the A/C system can be converted over to R-134a refrigerant (less environmentally harmful and expensive). Refer to Section 1 for additional information on R-12 to R-134a conversions, and for additional considerations dealing with your vehicle's A/C system.**

CRUISE CONTROL

General Information

When activated by the driver, the cruise control system is designed to maintain vehicle road speed without requiring further input from the accelerator pedal. To activate the cruise control system, the engine must be running and the vehicle speed must be greater than 30 mph (48 km/h).

The cruise control system consists of operator controls, a servo (throttle actuator) assembly, a speed sensor, a clutch switch, a Brake On/Off (BOO) switch, a vacuum dump valve, an amplifier assembly and the necessary wires and vacuum hoses.

Troubleshooting

To diagnose any malfunction with the cruise control system, first perform a thorough visual inspection. Begin by checking all items for abnormal conditions such as bare, broken or disconnected wires, and check for damaged or disconnected vacuum hoses as well. All vacuum hoses should be securely attached and routed with no kinks in them. The cruise control servo (throttle actuator) should operate freely and smoothly, and its cable should be adjusted as tightly as possible without opening the throttle plate or causing an increase in idle speed. Check for a sticking brake and clutch switch (if equipped), as this could keep the system from engaging.

Once it has been determined the system is not operating properly, and all obvious trouble sources have been ruled out, refer troubleshooting to a reputable repair facility.

CRUISE CONTROL TROUBLESHOOTING

Problem	Possible Cause
Will not hold proper speed	Incorrect cable adjustment
	Binding throttle linkage
	Leaking vacuum servo diaphragm
	Leaking vacuum tank
	Faulty vacuum or vent valve
	Faulty stepper motor
	Faulty transducer
	Faulty speed sensor
	Faulty cruise control module
Cruise intermittently cuts out	Clutch or brake switch adjustment too tight
	Short or open in the cruise control circuit
	Faulty transducer
	Faulty cruise control module
Vehicle surges	Kinked speedometer cable or casing
	Binding throttle linkage
	Faulty speed sensor
	Faulty cruise control module
Cruise control inoperative	Blown fuse
	Short or open in the cruise control circuit
	Faulty brake or clutch switch
	Leaking vacuum circuit
	Faulty cruise control switch
	Faulty stepper motor
	Faulty transducer
	Faulty speed sensor
	Faulty cruise control module

Note: Use this chart as a guide. Not all systems will use the components listed.

TCCA6C01

ENTERTAINMENT SYSTEMS

Radio Receiver/Tape Player

REMOVAL & INSTALLATION

Early Model Vehicles

1. Disconnect the negative battery cable.
2. Remove the heater or air conditioning floor ducts.
3. Disconnect the power lead, antenna, and speaker wires.
4. Pull the control knobs, discs, control shaft nuts and washers.
5. Remove the ashtray and bracket.
6. Working under the instrument panel, remove the support bracket nut from the radio chassis.
7. Carefully lower the radio down from behind the instrument panel.
8. Remove the radio.

To install:

9. Attach the radio to the support bracket and tighten retaining nut.
10. Place the radio into position.
11. Install the nuts and washers onto the control shafts. Tighten the nuts until they are snug.
12. Install the ashtray and bracket.
13. Install the heater or air conditioning floor ducts.
14. Attach the power lead, antenna, and speaker wires.
15. Pull the discs and control knobs.
16. Connect the negative battery cable.
17. Check the radio for proper operation.

Late Model Vehicles

BASE SYSTEM

♦ **See Figures 17 thru 22**

1. Disconnect the negative battery cable.
2. Remove the center instrument trim panel.
3. Unfasten the radio mounting bracket retaining screws.
4. Pull the radio out to disengage it from the lower rear bracket.
5. Unplug the wiring connectors and antenna cable.
6. Unfasten the screws from the two side mounting brackets and remove.
7. Unfasten the rear support retaining nut and remove the support.

To install:

8. Attach the rear support to the radio and tighten the retaining nut.
9. Place the mounting brackets on each side of the radio and install the screws.
10. Place the radio about a quarter of the way into the instrument panel, then attach the electrical connectors and the antenna.
11. Slide the radio in until it engages the rear support bracket. Install the radio-to-instrument panel retaining screws.
12. Install the center trim panel.
13. Connect the negative battery cable and check for proper operation.

ELECTRONIC SYSTEM

♦ **See Figures 23, 24, 25 and 26**

1. Disconnect the negative battery cable.
2. Remove the center instrument trim panel.

Fig. 17 Unfasten the center console's upper retaining screws

Fig. 18 Remove the shift console to access the center trim panel's lower screws

Fig. 19 Remove the radio control knobs

Fig. 20 Unfasten the lower center console screws and remove the console

Fig. 21 Unfasten the mounting screws and slide the radio assembly forward until its rear is accessible

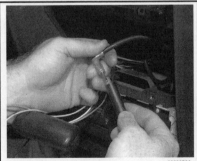

Fig. 22 Unplug the antenna and electrical connections, then remove the radio assembly from the vehicle

Fig. 23 The center instrument trim panel is secured by screws

Fig. 24 After the trim panel is removed, unfasten the four radio and mounting bracket retainers

Fig. 25 Pull the radio out and unplug the wiring connectors

Fig. 26 Don't forget to unplug the antenna wire

3. Unfasten the radio and mounting bracket retaining screws.

4. Pull the radio to the front and raise the back end of the radio slightly so the rear support bracket clears the clip in the instrument panel. Pull the radio out of the instrument panel slowly.

5. Unplug the wiring connectors and antenna cable.

6. Transfer the mounting brackets to the new radio, if necessary.

To install:

7. Attach the wiring connectors and the antenna to the radio.

8. Slide the radio into the radio into the instrument panel while keeping the rear of the radio slightly raised so you can engage the rear mounting bracket to the instrument panel clip.

9. Install and tighten the radio and bracket retaining screws to 14–16 inch lbs. (1.5–1.9 Nm).

10. Install the center trim panel.

11. Connect the negative battery cable and check the radio for proper operation.

Speakers

REMOVAL & INSTALLATION

Instrument Panel Mounted

MONAURAL SPEAKERS

1. If equipped, unfasten the lower air conditioner duct screws.
2. Unfasten the wire from the speaker.
3. Unplug the speaker lead.
4. Unfasten the speaker cover screws.

5. Unfasten the speaker retaining screws and remove the speaker.

To install:

6. Install the speaker and tighten its retaining screws.
7. Install the speaker cover and tighten the retaining screws.
8. Attach the speaker lead and wire.
9. If equipped, tighten the lower air conditioner duct screws.

STEREO SPEAKERS

1. Use an appropriate prytool to remove the speaker grille.

2. Unfasten the speaker-to-grille retaining screws and remove the speaker from the instrument panel.

3. Unplug the speaker electrical connection and remove the speaker from the vehicle.

4. Installation is the reverse of removal.

Door Mounted

♦ See Figures 27 and 28

1. Remove the door panel to gain access to the speaker.
2. Unfasten the speaker retaining screws and remove the speaker from the door.
3. Unplug the speaker wiring.

➡️Some of the speakers are set into a plastic sleeve or protector in the door. This protects the speaker from water and moisture in the door. Make sure the shield is in place when reinstalling the speakers.

4. Installation is the reverse of removal.

Fig. 27 Unfasten the speaker-to-door retaining screws

Rear Speakers

SEDAN MODELS

1. On sedans, the speakers are usually accessed through the trunk and removed as follows:

Fig. 28 Separate the speaker from the door and unplug the speaker electrical connection

a. Remove the speaker covers, then unplug the electrical connectors.
2. Unfasten the speaker retainers to remove the speaker.
  a. If the speakers are not accessible through the trunk, remove the speaker grilles from the rear shelf.
  b. Remove the retainers, then pull the speaker upwards slightly. Unplug the electrical connector and remove the speaker.

➥**Most of the rear speakers sit in some type of support or frame. This provides both a firm mount and isolates the speaker from its surroundings, preventing distortion. Make sure the frame is present when reinstalling the speaker.**

3. Installation of the speaker(s) is the reverse of removal.

HATCHBACKS AND WAGON MODELS

1. Unfasten the speaker grille or cover. Some are press-fit in place, others are held by plastic retaining pins. Look carefully before prying.
2. Once the speaker is exposed, unfasten the speaker retainers, remove the speaker and unplug its electrical connection.
3. Installation of the speaker(s) is the reverse of removal.

WINDSHIELD WIPERS AND WASHERS

Windshield Wiper Blade

REPLACEMENT

Trico® Type Blade

EXCEPT STATION WAGON REAR BLADE

♦ See Figure 29

1. Cycle the arm and blade assembly to a position on the windshield where the blade assembly can be easily removed, then turn the ignition switch **OFF**.
2. Grasp the wiper arm frame and pull it off the windshield.
3. Grasp the blade assembly and pull it off the pin on the wiper arm.
To install:
4. Place the new wiper blade into position and push the blade assembly onto the wiper arm pin. Make sure the blade is firmly attached to the pin.
5. Lower the blade and arm assembly onto the windshield.
6. Turn the wipers on and check for proper operation.

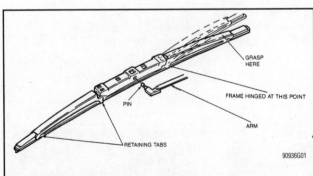

Fig. 29 Example of a Trico® type wiper blade assembly

Tridon® Type Blade

EXCEPT STATION WAGON REAR BLADE

♦ See Figure 30

1. Cylcle the arm and blade assembly to a position on the windshield where the blade assembly can be easily removed, then turn the ignition switch **OFF**.
2. Pull up on the spring lock and pull the blade assembly from the pin. Make sure the spring lock is not pulled excessively or it can become distorted.

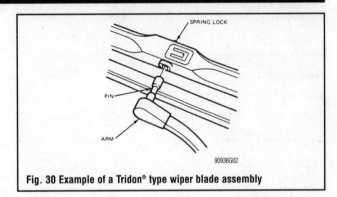

Fig. 30 Example of a Tridon® type wiper blade assembly

To install:
3. Place the new wiper blade into position and push the blade assembly onto the wiper arm pin until the spring lock engages the pin. Make sure the blade is firmly attached to the pin.
4. Turn the wipers on and check for proper operation.

STATION WAGON REAR BLADE

♦ See Figure 31

1. Press down on the arm to unlatch the top stud.
2. Depress the tab on the saddle below the arm to unlatch the top stud, then pull the blade from the arm.
To install:
3. Slide the blade assembly onto the arm, making sure the top stud and bottom saddle are securely latched.

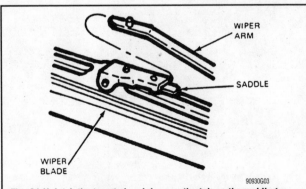

Fig. 31 Unlatch the top stud and depress the tab on the saddle to unlatch the stud, then remove the blade—station wagon rear blade

Windshield Wiper Arm

REMOVAL & INSTALLATION

1. Mark the position of the arm on the windshield with a grease pencil or tape.
2. Raise the blade end of the arm off the windshield and move the slide latch away from the pivot shaft.
3. The wiper arm can now be pulled off of the pivot shaft.

To install:

4. With the arm and blade assemblies removed from the pivot shafts, turn on the wiper switch and allow the motor to move the pivot shaft three or four cycles, then turn off the wiper switch. This will place the pivot shafts in the park position.
5. Align the arm with the marks made on the windshield earlier.
6. Hold the arm head on the pivot shaft and push it onto the shaft.
7. Hold the blade, then slide the latch into the groove under the pivot shaft. Lower the blade to the windshield.

➡**If the blade does not touch the windshield, the slide latch is not completely in place.**

8. Be sure the arm aligns with marks made earlier. If not, readjust.

Windshield Wiper Motor

REMOVAL & INSTALLATION

Front

▶ **See Figures 32, 33, 34 and 35**

1. Disconnect the negative battery cable.

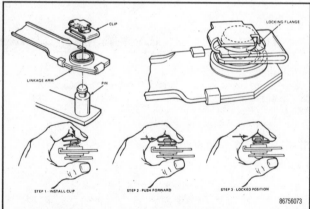

Fig. 32 Linkage retaining clip engaging/disengaging procedure

2. Unclip and lift the watershield cover from the cowl on the passenger's side.
3. Disconnect the power lead from the motor.
4. Remove the linkage retaining clip from the operating arm on the motor by lifting the locking tab up and pulling the clip away from the pin.
5. Unfasten the attaching bolts from the motor/bracket assembly, then remove the assembly.
6. If necessary, remove the operating arm from the motor, unfasten the three bolts and separate the motor from the bracket.

To install:

7. If removed, install the mounting bracket and the operating arm on the motor.
8. Position the motor and install the retaining bolts.

➡**Make sure you attach the ground wire.**

9. Attach the operating arm to the motor. Install the linkage retaining clip to the operating arm.
10. Engage the electrical lead to the motor.
11. Install the watershield cover to the cowl.
12. Connect the negative battery cable.

Rear

▶ **See Figure 36**

1. Disconnect the negative battery cable.
2. Remove the wiper arm.
3. Remove the pivot shaft attaching nut and spacers.
4. On hatchback vehicles, remove the liftgate inner trim panel.
5. On station wagons, remove the screws attaching the license plate housing. Disconnect the license plate light wiring and remove the housing.
6. Unplug the electrical connector to wiper motor.
7. On hatchback models, unfasten the three screws retaining the bracket to the door inner skin and remove the complete motor, bracket and linkage assembly.
8. On station wagon models, unfasten the motor and bracket assembly retaining screws and remove the motor and bracket assembly.

To install:

9. On station wagon models, Install the motor and bracket, then tighten the retaining screws.
10. On hatchback models, install the linkage, bracket and motor as an assembly, then tighten the retaining screws.
11. Attach the wiper motor electrical connector.
12. On station wagons, attach the light wiring, install the license plate housing and tighten the screws.
13. On hatchback models, install the liftgate inner trim panel.
14. Install the pivot shaft spacers and attaching nut.

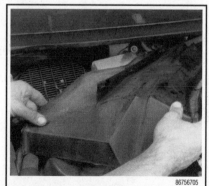

Fig. 33 Remove the watershield cover to access the wiper motor

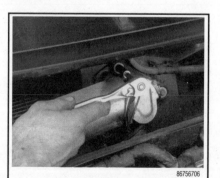

Fig. 34 After disengaging the linkage and unplugging the motor, remove the bolts that retain the wiper motor

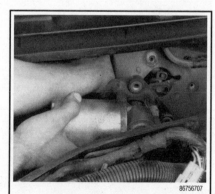

Fig. 35 Remove the motor while guiding the crank arm through the hole

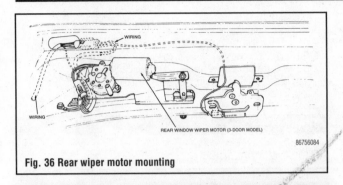

Fig. 36 Rear wiper motor mounting

Windshield Washer Motor

REMOVAL & INSTALLATION

Front

▶ See Figures 37 and 38

1. Disconnect the negative battery cable.
2. Unfasten the screws attaching the reservoir to the dash panel.
3. Unplug all electrical connections from the reservoir.
4. Unplug the hoses and remove the reservoir. The reservoir will drain with the hose disconnected.
5. Using a suitable prytool, pry out the washer motor retaining ring.
6. Grasp one wall of the motor with a suitable set of pliers as illustrated, then pull out the motor, seal and impeller assembly.

➡ If the impeller and seal come of when the motor is pulled out, they can be reassembled. Make sure the reservoir pump chamber is free of foreign material prior to reinstalling the motor.

To install:

7. Lubricate the outside of the seal with a dry lubricant such as powered graphite. This prevents the seal from sticking to the wall of the reservoir motor cavity and should make assembly easier.

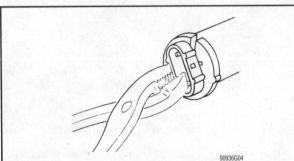

Fig. 37 Use pliers to remove the front washer pump from the fluid reservoir

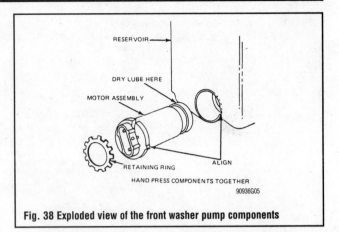

Fig. 38 Exploded view of the front washer pump components

8. Align the small projection on the motor end cap with the slot in the reservoir and assemble so that the seal is firmly seated against the bottom of the motor cavity.
9. Use a 1 inch socket (preferably a 12-point socket) and hand-press the motor retaining ring securely against the motor and plate.
10. Attach the electrical connection and the hoses to the reservoir.
11. Place the reservoir into position.
12. Install and tighten the reservoir retaining screws.
13. Fill the reservoir with fluid, check for leaks and repair as necessary.
14. Check the pump operation.

Rear

1. On station wagon models, remove the right-hand quarter trim panel.
2. On hatchback models, remove the left-hand quarter trim panel.
3. Unplug the reservoir electrical connector and hoses.
4. Unfasten the reservoir retaining screws and remove the reservoir from the vehicle.
5. Using an appropriate pry tool, pry the motor assembly from the reservoir.
6. Remove the pump screen and seal.
7. Flush the reservoir and clean any dirt from the reservoir or the pump motor cavity.

To install:

8. Lubricate the outside of the seal with a dry lubricant such as powered graphite. This prevents the seal from sticking to the wall of the reservoir motor cavity and should make assembly easier.
9. Install the screen and the seal. Make sure the seal is all the way down in the cavity.
10. Install the motor in the reservoir making sure it firmly seated in the seal.
11. Attach the electrical connection and the hoses to the reservoir.
12. Place the reservoir into position.
13. Install and tighten the reservoir retaining screws.
14. Fill the reservoir with fluid, check for leaks and repair as necessary.
15. Connect the negative battery cable.
16. Check the pump operation.
17. Install the trim panel.

INSTRUMENTS AND SWITCHES

Instrument Cluster

REMOVAL & INSTALLATION

1981–85 Models

▶ See Figure 39

1. Disconnect the negative battery cable.
2. Unfasten the bottom steering column cover screws and remove the cover.
3. Unfasten the cluster opening finish panel screws and remove the finish panel.

4. Unfasten the cluster-to-instrument panel retaining screws.
5. Reach up behind the instrument panel and disconnect the speedometer cable by pressing on the flat surface of the plastic connector.
6. Slide the cluster forward, unplug the cluster electrical connector and remove the cluster.

To install:

7. Attach the cluster electrical connector.
8. Install the cluster and tighten the cluster-to-instrument panel screws.
9. Reach up behind the instrument panel and connect the speedometer cable.
10. Install the cluster finish panel and tighten the screws.
11. Place the steering column cover into position and tighten the screws.
12. Connect the negative battery cable.

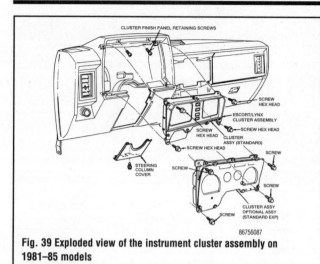

Fig. 39 Exploded view of the instrument cluster assembly on 1981–85 models

1986–90 Models

▶ **See Figures 40 thru 52**

1. Disconnect the negative battery cable.
2. Remove the two retaining screws at the bottom of the steering column opening and snap the steering column cover out.
3. Unfasten the 10 cluster opening finish panel retainer screws and remove the finish panel.
4. Remove the two upper and lower screws retaining the cluster to the instrument panel.
5. Reach under the instrument panel and disconnect the speedometer cable by pressing down on the flat surface of the plastic connector.
6. Pull the cluster away from the instrument panel. Disconnect the cluster feed plug from its receptacle in the printed circuit.

To install:

7. Attach the cluster electrical connector.
8. Install the cluster and tighten the cluster-to-instrument panel screws.
9. Reach up behind the instrument panel and connect the speedometer cable.
10. Install the cluster finish panel and tighten the screws.
11. Place the steering column cover into position and tighten the screws.
12. Connect the negative battery cable.

Gauges

REMOVAL & INSTALLATION

1. Disconnect the negative battery cable.
2. Remove the instrument cluster.

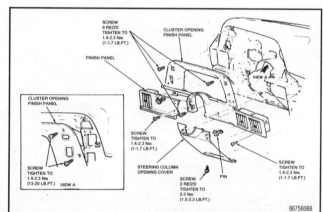

Fig. 40 Exploded view of the instrument cluster finish panel assembly on 1986–90 models

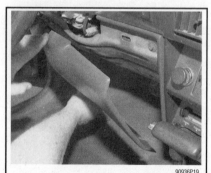

Fig. 41 Unfasten the steering column opening cover screws and remove the cover

Fig. 42 Remove the screws retaining the left-hand finish panel . . .

Fig. 43 . . . and remove the left side finish panel first

Fig. 44 Location of some of the finish panel retaining screws, as viewed from the passenger side of the vehicle

Fig. 45 Unfasten the remaining screws and pull the finish panel out . . .

Fig. 46 . . . then unplug any connectors from the finish panel, and remove the panel

Fig. 47 Location of some of the instrument cluster retaining screws

Fig. 48 After unfastening its retaining screws, slide the cluster out

Fig. 49 Make sure the speedometer cable is completely disconnected . . .

Fig. 50 . . . and unplug the cluster's electrical connection

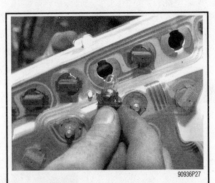

Fig. 51 If any of the cluster bulbs is defective, simply turn the bulb socket to remove it from the printed circuit board

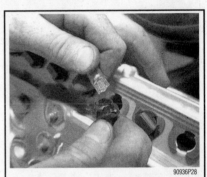

Fig. 52 To replace the bulb, pull the old one from the socket and push the new bulb into position

3. Unfasten the screws attaching the cluster mask to the backplate and remove the mask.

4. If equipped, unfasten the gauge-to-backplate retainers (always check that all the retainers are unfastened from the front and rear of the gauge).

5. Remove the gauge from the cluster.

To install:

6. Install the gauge.

7. If equipped, install and tighten the gauge-to-backplate retainers.

8. Install the cluster mask and tighten the retaining screws.

9. Install the instrument cluster.

10. Connect the negative battery cable.

Wiper Switch

REMOVAL & INSTALLATION

Windshield Wiper Switch

The front wiper switch is mounted on the steering column. Refer to and installation of this component.

Rear Window Wiper Switch

▶ See Figures 53 and 54

1. Unfasten the cluster opening finish panel screws and remove the panel by rocking the upper edge towards the driver.

2. Unplug the wiring connector from the rear washer switch.

3. Remove the washer switch from the instrument panel.

To install:

4. Engage the wiring connector.

5. Push the rear washer switch into the cluster finish panel until it snaps into place.

6. Install the cluster opening finish panel and tighten the screws.

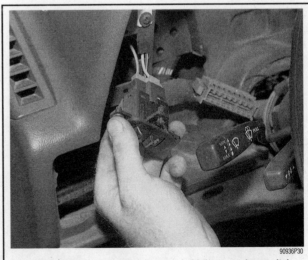

Fig. 53 After removing the finish panel, hold the rear wiper switch so that the electrical connector is accessible . . .

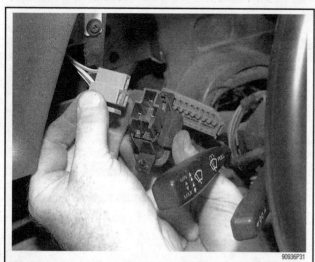

Fig. 54 . . . then unplug the electrical connector and remove the switch

Headlight Switch

REMOVAL & INSTALLATION

Knob Type

▶ See Figures 55, 56, 57, 58 and 59

1. Disconnect the negative battery cable.
2. On models without A/C, remove the left side air vent control cable retaining screws and let the cable hang.

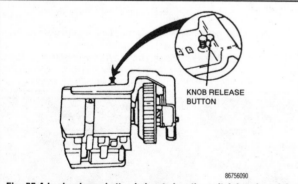

KNOB RELEASE BUTTON

Fig. 55 A knob release button is located on the switch housing of the knob type headlight switch

3. Remove the fuse panel bracket retaining screws. Move the fuse panel assembly aside to gain access to the headlight switch.
4. Pull the headlight knob out to the **ON** position. Depress the headlight knob and shaft retainer button and remove the knob and shaft assembly from the switch.
5. Remove the headlight switch retaining bezel.
6. Unplug the multiple connector plug and remove the switch from the instrument panel.

To install:

7. Install the headlight switch into the instrument panel.
8. Attach the multiple connector and install the headlight switch retaining bezel.
9. Install the knob and shaft assembly by inserting the shaft into the switch and gently pushing until the shaft locks in position.
10. Move the fuse panel back into position and attach fuse panel to the bracket with the two retaining screws.
11. On models without A/C, install the left side air vent control cable and bracket.
12. Connect the negative battery cable.

Rocker Type

▶ See Figure 60

1. Disconnect the negative battery cable.
2. Insert a thin flat bladed prytool under the flange at the side of the switch as illustrated, to depress the spring retaining clip. Twist the blade to remove the switch on one side.
3. Repeat the procedure on the other side of the switch with the blade.
4. Pull the switch and electrical connector from the instrument panel.

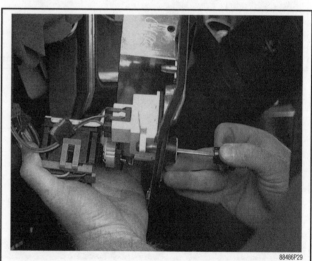

Fig. 56 While pressing the knob release button, remove the knob and shaft

Fig. 57 Unscrew the bezel assembly

Fig. 58 Separate the switch from its mounting on the trim piece

Fig. 59 Unplug the electrical connection and remove the switch

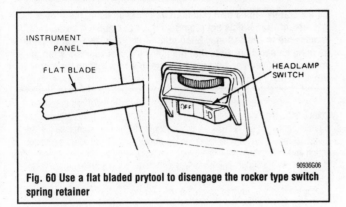

Fig. 60 Use a flat bladed prytool to disengage the rocker type switch spring retainer

5. Unplug the electrical connector and remove the switch.
To install:
6. Attach the switch electrical connector.
7. Place the switch into position and push on the front face of the switch until the spring clips are engaged.
8. Connect the negative battery cable and check for proper switch operation.

LIGHTING

Headlights

REMOVAL & INSTALLATION

Sealed Beam Type

♦ **See Figure 61**

1. Unfasten the headlight door mounted screws and pull the headlight forward.
2. Unplug the parking lamp socket and remove the headlight door.
3. Unfasten the retainer ring screws and remove the retainer ring.
4. Pull the headlight forward and unplug the headlight electrical connector.
5. Remove the headlight assembly.
To install:
6. Attach the headlight electrical connector.
7. Place the headlight into position making sure to align the headlight glass tabs into the positioning slots.
8. Install the retainer ring and tighten the retaining screws.

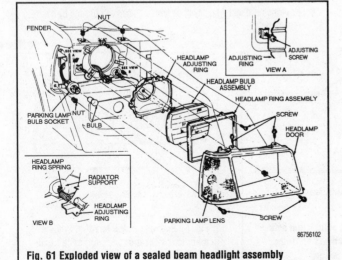

Fig. 61 Exploded view of a sealed beam headlight assembly

Back-up Light Switch

REMOVAL & INSTALLATION

Automatic Transaxle

The neutral safety switch controls the back-up lights on models with an automatic transaxle. Refer to Section 7 of this manual for switch removal and installation.

Manual Transaxle

1. Unplug the electrical connector from the back-up switch.
2. Place the transaxle in Reverse.
3. Using a suitable wrench, remove the back-up light switch.

➡**To prevent internal damage, do not shift the transaxle until the switch has been installed.**

To install:
4. Apply Teflon_ pipe sealant to the threads of the switch in a clockwise direction.
5. Install the switch and tighten to 14–18 ft. lbs. (19–24 Nm).
6. Attach the electrical connector to the back-up switch.
7. Place the transaxle in neutral.
8. Start the vehicle and check for proper switch operation.

➡**Remove the double sided tape on the outer edge of the headlight door and replace with new tape before installing the door.**

9. Attach the parking lamp socket to the parking lamp.
10. Install the headlight door and tighten the retaining screws.
11. Turn the headlights on and check for proper operation.
12. Adjust and aim the headlights as necessary.

Halogen Type

♦ **See Figures 62 and 63**

➡**The replaceable halogen headlamp bulb contains gas under pressure. The bulb may shatter if the glass envelope is scratched or the bulb is dropped. Handle the bulb carefully. Grasp the bulb ONLY by its plastic base. Do not touch the glass as deposits left by your fingers will cause hot spots when the bulb is illumined which may cause it to prematurely fail. Keep the bulb out of the reach of children.**

1. Check to see that the headlight switch is in the **OFF** position.
2. Raise the hood and locate the bulb installed in the rear of the headlight body.
3. Unplug the electrical connector by depressing the locktab and pulling the connector rearward.
4. Remove the bulb retaining ring by rotating it counterclockwise (when viewed from the rear) about ⅛ of a turn, then slide the ring off the plastic base.

➡**Keep the bulb retaining ring, it will be reused with the new bulb.**

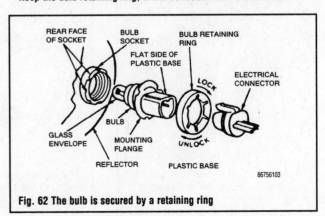

Fig. 62 The bulb is secured by a retaining ring

Fig. 63 Do not touch the glass portion of the bulb when removing or installing it

5. Carefully remove the headlight bulb from its socket in the reflector by gently pulling it straight backward out of the socket. Do not rotate the bulb while removing it.

To install:

6. With the flat side of the plastic base of the bulb facing upward, insert the glass envelope of the bulb into the socket. Turn the base slightly to the left or right, if necessary, to align the grooves in the forward part of the plastic base with the corresponding locating tabs inside the socket. When the grooves are aligned, push the bulb firmly into the socket until the mounting flange on the base contacts the rear face of the socket.

7. Slip the bulb retaining ring over the rear of the plastic base against the mounting flange. Lock the ring into the socket by rotating the ring clockwise. A stop will be felt when the retaining ring is fully engaged.

8. Push the electrical connector into the rear of the plastic until it snaps and locks into position.

9. Turn the headlights on and check for proper operation.

AIMING THE HEADLIGHTS

♦ See Figures 64, 65, 66, 67 and 68

The headlights must be properly aimed to provide the best, safest road illumination. The lights should be checked for proper aim and adjusted as necessary. Certain state and local authorities have requirements for headlight aiming; these should be checked before adjustment is made.

❋❋ CAUTION

About once a year, when the headlights are replaced or any time front end work is performed on your vehicle, the headlight should be accurately aimed by a reputable repair shop using the proper equipment. Headlights not properly aimed can make it virtually impossible to see and may blind other drivers on the road, possibly causing an accident. Note that the following procedure is a temporary fix, until you can take your vehicle to a repair shop for a proper adjustment.

Headlight adjustment may be temporarily made using a wall, as described below, or on the rear of another vehicle. When adjusted, the lights should not glare in oncoming car or truck windshields, nor should they illuminate the passenger compartment of vehicles driving in front of you. These adjustments are rough and should always be fine-tuned by a repair shop which is equipped with headlight aiming tools. Improper adjustments may be both dangerous and illegal.

For most of the vehicles covered by this manual, horizontal and vertical aiming of each sealed beam unit is provided by two adjusting screws which move the retaining ring and adjusting plate against the tension of a coil spring. There is no adjustment for focus; this is done during headlight manufacturing.

➡Because the composite headlight assembly is bolted into position, no adjustment should be necessary or possible. Some applications, however, may be bolted to an adjuster plate or may be retained by adjusting screws. If so, follow this procedure when adjusting the lights, BUT always have the adjustment checked by a reputable shop.

Before removing the headlight bulb or disturbing the headlamp in any way, note the current settings in order to ease headlight adjustment upon reassembly. If the high or low beam setting of the old lamp still works, this can be done using the wall of a garage or a building:

1. Park the vehicle on a level surface, with the fuel tank about ½ full and with the vehicle empty of all extra cargo (unless normally carried). The vehicle should be facing a wall which is no less than 6 feet (1.8m) high and 12 feet (3.7m) wide. The front of the vehicle should be about 25 feet from the wall.

2. If aiming is to be performed outdoors, it is advisable to wait until dusk in order to properly see the headlight beams on the wall. If done in a garage, darken the area around the wall as much as possible by closing shades or hanging cloth over the windows.

3. Turn the headlights **ON** and mark the wall at the center of each light's low beam, then switch on the brights and mark the center of each light's high beam. A short length of masking tape which is visible from the front of the vehicle may be used. Although marking all four positions is advisable, marking one position from each light should be sufficient.

4. If neither beam on one side is working, and if another like-sized vehicle is available, park the second one in the exact spot where the vehicle was and mark the beams using the same-side light. Then switch the vehicles so the one to be aimed is back in the original spot. It must be parked no closer to or farther away from the wall than the second vehicle.

5. Perform any necessary repairs, but make sure the vehicle is not moved, or is returned to the exact spot from which the lights were marked. Turn the headlights **ON** and adjust the beams to match the marks on the wall.

6. Have the headlight adjustment checked as soon as possible by a reputable repair shop.

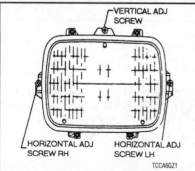

Fig. 64 Location of the aiming screws on most vehicles with sealed beam headlights

TCCA6GZ1

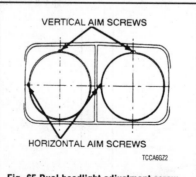

Fig. 65 Dual headlight adjustment screw locations—one side shown here (other side should be mirror image)

TCCA6GZ2

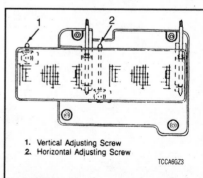

1. Vertical Adjusting Screw
2. Horizontal Adjusting Screw

Fig. 66 Example of the headlight adjustment screw location for composite headlamps

TCCA6GZ3

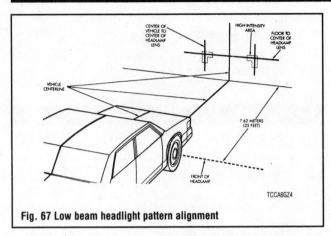

Fig. 67 Low beam headlight pattern alignment

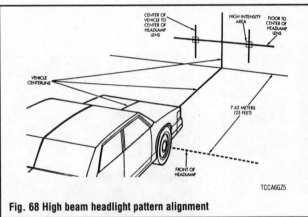

Fig. 68 High beam headlight pattern alignment

Front Turn Signal and Parking Lights

REMOVAL & INSTALLATION

Escort and Lynx Models

1981–85 MODELS

▶ **See Figure 61**

1. Remove the screws that retain the headlamp door.
2. Pull the headlight door forward and remove the parking light bulb socket from the light assembly.
3. Remove the bulb by pushing in and turning counterclockwise.
4. Installation is the reverse of removal.

1986–90 MODELS

▶ **See Figures 69 and 70**

1. Remove the three screws attaching the parking light to the headlight housing.
2. Hold the parking light with both hands and pull the lamp forward to release the upper hidden attachment.
3. From the side, remove the bulb socket and replace the bulb.
   To install:
4. Install a new bulb and attach the socket to the lens.
5. Place the parking light into position, then install and tighten the retaining screws.

EXP and LN7 Models

▶ **See Figure 71**

1. Remove the two parking light retaining screws and pull the light assembly forward.
2. Remove the bulb socket by twisting and remove the bulb.
3. To install, reverse the removal procedure.

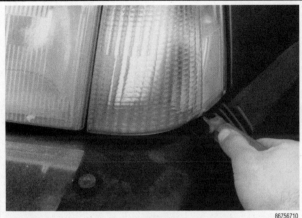

Fig. 69 Remove the screws that retain the parking light to the headlight housing

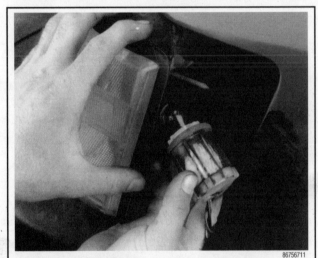

Fig. 70 Once the headlight is pulled forward, remove the parking light bulb socket from the light assembly

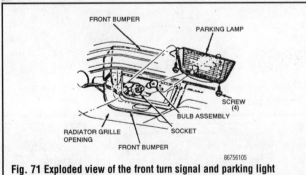

Fig. 71 Exploded view of the front turn signal and parking light mounting—EXP/LN7

Rear Turn Signal, Brake and Parking Lights

REMOVAL & INSTALLATION

Except Wagon Models

1. Remove the luggage compartment rear trim panel.
2. Remove the socket(s) from the lamp body and replace the bulb(s).
3. Installation is the reverse of removal.

Wagon Models

▶ See Figures 72, 73, 74 and 75

1. Remove the screws retaining the light assembly to the rear quarter opening.
2. Pull the light assembly out of the opening and remove the light socket to replace the bulb.
3. Installation is the reverse of removal.

High-Mount Brake Light

REMOVAL & INSTALLATION

Except Wagon Models

▶ See Figure 76

1. Remove the interior trim panel from the hatch.
2. Remove the socket and bulb from the lamp.
3. Remove the bulb from the socket.
4. Installation is the reverse of removal.

Wagon Models

▶ See Figures 77, 78, 79 and 80

1. Remove the two screws from the lens face.
2. Remove the socket and replace the bulb.
3. Installation is the reverse of procedure.

Back-Up Light

REMOVAL & INSTALLATION

▶ See Figures 81, 82, 83 and 84

1. Unfasten the lens retaining screws.
2. Pull the lens assembly away from the body until you can access the bulb socket assembly.
3. Turn the socket assembly to separate it from the lens.
4. Remove the bulb from the socket.
5. Installation is the reverse of removal.

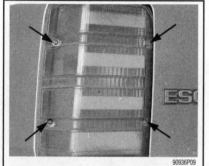

Fig. 72 Location of the rear turn signal, brake and parking light lens retaining screws—wagon models

Fig. 73 Separate the lens from the body to access the bulb's electrical connection

Fig. 74 Turn the socket assembly counter-clockwise to separate it from the lens

Fig. 75 Push the bulb in slightly, then turn the bulb to remove it from the socket

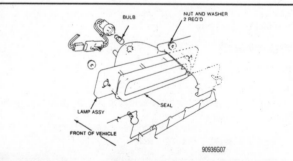

Fig. 76 High-mount brake light assembly—except wagon models

Fig. 77 Unfasten the high-mount brake light lens screws . . .

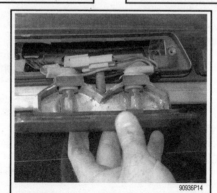

Fig. 78 . . . and separate the lens from the body to access the socket assemblies

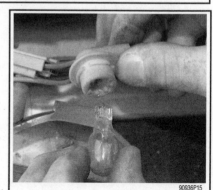

Fig. 79 Detach the socket from the lens and pull the bulb straight from the socket

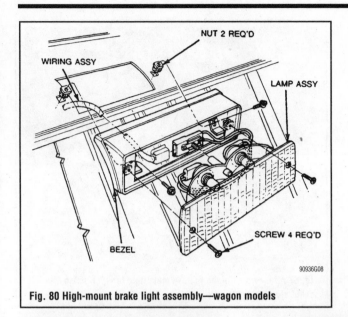

Fig. 80 High-mount brake light assembly—wagon models

Fig. 81 Unfasten the back-up light lens retaining screws . . .

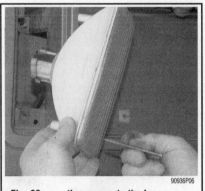

Fig. 82 . . . then separate the lens assembly from the body

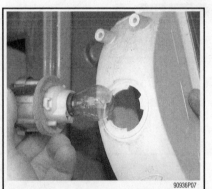

Fig. 83 Turn the socket assembly counterclockwise to separate it from the lens

Fig. 84 Push the bulb in slightly, then turn the bulb to remove it from the socket

Dome Light

REMOVAL & INSTALLATION

♦ See Figures 85 and 86

1. Carefully pry the dome light lens from the housing.
2. Pull the bulb from the housing.
3. Installation is the reverse of removal.

Courtesy/Map Lamp Combination

REMOVAL & INSTALLATION

1. Push the retainer forward and lower the lamp.
2. Unscrew the lens from the barrel.
3. Remove the bulb by turning it counterclockwise while pushing it in.
4. Installation is the reverse of removal.

Cargo Area Light

REMOVAL & INSTALLATION

1. Carefully remove the light lens from the housing by pulling it down on the right-hand side.

Fig. 85 Remove the dome light lens from its housing

✻✻ WARNING

If using needlenose pliers or its equivalent to remove the bulb, wear eye protection to prevent injury if the bulb should happen to break.

2. Using needlenose pliers or their equivalent, pull the bulb from the housing being careful not to break the bulb.
3. Installation is the reverse of removal.

Fig. 86 Grasp the dome light bulb and pull to remove

Fig. 87 After removing the license plate light lens, unfasten the socket assembly retainers

License Plate Lights

REMOVAL & INSTALLATION

Except EXP Models

▶ See Figures 87, 88, 89 and 90

1. Unfasten the license plate lens retaining screws or blind rivets.
2. Remove the lens assembly.

3. Unfasten the socket retainers.
4. Seperate the socket assembly from the lens.
5. Remove the bulb from the socket.
6. Installation is the reverse of removal.

EXP Models

The license plate lamp on the EXP model is part of the rear turn signal, brake and parking lamp assembly. Refer to the procedure in this section for the removal and installation of the bulb assembly.

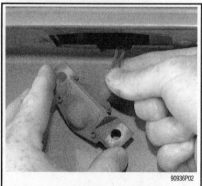

Fig. 88 Grasp the socket assembly and turn it counterclockwise . . .

Fig. 89 . . . to separate the socket assembly from the lens

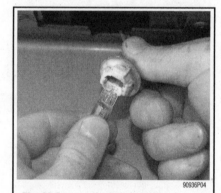

Fig. 90 Remove the bulb by pulling it straight from the socket

TRAILER WIRING

Wiring the vehicle for towing is fairly easy. There are a number of good wiring kits available and these should be used, rather than trying to design your own.

All trailers will need brake lights and turn signals as well as tail lights and side marker lights. Most areas require extra marker lights for overwide trailers. Also, most areas have recently required back-up lights for trailers, and most trailer manufacturers have been building trailers with back-up lights for several years.

Additionally, some Class I, most Class II and just about all Class III and IV trailers will have electric brakes. Add to this number an accessories wire, to operate trailer internal equipment or to charge the trailer's battery, and you can have as many as seven wires in the harness.

Determine the equipment on your trailer and buy the wiring kit necessary. The kit will contain all the wires needed, plus a plug adapter set which includes the female plug, mounted on the bumper or hitch, and the male plug, wired into, or plugged into the trailer harness.

When installing the kit, follow the manufacturer's instructions. The color coding of the wires is usually standard throughout the industry. One point to note: some domestic vehicles, and most imported vehicles, have separate turn signals. On most domestic vehicles, the brake lights and rear turn signals operate with the same bulb. For those vehicles without separate turn signals, you can purchase an isolation unit so that the brake lights won't blink whenever the turn signals are operated.

One, final point, the best kits are those with a spring loaded cover on the vehicle mounted socket. This cover prevents dirt and moisture from corroding the terminals. Never let the vehicle socket hang loosely; always mount it securely to the bumper or hitch.

CIRCUIT PROTECTION

Fuses

▶ **See Figures 91 and 92**

Fuses are a one-time circuit protection. If a circuit is overloaded or shorts, the thin metal fuse acts like a weak (and expendable) link in a chain by burning. This cuts off electrical flow before the circuit is damaged. Fuses inserted to replace blown fuses will continue to blow unless the circuit is first repaired.

The fuse panel is located below and to the left of the steering column.

Fig. 91 The fuse panel is located beneath the instrument panel, to the left of the steering column

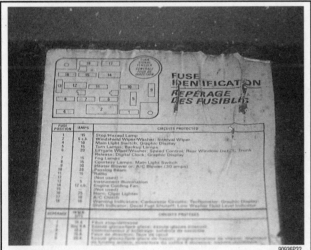

Fig. 92 This sticker outlining the fuse panel and fuse locations is located on the back of the glove box door

REPLACEMENT

1. If equipped, remove the fuse panel cover.
2. Locate the fuse to be removed.

3. If equipped with a small fuse removal tool (usually attached to the inside of the fuse panel cover), remove the fuse from its cavity and inspect it to see if its blown.
4. If the fuse is blown, replace it with a fuse of the same amperage rating.
5. If equipped, replace the cover.
6. If the fuse continues to blow, check the circuit or component that the fuse is protecting and repair as necessary.

Fusible Link

Fusible links are short lengths of special, Hypalon (high temperature) insulated wire, integral with the engine compartment wiring harness; they should not be confused with standard wire. A fusible link is several wire gauges smaller than the circuit which it protects. Under no circumstances should a fusible link replacement repair be made using a length of standard wire cut from bulk stock or from another wiring harness.

Fusible links are used to prevent major wire harness damage in the event of a short circuit or an overload condition in the wiring circuits that are normally not fused, due to carrying high amperage loads or because of their locations within the wiring harness. Each fusible link is of a fixed value for a specific electrical load and should a fusible link fail, the cause of the failure must be determine and repaired prior to installing a new fusible link of the same value. The following is a listing of fusible links wire gauges and their locations:

➡**The color coding of replacement fusible links may vary from the production color coding that is outlined in the text that follows.**

  • Black 16 Gauge Wire—one fusible link located in the wiring for the rear window defogger.
  • Brown 18 Gauge Wire—one fusible link is used to protect the heater fan motor circuit.
  • Blue 20 Gauge Wire—two fusible links in the wire between the starter relay and the EFE heater. On 1988–90 vehicles, a fusible link is installed in the engine compartment near the starter relay and protects the passive restraint module circuit.

➡**Always disconnect the negative battery cable before servicing the vehicle's electrical system.**

Circuit Breakers

RESETTING

Circuit breakers are used to protect the various components of the electrical system, such as headlights and windshield wipers. The circuit breakers for the vehicles this manual covers are located either in the control switch or mounted on or near the fuse panel.

Circuit breakers operate when an electrical circuit overloads, or exceeds its rated amperage. Once activated, they may be reset.

There are two kinds of circuit breakers. One type will automatically reset itself after a given length of time; the second will not reset itself until the problem in the circuit has been repaired.

Flashers

REPLACEMENT

The turn signal flasher is located on the front side of the fuse panel. The hazard warning flasher is located on the rear side of the fuse panel.
1. If equipped, remove the fuse panel cover.
2. Locate the flasher to be removed.
3. Grasp the flasher and pull it straight from the fuse panel.
4. Align the electrical contacts on the base of the replacement flasher with the fuse box, then push in the flasher until it seats fully.
5. If applicable, install the fuse panel cover.

WIRING DIAGRAMS

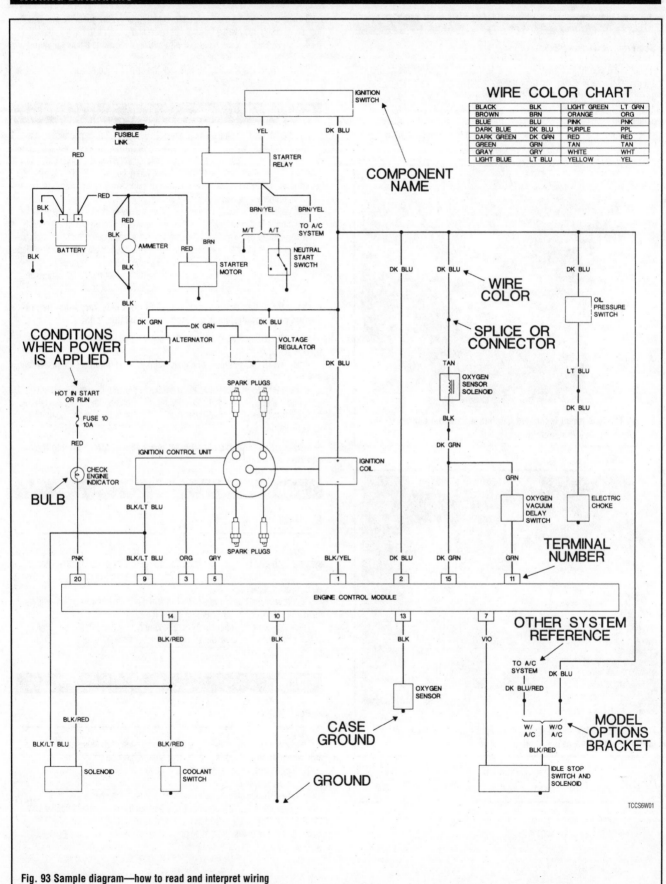

Fig. 93 Sample diagram—how to read and interpret wiring

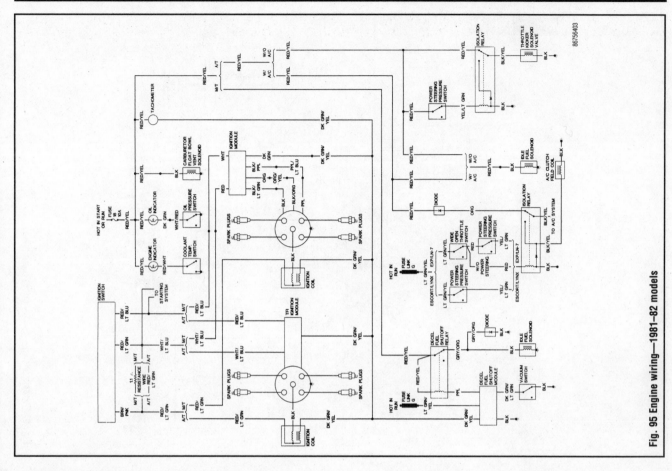

Fig. 95 Engine wiring—1981-82 models

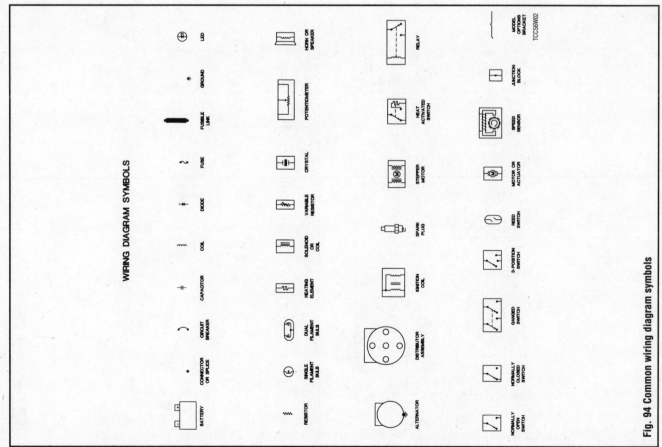

Fig. 94 Common wiring diagram symbols

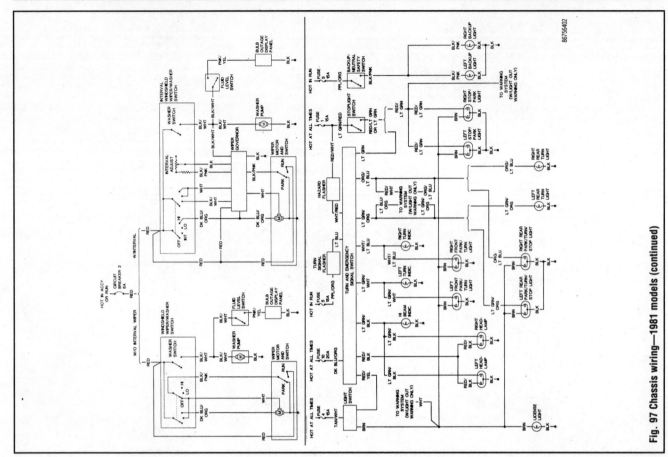

Fig. 97 Chassis wiring—1981 models (continued)

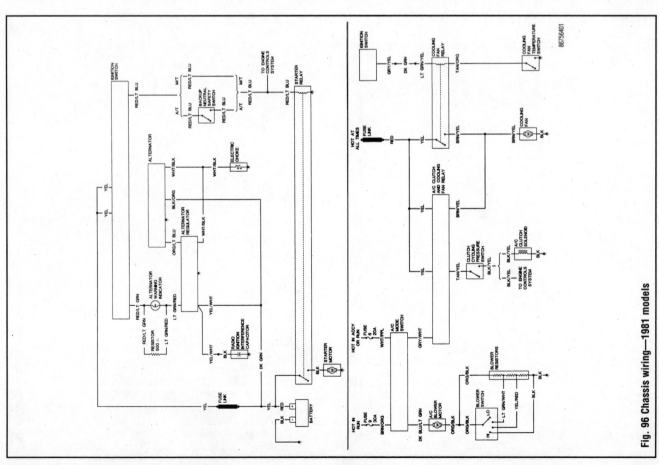

Fig. 96 Chassis wiring—1981 models

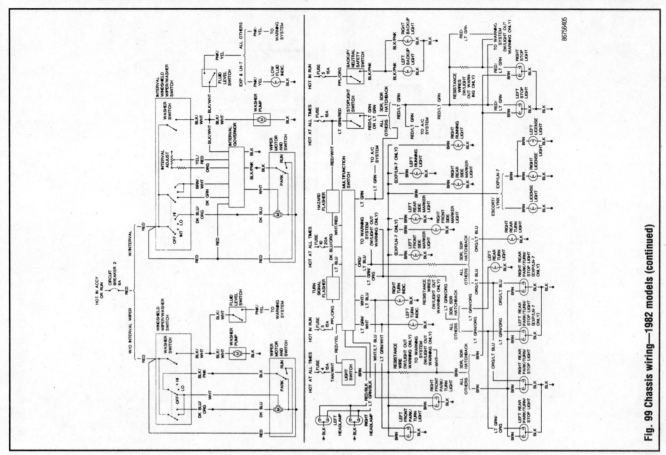

Fig. 99 Chassis wiring—1982 models (continued)

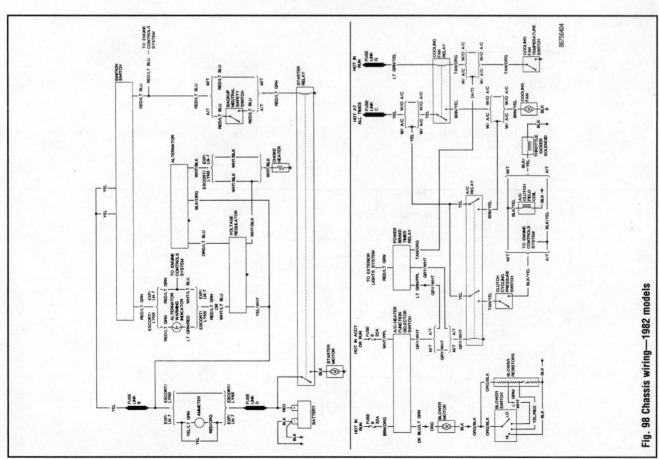

Fig. 98 Chassis wiring—1982 models

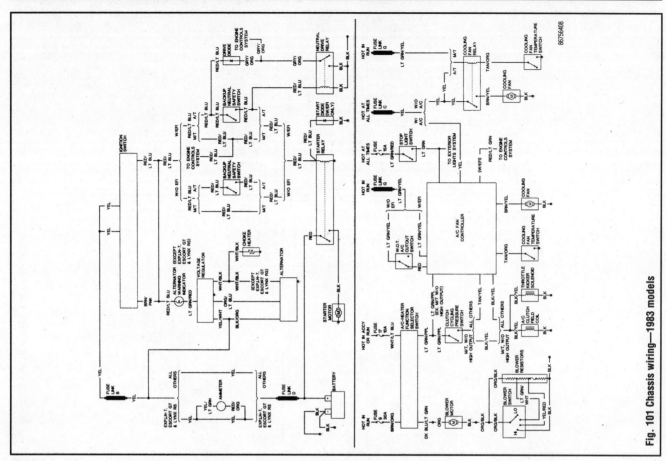

Fig. 101 Chassis wiring—1983 models

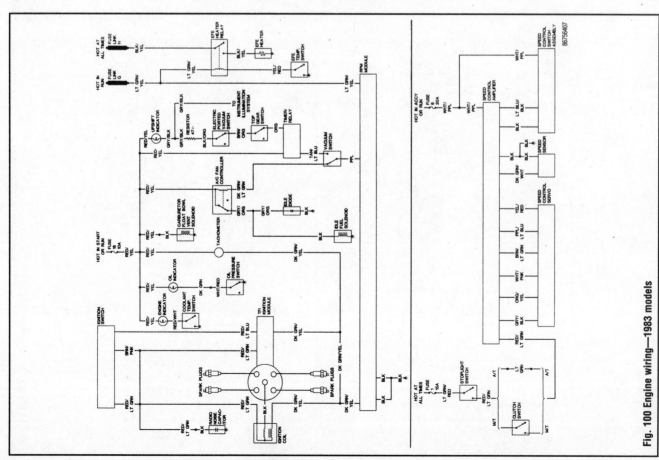

Fig. 100 Engine wiring—1983 models

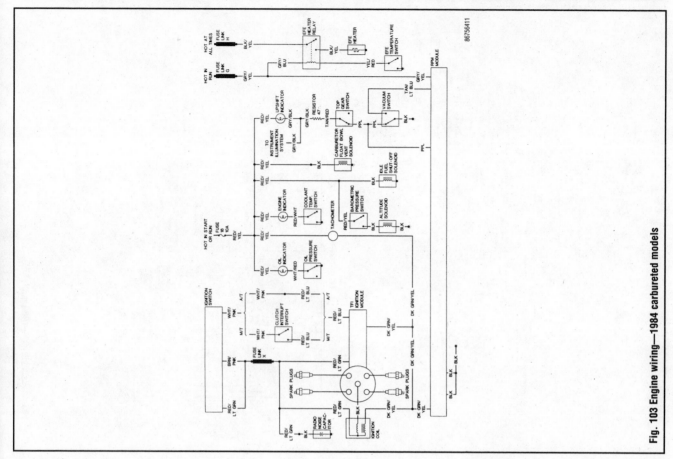

Fig. 103 Engine wiring—1984 carbureted models

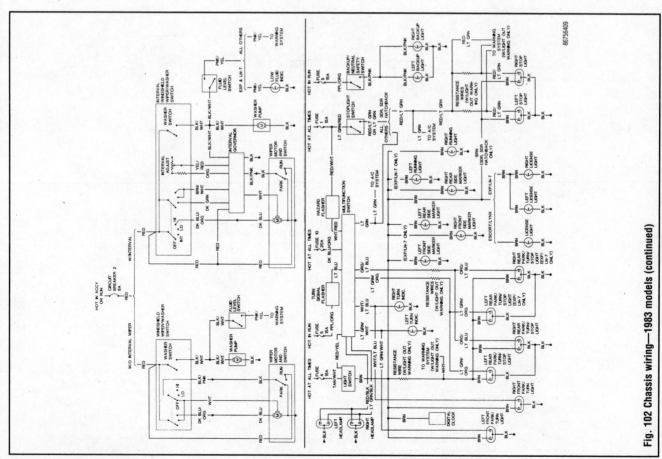

Fig. 102 Chassis wiring—1983 models (continued)

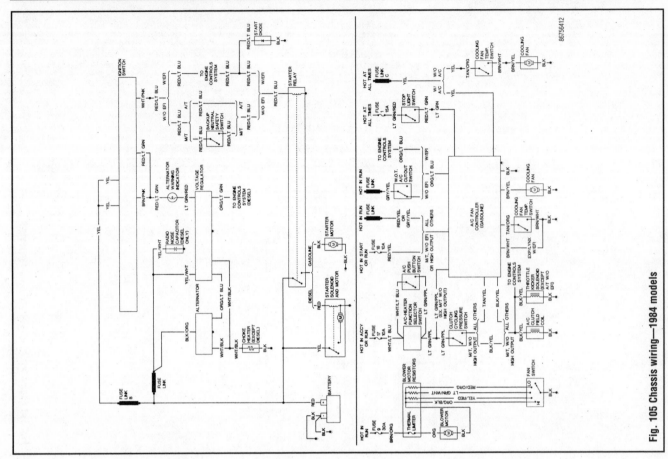

Fig. 105 Chassis wiring—1984 models

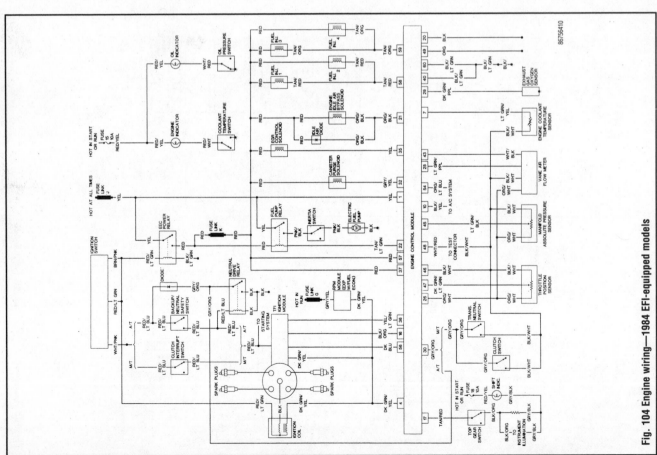

Fig. 104 Engine wiring—1984 EFI-equipped models

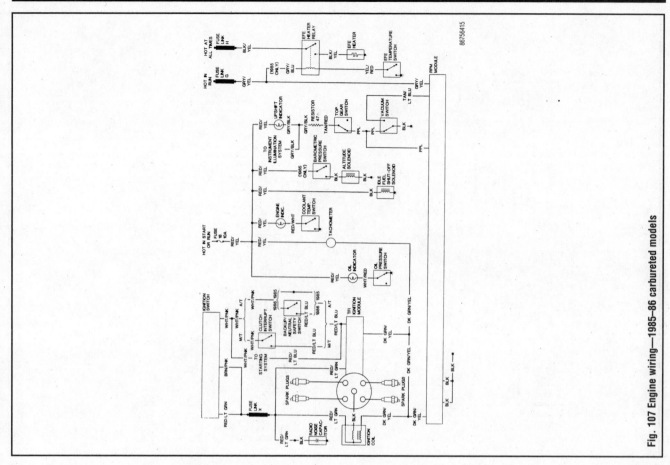

Fig. 107 Engine wiring—1985–86 carbureted models

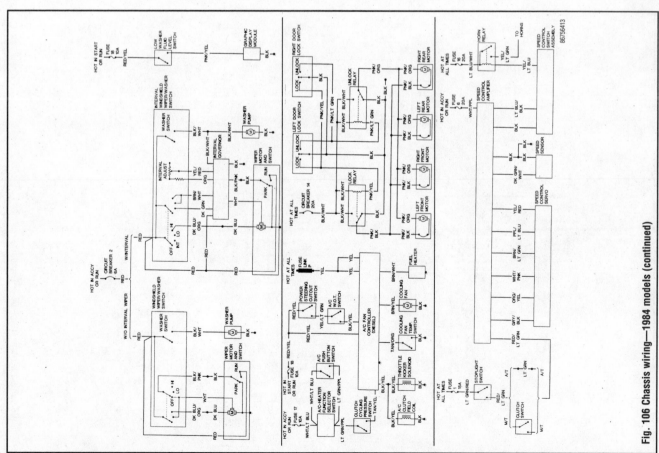

Fig. 106 Chassis wiring—1984 models (continued)

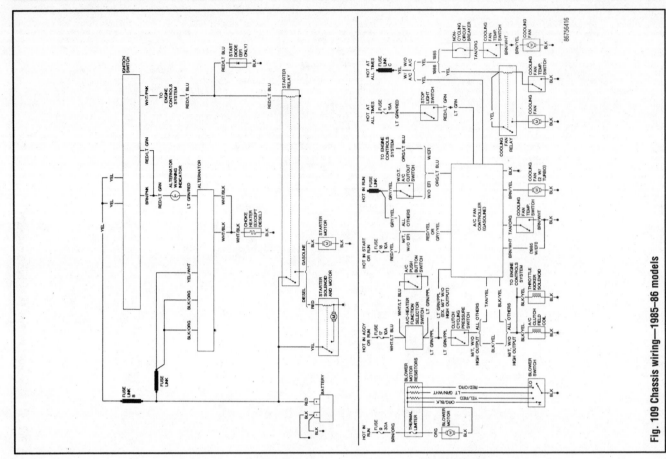

Fig. 109 Chassis wiring—1985-86 models

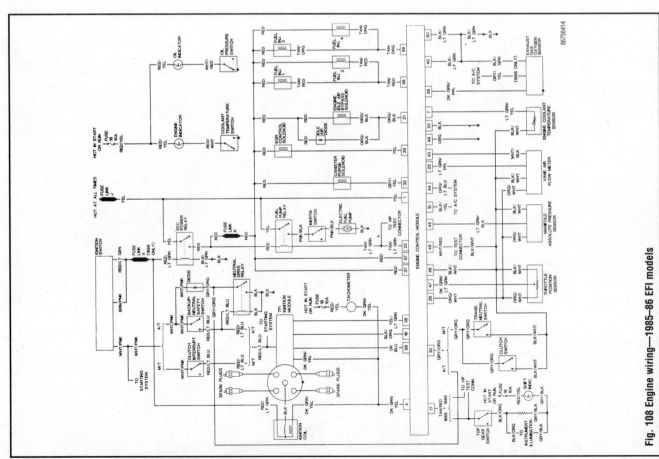

Fig. 108 Engine wiring—1985-86 EFI models

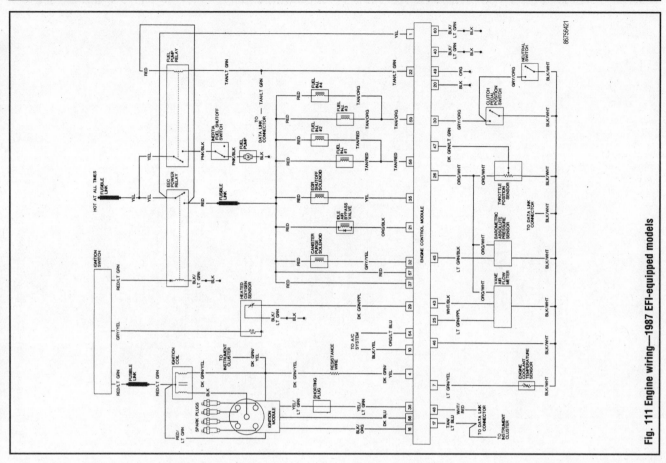

Fig. 111 Engine wiring—1987 EFI-equipped models

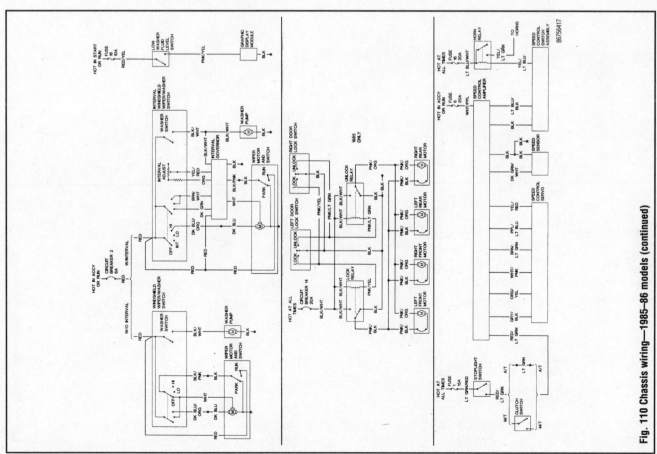

Fig. 110 Chassis wiring—1985–86 models (continued)

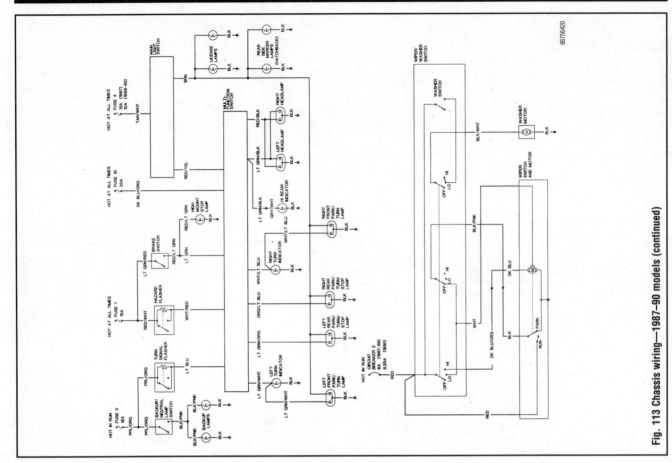

Fig. 113 Chassis wiring—1987–90 models (continued)

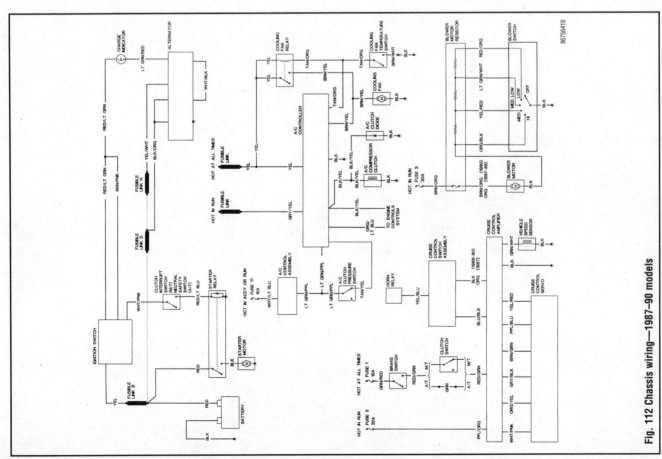

Fig. 112 Chassis wiring—1987–90 models

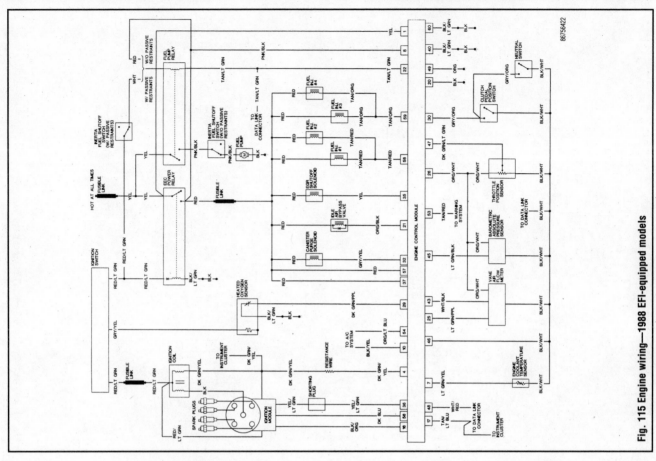

Fig. 115 Engine wiring—1988 EFI-equipped models

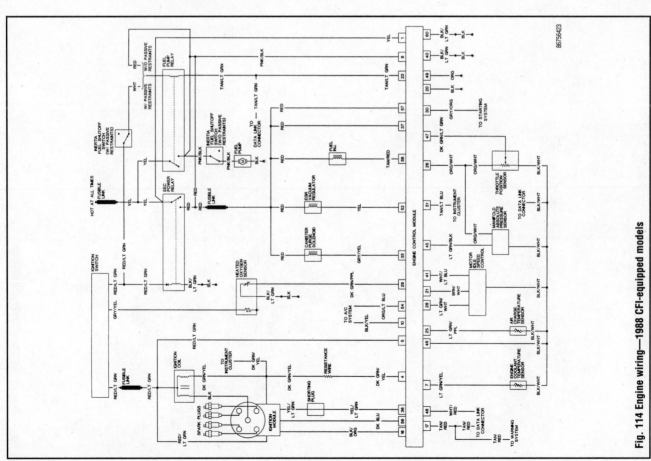

Fig. 114 Engine wiring—1988 CFI-equipped models

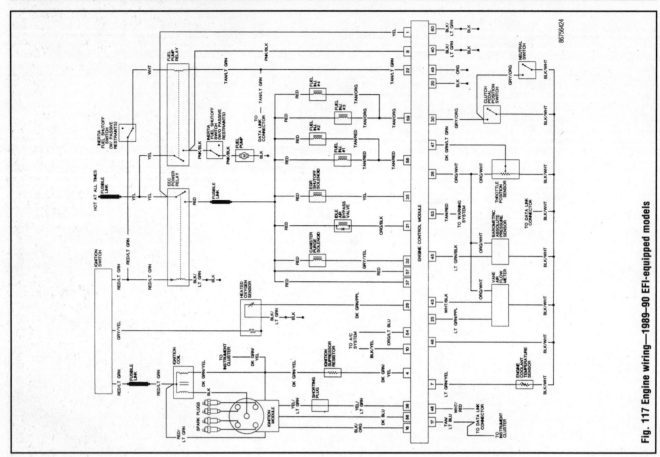

Fig. 117 Engine wiring—1989—90 EFI-equipped models

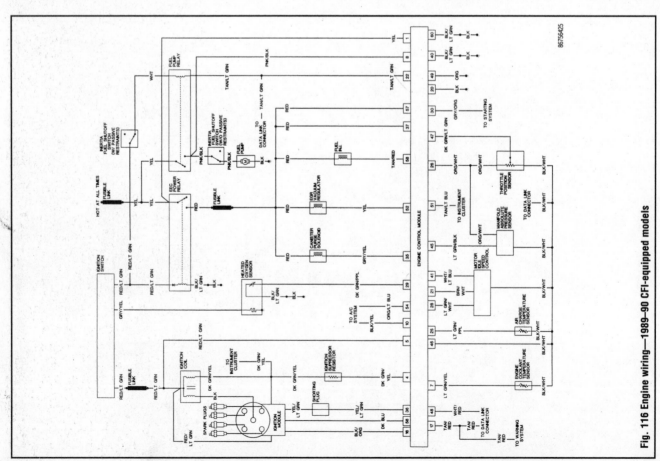

Fig. 116 Engine wiring—1989—90 CFI-equipped models

7

DRIVE TRAIN

MANUAL TRANSAXLE

Understanding the Manual Transaxle

Because of the way an internal combustion engine breathes, it can produce torque, or twisting force, only within a narrow speed range. Most modern, overhead valve pushrod engines must turn at about 2500 rpm to produce their peak torque. By 4500 rpm they are producing so little torque that continued increases in engine speed produce no power increases. The torque peak on overhead camshaft engines is generally much higher, but much narrower.

The manual transaxle and clutch are employed to vary the relationship between engine speed and the speed of the wheels so that adequate engine power can be produced under all circumstances. The clutch allows engine torque to be applied to the transaxle input shaft gradually, due to mechanical slippage. Consequently, the vehicle may be started smoothly from a full stop. The transaxle changes the ratio between the rotating speeds of the engine and the wheels by the use of gears. The gear ratios allow full engine power to be applied to the wheels during acceleration at low speeds and at highway/passing speeds.

In a front wheel drive transaxle, power is usually transmitted from the input shaft to a mainshaft or output shaft located slightly beneath and to the side of the input shaft. The gears of the mainshaft mesh with gears on the input shaft, allowing power to be carried from one to the other. All forward gears are in constant mesh and are free from rotating with the shaft unless the synchronizer and clutch is engaged. Shifting from one gear to the next causes one of the gears to be freed from rotating with the shaft and locks another to it. Gears are locked and unlocked by internal dog clutches which slide between the center of the gear and the shaft. The forward gears employ synchronizers; friction members which smoothly bring gear and shaft to the same speed before the toothed dog clutches are engaged.

Manual Transaxle Assembly

REMOVAL & INSTALLATION

1981–85 Models

1. Disconnect the negative battery terminal.
2. Remove the two transaxle-to-engine top mounting bolts.
3. Wedge a wood block about 7 in. (178mm) long under the clutch pedal to hold it slightly beyond its normal position.
4. Remove the clutch cable from the clutch release lever by pulling it forward to disconnect it from the clutch release lever.
5. If necessary, remove the clutch cable casing from the rib on top of the transaxle case.
6. On models equipped, unfasten the air management valve bracket-to-transaxle bolts.
7. Raise the vehicle and support it on jackstands.
8. If necessary, remove the brake line routing clamps from the front wheels.
9. Remove the bolt that secures the lower control arm ball joint to the steering knuckle assembly, and pry the lower control arm away from the knuckle. When installing, a new nut and bolt must be used.

➡**The plastic shield installed behind the rotor contains a molded pocket for the lower control arm ball joint. When removing the control arm from the knuckle, bend the shield toward the rotor to provide clearance.**

10. Use a suitable pryar to pry the right inboard CV-joint from the transaxle, then remove the CV-joint and halfshaft by pulling outward on the steering knuckle. Wire the CV-joint/halfshaft assembly in a level position to prevent it from expanding.

➡**When the CV-joint is pulled out of the transaxle fluid will leak out. Install shipping plugs T81P-1177-B or their equivalent to prevent dislocation of the differential side gears.**

11. Repeat the procedures and remove the left-hand CV-joint/halfshaft from the transaxle.

12. Remove the stabilizer bar.
13. Disconnect the speedometer cable and unplug the back-up light electrical connector at the transaxle.
14. On models equipped, unplug the neutral sensing switch.
15. Remove the three nuts from the starter mounting studs which hold the engine roll restrictor bracket.
16. Remove the roll restrictor and the starter stud bolts.
17. Unfasten the stiffener brace attaching bolts from the lower clutch housing.
18. Remove the shift mechanism crossover spring.
19. Remove the shift mechanism stabilizer bar-to-transaxle bolt.
20. Unfasten the shift mechanism-to-shift shaft mechanism bolt, then disconnect the shift mechanism from the shift shaft.
21. Place a transaxle jack under the transaxle.
22. Loosen the rear transaxle mount stud.
23. Unfasten the one upper and two lower rear transaxle bolts.
24. Unfasten the three front transaxle front mount bolts.

➡**Before supporting the engine with a jack under the oil pan, place a block of wood between the jack-to-engine contact surface.**

25. Lower the transaxle support jack until it clears the rear mount and support the engine with a jack, under the oil pan.
26. Remove the four remaining engine to transaxle bolts.

✳✳ CAUTION

The transaxle case may have sharp edges. Wear protective gloves when handling the transaxle.

27. Remove the transaxle assembly.
To install:
28. Using the transaxle jack, raise transaxle into position.
29. Engage the input shaft spline into the clutch disc and slowly work the transaxle onto the dowel sleeves.

➡**Make sure the transaxle is flush with the engine before installing the bolts.**

30. Install the four engine to transaxle bolts. Tighten the transaxle-to-engine bolts to 28–31 ft. lbs. (38–42 Nm).
31. Connect the speedometer cable.
32. Position the managed air valve bracket and rear mount over the rear mount bolt locations in the case.
33. Install the rear transaxle mount bolts and tighten them to 40–50 ft lbs. (55–70 Nm).
34. Install the rear mount stud nut and tighten the nut to 38–41 ft. lbs. (52–56 Nm).
35. Install the front transaxle mount bolts and tighten them to 40–50 ft lbs. (55–70 Nm).
36. Attach the back-up light switch and neutral sensing switch electrical connectors making sure the locking tabs are fully engaged.
37. Remove the transaxle jack from under the transaxle.
38. Install the stiffener brace bolts and tighten the bolts to 15–21 ft. lbs. (21–28 Nm).
39. Place the starter motor in position and install the motor retaining bolts. Tighten the bolts to 30–40 ft. lbs. (41–54 Nm).
40. Install the engine roll restrictor and its retaining nuts. Tighten the nuts to 25–30 ft. lbs. (34–40 Nm).
41. Install the shift mechanism stabilizer attaching bolt. Tighten the bolt to 23–32 ft. lbs. (38–44 Nm).
42. Attach the shift mechanism to the input shift rail. Tighten the bolt to 7–10 ft. lbs. (9–13 Nm).
43. Install the left and right CV-joint/halfshafts to the transaxle.

➡**When installing the CV-joint/halfshaft assemblies into the transaxle, install new circlips on the inner stub shaft, carefully install the assemblies into the transaxle to prevent damaging the oil seals, and insure that both joints are fully seated in the transaxle by lightly prying outward to confirm they are seated. If the circlips are not seated, the joints will move out of the transaxle.**

44. Install the bolt that secures the lower control arm ball joint to the steering knuckle assembly. When installing, a new nut and bolt must be used. Tighten the nut to 37–44 ft. lbs. (50–60 Nm).

45. Attach the brake line routing clamps from the front wheels. Tighten the clamp bolt to 8 ft. lbs. (11 Nm).

46. Install the stabilizer bar and its retainers. Tighten the bar mounting brackets to 40–44 ft. lbs. (54–60 Nm) and the stabilizer-to-control arm nuts to 59–73 ft. lbs. (80–90 Nm).

47. Fill the transaxle with the correct type and amount of fluid.

48. Tighten the transaxle filler plug to 9–15 ft. lbs. (12–20 Nm).

49. Lower the vehicle.

50. Connect and adjust the clutch.

51. Install the two transaxle-to-engine top mounting bolts. Tighten the bolts to 28–31 ft. lbs. (38–42 Nm).

52. Reconnect the negative battery terminal.

➡**Before starting the vehicle set the parking brake and pump the clutch pedal a minimum of two times to ensure proper clutch adjustment.**

53. Road test the vehicle and check for proper operation.

1985½–90 Models

1. Disconnect the negative battery cable. Wedge a 7 in. (178mm) wooden block under the clutch pedal to hold the pedal up slightly beyond its normal position. Grasp the clutch cable, pull it forward and disconnect it from the clutch release shaft assembly.

2. Remove the clutch casing from the rib on the top surface of the transaxle case.

3. Remove the upper two transaxle-to-engine bolts.

4. Remove the air management valve bracket-to-transaxle upper bolt.

5. Raise and safely support the vehicle.

6. Remove the lower control arm ball joint-to-steering knuckle nut/bolt and discard the nut/bolt; repeat this procedure on the opposite side.

7. Using a large prybar, pry the lower control arm from the steering knuckle; repeat this procedure on the opposite side.

➡**Be careful not to damage or cut the ball joint boot and do not contact the lower arm.**

8. Using a large prybar, pry the left-side inboard CV-joint assembly from the transaxle.

➡**Insert a shipping plug (tool number T81P-1177-B or equivalent) into the seal opening to prevent differential dislocation and lubricant leakage.**

9. Grasp the left-hand steering knuckle and swing it and the halfshaft outward from the transaxle; this will disconnect the inboard CV-joint from the transaxle.

➡**If the CV-joint assembly cannot be pried from the transaxle, insert a differential rotator tool through the left-side and tap the joint out; the tool can be used from either side of the transaxle.**

10. Using a wire, support the halfshaft in a near level position to prevent damage to the assembly during the remaining operations; repeat this removal procedure on the opposite side.

11. Disengage the locking tabs and remove the back-up light switch connector from the transaxle back-up light switch.

12. Remove the starter bolts.

13. Remove the shift mechanism-to-shift shaft nut/bolt, the control selector indicator switch arm and the shift shaft.

14. Remove the shift mechanism stabilizer bar-to-transaxle bolt, control selector indicator switch and bracket assembly.

15. Using a crow's foot wrench, remove the speedometer cable from the transaxle.

16. Remove two stiffener brace retaining bolts.

17. Using a floor jack and a transaxle support, position it under the transaxle and secure the transaxle to the jack.

18. Remove both rear mount-to-floor pan bolts, loosen the nut at the bottom of the front mount and remove the front mount-to-transaxle bolts.

19. Lower the floor jack, until the transaxle clears the rear insulator. Support the engine by placing wood under the oil pan.

20. Remove the engine-to-transaxle bolts and lower the transaxle from the vehicle.

To install:

21. Raise the transaxle into position and engage the input shaft with the clutch plate. Install the lower engine-to-transaxle bolts and tighten to 28–31 ft. lbs. (38–42 Nm).

➡**Never attempt to start the engine prior to installing the CV-joints or differential side gear dislocation and/or damage may occur.**

22. Install the front mount-to-transaxle bolts and tighten to 25–35 ft. lbs. (34–47 Nm); also, tighten the nut on the bottom of the front transaxle mount.

23. Install the air management valve-to-transaxle upper bolt, finger-tight and the bottom bracket bolt to 28–31 ft. lbs. (38–42 Nm).

24. Install both rear mount-to-floor pan brace bolts to 40–51 ft. lbs. (55–70 Nm).

25. Remove the floor jack and adapter.

26. Using a crow's foot wrench, install the speedometer cable, being careful not to cross-thread the cable nut.

27. Install the two stiffener brace bolts and tighten to 15–21 ft. lbs. (21–28 Nm).

28. Install the shifter stabilizer bar/control selector indicator switch-to-transaxle bolt and tighten to 23–35 ft. lbs. (31–47 Nm).

29. Install the shift mechanism-to-shift shaft, the switch actuator bracket clamp and tighten the bolt to 7–10 ft. lbs. (9–13 Nm); be sure to shift the transaxle into 4th for 4-speed or 5th for 5-speed and align the actuator.

30. Install the starter bolts and tighten to 30–40 ft. lbs. (41–54 Nm).

31. Install the back-up light switch connector to the transaxle switch.

32. Install the new circlip onto both inner joints of the halfshafts, then insert the inner CV-joints into the transaxle and fully seat them; lightly pry outward to confirm that the retaining rings are seated.

➡**When installing the halfshafts, be careful not to tear the oil seals.**

33. Connect the lower ball joint to the steering knuckle, insert a new pinch bolt and tighten the new nut to 37–44 ft. lbs. (50–60 Nm); be careful not to damage the boot.

34. Refill the transaxle and lower the vehicle.

35. Install the upper air management valve bracket-to-transaxle bolt and tighten to 28–31 ft. lbs. (38–42 Nm).

36. Install the both upper transaxle-to-engine bolts and tighten to 28–31 ft. lbs. (38–42 Nm).

37. Connect the clutch cable to the clutch release shaft assembly and remove the wooden block from under the clutch pedal. Connect the negative battery cable.

➡**Prior to starting the engine, set the hand brake and depress the clutch pedal several times to ensure proper clutch adjustment.**

Halfshafts

♦ **See Figures 1 and 2**

The front wheel drive halfshafts are a one-piece design. Constant Velocity (CV) joints are used at each end. The left-hand (driver's side) halfshaft is solid steel and is shorter than the right side halfshaft. The right-hand (passenger's side) halfshaft is depending on year and model, constructed of tubular steel or solid construction. The automatic and manual transaxles use similar halfshafts.

The halfshafts can be replaced individually. The CV-joint or boots can be cleaned or replaced. Individual parts of the CV-joints are not available. The inboard and outboard joints differ in size. CV-joint parts are fitted and should never be mixed or substituted with a part from another joint.

Inspect the boots periodically for cuts or splits. If a cut or split is found, inspect the joint, repack it with grease and install a new boot.

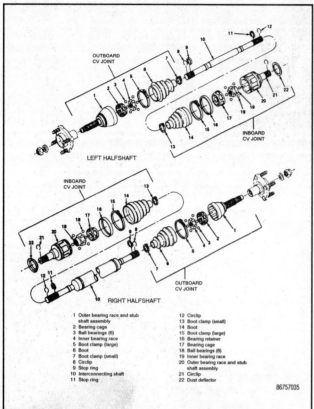

Fig. 1 Exploded view of common left and right halfshaft assemblies—1981–85 models

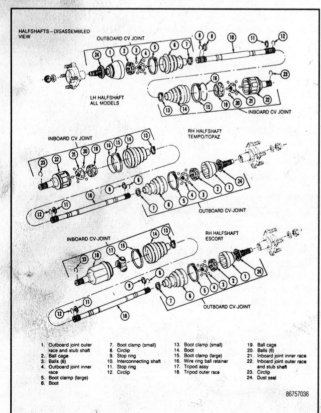

Fig. 2 Exploded view of common left and right halfshaft assemblies—1985½–90 models

REMOVAL & INSTALLATION

♦ See Figures 3 thru 9

Special tools are required for removing, installing and servicing halfshafts. They are listed by their descriptive names, with the Ford part numbers in parentheses: Front Hub Installer Adapter (T81P-1104-A), Wheel Bolt Adapters (T81P-1104-B or T83P-1104-BH), CV-Joint Separator (T81P-3514-A), Front Hub Installer/Remover (T81P-1104-C), Shipping Plug Tool (T81P-1177-B), Dust Deflector Installer (T83P-3425-AH), and Differential Rotator (T81P-4026-A).

It is necessary to have on hand new hub nuts and new lower control arm-to-steering knuckle attaching nuts and bolts. Once removed, these parts must not be reused, since their torque holding ability is destroyed during removal.

1. Loosen the front hub nut and the wheel lug nuts.
2. Raise and support the vehicle safely using jackstands.
3. Remove the tire and wheel assembly.
4. Remove and discard the front hub nut. Save the washers.

➡**Halfshaft removal and installation are the same for manual and automatic transaxles, except that the right-hand halfshaft assembly must be removed first on automatic transaxle equipped models. The differential service tool (T81P-4026-A or equivalent) is then inserted to drive the left-hand halfshaft from the transaxle. If only the left-hand halfshaft is to be serviced, remove the right-hand halfshaft from the transaxle and support it with a length of wire. Drive the left-hand halfshaft assembly from the transaxle.**

5. Remove the bolt that retains the brake hose to the strut.
6. Remove the nut and bolt securing the lower ball joint and separate the joint from the steering knuckle by inserting a prybar between the stabilizer and frame and pulling downward. Take care not to damage the ball joint boot.

➡**On some models, the lower control arm ball joint fits into a pocket formed in a plastic disc rotor shield. The shield must be carefully bent back away from the ball joint while prying the ball joint out of the steering knuckle. Do not contact or pry on the lower control arm.**

7. Remove the halfshaft from the differential housing using a prybar. Position the prybar between the case and the shaft and pry the joint away from the case. Do not damage the oil seal, the CV-joint boot or the dust deflector.
8. Install a shipping plug (tool number T81P-1177-B or equivalent) to prevent fluid loss and differential side gear misalignment.
9. Support the end of the shaft with a piece of wire, suspending it from a chassis member.
10. Separate the shaft from the front hub using the special remover/installer tool and adapters.

✳✳ WARNING

Never use a hammer to force the shaft from the wheel hub. Damage to the internal parts of the CV-joint may occur.

To install:

11. Install a new circlip on the inboard CV-joint stub shaft. Align the splines of the inboard CV-joint stub shaft with the splines in the differential. Push the CV-joint into the differential until the circlip seats on the side gear. Some force may be necessary to seat it.
12. Carefully align the splines of the outboard CV-joint stub shaft with the splines in the front wheel hub. Push the shaft into the hub as far as possible. Install the remover/installer tool and pull the CV-stub shaft through the hub.
13. Connect the control arm to the steering knuckle and install a new mounting bolt and nut. Tighten to 37–44 ft. lbs. (50–60 Nm) on 1981–85 models and 40–54 ft. lbs. (54–74 Nm) on 1986–90 models.
14. Connect the brake line to the strut.
15. Install the front hub washer and new hub nut. Install the tire and wheel assembly.
16. Lower the vehicle. Tighten the center hub nut to 180–200 ft. lbs. (244–271 Nm). Stake the nut using a blunt chisel.
17. Refill the transaxle, then road test the vehicle.

CV-JOINT OVERHAUL

There are two different types of inboard CV-joints (double offset and tripod), each of which requires a different removal procedure.

Fig. 3 Loosen, but do not remove, the axle nut while the vehicle is still on the ground

Fig. 4 Using two prybars, one on each side of the shaft, pry the halfshaft from the differential housing

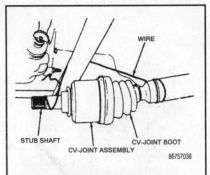

Fig. 5 When the halfshaft is detached, use sturdy wire to support its weight, rather than allowing it to hang loose

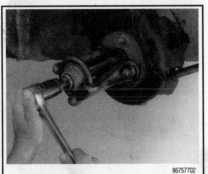

Fig. 6 Using a front hub removal tool, press the halfshaft's outboard CV-joint from the hub

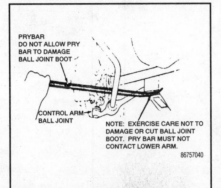

Fig. 7 Use a long prybar to separate the ball joint from the steering knuckle

Fig. 8 Once completely detached, remove the halfshaft from the vehicle

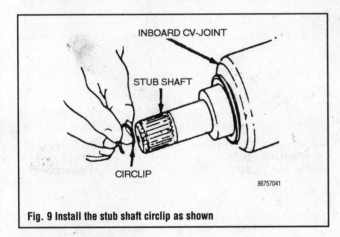

Fig. 9 Install the stub shaft circlip as shown

Double Offset Inboard Joint

▶ See Figures 10 thru 16

1. Disconnect the negative battery cable.
2. Remove halfshaft assembly from vehicle. Place the halfshaft in vise. Do not allow vice jaws to contact the boot or its clamp. The vise should be equipped with jaw caps to prevent damage to any machined surfaces.
3. Cut the large boot clamp using side cutters and peel away from the boot. After removing the clamp, roll the boot back over the shaft.
4. Remove the wire ring ball retainer.
5. Remove the outer race.
6. Pull inner race assembly out until it rests on the circlip. Using snapring pliers, spread the ring and move it back on the shaft.
7. Slide the inner race assembly down the shaft to allow access to the circlip. Remove circlip.
8. Remove the inner race assembly and boot.

➡ Circlips must not be reused. Replace with new circlips before assembly.

9. When replacing damaged CV-boots, the grease should be checked for contamination. If the CV-joints were operating satisfactorily and the grease does not appear to be contaminated, add grease and replace the boot. If the lubricant appears contaminated, proceed with a complete CV-joint disassembly and inspection.
10. Remove the balls by prying them from the cage.

➡ Exercise care to prevent scratching or other damage to the inner race or cage.

11. Rotate inner race to align lands with cage windows. Lift inner race out through the wider end of the cage.

To assemble:
12. Clean all parts (except boots) in a suitable solvent.
13. Inspect all CV-joint parts for excessive wear, looseness, pitting, rust and cracks.

➡ CV-joint components are matched during assembly. If inspection reveals damage or wear, the entire joint must be replaced as an assembly. Do not replace a joint merely because the parts appear polished. Shiny areas in ball races and on the cage spheres are normal.

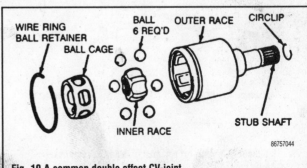

Fig. 10 A common double offset CV-joint

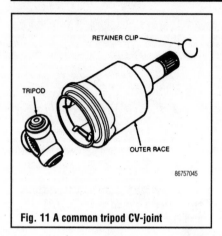

Fig. 11 A common tripod CV-joint

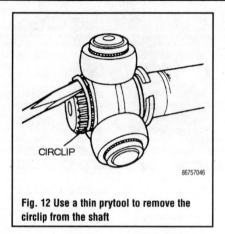

Fig. 12 Use a thin prytool to remove the circlip from the shaft

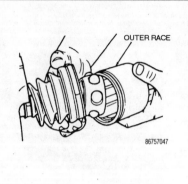

Fig. 13 The outer race assembly comes apart as shown

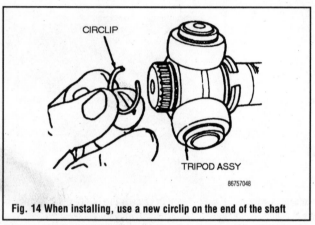

Fig. 14 When installing, use a new circlip on the end of the shaft

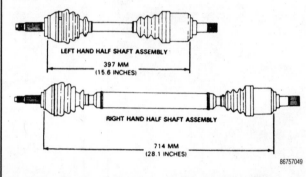

Fig. 15 Specified lengths for common halfshaft assemblies—1981–83 models

14. Install a new circlip in groove nearest end of the shaft. Do not over-expand or twist circlip during installation.

15. Install inner race in the cage. The race is installed through the large end of the cage with the circlip counterbore facing the large end of the cage.

16. With the cage and inner race properly aligned, install the balls by pressing through the cage windows with the heel of the hand.

17. Assemble inner race and cage assembly in the outer race.

18. Push the inner race and cage assembly by hand, into the outer race. Install with the inner race chamfer facing out.

19. Install the ball retainer into groove inside the outer race.

20. Install a new CV-boot.

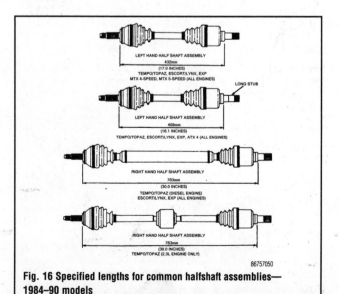

Fig. 16 Specified lengths for common halfshaft assemblies—1984–90 models

21. Position the stop ring and new circlip into grooves on the shaft.

22. Fill the CV-joint outer race with 3.2 oz. (90 grams) of grease, then spread 1.4 oz. (40 grams) of grease evenly inside the boot for a total combined fill of 4.6 oz. (130 grams).

23. With the boot peeled back, install the CV-joint using a soft-faced hammer. Ensure that the splines are aligned prior to installing the CV-joint onto the shaft.

24. Remove all excess grease from the CV-joint external surfaces.

25. Position the boot over the CV-joint. Before installing the boot clamp, move the CV-joint in or out, as necessary, to adjust to the proper length.

➡Insert a suitable tool between the boot and outer bearing race and allow the trapped air to escape from the boot. The air should be released from the boot only after adjusting to the proper dimensions.

26. Ensure boot is seated in its groove and clamp in position.

27. Tighten the clamp securely, but not to the point where the clamp bridge is cut or the boot is damaged.

28. Install the halfshaft assembly in the vehicle.

29. Connect the negative battery cable.

Inboard Tripod Joint

♦ **See Figures 17 thru 31**

1. Disconnect the negative battery cable.

2. Remove the halfshaft assembly from the vehicle. Place the halfshaft in a vice. Do not allow the vise jaws to contact the boot or its clamp. The vise should be equipped with jaw caps to prevent damage to any machined surfaces.

3. Cut the large boot clamp using side cutters and peel away from the boot. After removing the clamp, roll the boot back over the shaft.

4. Bend the retaining tabs back slightly to allow for tripod removal.

5. Separate the outer race from the tripod.

6. Move the stop ring back on the shaft using snapring pliers.

7. Move the tripod assembly back on the shaft to allow access to the circlip.

8. Remove the circlip from the shaft.

9. Remove the tripod assembly from the shaft. Remove the boot.

10. When replacing damaged CV-boots, the grease should be checked for contamination. If the CV-joints were operating satisfactorily and the grease does not appear to be contaminated, add grease and replace the boot. If the lubricant appears contaminated, proceed with a complete CV-joint disassembly and inspection.

11. Clean all parts (except boots) in a suitable solvent.

12. Inspect all CV-joint parts for excessive wear, looseness, pitting, rust and cracks.

➡ **CV-joint components are matched during assembly. If inspection reveals damage or wear the entire joint must be replaced as an assembly. Do not replace a joint merely because the parts appear polished. Shiny areas in ball races and on the cage spheres are normal.**

To assemble:

13. Install a new CV-boot.

14. Install the tripod assembly on the shaft with the chamfered side toward the stop ring.

15. Install a new circlip.

16. Compress the circlip and slide tripod assembly forward over the circlip to expose the stop ring groove.

17. Move stop ring into the groove using snapring pliers. Ensure that it is fully seated in the groove.

18. Fill CV-joint outer race with 3.5 oz. (100 grams) of grease and fill CV-boot with 2.1 oz. (60 grams) of grease.

19. Install outer race over tripod assembly and bend the six retaining tabs back into their original position.

20. Remove all excess grease from CV-joint external surfaces. Position boot over the CV-joint. Move the CV-joint in and out as necessary, to adjust to proper length.

➡ **Insert a suitable tool between the boot and outer bearing race and allow the trapped air to escape from the boot. The air should be released from the boot only after adjusting to the proper dimensions.**

Fig. 17 Install the tripod assembly by matching the splines and pushing until it seats on the shaft

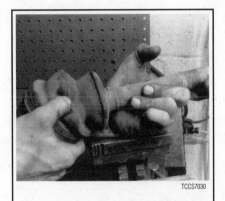

Fig. 18 Check the CV-boot for wear

Fig. 19 Removing the outer band from the CV-boot

Fig. 20 Removing the inner band from the CV-boot

Fig. 21 Removing the CV-boot from the joint housing

Fig. 22 Clean the CV-joint housing prior to removing the boot

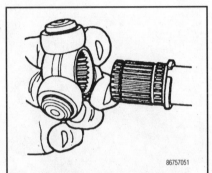

Fig. 23 Removing the CV-joint housing assembly

Fig. 24 Removing the CV-joint

Fig. 25 Inspecting the CV-joint housing

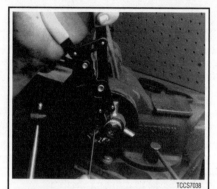

Fig. 26 Removing the CV-joint outer snapring

Fig. 27 Checking the CV-joint snapring for wear

Fig. 28 CV-joint snapring (typical)

Fig. 29 Removing the CV-joint assembly

Fig. 30 Removing the CV-joint inner snapring

Fig. 31 Installing the CV-joint assembly (typical)

21. Ensure boot is seated in its groove and clamp in position.
22. Tighten the clamp securely, but not to the point where the clamp bridge is cut or the boot is damaged.
23. Install a new circlip in the groove nearest end of the shaft by starting one end in the groove and working clip over the stub shaft end and into the groove.
24. Install the halfshaft assembly in the vehicle.
25. Connect the negative battery cable.

Outboard Joint

▶ **See Figures 32, 33, 34 and 35**

1. Disconnect the negative battery cable.
2. Remove the halfshaft assembly from the vehicle.
3. Place the halfshaft in a vice. Do not allow vise jaws to contact the boot or its clamp. The vise should be equipped with jaw caps or wood blocks to prevent the jaws from damaging any machined surfaces.

4. Cut the large boot clamp using side cutters and peel away from the boot. After removing the clamp, roll the boot back over shaft.
5. Support the interconnecting shaft in a soft jaw vise and angle the CV-joint to expose inner bearing race.
6. Using a brass drift and hammer, give a sharp tap to the inner bearing race to dislodge the internal circlip and separate the CV-joint from the interconnecting shaft. Take care not to drop the CV-joint at separation.
7. Remove the boot.
8. When replacing damaged CV-boots, the grease should be checked for contamination. If the CV-joints were operating satisfactorily and the grease does not appear to be contaminated, add grease and replace the boot. If the lubricant appears contaminated, proceed with a complete CV-joint disassembly and inspection.
9. Remove the circlip located near the end of the shaft. Discard the circlip.
10. Clamp CV-joint stub shaft in a vise with the outer face facing up. Care should be taken not to damage the dust seal. The vise must be equipped with jaw caps to prevent damage to the shaft splines.

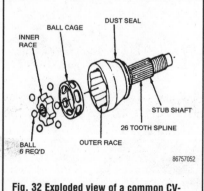

Fig. 32 Exploded view of a common CV-joint

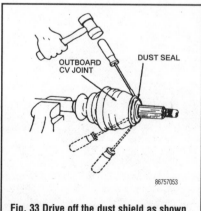

Fig. 33 Drive off the dust shield as shown

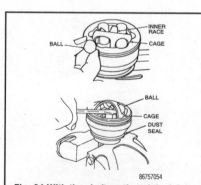

Fig. 34 With the shaft portion of the joint in a soft-jaw vise, remove the ball bearings for cleaning and inspection

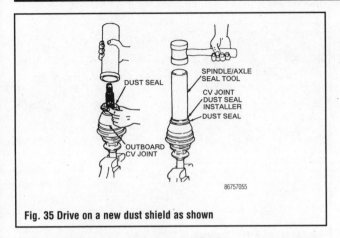

Fig. 35 Drive on a new dust shield as shown

11. Press down on the inner race until it tilts enough to allow removal of a ball. A tight assembly can be tilted by tapping the inner race with wooden dowel and hammer. Do not hit the cage.

12. With the cage sufficiently tilted, remove the ball from cage. Remove all 6 balls in this manner.

13. Pivot the cage and inner race assembly until it is straight up and down in outer race. Align cage windows with outer race lands while pivoting the bearing cage. With the cage pivoted and aligned, lift the assembly from the outer race.

14. Rotate the inner race up and out of the cage.

To assemble:

15. Clean all parts (except the boots) in a suitable solvent.

16. Inspect all CV-joint parts for excessive wear, looseness, pitting, rust and cracks.

➡ **CV-joint components are matched during assembly. If inspection reveals damage or wear the entire joint must be replaced as an assembly. Do not replace a joint merely because the parts appear polished. Shiny areas in ball races and on the cage spheres are normal.**

17. Apply a light coating of grease on the inner and outer ball races. Install the inner race in the cage.

18. Install the inner race and cage assembly in the outer race.

19. Install the assembly vertically and pivot 90 degrees into position.

20. Align the cage and inner race with the outer race. Tilt inner race and cage and install one of the six balls. Repeat this process until the remaining balls are installed.

21. Install a new CV-joint boot.

22. Install the stop ring, if removed.

23. Install a new circlip in the groove nearest the end of the shaft.

24. Pack the CV-joint with grease. Any grease remaining in tube should be spread evenly inside the boot.

25. With the boot peeled back, position CV-joint on shaft and tap into position using a plastic-faced hammer.

26. Remove all excess grease from the CV-joint external surfaces.

27. Position the boot over the CV-joint.

28. Ensure boot is seated in its groove and clamp into position.

29. Tighten the clamp securely, but not to the point where the clamp bridge is cut or the boot is damaged.

30. Install the halfshaft assembly in the vehicle.

31. Connect the negative battery cable.

CLUTCH

Understanding the Clutch

◆ See Figure 36

✳✳ CAUTION

The clutch driven disc may contain asbestos, which has been determined to be a cancer causing agent. Never clean clutch surfaces with compressed air! Avoid inhaling any dust from any clutch surface! When cleaning clutch surfaces, use a commercially available brake cleaning fluid.

The purpose of the clutch is to disconnect and connect engine power at the transaxle. A vehicle at rest requires a lot of engine torque to get all that weight moving. An internal combustion engine does not develop a high starting torque (unlike steam engines) so it must be allowed to operate without any load until it builds up enough torque to move the vehicle. Torque increases with engine rpm. The clutch allows the engine to build up torque by physically disconnecting the engine from the transaxle, relieving the engine of any load or resistance.

The transfer of engine power to the transaxle (the load) must be smooth and gradual; if it weren't, drive line components would wear out or break quickly. This gradual power transfer is made possible by gradually releasing the clutch pedal. The clutch disc and pressure plate are the connecting link between the engine and transaxle. When the clutch pedal is released, the disc and plate contact each other (the clutch is engaged) physically joining the engine and transaxle. When the pedal is pushed inward, the disc and plate separate (the clutch is disengaged) disconnecting the engine from the transaxle.

Most clutches utilize a single plate, dry friction disc with a diaphragm-style spring pressure plate. The clutch disc has a splined hub which attaches the disc to the input shaft. The disc has friction material where it contacts the flywheel and pressure plate. Torsion springs on the disc help absorb engine torque pulses. The pressure plate applies pressure to the clutch disc, holding it tight against the surface of the flywheel. The clutch operating mechanism consists of a release bearing, fork and cylinder assembly.

The release fork and actuating linkage transfer pedal motion to the release bearing. In the engaged position (pedal released) the diaphragm spring holds the pressure plate against the clutch disc, so engine torque is transmitted to the

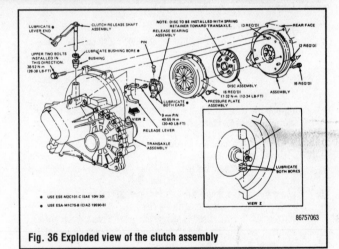

Fig. 36 Exploded view of the clutch assembly

input shaft. When the clutch pedal is depressed, the release bearing pushes the diaphragm spring center toward the flywheel. The diaphragm spring pivots the fulcrum, relieving the load on the pressure plate. Steel spring straps riveted to the clutch cover lift the pressure plate from the clutch disc, disengaging the engine drive from the transaxle and enabling the gears to be changed.

The clutch is operating properly if:

1. It will stall the engine when released with the vehicle held stationary.

2. The shift lever can be moved freely between 1st and reverse gears when the vehicle is stationary and the clutch disengaged.

Driven Disc and Pressure Plate

REMOVAL & INSTALLATION

1. Disconnect the negative battery cable.

2. Raise and safely support the vehicle.

3. Remove the transaxle.

4. Matchmark the pressure plate assembly and the flywheel so they can be assembled in the same position.

5. Loosen the pressure plate-to-flywheel bolts one turn at a time, in a crisscross sequence, until spring tension is relieved to prevent pressure plate cover distortion.

6. Support the pressure plate and remove the bolts. Remove the pressure plate and clutch disc from the flywheel.

7. Inspect the flywheel, clutch disc, pressure plate, throw-out bearing, pilot bearing and clutch fork for wear. Replace parts as required.

➠If the flywheel shows any signs of overheating (blue discoloration) or if it is badly grooved or scored, it should be refaced or replaced.

To install:

8. If removed, install a new pilot bearing using a suitable installation tool.

9. If removed, install the flywheel. Make sure the flywheel and crankshaft flange mating surfaces are clean. Tighten the flywheel bolts to 54–64 ft. lbs. (73–87 Nm).

10. Clean the pressure plate and flywheel surfaces thoroughly. Position the clutch disc and pressure plate into the installed position, aligning the matchmarks made previously; support them with a dummy shaft or clutch aligning tool.

11. Install the pressure plate-to-flywheel bolts. Tighten them gradually in a crisscross pattern to 12–24 ft. lbs. (17–32 Nm). Remove the alignment tool.

12. Lubricate the release bearing and install it in the fork.

13. To complete the installation, reverse the removal procedures. Lower the vehicle and connect the negative battery cable.

Clutch Cable

REMOVAL & INSTALLATION

▶ **See Figure 37**

1. Disconnect the negative battery cable.

2. Wedge a 7 in. (178mm) wood block under the clutch pedal to hold the pedal up slightly beyond its normal position.

3. Remove the air cleaner to gain access to the clutch cable.

4. Using a pair of pliers, grasp the clutch cable, pull it forward and disconnect it from the clutch release shaft assembly.

➠Do not grasp the wire strand portion of the inner cable since it may cut the wires and cause cable failure.

5. Remove the clutch casing from the insulator which is located on the rib on the top of the transaxle case.

6. Remove the rear screw and move the clutch shield away from the brake pedal support bracket.

7. Loosen the front retaining screw, located near the toe board, rotate the shield aside and snug the screw to retain the shield.

8. With the clutch pedal raised to release the pawl, rotate the gear quadrant forward, unhook the clutch cable and allow the quadrant to swing rearward. Do not allow the quadrant to snap back.

9. Pull the cable through the recess between the clutch pedal and the gear quadrant and from the insulator of the pedal assembly.

10. Remove the cable from the engine compartment.

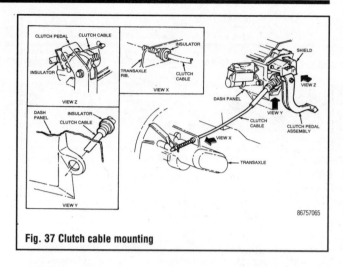

Fig. 37 Clutch cable mounting

To install:

11. Lift the clutch pedal to disengage the adjusting mechanism.

12. Insert the clutch cable through the dash panel and the dash panel grommet.

➠Be sure the clutch cable is routed under the brake lines and is not trapped at the spring tower by the brake lines. If equipped with power steering, route the cable inboard of the power steering hose.

13. Push the clutch cable through the insulator on the stop bracket and through the recess between the pedal and the gear quadrant.

14. Lift the clutch pedal to release the pawl. Rotate the gear quadrant forward and hook the cable into the gear quadrant.

15. Install the clutch shield on the brake pedal support bracket.

16. Using a piece of wire or tape, secure the pedal in its uppermost position.

17. Insert the clutch cable through the insulator and connect the cable to the clutch release lever in the engine compartment.

18. Remove the wooden block from under the clutch pedal.

19. Depress the clutch pedal several times. Install the air cleaner and connect the negative battery cable.

Adjustments

PEDAL HEIGHT AND FREE-PLAY

The pedal height and free-play are controlled by a self-adjusting feature. The self-adjusting feature should be checked every 5000 miles (8052 km). This is accomplished by insuring that the clutch pedal travels to the top of its upward position. Grasp the clutch pedal with your hand or put your foot under the clutch pedal, pull up on the pedal until it stops. Very little effort is required (about 10 lbs./4.5 kg). During the application of upward pressure, a click may be heard which means an adjustment was necessary and has been accomplished.

AUTOMATIC TRANSAXLE

Understanding the Automatic Transaxle

The automatic transaxle allows engine torque and power to be transmitted to the front wheels within a narrow range of engine operating speeds. It will allow the engine to turn fast enough to produce plenty of power and torque at very low speeds, while keeping it at a sensible rpm at high vehicle speeds (and it does this job without driver assistance). The transaxle uses a light fluid as the medium for the transmission of power. This fluid also works in the operation of various hydraulic control circuits and as a lubricant. Because the transaxle fluid performs all of these functions, trouble within the unit can easily travel from one part to another.

Neutral Safety Switch

REMOVAL & INSTALLATION

The neutral safety switch used on models equipped with a automatic transaxle also acts as the back-up light switch.

The mounting location of the neutral safety switch does not provide for adjustment of the switch position when installed. If the engine will not start in P or N, or if it will start in R or any of the D ranges, check the control linkage adjustment and/or replace with a known good switch.

1. Set the parking brake.
2. Disconnect the battery negative cable.
3. If necessary, remove the two managed air valve supply rear hoses and disconnect all necessary vacuum lines from the managed air valve.
4. If necessary, remove the managed air valve supply hose band-to-intermediate shift control bracket attaching screw.
5. If equipped, unfasten the throttle valve lever nut and washer, hold the lever stationary while loosening it to prevent internal damage, then remove the lever from the throttle valve shaft.
6. Unplug the wire connector from the neutral safety switch.
7. Unfasten the two retaining screws from the neutral start switch and remove the switch.

To install:

8. Place the switch on the manual shift shaft and loosely install the retaining bolts.
9. Use a No. 43 drill (0.089 in./2.26mm) and insert it into the switch to set the contacts.
10. Tighten the retaining screws of the switch and remove the drill.
11. Attach the switch electrical connector.
12. If removed, attach the throttle valve lever, lockwasher and nut. Hold the lever stationary while tightening the nut and tighten to 7.5–9.5 ft. lbs. (10–13 Nm).
13. If removed, install the managed air valve supply hose band-to-intermediate shift control bracket attaching screw.
14. If removed, attach all the hoses to the managed air valve that were disconnected during removal.
15. Connect negative battery cable.
16. Check the ignition switch for proper starting in **P** or **N**. Also make certain that the start circuit cannot be actuated in the **D** or **R** position and that the column is locked in the **LOCK** position.

Automatic Transaxle Assembly

REMOVAL & INSTALLATION

1981–85 Models

1. Disconnect the negative battery cable.
2. From under the hood, remove the bolts that attach the air manage valve to the automatic transaxle valve body cover.
3. Unplug the wiring harness connector from the neutral safety switch.
4. Disconnect the throttle valve linkage and the manual control lever cable at their levers.
5. Unfasten the two transaxle to engine upper attaching bolts. The bolts are located below and on either side of the distributor.
6. Loosen the front wheel lugs slightly. Jack up the front of the car and safely support it on jackstands. Remove the wheels.
7. Drain the transmission fluid.
8. Disconnect the brake hoses from the strut brackets on both sides.
9. Remove the pinch bolts that secure the lower control arms to the steering knuckles. Separate the ball joint from the steering knuckle.
10. Remove the stabilizer bar attaching bracket.
11. Unfasten the nuts that retain the stabilizer to the control arms. Remove the stabilizer bar. When removing the control arms from the steering knuckles, it will be necessary to bend the plastic shield slightly to gain ball joint clearance for removal.
12. Remove the tie rod ends from the steering knuckles. Use a special tie rod removing tool. Pry the right side halfshaft from the transaxle.
13. Remove the left side halfshaft from the transaxle. Support both the right and left side halfshafts out of the way with wire.
14. Install sealing plugs or the equivalent into the transaxle halfshaft mounting holes.
15. Remove the starter support bracket. Disconnect the starter cable. Unfasten the starter mounting studs and remove the starter motor.
16. Remove the transaxle support bracket.
17. Remove the torque converter dust cover.
18. Turn the converter for access to the converter-to-flywheel mounting nuts. Remove the nuts.
19. Position a transaxle jack under the transaxle and unfasten the rear support bracket nuts.
20. Unfasten the nuts that attach the left front insulator to the body bracket.
21. Unfasten the bracket-to-body bolts and remove the bracket.

22. Disconnect the transaxle cooler lines.
23. Remove the bolts that attach the manual lever bracket to the transaxle case.
24. Remove the four remaining transaxle to engine attaching bolts.

➡ **The torque converter mounting studs must be clear of the engine flywheel before the transaxle can be lowered from the vehicle.**

25. Take a small prybar and place it between the flywheel and the converter. Carefully move the transaxle away from the engine. When the converter mounting studs are clear, lower the transaxle about 3 in. (76mm).
26. Disconnect the speedometer cable from the transaxle.
27. Lower the transaxle to the ground.

➡ **When moving the transaxle away from the engine, watch the mount insulator. If it interferes with the transaxle before the converter mounting studs clear the flywheel, remove the insulator.**

To install:

28. Installation is the reverse order of the removal procedure. Be sure to pay strict attention to the following important steps:

a. Before installing the halfshaft into the transaxle, replace the circlip on the CV-joint stub shaft. Carefully work the clip over the end of the shaft, spreading it as little as possible.

b. To install the halfshaft into the transaxle, carefully align the splines of the CV-joint with the splines in the differential.

c. Exerting some force, push the CV-joint into the differential until the circlip is felt to seat the differential side gear. Be careful not to damage the differential oil seal.

➡ **A non-metallic, mallet may be used to aid in seating the circlip into the differential side gear groove. If a mallet is necessary, tap only on the outboard CV-joint stub shaft.**

d. Attach the lower ball joint to the steering knuckle, taking care not to damage or cut the ball joint boot. Insert a new service pinch bolt and attach a new nut. Tighten the nut to 37–44 ft. lbs. (50–60 Nm). Do not tighten the bolt.

e. Tighten the transaxle-to engine block bolts to 25–33 ft. lbs. (34–45 Nm).

f. Tighten the stabilizer U-clamp-to-bracket retainers to 60–70 ft. lbs. (81–95 Nm).

g. Tighten the stabilizer-to-control arm to 98–125 ft. lbs. (133–169 Nm).

h. Tighten the brake hose routing clip retainer to 8 ft. lbs. (11 Nm).

i. Tighten the manual cable bracket retainer to 10–20 ft. lbs. (14–27 Nm)

j. Tighten the starter motor bolts to 30–40 ft. lbs. (41–54 Nm).

k. Tighten the torque converter-to-flywheel bolts to 23–39 ft. lbs. (31–53 Nm).

l. Tighten the torque converter dust cover retainers to 15–21 ft. lbs. (20–28 Nm).

m. Tighten the insulator-to-bracket retainers to 55–70 ft. lbs. (75–90 Nm).

n. Tighten the insulator bracket-to-frame retainers to 40–50 ft. lbs. (55–70 Nm).

o. Tighten the insulator mount-to-transaxle bolts to 25–33 ft. lbs. (34–45 Nm).

1985½–90 Models

1. Disconnect the negative battery cable.

➡ **Due to automatic transaxle case configuration, the right-side halfshaft assembly must be removed first. The differential rotator tool or equivalent, is then inserted into the transaxle to drive the left-side inboard CV-joint assembly from the transaxle.**

2. Remove the air cleaner assembly.
3. Unplug the electrical harness connector from the neutral safety switch.
4. Disconnect the throttle valve linkage and the manual lever cable from their levers.

➡ **Failure to disconnect the linkage and allowing the transaxle to hang, will fracture the throttle valve cam shaft joint, which is located under the transaxle cover.**

5. To prevent contamination, cover the timing window in the converter housing.
6. If equipped, remove the bolts retaining the thermactor hoses.
7. If equipped, remove the ground strap, located above the upper engine mount.
8. If equipped, remove the coil and bracket assembly.

9. Remove both transaxle-to-engine upper bolts; the bolts are located below and on both ides of the distributor.

10. Raise and safely support the vehicle. Remove the front wheels.

11. Remove the control arm-to-steering knuckle nut, at the ball joint.

12. Using a hammer and a punch, drive the bolt from the steering knuckle; repeat this step on the other side. Discard the nut and bolt.

➡️**Be careful not to damage or cut the ball joint boot. The prybar must not contact the lower arm.**

13. Using a prybar, disengage the control arm from the steering knuckle; repeat this step on the other side.

➡️**Do not hammer on the knuckle to remove the ball joints. The plastic shield installed behind the rotor contains a molded pocket into which the lower control arm ball joint fits. When disengaging the control arm from the knuckle, clearance for the ball joint can be provided by bending the shield back toward the rotor. Failure to provide clearance for the ball joint can result in damage to the shield.**

14. Remove the stabilizer bar bracket-to-frame rail bolts and discard the bolts; repeat this step on the other side.

15. Remove the stabilizer bar-to-control arm nut/washer and discard the nut; repeat this step on the other side.

16. Pull the stabilizer bar from of the control arms.

17. Remove the brake hose routing clip-to-suspension strut bracket bolt; repeat this step on the other side.

18. Remove the steering gear tie rod-to-steering knuckle nut and disengage the tie rod from the steering knuckle; repeat this step on the other side.

19. Using a halfshaft removal tool, pry the halfshaft from the right side of the transaxle and support the end of the shaft with a wire.

➡️**It is normal for some fluid to leak from the transaxle when the halfshaft is removed.**

20. Using a differential rotator tool or equivalent, drive the left-side halfshaft from the differential side gear.

21. Pull the halfshaft from the transaxle and support the end of the shaft with a wire.

➡️**Do not allow the shaft to hang unsupported, as damage to the outboard CV-joint may result.**

22. Install seal plugs into the differential seals.

23. Remove the starter support bracket and disconnect the starter cable.

24. Remove the starter bolts and the starter.

25. If equipped with a throttle body, remove the hose and bracket bolts on the starter and a bolt at the converter and disconnect the hoses.

26. Remove the transaxle support bracket and the dust cover from the torque converter housing.

27. Remove the torque converter-to-flywheel nuts by turning the crankshaft pulley bolt to bring the nuts into position.

28. Position a suitable transaxle jack under the transaxle and remove the rear support bracket nuts.

29. Remove the left front insulator-to-body bracket nuts, the bracket-to-body bolts and the bracket.

30. Disconnect the transaxle cooler lines.

31. Remove the manual lever bracket-to-transaxle case bolts.

32. Support the engine. Make sure the transaxle is supported and remove the remaining transaxle-to-engine bolts.

33. Make sure the torque converter studs will clear the flywheel. Insert a prybar between the flywheel and the converter, then, pry the transaxle and converter away from the engine. When the converter studs are clear of the flywheel, lower the transaxle about 2–3 in. (51–76mm).

34. Disconnect the speedometer cable and lower the transaxle.

➡️**When moving the transaxle away from the engine, watch the No. 1 insulator. If it contacts the body before the converter studs clear the flywheel, remove the insulator.**

To install:

35. Raise the transaxle and align it with the engine and flywheel.

36. Install the No. 1 insulator, if removed. Tighten the transaxle-to-engine bolts to 25–33 ft. lbs. (34–45 Nm) and the torque converter-to-flywheel bolts to 23–39 ft. lbs. (31–53 Nm).

37. Install the manual lever bracket-to-transaxle case bolts and connect the transaxle cooler lines.

38. Install the left front insulator-to-body bracket nuts and tighten the nuts to 40–50 ft. lbs. (55–70 Nm).

39. Install the bracket-to-body bolts and tighten the bolts to 55–70 ft. lbs. (75–90 Nm).

40. Install the transaxle support bracket and the dust cover to the torque converter housing.

41. If equipped with a throttle body, install the hose and bracket bolts on the starter and a bolt to the converter and connect the hoses.

42. Install the starter and the support bracket. Tighten the starter-to-engine bolts to 30–40 ft. lbs. (41–54 Nm). Connect the starter cable.

43. Remove the seal plugs from the differential seals and install the halfshaft by performing the following procedures:

   a. Prior to installing the halfshaft in the transaxle, install a new circlip onto the CV-joint stub.

   b. Install the halfshaft in the transaxle by carefully aligning the CV-joint splines with the differential side gears. Be sure to push the CV-joint into the differential until the circlip is felt to seat in the differential side gear. Use care to prevent damage to the differential oil seal.

   c. Attach the lower ball joint to the steering knuckle, taking care not to damage or cut the ball joint boot. Insert a new pinch bolt and a new nut. While holding the bolt with a wrench, tighten the nut to 40–54 ft. lbs. (54–74 Nm).

44. Engage the tie rod with the steering knuckle and tighten the nut to 23–35 ft. lbs. (31–47 Nm).

45. Install the brake hose routing clip-to-suspension strut bracket and tighten the bolt to 8 ft. lbs. (11 Nm).

46. Install the stabilizer bar to control arm and using a new nut, tighten it to 98–125 ft. lbs. (133–169 Nm).

47. Install the stabilizer bar bracket-to-frame rail bolts and using new bolts, tighten them to 60–70 ft. lbs. (81–95 Nm).

48. Install the wheels and lower the vehicle. Install the upper transaxle-to-engine bolts and tighten to 25–33 ft. lbs. (34–45 Nm).

49. If equipped, install the ground strap, located above the upper engine mount, and the coil and bracket assembly.

50. If equipped, install the bolts retaining the thermactor hoses. Uncover the timing window in the converter housing.

51. Connect the throttle valve linkage and the manual lever cable to their levers.

52. Connect the electrical harness connector from the neutral safety switch.

53. Install the air cleaner assembly.

54. Connect the negative battery cable and road test the vehicle.

ADJUSTMENTS

Shift Linkage

1. Place the gear shift selector into **D**. The shift lever must be in the **D** position during linkage adjustment.

2. Working at the transaxle, loosen the transaxle lever-to-control cable nut.

3. Move the transaxle lever to the **D** position, 2nd detent from the most rearward position.

4. Tighten the adjusting nut to 10–15 ft. lbs. (14–20 Nm).

5. Make sure all gears engage correctly and the vehicle will only start in **P** or **D**.

Throttle Linkage

➡️**The Throttle Valve (TV) linkage adjustment is set at the factory and is critical in establishing automatic transaxle upshift and downshift timing and feel. Any time the engine, transaxle or throttle linkage components are removed, it is recommended that the TV linkage adjustment be reset after the component installation or replacement**

CARBURETED VEHICLES

▶ See Figure 38

The Throttle Valve (TV) control linkage is adjusted at the sliding trunnion block.

1. Adjust the curb idle speed to specification as shown on the under hood decal.

2. After the curb idle speed has been set, shut off the engine. Make sure the choke is completely opened. Check the carburetor throttle lever to make sure it is against the hot engine curb idle stop.

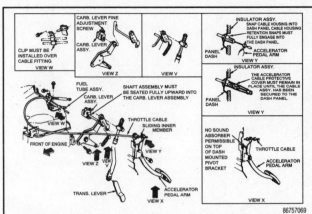

Fig. 38 Throttle linkage, cable and related components—carbureted models

3. Set the coupling lever adjustment screw at its approximate midrange. Make sure the TV linkage shaft assembly is fully seated upward into the coupling lever.

⚓ CAUTION

If adjustment of the linkage is necessary, allow the EGR valve to cool so you won't get burned.

4. To adjust, loosen the bolt on the sliding block on the TV control rod a minimum of one turn. Clean any dirt or corrosion from the control rod, free-up the trunnion block so that it will slide freely on the control rod.

5. Rotate the transaxle TV control lever up using a finger and light force, to insure that the TV control lever is against its internal stop. With reducing the pressure on the control lever, tighten the bolt on the trunnion block.

6. Check the carburetor throttle lever to be sure it is still against the hot idle stop. If not, repeat the adjustment steps.

1984–85 FUEL INJECTED VEHICLES

▶ See Figure 39

1. Disconnect the negative battery cable.
2. Remove the splash shield from the cable retainer bracket.
3. Loosen the trunnion bolt at the throttle valve rod.
4. Install a plastic clip to bottom the throttle valve rod; be sure the clip does not telescope.
5. Be sure the return spring is connected between the throttle valve rod and the retaining bracket to hold the transaxle throttle valve lever at its idle position.
6. Make sure the throttle lever is resting on the throttle return control screw.
7. Tighten the throttle valve rod trunnion bolt and remove the plastic clip.
8. Install the splash shield. Connect the negative battery cable and check the vehicle's operation.

REAR AXLE

Wheel Spindle

REMOVAL & INSTALLATION

1. Remove the wheel hub.

➡**If the vehicle is being raised using a hoist, a jackstand must be placed under the lower control arm to raise it to curb height.**

2. Remove the brake drum and wheel bearings.
3. Remove the brake backing plate.
4. Remove the tie rod end nut and washer.
5. Unfasten the strut-to-spindle nuts and bolts.
6. Unfasten the nut and bolt attaching the lower control arm to the spindle.
7. Remove the spindle.

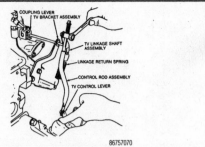

Fig. 39 Adjust the throttle valve linkage as shown on 1984–85 fuel injected models

1986–90 FUEL INJECTED VEHICLES

1. Set the parking brake and place the transaxle shift lever into **P**.
2. Loosen the sliding trunnion block bolt, located on the throttle valve control rod assembly, a minimum of one turn.
3. Make sure the trunnion block slides freely on the control rod.
4. Using a jumper wire, connect it between the STI connector and the signal return ground on the self-test connector.
5. Turn the ignition switch to the **RUN** position but do not start the engine. The Idle Speed Control (ISC) plunger should retract; wait until the plunger is fully retracted, about 10 seconds.
6. Turn the ignition switch **OFF** and remove the jumper wire.
7. Using light force, pull the throttle valve rod upward to ensure the control lever is against the internal stop.
8. Allow the trunnion to slide on the rod to its normal position.
9. Without relaxing the pressure on the throttle valve control lever, tighten the trunnion block bolt.
10. Connect the negative battery cable.

TRANSMISSION CONTROL LEVER

1. Position the selector lever in **D** against the rear stop.
2. Raise the vehicle and support it safely.
3. Loosen the manual lever-to-control lever nut.
4. Move the transaxle lever to the **D** position, second detent from the rearmost position. Tighten the attaching nut.
5. Check the operation of the transaxle in each selector position. Readjust if necessary.
6. Lower the vehicle.

Halfshafts

REMOVAL & INSTALLATION

Halfshaft removal, installation and overhaul procedures for automatic transaxle equipped models are covered in the manual transaxle portion of this section.

To install:

8. With new tie rod bushings in place in the spindle, and one new dished washer installed on the tie rod, position the spindle over the end of the tie rod.

9. Attach the strut to the spindle and install the retaining bolts and nuts. The bolts must be installed with their heads facing the rear of the vehicle. Tighten the bolts to 70–96 ft. lbs. (95–130 Nm).

10. Attach the lower control arm to the spindle and install a new bolt, washer and nut. Install the bolt with the head facing the front of the vehicle and tighten it to 60–80 ft. lbs. (81–109 Nm).

11. Install the tie rod to the spindle, then install a new dished washer and nut. Tighten the nut to 35–50 ft. lbs. (47–68 Nm).

12. Install the brake backing plate.
13. Install the brake drum and the bearings.
14. Install the wheel and lower the vehicle.

TORQUE SPECIFICATIONS

Components	Ft. Lbs.	Nm
Manual Transaxle		
1981-85 models		
Brake line routing clamp bolt	96 inch lbs.	11
Engine roll restrictor nuts	25-30	34-40
Engine-to-transaxle bolts	28-31	38-42
Front transaxle mount bolts	40-60	55-70
Lower control arm ball joint-to-steering knuckle nut	37-41	50-60
Rear mount stud nut	38-41	52-56
Rear transaxle mount bolts	40-60	55-70
Shift mechanism stabilizer attaching bolt	23-32	38-44
Shift mechanism-to-input shift rail bolt	83-120 inch lbs.	9-13
Stabilizer bar mounting bracket retainers	40-44	54-60
Stabilizer-to-control arm nuts	59-73	80-90
Starter motor bolts	30-40	41-54
Stiffener brace bolts	15-21	21-28
Transaxle filler plug	9-15	12-20
1985 1/2-90 models		
Engine-to-transaxle bolts	28-31	38-42
Front mount-to-transaxle bolts	25-35	34-47
Lower ball joint-to-steering knuckle nut	37-44	50-60
Rear mount-to-floor pan brace bolts	40-51	55-70
Shift mechanism-to-shift shaft	83-120 inch lbs.	9-13
Shifter stabilizer bar/control selector indicator switch-to-transaxle bolt	23-35	31-47
Starter bolts	30-40	41-54
Stiffener brace bolts	15-21	21-28
Upper air management valve bracket-to-transaxle bolt	28-31	38-42
Halfshafts		
Control arm-to-steering knuckle retainer		
1981-85 models	37-44	50-60
1986-90 models	40-54	54-74
Center hub nut	180-200	244-271
Clutch		
Driven disc and pressure plate		
Flywheel bolts	54-64	73-87
Pressure plate-to-flywheel bolts	12-24	17-32
Automatic Transaxle		
Neutral safety switch		
Throttle valve lever nut	84-120 inch lbs.	10-13
Transaxle		
1981-85 models		
Brake hose routing clip retainer	96 inch lbs.	11
Insulator bracket-to-frame retainers	40-60	55-70
Insulator-to-bracket retainers	55-70	75-90
Lower ball joint-to-steering knuckle pinch bolt and nut	37-44	50-60
Manual cable bracket retainer	10-20	14-27
Stabilizer U-clamp-to-bracket retainers	60-70	81-95
Stabilizer-to-control arm	98-125	133-169
Starter motor bolts	30-40	41-54
Torque converter dust cover retainers	15-21	20-28

90937C01

TORQUE SPECIFICATIONS

Components	Ft. Lbs.	Nm
Automatic Transaxle (cont.)		
Torque converter-to-flywheel bolts	23-39	31-53
Transaxle-to engine block bolts	25-33	34-45
1985 1/2-90 models		
Brake hose routing clip-to-suspension strut bracket bolt	96 inch lbs.	11
Insulator bracket-to-body bolts	55-70	75-90
Left front insulator-to-body bracket nuts	40-50	55-70
Lower ball joint-to-steering knuckle pinch bolt and nut	40-54	54-74
Stabilizer bar bracket-to-frame rail bolts	60-70	81-95
Stabilizer bar-to-control arm nut	98-125	133-169
Starter-to-engine bolts	30-40	41-54
Tie rod-to-steering knuckle nut	23-35	31-47
Torque converter-to-flywheel bolts	23-39	31-53
Transaxle-to-engine bolts	25-33	34-45
Shift linkage		
Adjusting nut	10-15	14-20
Rear Axle		
Wheel spindle		
Strut-to-spindle bolts and nuts	70-96	95-130
Lower control arm-to-spindle bolt	60-80	81-109
Tie rod-to-spindle nut	35-50	47-68

90937C02

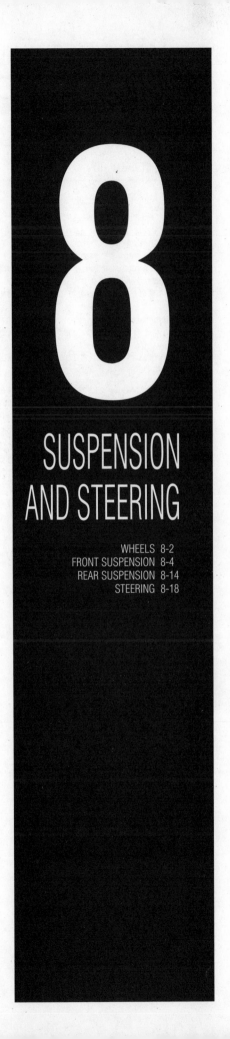

8

SUSPENSION AND STEERING

WHEELS

Wheels

REMOVAL & INSTALLATION

▶ **See Figures 1 thru 8**

1. Park the vehicle on a level surface.
2. Remove the jack, tire iron and, if necessary, the spare tire from their storage compartments.
3. Check the owner's manual or refer to Section 1 of this manual for the jacking points on your vehicle. Then, place the jack in the proper position.
4. If equipped with lug nut trim caps, remove them by either unscrewing or pulling them off the lug nuts, as appropriate. Consult the owner's manual, if necessary.
5. If equipped with a wheel cover or hub cap, unfasten the cover retaining screws or insert the tapered end of the tire iron in the groove and pry off the cover.
6. Apply the parking brake and block the diagonally opposite wheel with a wheel chock or two.

➡️**Wheel chocks may be purchased at your local auto parts store, or a block of wood cut into wedges may be used. If possible, keep one or two of the chocks in your tire storage compartment, in case any of the tires has to be removed on the side of the road.**

7. If equipped with an automatic transaxle, place the selector lever in **P** or Park; with a manual transmission/transaxle, place the shifter in Reverse.
8. With the tires still on the ground, use the tire iron/wrench to break the lug nuts loose.

➡️**If a nut is stuck, never use heat to loosen it or damage to the wheel and bearings may occur. If the nuts are seized, one or two heavy hammer blows directly on the end of the bolt usually loosens the rust. Be** careful, as continued pounding will likely damage the brake drum or rotor.

9. Using the jack, raise the vehicle until the tire is clear of the ground. Support the vehicle safely using jackstands.
10. Remove the lug nuts, then remove the tire and wheel assembly.

To install:

11. Make sure the wheel and hub mating surfaces, as well as the wheel lug studs, are clean and free of all foreign material. Always remove rust from the wheel mounting surface and the brake rotor or drum. Failure to do so may cause the lug nuts to loosen in service.
12. Install the tire and wheel assembly and hand-tighten the lug nuts.
13. Using the tire wrench, tighten all the lug nuts, in a crisscross pattern, until they are snug.
14. Raise the vehicle and withdraw the jackstand, then lower the vehicle.
15. Using a torque wrench, tighten the lug nuts in a crisscross pattern to 85–105 ft. lbs. (115–142 Nm). Check your owner's manual or refer to Section 1 of this manual for the proper tightening sequence.

✳️✳️ WARNING

Do not overtighten the lug nuts, as this may cause the wheel studs to stretch or the brake disc (rotor) to warp.

16. If so equipped, install the wheel cover or hub cap. Make sure the valve stem protrudes through the proper opening before tapping the wheel cover into position.
17. If equipped, install the lug nut trim caps by pushing them or screwing them on, as applicable.
18. Remove the jack from under the vehicle, and place the jack and tire iron/wrench in their storage compartments. Remove the wheel chock(s).
19. If you have removed a flat or damaged tire, place it in the storage compartment of the vehicle and take it to your local repair station to have it fixed or replaced as soon as possible.

Fig. 1 A common design wheel trim cover for 1980s models—remove by unfastening the Phillips screws

Fig. 2 Place the jack at the proper lifting point on your vehicle

Fig. 3 Before jacking the vehicle, block the diagonally opposite wheel with one or, preferably, two chocks

Fig. 4 With the vehicle still on the ground, break the lug nuts loose using the wrench end of the tire iron

Fig. 5 After the lug nuts have been loosened, raise the vehicle using the jack until the tire is clear of the ground

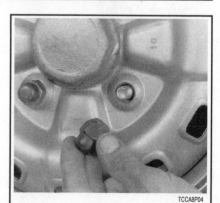

Fig. 6 Remove the lug nuts from the studs

Fig. 7 Remove the wheel and tire assembly from the vehicle

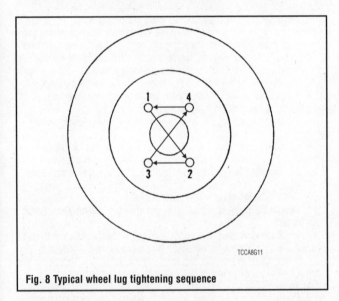

Fig. 8 Typical wheel lug tightening sequence

INSPECTION

Inspect the tires for lacerations, puncture marks, nails and other sharp objects. Repair or replace as necessary. Also check the tires for treadwear and air pressure as outlined in Section 1 of this manual. Check the wheel assemblies for dents, cracks, rust and metal fatigue. Repair or replace as necessary.

Wheel Lug Studs

REMOVAL & INSTALLATION

With Disc Brakes

▶ See Figures 9, 10 and 11

1. Raise and support the appropriate end of the vehicle safely using jackstands, then remove the wheel.
2. Remove the brake pads and caliper. Support the caliper aside using wire or a coat hanger. For details, please refer to Section 9 of this manual.
3. Remove the outer wheel bearing and lift off the rotor. For details on wheel bearing removal, installation and adjustment, please refer to Section 1 of this manual.
4. Properly support the rotor using press bars, then drive the stud out using an arbor press.

➡If a press is not available, CAREFULLY drive the old stud out using a blunt drift. MAKE SURE the rotor is properly and evenly supported or it may be damaged.

To install:

5. Clean the stud hole with a wire brush and start the new stud with a hammer and drift pin. Do not use any lubricant or thread sealer.
6. Finish installing the stud with the press.

➡If a press is not available, start the lug stud through the bore in the hub, then position about 4 flat washers over the stud and thread the lug nut. Hold the hub/rotor while tightening the lug nut, and the stud should be drawn into position. MAKE SURE THE STUD IS FULLY SEATED, then remove the lug nut and washers.

7. Install the rotor and adjust the wheel bearings.
8. Install the brake caliper and pads.
9. Install the wheel, then remove the jackstands and carefully lower the vehicle.
10. Tighten the lug nuts to the proper torque.

With Drum Brakes

▶ See Figures 12, 13 and 14

1. Raise the vehicle and safely support it with jackstands, then remove the wheel.
2. Remove the brake drum.
3. If necessary to provide clearance, remove the brake shoes, as outlined in Section 9 of this manual.
4. Using a large C-clamp and socket, press the stud from the axle flange.
5. Coat the serrated part of the stud with liquid soap and place it into the hole.

To install:

6. Position about 4 flat washers over the stud and thread the lug nut. Hold the flange while tightening the lug nut, and the stud should be drawn into position. MAKE SURE THE STUD IS FULLY SEATED, then remove the lug nut and washers.
7. If applicable, install the brake shoes.
8. Install the brake drum.
9. Install the wheel, then remove the jackstands and carefully lower the vehicle.
10. Tighten the lug nuts to the proper torque.

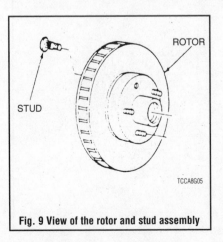

Fig. 9 View of the rotor and stud assembly

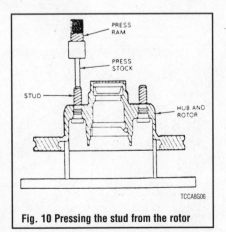

Fig. 10 Pressing the stud from the rotor

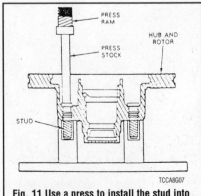

Fig. 11 Use a press to install the stud into the rotor

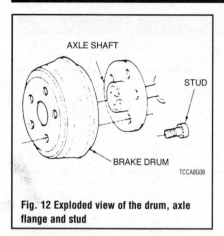

Fig. 12 Exploded view of the drum, axle flange and stud

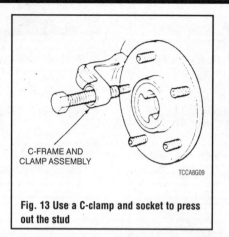

Fig. 13 Use a C-clamp and socket to press out the stud

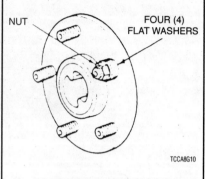

Fig. 14 Force the stud onto the axle flange using washers and a lug nut

FRONT SUSPENSION

♦ See Figure 15

The vehicles covered by this manual are equipped with a MacPherson strut front suspension. The strut acts upon a cast steering knuckle, which pivots on a ball joint mounted on a forged lower control arm. A stabilizer bar, which also acts as a locating link, is standard equipment. To maintain good directional stability, negative scrub radius is designed into the suspension geometry. This means that an imaginary line extended from the strut intersects the ground outside the tire patch. Caster and camber are preset and non-adjustable. The front suspension fittings are "lubed-for-life", so no grease fittings are provided.

MacPherson Struts

REMOVAL & INSTALLATION

1981–85 Models

♦ See Figures 16, 17 and 18

➡A coil spring compressor (such as Ford Tool number T81P5310-A, or equivalent) is required to compress the strut coil spring. DO NOT attempt to service the spring unless you are using a proper spring compressor tool.

1. Loosen the wheel lugs, raise the front of the car and safely support it on jackstands. Locate the jackstands under the frame jack pads, slightly behind the front wheels.
2. Remove the wheels.

3. Remove the brake line from the strut mounting bracket.
4. Place a floor jack or small hydraulic jack under the lower control arm. Raise the lower arm and strut as far as possible without raising the car.
5. Install the coil spring compressor. Place the top jaw of the compressor on the second coil from the top of the spring. Install the bottom jaw so that five coils will be gripped. Compress the spring evenly, from side to side, until there is about ⅛ in. (3mm) between any two spring coils. The coil spring must be compressed evenly. Always oil the compressor tool threads.
6. A pinch bolt retains the strut to the steering knuckle. Remove the pinch bolt.
7. Loosen, but do not remove, the two top mount-to-strut tower nuts. Lower the jack supporting the lower control arm.
8. Use a prybar and slightly spread the pinch bolt joint (knuckle to strut connection).
9. Place a piece of wood 2 in. x 4 in. x 7½ in. long (51mm x 102mm x 191mm), against the shoulder on the steering knuckle. Use a short prybar between the wooden block and the lower spring seat to separate the strut from the knuckle.
10. Remove the two strut upper mounting nuts.
11. Remove the MacPherson strut, spring and top mount assembly from the car.
To install:
12. Install the assembled strut, spring and upper mount into the car. If you have installed a new coil spring, be sure it has been compressed enough.
13. Position the two top mounting studs through the holes in the tower and install two new mounting nuts. Do not tighten the nuts completely.
14. Install the bottom of the strut fully into the steering knuckle pinch joint.
15. Install a new pinch bolt and tighten it to 68–81 ft. lbs. (92–110 Nm). Tighten the tow upper mount nuts to 22–29 ft. lbs. (30–40 Nm).

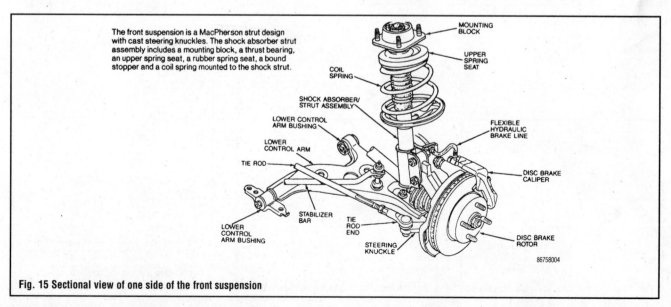

Fig. 15 Sectional view of one side of the front suspension

FRONT SUSPENSION AND STEERING COMPONENTS

1. MacPherson strut
2. Ball joint
3. Lower control arm
4. Stabilizer bar
5. Outer CV-joint
6. Tie rod end
7. Stabilizer bar insulator bushing

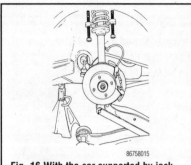

Fig. 16 With the car supported by jackstands and the wheel removed, raise the strut with a floor jack, then install a spring compressor

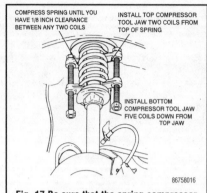

COMPRESS SPRING UNTIL YOU HAVE 1/8 INCH CLEARANCE BETWEEN ANY TWO COILS

INSTALL TOP COMPRESSOR TOOL JAW TWO COILS FROM TOP OF SPRING

INSTALL BOTTOM COMPRESSOR TOOL JAW FIVE COILS DOWN FROM TOP JAW

Fig. 17 Be sure that the spring compressor is situated as shown

Fig. 18 Separate the shock absorber strut from the knuckle using a short prybar as shown

16. Remove the coil spring compressor. Make sure the spring is fitting properly between the upper and lower seats.
17. Install the brake line to the strut bracket.
18. Install the front wheel(s). Lower the car and tighten the lugs.
19. Have the alignment checked at a reputable repair facility.

1985½–90 Models

▶ **See Figures 19 thru 24**

1. Loosen, but do not remove, the two top mount-to-shock tower nuts.
2. Raise and safely support the vehicle. Raise the vehicle to a point where it is possible to reach the two top mount-to-shock tower nuts and the strut-to-knuckle pinch bolt.
3. Remove the wheel and tire assembly.
4. Remove the brake flex line-to-strut bolt.
5. Remove the strut-to-knuckle pinch bolt.
6. Using a suitable prytool, spread the knuckle-to-strut pinch joint slightly.

7. Using a suitable prybar, place the top of the bar under the fender apron and pry down on the knuckle until the strut separates from the knuckle. Be careful not to pinch the brake hose.

➡**Do not pry against the caliper or brake hose bracket.**

8. Unfasten the two top mount-to-shock tower nuts and remove the strut from the vehicle.
   To install:
9. Install the strut assembly in the vehicle. Install the two top mount-to-shock tower nuts. Tighten to 25–30 ft. lbs. (37–41 Nm).
10. Slide the strut mounting flange onto the knuckle.
11. Install the strut-to-knuckle pinch bolt. Tighten to 55–81 ft. lbs. (75–110 Nm).
12. Install the brake flex line-to-strut bolt.
13. Install the wheel and tire assembly.
14. Lower the vehicle.
15. Have the alignment checked at a reputable repair facility.

Fig. 19 Remove the brake flex line-to-strut bolt with the correct wrench

Fig. 20 Remove the strut-to-knuckle pinch bolt

Fig. 21 Place the top of a prybar under fender apron and pry down on the knuckle until the strut separates from the knuckle

Fig. 22 Once loose at the bottom, go to the top of the strut to unbolt it from its shock tower mounts

Fig. 23 Remove the two top mount-to-shock tower nuts and remove the strut from the vehicle

Fig. 24 Once detached, remove the strut from the vehicle for disassembly, inspection or replacement

OVERHAUL

1981–85 Models

♦ See Figures 25, 26, 27, 28 and 29

➡A coil spring compressor (such as Ford Tool number T81P5310-A, or equivalent) is required to compress the strut coil spring. DO NOT attempt to service the spring unless you are using a proper spring compressor tool.

1. Place an 18mm deep socket that has an external hex drive top (Ford tool number D81P-18045-A1) over the strut shaft center nut. Insert a 6mm Allen wrench into the shaft end. With the edge of the strut mount clamped in a vise, remove the top shaft mounting nut from the shaft while holding the Allen wrench. Use locking pliers, if necessary, or a suitable extension to hold the Allen wrench.

➡Make a wooden holding device that will clamp the strut tube into the bench vise (see illustration). Do not clamp directly onto the strut tube, since damage may occur.

2. Clamp the strut into a bench vise. Remove the strut upper mount and the coil spring. If only the strut is to be serviced, do not remove the coil spring compressor from the spring.

To assemble:

3. If the coil spring is to be replaced, remove the compressor from the old spring and install it on the new.

4. Mount the strut (if removed) in the vise using the wooden fixture. Position the coil spring in the lower spring seat. Be sure that the pigtail of the spring is indexed in the seat, so that it follows the groove in the seat and fits flush. Be sure that the spring compressors are positioned 90 from the metal tab on the lower part of the strut.

5. Use a new nut and assemble the top mount to the strut. Tighten the shaft nut to 48–62 ft. lbs. (65–85 Nm).

1985½–90 Models

♦ See Figures 30, 31 and 32

1. Install a spring compressor in a bench mount, then position the strut in the compressor and compress the spring.

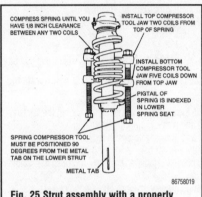

Fig. 25 Strut assembly with a properly installed spring compressor

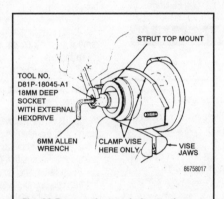

Fig. 26 Remove the top shaft retention nut as shown

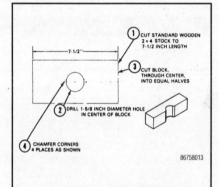

Fig. 27 Fabricate 2 wooden blocks as shown to secure the strut tube in a vise

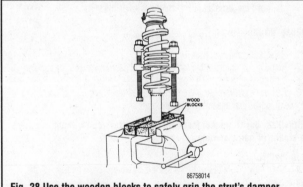

Fig. 28 Use the wooden blocks to safely grip the strut's damper unit—1981–85 models

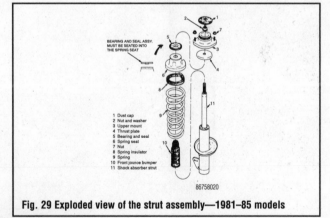

Fig. 29 Exploded view of the strut assembly—1981–85 models

Fig. 30 Install a spring compressor and alternately tighten both sides to relieve spring tension

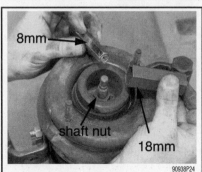

Fig. 31 Hold the shaft with an 8mm deep socket, while turning the nut with an 18mm deep socket and open end wrench

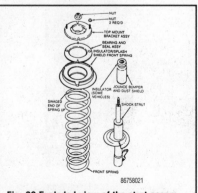

Fig. 32 Exploded view of the strut assembly—1985½–90 models

2. Place an 18mm deep socket on the strut shaft nut. Insert an 8mm deep socket with a ¼ in. drive wrench. Remove the top shaft mounting nut while holding the ¼ in. drive socket with a suitable extension.

➡ **Do not attempt to remove the shaft nut by turning the shaft and holding the nut. The nut must be turned and the shaft held to avoid possible damage to the shaft.**

3. Loosen the spring compressor tool and remove the top mount bracket assembly, bearing, insulator and spring.

To assemble:

4. Install the replacement strut in the spring compressor.

➡ **During reassembly of the strut/spring assembly, be certain to follow the correct sequence and properly position the bearing plate and seal assembly. If the bearing and seal assembly are improperly placed, damage to the bearing will result.**

5. Install the spring, insulator, bearing and top mount bracket assembly.

6. Install the top shaft mounting nut while holding the shaft with a ¼ drive 8mm deep socket and extension. Tighten nut to 35–50 ft. lbs. (48–68 Nm).

Lower Ball Joints

INSPECTION

▶ **See Figure 33**

1. Raise and safely support the vehicle so that the wheels are fully extended.
2. Have an assistant grasp the lower edge of the tire and move the wheel and tire assembly in and out.
3. As the wheel is being moved in and out, observe lower end of knuckle and lower control arm. Any movement indicates abnormal ball joint wear.
4. If any movement is observed, install new lower control arm assembly or the ball joint, as required.

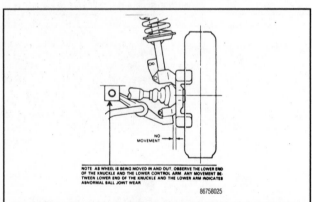

Fig. 33 There should be no lateral play in the ball joint—if there is, it should be replaced

REMOVAL & INSTALLATION

The lower ball joint is integral to the lower control assembly and cannot be serviced individually. Any movement of the lower ball joint detected as a result of inspection requires replacement of the lower control arm assembly.

Stabilizer Bar

REMOVAL & INSTALLATION

1981–85 Models

▶ **See Figures 34, 35 and 36**

1. Raise the vehicle and support it safely. The wheel(s) may be removed for convenience.
2. Unfasten the stabilizer bar insulator mounting bracket bolts. Remove the bar assembly.
3. Carefully cut any worn insulators from the stabilizer bar.
4. If necessary, with the bar removed, use the bushing tool illustrated to remove the old insulator bushings.

To install:

5. If removed, coat the new insulator bushing with a suitable vegetable oil.

➡ **Use only vegetable oil, since any other type of oil will deteriorate the bushing.**

6. Using the removal tool, install new bushings by tightening the C-clamp slowly until the bushing pops into place.
7. Coat the stabilizer bar and the insulators with a suitable lubricant and place them into position on the stabilizer bar.
8. Install washer spacers onto the stabilizer bar ends and push the mounting brackets over the insulators.
9. Install the stabilizer bar using new insulator mounting bracket bolts. Tighten to 50–60 ft. lbs. (68–81 Nm). Install new end nuts with the old dished washers. Tighten to 59–73 ft. lbs. (80–100 Nm).
10. If removed, install the wheel assembly,
11. Remove the jackstands and carefully lower the vehicle.

1985½–90 Models

1. Raise and safely support the vehicle.
2. Remove the nut from the stabilizer bar at each lower control arm and pull off the large dished washer. Discard nuts.
3. Remove stabilizer bar insulator U-bracket bolts and U-brackets and remove stabilizer bar assembly. Discard bolts.

➡ **Stabilizer bar U-bracket insulators can be serviced without removing the stabilizer bar assembly.**

To install:

4. Slide new insulators onto the stabilizer bar and position them in the approximate location.
5. Clean the stabilizer bar threads to remove dirt and contamination.

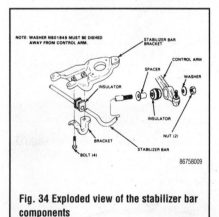

Fig. 34 Exploded view of the stabilizer bar components

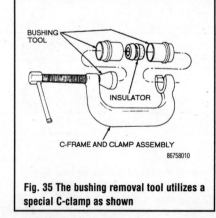

Fig. 35 The bushing removal tool utilizes a special C-clamp as shown

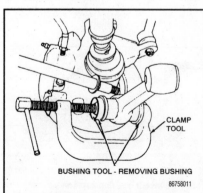

Fig. 36 Use the special C-clamp tool as shown to remove the stabilizer bar bushing

6. Install spacers into the control arm bushings from the forward side of the control arm, so that the washer end of the spacer will seat against the stabilizer bar machined shoulder, and push the mounting brackets over the insulators.

7. Insert the ends of the stabilizer bar into the lower control arms. Using new bolts, attach the stabilizer bar and the insulator U-brackets to the bracket assemblies. Hand start all four U-bracket bolts. Tighten all bolts halfway, then tighten bolts to 85–100 ft. lbs. (115–135 Nm).

8. Using new nuts and the original dished washers (dished side away from bushing), attach the stabilizer bar to the lower control arm. Tighten nuts to 98–115 ft. lbs. (132–156 Nm).

9. Lower the vehicle.

Lower Control Arm

REMOVAL & INSTALLATION

▶ **See Figures 37, 38, 39, 40 and 41**

1. Raise and safely support the vehicle.
2. Remove nut from stabilizer bar end. Pull off large dished washer.
3. Remove lower control arm inner pivot nut and bolt.
4. Remove lower control arm ball joint pinch bolt. Using a suitable prytool, slightly spread knuckle pinch joint and separate control arm from steering knuckle. A drift punch may be used to remove the bolt.

➡ **Do not allow the steering knuckle/halfshaft to move outward. Over-extension of the tripod CV-joint could result in separation of internal parts, causing failure of the joint.**

5. Remove the stabilizer bar spacer from the arm bushing.

➡ **Make sure the steering column is in the unlocked position. Do not use a hammer to separate the ball joint from knuckle.**

To install:

6. Assemble the lower control arm ball joint stud to the steering knuckle, ensuring that the ball stud groove is properly positioned.

7. Insert a new pinch bolt and nut. Tighten to 38–45 ft. lbs. (52–60 Nm).

8. Insert the stabilizer bar spacer into the arm bushing.

9. Clean the stabilizer bar threads to remove dirt and contamination.

10. Position the lower control arm onto the stabilizer bar and position the lower control arm to the inner underbody mounting. Install a new nut and bolt. Tighten to 48–55 ft. lbs. (65–74 Nm).

11. Assemble the stabilizer bar, dished washer and a new nut to the stabilizer. Tighten the nut to 98–115 ft. lbs. (132–156 Nm).

12. Lower the vehicle.

BUSHING REPLACEMENT

▶ **See Figure 42**

➡ **A C-clamp type remover/installer tool is necessary to replace the control arm to stabilizer mounting bushings. The Ford part number of this tool is T81P-5493-A and T74P-3044-A1.**

1. Raise the front of the car and safely support it on jackstands.
2. Remove the lower control arm.
3. Carefully cut away the retaining lip of the bushing. Use the special clamp type tool and remove the bushing.
4. Saturate the new bushing with vegetable oil or soapy water and install the bushing using the special tool.
5. Install the lower control arm to the vehicle.

Fig. 37 Remove the lower control arm inner pivot nut and bolt

Fig. 38 A drift punch may be used to remove the pivot bolt

Fig. 39 Once the bolt is out, the pivoting portion should slide out

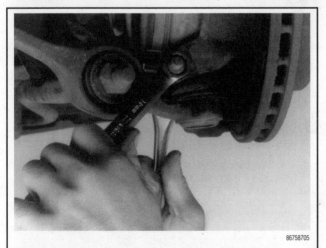

Fig. 40 Remove the lower control arm ball joint pinch bolt

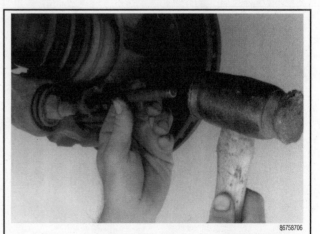

Fig. 41 A hammer and drift will probably be needed to push through the pinch bolt

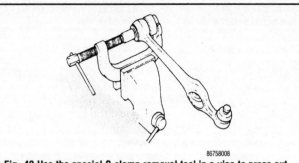

86758008

Fig. 42 Use the special C-clamp removal tool in a vise to press out the control arm bushing

Front Wheel Hub, Knuckle and Bearings

REMOVAL & INSTALLATION

1981–85 Models

♦ See Figure 43

➡The wheel hub and knuckle must be removed for bearing replacement or servicing. A special puller is required to remove and install the hub. (Ford Part Number T81P-1104-A, T81P-1104-C and adapters T81P-1104-B or T83P-1104-AH). The adapters screw over the lugs and attach to the puller, which uses a long screw attached to the end of the stub shaft to pull off or install the hub.

1. Remove wheel cover and slightly loosen the lugs.
2. Remove the hub retaining nut and washer. The nut is crimped staked to the shaft. Use a socket and sufficient torque to overcome the locking force of the crimp.
3. Raise the front of the car and support safely with jackstands. Remove the wheel(s).
4. Remove the brake caliper and disc rotor.

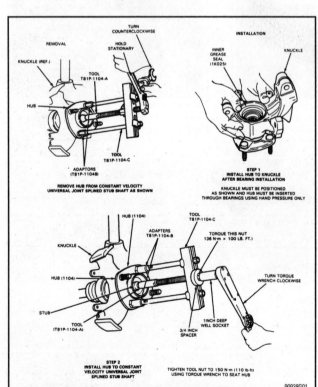

90938G01

Fig. 43 Removal and installation of the front wheel hub assembly— 1981–85 models

5. Disconnect the lower control arm and tie rod from the steering knuckle. Loosen the two top strut mounting nuts, but do not remove them.
6. Install a suitable hub remover/installer tool and remove the hub. If the outer bearing is seized on the hub remove it with a puller.
7. Unfasten the steering knuckle-to-lower control arm and the knuckle-to strut pinch bolts. Use a prytool, slightly spread the knuckle pinch joints and remove the knuckle.
8. On 1981–83 models:
9. After the front knuckle is removed, pull out the inner grease shield, the inner seal and bearing.
10. Remove the outer grease seal and bearing.
11. If you hope to reuse the bearings, clean them in a safe solvent. After cleaning the bearings and races, carefully inspect them for damage, pitting and heat coloring, etc. If damage etc. has occurred, replace all components (bearings, cups and seals). Always replace the seals with new ones.
12. If new bearings are to be used, remove the inner and outer races from the knuckle. A three jawed puller on a slide hammer will do the job.
13. Clean the interior bore of the knuckle.
14. On 1984–85 models:
    a. Remove the snapring that retains the bearing in the steering knuckle.
    b. Position the knuckle, outboard side up under a hydraulic press with appropriate adapters in place, and press the bearing from the knuckle.
    c. Clean the interior bore of the knuckle.

To install:

15. On 1981–83 models:
    a. Install the new bearing cups using a suitable driver. Be sure the cups are fully seated in the knuckle bore.
    b. Pack the wheel bearings with multi-purpose lubricant (Ford part number C1AZ-19590-B or the equivalent). If a bearing packer is not available, place a large portion of grease into the palm of your hand and slide the edge of the roller cage through the grease with your other hand. Work as much grease as you can between the bearing rollers.
    c. Put a sufficient amount of grease between the bearing cups in the center of the knuckle. Apply a thin film of grease on the bearing cups.
    d. Place the outer bearing and new grease seal into the knuckle. Place a thin film of grease on all three lips of the new outer seal.
    e. Turn the knuckle over and install the inner bearing and seal. Once again, apply a thin film of grease to the three lips of the seal.
    f. Install the inner grease shield. A small block of wood may be used to tap the seal into the knuckle bore.
    g. Keep the knuckle in the vertical position or the inner bearing will fall out. Start the wheel hub into the outer knuckle bore and push the hub as far as possible through the outer and inner bearings by hand.

➡Prior to installing the hub, make sure it is clean and free from burrs. Use crocus cloth to polish the hub if necessary. It is important to use only hand pressure when installing the hub, make sure the hub is through both the outer and inner bearings.

    h. With the hub as fully seated as possible through the bearings, position the hub and knuckle to the front strut.
16. On 1984–85 models:
    a. Position the knuckle outboard side down on the appropriate adapter and press in the new bearing. Be sure the bearing is fully seated. Install a new retainer snapring.
    b. Install the hub using tool T83T-1104-AH3 and press. Check that the hub rotates freely.
    c. Lubricate the stub shaft splines with a thin film of SAE 30 motor oil. Use hand pressure only and insert the splines into the knuckle and hub as far as possible.

➡Do not allow the hub to back out of the bearings while installing the stub shaft, otherwise it will be necessary to start all over.

17. Complete the installation of the suspension parts.
18. Install the hub remover/installer tool and tighten the center adapter to 120 ft. lbs. (163 Nm) to ensure the hub is fully seated.
19. Remove the installer tool and install the hub washer and nut. Finger-tighten the hub nut.
20. Install the disc (rotor) and caliper, etc.
21. Install the wheel(s) and snug the wheel lugs.
22. Lower the car to the ground, set the parking brake and block the wheels.
23. Tighten the wheel lugs to specification.

24. Tighten the center hub nut to 180–200 ft. lbs. (244–271 Nm). Do not use an impact wrench to tighten the hub nut!

25. Stake the hub nut using a chisel.

26. Have the alignment checked at a reputable repair facility.

1985½–90 Models

▶ **See Figures 44 thru 59**

1. Remove the wheel/hub cover from the wheel and tire assembly, then loosen the lug nuts.

2. Remove the hub nut and washer after applying sufficient torque to the nut to break the locking tab. The hub nut must be replaced with a new one upon installation.

3. Raise and safely support the vehicle. Remove the wheel(s).

4. Remove the brake caliper by loosening the caliper locating pins and rotating the caliper off the rotor, starting from the lower end of the caliper and lifting upward. Do not remove the caliper pins from the caliper assembly. Lift the caliper off the rotor and hang it free of the rotor. Do not allow the caliper assembly to hang from the brake hose. Support the caliper assembly with a length of wire.

5. Remove the rotor from the hub by pulling it off the hub bolts. If the rotor is difficult to remove from the hub, strike the rotor sharply between the studs with a rubber or plastic hammer. If the rotor will not pull off, apply a rust penetrating fluid to the inboard and outboard rotor hub mating surfaces. Install a three-jaw puller and remove the rotor by pulling on the rotor's outside diameter and pushing on the hub center. If excessive force is required for removal, check the rotor for lateral run-out.

6. If necessary, remove the rotor splash shield.

7. Disconnect the lower control arm and tie rod from the knuckle (leave the strut attached).

8. Loosen the two strut top mount-to-apron nuts.

9. Install a suitable hub removal tool and remove the hub/bearing/knuckle assembly by pushing out the CV-joint outer shaft until it is free of the assembly.

10. Support the knuckle with a length of wire, remove the strut bolt and slide the hub/knuckle assembly off the strut.

11. Carefully remove the support wire and transfer the hub/bearing assembly to the bench.

12. Install a suitable front hub puller with the jaws of the puller on the knuckle bosses and remove the hub.

➡ **Ensure that the shaft protector is centered, and that it clears the bearing inside diameter and rests on the end face of the hub journal.**

13. Remove the snapring which retains the bearing knuckle assembly, and discard.

14. Using a hydraulic press, place a suitable front bearing spacer (step side up) on the press plate and position the knuckle on the spacer with the outboard side up. Install the bearing removal tool on the bearing inner race and press the bearing out of the knuckle.

15. Discard the bearing.

16. Remove the halfshaft.

17. Place the halfshaft in a vise.

18. Remove the bearing dust seal by uniformly tapping on outer edge with a light-duty hammer and screwdriver. Discard the dust seal.

To install:

19. Place the halfshaft in a vise.

20. Install a new dust seal using a suitable seal installer. The seal flange must face outboard.

21. Install the halfshaft.

22. On the bench, remove all foreign material from the knuckle bearing bore and the hub bearing journal to ensure the correct seating of the new bearing.

➡ **If the hub bearing journal is scored or damaged, replace the hub with a new one. Do not attempt to service it. The front wheel bearings are of a cartridge design and are pre-greased, sealed and require no scheduled maintenance. The bearings are preset and cannot be adjusted. If a bearing is disassembled for any reason, it must be replaced as a unit. No individual service seals, rollers or races are available.**

23. Place the suitable bearing spacer, step side down, on a hydraulic press plate and position the knuckle on the spacer with the outboard side down. Position a new bearing in the inboard side of the knuckle. Install a suitable front

Fig. 44 Apply sufficient torque to break the hub nut retainer's locking tab . . .

Fig. 45 . . . then remove the hub nut and washer

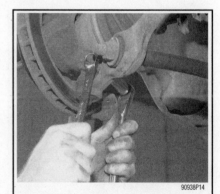

Fig. 46 Unfasten the lower control arm pinch bolt

Fig. 47 Remove the tie rod end's cotter pin using a pair of pliers

Fig. 48 Loosen the tie rod end nut, then use a puller to separate the tie rod end from the steering knuckle

Fig. 49 Lift the detached tie rod end from the steering knuckle

bearing installer on the bearing outer race face with undercut side facing bearing and press bearing into knuckle. Ensure that the bearing seats completely against the shoulder of the knuckle bore.

➡**Ensure proper positioning of the bearing installer during installation to prevent bearing damage.**

24. Install a new snapring in the knuckle groove using snapring pliers.

25. Place a suitable front bearing spacer on a press plate and position the hub on the tool with lugs facing downward. Position the knuckle assembly on the hub barrel with the outboard side down. Place a suitable front bearing remover on the inner race of the bearing and press down on the tool until the bearing moves freely in the knuckle after installation.

26. Suspend the hub/knuckle/bearing assembly on the vehicle with wire and attach the strut loosely to the knuckle.

27. Lubricate the CV-joint stub shaft splines with SAE 30 weight motor oil and insert the shaft into the hub splines as far as possible using hand pressure only. Check that the splines are properly engaged.

28. Install a suitable front hub installer and wheel bolt adapter to the hub and stub shaft. Tighten the hub installer tool to 120 ft. lbs. (162 Nm) to ensure that the hub is fully seated.

29. Remove the tool and install the washer and new hub nut retainer. Finger-tighten the hub nut retainer.

30. Complete the installation of the front suspension components.

31. Install the disc brake rotor to the hub assembly.

32. Install the disc brake caliper over the rotor.

33. Ensure that the outer brake shoe spring end is seated under the upper arm of the knuckle.

34. Install the wheel and tire assembly, tightening the wheel nuts finger-tight.

35. Lower the vehicle and block the wheels to prevent the vehicle from rolling.

36. Tighten the lug nuts to specification.

37. Manually thread the hub nut onto the CV-joint shaft as far as possible using a 30mm socket. Tighten the hub nut/retainer assembly to 180–200 ft. lbs. (244–271 Nm).

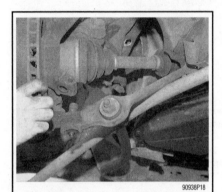

Fig. 50 Separate the lower control arm from the knuckle . . .

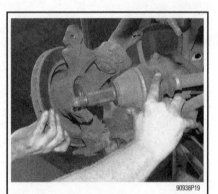

Fig. 51 . . . and pull the knuckle off the halfshaft/CV-joint assembly

Fig. 52 If the knuckle is hard to remove while still on the vehicle, loosen the upper strut retaining nuts . . .

Fig. 53 . . . and remove the knuckle and strut as an assembly

Fig. 54 Unfasten the steering knuckle and hub assembly-to-strut retainers . . .

Fig. 55 . . . then separate the knuckle from the strut

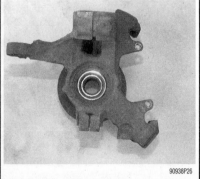

Fig. 56 View of the steering knuckle/hub and bearing assembly

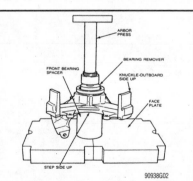

Fig. 57 Use an arbor press and a suitable bearing spacer to press the bearing from the knuckle

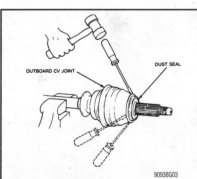

Fig. 58 Remove the bearing dust seal by uniformly tapping on its outer edge with a light-duty hammer and screwdriver

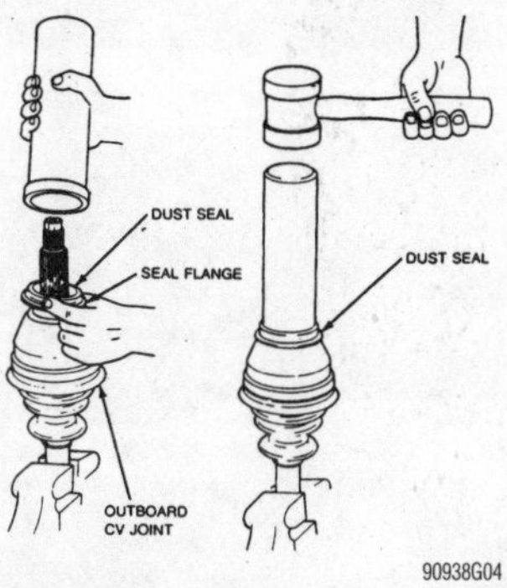

Fig. 59 Install a new dust seal with a suitable seal installer, making sure the seal flange faces outward

➡Do not use power or impact tools to tighten the hub nut. Do not move the vehicle before the retainer is tightened.

38. During tightening, an audible click sound will indicate the proper ratchet function of the hub nut retainer. As the hub nut retainer tightens, ensure that one of the three locking tabs is in the slot of the CV-joint shaft. If the hub nut retainer is damaged, or more than one locking tab is broken, replace the hub nut retainer.
39. Install the wheel, wheel cover or hub cover and lower the vehicle completely to ground.
40. Remove the wheel blocks.
41. Have the alignment checked at a reputable repair facility.

Wheel Alignment

If the tires are worn unevenly, if the vehicle is not stable on the highway or if the handling seems uneven in spirited driving, the wheel alignment should be checked. If an alignment problem is suspected, first check for improper tire inflation and other possible causes. These can be worn suspension or steering components, accident damage or even unmatched tires. If any worn or damaged components are found, they must be replaced before the wheels can be properly aligned. Wheel alignment requires very expensive equipment and involves minute adjustments which must be accurate; it should only be performed by a trained technician. Take your vehicle to a properly equipped shop.

Following is a description of the alignment angles which are adjustable on most vehicles and how they affect vehicle handling. Although these angles can apply to both the front and rear wheels, usually only the front suspension is adjustable.

CASTER

➧ **See Figure 60**

Looking at a vehicle from the side, caster angle describes the steering axis rather than a wheel angle. The steering knuckle is attached to a control arm or strut at the top and a control arm at the bottom. The wheel pivots around the line between these points to steer the vehicle. When the upper point is tilted back, this is described as positive caster. Having a positive caster tends to make the wheels self-centering, increasing directional stability. Excessive positive caster makes the wheels hard to steer, while an uneven caster will cause a pull to one side. Overloading the vehicle or sagging rear springs will affect caster, as will raising the rear of the vehicle. If the rear of the vehicle is lower than normal, the caster becomes more positive.

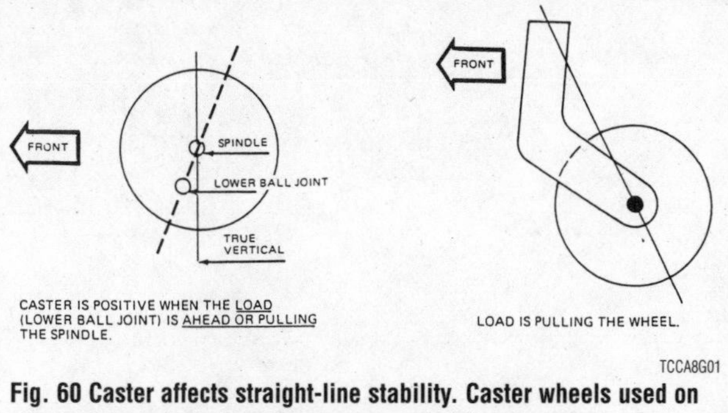

Fig. 60 Caster affects straight-line stability. Caster wheels used on shopping carts, for example, employ positive caster

CAMBER

➧ **See Figure 61**

Looking from the front of the vehicle, camber is the inward or outward tilt of the top of wheels. When the tops of the wheels are tilted in, this is negative camber; if they are tilted out, it is positive. In a turn, a slight amount of negative camber helps maximize contact of the tire with the road. However, too much negative camber compromises straight-line stability, increases bump steer and torque steer.

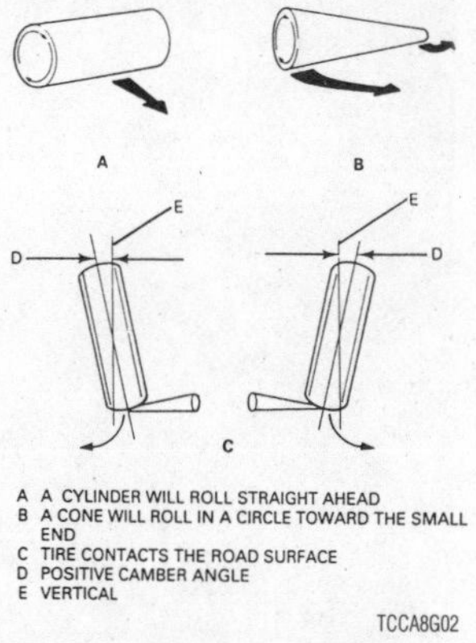

Fig. 61 Camber influences tire contact with the road

TOE

➧ **See Figure 62**

Looking down at the wheels from above the vehicle, toe angle is the distance between the front of the wheels, relative to the distance between the back of the wheels. If the wheels are closer at the front, they are said to be toed-in or to have negative toe. A small amount of negative toe enhances directional stability and provides a smoother ride on the highway.

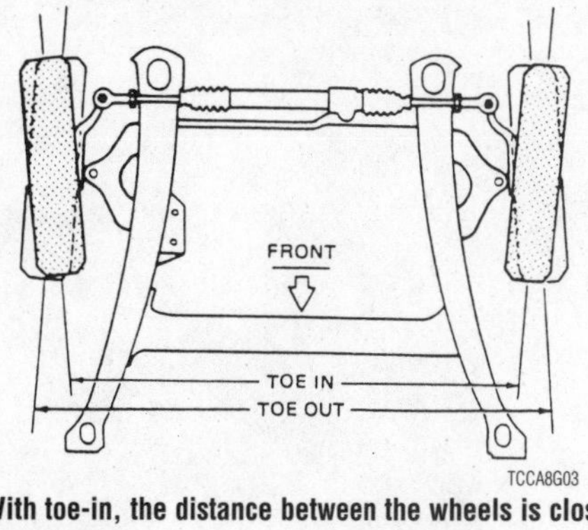

Fig. 62 With toe-in, the distance between the wheels is closer at the front than at the rear

REAR SUSPENSION

REAR SUSPENSION COMPONENTS

1. Shock absorber
2. Coil spring
3. Control arm
4. Tie rod

Coil Springs

REMOVAL & INSTALLATION

▶ **See Figures 63, 64 and 65**

1. Raise and support the vehicle safely. Position the jackstands beneath the frame pads slightly in front of the rear wheels.

2. Place a floor jack or small hydraulic jack under the rear control arm. Raise the control arm to its normal height with the jack, do not lift the car frame from the jackstands.

➡ **If a twin-post lift is used, vehicle must be supported on jackstands placed under the jack pads of the underbody.**

3. Remove the wheel(s).

4. Remove and discard nut, bolt and washers retaining lower control arm to spindle.

5. Slowly lower the jack under the control arm. The coil spring will relax as the control arm is lowered. Lower the control arm until the spring can be removed.

To install:

6. The spring insulator must be replaced when servicing the spring.

7. Index the insulator on the spring and press the insulator downward until it snaps into place. Check again to ensure the insulator is properly indexed against tip of the spring.

8. Install spring in control arm. Ensure spring is properly seated in control arm spring pocket.

9. Raise control arm and spring with a floor jack. Position the spring in the pocket on the underbody.

10. Using a new bolt, nut and washers, attach the control arm to the spindle. Install bolt with the head toward front of the vehicle. On the 1981–85 models, tighten the nut and bolt to 90–100 ft. lbs. (122–136 Nm). On the 1985½–90 models, tighten to 60–80 ft. lbs. (81–109 Nm).

11. Install the tire and wheel.

12. Remove the floor jack and lower the vehicle.

Shock Absorbers

REMOVAL & INSTALLATION

▶ **See Figures 66 thru 71**

1. Remove the rear compartment access panels. On 4-door models, remove the quarter trim panel.

➡ **Do not attempt to remove the shaft nut by turning the shaft and holding the nut. The nut must be turned while holding the shaft.**

2. Loosen, but do not remove, the top strut attaching nut using an 18mm deep socket while holding the strut rod with a 6mm Allen wrench (1981–85 vehicles) or a ¼ drive, 8mm deep socket and suitable extension (1985½–90 vehicles).

➡ **If the strut is to be reused, do not grip the shaft with pliers or locking pliers, as this will damage the shaft surface finish and may result in severe oil leakage.**

3. Raise and safely support the vehicle.

4. Remove the wheel(s).

➡ **If a frame contact lift is used, support the lower control arm with a floor jack. If a twin-post lift is used, support the body with floor jacks on lifting pads forward of the body bracket.**

5. Remove the stabilizer bar link from the shock bracket, if equipped.

6. Remove the clip retaining the brake line flexible hose to the rear shock and move it aside.

7. Loosen the two nuts and bolts retaining the shock to the spindle. Do not remove the bolts at this time.

8. Remove and discard the top mounting nut, washer and rubber insulator.

9. Remove and discard the two bottom mounting bolts.

10. Remove the shock from the vehicle.

To install:

11. Extend shock absorber to its maximum length.

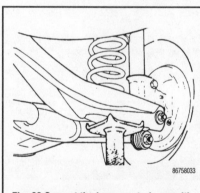

Fig. 63 Support the lower control arm with a jack

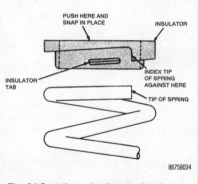

Fig. 64 Seat the spring into the insulator tab as shown

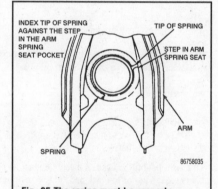

Fig. 65 The spring must be properly indexed into the arm spring seat pocket

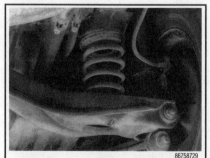

Fig. 66 On early model Escorts, shock absorption and rebound damping are handled by a side-by-side spring and shock absorber

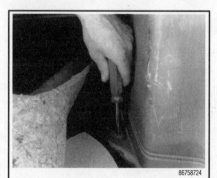

Fig. 67 Locate the fasteners and remove the rear compartment access panels—wagon model shown

Fig. 68 Without turning the shaft, loosen (but do not remove) the nut at the top of the strut with a deep socket

Fig. 69 If a frame contact lift is used, support the lower control arm with a floor jack

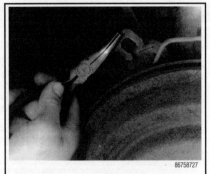

Fig. 70 Remove the clip retaining the brake line flexible hose to the rear shock strut and move it aside

Fig. 71 Loosen the nuts/bolts retaining the shock to the spindle, but do not remove until the top mounting nut is off

12. Install a new lower washer and insulator assembly, using tire mounting lubricant, or equivalent, to ease insertion into the quarter panel shock tower.

13. Position the upper part of the shock absorber shaft into the shock tower opening in the body and push slowly on the lower part of the shock until the mounting holes are lined up with the mounting holes in the spindle.

14. Install new lower mounting bolts and nuts. Do not tighten at this time.

→The heads of both bolts must be to the rear of the vehicle.

15. Place a new upper insulator and washer assembly and nut on the upper shock absorber shaft. Tighten the nut to 60–70 ft. lbs. (81–95 Nm) 1981–85 models and 35–55 ft. lbs. (48–75 Nm) on 1985½–90 models. Do not grip the shaft with pliers or locking pliers.

16. Tighten the two lower mounting bolts to 90–100 ft. lbs. (122–135 Nm) on 1981–85 models and 70–96 ft. lbs. (95–130 Nm) on 1985½–90 models.

17. Install stabilizer bar link to bracket on strut, if equipped. Tighten bolts to 40–55 ft. lbs. (55–75 Nm).

18. Install the brake line flex hose and retaining clip.

19. Install the wheel and tire assembly.

20. Install quarter trim and access panels, as required.

Control Arms

REMOVAL & INSTALLATION

1. Raise and safely support the vehicle.

2. Place a floor jack under the lower control arm. Raise the lower control arm to the curb position.

→If a twin-post lift is used, the vehicle must be supported on the jackstands placed under the jack pads of the underbody.

3. Remove the wheel(s).

4. Remove the nuts from the control arm-to-body mounting and the control arm-to-spindle mounting. Do not remove the bolts at this time.

5. Remove and discard the spindle end mounting bolt. Slowly the lower control arm with the floor jack until the spring insulator and spring can be removed.

6. Remove and discard the bolt from the body end and remove the control arm from vehicle.

To install:

7. Attach the lower control arm-to-body bracket using a new bolt and nut. The head of the bolt should face the front of the vehicle. Do not tighten the bolt at this time.

8. The spring insulator must be replaced when servicing the spring.

9. Index the insulator on the spring and press insulator downward until it snaps into place. Place spring in spring pocket in lower control arm. Make sure spring is properly indexed.

10. Using a floor jack, raise lower control arm until it is in line with mounting hole in the spindle.

11. Install lower control arm to spindle using a new bolt, nut and washers. Do not tighten at this time. Bolt head should face the front of the vehicle.

12. Using the floor jack, raise lower control arm to curb height.

13. Tighten control arm-to-spindle bolt to 90–100 ft. lbs. (122–135 Nm) on 1981–85 models and 60–80 ft. lbs. (81–109 Nm) on 1985½–90 models.

14. Tighten the control arm-to-body bolt to 65–75 ft. lbs. (88–102 Nm) on 1981–85 models and 52–74 ft. lbs. (70–100 Nm) on 1985½–90 models.

15. Install the tire and wheel.

16. Remove the floor jack and lower the vehicle.

Stabilizer Bar

REMOVAL & INSTALLATION

1. Raise the rear of the vehicle and support it with safety stands.

2. Remove the wheel and tire assembly.

3. Remove the nut and insulator that attaches the stabilizer bar end to the link assembly.

4. Unfasten the two stabilizer bar-to-body U-brackets. Remove the bar.

5. Unfasten the link assembly-to-shock bracket bolt and remove the link.

To install:

6. Inspect the stabilizer bar insulators and replace them if they are worn.

7. Attach the stabilizer bar to the body using the U-brackets. Tighten the bolts to 15–25 ft. lbs. (23–32 Nm).

8. Install the link assembly to the shock mounting bracket. Tighten the bolt to 41–55 ft. lbs. (55–75 Nm).

9. Pull down on the end of the stabilizer bar and insert the link assembly into the bar. Install the insulator and nut, then tighten the nut to 6–12 ft. lbs. (8–16 Nm).

10. Install the wheel and tire assembly.

11. Lower the vehicle.

Rear Wheel Bearings

REMOVAL & INSTALLATION

♦ See Figures 72 thru 79

1. Raise and safely support the vehicle.

2. Remove the wheel and tire assembly.

3. Remove the grease cap from the hub.

4. Remove the cotter pin, nut retainer, adjusting nut and flat washer from spindle. Discard the cotter pin.

5. Pull the hub and drum assembly off the spindle being careful not to drop outer bearing assembly.

6. Remove the outer bearing assembly.

7. Using a suitable seal remover, remove and discard grease seal.

8. Remove the inner bearing assembly from the hub.

9. Wipe all lubricant from the spindle and inside of the hub. Cover the spindle with a clean cloth and vacuum all loose dust and dirt from the brake assembly. Carefully remove cloth to prevent dirt from falling on spindle.

10. Clean both bearing assemblies and cups using solvent. inspect bearing assemblies and cups for excessive wear, scratches, pits or other damage. Replace all worn or damaged parts as required.

➡**Allow the solvent to dry before repacking bearings. Do not spin-dry bearings with air pressure.**

11. If the cups are replaced, remove them with Wheel Hub Cup Remover D80L-927-A and Bearing Cup Puller T77F-1102-A , or their equivalents.

To install:

12. If inner or outer bearing cups were removed, install replacement cups using driver handle T80T-4000-W and bearing cup replacers T77F-1202-A and T73T-1217-A or equivalent. Support drum hub on wood block to prevent damage. Ensure that the cups are properly seated in the hub.

➡**Do not use a cone and roller assembly to install the cup, as this will cause damage to the bearing cup and cone/roller assembly.**

13. Ensure all spindle and bearing surfaces are clean.

14. Using a bearing packer, pack bearing assemblies with a suitable wheel bearing grease. If a packer is not available, work in as much grease as possible between the rollers and the cages using your hand. Grease the cup surfaces.

15. Place inner bearing cone and roller assembly in the inner cup. Apply a light film of grease to the lips of a new grease seal and install seal with rear hub seal replacer T81P-1249-A or equivalent. Ensure that the retainer flange is seated all around.

16. Apply a light film of grease on the spindle shaft bearing surfaces.

17. Install a hub and drum assembly on the spindle. Keep the hub centered on the spindle to prevent damage to the grease seal and spindle threads.

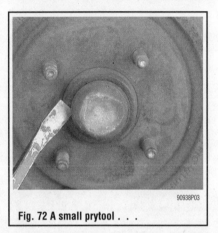

Fig. 72 A small prytool . . .

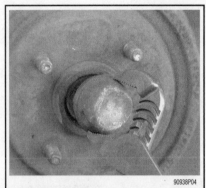

Fig. 73 . . . or a pair of pliers can be used to remove the grease cap from the hub

Fig. 74 A pair of needlenosed pliers can be used to remove the cotter pin from the hole in the spindle

Fig. 75 Use a ratchet and socket to loosen the wheel bearing retaining nut . . .

Fig. 76 . . . then remove the nut by hand

Fig. 77 Slide the drum slightly forward, then slide it back into position. This will allow you to grasp the washer and bearing

Fig. 78 After sliding the drum into position, remove the washer . . .

Fig. 79 . . . and the wheel bearing

18. Install the outer bearing assembly and keyed flat washer on the spindle. Install adjusting nut finger-tight. Adjust wheel bearings. Install a new cotter pin.

19. Install the wheel and tire on drum.

20. Lower the vehicle.

ADJUSTMENT

1. Raise and safely support the vehicle.

2. Remove the wheel covers or ornament and nut covers. Remove the grease cap from hub.

3. Remove the cotter pin and nut retainer. Discard the cotter pin.

4. Back off the adjusting nut one full turn. Ensure the nut turns freely on the spindle threads. Correct any binding condition.

5. Tighten the adjusting nut to 17–25 ft. lbs. (23–34 Nm) while rotating the hub and drum assembly to seat the bearings. Loosen the adjusting nut ½ turn and tighten the adjusting nut to 24–28 inch lbs. (2.7–3.2 Nm).

6. Position the adjusting nut retainer over the adjusting nut so the slots in the nut retainer flange are in line with the cotter pin hole in the spline.

7. Install a new cotter pin and bend ends around the retainer flange.

8. Check the hub rotation. If the hub rotates freely, install the grease cap. If not, check the bearings for damage and replace as necessary.

9. Install the wheel and tire assembly, wheel cover or ornaments, and the nut covers as required.

10. Lower the vehicle.

STEERING

Steering Wheel

REMOVAL & INSTALLATION

♦ **See Figures 80, 81, 82 and 83**

1. Disconnect the negative battery cable from the battery.

2. Unfasten the horn cover screws located on the back of the steering wheel assembly.

3. Unplug the horn electrical connection and remove the cover.

4. Loosen and remove the center mounting nut.

5. Scribe matchmarks on the steering wheel and shaft to assure installation in the proper alignment.

6. Remove the wheel with a steering wheel puller. DO NOT USE a knock-off type puller. It will cause damage to the collapsible steering column.

Fig. 80 Remove the steering wheel center hub by unscrewing it from the back of the wheel

To install:

7. Align the marks on the steering shaft and steering wheel. Place the wheel onto the shaft.

8. Install a new center mounting nut. Tighten the nut to 30–40 ft. lbs. (40–54 Nm) on 1981–85 models and 23–33 ft. lbs. (31–45 Nm) on 1986–90 models.

9. Attach the horn electrical connection and install the horn cover on the steering wheel. Tighten the horn pad screws until they are snug.

10. Connect the negative battery cable.

Turn Signal (Combination) Switch

The combination switch assembly is a multi-function switch comprising the controls for turn signals, hazard flasher, headlight dimmer and flash-to-pass functions. The switch lever is on the left side of the steering column, above the wiper switch lever; it controls the turn signal, headlight dimmer and flash-to-pass functions. The hazard flasher function is controlled by the actuating knob on the bottom part of the steering column.

REMOVAL & INSTALLATION

♦ **See Figures 84 and 85**

1. Disconnect the negative battery cable.

2. Remove the steering column shroud by unfastening the mounting screws.

3. Remove the upper shroud.

4. Remove the switch lever by using a twisting motion while pulling the lever straight out from the switch.

5. Peel back the foam cover to expose the switch.

6. Unplug the two switch electrical connectors.

7. Remove the two self-tapping screws that attach the switch to the lock cylinder housing and disengage the switch from the housing.

8. If your car is equipped with speed control, transfer the ground brush located in the turn signal switch canceling cam to the new switch.

Fig. 81 Once unscrewed, remove the cover to expose the wheel retaining nut

Fig. 82 Unbolt the retaining nut in order to pull the steering wheel

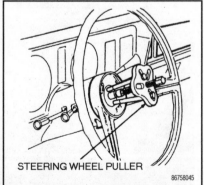

STEERING WHEEL PULLER

Fig. 83 Use only a crow's foot steering wheel puller to remove the steering wheel

To install:

9. To install the new switch, align the switch with the holes in the lock cylinder housing.

10. Install the two self-tapping screws.

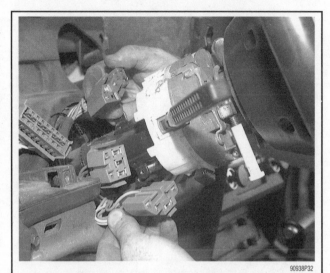

Fig. 84 Unplug the combination switch electrical connectors

Fig. 85 Unfasten the combination switch retaining screws and remove the switch assembly from the steering column

11. Install the foam covering the switch.

12. Install the handle by aligning the key on the lever with the keyway in the switch. Push the lever into the switch until it is fully engaged.

13. Attach the two switch electrical connectors.

14. Install the upper steering column shroud and tighten five attaching screws.

15. Connect the negative battery cable and check the switch for proper operation.

Windshield Wiper Switch

REMOVAL & INSTALLATION

♦ **See Figures 86, 87, 88, 89 and 90**

1. Disconnect the negative battery cable.
2. Remove the upper and lower trim shrouds.
3. Unplug the switch electrical connector.
4. Peel back the foam sight shield.
5. Unfasten the two hex head screws holding the switch and remove the wash/wipe switch.

To install:

6. Position the switch on the column and install the two hex head screws.
7. Reposition the foam sight shield over the switch.
8. Attach the switch electrical connector.
9. Install the upper and lower trim shrouds.
10. Connect the negative battery cable.
11. Check the switch for proper operation.

Fig. 86 Remove the steering column shroud

Fig. 87 Peel back or remove the foam sight shield from the wiper switch

Fig. 88 Unplug the wiper switch electrical connection

Fig. 89 Unfasten the two hex head screws holding the switch and remove the switch from the steering column

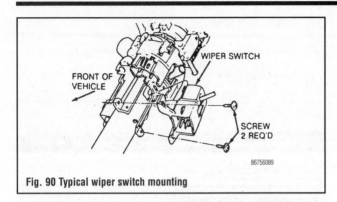

Fig. 90 Typical wiper switch mounting

Ignition Switch

REMOVAL & INSTALLATION

Early Model Vehicles

1. Remove the steering column upper and lower trim shroud by unfastening the self-tapping screws. The steering column attaching nuts may have to be loosened enough to allow removal of the upper shroud.
2. Unplug the electrical connector from ignition switch.
3. Remove the two bolts and nuts holding the steering column assembly to the steering column bracket assembly and lower the steering column to the seat.
4. Drill out the break-off head bolts that attach the switch to lock cylinder housing using a ⅛ in. (3.17mm) drill bit.
5. Remove the bolts using a suitable easy-out tool.
6. Disengage the switch from the actuator pin and remove the switch from the vehicle.
To install:
7. Adjust the switch by sliding the carrier to the switch **LOCK** position.
8. Insert a ¹⁄₁₆ inch drill bit or similar tool through the switch housing and into the carrier thereby preventing carrier movement with respect to the switch housing. It may be necessary to move the carrier slightly back and forth to align the carrier slightly back and forth to align the carrier and housing adjustment holes.

➡A new switch assembly includes an adjusting pin already installed.

9. Rotate the lock cylinder key to the **LOCK** position.
10. Install the ignition switch on the actuator pin.
11. Install and hand-tighten new brake-off head bolts.
12. Move the ignition switch up the steering column until all the travel in the screw slots is used. Hold the switch in this position and tighten the break-off head bolts until the heads break off.
13. Remove the drill bit or adjustment pin.
14. Align the holes in the outer tube assembly with the bolts in the steering column mounting bracket and hand tighten the nuts.
15. Attach the ignition switch electrical connection.
16. Install the upper and lower column covers, then tighten the switch retaining screws.

17. Tighten the steering column attaching fasteners to 15–25 ft. lbs. (20–30 Nm).
18. Connect the negative battery cable.
19. Check that the vehicle starts in **PARK** and **Neutral** only. The vehicle should not be able to be started in the **DRIVE** or **REVERSE** positions. Check the steering column locks when the switch is in the **LOCK** position.

Late Model Vehicles

▶ **See Figures 91, 92 and 93**

1. Disconnect the negative battery cable.
2. Remove the steering column upper and lower trim shroud by unfastening the self-tapping screws. The steering column attaching nuts may have to be loosened enough to allow removal of the upper shroud.
3. Remove the two bolts and nuts holding the steering column assembly to the steering column bracket assembly and lower the steering column to the seat.
4. Remove the steering column shrouds.
5. Unplug the electrical connector from ignition switch.
6. Rotate the ignition lock cylinder to the **RUN** position.
7. Remove the two screws attaching the switch to the lock cylinder housing.
8. Disengage the ignition switch from the actuator pin.
To install:
9. Check to see that the actuator pin slot in ignition switch is in the **RUN** position.

➡A new switch assembly will be pre-set in the **RUN** position.

10. Make certain that the ignition key lock cylinder is in approximately the **RUN** position. The **RUN** position is achieved by rotating the key lock cylinder approximately 90 from the **LOCK** position.
11. Install the ignition switch onto the actuator pin. It may be necessary to move the switch slightly back and fourth to align the switch mounting holes with the column lock housing threaded holes.
12. Install the new screws and tighten to 50–70 inch lbs. (5.6–7.9 Nm).
13. Plug in the electrical connector to the ignition switch.
14. Connect the negative battery cable.
15. Check the ignition switch for proper function including **START** and **ACC** positions. Also make certain that the steering column is locked when in the **LOCK** position.
16. Position the top half of the shroud on the steering column.
17. Install the two bolts and nuts attaching the steering column assembly to the steering column bracket assembly.
18. Position the lower shroud to the upper shroud and install the five self-tapping screws.

Ignition Lock Cylinder

REMOVAL & INSTALLATION

▶ **See Figure 94**

1. Disconnect the negative battery cable.
2. If equipped with a tilt steering column, remove the upper extension shroud by unsnapping the shroud from the retaining clip at the 9 o'clock position.

Fig. 91 Unplug the ignition switch electrical connection

Fig. 92 Unfasten the switch retainers using a security type Torx® bit

Fig. 93 After unfastening all the switch retainers, remove the switch from the steering column

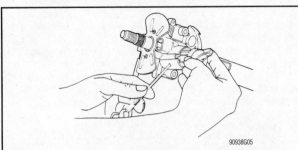

Fig. 94 Use a ⅛ in. (3.17mm) diameter pin or small wire punch to push on the lock cylinder retaining pin and remove the cylinder

3. Remove the steering column lower shroud.
4. Unplug the warning buzzer electrical connector.
5. With the lock cylinder key, rotate the cylinder to the **RUN** position.
6. Take a ⅛ in. (3.17mm) diameter pin or small wire punch and push on the cylinder retaining pin. The pin is visible through a hole in the mounting surrounding the key cylinder. Push on the pin and withdraw the lock cylinder from the housing.

To install:

7. Install the lock cylinder by turning it to the **RUN** position and depressing the retaining pin. Insert the lock cylinder into the housing. Be sure the lock cylinder is fully seated and aligned in the interlocking washer before turning the key to the **OFF** position. This action will permit the cylinder retaining pin to extend into the cylinder housing hole.
8. Rotate the lock cylinder, using the lock cylinder key, to ensure correct mechanical operation in all positions.
9. Attach the electrical connector for the key warning buzzer.
10. Install the lower steering column shroud or trim shroud halves.
11. Connect the negative battery cable.
12. Check for proper start in **P** or **N**, then make certain the start circuit cannot be actuated in the **D** and **R** positions and that the column is locked in the **LOCK** position.

Steering Linkage

REMOVAL & INSTALLATION

Tie Rod Ends

♦ See Figures 95, 96, 97 and 98

1. With paint or a marker pen, mark the tie rod end, jam nut and tie rod to make installation easier, without having to change the toe-in setting.
2. Remove and discard cotter pin and nut from the worn tie rod end ball stud.

➡**Although it is possible to remove the tie rod end first, loosening the jam nut is easier when the rod is still held in place.**

3. While holding the tie rod end with a suitable wrench, loosen the tie rod jam nut.
4. Disconnect the tie rod end from spindle, using a tie rod end remover tool such as 3290-D and adapter T81P-3504-W or suitable equivalents.
5. Grip the tie rod hex flats with a pair of locking pliers, and remove the tie rod end from the tie rod.

To install:

6. Clean the tie rod threads. Apply a light coating of disc brake caliper slide grease D7AZ-19590-A or equivalent, to the tie rod threads. Thread the new tie rod end to the same depth as the removed tie rod end. Tighten the jam nut.
7. Place the tie rod end stud into the steering spindle.
8. Install a new nut on tie rod end stud. Tighten the nut to 27–32 ft. lbs. (36–43 Nm), then continue tightening the nut to align the next castellation with the cotter pin hole in the stud. Install a new cotter pin.
9. Set the toe to specification and tighten the jam nuts to 35–50 ft. lbs. (47–68 Nm). Do not twist the bellows. Have the front end alignment (specifically the toe) checked by a reputable repair facility.

CHECKING

Tie Rod Articulation/Steering Effort

The yoke clearance is not adjustable except when overhauling the steering gear assembly. Pinion bearing preload is not adjustable because of the non-adjustable bearing usage. Tie rod articulation is preset and is not adjustable. If articulation is out of specification, replace the tie rod assembly. To check tie rod articulation, proceed as follows:

1. With the tie rod end disconnected from the steering knuckle, loop a piece of wire through the hole in the tie rod end stud.

Fig. 95 Remove and discard the cotter pin and nut from the worn tie rod end ball stud

Fig. 96 Holding the tie rod end with a suitable wrench (or locking pliers), loosen the tie rod jam nut

Fig. 97 Disconnect the tie rod end from the spindle, using a suitable tie rod end remover tool

Fig. 98 Matchmark its installed location to retain the same toe setting, then unscrew the tie rod end

2. Insert the hook of spring scale T74P-3504-Y or equivalent, through the wire loop. Effort to move the tie rod after initial breakaway should be 0.7–5.0 lbs. (0.3–2.25 Nm).

➡**Do not damage tie rod neck.**

3. Replace ball joint/tie rod assembly if effort falls outside this range. Save the tie rod end for use on the new tie rod assembly.

Manual Rack and Pinion

REMOVAL & INSTALLATION

▶ **See Figure 97 and 99**

1. Disconnect the negative battery cable.
2. Turn the ignition key to the **RUN** position.
3. Remove the access trim panel from below the steering column.
4. Remove the intermediate shaft bolts at the rack and pinion input shaft and the steering column shaft.
5. Using a suitable prytool, spread the slots enough to loosen the intermediate shaft at both ends. They cannot be separated at this time.
6. Raise the vehicle and support it safely.
7. Separate the tie rod ends from the steering knuckles, using a suitable tool. Turn the right wheel to the full left turn position.
8. Disconnect the speedometer cable at the transaxle on automatic transaxles only.
9. Disconnect the secondary air tube at the check valve.
10. Disconnect the exhaust system at the manifold and remove the system.
11. Remove the gear mounting brackets and insulators. Keep them separated as they are not interchangeable.
12. Turn the steering wheel full left so the tie rod will clear the shift linkage during removal.
13. Separate the gear intermediate shaft, with an assistant pulling upward on the shaft from the inside of the vehicle.

➡**Care should be taken during steering gear removal and installation to prevent tearing or damaging the steering gear bellows.**

14. Rotate the gear forward and down to clear the input shaft through the dash panel opening.
15. With the gear in the full left turn position, move the gear through the right (passenger side) apron opening until the left tie rod clears the shift linkage and other parts so it may be lowered.
16. Lower the left side of the gear assembly and remove from the vehicle.
To install:
17. Rotate the input shaft to a full left turn stop. Position the right wheel to a full left turn.

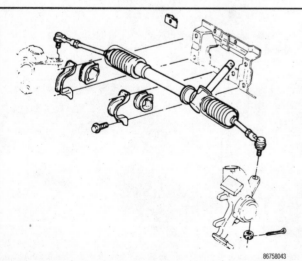

Fig. 99 Exploded view of the manual rack and pinion steering gear mounting

18. Start the right side of the gear through the opening in the right apron. Move the gear in until the left tie rod clears all parts so it may be raised up to the left apron opening.
19. Raise the gear and insert the left side through the apron opening. Rotate the gear so the joint shaft enters the dash panel opening.
20. With an assistant guiding the intermediate shaft from the inside of the vehicle, insert the input shaft into the intermediate shaft coupling. Insert the intermediate shaft clamp bolts finger-tight. Do not tighten at this time.
21. Install the gear mounting insulators and brackets in their proper places. Ensure the flat in the left mounting area is parallel to the dash panel. Tighten the bracket bolts to 40–55 ft. lbs. (54–75 Nm) in the sequence as described below:
    a. Tighten the left (driver's side) upper bolt halfway.
    b. Tighten the left side lower bolt.
    c. Tighten the left side upper bolt.
    d. Tighten the right side bolts.
    e. Do not forget that the right and left side insulators and brackets are not interchangeable side to side.
22. Attach the tie rod ends to the steering knuckles. Tighten the castellated nuts to 27–32 ft. lbs. (36–43 Nm), then tighten the nuts until the slot aligns with the cotter pin hole. Insert a new cotter pin.
23. Install the exhaust system.
24. Install the speedometer cable, if removed.
25. Tighten the gear input shaft to intermediate shaft coupling clamp bolt first. Then, tighten the upper intermediate shaft clamp bolt. Tighten both bolts to 20–37 ft. lbs. (28–50 Nm).
26. Install the access panel below the steering column. Turn the ignition key to the **OFF** position.
27. Check and adjust the toe. Tighten the tie rod end jam nuts, check for twisted bellows.

Power Rack and Pinion

REMOVAL & INSTALLATION

▶ **See Figures 97, 100, 101, 102, 103 and 104**

1. Disconnect the negative battery cable.
2. Turn the ignition key to the **RUN** position.
3. Remove the access panel from the dash below the steering column.
4. Remove the screws from the steering column boot at the dash panel and slide the boot up the intermediate shaft.
5. Remove the intermediate shaft bolt at the gear input shaft and loosen the bolt at the steering column shaft joint.
6. With a suitable tool, spread the slots enough to loosen the intermediate shaft at both ends. The intermediate shaft and gear input shaft cannot be separated at this time.
7. Remove the air cleaner, if necessary.
8. On vehicles equipped with air conditioning, secure the air conditioner liquid line above the dash panel opening. Doing so provides clearance for the gear input shaft removal and installation.
9. Separate the pressure and return lines at the intermediate connections.
10. Disconnect the exhaust secondary air tube at the check valve.
11. Raise the vehicle and support it safely.
12. Disconnect the exhaust system at the exhaust manifold.
13. Using a suitable tie rod end remover tool, separate the tie rod ends from the steering knuckles.

➡**Mark the location of the tie rod end prior to removal.**

14. Remove the left tie rod end from the tie rod on models equipped with a manual transaxle. This will allow the tie rod to clear the shift linkage.
15. Disconnect the speedometer cable at the transaxle, if equipped with a automatic transaxle. Remove the vehicle speed sensor.
16. Remove the transaxle shift cable assembly at the transaxle on vehicles equipped with a automatic transaxle.
17. Turn the steering wheel to the full left turn stop for easier gear removal.
18. Remove the screws holding the heater water tube to the shake brace below the oil pan.
19. Remove the nut from the lower of the two bolts holding the engine mount support bracket to the transaxle housing. Tap the bolt out as far as it will go.
20. Remove the gear mounting brackets and insulators.

Fig. 100 Detach the tie rod ends from the steering knuckles

Fig. 101 Remove the gear mounting brackets with the correct size socket

Fig. 102 Once the mounting bracket is free, remove the insulator behind it

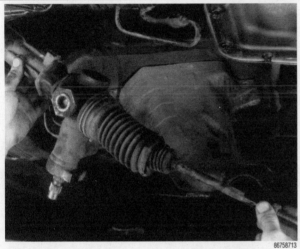

Fig. 103 Lower the left side of the steering gear and remove it from the vehicle

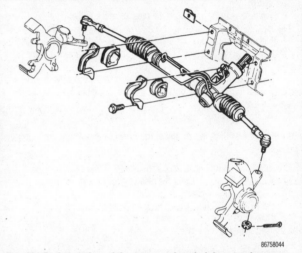

Fig. 104 Exploded view of the power rack and pinion steering gear mounting

21. Drape a cloth towel over both the apron opening edges to protect the bellows during gear removal.

22. Separate the gear from the intermediate shaft by either pushing up on the shaft with a bar from underneath the vehicle while pulling the gear down or with an assistant removing the shaft from inside the vehicle.

23. Rotate the gear forward and down to clear the input shaft through the dash panel opening.

24. Make sure the input shaft is in the full left turn position. Move the gear through the right (passenger) side apron opening until the left tie rod clears the left apron opening and the other parts so it may be lowered. Guide the power steering hoses around the nearby components as the gear is being removed.

25. Lower the left side of the gear and remove the gear out of the vehicle. Use care not to tear the bellows.

To install:

26. Rotate the input shaft to a full left turn stop. Position the right road wheel to a full left turn.

27. Start the right side of the gear through the opening in the right apron. Move the gear in until the left tie rod clears all parts so it may be raised up to the left apron opening.

28. Raise the gear and insert the left side through the apron opening. Move the power steering hoses into their proper positions at the same time. Rotate the gear so the joint shaft enters the dash panel opening.

29. With an assistant guiding the intermediate shaft from the inside of the vehicle, insert the input shaft into the intermediate shaft coupling.

30. Insert the intermediate shaft clamp bolts finger-tight. Do not tighten at this time.

31. Install the gear mounting insulators and brackets in their proper places. Ensure the flat in the left mounting area is parallel to the dash panel. Tighten the bracket bolts to 40–55 ft. lbs. (54–75 Nm) in the sequence as described below:

a. Tighten the left (driver's side) upper bolt halfway.
b. Tighten the left side lower bolt.
c. Tighten the left side upper bolt.
d. Tighten the right side bolts.

➡**Do not forget that the right and left side insulators and brackets are not interchangeable side-to-side.**

32. Attach the tie rod ends to the steering knuckles. Tighten the castellated nuts to 27–32 ft. lbs. (36–43 Nm), then tighten the nuts until the slot aligns with the cotter pin hole. Insert a new cotter pin.

33. Install the engine mount nut.

34. Install the heater water tube to the shake brace.

35. Install the exhaust system.

36. Install the speedometer cable, if removed.

37. Install the vehicle speed sensor and the transaxle shift cable.

38. Connect the secondary air tube at the check valve.

39. Attach the pressure and return lines at the intermediate connections or steering gear.

40. Install the air cleaner.

41. Tighten the gear input shaft-to-intermediate shaft coupling clamp bolt first. Then, tighten the upper intermediate shaft clamp bolt. Tighten to 20–30 ft. lbs. (27–40 Nm).

42. Install the access panel below the steering column.

43. Turn the ignition key to the **OFF** position.

44. Fill the system. Check and adjust the toe, then have the alignment checked by a qualified shop as soon as possible.

45. Tighten the tie rod end jam nuts to 40–50 ft. lbs. (54–68 Nm), check for twisted bellows.

46. Connect the negative battery cable.

Power Steering Pump

REMOVAL & INSTALLATION

1981–85 Models

1. Remove the air cleaner, air pump and belt.
2. Remove the reservoir filler extension and plug the hole with a clean rag.
3. From under the car, loosen one pump adjusting bolt.
4. Remove one pump-to-bracket mounting bolt and disconnect the fluid return line. Be prepared to catch any spilled fluid in a suitable container.
5. From above the car, loosen the adjusting bolt.
6. Loosen the pivot bolt and remove the drive belt.
7. Remove the two remaining pump-to-bracket mounting bolts.
8. Remove the pump by passing the pulley end through the adjusting bracket opening.
9. Remove the pressure hose from the pump.

To install:

10. From beneath the car, attach the pressure hose to the pump.
11. Pass the pulley through the opening in the adjusting bracket.
12. Install the mounting bolts and tighten to 30–45 ft. lbs. (41–61 Nm).
13. Make sure the air pump belt is on the inner power steering pump pulley groove.
14. Install the power steering pump belt. Insert a ½ inch drive socket wrench handle into the square hole at the bottom of the bracket to obtain the proper belt tension.
15. Tighten all the bolts to 30–45 ft. lbs. (41–61 Nm).

➡**Do not pry on the pump or any of the surrounding aluminum parts or brackets.**

16. Attach the return line to the pump.
17. Remove the rag and install the reservoir filler neck extension.
18. Install the air pump and the air cleaner.
19. Fill the pump with fluid and check for proper operation.

1985½–90 Models

1. Disconnect the negative battery cable.
2. Remove the air cleaner, thermactor air pump and belt.
3. Remove the reservoir filler extension and cover the hole to prevent dirt from entering.
4. If equipped with a remote reservoir, remove the reservoir supply hose at the pump, drain the fluid and plug or cap the opening at the pump to prevent entry of contaminants during removal.
5. From under the vehicle, loosen one pump adjusting bolt and one pump-to-bracket mounting bolt
6. Disconnect the fluid return line.
7. From above the vehicle, loosen one adjusting bolt and the pivot bolt.
8. Remove the drive belt and the two remaining pump-to-bracket mounting bolts.
9. Remove the pump by passing the pulley through the adjusting bracket opening.
10. Remove the pressure hose from the pump assembly.

To install:

11. From under the vehicle, connect the pressure hose to the pump. Pass the pulley through the opening in the adjusting bracket.
12. Install the mounting bolts and tighten to 30–45 ft. lbs. (40–62 Nm).
13. If applicable, make sure the air pump belt is on the inner power steering pump pulley groove. Install the power steering pump belt and adjust.

14. Tighten all bolts to 30–45 ft. lbs. (40–62 Nm).

➡**When adjusting belt tension, never pry on the pump or surrounding aluminum parts or brackets.**

15. If not equipped with a remote reservoir, install the return line to the pump.
16. From above the vehicle, install the reservoir filler neck extension, if applicable.
17. Install the air cleaner.
18. If applicable, install the remote reservoir supply to the pump.
19. Fill pump or remote reservoir with fluid and check operation.

BLEEDING

If air bubbles are present in the power steering fluid, bleed the system by performing the following:
1. Fill the reservoir to the proper level.
2. Operate the engine until it reaches normal operating temperature.
3. Turn the steering wheel all the way to the left then all the way to the right several times. Do not hold the steering wheel in the far left or far right position stops.
4. Check the fluid level and recheck the fluid for the presence of trapped air. If it is apparent that air is still in the system, fabricate or obtain a vacuum tester and purge the system as follows:

   a. Remove the pump dipstick cap assembly.
   b. Check and fill the pump reservoir with fluid to the COLD FULL mark on the dipstick.
   c. Disconnect the ignition wire and raise the front of the vehicle and support safely.
   d. Crank the engine with the starter and check the fluid level. Do not turn the steering wheel at this time.

❊❊ WARNING

DO NOT operate the starter for more than a few seconds at a time without stopping to allow the motor to cool down. Severe damage to the starter may occur if it is allowed to overheat by constant cranking.

   e. Fill the pump reservoir to the COLD FULL mark on the dipstick. Crank the engine with the starter while cycling the steering wheel lock-to-lock. Check the fluid level.
   f. Tightly insert a suitable size rubber stopper and air evacuator pump into the reservoir fill neck. Connect the ignition coil wire.
   g. With the engine idling, apply a 15 in. Hg (50.6 kPa) vacuum to the reservoir for three minutes. As air is purged from the system, the vacuum will drop off. Maintain the vacuum on the system as required throughout the three minutes.
   h. Remove the vacuum source. Fill the reservoir to the COLD FULL mark on the dipstick.
   i. With the engine idling, re-apply 15 in. Hg (50.6 kPa) vacuum source to the reservoir. Slowly cycle the steering wheel to lock-to-lock stops for approximately five minutes. Do not hold the steering wheel on the stops during cycling. Maintain the vacuum as required.
   j. Release the vacuum and disconnect the vacuum source. Add fluid, as required.
   k. Start the engine and cycle the wheel slowly and check for leaks at all connections.
   l. Lower the front wheels.
5. In cases of severe aeration, repeat the procedure.

TORQUE SPECIFICATIONS

Components	Ft. Lbs.	Nm
Wheels		
Lug nuts	85-105	115-142
Front Suspension		
MacPherson strut		
1981-85 models		
Strut-to-knuckle pinch bolt	68-91	92-110
Upper mount nuts	22-29	30-40
Shaft nut	48-62	65-85
1985 1/2-90 models		
Top mount-to-shock tower nuts	25-30	37-41
Strut-to-knuckle pinch bolt	55-81	75-110
Shaft nut	35-50	48-68
Stabilizer bar		
1981-85 models		
Insulator mounting bracket bolts	50-60	68-81
End nuts	59-73	80-100
1985 1/2-90 models		
U-bracket bolts	85-100	115-135
End nuts	98-115	132-156
Lower control arm		
Control arm ball joint pinch bolt	38-45	52-60
Front wheel hub, knuckle and bearings		
Center hub nut	180-200	244-271
Rear Suspension		
Coil springs		
Control arm-to-spindle nut and bolt		
1981-85 models	90-100	122-136
1985 1/2-90 models	60-80	81-109
Shock absorbers		
Upper insulator nut		
1981-85 models	60-70	81-95
1985 1/2-90 models	35-55	48-75
Lower mounting bolts		
1981-85 models	90-100	122-135
1985 1/2-90 models	70-96	95-130
Stabilizer bar link-to-bracket bolts	40-55	55-75
Rear control arms		
Control arm-to-spindle bolt		
1981-85 models	90-100	122-135
1985 1/2-90 models	60-80	81-109
Control arm-to-body bolt		
1981-85 models	65-75	88-102
1985 1/2-90 models	52-74	70-100
Stabilizer bar		
U-bracket bolts	15-25	23-32
Link assembly-to-shock mounting bracket bolt	41-55	55-75
Insulator nut	6-12	8-16

90938C01

TORQUE SPECIFICATIONS

Components	Ft. Lbs.	Nm
Steering		
Steering wheel		
Retaining nut		
1981-85 models	30-40	40-54
1985 1/2-90 models	23-33	31-45
Ignition switch		
Early model vehicles		
Steering column attaching fasteners	15-25	20-30
Late model vehicles		
Ignition switch screws	50-70	56-79
Tie rod ends		
Stud nuts	27-32	36-43
Jam nuts	35-50	47-68
Manual rack and pinion		
Bracket bolts	40-55	54-75
Power steering rack		
Bracket bolts	40-55	54-75
Power steering pump		
All bolts	30-45	41-61

90938C02

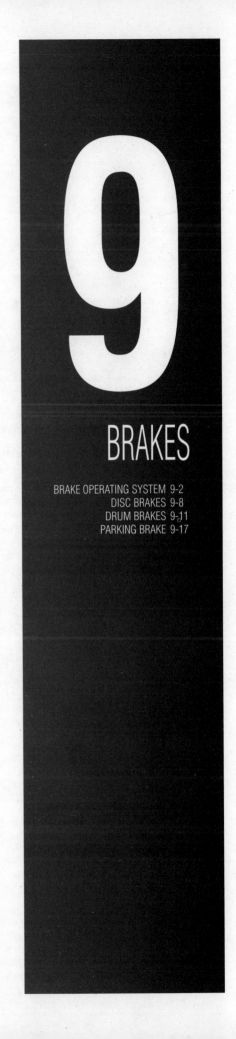

9

BRAKES

BRAKE OPERATING SYSTEM

Basic Operating Principles

Hydraulic systems are used to actuate the brakes of all modern automobiles. The system transports the power required to force the frictional surfaces of the braking system together from the pedal to the individual brake units at each wheel. A hydraulic system is used for two reasons.

First, fluid under pressure can be carried to all parts of an automobile by small pipes and flexible hoses without taking up a significant amount of room or posing routing problems.

Second, a great mechanical advantage can be given to the brake pedal end of the system, and the foot pressure required to actuate the brakes can be reduced by making the surface area of the master cylinder pistons smaller than that of any of the pistons in the wheel cylinders or calipers. The master cylinder consists of a fluid reservoir along with a double cylinder and piston assembly. Double type master cylinders are designed to separate the front and rear braking systems hydraulically in case of a leak.

The master cylinder coverts mechanical motion from the pedal into hydraulic pressure within the lines. This pressure is translated back into mechanical motion at the wheels by either the wheel cylinder (drum brakes) or the caliper (disc brakes).

Steel lines carry the brake fluid to a point on the vehicle's frame near each of the vehicle's wheels. The fluid is then carried to the calipers and wheel cylinders by flexible tubes in order to allow for suspension and steering movements.

In drum brake systems, each wheel cylinder contains two pistons, one at either end, which push outward in opposite directions and force the brake shoe into contact with the drum.

In disc brake systems, the cylinders are part of the calipers. At least one cylinder in each caliper is used to force the brake pads against the disc.

All pistons employ some type of seal, usually made of rubber, to minimize fluid leakage. A rubber dust boot seals the outer end of the cylinder against dust and dirt. The boot fits around the outer end of the piston on disc brake calipers, and around the brake actuating rod on wheel cylinders.

The hydraulic system operates as follows: When at rest, the entire system, from the piston(s) in the master cylinder to those in the wheel cylinders or calipers, is full of brake fluid. Upon application of the brake pedal, fluid trapped in front of the master cylinder piston(s) is forced through the lines to the wheel cylinders. Here, it forces the pistons outward, in the case of drum brakes, and inward toward the disc, in the case of disc brakes. The motion of the pistons is opposed by return springs mounted outside the cylinders in drum brakes, and by spring seals, in disc brakes.

Upon release of the brake pedal, a spring located inside the master cylinder immediately returns the master cylinder pistons to the normal position. The pistons contain check valves and the master cylinder has compensating ports drilled in it. These are uncovered as the pistons reach their normal position. The piston check valves allow fluid to flow toward the wheel cylinders or calipers as the pistons withdraw. Then, as the return springs force the brake pads or shoes into the released position, the excess fluid reservoir through the compensating ports. It is during the time the pedal is in the released position that any fluid that has leaked out of the system will be replaced through the compensating ports.

Dual circuit master cylinders employ two pistons, located one behind the other, in the same cylinder. The primary piston is actuated directly by mechanical linkage from the brake pedal through the power booster. The secondary piston is actuated by fluid trapped between the two pistons. If a leak develops in front of the secondary piston, it moves forward until it bottoms against the front of the master cylinder, and the fluid trapped between the pistons will operate the rear brakes. If the rear brakes develop a leak, the primary piston will move forward until direct contact with the secondary piston takes place, and it will force the secondary piston to actuate the front brakes. In either case, the brake pedal moves farther when the brakes are applied, and less braking power is available.

All dual circuit systems use a switch to warn the driver when only half of the brake system is operational. This switch is usually located in a valve body which is mounted on the firewall or the frame below the master cylinder. A hydraulic piston receives pressure from both circuits, each circuit's pressure being applied to one end of the piston. When the pressures are in balance, the piston remains stationary. When one circuit has a leak, however, the greater pressure in that circuit during application of the brakes will push the piston to one side, closing the switch and activating the brake warning light.

In disc brake systems, this valve body also contains a metering valve and, in some cases, a proportioning valve. The metering valve keeps pressure from traveling to the disc brakes on the front wheels until the brake shoes on the rear wheels have contacted the drums, ensuring that the front brakes will never be used alone. The proportioning valve controls the pressure to the rear brakes to lessen the chance of rear wheel lock-up during very hard braking.

Warning lights may be tested by depressing the brake pedal and holding it while opening one of the wheel cylinder bleeder screws. If this does not cause the light to go on, substitute a new lamp, make continuity checks, and, finally, replace the switch as necessary.

The hydraulic system may be checked for leaks by applying pressure to the pedal gradually and steadily. If the pedal sinks very slowly to the floor, the system has a leak. This is not to be confused with a springy or spongy feel due to the compression of air within the lines. If the system leaks, there will be a gradual change in the position of the pedal with a constant pressure.

Check for leaks along all lines and at wheel cylinders. If no external leaks are apparent, the problem is inside the master cylinder.

DISC BRAKES

Instead of the traditional expanding brakes that press outward against a circular drum, disc brake systems utilize a disc (rotor) with brake pads positioned on either side of it. An easily-seen analogy is the hand brake arrangement on a bicycle. The pads squeeze onto the rim of the bike wheel, slowing its motion. Automobile disc brakes use the identical principle but apply the braking effort to a separate disc instead of the wheel.

The disc (rotor) is a casting, usually equipped with cooling fins between the two braking surfaces. This enables air to circulate between the braking surfaces making them less sensitive to heat buildup and more resistant to fade. Dirt and water do not drastically affect braking action since contaminants are thrown off by the centrifugal action of the rotor or scraped off the by the pads. Also, the equal clamping action of the two brake pads tends to ensure uniform, straight line stops. Disc brakes are inherently self-adjusting. There are three general types of disc brake:

1. Fixed caliper
2. Floating caliper
3. Sliding caliper

The fixed caliper design uses two pistons mounted on either side of the rotor (in each side of the caliper). The caliper is mounted rigidly and does not move.

The sliding and floating designs are quite similar. In fact, these two types are often lumped together. In both designs, the pad on the inside of the rotor is moved into contact with the rotor by hydraulic force. The caliper, which is not held in a fixed position, moves slightly, bringing the outside pad into contact with the rotor. There are various methods of attaching floating calipers. Some pivot at the bottom or top, and some slide on mounting bolts. In any event, the end result is the same.

DRUM BRAKES

Drum brakes employ two brake shoes mounted on a stationary backing plate. These shoes are positioned inside a circular drum which rotates with the wheel assembly. The shoes are held in place by springs. This allows them to slide toward the drums (when they are applied) while keeping the linings and drums in alignment. The shoes are actuated by a wheel cylinder which is mounted at the top of the backing plate. When the brakes are applied, hydraulic pressure forces the wheel cylinder's actuating links outward. Since these links bear directly against the top of the brake shoes, the tops of the shoes are then forced against the inner side of the drum. This action forces the bottoms of the two shoes to contact the brake drum by rotating the entire assembly slightly (known as servo action). When pressure within the wheel cylinder is relaxed, return springs pull the shoes back away from the drum.

Most modern drum brakes are designed to self-adjust themselves during application when the vehicle is moving in reverse. This motion causes both shoes to rotate very slightly with the drum, rocking an adjusting lever, thereby causing rotation of the adjusting screw. Some drum brake systems are designed to self-adjust during application whenever the brakes are applied. This on-board adjustment system reduces the need for maintenance adjustments and keeps both the brake function and pedal feel satisfactory.

Clean, high quality brake fluid is essential to the safe and proper operation of the brake system. You should always buy the highest quality brake fluid that is available. If the brake fluid becomes contaminated, drain and flush the system, then refill the master cylinder with new fluid. Never reuse any brake fluid. Any brake fluid that is removed from the system should be discarded.

Brake Light Switch

REMOVAL & INSTALLATION

▶ See Figures 1 and 2

1. Disconnect the negative battery cable.
2. Unplug the wire harness at the connector from the switch.

➡The locking tab must be lifted before the connector can be removed.

3. Remove the hairpin retainer and white nylon washer. Slide the brake light switch and the pushrod away from the pedal. Remove the switch by sliding the switch up/down.

Fig. 1 The brake light switch is mounted on the brake pedal

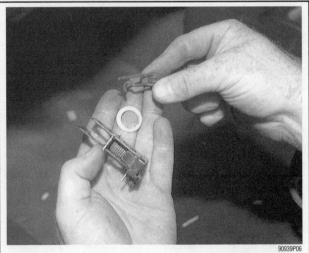

Fig. 2 View of the hairpin retainer, nylon washer and brake light switch

➡Since the switch side plate nearest the brake pedal is slotted, it is not necessary to remove the master cylinder pushrod's black bushing, or the white spacer washer nearest the pedal arm.

To install:
4. Position the switch so that the U-shaped side is nearest the pedal and directly over/under the pin. The black bushing must be in position in the pushrod eyelet with the washer face on the side closest to the retaining pin.
5. Slide the switch up/down, trapping the master cylinder pushrod and black bushing between the switch side plates. Push the switch and pushrod assembly firmly towards the brake pedal arm. Assemble the outside white plastic washer to the pin, then install the hairpin retainer to trap the whole assembly.

➡Do not substitute another type of pin retainer. Replace only with a production type hairpin retainer.

6. Plug in the wire harness connector to the switch.
7. Connect the negative battery cable.
8. Check the brake light switch for proper operation. Brake lights should illuminate with less than 6 lbs. (2.7 kg) of force applied to the brake pedal at the pad.

➡The brake light switch wire harness must have sufficient length to travel with the switch during full stroke of the pedal.

Master Cylinder

REMOVAL & INSTALLATION

Manual Brakes

Brake fluid contains polyglycol ethers and polyglycols. Avoid contact with the eyes and wash your hands thoroughly after handling brake fluid. If you do get brake fluid in your eyes, flush your eyes with clean, running water for 15 minutes. If eye irritation persists, or if you have taken brake fluid internally, IMMEDIATELY seek medical assistance.

1. Disconnect the negative battery cable.
2. Unplug the brake light switch wires at the connector. Remove the spring retainers and slide the brake light switch off the brake pedal pin far enough to clear the end of the pin.
3. Remove the brake light switch from the pin.
4. Loosen the two master cylinder retaining nuts inside the engine compartment, then slide the master cylinder pushrod, nylon washers and bushings off the brake pedal pin.
5. Using a flare nut wrench, unfasten the brake fluid lines from the master cylinder and cap the lines.
6. Unfasten the master cylinder-to-dash panel locknuts.
7. Remove the master cylinder from the engine compartment.

To install:
8. Carefully insert the master cylinder pushrod through the dash panel opening and place the master cylinder into position.
9. Install the master cylinder-to-dash panel locknuts but do not tighten them at this time.
10. Coat the nylon bushing and washer with 10W-40 engine oil. Install the washer and bushing on the brake pedal pin. On models equipped with cruise control, the washer next to the pedal arm is omitted and a snap-on adapter is used.
11. Place the brake light switch and the pushrod at the end of the brake pedal pin. Install the nylon bushing and washer, then secure them in position using the spring retainer.
12. Attach the brake light switch electrical connection.
13. Tighten the master cylinder-to-dash panel locknuts to 13–25 ft. lbs. (18–33 Nm).
14. Attach the brake fluid lines to the master cylinder and tighten the fittings using a flare nut wrench.
15. Fill the master cylinder with brake fluid and bleed the system.

Power Brakes

▶ See Figures 3, 4, 5, 6 and 7

✳✳ CAUTION

Brake fluid contains polyglycol ethers and polyglycols. Avoid contact with the eyes and wash your hands thoroughly after handling brake fluid. If you do get brake fluid in your eyes, flush your eyes with clean, running water for 15 minutes. If eye irritation persists, or if you have taken brake fluid internally, IMMEDIATELY seek medical assistance.

1. Disconnect the negative battery cable.
2. Disconnect the brake lines from the primary and secondary outlet ports of the master cylinder and pressure control valves. Be sure to plug all openings to prevent excessive fluid loss or system contamination.
3. Disconnect the brake warning light wire.
4. Remove the nuts attaching the master cylinder to the brake booster assembly.
5. Slide the master cylinder forward and upward from the vehicle.

To install:

6. Position the master cylinder over the booster pushrod and mounting studs. Install the nuts and tighten to 13–25 ft. lbs. (18–33 Nm).

Fig. 5 Disconnect the brake warning light wire

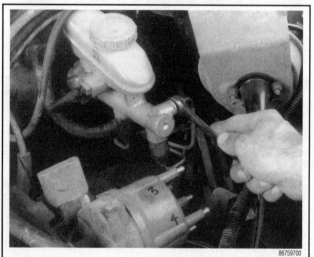
Fig. 3 Disconnect and plug the brake lines from the master cylinder ports

Fig. 6 Remove the nuts attaching the master cylinder to the brake booster assembly

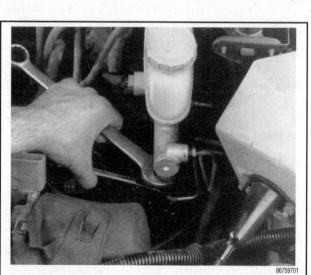
Fig. 4 Use the correct size wrenches to disconnect the brake line fittings

Fig. 7 Slide the master cylinder forward and upward from the vehicle

7. Remove the plugs and connect the brake lines. Tighten the fittings to 10–18 ft. lbs. (14–24 Nm).

8. Engage the brake warning indicator connector.

9. Make sure the master cylinder reservoir is full.

10. Bleed the brake system.

✳✳ CAUTION

Before attempting to test or operate the vehicle, make sure the bleeding procedure achieves a firm brake pedal.

11. Connect the negative battery cable. Check for fluid leaks and for proper brake system operation.

Power Brake Booster

REMOVAL & INSTALLATION

▶ **See Figure 8**

1. Disconnect the battery ground cable.
2. Remove the master cylinder.

3. From under the instrument panel, remove the brake light switch wiring connector from the switch.

4. Remove the pushrod retainer and outer nylon washer from the brake pin, slide the switch along the brake pedal pin, far enough for the outer hole to clear the pin.

5. Remove the switch by sliding it upward.

6. Remove the booster to dash panel retaining nuts. Slide the booster pushrod and pushrod bushing off the brake pedal pin.

7. Disconnect the manifold vacuum hose from the booster check valve and move the booster forward until the studs clear the dash panel, then remove the booster.

To install:

8. Align the pedal support and support spacer inside the vehicle, then place the booster in position on the dash panel. Hand-start the retaining nuts.

9. Working inside the vehicle, install the pushrod and pushrod bushing on the brake pedal pin. Tighten the booster-to-dash panel retaining nuts to 20–30 ft. lbs. (27–41 Nm).

10. Position the brake light switch so it straddles the booster pushrod with the switch slot toward the pedal blade and the hole just clearing the pin. Slide the switch down onto the pin.

11. Slide the assembly toward the pedal arm, being careful not to bend or deform the switch. Install the nylon washer on the pin and secure all parts to the

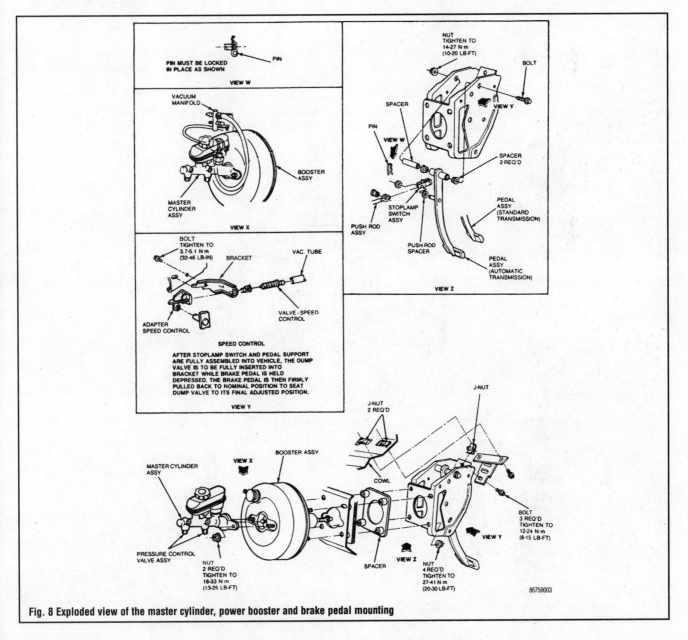

Fig. 8 Exploded view of the master cylinder, power booster and brake pedal mounting

pin with the hairpin retainer. Make sure the retainer is fully installed and locked over the pedal pin.

12. Install the brake light switch connector on the switch.

13. Connect the manifold vacuum hose to the booster check valve using a hose clamp.

14. Install the master cylinder according to the proper procedure.

15. Bleed the brake system.

16. Connect the negative battery cable and start the engine. Check the power brake function.

17. If equipped with speed control, adjust the dump valve as follows:

a. Firmly depress and hold the brake pedal.

b. Push in the dump valve until the valve collar bottoms against the retaining clip.

c. Place a 0.050–0.100 in. (1.27–2.54mm) shim between the white button of the valve and the pad on the brake pedal.

d. Firmly pull the brake pedal rearward to its normal position, allowing the dump valve to ratchet backward in the retaining clip.

Pressure Differential Valve

GENERAL INFORMATION

If a loss of brake fluid occurs on either side of the diagonally split system when the brakes are applied, a piston mounted in the valve moves off-center, allowing the brakes on the non-leaking side of the split system to operate. When the piston moves off-center, a brake warning switch, located in the center of the valve body, will turn on a dash-mounted warning light, indicating brake problems.

After repairs are made on the brake system and the system is bled, the warn-

ing switch will reset itself, once you pump the brake pedal. The dash light should also turn off.

Pressure Control Valve Assembly

➡**On some early model vehicles, a pressure differential valve was integral with the proportioning valves. Known as the brake control valve assembly, they performed the same functions as pressure control valves on later cars.**

On newer vehicles, there are two pressure control valves housed in the master cylinder assembly. The valves reduce rear brake system hydraulic pressure when the pressure exceeds a preset value. The rear brake hydraulic pressure is limited in order to minimize rear wheel skidding during hard braking.

REMOVAL & INSTALLATION

Early Model Vehicles

▶ **See Figure 9**

1. Unplug the brake warning light switch wire harness connector from the warning light switch.

2. Disconnect the front brake system inlet tube and the rear system inlet tube from the control valve assembly.

3. Disconnect the left and right front brake outlet tubes from the brake control valve system.

4. Disconnect the rear system outlet tube from the control valve assembly.

5. Unfasten the screw that attaches the valve to the fender apron bracket and remove the valve.

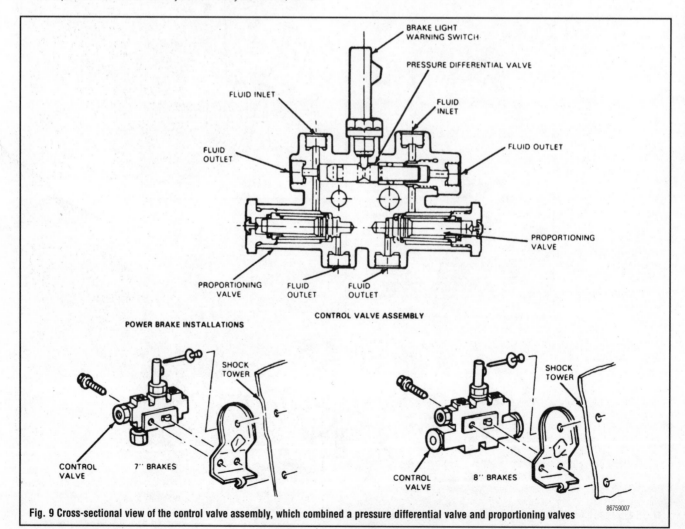

Fig. 9 Cross-sectional view of the control valve assembly, which combined a pressure differential valve and proportioning valves

86759007

→The control valve is not serviceable and must be replaced if any part of the assembly is defective.

To install:

6. Install the control valve onto the bracket on the fender apron, then install and tighten the mounting screw to 13–25 ft. lbs. (18–33 Nm).

7. Attach the rear brake outlet tube to the control valve assembly and tighten the tube nut to 10–18 ft. lbs. (14–24 Nm).

8. Attach the right and right front brake outlet tubes to the valve assembly and tighten the tube nuts to 10–18 ft. lbs. (14–24 Nm).

9. Attach the front brake inlet tube to the control valve assembly and tighten the tube nut to 10–18 ft. lbs. (14–24 Nm).

10. Attach the brake warning light switch electrical connection.

11. Bleed the brake system.

Late Model Vehicles

♦ **See Figure 10**

1. Disconnect the primary or secondary brake line, as necessary.

2. Loosen and remove the pressure control valve from the master cylinder housing.

To install:

3. Install the pressure control valve in the master cylinder housing port and tighten to 10–18 ft. lbs. (14–24 Nm).

4. Connect the brake line and tighten the fitting to 10–18 ft. lbs. (14–24 Nm).

5. Fill and bleed the brake system.

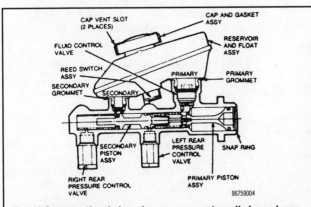

Fig. 10 Cross-sectional view of a common master cylinder and pressure control valve assembly

Bleeding the Brake System

♦ **See Figures 11 and 12**

It is necessary to bleed the brake system of air whenever a hydraulic component, of the system, has been rebuilt or replaced, or if the brakes feel spongy during application.

Your car has a diagonally split brake system. Each side of this system must be bled as an individual system, and there is a correct bleeding sequence to be followed. First bleed the right rear brake, second, bleed the left front brake, then follow with the left rear brake and lastly, bleed the right front brake.

✳✳ WARNING

When bleeding the brake system, never allow the master cylinder to run completely out of brake fluid. Always use DOT 3 heavy duty brake fluid, or equivalent. Never reuse brake fluid that has been drained from the system or that has been allowed to stand in an opened container for an extended period of time. If your car is equipped with power brakes, remove the reserve vacuum stored in the booster by pumping the pedal several times before bleeding.

1. Clean all dirt away from the master cylinder filler cap.

2. Start bleeding by filling the master cylinder reservoir to the MAX or FULL line with fresh brake fluid from a sealed container and keep it at least half full throughout the bleeding procedure.

3. Raise and support the car on jackstands. You may remove the wheel from the brake to be bled if this gives better access.

4. It is strongly recommended that any time bleeding is to be performed all wheels be bled rather than just one or two.

5. Starting with the right rear wheel cylinder. Remove the dust cover from the bleeder screw. Place the proper size box wrench over the bleeder fitting and attach a piece of rubber tubing (about three feet long and snug) over the end of the fitting.

6. Submerge the free end of the rubber tube into a container half filled with clean brake fluid.

7. Have a friend pump up the brake pedal and then push down to apply the brakes while you loosen the bleeder screw. When the pedal reaches the bottom of its travel close the bleeder fitting before your friend releases the brake pedal.

8. Repeat Step 7 until air bubbles cease to appear in the container in which the tubing is submerged. Tighten the fitting, remove the rubber tubing and install the dust cover.

9. Repeat the steps to the left front wheel, then to the left rear and right front until all the air is expelled from the system.

→**Refill the master cylinder after each wheel cylinder or caliper is bled. Be sure the master cylinder top gasket is mounted correctly and the brake fluid level is within ¼ in. (6mm) of the top.**

10. After bleeding the brakes, pump the brake pedal several times, this ensures proper seating of the rear linings and the front caliper pistons.

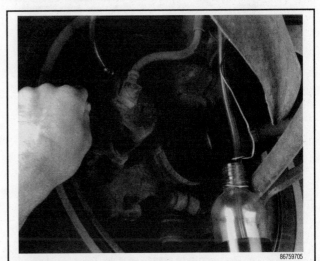

Fig. 11 Bleed the front brake caliper as shown—note the hanging plastic bottle of brake fluid

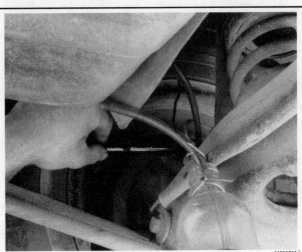

Fig. 12 Bleed the rear wheel cylinder as shown

DISC BRAKES

Brake Pads

REMOVAL & INSTALLATION

▶ **See Figures 13 and 14**

1. Remove the master cylinder cap and check fluid level in reservoir. Remove the brake fluid until reservoir is ½ full. Discard the removed fluid.
2. Raise and safely support the vehicle.
3. Remove the front wheel(s).
4. Back out, but do not remove, the caliper locating pins, unless new bushings are being installed.

➡ **A large C-clamp may be used to force the piston back into the caliper prior to the pad removal.**

5. Use a C-clamp or piston compressor tool to seat the piston in its bore.

➡ **Extra care must be taken during this procedure to prevent damage to the plastic piston. Metal or sharp objects cannot come into direct contact with the piston surface, or damage will result.**

Fig. 13 A large C-clamp can be used to force the piston back into the caliper prior to pad removal

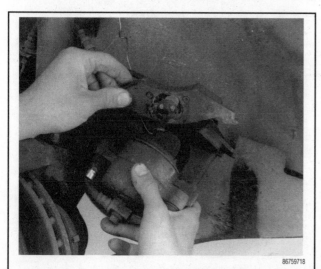

Fig. 14 Remove the inner and outer brake pads

6. Lift the caliper assembly from the rotor/integral knuckle and anchor plate using a rotating motion. Do not pry directly against plastic piston or damage will occur.
7. Remove the outer brake pad.
8. Remove the inner brake pad.
9. Inspect both rotor braking surfaces. Minor scoring or buildup of lining material does not require machining or replacement of rotor. Sand any glaze from both rotor braking surfaces using garnet paper 100-A (medium grit) or aluminum oxide 150-J (medium).
10. Suspend the caliper inside fender housing with a sturdy length of wire. Use care not to damage the caliper or stretch the brake hose.

To install:

11. Remove all rust buildup from inside the caliper legs where the outer shoe makes contact.
12. Install the inner shoe and lining assembly into the caliper piston(s). Do not bend the shoe clips during installation.
13. Install correct outer shoe and lining assembly. Ensure that the clips are properly seated.
14. Install the caliper over the rotor.
15. Install the wheel(s). Tighten the wheel nuts to 80–105 ft. lbs. (109–142 Nm).
16. Lower the vehicle.
17. Pump the brake pedal prior to moving the vehicle to position the brake linings. Check the fluid level in the master cylinder.
18. Connect the negative battery cable.
19. Road test to ensure correct operation.

INSPECTION

1. Loosen the front wheel lugs slightly, then raise the front of the car and safely support it on jackstands.
2. Remove the front wheel(s).
3. The cut out in the top of the front brake caliper allows visual inspection of the disc brake pad. If the lining is worn to within 0.125 inch (3.175mm) of the metal disc shoe (check local inspection requirements) replace all four pads (both sides).
4. While you are inspecting the brake pads, visually inspect the caliper for hydraulic fluid leaks. If a leak is visible the caliper will have to be rebuilt or replaced.

Brake Caliper

REMOVAL & INSTALLATION

▶ **See Figures 15, 16, 17, 18 and 19**

❊❊ CAUTION

Brake shoes may contain asbestos, which has been determined to be a cancer causing agent. Never clean the brake surfaces with compressed air! Avoid inhaling any dust from any brake surface! When cleaning brake surfaces, use a commercially available brake cleaning solvent.

1. Disconnect the negative battery cable.
2. Raise and safely support the vehicle.
3. Remove the wheel.
4. Disconnect the flexible brake hose from the caliper. Remove the hollow banjo bolt that connects hose fitting to caliper.
5. Remove the hose assembly from the caliper and plug the hose.
6. Remove the caliper locating pins using a Torx® T40 bit.

➡ **Do not remove the pins all the way. If fully removed, the pins are difficult to install and require new guide bushings.**

7. Lift the caliper off the rotor and integral knuckle/anchor plate using a rotating motion.

Fig. 15 Remove the front wheel for access to the caliper

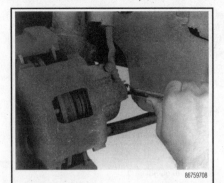

Fig. 16 Disconnect the flexible brake hose from the caliper

Fig. 17 Remove the caliper locating pins using the correct size and type of wrench

Fig. 18 Lift the caliper off the rotor and integral knuckle/anchor plate using a rotating motion

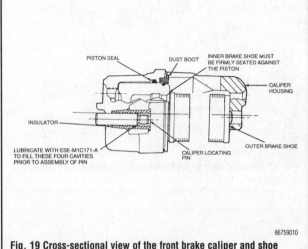

Fig. 19 Cross-sectional view of the front brake caliper and shoe (pad) assembly

➡ Do not pry directly against plastic piston or damage to piston will occur.

To install:

8. Position the caliper assembly above the rotor with the anti-rattle spring under the upper arm of the knuckle. Install the caliper over the rotor with a rotating motion. Ensure that the inner shoe is properly positioned.

➡ Ensure that the correct caliper assembly is installed on the correct knuckle. The caliper bleed screw should be positioned on top of the caliper when assembled on the vehicle.

9. Lubricate the locating pins and inside of insulators with silicone grease. Install the locating pins through the caliper insulators and into the knuckle attaching holes. The caliper locating pins must be inserted and the threads started by hand.

✳✳ CAUTION

Do not allow grease to come in contact with the braking surface or braking ability will be reduced and possible accident and personal injury may result.

10. Using the correct wrench and a Torx® T40 bit to tighten the caliper locating pins to 18–25 ft. lbs. (24–34 Nm).

11. Remove the plug or cap and install brake hose on caliper with a new gasket on each side of fitting outlet. Insert the attaching bolt through washers and fittings. Tighten the bolt to 30–40 ft. lbs. (40–54 Nm).

12. Bleed the brake system. Always install the rubber bleed screw cap after bleeding.

13. Top off the master cylinder, as required.

14. Install the wheel(s).
15. Connect negative battery cable.
16. Pump brake pedal prior to moving the vehicle to position brake linings.
17. Lower the vehicle and road test to ensure proper operation.

OVERHAUL

◗ **See Figures 20 thru 28**

✳✳ CAUTION

Brake shoes may contain asbestos, which has been determined to be a cancer causing agent. Never clean the brake surfaces with compressed air! Avoid inhaling any dust from any brake surface! When cleaning brake surfaces, use a commercially available brake cleaning solvent.

➡ Some vehicles may be equipped dual piston calipers. The procedure to overhaul the caliper is essentially the same with the exception of multiple pistons, O-rings and dust boots.

1. Remove the caliper from the vehicle and place on a clean workbench.

✳✳ CAUTION

NEVER place your fingers in front of the pistons in an attempt to catch or protect the pistons when applying compressed air! This could result in personal injury!

➡Depending upon the vehicle, there are two different ways to remove the piston from the caliper. Refer to the brake pad replacement procedure to make sure you have the correct procedure for your vehicle.

2. The first method is as follows:
   a. Stuff a shop towel or a block of wood into the caliper to catch the piston.
   b. Remove the caliper piston using compressed air applied into the caliper inlet hole. Inspect the piston for scoring, nicks, corrosion and/or worn or damaged chrome plating. The piston must be replaced if any of these conditions are found.

3. For the second method, you must rotate the piston to retract it from the caliper.

4. If equipped, remove the anti-rattle clip.

5. Use a prytool to remove the caliper boot, being careful not to scratch the housing bore.

6. Remove the piston seals from the groove in the caliper bore.

7. Carefully loosen the brake bleeder valve cap and valve from the caliper housing.

8. Inspect the caliper bores, pistons and mounting threads for scoring or excessive wear.

9. Use crocus cloth to polish out light corrosion from the piston and bore.

10. Clean all parts with denatured alcohol and dry with compressed air.

To assemble:

11. Lubricate and install the bleeder valve and cap.

12. Install the new seals into the caliper bore grooves, making sure they are not twisted.

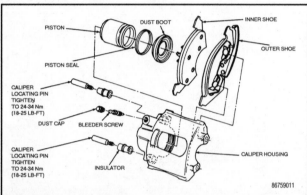

Fig. 20 Exploded view of the front brake caliper and shoe (pad) assembly

Fig. 21 For some types of calipers, use compressed air to drive the piston out of the caliper, but make sure to keep your fingers clear

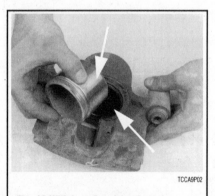

Fig. 22 Withdraw the piston from the caliper bore

Fig. 23 On some vehicles, you must remove the anti-rattle clip

Fig. 24 Use a prytool to carefully pry around the edge of the boot . . .

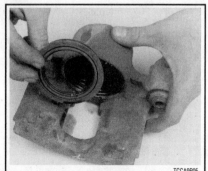

Fig. 25 . . . then remove the boot from the caliper housing, taking care not to score or damage the bore

Fig. 26 Use extreme caution when removing the piston seal; DO NOT scratch the caliper bore

Fig. 27 Use the proper size driving tool and a mallet to properly seal the boots in the caliper housing

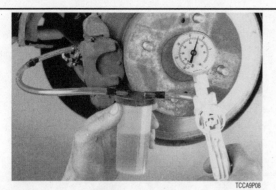

Fig. 28 There are tools, such as this Mighty-Vac, available to assist in proper brake system bleeding

13. Lubricate the piston bore.

14. Install the pistons and boots into the bores of the calipers and push to the bottom of the bores.

15. Use a suitable driving tool to seat the boots in the housing.

16. Install the caliper in the vehicle.

17. Install the wheel and tire assembly, then carefully lower the vehicle.

18. Properly bleed the brake system.

Brake Disc (Rotor)

REMOVAL & INSTALLATION

▶ See Figure 29

1. Raise and safely support the vehicle.

2. Remove the wheel(s).

3. Using a the correct wrench and Torx® T40 bit, unthread, but do not slide all the way out the caliper locating pins.

4. Lift the caliper assembly from the rotor/integral knuckle and anchor plate using a rotating motion. Do not pry directly against plastic piston or damage will occur.

5. Position the caliper aside and support it with a length of wire to avoid damage to the line or fitting.

6. Remove the rotor from hub assembly by pulling it off the hub studs.

Fig. 29 Remove the rotor from the hub assembly by pulling it off the hub studs

7. Inspect the rotor and refinish or replace, as necessary. If refinishing, check the minimum thickness specification.

To install:

8. If the rotor is being replaced, remove protective coating from new rotor with carburetor degreaser. If original rotor is being installed, make sure rotor braking and mounting surfaces are clean.

9. Install the rotor on the hub assembly.

10. Install the caliper assembly on the rotor.

11. Install the wheel(s).

12. Pump the brake pedal prior to moving vehicle to position brake linings.

13. Lower, then road test the vehicle.

INSPECTION

1. Using a brake rotor micrometer or Vernier caliper measure the rotor thickness in several places around the rotor.

2. The rotor thickness should not be less than the maximum wear specification. Refer to the brake specification chart in this section for the brake disc maximum wear specification.

3. If the rotor thickness exceeds the limit, replace the rotor.

4. Mount a magnetic base dial indicator to the strut member and zero the indicator stylus on the face of the rotor. Rotate the rotor 360 degrees by hand and record the run-out.

5. The rotor run-out should be a maximum of 0.002 inch (0.050mm). If the run-out exceeds the limit, replace the rotor.

DRUM BRAKES

REAR DRUM BRAKE COMPONENTS

1. Brake shoes	4. Lower return spring	7. Self-adjuster assembly
2. Adjuster lever	5. Parking brake cable	8. Upper return spring
3. Hold-down assemblies	6. Parking brake lever	9. Wheel cylinder

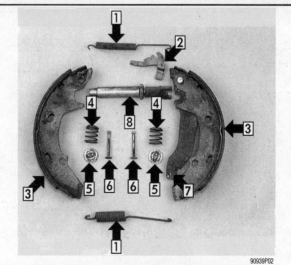

DISASSEMBLED DRUM BRAKE COMPONENTS

1. Return springs	4. Hold-down springs	7. Parking brake lever
2. Adjuster lever	5. Hold-down spring caps	8. Self-adjuster assembly
3. Brake shoes	6. Hold-down pins	

Brake Drums

REMOVAL & INSTALLATION

▶ See Figures 30, 31 and 32

1. Raise and safely support the vehicle.
2. Remove the rear wheel(s).
3. With a small prytool, remove the grease cap from the hub.
4. Remove the cotter pin with needlenose pliers.
5. Remove the nut and keyed flat washer from the spindle.
6. Remove the outer wheel bearing.
7. Remove the hub and drum assembly as a unit.

➡ If the hub/drum assembly will not come off, pry the rubber plug from the backing plate inspection hole. On vehicles with 7 inch brake drums, insert a long, thin prytool in the hole until it contacts the adjuster assembly pivot. Apply side pressure on this pivot point to allow the adjuster quadrant to ratchet and release the brake adjustment. On vehicles with 8 inch brake drums, remove the brake line-to-axle retention bracket. This will allow sufficient room for insertion of a long thin prytool to disengage the adjuster lever and back-off the adjusting screw.

8. Remove the brake drum.

Fig. 30 With a small prytool, carefully remove the grease cap from the hub

Fig. 31 Withdraw the cotter pin using needlenose pliers, then remove the nut and washer from the spindle

Fig. 32 With the bearing assembly removed, carefully pull off the hub and drum assembly as a unit

✴✴ CAUTION

Brake shoes may contain asbestos, which has been determined to be a cancer causing agent. Never clean the brake surfaces with compressed air! Avoid inhaling any dust from any brake surface! When cleaning brake surfaces, use a commercially available brake cleaning solvent.

9. Inspect the brake drum and refinish or replace, as necessary. If refinishing, check the maximum inside diameter specification.

To install:

10. Inspect and lubricate the bearings, as necessary. Replace the grease seal if any damage is visible.
11. Clean the spindle stem and apply a thin coat of wheel bearing grease.
12. Install the hub and drum assembly on the spindle.
13. Install the outer bearing into the hub on the spindle.
14. Install the keyed flat washer and adjusting nut. Finger-tighten the nut.
15. Adjust the wheel bearing (refer to Section 8 of this manual). Install the nut retainer and a new cotter pin.
16. Install the grease cap.
17. Install the wheel(s).
18. Pump brake pedal prior to moving vehicle to position brake linings.
19. Road test the vehicle.

INSPECTION

▶ See Figure 33

1. Use denatured alcohol to clean any dust, brake fluid or other contaminates from the drum.
2. Visually inspect the inside surface of the drum for scratches and uneven or abnormal wear.
3. Resurface the drum if the damage is minor and replace the drum if the damage is excessive.
4. Measure the inside diameter of the drum with a brake drum micrometer.

✴✴ CAUTION

Make sure to check the drum-to-shoe contact after repairing or replacing the drum.

5. If the drum diameter exceeds 7.145 inches (181.5mm) on three-door models or 8.059 inches (204.7mm) on four-door models, replace the drum.

Fig. 33 The drum's maximum diameter is usually stamped on the drum

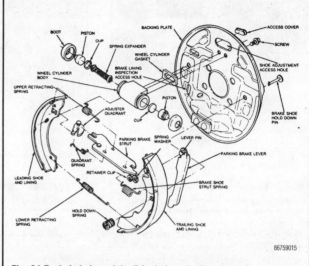

Fig. 34 Exploded view of the 7 inch drum brake assembly

Brake Shoes

✳✳ CAUTION

Brake shoes may contain asbestos, which has been determined to be a cancer causing agent. Never cleanÁhe brake surfaces with compressed air! Avoid inhaling any dust from any brake surface! When cleaning brake surfaces, use a commercially available brake cleaning solvent.

INSPECTION

1. Check the brake linings for peeling, cracks or extremely uneven wear.
2. Use a Vernier caliper to measure the lining thickness.
3. If the lining thickness is less than shown in the brake specifications chart in this manual, replace the brake shoes.
4. If their is evidence of the lining being contaminated by brake fluid or oil, replace the shoes.
5. Always replace the brake shoe assemblies on both sides.

REMOVAL & INSTALLATION

7 Inch (180mm) Brake Drum

▶ **See Figures 34 thru 39**

1. Raise and safely support the vehicle.
2. Remove the rear wheel(s).
3. Remove the hub and drum assembly.

➡**A special hold-down spring retainer tool is available to ease removal and installation of the retainers. Position the tool over the retainer, press in lightly and twist a quarter turn to disengage the retainer.**

4. Remove the hold-down spring retainers, followed by the springs and pins.
5. Lift the brake shoe and adjuster assembly up and away from the anchor block and shoe guide. Do not damage the boots when rotating shoes off the wheel cylinder.
6. Remove the parking brake cable end from the parking brake lever to allow removal of the brake shoe and adjuster assembly from the vehicle.
7. Remove the lower shoe-to-shoe spring from the leading and trailing shoe slots.
8. Hold the brake shoe/adjuster assembly, remove the leading shoe-to-adjuster strut retracting spring. This can be done by rotating shoe over adjuster quadrant until spring is slack and then disconnecting spring. The leading shoe should now be free.

Fig. 35 Use a suitable brake cleaner spray to remove any gunk from the brake assembly

Fig. 36 Use a special hold-down spring retainer removal tool

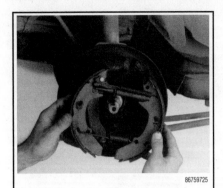

Fig. 37 Be careful not to bend adjuster components when removing the assembly

Fig. 38 Use a spring plier tool to remove the retracting springs from the brake shoes

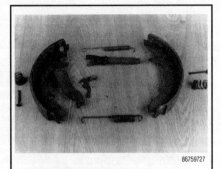

Fig. 39 As you remove the components, lay them out to remind yourself of their proper positions

9. Remove the trailing shoe-to-parking brake strut retracting spring by pivoting the strut downward until it disengages from the trailing shoe.

10. Disassemble the adjuster, if necessary, by pulling the quadrant away from the knurled pin in the strut and rotating the quadrant in either direction until its teeth are no longer meshed with the pin. Remove the spring and slide the quadrant out of the slot. Do not over stress the spring during disassembly.

11. Remove the parking brake lever from the trailing shoe and lining assembly by removing the horseshoe retaining clip and the spring washer, then lift the lever off the pin on the brake shoe.

To install:

12. Apply a light coating of high temperature grease at points where the brake shoes contact the backing plate.

✳✳ CAUTION

Do not allow the grease to come in contact with the braking surface or braking ability will be reduced and possible accident or personal injury may result.

13. Apply a light uniform coating of multi-purpose lubricant to the strut at contact surface between the strut and the adjuster quadrant.

14. Install the adjuster quadrant pin into the slot in the strut and install the adjuster spring. Pivot the quadrant until it meshes with the knurled pin in the third and fourth notch of the outboard end of the quadrant.

15. Assemble the parking brake lever to the trailing shoe. Install the spring washer and a new horseshoe clip. Crimp the clip until the lever is securely fastened.

16. Install the trailing shoe-to-parking brake strut retracting spring by attaching the spring to slots in each part and pivoting the strut into position to tension the spring. Make sure the end of the spring with the hook that is parallel to the center line of the coils is installed in the hole in the shoe web. The installed spring should be flat against the shoe web and parallel to the strut.

17. Install the lower shoe-to-shoe retracting spring between the leading and trailing shoes. The spring hook with the longest straight section fits into the hole in the trailing shoe.

18. Install the leading shoe-to-adjuster/strut retracting spring by installing the spring to both parts and pivoting the leading shoe over the quadrant into position to tension the spring.

19. Expand the shoe and strut assembly to fit over the anchor plate and wheel cylinder piston inserts.

20. Attach the parking brake cable to the parking brake lever.

21. Insert the hold-down pins through the backing plate and brake shoes. Install the hold-down springs and secure the retainers.

22. Set the brake shoe diameter using a suitable brake adjusting gauge.

23. Install the hub/drum and correctly adjust the wheel bearings (refer to Section 8 of this manual).

24. Install the wheel(s).

25. Lower the vehicle and check brake operation.

8 Inch (203mm) Brake Drum

▶ See Figures 35 thru 40

1. Raise and safely support the vehicle.
2. Remove the rear wheel(s).
3. Remove the hub and drum assembly.

➡Use a suitable brake cleaner spray the brake components to remove any unwanted gunk from the brake assembly before or during service.

➡A special hold-down spring retainer tool is available to ease removal and installation of the retainers. Position the tool over the retainer, press in lightly and twist a quarter turn to disengage the retainer.

4. Remove the hold-down spring retainers, followed by the springs and pins.

5. Lift the brake shoes, springs and adjuster assembly off backing plate and wheel cylinder. Be careful not to bend the adjusting lever during removal.

6. Remove the cable from the parking brake lever.

7. Remove the retracting springs from the lower brake shoe attachments and upper shoe-to-adjusting lever attachment points. This will separate the brake shoes and disengage the adjuster mechanism.

8. Remove the horseshoe retaining clip and spring washer, then slide the lever off the pin on the trailing shoe.

To install:

9. Apply a light coating of high temperature grease at the points where the brake shoes contact the backing plate.

10. Apply a light coating of lubricant to the adjuster screw threads and the socket end of the adjusting screw. Install the stainless steel washer over the

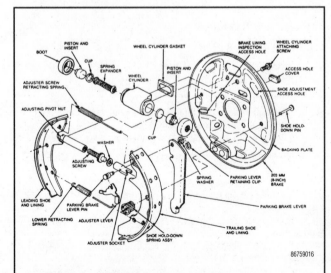

Fig. 40 Exploded view of the 8 inch drum brake assembly

socket end of the adjusting screw and install the socket. Turn the adjusting screw into the adjusting pivot nut to the limit of the threads and then back-off ½ turn.

11. Assemble the parking brake lever to the trailing shoe by installing the spring washer and a new horseshoe retaining clip. Crimp the clip until it retains the lever to the shoe securely.

12. Attach the cable to the parking brake lever.

13. Attach the lower shoe retracting spring to the leading and trailing shoes and install this assembly to the backing plate. It will be necessary to stretch the retracting spring (as the shoes are installed) downward over the anchor plate to the inside of shoe retaining plate.

14. Insert the hold-down pins through the backing plate and brake shoes. Install the hold-down springs and secure the retainers.

15. Install the adjuster screw assembly between the leading shoe slot and the slot in the trailing shoe and parking brake lever. The adjuster socket end slot must fit into the trailing shoe parking brake lever.

➡The adjuster socket blade is marked R or L for the right-hand or left-hand brake assemblies. The R or L adjuster blade must be installed with the letter R or L in the upright position, facing the wheel cylinder, on the correct side to ensure that the deeper of the two slots in the adjuster sockets fits into the parking brake lever.

16. Assemble the adjuster lever in the groove located in the parking brake lever pin and into the slot of the adjuster socket that fits into the trailing shoe web.

17. Attach the upper retracting spring to the leading shoe slot. Using a suitable spring tool, stretch the other end of the spring into the notch on the adjuster lever. If the adjuster lever does not contact the star wheel after installing the spring, it is possible that the adjuster socket is installed incorrectly.

18. Set the brake shoe diameter using a suitable brake adjusting gauge.

19. Install the hub/drum. Refer to Section 8 to adjust the wheel bearing(s).

20. Install the wheel(s).

21. Lower the vehicle and check brake operation.

ADJUSTMENTS

7 Inch (180mm) Brake Drum

1. Raise and safely support the vehicle.
2. Remove the wheel and tire assembly.
3. Remove the brake drum.
4. Check the parking brake cables for proper adjustment. Make sure the equalizer operates freely with the brake shoes centered on the backing plate.
5. Apply a small quantity of disc brake caliper slide grease or equivalent to the points where the shoes contact the backing plate. Ensure that the grease does not contact the shoe linings.
6. Pivot the adjuster quadrant until it meshes with the knurled pin and is in the third or fourth notch on the outboard end of the quadrant.
7. Install the brake drum.
8. Install the wheel and tire assembly.
9. Adjust the wheel bearings.
10. Lower the vehicle.
11. Apply the brakes several times before driving the vehicle.

12. Check the brake system operation by making several stops while driving slowly forward.

8-Inch (203mm) Brake Drum

1. Raise and safely support the vehicle.
2. Remove the wheel and tire assembly.
3. Remove the brake drum.
4. Check the parking brake cables for proper adjustment. Make sure the equalizer operates freely with the brake shoes centered on the backing plate.
5. Apply a small quantity of disc brake caliper slide grease or equivalent to the points where the shoes contact the backing plate. Ensure that the grease does not contact the shoe linings.
6. Using a brake adjusting gauge, measure the inside diameter of the brake drum.
7. Compare the brake drum measurement to the brake shoes.
8. Adjust the brake shoe diameter to fit the gauge. Line up the brake shoes vertically so that the flats on the bottom of the shoes are with the bottom of the anchor pin and shoe retainer before setting the gauge diameter.
9. Hold the automatic adjusting lever out of engagement while rotating the adjusting screw. Make sure the adjusting screw turns freely.
10. Rotate the shoe gauge around the shoes to ensure proper seating
11. Install the brake drum.
12. Install the wheel and tire assembly.
13. Adjust the wheel bearings.
14. Lower the vehicle.
15. Apply the brakes several times before driving the vehicle.
16. Check the brake system operation by making several stops while driving slowly forward.

Wheel Cylinders

REMOVAL & INSTALLATION

▶ **See Figures 41, 42 and 43**

1. Raise and safely support the vehicle.
2. Remove the wheel(s), then the hub/drum assemblies.

☼☼ CAUTION

Brake shoes may contain asbestos, which has been determined to be a cancer causing agent. Never clean the brake surfaces with compressed air! Avoid inhaling any dust from any brake surface! When cleaning brake surfaces, use a commercially available brake cleaning solvent.

3. Remove the brake shoe assembly.

➡Use caution to prevent brake fluid from contacting the brake linings and drum braking surface. Contaminated linings must be replaced.

4. Disconnect the brake tube from the wheel cylinder.
5. Unfasten the wheel cylinder attaching bolts and remove the wheel cylinder.

86759728

Fig. 41 A special clamp makes it a simple matter to prevent fluid leakage

86759729

Fig. 42 Remove the brake line fitting from the wheel cylinder using the proper wrench

86759730

Fig. 43 Remove the disconnected wheel cylinder from the vehicle

To install:

6. Ensure the ends of the hydraulic fittings are free of foreign matter before making the connections.

7. Position the wheel cylinder and foam seal on the backing plate, then finger-tighten the brake tube to the cylinder.

8. Secure the cylinder to the backing plate by installing attaching bolts. Tighten the bolts to 8–10 ft. lbs. (10–14 Nm).

9. Tighten the tube nut fitting.

10. Install and adjust the brakes.

11. Install the hub/drum assemblies and the wheel(s).

12. Bleed the brake system and lower the vehicle.

13. Road test the vehicle.

OVERHAUL

▶ **See Figures 44 thru 53**

Wheel cylinder overhaul kits may be available, but often at little or no savings over a reconditioned wheel cylinder. It often makes sense with these components to substitute a new or reconditioned part instead of attempting an overhaul.

If no replacement is available, or you would prefer to overhaul your wheel cylinders, the following procedure may be used. When rebuilding and installing wheel cylinders, avoid getting any contaminants into the system. Always use clean, new, high quality brake fluid. If dirty or improper fluid has been used, it will be necessary to drain the entire system, flush the system with proper brake fluid, replace all rubber components, then refill and bleed the system.

1. Remove the wheel cylinder from the vehicle and place on a clean workbench.

2. First remove and discard the old rubber boots, then withdraw the pistons. Piston cylinders are equipped with seals and a spring assembly, all located behind the pistons in the cylinder bore.

3. Remove the remaining inner components, seals and spring assembly. Compressed air may be useful in removing these components. If no compressed air is available, be VERY careful not to score the wheel cylinder bore when removing parts from it. Discard all components for which replacements were supplied in the rebuild kit.

4. Wash the cylinder and metal parts in denatured alcohol or clean brake fluid.

※※ **WARNING**

Never use a mineral-based solvent such as gasoline, kerosene or paint thinner for cleaning purposes. These solvents will swell rubber components and quickly deteriorate them.

5. Allow the parts to air dry or use compressed air. Do not use rags for cleaning, since lint will remain in the cylinder bore.

6. Inspect the piston and replace it if it shows scratches.

7. Lubricate the cylinder bore and seals using clean brake fluid.

8. Position the spring assembly.

9. Install the inner seals, then the pistons.

10. Insert the new boots into the counterbores by hand. Do not lubricate the boots.

11. Install the wheel cylinder.

Fig. 44 Remove the outer boots from the wheel cylinder

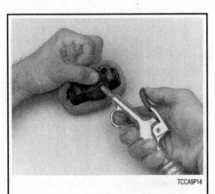

Fig. 45 Compressed air can be used to remove the pistons and seals

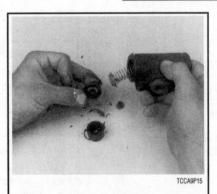

Fig. 46 Remove the pistons, cup seals and spring from the cylinder

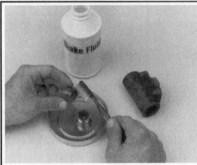

Fig. 47 Use brake fluid and a soft brush to clean the pistons . . .

Fig. 48 . . . and the bore of the wheel cylinder

Fig. 49 Once cleaned and inspected, the wheel cylinder is ready for assembly

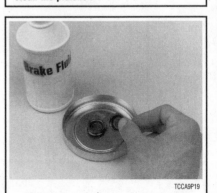

Fig. 50 Lubricate the cup seals with brake fluid

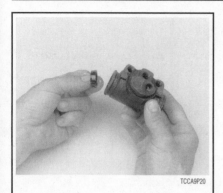

Fig. 51 Install the spring, then the cup seals in the bore

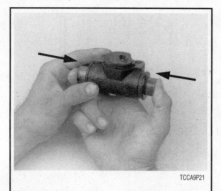

Fig. 52 Lightly lubricate the pistons, then install them

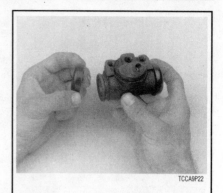

Fig. 53 The boots can now be installed over the wheel cylinder ends

PARKING BRAKE

The parking brake control is hand operated and mounted on the floor between the front seats. When the control lever is pulled up (from the floor) an attached cable applies the rear brakes.

Parking Brake Control Assembly

REMOVAL & INSTALLATION

▶ **See Figures 54, 55, 56 and 57**

1. Place the control assembly in the seventh notch position and remove the adjusting nut. Completely release the control assembly.
2. Remove the two screws or bolts that attach the control assembly to the floor pan.

Fig. 54 Remove the armrest if it obstructs the adjuster mechanism

3. Disconnect the brake light and ground wire from the control assembly.
4. Remove the control assembly from the vehicle.

To install:

5. Install the adjusting rod into the control assembly clevis and position the control assembly on the floor pan.
6. Install the brake light and ground wire.
7. Install the two screws or bolts that attach the control assembly to the floor pan. Tighten the bolts to 13–20 ft. lbs. (17–28 Nm).
8. Install the adjusting nut and adjust the parking brake.
9. Connect the negative battery cable.

Cables

REMOVAL & INSTALLATION

1981–85 Models

▶ **See Figures 58 and 59**

1. Pull up slowly on the control lever and stop at the seventh notch position, count the clicks as you pull up on the handle. The adjusting nut is now accessible.
2. Remove the adjusting nut. Completely release the control handle (push the release button and lower the lever to the floor.
3. Raise the car and safely support on jackstands.
4. Disconnect the parking brake cable from the equalizer.
5. Remove the hairpin clip that holds the cable to the floor pan tunnel bracket.
6. Remove the wire retainer that holds the cable to the fuel tank mounting bracket.
7. Remove the cable from the wire retainer.

Fig. 55 Place the control assembly in the seventh notch position and remove the adjusting nut

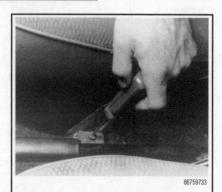

Fig. 56 Unscrew the control assembly from the floor pan

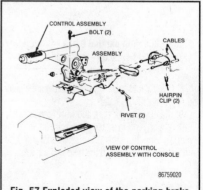

Fig. 57 Exploded view of the parking brake assembly

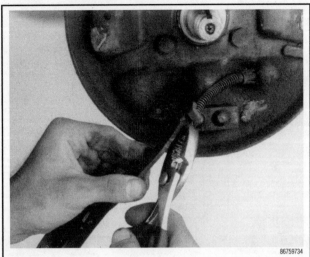

Fig. 58 Disconnect the parking brake cable from the trailing shoe parking brake lever

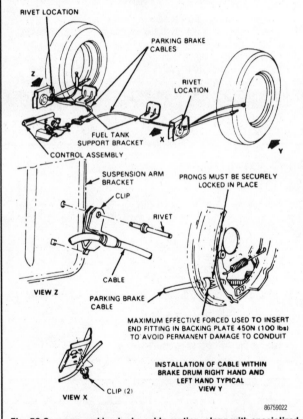

Fig. 59 Common parking brake cable routing, along with specialized brackets and hardware—1981–85 models

8. Drill out the pop rivet that attaches the cable retaining clip to the rear tie rod end bracket.

9. Remove the rear tire and wheel assemblies and the brake drums.

10. Disconnect the parking brake cable from the trailing shoe parking brake levers. Depress the cable prongs that hold the cable in the backing plate hole. Remove the cable through the hole in the backing plate.

To install:

11. Insert the cable through the hole in the backing plate. Make sure the retention prongs are securely locked in place.

12. Connect the parking brake cable to the trailing shoe parking brake levers.

13. Attach the cable to the rear clip on the tie rod end bracket and install a new rivet.

14. Route the cable through the floor pan bracket and install the hairpin retaining clip.

15. Attach the cable to the equalizer.

16. Insert the cable into the wire retainer and snap retainer into the hole in the fuel tank mounting bracket.

17. Install the brake drums and the tire assemblies.

18. Adjust the parking brake and lower the vehicle.

1985½–90 Models

◆ See Figure 60

1. Place the control assembly in the seventh applied notch position and loosen the adjusting nut, then completely release control assembly.

2. Raise and safely support vehicle. Remove parking brake cable from equalizer.

3. Remove hairpin clip holding cable to floor pan tunnel bracket.

4. Remove wire retainer holding cable to fuel tank mounting bracket.

5. Remove cable from wire retainer.

6. Remove cable and clip from the fuel pump bracket.

7. Unfasten the screw holding the cable retaining clip to the rear sidemember. Remove the cable from the clip.

8. Remove the wheel and rear brake drum.

➡**A box wrench slightly smaller than the cable end can be used to ease its removal from the backing plate by sliding it over and depressing the splayed prongs.**

9. Disengage cable end from brake assembly parking brake lever. Depress prongs holding cable to backing plate. Remove cable through the hole in the backing plate.

To install:

10. Insert the cable through hole in the backing plate. Attach the cable end to the rear brake assembly parking brake lever.

11. Insert conduit end fitting into backing plate. Ensure retention prongs are locked into place.

12. Insert cable into rear attaching clip and attach clip to rear sidemember with screw.

13. Route cable through bracket in floor pan tunnel and install hairpin retaining clip.

14. Install cable end into equalizer.

15. Insert cable into wire retainer and snap retainer into hole in fuel tank mounting bracket. Insert cable and install clip into fuel pump bracket.

16. Install rear drum, wheel and wheel cover.

17. Lower vehicle.

18. Adjust parking brake.

ADJUSTMENT

◆ See Figures 61 and 62

➡**The rear brake shoes should be properly adjusted before adjusting the parking brake. Although ordinarily the shoes are only adjusted initially upon setup, if you believe you may have disturbed the adjustment, refer to the brake shoe adjustment procedure in this section.**

1. With the engine running, apply approximately 100 lbs. (450 N) pedal effort to the hydraulic service brake three times before adjusting the parking brake.

2. Block the front wheel(s) and place the transaxle in Neutral. Raise and safely support the rear of the vehicle just enough to rotate the wheel.

3. Place the parking brake control assembly in the 12th notch position,

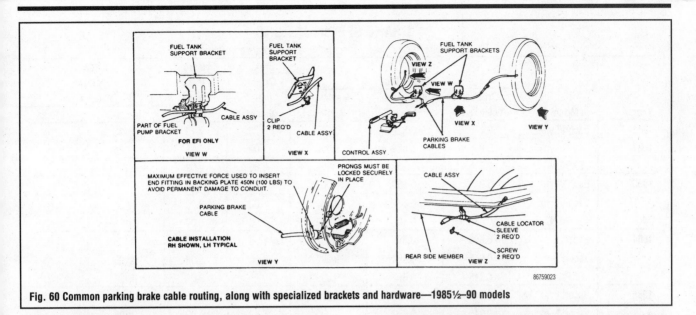

Fig. 60 Common parking brake cable routing, along with specialized brackets and hardware—1985½–90 models

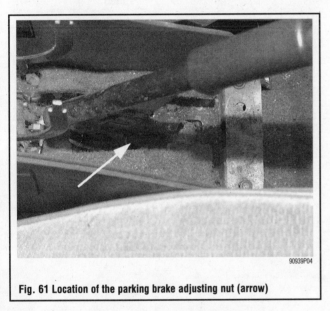

Fig. 61 Location of the parking brake adjusting nut (arrow)

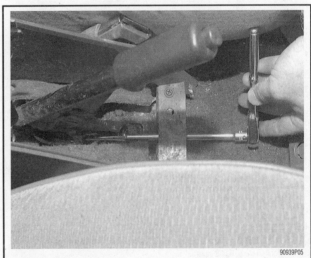

Fig. 62 Adjust the parking brake using a socket, extension and ratchet

just two notches from full application. Tighten the adjusting nut until approximately 1 in. (25mm) of threaded rod is exposed beyond the nut. Release the parking brake control and rotate the rear wheels by hand. There should be no brake drag.

4. If the brakes drag when the control assembly is fully released, or the handle travels too far upward on full, repeat the procedure and adjust the nut accordingly.

BRAKE SPECIFICATIONS
All specifications given in inches unless otherwise indicated

Year	Model		Brake Disc			Brake Drum Diameter		Minimum Lining Thickness	
			Original Thickness	Maximum Wear	Maximum Run-out	Original Inside Diameter	Max. Wear Limit	Front	Rear
1981	Escort/Lynx		0.945	0.882	0.002	7.09	7.18	0.125	①
1982	Escort/Lynx		0.945	0.882	0.002	7.09	7.18	0.125	①
	EXP/LN7		0.945	0.882	0.002	8.00	8.09	0.125	①
1983	Escort/Lynx	②	0.945	0.882	0.002	7.09	7.18	0.125	①
	Escort/Lynx	③	0.945	0.882	0.002	8.00	8.09	0.125	①
	EXP/LN7		0.945	0.882	0.002	8.00	8.09	0.125	①
1984	Escort/Lynx	②	0.945	0.882	0.002	7.09	7.18	0.125	①
	Escort/Lynx	③	0.945	0.882	0.002	8.00	8.09	0.125	①
	EXP/LN7		0.945	0.882	0.002	8.00	8.09	0.125	①
1985	Escort/Lynx	②	0.945	0.882	0.002	7.09	7.18	0.125	①
	Escort/Lynx	③	0.945	0.882	0.002	8.00	8.09	0.125	①
	EXP		0.945	0.882	0.002	8.00	8.09	0.125	①
1986	Escort/Lynx	②	0.945	0.882	0.002	7.09	7.18	0.125	①
	Escort/Lynx	③	0.945	0.882	0.002	8.00	8.09	0.125	①
	EXP		0.945	0.882	0.002	8.00	8.09	0.125	①
1987	Escort/Lynx	②	0.945	0.882	0.002	7.09	7.18	0.125	①
	Escort/Lynx	③	0.945	0.882	0.002	8.00	8.09	0.125	①
1988	Escort	②	0.945	0.882	0.002	7.09	7.18	0.125	①
	Escort	③	0.945	0.882	0.002	8.00	8.09	0.125	①
1989	Escort	②	0.945	0.882	0.002	7.09	7.18	0.125	①
	Escort	③	0.945	0.882	0.002	8.00	8.09	0.125	①
1990	Escort	②	0.945	0.882	0.002	7.09	7.18	0.125	①
	Escort	③	0.945	0.882	0.002	8.00	8.09	0.125	①

① Over rivet head: 0.030 inch

　Bonded lining: 0.062 inch

② 7 inch rear drum

③ 8 inch rear drum

90939C01

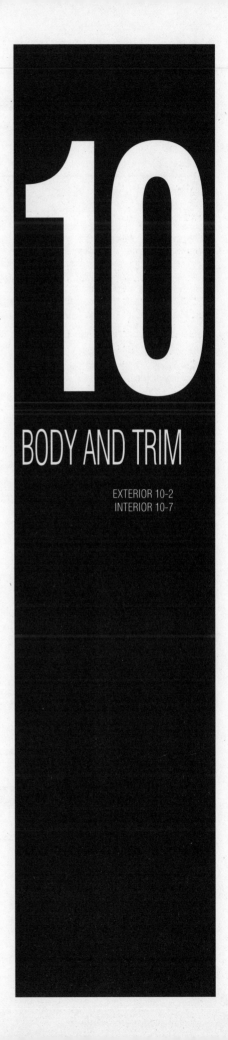

10

BODY AND TRIM

EXTERIOR

Doors

ADJUSTMENT

▶ **See Figure 1**

Adjusting the hinge affects the positioning of the outside surface of the door frame. Adjusting the latch striker affects the alignment of the door relative to the weatherstrip and the door closing characteristics.

The door latch striker pin can be adjusted laterally and vertically as well as for and aft. The latch striker should not be adjusted to correct the door sag.

The latch striker should be shimmed to get the clearance shown in the illustration, between the striker and the latch. To check this clearance, clean the latch jaws and striker area. Apply a thin layer of dark grease to the striker. As the door is closed and opened, a measurable pattern will result on the latch striker.

➡ **Use a maximum of two shims under the striker.**

The door hinges provide sufficient adjustment to correct most door misalignment conditions. The holes of the hinge and/or the hinge attaching points are enlarged or elongated to provide for hinge and door alignment.

➡ **DO NOT cover up a poor alignment with a latch striker adjustment.**

1. Refer to the illustration to determine which hinge screws must be loosened to move the door in the desired direction.
2. Loosen the hinge screws just enough to permit movement of the door with a padded prybar.
3. Move the door the distance estimated to be necessary for a correct fit. Tighten the hinge bolts to 18–26 ft. lbs. (25–35 Nm), then check the door fit to be sure there is no bind or interference with the adjacent panel.

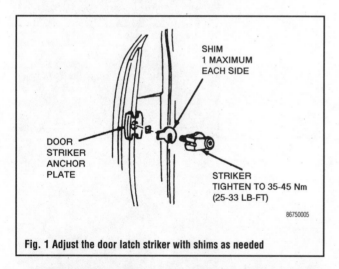

Fig. 1 Adjust the door latch striker with shims as needed

Hood

REMOVAL & INSTALLATION

▶ **See Figures 2, 3 and 4**

➡ **The help of an assistant is recommended, when removing or installing the hood.**

1. Open and support the hood.
2. Protect the body with fender covers to prevent damage to the paint.
3. Scribe marks around the hinge locations for reference during installation.
4. Remove the hinge attaching bolts, being careful not to let the hood slip as the bolts are removed.
5. Remove the hood and place it in a safe location.

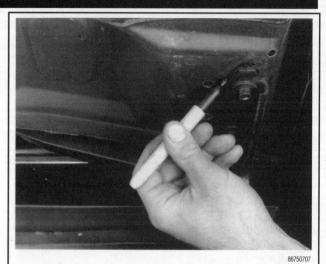

Fig. 2 Scribe marks around the hinge locations for reference during installation

Fig. 3 While a helper holds the hood, carefully remove the hinge attaching bolts

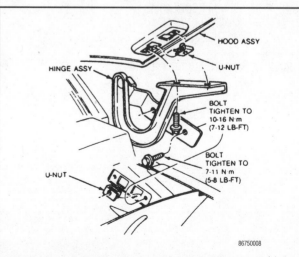

Fig. 4 Common hood hinge alignment and torque specifications

To install:

6. Place the hood into position. Install and partially tighten the attaching bolts.

7. Adjust the hood with the reference marks and tighten the attaching bolts to 7–12 ft. lbs. (10–16 Nm).

8. Check the hood for an even fit between the fenders and for flush fit with the front of the fenders. Also, check for a flush fit with the top of the cowl and fenders. If necessary, adjust the hood latch.

ALIGNMENT

The hood can be adjusted fore and aft and side to side by loosening the hood-to-hinge attaching bolts and reposition the hood. To raise or lower the hood, loosen the hinge hood on body attaching bolts and raise or lower the hinge as necessary.

The hood lock can be moved from side-to-side and up and down and laterally to obtain a snug hood fit by loosening the lock attaching screws and moving as necessary.

Hatch/Liftgate

REMOVAL & INSTALLATION

➡**The help of an assistant is recommended, when removing or installing the hatch/liftgate.**

1. Open and support the hatchback assembly.

2. If necessary, pull down on the weatherstrip across the entire top edge of the hatchback opening. Carefully loosen and pull down the headlining to expose the access holes to the hinge screws.

3. Using a scribe, mark the location of the hinge-to-roof frame attachments at both hinges.

4. Remove the hinge-to-roof frame attaching screw and washer assembly from each hinge.

5. Remove the hatch/liftgate.

6. Installation is the reverse of removal. Check and perform alignment as necessary and tighten the hinge retainers to 16–20 ft. lbs. (22–27 Nm).

ALIGNMENT

Hatchback Hinge

ESCORT/LYNX AND EXP/LN7

The hatchback can be adjusted fore-and-aft, and side-to-side by loosening the hinge to roof frame attaching screw at each hinge.

1. To adjust the hinge, pull down on the weatherstrip across the entire top edge of the hatchback opening.

2. Carefully loosen and pull down the headlining to expose the access holes to the hinge screws. Adjust the hinge as necessary. Seal the hinge after adjustment with clear silicone sealer. Apply trim cement to the sheet metal flange, and install the headlining and smooth out any wrinkles. Install the weatherstrip.

The hatchback can be adjusted in and out by shimming the hinge at the header roof frame.

The hatchback should be adjusted for an even and parallel fit with the hatchback opening and shrouding panels.

Liftgate Hinge

ESCORT/LYNX

On the four-door liftgate models, the liftgate can be adjusted up and down and side-to-side by loosening the header roof frame attaching screw and washer assembly.

The liftgate can be adjusted in and out by shimmering the hinges at the header roof frame. The liftgate should be adjusted for an even parallel fit with the liftgate opening and surrounding panels.

1. To adjust a hinge, or hinges, remove the weatherstrip and pull down the headliner to gain access to the hinge attachment(s).

2. Adjust the hinge(s) as necessary. Seal the hinge after adjustment with clear silicone sealer. Apply trim cement to the sheet metal flange, then install the headlining and smooth out any wrinkles.

3. Install the weatherstrip.

Grille

REMOVAL & INSTALLATION

1981–85 Models

➡ See Figure 5

1. Unfasten the five radiator grille attaching screws (two on each side and one in the center).

2. Remove the grille from the mounting brackets on the radiator support.

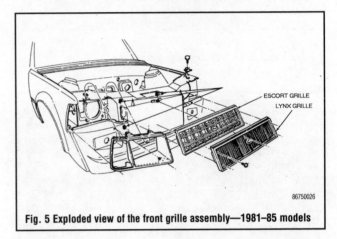

Fig. 5 Exploded view of the front grille assembly—1981–85 models

To install:

3. Position the grille to the vehicle and loosely install the grille attaching screws. The grille should rest on the locating tabs that extend from the headlamp doors.

4. Adjust the grille side to side so there is a uniform gap between the grille and the headlamp doors. Tighten the retaining bolts.

1985½–90 Models

EXCEPT ESCORT GT

➡ See Figures 6, 7 and 8

1. Unfasten the grille retaining screws.

2. Push down on the top side of lower snap-in retainer at both sides of grille and pull the grille out at the bottom.

3. Push up on the bottom side of the upper snap-in retainer at both sides of the grille and pull the grille out at the top.

4. Pull the grille forward out of the grille opening panel.

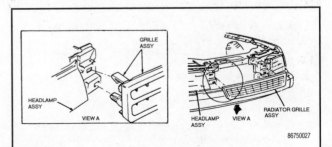

Fig. 6 Mounting points of the front grille assembly—1985½–90 models

Fig. 7 Unfasten the grille retaining screws

Fig. 8 Unfasten all the grille retainers and remove the grille

To install:
5. Position the grille to the vehicle and align the snap-in retainers with appropriate slots and push in on the grille until all the retainers are seated.
6. Install the grille retaining screws.

1985½–87 *ESCORT GT*

▶ See Figure 9

1. Unfasten the retaining screws(s) on the top of the grille assembly at both sides and pull the grille out at the top.
2. Push up on the bottom side of the upper snap-in retainer at both sides of the grille out at the top.
3. Put grille forward out of the grille opening panel.
To install:
4. Position the grille to align the lower snap-in retainers and upper tabs over the U-nuts at both sides.
5. Align the snap-in retainers with appropriate slots and push in on the grille until all the retainers are seated.
6. Install the upper retaining screw at both sides.

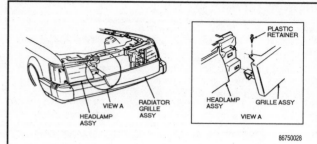

Fig. 9 Mounting points of the front grille assembly—1985½–87 Escort GT

1988–90 *ESCORT GT*

▶ See Figure 10

1. Remove the lower grille bar by pushing up on the three retaining tabs located on the back side of the grille. Pull the grille bar forward to remove it.
2. Remove the two screws retaining the grille at the top ends to mounting brackets.
3. Pull grille forward to remove it.
4. Remove the mounting brackets from the headlamp housing by pushing down on the top side of the lower snap-in retainers at both sides and push up on the bottom of the top snap-in retainers.

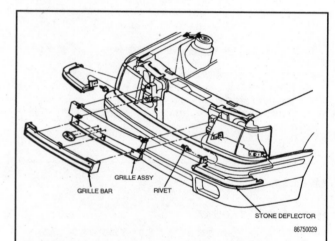

Fig. 10 Mounting points of the front grille assembly—1988–90 Escort GT

To install:
5. Position the grille to align the upper and lower snap-in retainers.
6. Push the grille in, to the seat retainers.
7. Align grille bar retainers with the holes in the grille and push in until seated.
8. Install the retaining screws. Tighten the screws to 6–14 ft. lbs. (8–19 Nm).

Outside Mirrors

REMOVAL & INSTALLATION

Manual Mirrors

▶ See Figure 11

1. Remove the inside door trim panel from the door in which the mirror is to be taken from.

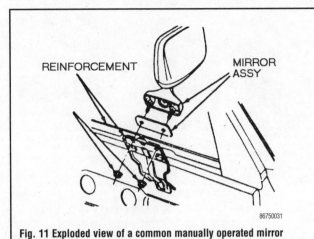

Fig. 11 Exploded view of a common manually operated mirror assembly

2. Remove the retaining nuts and washers from the mirror.
3. Lift the mirror up and out of the door and discard the gasket.

To install:
4. Install the mirror and gasket onto the door.
5. Install the nuts and washers and tighten the nuts to 25–36 inch lbs. (2.8–4.0 Nm)
6. Reinstall the door trim panel.

Remote Control Mirrors

◗ See Figures 12 and 13

1. Remove the set screw fastening the control lever end of the cable assembly to the control lever bezel on the door trim panel.
2. Remove the inside door trim panel and weather insulator from the door in which the mirror is to be taken from.
3. Disengage the cable from the routing clips and guides located inside the door.
4. Remove the mirror attaching nuts and washers.
5. Remove the mirror and cable assembly from the door.

To install:
6. Place the remote cable into the hole and the door and position the mirror to the door. Install the nuts and washers and tighten them to 21–39 inch lbs. (2.3–4.4 Nm).
7. Route the cable through the door into the cable guides and engage the cable into the locating clips.
8. Check the operation of the mirror and operate the mirror up and down to insure that the mirror cables do not interfere with the window mechanism.

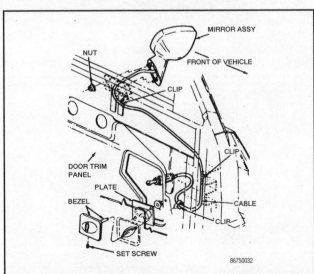

Fig. 12 Exploded view of a common remote control mirror assembly

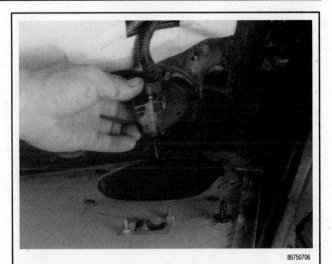

Fig. 13 The mirror control is accessible once the door panel is removed

9. Install the weather insulator and door trim panel.
10. Place the control lever bezel onto the door trim panel and install the setscrew.

Power Mirrors

◗ See Figures 14, 15 and 16

1. Disconnect the negative battery cable.
2. Remove the inside door trim panel and weather insulator from the door in which the mirror is to be taken from.
3. Unplug the electrical connector from the mirror unit.
4. Disengage the wire harness cable from the routing clips and guides located inside the door.
5. Unfasten the mirror attaching nuts and washers.
6. Remove the mirror and wire assembly from the door.

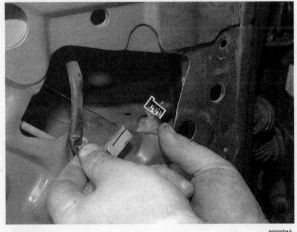

Fig. 14 Remove the door trim panel and watershield to access and unplug the mirror electrical connection

To install:
7. Place the wire harness into the hole in the door and position the mirror on the door. Install the nuts and washers and tighten them to 35–51 inch lbs. (4–6 Nm).
8. Route the wire harness through the door into the harness guides and engage the wire harness connector into the mirror unit.
9. Connect the negative battery cable.

Fig. 15 To unfasten the mirror-to-door retainers, use the proper size socket, extension and ratchet

Fig. 16 After the retainers have been unfastened, remove the mirror and wire assembly from the door

10. Check the operation of the mirror and operate the mirror up and down to insure that the mirror wires do not interfere with the window mechanism.

11. Install the weather insulator and door trim panel.

Antenna

REMOVAL & INSTALLATION

▶ See Figures 17, 18, 19, 20 and 21

1. Disconnect the negative battery cable.
2. Remove the snap cap from the antenna, if so equipped.
3. Remove the base attaching screws.
4. Pull (do not pry) the antenna up through the fender.
5. Push in on the sides of the glove box door and place the door in the hinged downward position.
6. Disconnect the antenna lead from the rear of the radio and remove the antenna cable from the heater or air conditioning cable retaining clips.

➡On some models, it may be necessary to remove the right-hand side kick panel in order to gain access to some of the antenna cable retaining clips.

Fig. 17 Use a wrench to loosen the antenna mast from the base . .

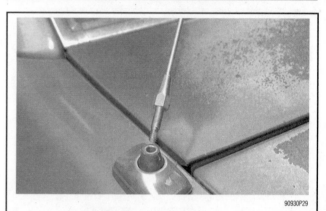

Fig. 18 . . . then unscrew the mast by hand

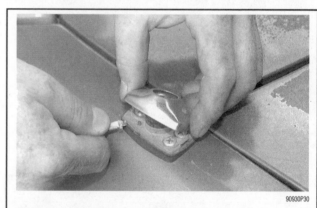

Fig. 19 Pry or snap off the antenna base trim cap

Fig. 20 Unfasten the antenna base-to-fender attaching screws, then remove the base from the fender

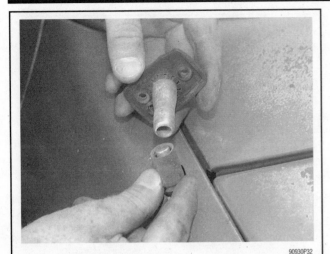

Fig. 21 Disconnect the antenna cable from the base and remove the base

7. Pull the antenna cable through the hole in the door hinge pillar and fender and remove the antenna assembly from the vehicle.

To install:

8. With the right front door open, put the gasket on the antenna and position the antenna base and wire harness assembly into the fender opening.

9. Install the antenna base onto the fender using the retaining screws.

10. Install the antenna base cap and antenna mast assembly, if so equipped.

11. Pull the antenna lead through the door hinge pillar opening. Seat the grommet by pulling the antenna wiring harness cable through the hole from the inside of the vehicle.

12. Route the antenna cable behind the glove box, along the instrument panel and install the cable in the retaining clips from which they were removed.

13. Attach the antenna wiring connector into the back of the radio.

14. Install the right-hand kick panel, if removed.

15. Push in on the sides of the glove box door and place in the hinged upward position.

16. Connect the negative battery cable.

INTERIOR

Instrument Panel and Pad

REMOVAL & INSTALLATION

1981–90 Models

▶ **See Figures 22, 23 and 24**

1. Disconnect the negative battery cable.
2. Unfasten the steering column opening cover retaining screws and remove the cover.
3. If equipped on later model vehicles, unfasten the bolts at the top of the steering column opening cover and disengage the two clips on top of the cover, then remove the cover.
4. Unfasten the steering column-to-support bracket retainers and lower the steering column.
5. Remove the steering column trim shrouds.
6. Disengage all electrical connections from the steering column switches.
7. If necessary, unfasten the left-hand instrument finish panel screw and remove the panel.
8. If applicable, remove the six cluster finish panel screws, pull the finish panel rearward, unplug the fog lamp switch (if equipped) and remove the panel.
9. Disconnect the speedometer cable by reaching up under the instrument panel and pressing on the flat surface of the plastic connector.
10. Remove the instrument cluster.
11. If necessary, remove the radio knobs, unfasten the center finish panel screws and remove the panel.
12. If necessary, unfasten the right-hand finish panel screws. Pull out the bin side first and pull to the left to disengage the clip on the right side of the register.
13. Unfasten the glove box hinge support screws. Depress the sides of the glove box bin and remove the glove box assembly.
14. Tag and disengage all vacuum hoses and electrical connectors, heater, A/C control cables and radio antenna cable.
15. Unplug all necessary underhood electrical connectors to the main wire loom. Disengage the rubber grommet from the dash panel and feed wire and connectors into the instrument panel area.
16. Remove the steering column support bracket retainers.
17. If necessary, remove the speaker covers.
18. Remove the instrument panel brace retainers.
19. If necessary, unfasten the upper and lower instrument panel to cowl side retaining screws.
20. Unfasten the instrument panel upper retaining screws and remove the instrument panel from the vehicle.
21. Transfer all attaching components to the replacement panel.

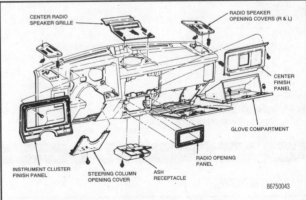

Fig. 22 A common instrument panel and pad—1988 Escort shown

Fig. 23 Exploded view of common instrument panel components

To install:

22. Install the glove box assembly.

23. Place the instrument panel in the vehicle and into position.

24. Install the instrument panel upper retaining screws and tighten them to 20.4–30 inch lbs. (2.3–3.4 Nm) on 1981–87 models and 18–25 ft. lbs. (2.0–2.9 Nm).

25. If removed, install the upper and lower instrument panel to cowl side retaining screws. Tighten the screws to 5–8 ft. lbs. (7–11 Nm).

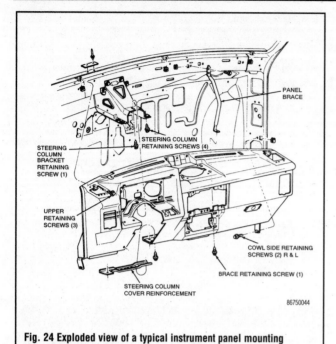

Fig. 24 Exploded view of a typical instrument panel mounting

26. Install the instrument panel brace retainers. Tighten to 60–96 inch lbs. (7–11 Nm).

27. Install the steering column support bracket and tighten the nut to 36–48 inch lbs. (4–6 Nm).

28. If removed, install the speaker covers.

29. Push the wiring harness and connectors through the dash panel into the engine compartment.

30. Attach all underhood electrical connectors that were unplug during instrument panel removal.

31. Attach all vacuum hoses and electrical connectors, heater, A/C control cables and radio antenna cable.

32. Connect the speedometer cable to the speedometer head.

33. Install the instrument cluster.

34. Connect the speedometer to the transaxle, if required.

35. If removed, install the cluster opening finish panel and screws. Tighten the screws to 18–25 inch lbs. (2–2.9 Nm).

36. If removed, install the radio knobs, the center finish panel and its retaining screws.

37. Raise the steering column and tighten the column-to-support bracket retainers.

38. If removed, install the steering column opening reinforcement and its bolts. Tighten the bolts to 80–124 inch lbs. (2–2.9 Nm).

39. Attach all electrical connections to the steering column switches.

40. Install the left-hand finish panel and tighten the retaining screws.

41. Install the steering column trim shrouds.

42. Install the steering column opening cover.

43. Connect the negative battery cable.

Floor Consolette

REMOVAL & INSTALLATION

♦ See Figure 25

1. Unfasten the screw located in the console tray.

2. Using a suitable prytool, pry up the console top from the console bottom at the rear of the console top.

3. Unfasten the three remaining console screws and remove the console bottom.

4. Installation is the reverse of removal.

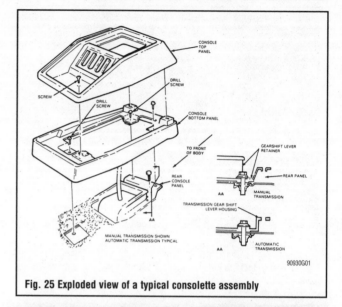

Fig. 25 Exploded view of a typical consolette assembly

Floor Console

REMOVAL & INSTALLATION

1981–84 Models

♦ See Figure 26

1. Move the parking brake lever forward enough to insert a finger into the lever slot of the finish panel.

2. Using your finger, pull upward at the rear of the finish panel through the slot opening.

3. Pull the parking brake lever fully rearward to the set position. Remove the finish panel over the brake and gear shift levers.

4. Unfasten the four screws holding the console base.

5. Unfasten the screws attaching the console to the instrument panel.

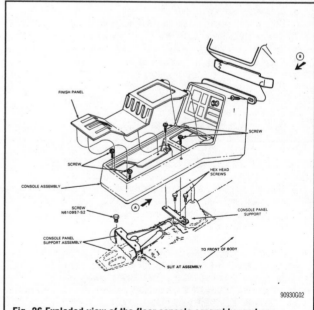

Fig. 26 Exploded view of the floor console assembly used on 1981–84 models

6. Place the parking brake lever in the released position.

7. Move the shift lever into the low gear position on models with an automatic transaxle or fourth gear on models with a manual transaxle.

8. Raise the console to gain access to any electrical connectors.

9. Unplug the connectors and remove the console.

To install:

10. Attach the console electrical connectors.

11. Place the console into position.

12. Install the console retaining screws.

13. Install the console finish panel.

1985–87 Models

▶ **See Figure 27**

1. Unfasten the two screw trim covers at the rear and the four screw trim covers at the sides of the console.

➡**You may need to move the seats to access the screw trim covers.**

2. Unfasten the two screws attaching the rear of the console to the armrest.

3. Unfasten the four armrest-to-rear floor bracket bolts.

4. Lift the armrest from the console.

5. Unfasten the three rear finish panel-to-console screws. Slip the finish panel off the parking brake through the hole in the end of the panel.

6. Unfasten the console-to-front support bracket screws.

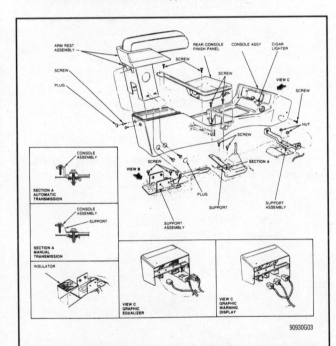

Fig. 27 Exploded view of the console components—1985–87 models

7. Remove the two screws retaining console to the transaxle shift casting (automatic transaxle) or console mounting bracket (manual transaxle).

8. Unfasten the main wiring harness from the front of the console.

9. Remove the console.

To install:

10. Attach the main wiring harness to the front of the console.

11. Install the console into position.

12. Install the two screws retaining console to the transaxle shift casting (automatic transaxle) or console mounting bracket (manual transaxle).

13. Install the console-to-front support bracket screws.

14. Place the rear finish panel into position and tighten its retaining screws.

15. Install the armrest and tighten its retaining bolts.

16. Install the two screws attaching the rear of the console to the armrest.

17. Install the two screw trim covers at the rear and the four screw trim covers at the sides of the console.

1988–90 Models

WITH PASSIVE RESTRAINT SYSTEM

▶ **See Figures 28, 29 and 30**

1. Cycle the shoulder belts to the A-pillar position.

2. Remove the safety belt anchor plug buttons and bolts. Allow the belts to retract into the console.

3. Remove the access hole covers that snap out of the rear on the console.

4. If applicable, unfasten the two armrest-to-console screws.

5. Snap out the shoulder belt bevels from the console.

➡**Access to the armrest screws can be gained through the safety belt openings.**

6. Unfasten the armrest screws (two on each side), and remove the armrest.

7. Carefully pull off the two emergency release lever handles by relieving the pressure from the retaining clips on the underside of the handle and gently pull the handle off.

8. Unfasten the three finish panel-to-console screws, then lift the panel out of the console and unplug the electrical connectors.

Fig. 28 Remove the rear console trim panel

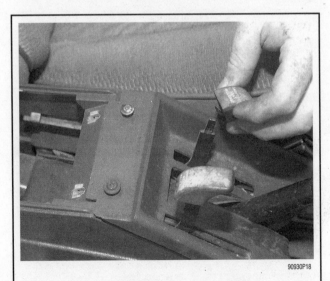

Fig. 29 Remove the seat belt retractor assembly knobs

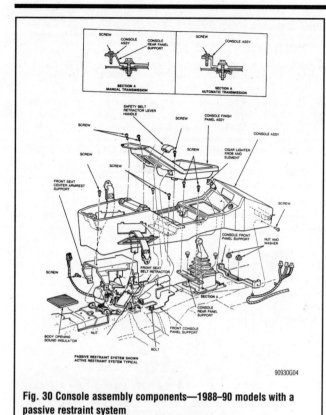

Fig. 30 Console assembly components—1988–90 models with a passive restraint system

9. Unfasten the seven console-to-floor screws.
10. Lift the console up and unplug all necessary connectors.
11. Unfasten the rear console support bracket retainers and remove the bracket.
12. Unfasten the retaining retractor assembly-to-floor brace bolts. Unplug the electrical connector and remove the retractor.

To install:
13. Install the retractor and attach the electrical connector.
14. Install the retractor-to-floor brace bolts and tighten the bolts to 22–32 ft. lbs. (30–43 Nm).
15. Install the support bracket and tighten the retainers.
16. Attach the console electrical connections and place the console into position.
17. Install and tighten the seven console-to-floor screws.
18. Attach the electrical connectors to the finish panel, install the panel and tighten the screws.
19. Install the two emergency release lever handles making sure the clips engage.
20. Install the armrest and its retainers.
21. Snap the shoulder belt bevels into the console.
22. Install the safety belt anchor bolts and plugs.
23. Check that the safety belt is functioning properly.

Mini-Console

REMOVAL & INSTALLATION

1988–90 Models

WITH ARMREST

▶ See Figure 31

1. Cycle the shoulder belts to the A-pillar position.
2. Remove the safety belt anchor plug buttons and bolts. Allow the belts to retract into the console.
3. Remove the access hole covers that snap out of the rear on the console.

4. If applicable, snap out the two plug buttons at the rear of the console and unfasten the two armrest-to-console screws.
5. Snap out the shoulder belt bevels from the console.

➡**Access to the armrest screws can be gained through the safety belt openings.**

6. Unfasten the armrest screws (two on each side), and remove the armrest.
7. Carefully pull off the two emergency release lever handles by relieving the pressure from the retaining clips on the underside of the handle and gently pull the handle off.
8. Unfasten the two console-to-floor support screws and remove the console.
9. Unfasten the rear console support bracket retainers and remove the bracket.
10. Unfasten the retaining retractor assembly-to-floor brace bolts. Unplug the electrical connector and remove the retractor.

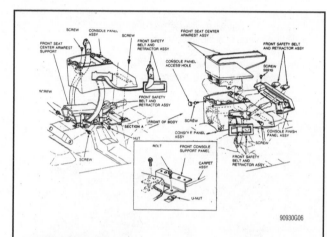

Fig. 31 Mini-console assembly components—1988–90 models with armrest

To install:
11. Install the retractor and attach the electrical connector.
12. Install the retractor-to-floor brace bolts and tighten the bolts to 22–32 ft. lbs. (30–43 Nm).
13. Install the support bracket and tighten the retainers.
14. Attach the console electrical connections and place the console into position.
15. Install and tighten the console-to-floor support screws.
16. Install the two emergency release lever handles making sure the clips engage.
17. Install the armrest and its retainers.
18. Snap the shoulder belt bevels into the console.
19. Install the safety belt anchor bolts and plugs.
20. Check that the safety belt is functioning properly.

WITHOUT ARMREST

▶ See Figure 32

1. Cycle the shoulder belts to the A-pillar position.
2. Remove the safety belt anchor plug buttons and bolts. Allow the belts to retract into the console.
3. Remove the access hole covers that snap out of the rear on the console.
4. If applicable, snap out the two plug buttons at the rear of the console and unfasten the two rear finish panel-to-console screws. Remove the finish panel.
5. Carefully pull off the two emergency release lever handles by relieving the pressure from the retaining clips on the underside of the handle and gently pull the handle off.
6. Unfasten the two front finish panel-to-console screws. Remove the finish panel and unplug any necessary electrical connectors.

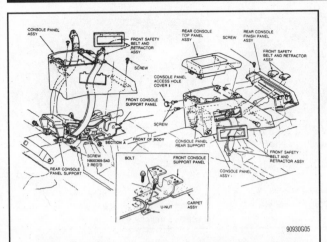

Fig. 32 Mini-console assembly components—1988–90 models without armrest

7. Unfasten the two console-to-floor support screws and remove the console.

8. Unfasten the rear console support bracket retainers and remove the bracket.

9. Unfasten the retaining retractor assembly-to-floor brace bolts. Unplug the electrical connector and remove the retractor.

To install:

10. Install the retractor and attach the electrical connector.

11. Install the retractor-to-floor brace bolts and tighten the bolts to 22–32 ft. lbs. (30–43 Nm).

12. Install the support bracket and tighten the retainers.

13. Attach the console electrical connections and place the console into position.

14. Install and tighten the console-to-floor support screws.

15. Install the two emergency release lever handles making sure the clips engage.

16. Install the finish panels and their retainers.

17. Snap the plug buttons into their locations at the rear of the console.

18. Install the safety belt anchor bolts and plugs.

19. Check that the safety belt is functioning properly.

Roof Console

REMOVAL & INSTALLATION

▶ **See Figure 33**

1. Remove the lamp lenses by inserting a small prytool into one of the notches on the sides of the lens.

2. Remove the screw located in each lens opening.

3. Support the console and unfasten the front screw.

4. Lower the console from the roof and unplug all the electrical connections from the console.

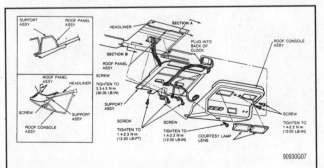

Fig. 33 Typical roof console components

5. Remove the console.

6. Installation is the reverse of removal.

Door Panels

REMOVAL & INSTALLATION

▶ **See Figures 34 thru 40**

1. Remove the window regulator handle retaining screw and the handle.

2. Remove the door handle pull cup.

3. Unfasten the retaining screws from the armrest assembly. Remove the armrest.

4. On vehicles with power door locks, unplug the wiring connector.

5. Remove the trim panel retaining screws from the bottom of the map compartment, if so equipped.

6. Remove the retaining setscrew from the remote control mirror bezel, if so equipped.

7. Using a suitable push pin tool, pry the trim panel retaining push pins from the door interior panel.

➡**Do not use the trim panel to pull the push pins from the door inner panel holes.**

8. If the trim panel is to be replaced, transfer the trim panel retaining push pins to the new panel assembly.

To install:

9. Replace any bent, broken or missing push pins.

➡**If the watershield has been removed, be sure to position it correctly before installing the trim panel.**

10. Be sure that the armrest retaining clips are properly positioned on the door inner panel. If they have been dislodged, they must be installed before installing the watershield.

11. Position the trim panel to the door inner panel. Route the remote control outside mirror cable through the bezel, if so equipped.

12. Position the trim panel to the door inner panel and locate the push pins in the countersunk holes. Firmly push the trim panel at the push pin locations to set each push pin.

13. Install the set screw from the remote control outside mirror bezel, if so equipped.

14. Install the trim panel retaining screws at the bottom of the map pocket, if so equipped.

15. On vehicles with power door locks, attach the wiring connector.

16. Position the armrest to the trim panel and install the retaining screws.

17. Install the door handle pull cup.

18. Install the window regulator handle.

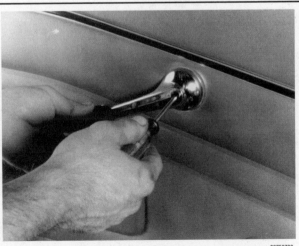

Fig. 34 Use a Phillips screwdriver to remove the retaining screw and window regulator handle

Fig. 35 Unfasten the Phillips screw and remove the door handle pull cup

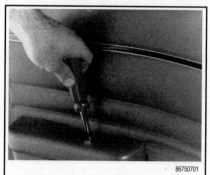

Fig. 36 Remove the retaining screws from the armrest assembly, then remove the armrest

Fig. 37 Remove the trim panel screws beneath the map compartment, then remove the compartment

Fig. 38 Use a suitable tool to pry the trim panel push pins from the interior door panel

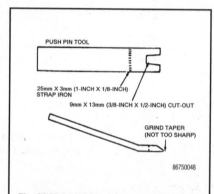

Fig. 39 If necessary, fabricate a push pin tool to the dimensions shown

Fig. 40 When fully detached, remove the door panel

Door Lock Cylinder

REMOVAL & INSTALLATION

♦ See Figures 41, 42, 43 and 44

➡When a lock cylinder must be replaced, replace both locks in the set to avoid carrying an extra key which fits only one lock.

1. Remove the door trim panel and the watershield.
2. Remove the clip attaching the lock cylinder rod to the lock cylinder.
3. Pry the lock cylinder retainer out of the slot in the door.
4. Remove the lock cylinder from the door.

To install:

5. Position the cylinder lock assembly into the outer door panel.

6. Install the cylinder retainer into its slot and push the retainer onto the lock cylinder.
7. Install the lock cylinder rod with the clip onto the lock assembly.
8. Lock and unlock the door to check the lock cylinder operation.
9. Install the watershield and door trim panel.

Power Door Lock Actuator Motor

REMOVAL & INSTALLATION

1. Disconnect the negative battery cable.
2. Remove the door trim panel and the watershield.
3. Using a ¼ in. (6mm) diameter drill bit, remove the pop rivet attaching the actuator motor to the door. Unplug the wiring at the connector.

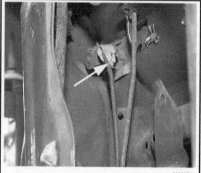

Fig. 41 Location of the lock cylinder rod-to-lock cylinder retaining clip (arrow)

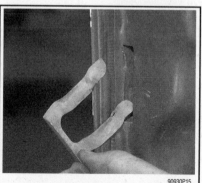

Fig. 42 Remove the lock cylinder retainer through the slot in the door . . .

Fig. 43 . . . then remove the lock cylinder from the door

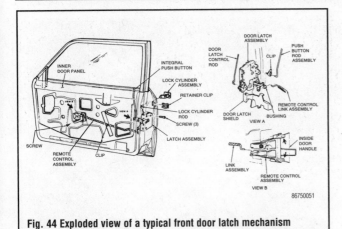

Fig. 44 Exploded view of a typical front door latch mechanism

4. Disconnect the actuator motor link from the door latch and remove the motor.

To install:
5. Connect the actuator motor link to the door latch.
6. Attach the wiring at the connector.
7. Install the door lock actuator motor to the door with a pop rivet, using a suitable rivet gun.

➡Make sure that the actuator boot is not twisted during installation. The pop rivet must be installed with the bracket base tight to the inner panel.

8. Install the door trim panel and water shield.
9. Reconnect the negative battery cable.

Door Glass

REMOVAL & INSTALLATION

Front Door

▶ **See Figures 45 and 46**

1. Remove the door trim panel and watershield.
2. Remove the two rivets attaching the glass to the run and bracket assembly.

➡Prior to the removing center pins from the rivet, it is recommended that a suitable block support be inserted between the door outer panel and the glass bracket to stabilize the glass during the rivet removal. Remove the center pin from each rivet with a drift punch. Then, using a ¼ in. (6mm) diameter drill, carefully drill out the remainder of each rivet, as damage to the plastic glass retainer and spacer could result.

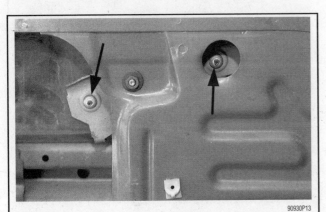

Fig. 45 Location of the door glass-to-regulator run and bracket assembly rivets

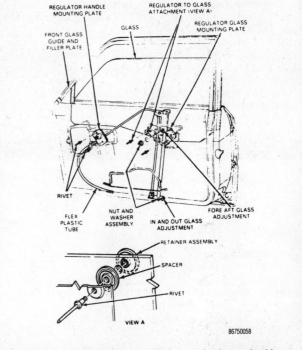

Fig. 46 Exploded view of the front window mechanism and cable drive system

3. Remove the glass.
4. Remove the drillings and pins from the bottom of the door.

To install:
5. Snap the plastic retainer and spacer into the two glass retainer holes. Make certain that the metal washer in the retainer assembly is on the outboard side of the glass.
6. Insert the glass into the door.
7. Position the door glass to the door glass bracket and align the glass and glass bracket retaining holes
8. Install the retaining rivets.

➡Two ¼-20 x 1 inch bolts and two ¼-20 x 1 inch nut and washer assemblies may be used to as an alternative to rivets for glass retention. When installing the bolts and nuts, they cannot be tightened more than 36–60 inch lbs. (4–7 Nm).

9. Check the operation of the window.
10. Install the trim panel and watershield.

Rear Door

1. Remove the door trim panel and watershield.
2. Remove the glass-to-glass bracket attaching rivets and lower the glass to the bottom of the door.

➡Prior to the removing center pins from the rivet, it is recommended that a suitable block support be inserted between the door outer panel and the glass bracket to stabilize the glass during the rivet removal. Remove the center pin from each rivet with a drift punch. Then, using a ¼ in. (6mm) diameter drill carefully drill out the remainder of each rivet as damage to the plastic glass retainer and spacer could result.

3. Remove the glass run from the top of door frame and the front of the division bar.
4. Remove the screw and washer at the top and bottom of the division bar. Tilt the division bar forward to remove it.
5. Lift the glass up between the door belt moldings and remove the glass.

To install:
6. Install plastic spacers into the glass.
7. Insert the glass into the door.

8. Install the subassembly rear glass and weatherstrip , make certain that the weatherstrip is seated properly for proper sealing.

9. Install the division bar and tighten the top screw and washer, then loosely tighten the bottom screw and washer.

10. Install the door glass run assembly.

11. Install the glass-to-regulator mounting bracket, raise the glass from the bottom of the door and install two ¼ (6mm) blind rivets or two ¼-20 x 1 inch bolt and nut assemblies.

12. Check the operation of the window.

13. Tighten the screw and washer at the lower division bar.

14. Install the trim panel and watershield.

Window Regulator

REMOVAL & INSTALLATION

Front Door

▶ **See Figures 46, 47, and 48**

1. Remove the door trim panel and watershield.

2. Prop the glass if the full-up position.

3. Remove the four pop rivets attaching the regulator mounting plate assembly to the inner door panel. Remove the center pin from each rivet with a drift punch. Using a ¼ in. (6mm) diameter drill, drill out the remainder of the rivet, using care not to enlarge the sheet metal retaining holes.

4. Remove the two nut and washer assemblies attaching the regulator tube to the inner panel and door sill.

5. Slide the run and bracket rearward at the bottom.

6. Remove the window regulator arm slide/roller from the glass bracket C-channel and remove the regulator.

To install:

7. With glass in the full-up position, install the window regulator through the access hole in the door and insert the slide roller into the glass bracket channel.

8. Slide the tube assembly forward into position, loosely install the two nut and washer assemblies to the regulator tube guide.

9. Install the four rivets or four, ¼ in.–20 x ½ in. screws and washer assemblies and two, ¼ in.–20 nut/washer assemblies to secure the regulator handle mounting plate to door inner panel. Equivalent metric retainers may be used.

10. Tighten loosely assembled nut and washer assemblies from Step 9.

11. Cycle the glass to ensure smooth operation. Install the watershield and door trim panel.

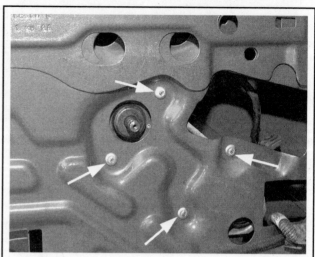

Fig. 48 Location of the four window regulator-to-door pop rivets

Rear Door

▶ **See Figure 49**

1. Remove the door trim panel and watershield.

2. Remove the two rivets attaching the main glass-to-glass bracket.

3. Remove the rivets attaching the regulator mounting plate assembly to the inner door panel.

4. Remove the two nut and washer assemblies retaining the run and bracket assembly to the inner panel.

5. Disconnect the door latch remote rods at the door latch.

6. Remove the window regulator from the door. Be sure to use the access hole in the inner door panel for removal and installation of the regulator.

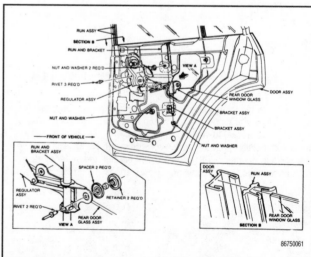

Fig. 49 Exploded view of the rear window mechanism

To install:

7. Install the window regulator through the access hole in the rear door.

8. Loosely assemble the two nut and washer assemblies to the run and bracket assembly studs on the door inner panel.

9. Install rivets or equivalent screw, washer and nut assemblies to secure the regulator mounting plate to the inner door panel.

10. Install the rear door window glass bracket. Position the glass in the full up position and tighten loosely assembles nut from Step 8.

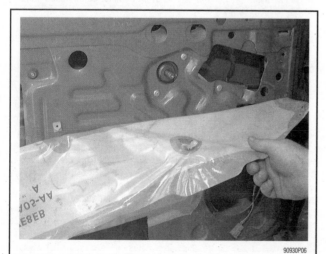

Fig. 47 Remove the trim panel and watershield to access the regulator retaining pop rivets

11. Connect the door latch remote rods at the door latch.

12. Cycle the glass up and down to check for smooth operation. Install the watershield and trim panel.

Electric Window Motor

REMOVAL & INSTALLATION

2-Door Models

▶ **See Figure 50**

1. Raise the window to the full up position, if possible. If the glass cannot be raised and is partially down or in the full down position, it must be supported so that it will not fall into the door well during motor removal.

2. Disconnect the negative battery cable.

3. Remove the door trim panel and watershield.

4. Unplug the electric window motor wire from the wire harness connector and move the motor away from the area to be drilled.

5. Using a ¾ in. hole saw with a ¼ in. pilot, drill the hole at point A and point B dimples. Remove the drillings.

➡ **Before the removal of the motor drive assembly, make certain that the regulator arm is in a fixed position to prevent counterbalance spring unwind.**

6. Remove the three window motor mounting screws and disengage the motor and drive assembly from the regulator quadrant gear.

7. Install the new motor and drive assembly. Tighten the three motor mounting screws to 50–85 inch lbs. (5.5–9.5 Nm).

8. Connect window motor wiring harness leads.

9. Connect the negative battery cable.

10. Check the power window for proper operation.

11. Install the door trim panel and watershield. Check that all drain holes at the bottom of the doors are open to prevent water accumulation over the motor.

4-Door Models

FRONT DOOR

▶ **See Figure 51**

1. Raise the window to the full up position, if possible. If the glass cannot be raised and is partially down or in the full down position, it must be supported so that it will not fall into the door well during motor removal.

2. Disconnect the negative battery cable.

3. Remove the door trim panel and watershield.

4. Unplug the electric window motor wire from the wire harness connector and move the motor away from the area to be drilled.

5. Using a ¾ in. hole saw with a ¼ in. pilot, drill the hole at the existing dimple (point A) adjacent to the radio speaker opening. Remove the drillings.

6. At the upper motor mount screw head, the sheet metal interference can be removed by grinding out the inner panel surface sufficiently to clear the screw head for easy removal. Remove the drillings.

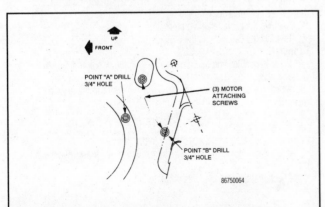

Fig. 50 Drill holes at the existing dimples—2-door models

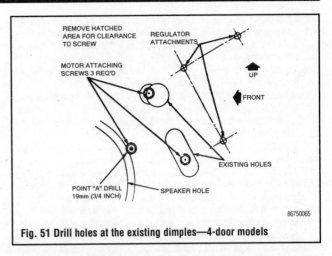

Fig. 51 Drill holes at the existing dimples—4-door models

➡ **Before the removal of the motor drive assembly, make certain that the regulator arm is in a fixed position to prevent counterbalance spring unwind.**

7. Remove the three window motor mounting screws and disengage the motor and drive assembly from the regulator quadrant gear.

8. Install the new motor and drive assembly. Tighten the three motor mounting screws to 50–85 inch lbs. (5.5–9.5 Nm).

9. Connect window motor wiring harness leads.

10. Connect the negative battery cable.

11. Check the power window for proper operation.

12. Install the door trim panel and watershield. Check that all drain holes at the bottom of the doors are open to prevent water accumulation over the motor.

REAR DOOR

1. Raise the window to the full up position, if possible. If the glass cannot be raised and is partially down or in the full down position, it must be supported so that it will not fall into the door well during motor removal.

2. Disconnect the negative battery cable.

3. Remove the door trim panel and watershield.

4. Disconnect the electric window motor wire from the wire harness connector and move the motor away from the area to be drilled.

5. Using a ¾ in. hole saw with a ¼ in. pilot, drill three holes in the door inner panel at the three existing dimples to gain access to the three motor and drive attaching screws. Remove the drillings.

➡ **Before the removal of the motor drive assembly, make certain that the regulator arm is in a fixed position to prevent counterbalance spring unwind.**

6. Remove the three window motor mounting screws and disengage the motor and drive assembly from the regulator quadrant gear.

7. Install the new motor and drive assembly. Tighten the three motor mounting screws to 50–85 inch lbs. (5.5–9.5 Nm).

8. Connect window motor wiring harness leads.

9. Connect the negative battery cable.

10. Check the power window for proper operation.

11. Install the door trim panel and watershield. Check that all drain holes at the bottom of the doors are open to prevent water accumulation over the motor.

Windshield and Fixed Glass

REMOVAL & INSTALLATION

If your windshield, or other fixed window, is cracked or chipped, you may decide to replace it with a new one yourself. However, there are two main reasons why replacement windshields and other window glass should be installed only by a professional automotive glass technician: safety and cost.

The most important reason a professional should install automotive glass is for safety. The glass in the vehicle, especially the windshield, is designed with safety in mind in case of a collision. The windshield is specially manufactured from two panes of specially-tempered glass with a thin layer of transparent plastic between them. This construction allows the glass to "give" in the event that a part of your body hits the windshield during the collision, and prevents the glass from shattering, which could cause lacerations, blinding and other harm to passengers of the vehicle. The other fixed windows are designed to be tempered so that if they break during a collision, they shatter in such a way that there are no large pointed glass pieces. The professional automotive glass technician knows how to install the glass in a vehicle so that it will function optimally during a collision. Without the proper experience, knowledge and tools, installing a piece of automotive glass yourself could lead to additional harm if an accident should ever occur.

Cost is also a factor when deciding to install automotive glass yourself. Performing this could cost you much more than a professional may charge for the same job. Since the windshield is designed to break under stress, an often life saving characteristic, windshields tend to break VERY easily when an inexperienced person attempts to install one. Do-it-yourselfers buying two, three or even four windshields from a salvage yard because they have broken them during installation are common stories. Also, since the automotive glass is designed to prevent the outside elements from entering your vehicle, improper installation can lead to water and air leaks. Annoying whining noises at highway speeds from air leaks or inside body panel rusting from water leaks can add to your stress level and subtract from your wallet. After buying two or three windshields, installing them and ending up with a leak that produces a noise while driving and water damage during rainstorms, the cost of having a professional do it correctly the first time may be much more alluring. We here at Chilton, therefore, advise that you have a professional automotive glass technician service any broken glass on your vehicle.

WINDSHIELD CHIP REPAIR

▶ See Figures 52 and 53

➡Check with your state and local authorities on the laws for state safety inspection. Some states or municipalities may not allow chip repair as a viable option for correcting stone damage to your windshield.

Although severely cracked or damaged windshields must be replaced, there is something that you can do to prolong or even prevent the need for replacement of a chipped windshield. There are many companies which offer windshield chip repair products, such as Loctite's® Bullseye™ windshield repair kit. These kits usually consist of a syringe, pedestal and a sealing adhesive. The syringe is mounted on the pedestal and is used to create a vacuum which pulls the plastic layer against the glass. This helps make the chip transparent. The adhesive is then injected which seals the chip and helps to prevent further stress cracks from developing

➡Always follow the specific manufacturer's instructions.

Inside Rear View Mirror

REMOVAL & INSTALLATION

▶ See Figures 54 and 55

1. Loosen the mirror assembly-to-mounting bracket setscrew.
2. Remove the mirror assembly by sliding upward and away from the mounting bracket.
3. Install the mirror by attaching it to the mounting bracket, then tighten the set screw to 10–20 inch lbs. (1–2 Nm).

Power Seat Motor and Drive Cables

REMOVAL & INSTALLATION

1. Remove the seat and track assembly.
2. Unfasten the motor-to-assembly mounting bolts.
3. Remove the hose clamps attaching the cables to the seat tracks.

Fig. 52 Small chips on your windshield can be fixed with an aftermarket repair kit, such as the one from Loctite®

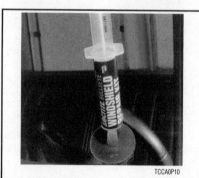

Fig. 53 Most kits use a self-stick applicator and syringe to inject the adhesive into the chip or crack

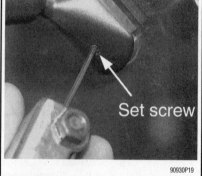

Fig. 54 Unfasten the rear view mirror setscrew

4. Open the wire retaining straps and remove the motor assembly and cable from the seat track assembly.
5. Remove the cable retaining brackets.
6. Remove the cables from the motor.
To install:
7. Place the cables and retaining brackets on the motor and tighten the retaining screws.
8. Attach the cables to the seat tracks and the motor to the housing bracket.
9. Install and tighten the motor attaching bolts.
10. Install the cable-to-seat track clamps.
11. Install the seat and track assembly in the vehicle.
12. Insert the motor wire in the wire straps and attach the wire at the connector.
13. Check that the seat operates properly.

Fig. 55 Slide the mirror up and off the mounting bracket to remove it

TORQUE SPECIFICATIONS

Components	Ft. Lbs.	Nm
Exterior		
Door hinge bolts	18-26	25-35
Hood hinge bolts	84-144 inch lbs.	10-16
Hatchback and liftgate hinge retainers	16-20	22-27
Outside mirrors		
Manual mirrors		
Mirror nuts	25-36 inch lbs.	2.8-4.0
Remote control mirrors		
Mirror nuts	21-39 inch lbs.	2.3-4.4
Power mirrors		
Mirror nuts	36-48 inch lbs.	4-6
Interior		
Instrument panel and pad		
Instrument panel upper retaining screws		
1981-87 models		
1988-90 models		
Upper and lower instrument panel-to-cowl side screws	60-96 inch lbs.	7-11
Instrument panel brace retainers	60-96 inch lbs.	7-11
Steering column support bracket nut	36-48 inch lbs.	4-6
Cluster opening finish panel screws	18-25 inch lbs.	2-2.9
Steering column opening reinforcement bolts	80-124 inch lbs.	9-14
Floor console		
Retractor-to-floor brace bolts	22-32	30-43
Door glass		
1/4-20 x 1 inch bolts and nuts	36-60 inch lbs.	4-7
Electric window motor		
Motor retainers	50-85 inch lbs.	5.5-9.5
Inside rear view mirror		
Mirror setscrew	10-20 inch lbs.	1-2
Seats		
Front		
Seat-track-to-seat cushion screws	9-18	12.2-24.5
Seat track screws, studs and/or nuts	9-18	12.2-24.5
Rear fold-down type		
Hinge attaching screws	13-20	17.6-27
Articulating arm mounting bolt	14-16	19-21.5

90930C01

GLOSSARY

AIR/FUEL RATIO: The ratio of air-to-gasoline by weight in the fuel mixture drawn into the engine.

AIR INJECTION: One method of reducing harmful exhaust emissions by injecting air into each of the exhaust ports of an engine. The fresh air entering the hot exhaust manifold causes any remaining fuel to be burned before it can exit the tailpipe.

ALTERNATOR: A device used for converting mechanical energy into electrical energy.

AMMETER: An instrument, calibrated in amperes, used to measure the flow of an electrical current in a circuit. Ammeters are always connected in series with the circuit being tested.

AMPERE: The rate of flow of electrical current present when one volt of electrical pressure is applied against one ohm of electrical resistance.

ANALOG COMPUTER: Any microprocessor that uses similar (analogous) electrical signals to make its calculations.

ARMATURE: A laminated, soft iron core wrapped by a wire that converts electrical energy to mechanical energy as in a motor or relay. When rotated in a magnetic field, it changes mechanical energy into electrical energy as in a generator.

ATMOSPHERIC PRESSURE: The pressure on the Earth's surface caused by the weight of the air in the atmosphere. At sea level, this pressure is 14.7 psi at 32°F (101 kPa at 0°C).

ATOMIZATION: The breaking down of a liquid into a fine mist that can be suspended in air.

AXIAL PLAY: Movement parallel to a shaft or bearing bore.

BACKFIRE: The sudden combustion of gases in the intake or exhaust system that results in a loud explosion.

BACKLASH: The clearance or play between two parts, such as meshed gears.

BACKPRESSURE: Restrictions in the exhaust system that slow the exit of exhaust gases from the combustion chamber.

BAKELITE: A heat resistant, plastic insulator material commonly used in printed circuit boards and transistorized components.

BALL BEARING: A bearing made up of hardened inner and outer races between which hardened steel balls roll.

BALLAST RESISTOR: A resistor in the primary ignition circuit that lowers voltage after the engine is started to reduce wear on ignition components.

BEARING: A friction reducing, supportive device usually located between a stationary part and a moving part.

BIMETAL TEMPERATURE SENSOR: Any sensor or switch made of two dissimilar types of metal that bend when heated or cooled due to the different expansion rates of the alloys. These types of sensors usually function as an on/off switch.

BLOWBY: Combustion gases, composed of water vapor and unburned fuel, that leak past the piston rings into the crankcase during normal engine operation. These gases are removed by the PCV system to prevent the buildup of harmful acids in the crankcase.

BRAKE PAD: A brake shoe and lining assembly used with disc brakes.

BRAKE SHOE: The backing for the brake lining. The term is, however, usually applied to the assembly of the brake backing and lining.

BUSHING: A liner, usually removable, for a bearing; an anti-friction liner used in place of a bearing.

CALIPER: A hydraulically activated device in a disc brake system, which is mounted straddling the brake rotor (disc). The caliper contains at least one piston and two brake pads. Hydraulic pressure on the piston(s) forces the pads against the rotor.

CAMSHAFT: A shaft in the engine on which are the lobes (cams) which operate the valves. The camshaft is driven by the crankshaft, via a belt, chain or gears, at one half the crankshaft speed.

CAPACITOR: A device which stores an electrical charge.

CARBON MONOXIDE (CO): A colorless, odorless gas given off as a normal byproduct of combustion. It is poisonous and extremely dangerous in confined areas, building up slowly to toxic levels without warning if adequate ventilation is not available.

CARBURETOR: A device, usually mounted on the intake manifold of an engine, which mixes the air and fuel in the proper proportion to allow even combustion.

CATALYTIC CONVERTER: A device installed in the exhaust system, like a muffler, that converts harmful byproducts of combustion into carbon dioxide and water vapor by means of a heat-producing chemical reaction.

CENTRIFUGAL ADVANCE: A mechanical method of advancing the spark timing by using flyweights in the distributor that react to centrifugal force generated by the distributor shaft rotation.

CHECK VALVE: Any one-way valve installed to permit the flow of air, fuel or vacuum in one direction only.

CHOKE: A device, usually a moveable valve, placed in the intake path of a carburetor to restrict the flow of air.

CIRCUIT: Any unbroken path through which an electrical current can flow. Also used to describe fuel flow in some instances.

CIRCUIT BREAKER: A switch which protects an electrical circuit from overload by opening the circuit when the current flow exceeds a predetermined level. Some circuit breakers must be reset manually, while most reset automatically.

COIL (IGNITION): A transformer in the ignition circuit which steps up the voltage provided to the spark plugs.

COMBINATION MANIFOLD: An assembly which includes both the intake and exhaust manifolds in one casting.

COMBINATION VALVE: A device used in some fuel systems that routes fuel vapors to a charcoal storage canister instead of venting them into the atmosphere. The valve relieves fuel tank pressure and allows fresh air into the tank as the fuel level drops to prevent a vapor lock situation.

COMPRESSION RATIO: The comparison of the total volume of the cylinder and combustion chamber with the piston at BDC and the piston at TDC.

CONDENSER: 1. An electrical device which acts to store an electrical charge, preventing voltage surges. 2. A radiator-like device in the air conditioning system in which refrigerant gas condenses into a liquid, giving off heat.

CONDUCTOR: Any material through which an electrical current can be transmitted easily.

CONTINUITY: Continuous or complete circuit. Can be checked with an ohmmeter.

COUNTERSHAFT: An intermediate shaft which is rotated by a mainshaft and transmits, in turn, that rotation to a working part.

CRANKCASE: The lower part of an engine in which the crankshaft and related parts operate.

CRANKSHAFT: The main driving shaft of an engine which receives reciprocating motion from the pistons and converts it to rotary motion.

CYLINDER: In an engine, the round hole in the engine block in which the piston(s) ride.

CYLINDER BLOCK: The main structural member of an engine in which is found the cylinders, crankshaft and other principal parts.

CYLINDER HEAD: The detachable portion of the engine, usually fastened to the top of the cylinder block and containing all or most of the combustion chambers. On overhead valve engines, it contains the valves and their operating parts. On overhead cam engines, it contains the camshaft as well.

DEAD CENTER: The extreme top or bottom of the piston stroke.

DETONATION: An unwanted explosion of the air/fuel mixture in the combustion chamber caused by excess heat and compression, advanced timing, or an overly lean mixture. Also referred to as "ping".

DIAPHRAGM: A thin, flexible wall separating two cavities, such as in a vacuum advance unit.

DIESELING: A condition in which hot spots in the combustion chamber cause the engine to run on after the key is turned off.

DIFFERENTIAL: A geared assembly which allows the transmission of motion between drive axles, giving one axle the ability to turn faster than the other.

DIODE: An electrical device that will allow current to flow in one direction only.

DISC BRAKE: A hydraulic braking assembly consisting of a brake disc, or rotor, mounted on an axle, and a caliper assembly containing, usually two brake pads which are activated by hydraulic pressure. The pads are forced against the sides of the disc, creating friction which slows the vehicle.

DISTRIBUTOR: A mechanically driven device on an engine which is responsible for electrically firing the spark plug at a predetermined point of the piston stroke.

DOWEL PIN: A pin, inserted in mating holes in two different parts allowing those parts to maintain a fixed relationship.

DRUM BRAKE: A braking system which consists of two brake shoes and one or two wheel cylinders, mounted on a fixed backing plate, and a brake drum, mounted on an axle, which revolves around the assembly.

DWELL: The rate, measured in degrees of shaft rotation, at which an electrical circuit cycles on and off.

ELECTRONIC CONTROL UNIT (ECU): Ignition module, module, amplifier or igniter. See Module for definition.

ELECTRONIC IGNITION: A system in which the timing and firing of the spark plugs is controlled by an electronic control unit, usually called a module. These systems have no points or condenser.

END-PLAY: The measured amount of axial movement in a shaft.

ENGINE: A device that converts heat into mechanical energy.

EXHAUST MANIFOLD: A set of cast passages or pipes which conduct exhaust gases from the engine.

FEELER GAUGE: A blade, usually metal, or precisely predetermined thickness, used to measure the clearance between two parts.

FIRING ORDER: The order in which combustion occurs in the cylinders of an engine. Also the order in which spark is distributed to the plugs by the distributor.

FLOODING: The presence of too much fuel in the intake manifold and combustion chamber which prevents the air/fuel mixture from firing, thereby causing a no-start situation.

FLYWHEEL: A disc shaped part bolted to the rear end of the crankshaft. Around the outer perimeter is affixed the ring gear. The starter drive engages the ring gear, turning the flywheel, which rotates the crankshaft, imparting the initial starting motion to the engine.

FOOT POUND (ft. lbs. or sometimes, ft.lb.): The amount of energy or work needed to raise an item weighing one pound, a distance of one foot.

FUSE: A protective device in a circuit which prevents circuit overload by breaking the circuit when a specific amperage is present. The device is constructed around a strip or wire of a lower amperage rating than the circuit it is designed to protect. When an amperage higher than that stamped on the fuse is present in the circuit, the strip or wire melts, opening the circuit.

GEAR RATIO: The ratio between the number of teeth on meshing gears.

GENERATOR: A device which converts mechanical energy into electrical energy.

HEAT RANGE: The measure of a spark plug's ability to dissipate heat from its firing end. The higher the heat range, the hotter the plug fires.

HUB: The center part of a wheel or gear.

HYDROCARBON (HC): Any chemical compound made up of hydrogen and carbon. A major pollutant formed by the engine as a byproduct of combustion.

HYDROMETER: An instrument used to measure the specific gravity of a solution.

INCH POUND (inch lbs.; sometimes in.lb. or in. lbs.): One twelfth of a foot pound.

INDUCTION: A means of transferring electrical energy in the form of a magnetic field. Principle used in the ignition coil to increase voltage.

INJECTOR: A device which receives metered fuel under relatively low pressure and is activated to inject the fuel into the engine under relatively high pressure at a predetermined time.

INPUT SHAFT: The shaft to which torque is applied, usually carrying the driving gear or gears.

INTAKE MANIFOLD: A casting of passages or pipes used to conduct air or a fuel/air mixture to the cylinders.

JOURNAL: The bearing surface within which a shaft operates.

KEY: A small block usually fitted in a notch between a shaft and a hub to prevent slippage of the two parts.

MANIFOLD: A casting of passages or set of pipes which connect the cylinders to an inlet or outlet source.

MANIFOLD VACUUM: Low pressure in an engine intake manifold formed just below the throttle plates. Manifold vacuum is highest at idle and drops under acceleration.

MASTER CYLINDER: The primary fluid pressurizing device in a hydraulic system. In automotive use, it is found in brake and hydraulic clutch systems and is pedal activated, either directly or, in a power brake system, through the power booster.

MODULE: Electronic control unit, amplifier or igniter of solid state or integrated design which controls the current flow in the ignition primary circuit based on input from the pick-up coil. When the module opens the primary circuit, high secondary voltage is induced in the coil.

NEEDLE BEARING: A bearing which consists of a number (usually a large number) of long, thin rollers.

OHM: (Ω) The unit used to measure the resistance of conductor-to-electrical flow. One ohm is the amount of resistance that limits current flow to one ampere in a circuit with one volt of pressure.

OHMMETER: An instrument used for measuring the resistance, in ohms, in an electrical circuit.

OUTPUT SHAFT: The shaft which transmits torque from a device, such as a transmission.

OVERDRIVE: A gear assembly which produces more shaft revolutions than that transmitted to it.

OVERHEAD CAMSHAFT (OHC): An engine configuration in which the camshaft is mounted on top of the cylinder head and operates the valve either directly or by means of rocker arms.

OVERHEAD VALVE (OHV): An engine configuration in which all of the valves are located in the cylinder head and the camshaft is located in the cylinder block. The camshaft operates the valves via lifters and pushrods.

OXIDES OF NITROGEN (NOx): Chemical compounds of nitrogen produced as a byproduct of combustion. They combine with hydrocarbons to produce smog.

OXYGEN SENSOR: Use with the feedback system to sense the presence of oxygen in the exhaust gas and signal the computer which can reference the voltage signal to an air/fuel ratio.

PINION: The smaller of two meshing gears.

PISTON RING: An open-ended ring with fits into a groove on the outer diameter of the piston. Its chief function is to form a seal between the piston and cylinder wall. Most automotive pistons have three rings: two for compression sealing; one for oil sealing.

PRELOAD: A predetermined load placed on a bearing during assembly or by adjustment.

PRIMARY CIRCUIT: the low voltage side of the ignition system which consists of the ignition switch, ballast resistor or resistance wire, bypass, coil, electronic control unit and pick-up coil as well as the connecting wires and harnesses.

PRESS FIT: The mating of two parts under pressure, due to the inner diameter of one being smaller than the outer diameter of the other, or vice versa; an interference fit.

RACE: The surface on the inner or outer ring of a bearing on which the balls, needles or rollers move.

REGULATOR: A device which maintains the amperage and/or voltage levels of a circuit at predetermined values.

RELAY: A switch which automatically opens and/or closes a circuit.

RESISTANCE: The opposition to the flow of current through a circuit or electrical device, and is measured in ohms. Resistance is equal to the voltage divided by the amperage.

RESISTOR: A device, usually made of wire, which offers a preset amount of resistance in an electrical circuit.

RING GEAR: The name given to a ring-shaped gear attached to a differential case, or affixed to a flywheel or as part of a planetary gear set.

ROLLER BEARING: A bearing made up of hardened inner and outer races between which hardened steel rollers move.

ROTOR: 1. The disc-shaped part of a disc brake assembly, upon which the brake pads bear; also called, brake disc. 2. The device mounted atop the distributor shaft, which passes current to the distributor cap tower contacts.

SECONDARY CIRCUIT: The high voltage side of the ignition system, usually above 20,000 volts. The secondary includes the ignition coil, coil wire, distributor cap and rotor, spark plug wires and spark plugs.

SENDING UNIT: A mechanical, electrical, hydraulic or electro-magnetic device which transmits information to a gauge.

SENSOR: Any device designed to measure engine operating conditions or ambient pressures and temperatures. Usually electronic in nature and designed to send a voltage signal to an on-board computer, some sensors may operate as a simple on/off switch or they may provide a variable voltage signal (like a potentiometer) as conditions or measured parameters change.

SHIM: Spacers of precise, predetermined thickness used between parts to establish a proper working relationship.

SLAVE CYLINDER: In automotive use, a device in the hydraulic clutch system which is activated by hydraulic force, disengaging the clutch.

SOLENOID: A coil used to produce a magnetic field, the effect of which is to produce work.

SPARK PLUG: A device screwed into the combustion chamber of a spark ignition engine. The basic construction is a conductive core inside of a ceramic insulator, mounted in an outer conductive base. An electrical charge from the spark plug wire travels along the conductive core and jumps a preset air gap to a grounding point or points at the end of the conductive base. The resultant spark ignites the fuel/air mixture in the combustion chamber.

SPLINES: Ridges machined or cast onto the outer diameter of a shaft or inner diameter of a bore to enable parts to mate without rotation.

TACHOMETER: A device used to measure the rotary speed of an engine, shaft, gear, etc., usually in rotations per minute.

THERMOSTAT: A valve, located in the cooling system of an engine, which is closed when cold and opens gradually in response to engine heating, controlling the temperature of the coolant and rate of coolant flow.

TOP DEAD CENTER (TDC): The point at which the piston reaches the top of its travel on the compression stroke.

TORQUE: The twisting force applied to an object.

TORQUE CONVERTER: A turbine used to transmit power from a driving member to a driven member via hydraulic action, providing changes in drive ratio and torque. In automotive use, it links the driveplate at the rear of the engine to the automatic transmission.

TRANSDUCER: A device used to change a force into an electrical signal.

TRANSISTOR: A semi-conductor component which can be actuated by a small voltage to perform an electrical switching function.

TUNE-UP: A regular maintenance function, usually associated with the replacement and adjustment of parts and components in the electrical and fuel systems of a vehicle for the purpose of attaining optimum performance.

TURBOCHARGER: An exhaust driven pump which compresses intake air and forces it into the combustion chambers at higher than atmospheric pressures. The increased air pressure allows more fuel to be burned and results in increased horsepower being produced.

VACUUM ADVANCE: A device which advances the ignition timing in response to increased engine vacuum.

VACUUM GAUGE: An instrument used to measure the presence of vacuum in a chamber.

VALVE: A device which control the pressure, direction of flow or rate of flow of a liquid or gas.

VALVE CLEARANCE: The measured gap between the end of the valve stem and the rocker arm, cam lobe or follower that activates the valve.

VISCOSITY: The rating of a liquid's internal resistance to flow.

VOLTMETER: An instrument used for measuring electrical force in units called volts. Voltmeters are always connected parallel with the circuit being tested.

WHEEL CYLINDER: Found in the automotive drum brake assembly, it is a device, actuated by hydraulic pressure, which, through internal pistons, pushes the brake shoes outward against the drums.

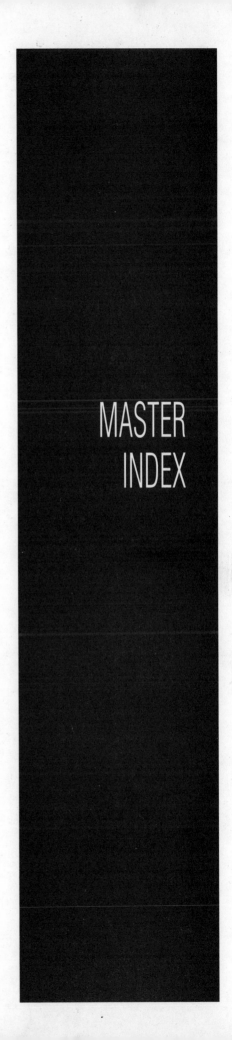

MASTER

INDEX

Total Car Care, continued

Sentra/Pulsar/NX 1982-96
PART NO. 8263/52700
Stanza/200SX/240SX 1982-92
PART NO. 8262/52750
240SX/Altima 1993-98
PART NO. 52752
Datsun/Nissan Z and ZX 1970-88
PART NO. 8846/52800

RENAULT
Coupes/Sedans/Wagons 1975-85
PART NO. 58300

SATURN
Coupes/Sedans/Wagons 1991-98
PART NO. 8419/62300

SUBARU
ff-1/1300/1400/1600/1800/Brat 1970-84
PART NO. 8790/64300
Coupes/Sedans/Wagons 1985-96
PART NO. 8259/64302

SUZUKI
Samurai/Sidekick/Tracker 1986-98
PART NO. 66500

TOYOTA
Camry 1983-96
PART NO. 8265/68200
Celica/Supra 1971-85
PART NO. 68250
Celica 1986-93
PART NO. 8413/68252
Corolla 1970-87
PART NO. 8586/68300
Corolla 1988-97
PART NO. 8414/68302
Cressida/Corona/Crown/MkII 1970-82
PART NO. 68350
Cressida/Van 1983-90
PART NO. 68352
Toyota Trucks 1970-88
PART NO. 8578/68600
Pick-Ups/Land Cruiser/4Runner
1989-96
PART NO. 8163/68602

Previa 1991-98
PART NO. 68640
Tercel 1984-94
PART NO. 8595/68700

VOLKSWAGEN
Air-Cooled 1949-69
PART NO. 70200
Air-Cooled 1970-81
PART NO. 70202
Front Wheel Drive 1974-89
PART NO. 8663/70400
Golf/Jetta/Cabriolet 1990-93
PART NO. 8429/70402

VOLVO
Coupes/Sedans/Wagons 1970-89
PART NO. 8786/72300
Coupes/Sedans/Wagons 1990-98
PART NO. 8428/72302

Collector's Hard-Cover Manuals

Auto Repair Manual 1993-97
PART NO. 7919
Auto Repair Manual 1988-92
PART NO. 7906
Auto Repair Manual 1980-87
PART NO. 7670
Auto Repair Manual 1972-79
PART NO. 6914
Auto Repair Manual 1964-71
PART NO. 5974
Auto Repair Manual 1954-63
PART NO. 5652

Auto Repair Manual 1940-53
PART NO. 5631
Import Car Repair Manual 1993-97
PART NO. 7920
Import Car Repair Manual 1988-92
PART NO.7907
Import Car Repair Manual 1980-87
PART NO. 7672
Truck and Van Repair Manual 1993-97
PART NO. 7921
Truck and Van Repair Manual 1991-95
PART NO. 7911

Truck and Van Repair Manual 1986-90
PART NO. 7902
Truck and Van Repair Manual 1979-86
PART NO. 7655
Truck and Van Repair Manual 1971-78
PART NO. 7012
Truck Repair Manual 1961-71
PART NO. 6198
Motorcycle and ATV Repair Manual
1945-85
PART NO. 7635

System-Specific Manuals

Guide to Air Conditioning Repair and
Service 1982-85
PART NO. 7580
Guide to Automatic Transmission
Repair 1984-89
PART NO. 8054
Guide to Automatic Transmission
Repair 1984-89
Domestic cars and trucks
PART NO. 8053

Guide to Automatic Transmission
Repair 1980-84
Domestic cars and trucks
PART NO. 7891
Guide to Automatic Transmission
Repair 1974-80
Import cars and trucks
PART NO. 7645
Guide to Brakes, Steering, and
Suspension 1980-87
PART NO. 7819

Guide to Fuel Injection and Electronic
Engine Controls 1984-88
Guide to Electronic Engine Controls
1978-85
PART NO. 7535
Guide to Engine Repair and Rebuilding
PART NO. 7643
Guide to Vacuum Diagrams 1980-86
Domestic cars and trucks
PART NO. 7821